혼공

유형독해

실력(매운맛)

저자 허준석 김상근

랭기지플러스

초판인쇄	2017년 10월 23일
초판발행	2017년 11월 13일
저자	허준석, 김상근
펴낸이	엄태상
책임 편집	이효리, 장은혜, 김효은, 정유항
표지 디자인	이미애
내지 디자인	박경미
마케팅	이상호, 오원택, 이승욱, 전한나, 왕성석
온라인마케팅	김마선, 유근혜, 심유미
펴낸곳	랭기지플러스
주소	서울시 종로구 자하문로 300 시사빌딩
주문 및 교재 문의	1588-1582
팩스	(02)3671-0500
홈페이지	www.sisabooks.com
이메일	sisabooks@naver.comm
등록일자	2000년 8월 17일
등록번호	1-2718호

ISBN 978-89-5518-401-3 (53740)

혼공

유형독해

실력(매운맛)

저자 허준석 김상근

랭기지플러스

구성과 특징

1. 최신 학평, 수능 유형을 분석해 학생들의 오답률이 가장 높았던 문제들을 엄선하여 구성했습니다. 고난도의 문제들을 풀어보며 독해 실력을 한층 향상시킬 수 있습니다.

2. 각 유형별 필승 해결 전략을 실었습니다. 유형별 특징과 해결 방법 및 정답을 찾아가는 과정을 자세히 설명했습니다.

3. 혼자 공부하기에 어려움이 없도록 친절하게 해설을 구성했습니다.

1단계 개념 요리하기

학습날짜 :   월   일

01 문항 특징

- 비교적 쉬운 유형에 속한 문항이지만, 제목/주제 문제가 어려워지는 추세임
- 글의 요지의 경우 지문이 어려운 문항도 출제되지만, 선택지가 우리말이라서 정답률은 높은 편임
- 제목/주제 문제가 어려운 이유는 선택지가 영어로 제시되기 때문임
- 특히 제목의 경우 50%대의 정답률을 보이는 문제가 출제되기도 함
- 주제는 키워드가 선택지에 제시되나, 제목의 경우는 그렇지 않은 경우가 많음

02 혼공 전략

1단계 개념 요리하기

각 문항에 대한 비법이라고 할 수 있는 혼공 전략이 1단계에서 여러분을 맞이합니다. 각 문항별 학습 전략을 제공합니다.

2단계 문항 맛보기

다음 글의 제목으로 가장 적절한 것은?

2013년 수능 25번

The names of pitches are associated with particular frequency values. Our current system is called A440 because the note we call 'A' that is in the middle of the piano keyboard has been fixed to have a frequency of 440 Hz. This is entirely arbitrary. We could fix 'A' at any frequency, such as 439 or 424; different standards were used in the time of Mozart than today. Some people claim that the precise frequencies affect the overall sound of a musical piece and the sound of instruments. Led Zeppelin, a band popular in the 70s, often tuned their instruments away from the modern A440 standard to give their music an uncommon sound, and perhaps to link it with the European children's

2단계 문항 맛보기

2단계에는 맛보기 문항을 통해 유형을 파악하고 바로 뒤 페이지에서 정답과 오답의 이유, 지문에 숨겨져 있는 정답에 대한 힌트를 확인할 수 있습니다.

3단계 고난도 문항 요리하기

1. 다음 글의 요지로 가장 적절한 것은?

2012년 수능 36번

What's dangerous about the Internet is, because it has the aura of technology around it, it has a totally undeserved instant credibility. The fact that information is conveyed in this high-tech manner somehow adds authority to what is conveyed, when in fact the Internet is a global conveyer of unfiltered, unedited, untreated information. It is the greatest tool we have not

2. 다음 글의 주제로 가장 적절한 것은?

2016년 6월 22번

When we hear a story, we look for beliefs that are being commented upon. Any story has many possible beliefs inherent in it. But how does someone listening to a story find those beliefs? We find them by looking through the beliefs we already have. We are not as concerned with what we are hearing as we are with finding what we already know that is relevant. Picture it in this way.

3단계 고난도 문항 요리하기

3단계에서는 2단계에서 학습한 전략을 실제로 적용해 볼 수 있도록 실전 문항을 준비했습니다. 하루에 풀기 적당한 8문항으로 고난도 유형에 완벽 적응할 수 있습니다.

4단계 혼공 개념 마무리

★ 혼공 1일차에 나온 문장들을 해석해 보자.

1 The fact that information is conveyed in this high-tech manner somehow adds authority to what is conveyed, when in fact the Internet is a global conveyer of unfiltered, unedited, untreated information.

2 It would be difficult for a vision statement to provide direction to decision makers and energize employees toward achieving long-term strategic intent unless they know of the vision and observe management's

단어 ⁺ PLUS

1
· convey 전달하다
· authority 권위
· unfiltered 걸러지지 않은
· untreated 처리되지 않은

2
· decision maker 의사결정권자
· strategic 전략적인
· intent 의도
· commitment 헌신

4단계 혼공 개념 마무리

독해 공부를 하고 나면 늘 단어, 그리고 막혔던 문장을 복습하느라 시간이 많이 걸리는 점을 보완하기 위해 다시 공부해봐야 할 문장, 복습할 가치가 있는 표현이 들어간 부분을 선별해서 정리했습니다.

1단계 모의고사 1회

1. 다음 글의 제목으로 가장 적절한 것은?

When we lived as foragers with earthbound religions, animals were the first beings, world-shapers, and the teachers and ancestors of people. When we became agriculturalists and looked to the heavens for instruction about the seasons and bad weather, we saw animal forms among the stars. Of the forty-eight Ptolemaic constellations, all but a few are organic, and twenty-five are named for animals. Of the twenty-two more

2. (A), (B), (C)의 각 네모 안에서 어법에 맞는 표현으로 가장 적절한 것은?

Sometimes perfectionists find that they are troubled because (A) what / whatever they do it never seems good enough. If I ask, "For whom is it not good enough?" they do not always know the answer. After giving it some thought they usually conclude that it is not good enough for them and not good enough for other important people in their lives. This is a key point, because it

승부수 문항 모의고사

앞서 학습한 내용들을 최종적으로 확인할 수 있는 모의고사 부분으로 1일차당 10문제로 구성하였습니다. 어려운 문항들로만 구성되어 있는 모의고사 부분을 마치고 나면 한층 독해 실력이 업그레이드 될 것입니다.

혼공 01일차 대의 파악 문제

3단계 고난도 문항 요리하기　　p.17

●정답

1. ⑤　2. ⑤　3. ①　4. ①　5. ③　6. ①　7. ⑤　8. ③

1. ⑤

●전체 해석

인터넷에 있어서 위험한 점은, 그것이 기술이라는 분위기를 두르고 있어서 그것이 전혀 자격도 없으면서 즉각적인 신빙성을 지닌다는 것이다. 정보가 이런 첨단 기술 방식으로 전달된다는 사실이 웬일인지 전달되는 내용에 권위를 더해준다 할지라도, 사실 인터넷은 여과되지 않고, 편집되지 않고, 처리되지 않은 정보를 전 세계에 전하고 있다. 그것은 사람들을 더 빨리 더 똑똑하게 만들기 위한 우리가 가진 가장 좋은 도구에만 그치지 않는다. 그것은 또한 사람들을 더 빨리 더 멍청하게 만들기 위한 우리가 가진 가장 좋은 도구이기도 하다. 인터넷에 발표된 소문들은 오늘날

have access.

이것은 특히 사실이다 / 사람들 사이에 / 인터넷에 접속하지 않고 / 뉴스나 소문의 조각을 듣는 / 주변의 사람들로부터 / 접속하는

●해설

1. 다음 글의 요지로 가장 적절한 것은?

What's dangerous about the Internet is, because it has the au~ of technology around it, it has a totally undeserved insta~ credibility. The fact that information is conveyed in this high~ tech manner somehow adds authority to what is conveye~ when in fact the Internet is a global conveyer of unfilter~ unedited, untreated information. It is the greatest tool w~ have not only for making people smarter quicker, but al~ for making people dumber faster. Rumors published on t~ Internet now have a way of immediately becoming facts. T~ is particularly true among people who might not themselv~ have access to the Internet but hear a piece of news or gos~ from the people around them who do have access.

정답 및 해설

독해 문제를 풀 때 필요한 모든 설명을 친절하게 담아냈습니다. 단락을 나누어 문장을 분석하고, 놓치지 말아야 할 문법사항까지 정리해 놓아 독해 학습에 최적화 된 해설집이라고 할 수 있습니다.

5

혼공 유형독해 메뉴판
실력(매운맛)

독해 잘하는 법

영어 독해를 잘하는 법은 과연 있을까? 물론 당연히 존재하지. 영어를 비롯한 모든 언어는 쓰면 쓸수록 실력이 늘게 되어 있어. 그렇다면 영어는 어떻게 하면 독해력이 늘 수 있을까? 지금부터 알려주는 방법은 고등학교 때 뿐만 아니라 대학이나 사회에 나가서도 영어 독해를 늘릴 수 있는 최상의 방법이야.

Step 1

독해를 할 때 일단 모르는 문장구조나 해석이 안되는 문장에 무조건 줄을 쳐야 해. 나중에 해석을 보고 해야지라고 마음먹는다면, 그것은 영어 독해 공부를 하지 않겠다고 선언하는 것과 같아. 연필도 좋고, 펜도 좋아. 개인적으로는 형광펜을 추천하지. 일단 해석이 안 되면 밑줄을 치는 거야.

Most often, you will find or meet people who introduce themselves in terms of their work or by what they spend time on. These people introduce themselves as a salesman or an executive. There is nothing criminal in doing this, but psychologically, we become what we believe. Identifying what we can do in the workplace serves to enhance the quality of our professional career. People who follow this practice tend to lose their individuality and begin to live with the notion that they are recognized by the job they do. However, jobs may not be permanent, and you may lose your job for countless reasons, some of which you may not even be responsible for. In such a case, these people suffer from an inevitable social and mental trauma, leading to emotional stress and a feeling that all of a sudden they have been disassociated from what once was their identity.

Step 2

문제를 풀고 해설지를 보면서 전체 지문을 해석을 하겠지? 그러면 형광펜으로 밑줄 친 부분은 더욱 신경써서 봐야 해. 그리고 나서 할 일은 바로 그 문장들을 위한 노트를 만드는 것이지. 즉, 나만의 독해노트를 만드는 거야.

1. Identifying / what we can do in the workplace / serves to enhance / the quality of our professional career.
   확인하는 것은 / 우리가 직장에서 할 수 있는 것을 / 높이는 데 도움을 줘 / 우리의 전문적 일의 질을

   직장에서 우리가 할 수 있는 것을 확인하는 것은 우리가 하는 전문적 일의 질을 높이는 데 도움이 된다.

1. Identifying what we can do in the workplace serves to enhance the quality of our professional career.

2. these people / suffer from an inevitable social and mental trauma, / leading to emotional stress and a feeling / that all of a sudden / they have been disassociated / from what once was their identity.

이 사람들은 / 피할 수 없는 사회적 정신적 트라우마로부터 고통을 받아 / 이는 감정적 스트레스와 감정을 유발하지 / 갑작스럽게 / 그들이 단절되어 왔다는 / 한 때 그들의 정체성이었던 것으로부터

이러한 사람들은 피할 수 없는 사회적, 정신적 외상 때문에 고통을 받고 이것은 감정적 스트레스와 한때 그들의 정체성이었던 것과 자신들이 갑자기 단절되어 왔다는 느낌을 유발한다.

2. these people suffer from an inevitable social and mental trauma, leading to emotional stress and a feeling that all of a sudden they have been disassociated from what once was their identity.

노트는 스프링 노트를 추천해. 이게 보기가 편하거든. 화면에서 보는 것처럼 오른쪽에는 이해가 안되거나 해석이 안되는 영어 문장을 쓰는 거야. 그리고 왼쪽에는 우리말 해석을 쓰는 거지. 이때 해석을 쓸 때는 직독직해 하나와, 해설지에 있는 해석 둘 다를 쓰면 더 좋아.

Step 3

이제 남은 일은 자기 전이건, 주말이건, 이렇게 모아놓은 '나만의 독해노트'를 계속 보는 거지. 해석이 안 되면 체크 표시를 하고, 나중에 볼 때는 또 그 부분을 위주로 보는 거야. 그렇게 되면, 해석이 안 되는 부분을 자주 보게 되므로, 비슷한 구조의 문장을 다시 보게 될 때, 자연스럽게 해석이 되겠지. 나의 약점이 어느덧 강점이 되는 구조랄까?

Bonus!

어법 문제도 마찬가지 방법을 사용하면 좋아. 나만의 어법노트를 만드는 거지. 왼쪽에는 자신이 틀리거나 잘 모르는 어법 문제를, 오른쪽에는 정답과 해설을 적는 거지. 이런 식으로 차곡차곡 정리하다보면, 그 어떤 어법 문제집 보다 나에게 딱 맞는 '나만의 어법 노트'가 탄생하게 되겠지. 그러다 보면 어느덧 나는 어법의 신이 되어 있을 거야.

1. for whom
   뒤에 완전한 문장이 와서
   * 전치사+관계대명사 + 완전한 문장

1. I remember one of the smartest I.T. executives [whom / for whom] I ever worked strongly resisting the movement to measure programmer productivity that was popular at the time.

머리말

안녕하세요? 혼공지기 허준석, 김상근입니다. 2018 수능부터 영어는 절대평가로 치러집니다. 영어 과목의 경우 예전처럼 표준점수와 백분위가 성적표에 나오는 것이 아니라 등급만 기재된 다는 뜻이지요. 상대평가일 경우 수능 응시인원의 4%만이 1등급을 받았고, 11%만이 2등급을 받게 되는 구조여서 좋은 등급을 받기 위해서는 100점을 목표로 영어 공부를 해야 했습니다. 그런데 절대평가의 경우 90점만 넘기면 1등급이고, 80점만 넘기면 2등급을 받게 되니 내 점수와는 상관없이 남들과의 비교로 등급이 결정되었던 상대평가와 달리 내가 받은 점수로만 등급이 결정됩니다.

이처럼 절대평가는 순전히 자기 자신과의 싸움이라고 할 수 있지요. 자신이 원하는 대학을 가기 위해서 영어 과목은 다른 과목과는 달리 스스로 열심히만 한다면 충분히 좋은 결과를 얻을수 있습니다. 하지만, 여기서 문제가 한 가지 있습니다. 절대평가가 되면서 1, 2등급의 인원이 많게는 2배 정도 늘게 됩니다. 따라서 특히 서울권 대학들은 수시에서의 수능 최저기준을 올리거나, 정시에서 영어 1등급이 아니면 합격하게 어렵게 만들어놓고 있는 실정이지요.

영어 1등급. 위에서도 언급했듯이 90점을 넘겨야 받을 수 있는 등급입니다. 쉬운 문항은 최대한 많이 맞고, 어려운 문항에서 승부를 걸어야 한다는 뜻이지요. 특히나 어법, 어휘, 빈칸추론, 문장삽입, 순서배열, 장문독해처럼 3점으로 출제되는 문항을 3개 이상 틀리게 되면 1등급을 받기가 상당히 힘들어집니다. 어려운 문항이라고 할 수 있는 이 문항에서 최대한 많은 득점을 해야 합니다.

그래서 준석 샘과 상근 샘이 여러분을 위해서 유형독해 순한맛에 이어 어려운 문항에 대비할 수 있는 유형독해 실력(매운맛) 교재를 준비했습니다. 고3 학평과 평가원 출제 문항에서 오답률이 높았던 문항을 중심으로 어려운 문항을 충분히 연습하도록 구성하여 20일이면 한권의 어려운 독해 교재를 끝내도록 만들었습니다. 물론 문항 자체가 어려워서 혼자하기에는 어려울 수도 있기 때문에 해설집도 꼼꼼하게 하나하나 정성스레 집필했습니다. 그리고 공부하다가 궁금한 것이 있다면, 준석 샘의 혼공카페(http://cafe.naver.com/junteacherfan)나 상근 샘의 블로그(http://blog.naver.com/sangpia)에서 질문을 맘껏 해도 좋습니다.

승부수 문항을 중심으로 연습해서 꼭 영어 1등급을 맞을 수 있기를 바랍니다. 혼공!

2017년 서서히 추위가 몰려올 즈음

허준석, 김상근샘

혼공 Study Plan

	차시	내용	학습/복습	날짜	완료
01 일차		대의 파악 문제	학습날짜 (/)		완료 ☐
			복습날짜 (/)		완료 ☐
02 일차		어법 1(선택형)	학습날짜 (/)		완료 ☐
			복습날짜 (/)		완료 ☐
03 일차		어법 2(밑줄형)	학습날짜 (/)		완료 ☐
			복습날짜 (/)		완료 ☐
04 일차		어휘 1(선택형)	학습날짜 (/)		완료 ☐
			복습날짜 (/)		완료 ☐
05 일차		어휘 2(밑줄형)	학습날짜 (/)		완료 ☐
			복습날짜 (/)		완료 ☐
06 일차		주어진 문장 넣기	학습날짜 (/)		완료 ☐
			복습날짜 (/)		완료 ☐
07 일차		글의 순서	학습날짜 (/)		완료 ☐
			복습날짜 (/)		완료 ☐
08 일차		요약문 완성	학습날짜 (/)		완료 ☐
			복습날짜 (/)		완료 ☐
09 일차		장문독해(2문항형)	학습날짜 (/)		완료 ☐
			복습날짜 (/)		완료 ☐
10 일차		빈칸추론(단어)	학습날짜 (/)		완료 ☐
			복습날짜 (/)		완료 ☐
11 일차		빈칸추론(구/문장)	학습날짜 (/)		완료 ☐
			복습날짜 (/)		완료 ☐
12 일차		빈칸추론(앞부분)	학습날짜 (/)		완료 ☐
			복습날짜 (/)		완료 ☐
13 일차		빈칸추론(뒷부분)	학습날짜 (/)		완료 ☐
			복습날짜 (/)		완료 ☐
14 일차		승부수 문항 모의고사 1회	학습날짜 (/)		완료 ☐
			복습날짜 (/)		완료 ☐
15 일차		승부수 문항 모의고사 2회	학습날짜 (/)		완료 ☐
			복습날짜 (/)		완료 ☐
16 일차		승부수 문항 모의고사 3회	학습날짜 (/)		완료 ☐
			복습날짜 (/)		완료 ☐
17 일차		승부수 문항 모의고사 4회	학습날짜 (/)		완료 ☐
			복습날짜 (/)		완료 ☐
18 일차		승부수 문항 모의고사 5회	학습날짜 (/)		완료 ☐
			복습날짜 (/)		완료 ☐
19 일차		승부수 문항 모의고사 6회	학습날짜 (/)		완료 ☐
			복습날짜 (/)		완료 ☐
20 일차		승부수 문항 모의고사 7회	학습날짜 (/)		완료 ☐
			복습날짜 (/)		완료 ☐

A course

승부수 문항 |

혼공

01일차

대의 파악 문제

#생각보다_어려워지는_제목문제에_주의하라

난이도 🌶️🌶️🌶️

Accept challenges, so that you may feel the exhilaration of victory.
by George S. Patton

도전을 받아들여라. 그러면 승리의 쾌감을 맛볼 지도 모른다.

1 단계 개념 요리하기

01 문항 특징

- 🌶 비교적 쉬운 유형에 속한 문항이지만, 제목/주제 문제가 어려워지는 추세임
- 🌶 글의 요지의 경우 지문이 어려운 문항도 출제되지만, 선택지가 우리말이라서 정답률은 높은 편임
- 🌶 제목/주제 문제가 어려운 이유는 선택지가 영어로 제시되기 때문임
- 🌶 특히 제목의 경우 50%대의 정답률을 보이는 문제가 출제되기도 함
- 🌶 주제는 키워드가 선택지에 제시되나, 제목의 경우는 그렇지 않은 경우가 많음

02 혼공 전략

1 '예시 앞'에 주제문이 있는 경우가 많아.

주제문 ┄┄┄

Give children options and allow them to make their own decisions – on how much they would like to eat, whether they want to eat or not, and what they would like to have. For example, include them in the decision-making process of what you are thinking of making for dinner.

예시문

2 통념에 대한 반박하는 부분에 필자의 의도가 나타나지.

통념 ┄┄┄   반론 → 주제문일 가능성이 높아.

Many people seem to agree that exercise should be painful. But the truth of the matter is that this is a very dangerous idea.

3 역시 중요한 건 연결어지. 반론을 나타내는 however, 결론을 나타내는 therefore 같은 연결어가 결정적인 키(key)가 될 수 있어.

4 선택지를 선택할 때 범위 설정에 주의해야 해.

주제문

Communication means a sharing of information. People communicate with each other in many ways including words, letters and so on. Much communication is face-to-face and silent. People smile and laugh. They shake hands. They wave.

① **What Information Means** → 적절한 범위에 해당하지. 이것이 바로 정답!!
② How People Communicate → 너무 범위가 포괄적이야.
③ Why Words Are Important → 본문에 words라는 단어에 혹하면 안 돼.

다음 글의 제목으로 가장 적절한 것은?

2013년 수능 25번

The names of pitches are associated with particular frequency values. Our current system is called A440 because the note we call 'A' that is in the middle of the piano keyboard has been fixed to have a frequency of 440 Hz. This is entirely arbitrary. We could fix 'A' at any frequency, such as 439 or 424; different standards were used in the time of Mozart than today. Some people claim that the precise frequencies affect the overall sound of a musical piece and the sound of instruments. Led Zeppelin, a band popular in the 70s, often tuned their instruments away from the modern A440 standard to give their music an uncommon sound, and perhaps to link it with the European children's folk songs that inspired many of their compositions. Many purists insist on hearing baroque music on period instruments, both because the instruments have a different sound and because they are designed to play the music in its original tuning standard, something that purists deem important.

① Should 'A' Always Be Tuned at 440 Hz?
② Arbitrary Tuning: A New Trend in Music
③ How to Correctly Measure Frequency Values.
④ How Do Musicians Detect Pitch Differences?
⑤ Unstable Pitches: A Common Thread in Music

WORD

pitch 음 높이   **be associated with** ~과 연관이 있다   **frequency value** 진동수   **note** 음   **arbitrary** 자의적인, 임의의   **precise** 정밀한   **overall** 전반적인   **tune** 음을 맞추다   **uncommon** 흔하지 않은   **inspire** 영감을 주다   **composition** 작품, 작곡   **purist** 순수주의자   **period instrument** 시대 악기   **deem** 여기다   **unstable** 불안정한   **thread** 가닥, 맥락, 실

The names of pitches are associated with particular frequency values. Our current system is called A440 because the note we call 'A' that is in the middle of the piano keyboard has been fixed to have a frequency of 440 Hz. This is entirely arbitrary. We could fix 'A' at any frequency, such as 439 or 424; different standards were used in the time of Mozart than today. Some people claim that the precise frequencies affect the overall sound of a musical piece and the sound of instruments. Led Zeppelin, a band popular in the 70s, often tuned their instruments away from the modern A440 standard to give their music an uncommon sound, and perhaps to link it with the European children's folk songs that inspired many of their compositions. Many purists insist on hearing baroque music on period instruments, both because the instruments have a different sound and because they are designed to play the music in its original tuning standard, something that purists deem important.

This(진동수가 고정되어 있다는 사실)이 임의적이라는 이야기는 그러한 사실이 바뀔 수 있다는 뜻이야. 맨 처음 문장을 바로 반박하는 문장에 해당되지.

'정확한 진동수'를 A440으로 착각하면 안 돼. 여기서 말하는 '정확한 진동수'가 악곡과 악기의 소리에 영향을 준다는 거지. 즉 악곡과 악기에 따라 진동수가 다르다는 거야. 한마디로 상대적인 기준을 말하는 거지.

진동수의 절대성을 부정하는 예가 나오고 있어. Led Zeppelin은 A440이 아닌 다른 기준을 적용했고, 순수주의자들은 A440과는 다른 바로크 음악을 기준으로 삼아야 한다고 주장하고 있지.

A440의 절대성에 대한 의문을 표하고 있어. 정확하게 제목에 가깝다고 할 수 있지.

① Should 'A' Always Be Tuned at 440 Hz?
'A'가 늘 440 Hz에 맞춰져야 하는가?

본문에 나온 'Arbitrary'를 이용한 매력적인 오답이지. '절대성'을 부정하는 내용이기도 해. 하지만, 새로운 경향을 추구하지는 않아. 본문에 나온 예는 새로운 것이 아닌 절대성만 부정하는 예라는 걸 조심해야 해.

② Arbitrary Tuning: A New Trend in Music
자의적인 음 조율: 음악에서의 새로운 경향

③ How to Correctly Measure Frequency Values
진동수 값을 바르게 측정하는 방법

④ How Do Musicians Detect Pitch Differences?
음악가들은 어떻게 음 높이 차이를 찾아내는 가

⑤ Unstable Pitches: A Common Thread in Music
불안정한 음 높이: 음악에서의 공통된 맥락

Solution 첫 문장에 나오는 A440에 대한 절대성을 뒤에 나오는 문장들이 반박하고 있는 형태를 띄고 있지. A440은 절대적인 것이 아니고 시대에 따라, 악기에 따라, 악곡에 따라 달라진다는 거야. 뒤에 나오는 Led Zeppelin과 순수주의자들의 예에서 다시 한 번 이를 이야기 해주고 있어. 중간에 나오는 the precise frequencies의 의미를 'A440의 절대성'으로 혼동 하지 않으면 ① Should 'A' Always Be Tuned at 440Hz?를 정답으로 고를 수 있어.

해석 음 높이의 명칭은 특정한 진동값과 관련이 있다. 현재 체계는 A440이라고 불리는데, (그것은) 우리가 A라고 부르는, 피아노 건반의 가운데에 있는 음이 440 Hz의 진동수를 가지도록 고정이 되었기 때문이다. 이것은 전적으로 자의적이다. 가령 439나 424처럼 어떤 진동수에도 'A'를 고정할 수 있을 것이고, (실제로) 오늘날과는 다른 기준이 모차르트가 살았던 시대에 사용되었다. 어떤 이들은 정확한 진동수가 악곡의 전반적인 소리와 악기의 소리에 영향을 끼친다고 주장한다. 70년대의 인기 밴드였던 Led Zeppelin은 자신들의 음악에 흔하지 않은 소리를 입히고 아마도 그것(자신들의 음악)을 자신들의 많은 작품에 영감을 주었던 유럽의 민속 동요와 연관시키려고 현대 A440 표준에서 벗어나 악기의 음을 맞추었다. 많은 순수주의자들은 시대 악기로 바로크 음악을 들어야 한다고 주장하는데, (그것은) 그 악기가 다른 소리를 지니고 있기 때문이고 그 악기들이 원래의 조율 기준, 즉 순수주의자들이 중요하다고 여기는 것으로 음악을 연주하도록 설계되어 있기 때문이다.

1. 다음 글의 요지로 가장 적절한 것은?

2012년 수능 36번

What's dangerous about the Internet is, because it has the aura of technology around it, it has a totally undeserved instant credibility. The fact that information is conveyed in this high-tech manner somehow adds authority to what is conveyed, when in fact the Internet is a global conveyer of unfiltered, unedited, untreated information. It is the greatest tool we have not only for making people smarter quicker, but also for making people dumber faster. Rumors published on the Internet now have a way of immediately becoming facts. This is particularly true among people who might not themselves have access to the Internet but hear a piece of news or gossip from the people around them who do have access.

① 신속한 정보 보급을 위해 인터넷 접근성의 개선이 요구된다.

② 인터넷은 근거 없는 소문을 유포하여 사회 불안을 조장한다.

③ 인터넷은 다양한 정보를 빠르게 제공하는 훌륭한 도구이다.

④ 인터넷은 지적 능력의 향상과 저하를 동시에 가져온다.

⑤ 인터넷은 검증되지 않은 정보를 사실처럼 믿게 만든다.

2. 다음 글의 주제로 가장 적절한 것은?

2016년 6월 22번

When we hear a story, we look for beliefs that are being commented upon. Any story has many possible beliefs inherent in it. But how does someone listening to a story find those beliefs? We find them by looking through the beliefs we already have. We are not as concerned with what we are hearing as we are with finding what we already know that is relevant. Picture it in this way. As understanders, we have a list of beliefs, indexed by subject area. When a new story appears, we attempt to find a belief of ours that relates to it. When we do, we find a story attached to that belief and compare the story in our memory to the one we are processing. Our understanding of the new story becomes, at that point, a function of the old story. Once we find a belief and connected story, we need no further processing; that is, the search for other beliefs stops.

① the use of a new story in understanding an old story

② the limits of our memory capacity in recalling stories

③ the influence of new stories on challenging our beliefs

④ the most efficient strategy to improve storytelling skills

⑤ the role of our existing beliefs in comprehending a new story

3. 다음 글의 제목으로 가장 적절한 것은?

2016년 9월 23번

A strategic vision has little value to the organization unless it's effectively communicated down the line to lower-level managers and employees. It would be difficult for a vision statement to provide direction to decision makers and energize employees toward achieving long-term strategic intent unless they know of the vision and observe management's commitment to that vision. Communicating the vision to organization members nearly always means putting "where we are going and why" in writing, distributing the statement organizationwide, and having executives personally explain the vision and its justification to as many people as possible. Ideally, executives should present their vision for the company in a manner that reaches out and grabs people's attention. An engaging and convincing strategic vision has enormous motivational value – for the same reason that a stone mason is inspired by building a great cathedral for the ages.

* stone mason: 석공 ** cathedral: 대성당

① What Makes a Strategic Vision Successful?
② Why Is Creating a Vision Statement Difficult?
③ Building a Future: Innovative Leadership Training
④ Effective Decision-Making Processes in Organizations
⑤ Motivating Employees through Organizational Development

4. 다음 글의 주제로 가장 적절한 것은?

2012년 6월 33번

What everyday rules for behavior guide parents' efforts to socialize their toddlers and preschool-age children? To answer this question, Gralinski and Kopp observed and interviewed mothers and their children in these age groups. They found that for fifteen-month-olds, mothers' rules and requests centered on ensuring the children's safety and, to a lesser extent, protecting the families' possessions from harm; respecting basic social niceties ("Don't bite"; "No kicking"); and learning to delay getting what they wanted. As children's ages and cognitive sophistication increased, the numbers and kinds of prohibitions and requests expanded from the original focus on child protection and interpersonal issues to family routines, self-care, and other concerns regarding the child's independence. By the time children were three, a new quality of rule emerged: "Do not scream in a restaurant, run around naked in front of company, or pick your nose."

① changes in maternal rules according to children's age
② limitations of discipline for children's socialization
③ parents' concerns about children's independence
④ importance of parents' anger management skills
⑤ effects of thinking ability on children's socialization

WORD

strategic 전략적인 organization 조직 statement 성명, 진술 decision maker 의사결정자 intent 의도 observe 관찰하다 commitment 헌신 distribute 분배하다, 퍼뜨리다 organizationwide 조직 전체에 executive 간부 justification 정당성 attention 관심 engaging 마음을 잡는 convincing 설득력 있는 enormous 엄청난

WORD

socialize 사회화하다 observe 관찰하다 ensure 보장하다 extent 정도 protect 보호하다 possession 재산 nicety 세부 사항 bite 물다 cognitive 인지적인 sophistication 정교함 prohibition 금지 expand 확장하다 interpersonal 대인관계와 관련된 regarding ~에 관한 family routine 가족의 일상적인 일 emerge 나타나다 scream 소리치다 naked 벌거벗은

5. 다음 글의 제목으로 가장 적절한 것은?

2012년 수능 40번

In the early 1990s Norway introduced a carbon tax on emissions from energy, and it did seem to encourage environmental innovation. However, unexpected circumstances came when they tried to apply this approach globally. Agreeing on international taxes on emissions was notoriously hard, as we already know that the European Union has experienced terrible difficulties in trying to regularize the complex and myriad differences in its members' sales taxes. Besides, although Sweden, Finland, and Denmark barely decided to introduce carbon taxes during the 1990s, they have not harmonized their approaches with Norway or with each other. If such similar countries can't come to an agreement, there is little hope for doing so with the vastly more diverse countries in the rest of the world.

① Reduce Carbon Emission, Rescue Earth
② No Exit Out of Fatal Carbon Emissions
③ Global Carbon Tax: A Long Way to Go
④ Carbon Emissions: Not in My Backyard
⑤ Everlasting Conflict: Taxpayers vs. Collectors

6. 다음 글의 제목으로 가장 적절한 것은?

2015년 수능 23번

When we remark with surprise that someone "looks young" for his or her chronological age, we are observing that we all age biologically at different rates. Scientists have good evidence that this apparent difference is real. It is likely that age changes begin in different parts of the body at different times and that the rate of annual change varies among various cells, tissues, and organs, as well as from person to person. Unlike the passage of time, biological aging resists easy measurement. What we would like to have is one or a few measurable biological changes that mirror all other biological age changes without reference to the passage of time, so that we could say, for example, that someone who is chronologically eighty years old is biologically sixty years old. This kind of measurement would help explain why one eighty-year-old has so many more youthful qualities than does another eighty-year-old, who may be biologically eighty or even ninety years old.

① In Search of a Mirror Reflecting Biological Aging
② Reasons for Slow Aging in the Modern Era
③ A Few Tips to Guess Chronological Age
④ Secrets of Biological Aging Disclosed
⑤ Looking for the Fountain of Youth

WORD

emission 배출   encourage 장려하다   innovation 혁신   notoriously 악명 높게   regularize 합법화하다   myriad 무수한   barely 거의 ~ 하지 않다   harmonize 일치시키다   vastly 거대하게   diverse 다양한   everlasting 영원한

WORD

chronological age 생활 연령   biologically 생물학적으로   rate 속도, 비율   apparent 외관상의, 겉보기의   tissue 조직   organ 기관, 장기   mirror 반영하다   without reference to ~에 관계없이   quality 특징, 특성   Fountain of Youth 청춘의 샘

7. 다음 글의 제목으로 가장 적절한 것은?

2016년 6월 23번

Savannas pose a bit of a problem for ecologists. There is an axiom in ecology that 'complete competitors cannot coexist': in other words, where two populations of organisms use exactly the same resources, one would be expected to do so slightly more efficiently than the other and therefore come to dominate in the long term. In temperate parts of the world, either trees dominate (in forests) or grasses dominate (in grasslands). Yet, in savannas grasses and trees coexist. The classic explanation proposes that trees have deep roots while grasses have shallow roots. The two plant types are therefore able to coexist because they are not in fact competitors: the trees increase in wetter climates and on sandier soils because more water is able to penetrate to the deep roots. Trees do indeed have a few small roots which penetrate to great depth, but most of their roots are in the top half-metre of the soil, just where the grass roots are.

* axiom: 원리, 공리

① A War at Hand Between Plants in Savannas
② A Rivalry for Wetter Soils among Savanna Trees
③ Are Savannas a Hidden Treasure of Bio-Diversity?
④ Cyclic Dominance of Trees over Grasses in Savannas
⑤ Strange Companions: Savanna Plants Confuse Ecologists

8. 다음 글의 제목으로 가장 적절한 것은?

2012년 수능 38번

Scientists should be careful to reduce bias in their experiments. A bias occurs when what the scientist expects changes how the results are viewed. This expectation might cause a scientist to select a result from one trial over those from other trials. Scientists can lessen bias by running as many trials as possible and by keeping accurate notes of each observation made. Valid experiments also must have data that are measurable. This allows others to compare the results to data they obtain from a similar experiment. Most importantly, the experiment must be repeatable. Findings are supportable when other scientists perform the same experiment and get the same results.

① necessary conditions of repeatable experiments
② importance of identifying bias in scientific research
③ requirements for objective scientific experiments
④ guidelines for collecting measurable data in experiments
⑤ effective strategies for keeping accurate notes on data

WORD

pose 야기하다 ecologist 생태학자 ecology 생태계 coexist 공존하다 dominate 지배하다 temperate 온화한 shallow 얕은 explanation 설명 competitor 경쟁자 penetrate 침투하다 cyclic 순환하는 companion 동반자 confuse 혼동시키다

WORD

bias 선입견 expectation 예상, 기대 trial 시도 lessen 줄이다 accurate 정확한 observation 관찰 valid 유효한, 타당한 measurable 측정 가능한 compare 비교하다 supportable 지지될 수 있는

★ 혼공 1일차에 나온 문장들을 해석해 보자.

1 The fact that information is conveyed in this high-tech manner somehow adds authority to what is conveyed, when in fact the Internet is a global conveyer of unfiltered, unedited, untreated information.

1
+ **convey** 전달하다
+ **authority** 권위
+ **unfiltered** 걸러지지 않은
+ **untreated** 처리되지 않은

2 It would be difficult for a vision statement to provide direction to decision makers and energize employees toward achieving long-term strategic intent unless they know of the vision and observe management's commitment to that vision.

2
+ **decision maker**
  의사결정권자
+ **strategic** 전략적인
+ **intent** 의도
+ **commitment** 헌신

3 As children's ages and cognitive sophistication increased, the numbers and kinds of prohibitions and requests expanded from the original focus on child protection and interpersonal issues to family routines, self-care, and other concerns regarding the child's independence.

3
+ **cognitive** 인지적인
+ **sophistication** 정교함
+ **prohibition** 금지
+ **expand** 확장하다
+ **interpersonal** 대인관계의
+ **regarding** ～에 관한

4 It is likely that age changes begin in different parts of the body at different times and that the rate of annual change varies among various cells, tissues, and organs, as well as from person to person.

4
+ **annual** 연간의
+ **various** 다양한
+ **tissue** 조직

5 There is an axiom in ecology that 'complete competitors cannot coexist': in other words, where two populations of organisms use exactly the same resources, one would be expected to do so slightly more efficiently than the other and therefore come to dominate in the long term.

5
+ **axiom** 격언, 공리
+ **complete** 완전한
+ **competitor** 경쟁자
+ **coexist** 공존하다

6 What we would like to have is one or a few measurable biological changes that mirror all other biological age changes without reference to the passage of time, so that we could say, for example, that someone who is chronologically eighty years old is biologically sixty years old.

6
+ **measurable** 측정 가능한
+ **biological** 생물학적인
+ **without reference to**
  ～에 관계없이

독서 잘하는 비법 #1

샘은 학창 시절에 독서가 참 어려웠어. 진득하게 책을 읽는 모습을 그리고 또 그렸지만 내 집중력은 10분을 넘기기가 힘들었어. 샘 시절에도 그랬는데, 요즘같이 재미있는 볼거리가 휴대폰에 넘쳐나는 너희들은 얼마나 독서가 힘들까?

그래서 샘과 친한 파워 블로거 중에 독서 관련 전문가 분에게 독서 잘하는 비법을 좀 달라고 졸랐어. 몇 차례에 걸쳐 내용을 알려주도록 할게. 그나저나 자료를 주다니 우리 친하긴 친한가봐. 하하.

〈조급함을 버리자〉

'책을 빨리 읽고 싶어요~'

'책을 많이 볼 수 있는 방법이 없을까요?'

강연을 나가면 위와 같은 질문을 자주 받는다.

책을 빨리 읽고 싶어 하는 분들이 많다.

권 수에만 집착하는 사람 또한 많다.

책에 담긴 의미를 깊이 있게 생각하지 않고

제대로 곱씹지 않으니 변화가 있겠는가...

페이지 넘기기에만 급급해 하지 말자.

권 수에만 집착하지 말자.

책을 많이 읽는 것보다

책을 빨리 읽는 것보다

한 권의 책이라도 제대로 읽고

중요한 내용을 한 가지라도 기록하고 기록한 것을 자신의 삶에

적용해 보는 것이 그 무엇보다 중요하다.

실천 없는 독서를 통해 성공한 사람을 본 적이 있는가?

난 아직까지 단 한 명도 만나지 못했다.

〈세상은 넓고 읽을 책은 많다. 완독의 부담감을 버리자!〉

독서 노하우 – 세상은 넓고 읽을 책은 많다.

완독의 부담감을 버리자!

혼공

02일차

어법 1 (선택형)

#어법문제를_포기하지_마라 #1등급을_좌우한다

난이도 🌶️🌶️🌶️

The most wasted of all days is one without laughter.
by E. E. Cummings

인생에서 가장 의미 없이 보낸 날은 웃지 않고 보낸 날이다.

개념 요리하기

01 문항 특징

- 🌶 어법상 맞는 것 혹은 틀린 부분을 고르는 문항(2017학년도 기준 1문항 출제)
- 🌶 둘 중 하나를 고르는 문항이나 밑줄 친 부분 중 틀린 부분을 고르는 문항으로 출제 됨
- 🌶 2012년 이후 밑줄 어법만 수능에서 출제되고 있음
- 🌶 긴주어 문장의 동사의 수 일치, 본동사 vs 준동사, ing vs ed, 형용사 vs 부사, what vs that, 관계
  부사 vs 관계대명사 등의 문제가 단골로 출제 됨
- 🌶 기출 문항 분석으로 자주 나오는 유형 위주로 공부하는 것이 효과적임

02 혼공 전략

1 긴 주어 + 동사 유형: 수 일치, 동사의 유형(본동사 vs 준동사)
   → 웬만하면 맨 앞이 주어

주어	수식어구(관계사, 전치사구, 동격절, to부정사, 분사, 삽입절)	동사

주어와 수 일치(단수 주어–단수 동사, 복수 주어–복수 동사)와 동사 자리에 to부정사나 –ing형의 준동사가 오지 않으니 주의하자.

2 능동태 vs 수동태(ing vs ed): 주어와 동사의 관계 파악, 동사의 종류 파악
❶ 동사의 종류 파악: 자동사 vs 타동사
❷ 타동사일 경우 목적어 유무 판단
❸ 4/5형식 동사일 경우 해석 필수

동사의 종류파악
- 타동사(을/를)
  - 목적어 O
    - 4형식
      - '주다' → 능
      - '받다' → 수
    - 3형식 → 능
  - 목적어 X → 수
- 자동사 → 능

3 형용사 vs 부사: 수식 받는 녀석으로 판단 (명사 수식-형용사 / 나머지 수식-부사)

형용사
① 명사/대명사 수식
② 2형식 동사 뒤
  be, seem, appear,
  look, sound, feel
③ 5형식 동사의 O.C.
  make, keep, find, ← '~하게'로 해석
  consider, leave

2형식 동사
be동사, appear, seem
[감각동사] look, sound, feel
[~이 되다] become, grow,
get, turn

+ 형용사
주격 보어

(A), (B), (C)의 각 네모 안에서 어법에 맞는 표현으로 가장 적절한 것은?

2012학년도 수능 20번

On January 10, 1992, a ship (A) traveled / traveling through rough seas lost 12 cargo containers, one of which held 28,800 floating bath toys. Brightly colored ducks, frogs, and turtles were set adrift in the middle of the Pacific Ocean. After seven months, the first toys made landfall on beaches near Sitka, Alaska, 3,540 kilometers from (B) what / where they were lost. Other toys floated north and west along the Alaskan coast and across the Bering Sea. Some toy animals stayed at sea (C) even / very longer. They floated completely along the North Pacific currents, ending up back in Sitka.

	(A)		(B)		(C)
①	traveled	‥‥‥	what	‥‥‥	even
②	traveled	‥‥‥	what	‥‥‥	very
③	traveling	‥‥‥	what	‥‥‥	even
④	traveling	‥‥‥	where	‥‥‥	even
⑤	traveling	‥‥‥	where	‥‥‥	very

WORD

cargo 화물   **adrift** 표류하는   **landfall** 육지 도착   **completely** 완전히   **current** 해류   **float** 떠다니다

On January 10, 1992, a ship (A) [traveled / traveling] through rough seas lost 12 cargo containers, one of which held 28,800 floating bath toys. Brightly colored ducks, frogs, and turtles were set adrift in the middle of the Pacific Ocean. After seven months, the first toys made landfall on beaches near Sitka, Alaska, 3,540 kilometers from (B) [what / where] they were lost. Other toys floated north and west along the Alaskan coast and across the Bering Sea. Some toy animals stayed at sea (C) [even / very] longer. They floated completely along the North Pacific currents, ending up back in Sitka.

Solution 뒤에 lost라는 문장의 본동사가 나와. 따라서 주어진 자리는 주어인 a ship을 수식하는 분사라는 거지. 그렇다면 능동 vs 수동 개념으로 가야하는데, ship과 travel(항해하다)의 관계는 능동 관계가 성립되지. 따라서 능동을 의미하는 현재분사 traveling이 정답이야.

Solution what 뒤에는 불완전한 문장, where 뒤에는 완전한 문장이 와야 하지, 뒤에 오는 they were lost는 완전한 문장이므로 where이 정답이야. 참고로 where은 여기서 '~인 곳'을 의미해.

Solution 비교급을 강조하는 것을 물어보고 있어. 어렵지 않게 정답을 선택할 수 있겠지? 바로 정답은 even이야. 참고로 비교급을 강조하는 것은 even, far, even, still, a lot, a little이 있어.

해석 1992년 1월 10일, 거친 바다를 항해하던 배 한 척이 12개의 화물 컨테이너를 잃었는데, 그 중 하나는 28,800개의 물에 뜨는 욕실 장난감을 담고 있었다. 밝은 색의 오리, 개구리, 그리고 거북이 모양의 장난감들은 태평양 한가운데에 표류하게 되었다. 7개월 후에 잃어버린 장소에서 3,540킬로미터 떨어진 알래스카의 Sitka 근처 해변 육지에 첫 번째 장난감들이 도달했다. 다른 장난감들은 알래스카 해안을 따라 그리고 베링 해를 가로질러 북쪽과 서쪽으로 떠다녔다. 어떤 장난감들은 바다에 훨씬 더 오래 있었다. 그것들은 완전히 북태평양 해류를 따라 떠다녔고, 결국에는 Sitka로 되돌아갔다.

고난도 문항 요리하기

1. (A), (B), (C)의 각 네모 안에서 어법에 맞는 표현으로 가장 적절한 것은? 2012학년도 6월 20번

When induced to give spoken or written witness to something they doubt, people will often feel bad about their deceit. Nevertheless, they begin to believe (A) what / that they are saying. When there is no compelling external explanation for one's words, saying becomes believing. Tory Higgins and his colleagues had university students read a personality description of someone and then (B) summarize / summarized it for someone else who was believed either to like or to dislike this person. The students wrote a more positive description when the recipient liked the person. Having said positive things, they also then liked the person more themselves. (C) Asked / Asking to recall what they had read, they remembered the description as being more positive than it was. In short, it seems that we are prone to adjust our messages to our listeners, and, having done so, to believe the altered message.

	(A)		(B)		(C)
①	what	·····	summarize	·····	Asked
②	what	·····	summarize	·····	Asking
③	what	·····	summarized	·····	Asked
④	that	·····	summarized	·····	Asking
⑤	that	·····	summarized	·····	Asked

2. (A), (B), (C)의 각 네모 안에서 어법에 맞는 표현으로 가장 적절한 것은? 2013학년도 수능 20번

In many countries, amongst younger people, the habit of reading newspapers has been on the decline and some of the dollars previously (A) spent / were spent on newspaper advertising have migrated to the Internet. Of course some of this decline in newspaper reading has been due to the fact that we are doing more of our newspaper reading online. We can read the news of the day, or the latest on business, entertainment or (B) however / whatever news on the websites of the *New York Times*, the *Guardian* or almost any other major newspaper in the world. Increasingly, we can access these stories wirelessly by mobile devices as well as our computers. Advertising dollars have simply been (C) followed / following the migration trail across to these new technologies.

	(A)		(B)		(C)
①	spent	·····	however	·····	followed
②	spent	·····	whatever	·····	following
③	were spent	·····	however	·····	following
④	were spent	·····	whatever	·····	followed
⑤	were spent	·····	whatever	·····	following

WORD

induce 유도하다   deceit 사기, 속임수   compelling 강력한, 설득력 있는   summarize 요약하다   recipient 수령자   be prone to부정사 ~하는 경향이 있다   alter 바꾸다

WORD

decline 감소, 감소하다   previously 이전에   increasingly 점차   wirelessly 무선으로   device 기기   migration 이동   trail 경로

3. (A), (B), (C)의 각 네모 안에서 어법에 맞는 표현으로 가장 적절한 것은?
2012학년도 9월 20번

You have to pay close attention to someone's normal pattern in order to notice a deviation from it when he or she lies. Sometimes the variation is as (A) subtle / subtly as a pause. Other times it is obvious and abrupt. I recently saw a news interview with an acquaintance (B) who / whom I was certain was going to lie about a few particularly sensitive issues, and lie she did. During most of her interview she was calm and direct, but when she started lying, her manner changed dramatically: she threw her head back, laughed in 'disbelief,' and shook her head back and forth. It is true that the questions (C) dealt / dealing with very personal issues, but I have found that in general, no matter how touchy the question, if a person is telling the truth his or her manner will not change significantly or abruptly.

	(A)	(B)	(C)
①	subtle	who	dealt
②	subtle	who	dealing
③	subtle	whom	dealt
④	subtly	who	dealt
⑤	subtly	whom	dealing

4. (A), (B), (C)의 각 네모 안에서 어법에 맞는 표현으로 가장 적절한 것은?
2011학년도 6월 21번

There is an old Japanese legend about a man renowned for his flawless manners visiting a remote village. Wanting to honor as well as observe him, the villagers prepared a banquet. As they sat to eat, all eyes were on their noble guest. Everyone looked at (A) what / how the man held his chopsticks, so that they could imitate him. But then, by an unfortunate accident, as the mannered man raised a slippery slice of tofu to his lips, he (B) placed / was placed the tiniest bit of excess pressure on his chopsticks, propelling his tofu through the air and onto his neighbor's lap. After a brief moment of surprise, in order to preserve the myth of their guest's perfection and keep (C) him / himself from any embarrassment, all the villagers at the banquet began to fling tofu into each other's laps.

	(A)	(B)	(C)
①	what	placed	him
②	what	was placed	himself
③	how	placed	him
④	how	placed	himself
⑤	how	was placed	himself

deviation 벗어남, 탈선 **subtle** 미묘한, 포착하기 힘든 **pause** 중단, 한숨 돌림 **acquaintance** 아는 사람 **dramatically** 극적으로 **disbelief** 불신감 **touchy** 까다로운 **abruptly** 갑자기

legend 전설 **renowned** 유명한 **flawless** 흠잡을 데 없는, 완벽한 **observe** 관찰하다 **banquet** 연회, 축하연 **slippery** 미끄러운 **tofu** 두부 **propel** 나아가게 하다, 움직이게 하다 **preserve** 지키다, 유지하다 **embarrassment** 당황 **fling** 내던지다 **lap** 무릎

5. (A), (B), (C)의 각 네모 안에서 어법에 맞는 표현으로 가장 적절한 것은?

2015학년도 9월 28번

The term *objectivity* is important in measurement because of the scientific demand that observations be subject to public verification. A measurement system is objective to the extent that two observers (A) evaluate / evaluating the same performance arrive at the same (or very similar) measurements. For example, using a tape measure to determine the distance a javelin (B) threw / was thrown yields very similar results regardless of who reads the tape. By comparison, evaluation of performances such as diving, gymnastics, and figure skating is more subjective – although elaborate scoring rules help make (C) it / them more objective. From the point of view of research in motor behavior, it is important to use performances in the laboratory for which the scoring can be as objective as possible.

*javelin: 투창

	(A)	(B)	(C)
①	evaluate	threw	it
②	evaluate	threw	them
③	evaluating	threw	it
④	evaluating	was thrown	them
⑤	evaluating	was thrown	it

term 용어 objectivity 객관성 be subject to ~을 받아야 하다, ~을 필요로 하다 verification 검증 objective 객관적인 tape measure 줄자 yield 산출하다, 생산하다 regardless of ~에 상관없이 gymnastics 체조, 체육 elaborate 정교한 motor behavior 운동, 행동 laboratory 실험실

6. (A), (B), (C)의 각 네모 안에서 어법에 맞는 표현으로 가장 적절한 것은?

2014학년도 9월 27번

It had long been something of a mystery where, and on what, the northern fur seals of the eastern Pacific feed during the winter, (A) when / which they spend off the coast of North America from California to Alaska. There is no evidence that they are feeding to any great extent on sardines, mackerel, or other commercially important fishes. Presumably four million seals could not compete with commercial fishermen for the same species without the fact (B) being / is known. But there is some evidence on the diet of the fur seals, and it is highly significant. Their stomachs have yielded the bones of a species of fish that has never been seen alive. Indeed, not even its remains (C) has / have been found anywhere except in the stomachs of seals. Ichthyologists say that this 'seal fish' belongs to a group that typically inhabits very deep water, off the edge of the continental shelf.

* ichthyologist: 어류학자

	(A)	(B)	(C)
①	when	is	have
②	when	being	have
③	which	being	have
④	which	being	has
⑤	which	is	has

to any great extent 얼마큼이나 많이 sardine 정어리 mackerel 고등어 presumably 추측컨대 compete 경쟁하다 significant 의미심장한, 중대한 yield 산출하다 remains 잔존물, 잔해, 유적 inhabit ~에 살다, 서식하다 continental shelf 대륙붕

7. (A), (B), (C)의 각 네모 안에서 어법에 맞는 표현으로 가장 적절한 것은?
2013학년도 9월 20번

Remember what it was like to report on a daily deadline for the first time? Or to interview a city official for the first time? Or to begin to maneuver a desktop publishing program? We know that the journalism program at our college was a source of (A) many / much of these firsts for you. We're still providing these important first experiences to budding young writers and editors. And we're hoping you'll be willing to help these students make it through the program. As you know, the costs of providing first-rate education just keep going up. We've done everything we can (B) contain / to contain costs without compromising quality. One of those things is to set up a scholarship fund for students with special financial needs. We hope you would consider contributing generously to our fund. You'll get a great feeling (C) known / knowing you're helping support the formation of future leaders in the profession.

	(A)	(B)	(C)
①	many	contain	known
②	many	contain	knowing
③	many	to contain	knowing
④	many	contain	knowing
⑤	many	to contain	known

8. (A), (B), (C)의 각 네모 안에서 어법에 맞는 표현으로 가장 적절한 것은?
2017학년도 9월 28번

Like life in traditional society, but unlike other team sports, baseball is not governed by the clock. A football game is comprised of exactly sixty minutes of play, a basketball game forty or forty-eight minutes, but baseball has no set length of time within which the game must be completed. The pace of the game is therefore leisurely and (A) unhurried / unhurriedly , like the world before the discipline of measured time, deadlines, schedules, and wages paid by the hour. Baseball belongs to the kind of world (B) which / in which people did not say, "I haven't got all day." Baseball games do have all day to be played. But that does not mean that they can go on forever. Baseball, like traditional life, proceeds according to the rhythm of nature, specifically the rotation of the Earth. During its first half century, games were not played at night, which meant that baseball games, like the traditional work day, (C) ending / ended when the sun set.

	(A)	(B)	(C)
①	unhurried	in which	ended
②	unhurried	which	ending
③	unhurriedly	which	ended
④	unhurriedly	which	ending
⑤	unhurriedly	in which	ended

WORD

maneuver 기동시키다, 교묘히 다루다   desktop publishing program 컴퓨터 출판 프로그램   budding 신진의, 싹이 트는   contain 억제하다   compromise 훼손하다, 타협하다   generously 후하게

WORD

govern 좌우하다, 지배하다   leisurely 여유로운   unhurried 느긋한, 서두르지 않는   discipline 규율   measured 정확히 잰   belong to ~에 속하다   proceed 진행하다   rotation 자전, 회전

4 단계 혼공 개념 마무리

★ 혼공 2일차에 나온 문장들을 해석해 보자.

1 Asked to recall what they had read, they remembered the description as being more positive than it was.

1
+ **recall** 기억하다
+ **description** 설명, 묘사

2 I recently saw a news interview with an acquaintance who I was certain was going to lie about a few particularly sensitive issues, and lie she did.

2
+ **acquaintance** 아는 사람
+ **particularly** 상당히
+ **sensitive** 예민한

3 It is true that the questions dealt with very personal issues, but I have found that in general, no matter how touchy the question, if a person is telling the truth his or her manner will not change significantly or abruptly.

3
+ **in general** 일반적으로
+ **touchy** 예민한
+ **abruptly** 갑자기

4 But then, by an unfortunate accident, as the mannered man raised a slippery slice of tofu to his lips, he placed the tiniest bit of excess pressure on his chopsticks, propelling his tofu through the air and onto his neighbor's lap.

4
+ **slippery** 미끄러운
+ **tofu** 두부
+ **excess** 초과된
+ **pressure** 압력
+ **propel** 나아가게 하다

5 It had long been something of a mystery where, and on what, the northern fur seals of the eastern Pacific feed during the winter, which they spend off the coast of North America from California to Alaska.

5
+ **seal** 물개
+ **feed** 먹이를 먹다

6 A football game is comprised of exactly sixty minutes of play, a basketball game forty or forty-eight minutes, but baseball has no set length of time within which the game must be completed.

6
+ **be comprised of** ～으로 구성되다
+ **be completed** 끝나다

7 During its first half century, games were not played at night, which meant that baseball games, like the traditional work day, ended when the sun set

7
+ **traditional** 전통적인
+ **the sun sets** 해가 지다

독서 잘하는 비법 #2

「비법 1」에 이어서 파워 블로거 '유근용' 샘의 글을 옮겨왔어.

〈세상은 넓고 읽을 책은 많다〉

군대에서 책을 꾸준히 읽다 보니 선, 후임병들에게 책에 대한 질문들을 많이 받았다. 그중에서 공통된 질문 중 하나는 '책을 처음부터 끝까지 다 읽어야 하는가'에 대한 것이었다. 주변에 '책 한 권을 다 읽지 않고 다른 책을 읽으면 두 권 다 제대로 읽은 것 같지 않다' 이 책, 저 책 옮겨 읽다 보면 내용이 제대로 기억나지 않아서 다시 처음부터 읽게 된다'는 고민을 털어놓는 사람도 꽤 많았다. 나 역시 군대에서 처음 책을 읽었을 때는 '책은 무조건 한 권 한 권 완독해야 해'라는 생각에 빠져있었다. 책을 읽을 때만큼은 완벽주의자가 되어야 한다는 생각이 강했던 것이다. 활자 중독증 환자처럼 책의 모든 글자를 읽어야 직성이 풀렸다. 하지만 어느 순간 이런 생각이 들었다.

'내가 읽는 방식이 과연 옳은 방식일까?'

'완벽하게 읽는다는 것은 어떤 의미일까?'

'이런 식으로 책을 읽는다면 평생 몇 권이나 읽을 수 있을까?'

책마다 중요한 부분과 집중해서 읽어야 할 부분은 따로 있고 모든 페이지가 무조건 유익한 것은 아니라는 걸 오랜 시간이 지난 뒤에야 깨닫게 되었다. 서점을 가보면 하루에도 수십, 수백 종류의 책이 쏟아져 나오고 있다. 읽어야 할 책들은 산더미처럼 쌓이고 있고 평생 책만 읽고 산다 해도 우리가 읽을 수 있는 책은 극히 제한적일 수밖에 없다. 때문에 자신에게 정말 필요한 부분을 골라 읽을 수 있다면 책을 좀 더 빠르고 재미있게 읽을 수 있을 것이다.

나는 두 가지 방법을 제안하고 싶다.

첫 번째는 목차를 먼저 살피는 것이다. 가장 먼저 목차를 살펴보고 가장 끌리는 제목을 체크 한 후에 먼저 읽는다. 내가 관심 있는 부분이라 몰입도와 집중력이 향상된다. 그런 후에 나머지 부분을 읽고 나에게 맞지 않거나 굳이 알 필요가 없는 내용은 넘어가도 좋다. 내가 알고자 하는 것, 느끼고자 하는 것을 받아들이기에도 시간은 부족하기 때문이다.

두 번째는 완독에 대한 부담감과 의무감을 떨쳐버리는 것이다. 내용도 잘 모르겠고, 재미도 없고, 감동도 없는 책을 읽어야 하는 것보다 더한 고역은 없다. 나는 하루에 한 권 이상 책을 읽기로 다짐하면서 무조건 완독을 목표로 했었다. 목표였기 때문에 그걸 지키려고 애썼다. 하지만 어느 순간 완독에 대한 부담감과 의무감을 완전히 내려놓았다. 꼼꼼히 읽는 책도 읽지만 목차를 보고 필요한 부분만 찾아서 읽는 독서도 함께 하고 있다.

군대에서나 사회에서는 책 읽을 시간이 절대적으로 부족할 수밖에 없다. 독서 초보일수록, 책 읽는 요령이 없는 사람일수록 책 한 권을 완독해야 한다는 부담감이 클 것이다. 지금부터라도 마음의 부담을 조금만 내려놓자. 물론 독서 습관을 제대로 잡기까지는 어렵지 않은 책들을 읽으며 완독을 하는 것이 좋다. 책 근육을 만들어야 하기 때문이다. 하지만 어느 정도 책 읽기에 익숙해졌다면 자신에게 꼭 필요한 부분을 찾아 읽고, 그것을 흡수해서 자기화 시키려는 노력을 해 나가보자. 한 권의 책에서 나를 일깨우고 피와 살이 되는 단 하나의 문장을 얻었다면 그것만으로도 충분하니 말이다.

03일차

어법 2 (밑줄형)

#어법은_1문제 #밑줄형이_대세

난이도 🌶🌶🌶

If we take care of the moments, the years will take care of themselves.
by Maria Edgeworth

순간들을 소중히 여기다 보면, 긴 세월은 저절로 흘러간다.

01 문항 특징

🌶 어법 문제는 1등급을 결정하는 문항으로 주로 고난도 3점 문항으로 출제되고 있음

🌶 단순한 어법적 지식을 묻는 문항도 출제가 되지만, 대체로 독해를 위한 어법 문제 출제가 증가하고 있음

🌶 2013~2017학년도 수능 평균 정답률 52%를 보여주고 있음

🌶 5년간 출제 어법 포인트

2013	주어 동사 일치, other, 관계사, 동명사 주어, 형용사 보어, 분사 vs 동사, 복합관계형용사 vs 복합관계부사, ing vs ed
2014	관계사 that, 본동사, to부정사의 부사적 용법, 동사 수식 부사, 명사 수식-ed
2015	본동사, 형용사, 관계부사 where, 주어-동사 수 일치
2016	소유격대명사, 명사 수식-ed, 부사, 본동사, 접속사 that
2017	those, 형용사, 과거분사-ed, what, 주어-동사 수 일치

02 혼공 전략

1 what vs that

❶ 명사 + [what / that]: 선행사가 존재하므로 that

❷ [what / that] + 문장 → 완전한 문장이면 that / 불완전한 문장이면 what

2 which vs where (관계대명사 vs 관계부사)

뒤에 오는 문장이 완전한 문장이면 관계부사 where, 불완전한 문장이면 which

3 단수 취급 주어

❶ 동명사, to부정사, what절, that절, whether절, 의문사절

❷ 추상명사: information, beauty, importance, evidence, advice, knowledge, news, work

❸ 과목, 병명, 나라명 : economics, economics, electronics, ethics, literature, mathematics, mumps (볼거리), the Unite States, The United Nations

❹ 시간, 거리, 중량, 가격

❺ every, each, much, little

문항 맛보기

다음 글의 밑줄 친 부분 중, 어법상 틀린 것은?

   We take it for granted that film directors are in the game of recycling. Adapting novels ① is one of the most respectable of movie projects, while a book that calls itself the novelization of a film is considered barbarous. Being a hybrid art as well as a late one, film has always been in a dialogue with ② other narrative genres. Movies were first seen as an exceptionally potent kind of illusionist theatre, the rectangle of the screen corresponding to the proscenium of a stage, ③ which appear actors. Starting in the early silent period, plays were regularly "turned into" films. But ④ filming plays did not encourage the evolution of what truly was distinctive about a movie: the intervention of the camera – its mobility of vision. As a source of plot, character, and dialogue, the novel seemed more ⑤ suitable. Many early successes of cinema were adaptations of popular novels.

*proscenium: 앞 무대

WORD

take A for granted A를 당연히 여기다   **adapt** 각색하다   **barbarous** 상스러운   **petent** (영향력이) 강한   **distinctive** 독특한   **adaptation** 각색

We take it for granted that film directors are in the game of recycling. Adapting novels ① is one of the most respectable of movie projects, while a book that calls itself the novelization of a film is considered barbarous. Being a hybrid art as well as a late one, film has always been in a dialogue with ② other narrative genres. Movies were first seen as an exceptionally potent kind of illusionist theatre, the rectangle of the screen corresponding to the proscenium of a stage, ③ which appear actors. Starting in the early silent period, plays were regularly "turned into" films. But ④ filming plays did not encourage the evolution of what truly was distinctive about a movie: the intervention of the camera – its mobility of vision. As a source of plot, character, and dialogue, the novel seemed more ⑤ suitable. Many early successes of cinema were adaptations of popular novels.

Solution 문장의 주어는 동사 앞에 있는 novels가 아닌 동명사 Adapting이야. 동명사 주어는 무조건 단수 취급하지. 따라서 단수 동사 is는 OK.

Solution other은 뒤에 복수 명사가 오고, 혼자서는 쓰일 수 없어. 뒤에는 narrative genres라는 복수 명사가 왔으니 OK.

Solution 얼핏 보면 appear의 주어가 없어서 불완전한 문장이니까 which가 맞는 것처럼 보여. 그런데 자세히 보면 appear은 '~에 나타나다'를 나타내는 자동사야. 뒤에 목적어가 나오면 안 되지. 따라서 actors는 목적어가 아닌 주어인거야. 한마디로 주어와 동사가 도치된 문장이라는 거지. actors appear이 원래 문장이야. 완전한 문장이 왔으니 which는 틀려. 내용상 '배우가 앞 무대로 출연하다'가 되어야 하니 on which가 되어야겠지.

Solution seem이라는 자동사 뒤에 보어로 형용사인 suitable이 왔으니 OK.

Solution 뒤에 나오는 did not encourage의 주어 역할을 하는 동명사가 나왔고, 내용상 '영화화 하는 것'이 되므로 OK.

해석 우리는 영화 감독들이 재활용 게임을 하고 있다는 것을 당연시 한다. 소설을 각색하는 것은 가장 훌륭한 영화 프로젝트들 중에서 하나인 반면, 영화를 소설화했다고 하는 책은 당연히 상스럽게 보인다. 후발 예술이면서 동시에 혼합 예술이기도 한 영화는 다른 서사 장르와 항상 대화를 해왔다. 직사각형 모양의 화면이 배우가 출연하는 앞무대와 유사하게 보이면서, 초기에 영화는 특별히 유력한 일종의 마술 공연장으로 보였다. 초창기 무성 영화기를 시발점으로 연극은 자주 영화로 '전환'되었다. 하지만 연극을 영화화하는 것은 영화의 진정한 독특함, 즉 카메라의 개입, 다시 말해 그것의 시각적 기동성의 발전을 조장하지 못했다. 줄거리, 등장인물, 대화의 공급원으로서 소설이 (연극보다 영화에) 더 적합해 보였다. 영화의 초기 성공작의 다수가 유명 소설의 각색물이었다.

3단계 고난도 문항 요리하기

1. 다음 글의 밑줄 친 부분 중, 어법상 틀린 것은?

2015학년도 6월 27번

In the twentieth century, advances in technology, from refrigeration to sophisticated ovens to air transportation ① that carries fresh ingredients around the world, contributed immeasurably to baking and pastry making. At the beginning of the twenty-first century, the popularity of fine breads and pastries ② are growing even faster than new chefs can be trained. Interestingly enough, many of the technological advances in bread making have sparked a reaction among bakers and consumers ③ alike. They are looking to reclaim some of the flavors of old-fashioned breads that ④ were lost as baking became more industrialized and baked goods became more refined, standardized, and – some would say – flavorless. Bakers are researching methods for ⑤ producing the handmade sourdough breads of the past, and they are experimenting with specialty flours in their search for flavor.

2. 다음 글의 밑줄 친 부분 중, 어법상 틀린 것은?

2014학년도 6월 27번

Given that music appears to enhance physical and mental skills, are there circumstances where music is ① damaging to performance? One domain ② which this is of considerable significance is music's potentially damaging effects on the ability to drive safely. Evidence suggests an association between loud, fast music and reckless driving, but how might music's ability to influence driving in this way ③ be explained? One possibility is that drivers adjust to temporal regularities in music, and ④ that their speed is influenced accordingly. In other words, just as faster music causes people to eat faster, ⑤ so it causes people to drive at faster speeds, as they engage mentally and physically with ongoing repeated structures in the music.

WORD

refrigeration 냉장   sophisticated 고성능의, 정교한   transportation 수송   ingredient 재료   immeasurably 헤아릴 수 없을 정도로   spark 촉발하다, 유발하다   look to do ~하기를 원하다   reclaim 되찾다, 환원하다   refined 세련된, 정제된   standardized 표준화된   sourdough 시큼한 맛이 나는 반죽

WORD

given 고려할 때   enhance 향상시키다   circumstance 환경   domain 분야   of significance 중요한   association 연관성   reckless 난폭한, 무모한   adjust 적응하다   temporal 박자의   regularity 규칙성   accordingly 그에 따라

3. 다음 글의 밑줄 친 부분 중, 어법상 틀린 것은?

2017학년도 수능 28번

When people face real adversity – disease, unemployment, or the disabilities of age – affection from a pet takes on new meaning. A pet's continuing affection becomes crucially important for ① those enduring hardship because it reassures them that their core essence has not been damaged. Thus pets are important in the treatment of ② depressed or chronically ill patients. In addition, pets are ③ used to great advantage with the institutionalized aged. In such institutions it is difficult for the staff to retain optimism when all the patients are declining in health. Children who visit cannot help but remember ④ what their parents or grandparents once were and be depressed by their incapacities. Animals, however, have no expectations about mental capacity. They do not worship youth. They have no memories about what the aged once ⑤ was and greet them as if they were children. An old man holding a puppy can relive a childhood moment with complete accuracy. His joy and the animal's response are the same.

4. 다음 글의 밑줄 친 부분 중, 어법상 틀린 것은?

2016학년도 수능 28번

The Greeks' focus on the salient object and its attributes led to ① their failure to understand the fundamental nature of causality. Aristotle explained that a stone falling through the air is due to the stone having the property of "gravity." But of course a piece of wood ② tossed into water floats instead of sinking. This phenomenon Aristotle explained as being due to the wood having the property of "levity"! In both cases the focus is ③ exclusively on the object, with no attention paid to the possibility that some force outside the object might be relevant. But the Chinese saw the world as consisting of continuously interacting substances, so their attempts to understand it ④ causing them to be oriented toward the complexities of the entire "field," that is, the context or environment as a whole. The notion ⑤ that events always occur in a field of forces would have been completely intuitive to the Chinese.

* salient: 현저한, 두드러진 ** levity: 가벼움

WORD

adversity 역경 disability 장애 affection 애정 chronically 만성적
으로 to advantage 유익하게, 유리하게 institutionalize 시설에 수용하
다 retain 유지하다 optimism 낙관주의 worship 숭배하다 relive
다시 체험하다 complete 완전한 accuracy 정확성

WORD

attribute 속성, 자질 causality 인과 관계 property 성질, 속
성 gravity 중력 toss 던지다 phenomenon 현상 exclusively
오로지, 배타적으로 relevant 관련 있는 substance 물질 oriented
toward ~을 지향하는 complexity 복잡성 context 맥락, 전후 사정
notion 개념, 관념 intuitive 직관적인

5. 다음 글의 밑줄 친 부분 중, 어법상 틀린 것은?

2014학년도 수능 27번

Oxygen is what it is all about. Ironically, the stuff that gives us life eventually kills it. The ultimate life force lies in tiny cellular factories of energy, called mitochondria, ① that burn nearly all the oxygen we breathe in. But breathing has a price. The combustion of oxygen that keeps us alive and active ② sending out by-products called oxygen free radicals. They have Dr. Jekyll and Mr. Hyde characteristics. On the one hand, they help guarantee our survival. For example, when the body mobilizes ③ to fight off infectious agents, it generates a burst of free radicals to destroy the invaders very efficiently. On the other hand, free radicals move ④ uncontrollably through the body, attacking cells, rusting their proteins, piercing their membranes and corrupting their genetic code until the cells become dysfunctional and sometimes give up and die. These fierce radicals, ⑤ built into life as both protectors and avengers, are potent agents of aging.

* oxygen free radical: 활성 산소

** membrane: (해부학) 얇은 막

6. 다음 글의 밑줄 친 부분 중, 어법상 틀린 것은?

2015학년도 수능 28번

During the early stages when the aquaculture industry was rapidly expanding, mistakes were made and these were costly both in terms of direct losses and in respect of the industry's image. High-density rearing led to outbreaks of infectious diseases that in some cases ① devastated not just the caged fish, but local wild fish populations too. The negative impact on local wildlife inhabiting areas ② close to the fish farms continues to be an ongoing public relations problem for the industry. Furthermore, a general lack of knowledge and insufficient care being taken when fish pens were initially constructed ③ meaning that pollution from excess feed and fish waste created huge barren underwater deserts. These were costly lessons to learn, but now stricter regulations are in place to ensure that fish pens are placed in sites ④ where there is good water flow to remove fish waste. This, in addition to other methods that decrease the overall amount of uneaten food, ⑤ has helped aquaculture to clean up its act.

7. 다음 글의 밑줄 친 부분 중, 어법상 틀린 것은?

2011학년도 수능 20번

The word 'courage' takes on added meaning if you keep in mind that it is derived from the Latin word 'cor' ① meaning 'heart.' The dictionary defines courage as a 'quality which enables one to pursue a right course of action, through ② which one may provoke disapproval, hostility, or contempt.' Over 300 years ago La Rochefoucauld went a step further when he said: "Perfect courage is to do unwitnessed what we should be capable of doing before all men." It is not easy ③ to show moral courage in the face of either indifference or opposition. But persons who are daring in taking a wholehearted stand for truth often ④ achieving results that surpass their expectations. On the other hand, halfhearted individuals are seldom distinguished for courage even when it involves ⑤ their own welfare. To be courageous under all circumstances requires strong determination.

* provoke: 유발하다

8. 다음 글의 밑줄 친 부분 중, 어법상 틀린 것은?

2016학년도 9월 28번

The Internet and communication technologies play an ever-increasing role in the social lives of young people in developed societies. Adolescents have been quick to immerse themselves in technology with most ① using the Internet to communicate. Young people treat the mobile phone as an essential necessity of life and often prefer to use text messages to communicate with their friends. Young people also ② increasingly access social networking websites. As technology and the Internet are a familiar resource for young people, it is logical ③ what they would seek assistance from this source. This has been shown by the increase in websites that provide therapeutic information for young people. A number of 'youth friendly' mental health websites ④ have been developed. The information ⑤ presented often takes the form of Frequently Asked Questions, fact sheets and suggested links. It would seem, therefore, logical to provide online counselling for young people.

★ 혼공 3일차에 나온 문장들을 해석해 보자.

단어 PLUS

1 In the twentieth century, advances in technology, from refrigeration to sophisticated ovens to air transportation that carries fresh ingredients around the world, contributed immeasurably to baking and pastry making.

1
+ advance 발전
+ sophisticated 정교한
+ transportation 이동
+ ingredient 재료
+ immeasurably
헤아릴 수 없을 정도로

2 In other words, just as faster music causes people to eat faster, so it causes people to drive at faster speeds, as they engage mentally and physically with ongoing repeated structures in the music.

2
+ engage with 관계를 맺다
+ ongoing 지속적인

3 Children who visit cannot help but remember what their parents or grandparents once were and be depressed by their incapacities.

3
+ cannot help but
~하지 않을 수 없다
+ depressed 우울한

4 In both cases the focus is exclusively on the object, with no attention paid to the possibility that some force outside the object might be relevant.

4
+ exclusively 배타적으로
+ object 대상, 물건
+ relevant 관련된

5 Furthermore, a general lack of knowledge and insufficient care being taken when fish pens were initially constructed meant that pollution from excess feed and fish waste created huge barren underwater deserts.

5
+ insufficient 불충분한
+ initially 우선적으로
+ constructed 구성된

6 The dictionary defines courage as a 'quality which enables one to pursue a right course of action, through which one may provoke disapproval, hostility, or contempt.'

6
+ define 정의하다
+ courage 용기
+ quality 성질, 품질
+ pursue 추구하다
+ provoke 유발하다

7 But the Chinese saw the world as consisting of continuously interacting substances, so their attempts to understand it caused them to be oriented toward the complexities of the entire "field," that is, the context or environment as a whole.

7
+ continuously 지속적으로
+ interact 관계를 맺다

오늘은 독서분야 파워 블로거인 샘의 친한 지인 '유근용'님의 마지막 글이야. 더 많은 글이 궁금하다면 네이버에서 '유근용' 또는 '일독일행'이라고 검색해 봐. 샘에게 큰 영감을 주신 분이지. 그 분의 독서 잘하는 비법 3번째를 공개할게.

〈읽고 싶을 때 읽어라.〉

> 책이 잘 읽히지 않을 때가 있고 잘 읽힐 때가 있다.
>
> 안 읽힐 때는 그만 읽는 게 맞다.
>
> 억지로 읽으려 하지 마라. 억지로 되지 않으니 말이다.
>
> 대신 잘 읽힐 때 계속 읽어나가라. 쉼 없이 말이다.
>
> 읽고자 하는 마음이 용솟음칠 때 몰아쳐 읽어나가라.
>
> 매일 꾸준히 책을 읽는 것이 가장 좋지만, 또 그것이 정답이지만
>
> 자신의 컨디션과 상황에 따라 조절해서 읽는 것도 좋은 방법이다.
>
> 명심하자!

〈책을 읽는 것이 왜 중요할까?〉

주변에 사업하시는 분들이 많다. 1년 매출만 해도 최소 50억이 넘는 분들이다. 가끔씩 이분들의 회사에 방문해보면 사무실에 눈에 띄는 한 가지가 있다. 바로 책장이다. 누구 할 것 없이 다양한 책들로 서재가 가득 채워져 있다. 어디 사무실 뿐일까, 그 분들의 집에는 더 크고 많은 책들로 채워져 있다.

책을 읽어야 성공한다고 말한다. 독서불패라 말한다. 책을 읽는다고 전부 성공할 수는 없지만 성공한 사람들은 모두 책을 읽는 사람들이라고 말한다. 도대체 왜! 왜 이렇게 책이 중요한 것일까? 간략하게 2가지 이유를 적어보겠다.

❶ 책을 읽다 보면 자연스럽게 새로운 아이디어를 얻게 된다. 보도새퍼의 '돈'이란 책을 보면 이런 말이 나온다. '우리가 습득하는 새로운 단어는 모두 새로운 아이디어를 의미한다.' 즉 아이디어야말로 돈으로 환산할 수 없는 그 이상의 가치를 지닌다는 것이다. 엄청난 재산이라 할 수 있다. 이런 아이디어를 얻기 위해 가장 빠르고 좋은 방법은 책을 읽는 것이다.

❷ 두 번째 이유는 우리의 수입이 읽은 책의 양에 비례해서 늘어나기 때문이다. 이 말에 의구심을 갖는 사람도 있을 것이다. 하지만 주변을 보라. 자신 보다 더 나은 삶을 사는 사람들을 보면 분명 본인보다 책을 더 많이 읽는 사람일 것이다. 우리는 자신보다 책을 더 많이 읽고 경험이 많은 사람들에게 돈을 주고 배울 수밖에 없다. 링컨의 말을 기억하자. '책을 한 권 읽은 사람은 책을 두 번 읽은 사람의 지배를 당한다'

04일차

어휘1(선택형)

#어휘은 1문제 #반의어가 대세

난이도 🌶🌶🌶

It is possible to store the mind with a million facts
and still be entirely uneducated.
by Alec Bourne

백만 가지 사실을 머릿속에 집어넣고도 여전히 완전히 무지할 수 있다.

1 단계 개념 요리하기

01 문항 특징

- 문맥상 어울리는 어휘 혹은 어색한 어휘를 고르는 문항(2017학년도 기준 1문항 출제)
- 어법과 마찬가지로 선택형과 밑줄형 문항으로 출제됨
- 5년 평균 66%의 정답률을 보여주고 있어 생각보다 까다로운 유형임
- 3년 연속 선택형으로 출제되지만, 정확한 지문의 이해가 되지 않으면 어려움
- 선택형은 대부분 반의어로 짝지어지고 있음
- 글의 전체 흐름을 고려해서 주어진 어휘를 선택해야 함

02 혼공 전략

1 전체 주제를 파악하고 바로 앞 문장과의 관계를 살펴보자.

New technologies create new interactions and cultural rules. As a way to encourage TV viewing, social television systems now enable social interaction among TV viewers in different locations. These systems are known to build a greater sense of (A) connectedness / isolation among TVusing friend.

Solution 이 글의 주제는 새로운 기술이 새로운 관계와 문화 역할을 만든다는 거야. 문단 첫 문장이 이 글의 주제문이고 그 뒤로 아무런 반전 없이 내용이 이어지고 있어. 예로 소셜 TV를 들고 있는데, 상호작용을 일으킨다고 나오지. 선택형에서 비교되는 어휘는 거의 반의어야. '유대감 vs 고립'의 대결이지. 따라서 이어지는 어휘는 상호작용과 비슷한 유대감(connectedness)이 와야 해.

2 앞 문장도 중요하지만, 뒤에 오는 문장도 역시 관계 파악을 해야 해.

In most people, emotions are situational. Something in the here and now makes you mad. The emotion itself is tied / unrelated to the situation in which it originates. As long as you remain in that emotional situation, you're likely to stay angry.

Solution 앞에서는 감정이 상황적이라고 나오지. 그런데 이 문장만으로 올바른 어휘를 선택하기에는 부족함이 있어. 감정을 유발하는 상황과 묶여 있다는 건지, 관련이 없고 다른 요소가 개입된다는 건지 애매하지. 이때, 바로 뒤에 예시가 나오는데, 상황에 머무르면 감정이 안 좋아진다고 나와. 한마디로 감정과 상황은 연결(tied)되어 있다는 거지.

2 단계 문항 맛보기

(A), (B), (C)의 각 네모 안에서 문맥에 맞는 낱말로 가장 적절한 것은?

One of the most commonly cited reasons for keeping a pet animal is for the companionship it can provide. The general term companionship usually translates into partaking in shared activities, such as walking the dog, playing with the cat. However, such behavioral interactions between humans and pet animals are usually asymmetrically organized. Humans tend to interact with their pets when they feel like it, rather than (A) consistently / occasionally responding to the animal's demands for attention. In addition, it is often observed that once interaction between humans and pets has arisen, the termination of such interactional sequences invariably (B) originates / separates from the human. This suggests that activities like walking the dog and playing with the cat only arise when time can be spared from the human owner's other commitments. Therefore, if one views activity as a global concept – involving instigation, performance, and termination – labeling certain forms of human-pet interaction as shared activities may be (C) appealing / misleading .

* instigation: (~하도록) 부추김

	(A)	(B)	(C)
①	consistently	⋯⋯ originates	⋯⋯ appealing
②	consistently	⋯⋯ originates	⋯⋯ misleading
③	consistently	⋯⋯ separates	⋯⋯ appealing
④	occasionally	⋯⋯ originates	⋯⋯ misleading
⑤	occasionally	⋯⋯ separates	⋯⋯ appealing

WORD

cited 인용된 **companionship** 동반자 관계 **translate** 번역하다 **behavioral** 행동적 **interaction** 상호관계 **partake** 같이 하다, 참여하다 **asymmetrically** 비대칭으로 **termination** 종료, 폐지 **invariably** 명확히 **be spared from** ~을 모면하다 **commitment** 책임

One of the most commonly cited reasons for keeping a pet animal is for the companionship it can provide. The general term companionship usually translates into partaking in shared activities, such as walking the dog, playing with the cat. However, such behavioral interactions between humans and pet animals are usually asymmetrically organized. Humans tend to interact with their pets when they feel like it, rather than (A) [consistently/occasionally] responding to the animal's demands for attention. In addition, it is often observed that once interaction between humans and pets has arisen, the termination of such interactional sequences invariably (B) [originates/separates] from the human. This suggests that activities like walking the dog and playing with the cat only arise when time can be spared from the human owner's other commitments. Therefore, if one views activity as a global concept – involving instigation, performance, and termination – labeling certain forms of human-pet interaction as shared activities may be (C) [appealing/misleading].

Solution (A) consistently: 바로 앞 문장에서 인간은 자기가 하고 싶을 때만 애완동물과 상호관계를 맺는다는 말이 나오지. rather than은 '~라기 보다는'이므로 이와 반대되는 상황을 나타내는 consistently(꾸준하게)를 써야 해. occasionally는 '이따금씩'이라는 뜻이야.

Solution (B) originates: 앞의 내용은 인간과 애완동물의 관계는 인간중심이라는 거야. 이런 관계의 종결도 역시 인간중심이라는 내용이니까 인간으로부터 '발생하다(originates)'가 되어야 겠지. separate는 '분리하다'를 의미해. 내용상 인간과 분리되는 건 아니지.

Solution (C) misleading: 앞에서 언급된 것은 인간과 애완동물의 관계는 철저하게 인간중심이라는 거야. 이 문장은 결론을 내리는 부분인데, 인간과 애완동물의 관계를 공유된 활동으로 보는 것은 인간중심의 관계와는 다르지. 따라서 이를 부인하는 '잘못된(misleading)'이 적절해. appealing은 '마음을 끄는'을 의미하지.

해석 애완동물을 키우는 가장 흔하게 언급되는 이유 중 하나가 그것(애완동물을 키우는 것)이 줄 수 있는 동반자 관계를 위해서라는 것이다. 동반자 관계라는 일반 용어는 보통 개를 산책시키거나 고양이와 놀아 주는 것 같이 공유하는 활동에 참여하는 것으로 해석된다. 그러나 인간과 애완동물의 그러한 행동적 상호 관계는 보통 불균형적으로 구성된다. 인간은 관심을 받고자 하는 (애완)동물의 요구에 지속적으로 응하기보다는 그들이 그렇게 하고 싶을 때 애완동물과 상호 작용을 하는 경향이 있다. 게다가, 인간과 애완동물의 상호 작용이 발생하고 나면 그러한 상호 작용 절차의 종료는 항상 사람으로부터 비롯되는 것이 자주 목격된다는 것이다. 이것은 개를 산책시키거나 고양이와 놀아 주는 활동이 인간 주인의 다른 책임으로부터 시간이 날 수 있을 때만 이루어진다는 것을 시사한다. 그러므로 활동이란 것을 선동, 수행, 그리고 종료를 포함한 보편적인 개념으로 본다면 인간과 애완동물의 상호 작용의 특정 형태를 공유하는 활동이라고 이름 짓는 것은 잘못된 것일 수 있다.

고난도 문항 요리하기

1. (A), (B), (C)의 각 네모 안에서 문맥에 맞는 낱말로 가장 적절한 것은? `2018학년도 6월 29번`

Some coaches erroneously believe that mental skills training (MST) can only help perfect the performance of highly skilled competitors. As a result, they shy away from MST, (A) denying/rationalizing that because they are not coaching elite athletes, mental skills training is less important. It is true that mental skills become increasingly important at high levels of competition. As athletes move up the competitive ladder, they become more homogeneous in terms of physical skills. In fact, at high levels of competition, all athletes have the physical skills to be successful. Consequently, any small difference in (B) physical/mental factors can play a huge role in determining performance outcomes. However, we can anticipate that personal growth and performance will progress faster in young, developing athletes who are given mental skills training than in athletes not exposed to MST. In fact, the optimal time for introducing MST may be when athletes are first beginning their sport. Introducing MST (C) early/later in athletes' careers may lay the foundation that will help them develop to their full potential.

* homogeneous: 동질적인 ** optimal: 최적의

	(A)	(B)	(C)
①	denying	…… physical	…… later
②	denying	…… mental	…… early
③	rationalizing	…… physical	…… early
④	rationalizing	…… physical	…… later
⑤	rationalizing	…… mental	…… early

WORD

erroneously 잘못되게 **perfect** 완벽하게 하다 **performance** 기량 **shy away from** ~을 피하다 **factor** 요인 **expose ~ to** … ~이 …을 경험하게 하다 **lay the foundation** 기초를 놓다 **potential** 잠재 능력

2. (A), (B), (C)의 각 네모 안에서 문맥에 맞는 낱말로 가장 적절한 것은? `2012학년도 수능 33번`

Even those of us who claim not to be materialistic can't help but form attachments to certain clothes. Like fragments from old songs, clothes can (A) evoke/erase both cherished and painful memories. A worn-thin dress may hang in the back of a closet even though it hasn't been worn in years because the faint scent of pine that lingers on it is all that remains of someone's sixteenth summer. A(n) (B) impractical/brand-new white scarf might be pulled out of a donation bag at the last minute because of the promise of elegance it once held for its owner. And a ripped T-shirt might be (C) rescued/forgotten from the dust rag bin long after the name of the rock band once written across it has faded. Clothes document personal history for us the same way that fossils chart time for archaeologists.

	(A)	(B)	(C)
①	evoke	…… impractical	…… rescued
②	evoke	…… impractical	…… forgotten
③	evoke	…… brand-new	…… forgotten
④	erase	…… impractical	…… rescued
⑤	erase	…… brand-new	…… forgotten

WORD

materialistic 유물주의적인 **attachment** 애착, 집착 **promise** 기대, 약속 **document** ~로 증명하다, (상세히) 보도하다 **chart** (도표로) 나타내다

3. (A), (B), (C)의 각 네모 안에서 문맥에 맞는 낱말로 가장 적절한 것은?

2011학년도 9월 31번

When it comes to food choices, young people are particularly (A) vulnerable / immune to peer influences. A teenage girl may eat nothing but a lettuce salad for lunch, even though she will become hungry later, because that is what her friends are eating. A slim boy who hopes to make the wrestling team may routinely overload his plate with foods that are (B) dense / deficient in carbohydrates and proteins to 'bulk up' like the wrestlers of his school. An overweight teen may eat (C) greedily / moderately while around his friends but then devour huge portions when alone. Few young people are completely free of food-related pressures from peers, whether or not these pressures are imposed intentionally.

* carbohydrate: 탄수화물

	(A)	(B)	(C)
①	vulnerable	dense	greedily
②	vulnerable	dense	moderately
③	vulnerable	deficient	greedily
④	immune	deficient	moderately
⑤	immune	dense	greedily

4. (A), (B), (C)의 각 네모 안에서 문맥에 맞는 낱말로 가장 적절한 것은?

2016학년도 수능 29번

The Atitlán Giant Grebe was a large, flightless bird that had evolved from the much more widespread and smaller Pied-billed Grebe. By 1965 there were only around 80 birds left on Lake Atitlán. One immediate reason was easy enough to spot: the local human population was cutting down the reed beds at a furious rate. This (A) accommodation / destruction was driven by the needs of a fast growing mat-making industry. But there were other problems. An American airline was intent on developing the lake as a tourist destination for fishermen. However, there was a major problem with this idea: the lake (B) lacked / supported any suitable sporting fish! To compensate for this rather obvious defect, a specially selected species of fish called the Large-mouthed Bass was introduced. The introduced individuals immediately turned their attentions to the crabs and small fish that lived in the lake, thus (C) competing / cooperating with the few remaining grebes for food. There is also little doubt that they sometimes gobbled up the zebra-striped Atitlán Giant Grebe's chicks.

* reed: 갈대

** gobble up: 게걸스럽게 먹다

	(A)	(B)	(C)
①	accommodation	lacked	competing
②	accommodation	supported	cooperating
③	destruction	lacked	competing
④	destruction	supported	cooperating
⑤	destruction	lacked	cooperating

WORD

when it comes to ~에 관한 한　**lettuce** 상추　**overload** 짐을 너무 많이 싣다　**protein** 단백질　**bulk up** 커지다, 크게 하다　**devour** 게걸스럽게 먹다

WORD

flightless 날지 못하는　**evolve** 진화하다　**spot** 발견하다　**reed bed** 갈대밭　**furious** 맹렬한, 몹시 화가 난　**intent** 강한 관심을 보이는　**tourist destination** 관광지　**compensate for** ~을 보충[보상]하다　**obvious** 분명한　**defect** 결함　**chick** 새끼 새

5. (A), (B), (C)의 각 네모 안에서 문맥에 맞는 낱말로 가장 적절한 것은?

2016학년도 6월 29번

In 2001, researchers at Wayne State University asked a group of college volunteers to exercise for twenty minutes at a (A) preset / self-selected pace on each of three machines: a treadmill, a stationary bike, and a stair climber. Measurements of heart rate, oxygen consumption, and perceived effort were taken throughout all three workouts. The researchers expected to find that the subjects unconsciously targeted the same relative physiological intensity in each activity. Perhaps they would (B) automatically / intentionally exercise at 65 percent of their maximum heart rate regardless of which machine they were using. Or maybe they would instinctively settle into rhythm at 70 percent of their maximum rate of oxygen consumption in all three workouts. But that's not what happened. There was, in fact, no (C) consistency / variation in measurements of heart rate and oxygen consumption across the three disciplines. Instead, the subjects were found to have chosen the same level of perceived effort on the treadmill, the bike, and the stair climber.

* treadmill: 러닝머신
** physiological: 생리학적인

	(A)	(B)	(C)
①	preset	...... intentionally	...... consistency
②	preset	...... automatically	...... variation
③	self-selected	...... intentionally	...... variation
④	self-selected	...... intentionally	...... consistency
⑤	self-selected	...... automatically	...... consistency

WORD
stationary 정지된   **consumption** 소비, 소모   **physiological** 생리적인
intensity 강도   **instinctively** 본능적으로

6. (A), (B), (C)의 각 네모 안에서 문맥에 맞는 낱말로 가장 적절한 것은?

2017학년도 수능 29번

When teachers work in isolation, they tend to see the world through one set of eyes – their own. The fact that there might be someone somewhere *in the same building or district* who may be more successful at teaching this or that subject or lesson is (A) based / lost on teachers who close the door and work their way through the school calendar virtually alone. In the absence of a process that (B) allows / forbids them to benchmark those who do things better or at least differently, teachers are left with that one perspective – their own. I taught various subjects under the social studies umbrella and had very little idea of how my peers who taught the same subject did what they did. The idea of meeting regularly to compare notes, plan common assessments, and share what we did well (C) mostly / never occurred to us. Rather, we spent much time in the social studies office complaining about a lack of time and playing the blame game.

	(A)	(B)	(C)
①	based	...... allows	...... never
②	based	...... forbids	...... mostly
③	lost	...... allows	...... mostly
④	lost	...... allows	...... never
⑤	lost	...... forbids	...... never

WORD
isolation 고립, 격리   **district** 지역, 구역   **be lost on** ~에게 이해되지 않다   **in the absence of** ~이 없는 상태에서   **benchmark** 벤치마킹하다   **perspective** 시각, 관점   **compare notes** 의견이나 정보를 교환하다
assessment 평가   **blame game** 비난 게임

7. (A), (B), (C)의 각 네모 안에서 문맥에 맞는 낱말로 가장 적절한 것은?
2017학년도 9월 29번

You can't have a democracy if you can't talk with your neighbors about matters of mutual interest or concern. Thomas Jefferson, who had an enduring interest in democracy, came to a similar conclusion. He was prescient in understanding the dangers of (A) concentrated / limited power, whether in corporations or in political leaders or exclusionary political institutions. Direct involvement of citizens was what had made the American Revolution possible and given the new republic vitality and hope for the future. Without that involvement, the republic would die. Eventually, he saw a need for the nation to be (B) blended / subdivided into "wards" – political units so small that everyone living there could participate directly in the political process. The representatives for each ward in the capital would have to be (C) resistant / responsive to citizens organized in this way. A vibrant democracy conducted locally would then provide the active basic unit for the democratic life of the republic. With that kind of involvement, the republic might survive and prosper.

* prescient: 선견지명이 있는
** vibrant: 활력이 넘치는

	(A)	(B)	(C)
①	concentrated	blended	resistant
②	concentrated	subdivided	responsive
③	concentrated	subdivided	resistant
④	limited	subdivided	resistant
⑤	limited	blended	responsive

8. (A), (B), (C)의 각 네모 안에서 문맥에 맞는 낱말로 가장 적절한 것은?
2014학년도 6월 28번

England's plan to establish colonies in North America, starting in the late sixteenth century, was founded on a (A) false / valid idea. It was generally assumed that Virginia, the region of the North American continent to which England laid claim, would have the same climate as the Mediterranean region of Europe, since it lay at similar latitudes. As a result, the English hoped that the American colonies, once established, would be able to supply Mediterranean goods such as olives and fruit and reduce England's (B) dependence / restriction on imports from continental Europe. One prospectus claimed that the colonies would provide "the wines, fruit and salt of France and Spain ... the silks of Persia and Italy." Similarly, (C) abundant / scarce timber would do away with the need to import wood from Scandinavia. In short, America was mistakenly expected to be a land of plenty that would quickly turn a profit.

*latitude: 위도
**prospectus: 사업 설명서, 투자 설명서

	(A)	(B)	(C)
①	false	dependence	abundant
②	false	dependence	scarce
③	false	restriction	abundant
④	valid	restriction	scarce
⑤	valid	restriction	abundant

WORD

democracy 민주주의 체제 mutual 상호적인 enduring 지속적인 concentrated 집중된 exclusionary 배타적인 involvement 참여 republic 공화국 vitality 활력 subdivide 세분하다 blend 섞다 ward (지방 의회 구성단위가 되는) 구(區) representative 대표 responsive 반응하는

WORD

establish 설립하다 colony 식민지 valid 타당한 assume 추정하다 continent 대륙 the Mediterranean region 지중해 지역 goods 물품 continental 대륙의 timber 목재 do away with ~을 없애버리다

★ 혼공 4일차에 나온 문장들을 해석해 보자.

단어 PLUS

1 Few young people are completely free of food-related pressures from peers, whether or not these pressures are imposed intentionally.

1
+ **completely** 완전히
+ **pressure** 압박, 압력
+ **impose** 부여하다

2 However, we can anticipate that personal growth and performance will progress faster in young, developing athletes who are given mental skills training than in athletes not exposed to MST.

2
+ **anticipate** 기대하다
+ **performance** 수행
+ **progress** 진행하다
+ **expose** 노출시키다

3 A worn-thin dress may hang in the back of a closet even though it hasn't been worn in years because the faint scent of pine that lingers on it is all that remains of someone's sixteenth summer.

3
+ **closet** 옷장
+ **scent** 냄새
+ **linger** 남다

4 A teenage girl may eat nothing but a lettuce salad for lunch, even though she will become hungry later, because that is what her friends are eating.

4
+ **nothing but** 오직
+ **lettuce** 상추

5 The fact that there might be someone somewhere *in the same building or district* who may be more successful at teaching this or that subject or lesson is lost on teachers who close the door and work their way through the school calendar virtually alone.

5
+ **district** 구역
+ **virtually** 실제로

6 Direct involvement of citizens was what had made the American Revolution possible and given the new republic vitality and hope for the future.

6
+ **republic** 공화국의
+ **vitality** 활력

7 It was generally assumed that Virginia, the region of the North American continent to which England laid claim, would have the same climate as the Mediterranean region of Europe, since it lay at similar latitudes.

7
+ **assume** 추정하다
+ **region** 지역
+ **continent** 대륙
+ **Mediterranean** 지중해의
+ **latitude** 위도

영어가 안 돼서 슬플 때 이야기

샘은 하와이를 정말 좋아해. 왜냐고? 개인적으로 두 번 가봤는데. 한 번은 10일, 다른 한번은 두 달이었어. 어마어마하지?

첫 번째는 신혼여행이었어. 정말 하와이라는 곳에 대해 엄청난 환상을 가지고 있었기 때문에 막상 도착하니 정말 10일은 너무나 빨리 흘러버려서 아쉽고 또 아쉬웠지. 그래서 기회를 노리고 노리다가 결국 출장으로 두 달을 가게 되었어. 말이 두 달이지 꽤나 긴 시간이었어. 많은 것들을 체험했지.

샘은 다행히 영어회화를 좋아하고 외국인 친구가 많은 편이라 현지 생활이 어렵지 않았어. 하지만 같이 출장 간 분들은 꽤 힘들어 하셨어. 심지어 영어를 전공한 분들도 현지 영어의 속사포 랩 같은 속도에 당황하곤 했었지.

때는 출장간지 두 달째가 되는 주말이었어. 근처 섬으로 놀러가기로 했어. 하와이에는 섬이 총 6개가 있거든. 그 중에서 '마우이'라는 섬으로 놀러갔어. 하룻밤을 자고 어느 식당에서 아침 식사를 주문하려던 차였어. 한 한국인 신혼 부부가 있더군. 내심 반가웠지만 주제 넘게 아는 척 할 수가 없었어. 그냥 바라볼 수 밖에. 우리는 주문을 끝냈고 음식을 기다리고 있었어. 마침 그 신혼 부부가 주문을 하고 있더라고. 서버가 주문을 받느라 이것저것 자세하게 영어로 물어보는 중이었어.

부부는 질린 표정이었어. 왜냐하면 우리 나라처럼 메뉴 하나 시키면 반찬이 알아서 나오는 시스템이 아니거든. 계란부터 빵의 종류, 샐러드 소스까지도 물어보기도 해. 한국인의 정서에는 안 맞는 스타일이야. 하하. 여튼 나는 흥미롭게 그들의 대화를 듣고 있었어.

"오빠가 주문 좀 해봐."

"아니, 네 차례잖아. 네가 하고 나면 나도 할게."

"아니, 나 이 여자가 뭐라고 하는지 정말 모르겠어."

"야, 너 토익 800점 받았다고 했잖아?"

"오빠, 이러기야!"

서버는 무슨 대화인지도 모르고 서서 눈만 멀뚱멀뚱 하고 있었다. 대화는 점점 심각해졌고 급기야 주문을 하고 나서 두 사람은 대화가 없어졌다.

아.. 내가 나섰어야 하나? 그렇다고 신혼 부부 식사 주문하는데 '제가 도와드릴까요?'라고 하는 것도 참 모양 빠지는 행동이다.

결론 : 영어 공부는 해 놓으면 결국 써먹을 곳이 있다.

혼공

05일차

어휘2(밑줄형)

#전체적인_주제파악_밑줄_친_어휘의_반의어_생각하기

난이도 🌶🌶🌶

In this life he laughs longest who laughs last.
by John Masefield

이 인생에서는 마지막에 웃는 자가 가장 오래 웃는 자다.

01 문항 특징

🌶 밑줄형 어휘의 경우 밑줄 친 어휘의 반의어를 항상 고려해야 함

🌶 글의 흐름의 포인트가 되는 부분에 밑줄을 긋는 경향이 있음

🌶 밑줄 친 어휘의 정확한 의미를 알고 독해를 하는 것이 가장 중요함

🌶 선택형이 대세지만, 항상 밑줄형도 출제될 수 있음을 인지해야 함

🌶 글의 흐름과 어휘의 정확한 의미 파악이 꼭 필요함

02 혼공 전략

1 두 가지 상황을 비교할 때, +/- 관계를 파악해야 해.

> The study showed **a strong preference for text over voice**. Users offered two key <u>reasons</u> for ③ <u>disliking</u> text chat. First, text chat required less effort and attention, and was more enjoyable than voice chat. Second, study participants viewed text chat as more polite.

Solution 바로 앞 문장에서 text vs voice의 관계 설정이 언급되고 있어. preference for text over voice라고 표현된 부분에서 text가 voice보다 우위에 있는 관계를 파악을 해야 해. 뒤에 밑줄 친 dislike는 text chat에 대해서 (−)인 관계를 드러내므로 앞에서 언급한 것과는 정반대를 의미하지. 따라서 disliking은 틀린 거야. favoring이 나와야겠지.

2 반의어의 가능성이 열려있다면 그 반의어도 해석 시 고려해야 하지.

> But, don't worry! Your kids just want to be like the celebrities in their performance as professionals, not in their private behavior. They are just ④ <u>uncommon</u> people except that they have excellent skills in their field.

Solution 아이들이 유명인을 좋아하는 것은 그들의 사생활이 아닌 프로로서 뛰어나기 때문이라고 언급하고 있어. 밑줄 친 어휘인 uncommon(특별한)을 보자마자 common(평범한)이 생각나야 해. 그리고 이 둘을 모두 넣어보고 더 자연스러운 것을 찾아야겠지. 바로 뒤에 오는 문구에서 자기 분야에서 뛰어난 것을 제외하면 별거 없는 사람들이라는 내용이 자연스러워. 따라서 uncommon이 아닌 common이 나와야 해.

다음 글의 밑줄 친 부분 중, 문맥상 낱말의 쓰임이 적절하지 <u>않은</u> 것은?

2014학년도 9월 28번

Occasionally, there are children who have trouble understanding that their clothing choice is inappropriate or even unhealthy. Some children ① <u>follow</u> the suggestion that sandals may not be the best option for a snowy day. For those kids, ② <u>experience</u> may be the best teacher. For example, when Lydia was eight years old, she insisted on wearing her favorite sandals to school despite ③ <u>warnings</u> that the sidewalks were covered in snow and slush. Her mom ④ <u>worried</u> that she would arrive at school with cold, wet feet, but Lydia would not change her mind. Of course, her mother was right. While Lydia did have some very uncomfortable toes because they became soaked and frozen on her way to and from school, she learned that sometimes fashion isn't ⑤ <u>worth</u> the price of serious discomfort.

WORD

occasionally 가끔   **have trouble ~ing** ~하는 데 어려움이 있다   **inappropriate** 적절하지 않은   **suggestion** 제안   **option** 선택, 선택권   **slush** 진 창 눈, 진창길   **soaked** 젖은   **discomfort** 불편, 불쾌

Occasionally, there are children who have trouble understanding that their clothing choice is inappropriate or even unhealthy. Some children ① follow the suggestion that sandals may not be the best option for a snowy day. For those kids, ② experience may be the best teacher. For example, when Lydia was eight years old, she insisted on wearing her favorite sandals to school despite ③ warnings that the sidewalks were covered in snow and slush. Her mom ④ worried that she would arrive at school with cold, wet feet, but Lydia would not change her mind. Of course, her mother was right. While Lydia did have some very uncomfortable toes because they became soaked and frozen on her way to and from school, she learned that sometimes fashion isn't ⑤ worth the price of serious discomfort.

Solution 여기서 언급된 아이들은 자신들이 선택한 옷이 건강에는 좋지 않다는 예에 해당하는 아이들야. 뒤에 나오는 예시는 고집을 피우다가 고생을 하게 되는 아이에 대한 거지. 따라서 그 아이들은 눈이 오는 날 샌들을 신는 것이 적절치 못하다는 제안을 받아들이지 않는다고 하는 것이 글의 흐름상 자연스러워. 따라서 follow(따르다) 보다는 resist(저항하다)와 같은 부정적인 어휘가 적절하지.

Solution 뒤에 나오는 예시로 봐서 직접 경험을 해봐야 패션으로 인해 겪는 불편함을 알게 되지. 따라서 experience(경험)는 적절해.

Solution 바로 뒤에 인도가 눈으로 덮여있다는 내용이 나오는데, 조심하라는 '경고'니까 warnings은 적절한 어휘야.

Solution 추운 날 경고를 무시한 채 샌들을 신고 가다가 고생한 경험으로 인해서 패션보다 불편함이 더 크다는 교훈을 얻게 되었으므로 앞의 부정어까지 고려해서 '가치가 없다(isn't worth)'는 적절하지.

Solution 발이 차갑고 젖은 상태로 학교에 도착하는 걸 걱정(worried)하는 것은 자연스럽지.

해석 이따금 자신들의 의복 선택이 적절하지 않거나 심지어 건강에 좋지 않다는 사실을 이해하는 데 어려움을 겪는 아이들이 있다. 어떤 아이들은 눈이 오는 날 샌들을 신는 것은 최선의 선택이 아닐 것이라는 제안을 따른다.(→ 받아들이지 않는다.) 그러한 아이들에게는 경험이 가장 좋은 교사가 될 수 있다. 예를 들어, Lydia는 여덟살 때, 인도가 눈과 진창으로 덮여 있다는 경고에도 불구하고, 자기가 제일 좋아하는 샌들을 신고 학교에 가겠다고 고집을 부렸다. 그녀의 엄마는 그녀가 발이 차갑게 젖은 상태로 학교에 도착하게 될까 봐 걱정했으나, Lydia는 자신의 마음을 바꾸려 하지 않았다. 물론, 어머니의 생각이 옳았다. Lydia는 등하굣길에 발가락들이 물에 젖고 얼어서 실제로 몇 개의 발가락이 정말 매우 불편했지만, 때때로 패션은 심한 불편함의 대가를 치를 만큼 가치가 있는 것이 아니라는 것을 배웠다.

3 단계 고난도 문항 요리하기

1. 다음 글의 밑줄 친 부분 중, 문맥상 낱말의 쓰임이 적절하지 <u>않은</u> 것은?

`2014학년도 수능 28번`

When people started to plant stored seed stock deliberately, they also began protecting their plants. This changed the evolutionary ① <u>pressure</u> that these food plants experienced, as they no longer had to survive in a natural environment. Instead, people created a new environment for them, and selected for other characteristics than nature previously had. Seeds recovered at archaeological sites clearly show that farmers selected for larger seeds and ② <u>thinner</u> seed coats. Thick seed coats are often ③ <u>essential</u> for seeds to survive in a natural environment because the seeds of many wild plants remain dormant for months until winter is over and rain sets in. But under human management thick seed coats are unnecessary, as farmers ④ <u>evade</u> responsibility for storing seeds away from moisture and predators. In fact, seeds with thinner coats were ⑤ <u>preferred</u> as they are easier to eat or process into flour, and they allow seedlings to sprout more quickly when sown.

2. 다음 글의 밑줄 친 부분 중, 문맥상 낱말의 쓰임이 적절하지 <u>않은</u> 것은?

`2012학년도 9월 33번`

Life is full of hazards. Disease, enemies and starvation are always menacing primitive man. Experience teaches him that medicinal herbs, valor, the most strenuous labor, often come to naught, yet normally he wants to ① <u>survive</u> and enjoy the good things of existence. Faced with this problem, he takes to any method that seems ② <u>adapted</u> to his ends. Often his ways appear incredibly ③ <u>crude</u> to us moderns until we remember how our next-door neighbor acts in like emergencies. When medical science pronounces him ④ <u>curable</u>, he will not resign himself to fate but runs to the nearest quack who holds out hope of recovery. His urge for self-preservation will not down, nor will that of the illiterate peoples of the world, and in that overpowering will to live is anchored the belief in supernaturalism, which is absolutely ⑤ <u>universal</u> among known peoples, past and present.

* quack: 돌팔이 의사

WORD

seed stock 씨앗 종자 deliberately 의도적으로, 일부러 archaeological 고고학의 evolutionary 진화의 pressure 압박, 압력 dormant 휴지기의 set in 시작되다 seedling 묘목, 모종 sprout 발아하다, 발육하다

WORD

starvation 기아 menace 위협하다 primitive 원시적인 medicinal herb 약초 valor 용기 strenuous 근면한 come to naught 허사로 돌아가다 take to ~에 매달리다 end 목적 crude 투박한 resign oneself to 체념하고 받아들이다 illiterate 무지한 anchor 고정하다

3. 다음 글의 밑줄 친 부분 중, 문맥상 낱말의 쓰임이 적절하지 않은 것은?

2016학년도 9월 29번

An Egyptian executive, after entertaining his Canadian guest, offered him joint partnership in a new business venture. The Canadian, delighted with the offer, suggested that they meet again the next morning with their ① respective lawyers to finalize the details. The Egyptian never showed up. The surprised and disappointed Canadian tried to understand what had gone wrong: Did Egyptians ② lack punctuality? Was the Egyptian expecting a counter-offer? Were lawyers unavailable in Cairo? None of these explanations proved to be correct; rather, the problem was ③ caused by the different meaning Canadians and Egyptians attach to inviting lawyers. The Canadian regarded the lawyers' ④ absence as facilitating the successful completion of the negotiation; the Egyptian interpreted it as signaling the Canadian's mistrust of his verbal commitment. Canadians often use the impersonal formality of a lawyer's services to finalize ⑤ agreements. Egyptians, by contrast, more frequently depend on the personal relationship between bargaining partners to accomplish the same purpose.

* punctuality: 시간 엄수

4. 다음 글의 밑줄 친 부분 중, 문맥상 낱말의 쓰임이 적절하지 않은 것은?

2015학년도 9월 29번

A special feature of the real estate rental market is its tendency to undergo a severe and prolonged contraction phase, more so than with manufactured products. When the supply of a manufactured product ① exceeds the demand, the manufacturer cuts back on output, and the merchant reduces inventory to balance supply and demand. However, ② property owners cannot reduce the amount of space available for rent in their buildings. Space that was constructed to accommodate business and consumer needs at the peak of the cycle ③ remains, so vacancy rates climb and the downward trend becomes more severe. Rental rates generally do not drop below a certain point, the ④ maximum that must be charged in order to cover operating expenses. Some owners will take space off the market rather than lose money on it. A few, unable to subsidize the property, will sell at distress prices, and lenders will repossess others. These may then be placed on the market at lower rental rates, further ⑤ depressing the market.

*contraction phase: 경기 수축기(후퇴기)
**distress price: 투매 가격(판매자가 손해를 감수하는 매우 싼 가격)

WORD

joint partnership 합작 제휴　venture 벤처 사업　counter-offer 수정 제안　explanation 설명　absence 결여　facilitate 용이하게 하다　interpret 해석하다, 이해하다　completion 완료　negotiation 협상　impersonal 사사롭지 않은　formality 형식상의 절차

WORD

real estate 부동산　tendency 경향　undergo 겪다　manufactured product 공산품(공장에서 제조된 상품)　exceed 초과하다, 넘다　cut back on ~을 줄이다　output 생산량　inventory 재고　property 부동산　accommodate 수용하다　vacancy rate 공실률　subsidize ~의 비용의 일부를 지급하다, ~에 보조금을 지급하다　lender 대출기관, 빌려주는 사람　repossess (임대료를 치르지 않은 부동산을) 회수[압류]하다

5. 다음 글의 밑줄 친 부분 중, 문맥상 낱말의 쓰임이 적절하지 <u>않은</u> 것은?

2011학년도 수능 32번

Many people take numerous photos while traveling or on vacation or during significant life celebrations to ① <u>preserve</u> the experience for the future. But the role of photographer may actually detract from their ② <u>delight</u> in the present moment. I know a father who devoted himself earnestly to photographing the birth of his first and only child. The photos were beautiful but, he ③ <u>lamented</u> afterward he felt that he had missed out on the most important first moment of his son's life. Looking through the camera lens made him ④ <u>detached</u> from the scene. He was just an observer, not an experiencer. Teach yourself to use your camera in a way that ⑤ <u>neglects</u> your ongoing experiences, by truly looking at things and noticing what is beautiful and meaningful.

6. 다음 글의 밑줄 친 부분 중, 문맥상 낱말의 쓰임이 적절하지 <u>않은</u> 것은?

2013학년도 6월 32번

Organic food production is growing by leaps and bounds. Many consumers are willing to pay premium prices for organic foods, convinced that they are helping the earth and eating healthier. Some experts say, however, that organic farming has some ① <u>drawbacks</u>. One of the most frequent criticisms is that the crop yields of organic farms are much ② <u>lower</u> than those of traditional farms. That's because organic fields suffer more from weeds and insects than ③ <u>conventional</u> fields. Another argument often offered by experts is that organic farming can supply food for niche markets of ④ <u>wealthy</u> consumers but cannot feed billions of hungry people around the globe. Only the careful use of chemical inputs, not the costly organic methods, can help ⑤ <u>reduce</u> food production significantly in the countries facing hunger.

[*] niche market: 틈새시장

WORD

celebration 축하, 기념   preserve 보존하다   detract from ~을 손상시키다   lament 슬퍼하다   detached 떨어진, 분리된   neglect 소홀히 하다, 무시하다   ongoing 진행하는

WORD

by leaps and bounds 급속도로   drawback 결점   criticism 비판, 비난   yield 산출량, 생산량   conventional 전통적인   argument 주장, 논쟁, 언쟁   costly 비용이 드는   significantly 상당히

7. 다음 글의 밑줄 친 부분 중, 문맥상 낱말의 쓰임이 적절하지 <u>않은</u> 것은?

2013학년도 6월 31번

Over the course of the past forty years, no country on earth has cut its alcohol consumption more than France. While consumption of beer and spirits has stayed basically steady in France, the per capita consumption of alcohol from wine ① <u>fell</u> from 20 liters in 1962 to about 8 in 2001. One reason for the dwindling wine consumption is the ② <u>acceleration</u> of the French meal. In 1978, the average French meal lasted 82 minutes. ③ <u>Plenty</u> of time for half a bottle, if not a whole bottle. Today, the average French meal has been slashed down to 38 minutes. Wine is a ④ <u>victim</u> of the disappearance of the leisurely meal. It is not the target of the change, but the decline in wine consumption is a ⑤ <u>cause</u> of the emergence of the faster, more modern, on-the-go lifestyle.

* spirits: 독한 술

8. 다음 글의 밑줄 친 부분 중, 문맥상 낱말의 쓰임이 적절하지 <u>않은</u> 것은?

2012학년도 6월 33번

According to Cambodian legends, lions once roamed the countryside attacking villagers and their precious buffalo, and long before the great Khmer Empire began in the 9th century, farmers developed a fierce martial art to defend themselves against the ① <u>predator</u>. These techniques became *bokator*. Meaning 'to fight a lion,' *bokator* is a martial art ② <u>depicted</u> on the walls of Angkor Wat. There are 10,000 moves to master, ③ <u>mimicking</u> animals such as monkeys, elephants and even ducks. King Jayavarman VII, the warrior king who united Cambodia in the 12th century, made his army train in *bokator*, turning it into a ④ <u>fearsome</u> fighting force. Despite its long tradition in Cambodia, *bokator* ⑤ <u>flourished</u> when the Khmer Rouge took power in 1975 and executed most of the discipline's masters over the next four years.

WORD

consumption 소비 **per capita** 1인당 **slash** 깎아 내리다, 베다 **acceleration** 가속 **leisurely** 여유 있는, 느긋한 **emergence** 출현 **modern** 현대의

WORD

roam 배회하다 **fierce** 격렬한 **martial art** 무술 **predator** 포식자 **depict** 묘사하다 **mimic** 모방하다 **fearsome** 무서운 **execute** 처형하다

혼공 개념 마무리

★ 혼공 5일차에 나온 문장들을 해석해 보자.

1 Seeds recovered at archaeological sites clearly show that farmers selected for larger seeds and thinner seed coats.

1
+ **recover** 회복하다
+ **archaeological** 고고학의

2 His urge for self-preservation will not down, nor will that of the illiterate peoples of the world, and in that overpowering will to live is anchored the belief in supernaturalism, which is absolutely universal among known peoples, past and present.

2
+ **urge** 욕구
+ **self-preservation** 자기보존
+ **illiterate** 문맹의
+ **anchor** 닻을 내리다
+ **supernaturalism** 미신
+ **absolutely** 절대적으로

3 Space that was constructed to accommodate business and consumer needs at the peak of the cycle remains, so vacancy rates climb and the downward trend becomes more severe.

3
+ **accommodate** 수용하다
+ **at the peak of** ~의 정점에서
+ **vacancy** 비어 있음
+ **severe** 심각한

4 Teach yourself to use your camera in a way that enhances your ongoing experiences, by truly looking at things and noticing what is beautiful and meaningful.

4
+ **enhance** 향상시키다
+ **ongoing** 지속적인

5 Many consumers are willing to pay premium prices for organic foods, convinced that they are helping the earth and eating healthier.

5
+ **organic** 유기농의
+ **convince** 확신시키다

6 King Jayavarman VII, the warrior king who united Cambodia in the 12th century, made his army train in *bokator*, turning it into a fearsome fighting force.

6
+ **fearsome** 무시무시한

7 Thick seed coats are often essential for seeds to survive in a natural environment because the seeds of many wild plants remain dormant for months until winter is over and rain sets in.

7
+ **dormant** 휴면기의

B

course

승부수 문항 II

06일차

주어진 문장 넣기

#극강의_난이도 #언어의_감 #논리력이_필요

난이도 🌶🌶🌶

I show you doubt, to prove that faith exists.
by Robert Browning

나는 믿음이 존재함을 보여주기 위해 의구심을 보인다.

01 문항 특징

- 2015학년도 수능 이후 2문제씩 출제 (2017 수능 2문제 출제)
- 1문항은 쉽고 1문항은 어렵게 출제되는 추세임
- 빈칸 추론과 더불어 올해의 고난도 문항으로 꼽힘
- 5년 평균 정답률 59%
- 급격한 반전, 갑작스런 대명사 등장, 연결어 등이 힌트로 주어짐
- 힌트가 없는 경우 문장들 사이의 논리성으로 해결해야 함

02 혼공 전략

1 문장 사이에 갑작스런 방향 전환이 있는 부분이 정답이야.

> 역접, 즉 방향 전환

> 부정적 내용

But there will be times in your life when there is no one around to stand up and cheer you on.

> 긍정적 내용

Each of us needs people in our lives who encourage us so that we can feel confident in our capabilities and move forward toward our goals. (） When this happens, don't get depressed. Instead, become your own cheerleader.

> 부정적 내용

Solution 주변에 우리를 격려해 주는 사람이 필요하고, 그들로 인해서 우리는 긍정적인 결과를 본다는 내용이야. 그런데 뒤에 나오는 this happens에 대해서는 실망하지 말라는 내용이 나와. 분명히 앞에는 긍정적인 내용인데, 뒤에 이어지는 내용은 부정적인 내용이야. 논리적 비약이 느껴지지. 주어진 문장은 부정적인 내용이 나오니 바로 이 부분이 들어갈 공간이 되는 거지. 주어진 문장에 however, but 등의 역접을 나타내는 연결어가 나온다면 이런 방향 전환 포인트를 찾아야 해.

2 논리적 비약점을 찾아라. 갑작스런 인물/사건(대명사)의 등장이 포인트!

> 이 대명사가 지칭하는 것을 정확하게 파악해야 해. 여기서는 교외에 사는 사람들한테는 별로인 거지.

This is not the case for people who live in the suburbs.

It's often easier and cheaper to walk a few blocks than to wait for a taxi or subway. In this way, exercise can be structured into the daily routine. (） Because the suburbs are spread out, it's too far to walk to the office or run to the store.

> 갑자기 교외 지역이 등장하지.

Solution 앞부분은 교통수단을 이용하는 것보다 걷는 것이 좋다는 거야. 그런데 교외 지역이 확산되니 걷는 것은 별로라는 내용이야. 중간에 교외 지역(the suburbs)이 갑자기 등장하지. 이 앞에서는 한 번도 나오지 않았어. 따라서 주어진 문장은 이 앞에 나와야겠지.
문단에서 갑자기 대명사나 「the + 명사」가 등장할 때 그것이 지칭하는 것이 앞에 나오는지도 잘 살펴봐야 해. 없는 것이 등장한다면, 분명 주어진 문장에서 언급한 녀석일 가능성이 높아.

글의 흐름으로 보아, 주어진 문장이 들어가기에 가장 적절한 곳은?

2016학년도 6월 39번

They quickly pick out a whole series of items of the same type, making a handful of, say, small screws.

People make extensive use of searching images. One unexpected context is sorting. Suppose you have a bag of small hardware – screws, nails, and so on – and you decide to organize them into little jars. You dump the stuff out on a table and begin separating the items into coherent groups. (①) It is possible to do this by randomly picking up individual objects, one by one, identifying each one, and then moving it to the appropriate jar. (②) But what most people do is very different. (③) They put them in the jar and then go back and do the same for a different kind of item. (④) So the sorting sequence is nonrandom, producing runs of items of a single type. (⑤) It is a faster, more efficient technique, and much of the increased efficiency is due to the use of searching images.

WORD

a series of 일련의   a handful of 적은   extensive 광범위한   context 상황, 환경   sorting 분리   hardware 철물   screw 나사   dump out 쏟다
separate 분류하다, 나누다   coherent 일관성 있는   identify 구별하다   appropriate 적절한   sequence 순서   efficiency 효율성

They quickly pick out a whole series of items of the same type, making a handful of, say, small screws.

Solution 물건을 분류하는 법이 나와. 이것만 가지고는 이 문장의 성격을 알 수가 없을 거야. 즉, 아래 나오는 전체적인 지문의 문맥을 파악해야 한다는 이야기야. 여하튼 주어진 문장은 같은 물건끼리 분류한다는 내용이야.

People make extensive use of searching images. One unexpected context is sorting. Suppose you have a bag of small hardware – screws, nails, and so on – and you decide to organize them into little jars. You dump the stuff out on a table and begin separating the items into coherent groups. (①) It is possible to do this by randomly picking up individual objects, one by one, identifying each one, and then moving it to the appropriate jar. (②) But what most people do is very different. (③) They put them in the jar and then go back and do the same for a different kind of item. (④) So the sorting sequence is nonrandom, producing runs of items of a single type. (⑤) It is a faster, more efficient technique, and much of the increased efficiency is due to the use of searching images.

Solution 당신이 생각하는 무작위적인 물건 분류법을 설명하고 있어. 여기까지는 논리적인 허점이 보이지 않아.

Solution 글의 흐름이 바뀌고 있어. 앞에서는 무작위적인 분류법인데, 대부분의 사람들은 다른 방법을 사용한다고 하지. 그렇다면, 이후의 내용은 무작위적인 것이 아닌 어떤 기준을 중심으로 분류한다는 내용이 나와야겠지.

Solution 뒤에 'them'이 지칭하는 것이 과연 무엇일까? 파란색 부분에 있는 쏟아 놓은 물건일까? 그렇다고 하기에는 다시 단지에 넣으니까 이상하지? 바로 무언가가 이 문장 앞에 나와야 한다는 거지. 그게 바로 주어진 문장에 있는 'a whole series of times'를 가리키고 있어. 따라서 주어진 문장은 바로 ③번에 들어가야 하겠지.

정답: ③

해석 사람들은 광범위하게 검색 이미지를 사용한다. 예상치 못한 상황은 분리이다. 당신은 나사, 못 등의 작은 철물을 가방 가득 가지고 있고 이것을 작은 단지에 분리하기로 했다고 하자. 당신은 책상 위에 이 물건을 쏟아 놓고 물건을 일관된 그룹으로 분리한다. 개별적인 물건을 하나씩 무작위로 집고 확인하고, 적절한 단지로 옮기는 것은 가능하다. 하지만 대부분의 사람들은 매우 다르게 한다. 그들은 빠르게 같은 유형의 일련의 물건, 말하자면 한 줌의 나사 같은 것을 골라낸다. 그들은 이 물건을 단지에 넣고 다시 돌아가 다른 좋은 물건에게 유사한 일을 한다. 그래서 분류 순서는 무작위로 행해지는 것이 아니고, 하나의 유형의 연속적인 항목을 만들어 낸다.

고난도 문항 요리하기

1. 글의 흐름으로 보아, 주어진 문장이 들어가기에 가장 적절한 곳은? 2013학년도 수능 44번

Despite such evidence of favoritism toward handsome politicians, follow-up research demonstrated that voters did not realize their bias.

Research has shown that we automatically assign to good-looking individuals such favorable traits as talent, kindness, honesty, and intelligence. (①) Furthermore, we make these judgements without being aware that physical attractiveness plays a role in the process. (②) Some consequences of this unconscious assumption that "good-looking equals good" scare me. (③) For example, a study of the 1974 Canadian federal elections found that attractive candidates received more than two and a half times as many votes as unattractive candidates. (④) In fact, 73 percent of Canadian voters surveyed denied in the strongest possible terms that their votes had been influenced by physical appearance; only 14 percent even allowed for the possibility of such influence. (⑤) Voters can deny the impact of attractiveness on electability all they want, but evidence has continued to confirm its troubling presence.

2. 글의 흐름으로 보아, 주어진 문장이 들어가기에 가장 적절한 곳은? 2017학년도 9월 38번

Even so, research confirms the finding that nonverbal cues are more credible than verbal cues, especially when verbal and nonverbal cues conflict.

Researchers have reported various nonverbal features of sarcasm. (①) Most disagree as to whether nonverbal cues are essential to the perception of sarcasm or the emotion that prompts it. (②) Also, nonverbal cues are better indicators of speaker intent. (③) As the nature of sarcasm implies a contradiction between intent and message, nonverbal cues may "leak" and reveal the speaker's true mood as they do in deception. (④) Ostensibly, sarcasm is the opposite of deception in that a sarcastic speaker typically intends the receiver to recognize the sarcastic intent; whereas, in deception the speaker typically intends that the receiver not recognize the deceptive intent. (⑤) Thus, when communicators are attempting to determine if a speaker is sarcastic, they compare the verbal and nonverbal message and if the two are in opposition, communicators may conclude that the speaker is being sarcastic.

* sarcasm: 비꼼
** ostensibly: 표면상

WORD

evidence 증거 favoritism 편애 follow-up 다음의, 후속의 demonstrate 증명하다, 설명하다 assign 부여하다, 배정하다 attractiveness 매력 요소 consequence 결과 term 어조, 용어 appearance 외모 electability 선출 가능성 confirm 확인하다 presence 존재

WORD

confirm 확증하다, 확인해 주다 nonverbal 비언어적인, 말을 쓰지 않는 credible 신빙성이 있는, 믿을 수 있는 conflict 상충하다, 충돌하다 perception 인지, 지각 prompt 촉발하다, 자극하다 indicator 보여 주는 것, 지표 intent 의도 imply 암시하다 contradiction 모순 deception 속임, 사기

3. 글의 흐름으로 보아, 주어진 문장이 들어가기에 가장 적절한 곳은?

2014학년도 9월 39번

The experimenter then changed the context so that the participants had to do a subtly different task.

By changing the focus or context of a task, we can get renewed energy even when we feel that we are completely out of energy. To demonstrate this, a psychologist asked people to take part in what she called 'semi-free tasks'. The tasks included drawing, repeatedly writing 'ababababababab...', or reading a short poem. (①) The participants were asked to do these tasks until they felt exhausted. The experimenter then changed the context so that the participants had to do a subtly different task. (②) Those drawing were asked to redraw their last picture to demonstrate how quickly they could draw. (③) Those writing 'abab' were asked to sign their name and address. (④) In this new context their fatigue disappeared. (⑤) This phenomenon of creating a second wind can be seen in action at airports where security officers rotate around different stations to stop routine-induced fatigue from settling in.

4. 글의 흐름으로 보아, 주어진 문장이 들어가기에 가장 적절한 곳은?

2017학년도 6월 39번

For example, the first step in servicing or installing equipment is talking with the clients to understand how they used the equipment.

The customer service representatives in an electronics firm under major restructuring were told they had to begin selling service contracts for their equipment in addition to installing and repairing them. This generated a great deal of resistance. (①) To the service representatives, learning to sell was a very different game from what they had been playing. (②) But it turned out they already knew a lot more about sales than they thought. (③) The same is true in selling. (④) The salesperson first has to learn about the customer's needs. (⑤) The service representatives also had a great deal of product knowledge and hands-on experience, which is obviously important in sales.

5. 글의 흐름으로 보아, 주어진 문장이 들어가기에 가장 적절한 곳은?

2014학년도 수능 39번

So, when someone is threatening to go to war, or trying to convince us and mounting a huge public relations campaign to justify it, the news media have a responsibility to question everything.

It's important that the media provide us with diverse and opposing views, so we can choose the best available options. Let's take the example of going to war. (①) War should be a last resort, obviously, undertaken when all other options have failed. (②) They should be providing the most intense scrutiny on our behalf, so the public can see the other side of things. (③) Otherwise, we may be drawn into unnecessary wars, or wars fought for reasons other than those presented by governments and generals. (④) Most of the time, the media fail to perform this crucial role. (⑤) Even the large, so-called 'liberal' American media have admitted that they have not always been watchdogs for the public interest, and that their own coverage on some major issues "looks strikingly one-sided at times."

* scrutiny: 면밀한 조사

6. 글의 흐름으로 보아, 주어진 문장이 들어가기에 가장 적절한 곳은?

2018학년도 6월 38번

The net effect of this was that, although customers benefited, the banks lost out as their costs increased but the total number of customers stayed the same.

In mature markets, breakthroughs that lead to a major change in competitive positions and to the growth of the market are rare. (①) Because of this, competition becomes a zero sum game in which one organization can only win at the expense of others. (②) However, where the degree of competition is particularly intense a zero sum game can quickly become a negative sum game, in that everyone in the market is faced with additional costs. (③) As an example of this, when one of the major high street banks in Britain tried to gain a competitive advantage by opening on Saturday mornings, it attracted a number of new customers who found the traditional Monday-Friday bank opening hours to be a constraint. (④) However, faced with a loss of customers, the competition responded by opening on Saturdays as well. (⑤) In essence, this proved to be a negative sum game.

WORD

threaten 위협하다　convince 납득시키다　mount 벌이다, 시작하다　diverse 다양한　last resort 최후의 수단　obviously 명백히　undertake 착수하다　on one's behalf ~를 대신하여　crucial 결정적인, 중대한　watchdog 지키는 사람, 파수꾼　coverage 보도

WORD

net 최종적인, 근본적인　lose out 손해를 보다　mature 충분히 발달한　breakthrough 획기적인 발전, 돌파구　at the expense of ~의 희생으로, ~의 비용으로　negative sum game 참가자 모두가 손해를 보는 게임　competitive advantage 경쟁 우위　constraint 제약

7. 글의 흐름으로 보아, 주어진 문장이 들어가기에 가장 적절한 곳은? [2017학년도 6월 38번]

That is why people experience jet lag when traveling across time zones.

In humans, body clocks are responsible for daily changes in blood pressure, body temperature, hormones, hunger, and thirst, as well as our sleep-wake cycles. (①) These biological rhythms, which we experience as internal time, are probably older than sleep, developed over the course of millions of years of evolution. (②) They facilitate physiological and behavioral changes on a roughly twenty-four-hour cycle no matter what is happening outside, whether a cold front moves in or clouds block the light of the sun. (③) Their internal clocks continue to run in accordance with the place they left behind, not the one to which they have come, and it can take some time to realign the two. (④) The most remarkable thing is that our internal body clocks can be readjusted by environmental cues. (⑤) We may get jet lag for a few days when we ask our body clocks to adapt to a vastly different schedule of day and night cycles on the other side of the Earth, but they can do it.

* facilitate: 쉽게 하다
** realign: 재조정하다

8. 글의 흐름으로 보아, 주어진 문장이 들어가기에 가장 적절한 곳은? [2016학년도 수능 38번]

Even so, it is not the money *per se* that is valuable, but the fact that it can potentially yield more positive experiences.

Money – beyond the bare minimum necessary for food and shelter – is nothing more than a means to an end. Yet so often we confuse means with ends, and sacrifice happiness (end) for money (means). It is easy to do this when material wealth is elevated to the position of the ultimate end, as it so often is in our society. (①) This is not to say that the accumulation and production of material wealth is in itself wrong. (②) Material prosperity can help individuals, as well as society, attain higher levels of happiness. (③) Financial security can liberate us from work we do not find meaningful and from having to worry about the next paycheck. (④) Moreover, the desire to make money can challenge and inspire us. (⑤) Material wealth in and of itself does not necessarily generate meaning or lead to emotional wealth.

* *per se*: 그 자체로

WORD

jet lag 시차증　thirst 갈증　biological 생물학적　physiological 생리학적　behavioral 행동의　roughly 대략　in accordance with ~과 일치하여　cold front 한랭전선　readjust 재조정하다, 재적응하다

WORD

valuable 가치있는　potentially 잠재적으로　nothing more than ~ ~에 불과하다　means 수단　elevate 올리다　accumulation 축적　confuse ~ with ... ~을 …과 혼동하다　ultimate 궁극적인　liverate 자유롭게 하다

★ 혼공 6일차에 나온 문장들을 해석해 보자.

단어 PLUS

1 Despite such evidence of favoritism toward handsome politicians, follow-up research demonstrated that voters did not realize their bias.

1
+ evidence 증거
+ favoritism 편애
+ bias 편견

2 Ostensibly, sarcasm is the opposite of deception in that a sarcastic speaker typically intends the receiver to recognize the sarcastic intent; whereas, in deception the speaker typically intends that the receiver not recognize the deceptive intent.

2
+ ostensibly 표면상
+ sarcasm 비아냥
+ intent 의도
+ whereas 반면에
+ deception 속임수

3 This phenomenon of creating a second wind can be seen in action at airports where security officers rotate around different stations to stop routine-induced fatigue from settling in.

3
+ security 정밀조사
+ routine-induced
  일상에 의해 생기는
+ fatigue 피로

4 The customer service representatives in an electronics firm under major restructuring were told they had to begin selling service contracts for their equipment in addition to installing and repairing them.

4
+ representatives 대표자
+ restructuring 구조조정
+ contract 계약

5 So, when someone is threatening to go to war, or trying to convince us and mounting a huge public relations campaign to justify it, the news media have a responsibility to question everything.

5
+ convince 납득시키다
+ mount 벌이다

6 In mature markets, breakthroughs that lead to a major change in competitive positions and to the growth of the market are rare.

6
+ breakthrough 혁신
+ competitive 경쟁의

7 They facilitate physiological and behavioral changes on a roughly twenty-four-hour cycle no matter what is happening outside, whether a cold front moves in or clouds block the light of the sun.

7
+ facilitate 쉽게하다, 촉진하다
+ physiological 생리학적인
+ roughly 거의, 대략

영어 모의고사 성적이 안 올라요

샘도 학생 시절이 있었어. 어린이에서 갑자기 어른이 된 게 아니라구. 여튼 귀엽던 학생시절 때는 고1이었어. 초등학교 동창 친구가 있었는데 중학교는 다른 곳에 다녔거든. 그 친구를 고등학교 1학년 때 다시 만나게 된 거야. 초등학교 때 나름 라이벌이었기 때문에 성적으로 지기 싫었어. 그런데, 첫 모의고사를 보니 성적차이가 너무 많이 나더라고. 물론 내 패배였어.

특히 내가 지고 싶지 않았던 영어 성적이 너무 많이 차이나더라고. 일단 단어장을 사서 외우고 또 외웠지. 이를 갈면서 다음 모의고사를 기다렸어. 하지만, 시험을 보는데 막상 중간에 좀 어려운 문제가 나오니까 꼬이기 시작했어. 그리고 그 문제 때문에 마지막 독해에 가지도 못하고 집중력이 마구마구 흔들렸어. 모의고사가 끝나고 채점을 하는데 사람 마음이 참 간사하더라. 혹시나 찍은 게 맞지 않을까 조마조마하면서 답지를 가린 손을 서서히 들어 올렸어. 그런데 역시나 기적은 일어나지 않았어. 그렇게 1년을 그 녀석에게 완패 당했어.

2학년이 되었고 그 친구는 이과로 나는 문과로 갔어. 그 친구는 나를 라이벌로 아예 생각하지 않았겠지만 나는 집에서 혼자 원인을 분석해봤어. 나의 보이지 않는 경쟁은 계속되고 있었거든.

단어는 어느 정도 외운 거 같은데 왜 안 되는 걸까? 일단 독해집을 샀어. 다양한 분야의 소재를 다룬 독해 문제가 많이 수록 되어있더군. 게다가 그리 두껍지 않은 분량이었어. 딱 1달 만에 다 풀었어. 파이팅이 엄청났거든. 다행히 모의고사가 다가왔어. 시험을 치는데 1학년 때보다는 확실히 낫더라고. 느낌이 좋았어. 하지만 채점을 하는데 맞았다고 생각했던 문제 몇 개가 틀리더라고. 아! 탄식이 흘러나왔지. A형이라 마음 속으로 고함을 질렀어.

며칠이 지나서 모의고사 성적 우수자 명단을 게시판에 공고했어. 참 잔인하지만 샘이 학교 다닐 때에는 문·이과 탑랭커들의 성적을 모든 학생들이 다 볼 수 있었어. 그 친구는 이과 명단에 있었고, 나는 문과 명단에 없었어. 영어 성적만 비교했는데도 아직 원점수 10점 정도 차이가 났어. 정말 미칠 것 같았지. 이러다가 2학년이 다 지나갈 것 같다는 두려움도 들었어.

집에 와서 평정을 다시 찾은 나는, 나름의 시스템을 구축했어. 단어는 쉬는 시간 5분씩 하루에 8번 이상씩 계속 보고, 어려운 문장을 정리해서 점심 시간 등 조금 긴 자투리 시간에 10~15분씩 읽고 직독직해 했어. 그리고 자습시간처럼 긴 시간에는 5~6문제를 매일 시간 재고 풀었어. 이렇게 2~3달 지나니까 15~16문제도 거뜬하게 풀 수 있겠더라고. 그렇게 다시 모의고사가 찾아왔어.

'다른 건 몰라도 영어는 이긴다'라는 생각이 강했지. 초집중해서 듣기 문제부터 풀었어. 듣기는 스피커 위치가 안 좋으면 불리할까봐 평소 화장실에 갈 때마다 라디오를 가지고 갔어. 미친 것 같지만 울리는 소리에 적응하기 위함이었어. 여튼 듣기를 무사히 넘기고, 독해를 풀다보니 생각지 못한 문항이 중간에 등장하더라고. 내가 어려우면 다른 친구들도 어려울 것이라 생각했지. 심호흡 크게 하고 문제를 다시 읽어보았어. 갑자기 답이 쑥~ 떠오르더라고. 그렇게 고비를 넘기고 빠듯하지만 시간 내에 문제를 다 풀었어.

채점을 하는데 정말 눈물이 나오는 줄 알았어. 처음 100점을 받았거든. 그 친구를 처음 이긴 시험이기도 하고.

혼공

07일차

글의 순서

#생각보다_쉽다

난이도 🌶🌶🌶

It is a great ability to be able to conceal one's ability.
by Francois de La Rochefoucauld

자신의 능력을 숨길 수 있는 것은 대단한 능력이다.

- 매년 2문제씩 출제 (2017 수능 2문제 출제)
- 주어진 글 다음에 (A), (B), (C) 세 개의 단락을 배열하는 문제임
- 여러 실마리를 사용하여 문장의 전후관계를 맞춰야 함
- 대명사와 연결사, 논리적 독해 능력이 필요함
- 실제로는 두 문단의 순서만 맞춰도 답이 나오는 유형임
- 선택지에서 첫 문단으로 하나만 제시되어 있는 것은 제거(주로 (A)) → 대부분 (B) or (C)가 첫 문단

1 선택지에서 시작점 1개는 제거하자.

① (A) – (C) – (B) 　② (B) – (A) – (C) 　③ (B) – (C) – (A)

④ (C) – (A) – (B) 　⑤ (C) – (B) – (A)

> **Solution** 절대적이지는 않지만 확률적으로 (A)로 시작하는 보기가 하나인데 이게 정답이면 첫 번째 단락만 파악하면 답이 나와 버리잖아. 그럼 나머지 2개의 단락은 읽어보지도 않는 사태가 발생하지. 그래서 웬만하면 1개짜리는 제거하는 게 좋지. 보통은 (B) vs (C)의 대결이라고 보면 돼.

2 대명사, 연결어, 혹은 부정/긍정 관계를 파악하자.

> The Internet has several big advantages: there's lots of information, and it can be totally up-to-date.

> **Solution** 일단 시작점은 인터넷의 장점인데 이어지는 내용은 이걸 뒷받침할 수도 있고, 반박할 수도 있어. 둘 다 염두에 두어야겠지.

❸ (A) **Therefore**, avoid using the Internet as your first or only source of information.

❶ (B) **However**, it's not always a reliable source.

❷ (C) There are often no editors to make sure the facts are straight, and anyone with a computer can post his or her own opinions as fact.

> **Solution** 결론에 해당하는 Therefore가 쓰이고 있어. 무엇에 대한 결론인가 봤더니 인터넷을 너무 의지하지 말라는 거네? 부정적인 내용에 대한 결론이지. 결국 (A)가 마지막이네.

> **Solution** However라는 역접을 의미하는 연결어가 나오지. 뒤에 보니 항상 믿을만 한건 아니래. 바로 인터넷의 단점을 말하고 있어. 남은 건 다른 단락의 성격을 보면 돼. 인터넷에 대해 긍정인지 부정인지 말이야.

> **Solution** 역시 인터넷의 단점을 언급하고 있어. 당연히 (B) 뒤에 나와야겠지.

주어진 글 다음에 이어질 글의 순서로 가장 적절한 것은?

2016학년도 6월 37번

The timing of positive versus negative behavior seems to influence attraction. Several studies have identified what has been called the loss-gain effect.

(A) Studies suggest that you would not. In fact, people are more attracted to individuals who are consistently negative than to people who initially behave positively and then switch to negative behavior.

(B) The reason is this: people who start out being nice get our hopes up, so the letdown we experience when we discover that they are not nice makes it worse than if they had acted badly from the start.

(C) This effect reflects what happens to attraction when a person's behavior moves from positive to negative or from negative to positive. For example, if someone seemed very nice to you early in the interaction, but then began to act like a fool, would you be more attracted to that person than if that person were a fool from the start?

① (A) – (C) – (B)　　② (B) – (A) – (C)　　③ (B) – (C) – (A)

④ (C) – (A) – (B)　　⑤ (C) – (B) – (A)

WORD

versus 대 (對)　　**behavior** 행동　　**attraction** 매력(도)　　**identify** 확인하다, 식별하다　　**loss-gain effect** 득실 효과　　**consistently** 일관되게　　**switch** 전환하다　　**letdown** 감소, 쇠퇴　　**discover** 발견하다　　**from the start** 처음부터　　**reflect** 반영하다　　**interaction** 상호작용

The timing of positive versus negative behavior seems to influence attraction. Several studies have identified what has been called the loss-gain effect.

(A) Studies suggest that you would not. In fact, people are more attracted to individuals who are consistently negative than to people who initially behave positively and then switch to negative behavior.

(B) The reason is this: people who start out being nice get our hopes up, so the letdown we experience when we discover that they are not nice makes it worse than if they had acted badly from the start.

(C) This effect reflects what happens to attraction when a person's behavior moves from positive to negative or from negative to positive. For example, if someone seemed very nice to you early in the interaction, but then began to act like a fool, would you be more attracted to that person than if that person were a fool from the start?

① (A) – (C) – (B)   ② (B) – (A) – (C)   ③ (B) – (C) – (A)
④ (C) – (A) – (B)   ⑤ (C) – (B) – (A)

정답: ④

해석 긍정적 행동 대(對) 부정적 행동의 타이밍은 느껴지는 매력도에 영향을 미치는 것처럼 보인다. 몇몇의 연구에 의해 득실 효과라는 것이 확인 되었다. (C) 이 효과는 어떤 이의 행동이 긍정적 행동에서 부정적 것으로 혹은 부정적 행동에서 긍정적인 것으로 변화할 때 매력도에 어떤 일이 일어나는지를 반영한다. 예를 들면, 어떤 사람이 상호 작용 초기에는 여러분에게 매우 친절해 보이지만, 그 후에 바보처럼 행동하기 시작한다면 당신은 그 사람이 처음부터 바보처럼 행동할 때보다 그 사람에게 더 끌리게 될까? (A) 연구에 따르면, 당신이 그렇지 않을 것이다. 사실, 사람들은 처음에 긍정적으로 행동한 후 부정적 행동으로 전환하는 사람들보다 일괄되게 부정적인 사람들에게 더 끌린다. (B) 그 이유는 다음과 같다. 초기에 친절한 사람들은 우리의 기대감을 높여 주어, 그들이 친절하지 않다는 것을 알게 되었을 때 우리가 경험하는 실망은 그들이 처음부터 나쁘게 행동했을 때보다 상황이 더 악화시킨다.

3 단계 고난도 문항 요리하기

1. 주어진 글 다음에 이어질 글의 순서로 가장 적절한 것은?

2016학년도 9월 36번

According to one traditional definition, *aesthetics* is the branch of philosophy that deals with beauty, especially beauty in the arts. Examining the pleasing features of the *Mona Lisa* or a snow-capped mountain, for example, would come under aesthetics.

(A) Consider Picasso's *Guernica*, a huge (11-ft. × 25.6-ft.) painting in black, white, and grey that he made in response to the slaughter of Spanish civilians by German and Italian warplanes during the Spanish Civil War. Images of a cruel war dominate the canvas.

(B) That definition seems too narrow, however, since works of art and natural objects may interest us in other ways than by being beautiful. Instead of evoking admiration of beauty, artists may evoke puzzlement, shock, and even disgust.

(C) This work is widely admired but not for being beautiful. So a better definition of aesthetics would be that it is the branch of philosophy that deals with the ways things please people in being experienced.

* slaughter: 대량 학살

① (A) – (C) – (B) ② (B) – (A) – (C)
③ (B) – (C) – (A) ④ (C) – (A) – (B)
⑤ (C) – (B) – (A)

2. 주어진 글 다음에 이어질 글의 순서로 가장 적절한 것은?

2008학년도 6월 38번

When we look at the world and ourselves, we do it through a set of filters. Think about what a filter is. A filter is a mechanism that lets some things flow in but screens other things out.

(A) Through them, we process and assign a weight and meaning to every event in our lives. Some things flow in, others are screened out, but everything is affected: not just what we 'see,' but what we 'hear' and 'believe.'

(B) Depending on what the filter is made up of, it can also alter whatever is looked at or passes through it. Sunglasses are a good example of a visual filter.

(C) But, obviously, I am not talking here about some physical apparatus that we can put on and take off, like a pair of glasses. In fact, the filters I am mentioning are internal, mental, emotional, verbal, and perceptual in nature.

① (A) – (B) – (C) ② (A) – (C) – (B)
③ (B) – (A) – (C) ④ (B) – (C) – (A)
⑤ (C) – (B) – (A)

3. 주어진 글 다음에 이어질 글의 순서로 가장 적절한 것은?

2015학년도 6월 37번

Mom and Dad went to dinner at a nice restaurant. On that first night to myself, Dad entrusted me with his movie projector and all the reels of film.

(A) Then I can play the film backward and watch the cat fly down to the floor and see all the splashes of ice cream slurp themselves back into the dish. I made Simon jump in and out several times before I watched the rest of the film.

(B) He said I could do everything myself that night. So I set up the screen at one end of the living room. I turned on the projector, turned off the light, put the bowl of popcorn in my lap, and settled in to watch the film labeled HATTIE-1951.

(C) It's one of my favorites because my third birthday party is on it and I can watch our old cat Simon jump up on the dining room table and land in a dish of ice cream.

* slurp: 후루룩 소리를 내다

① (A) – (C) – (B)   ② (B) – (A) – (C)
③ (B) – (C) – (A)   ④ (C) – (A) – (B)
⑤ (C) – (B) – (A)

4. 주어진 글 다음에 이어질 글의 순서로 가장 적절한 것은?

2012학년도 9월 43번

One reason why the definitions of words have changed over time is simply because of their misuse. There are a growing number of examples where the incorrect meaning of relatively commonplace language has become more widespread than the original intention or definition.

(A) Now, imagine that an angry customer sent you a letter about the service he received in one of your stores. If your reply is that you 'perused his letter,' he is likely to get even more angry than he was before.

(B) The word 'peruse' is one of them. Most people think that to 'peruse' something means to 'scan or skim it quickly, without paying much attention.' In fact, this is the exact opposite of what 'peruse' really means: 'to study or read something carefully, in detail.'

(C) But the word has been misused so often by so many people, that this second sense of it – the exact opposite of what it actually means – has finally been accepted as a secondary definition and as far as most people know, it is the only definition.

① (A) – (C) – (B)   ② (B) – (A) – (C)
③ (B) – (C) – (A)   ④ (C) – (A) – (B)
⑤ (C) – (B) – (A)

WORD

to oneself 혼자, 홀로   **entrust** 맡기다   **reel** (필름) 통   **splash** (떨어지는) 방울, (방울로 인한) 얼룩, 철벅하는 소리   **settle in** 자리를 잡다, 거처를 정하다

WORD

definition 정의   **misuse** 오용   **commonplace** 진부한, 흔한   **peruse** 정독하다   **scan** 훑어보다   **skim** 대충 지나치다   **secondary** 부차적인, 두 번째의

5. 주어진 글 다음에 이어질 글의 순서로 가장 적절한 것은?

2013학년도 9월 43번

Studying history is not about memorizing what we have been told – it requires us to investigate the past. Like a detective, we start with the easy, known pieces of information.

(A) You have to go further to ask questions such as, "Why was he cruel?" and "What were the results of his rule?" Hence, studying history trains us not to accept everything we read or hear as the truth. Instead, it trains us to use our critical thinking skills to get the full picture of the past.

(B) For example, if someone told you that Chinese Emperor Qin Shihuang was a cruel ruler, would you simply accept this as the truth? Or, would you ask questions about the statement and look for information or evidence to support it?

(C) We then shuffle the pieces around to see how they fit together. Once all the pieces fit, we have the full picture. As we put the pieces together, we challenge ourselves to think of other ways to describe what we know.

① (A) – (C) – (B) ② (B) – (A) – (C)
③ (B) – (C) – (A) ④ (C) – (A) – (B)
⑤ (C) – (B) – (A)

6. 주어진 글 다음에 이어질 글의 순서로 가장 적절한 것은?

2014학년도 6월 38번

Organic farmers grow crops that are no less plagued by pests than those of conventional farmers; insects generally do not discriminate between organic and conventional as well as we do.

(A) However, most organic farmers have no choice but to rely on chemicals as necessary supplements to their operations. With pests often consuming up to 40 percent of the crops grown in the United States, they do so as a matter of course.

(B) They might refer to these substances as "botanical extracts." But according to Ned Groth, a senior scientist at Consumers Union, these toxins "are not necessarily less worrisome because they are natural."

(C) It is true that they are far more likely than conventional farmers to practice environmentally beneficial forms of biological control, and that they are also more likely to sensibly diversify their crops to reduce infestation.

* infestation: 횡행, 만연

① (A) – (C) – (B) ② (B) – (A) – (C)
③ (B) – (C) – (A) ④ (C) – (A) – (B)
⑤ (C) – (B) – (A)

WORD

memorize 암기하다 investigate 조사하다 detective 탐정 hence 따라서, 그런 이유로 get the picture 이해하다 emperor 황제 statement 진술 evidence 증거 shuffle 이리저리 바꾸다 put ~ together ~을 모으다, 짜 맞추다

WORD

organic 유기농법의 plague 괴롭히다, 고통을 주다 pest 해충 conventional 재래식의, 전통적인 discriminate 구별하다 have no choice but to부정사 ~할 수밖에 없다 supplement 보충물 substance 물질 botanical 식물의 extract 추출물 Consumers Unions 미국 소비자 동맹 diversify 다양화하다

7. 주어진 글 다음에 이어질 글의 순서로 가장 적절한 것은?

2017학년도 6월 36번

The ancient Greeks sought to improve memory through brain training methods such as memory palaces and the method of loci. At the same time, they and the Egyptians became experts at externalizing information, inventing the modern library, a grand storehouse for externalized knowledge.

(A) This need isn't simply learned; it is a biological imperative — animals organize their environments instinctively. Most mammals are biologically programmed to put their digestive waste away from where they eat and sleep.

(B) We don't know why these simultaneous explosions of intellectual activity occurred when they did (perhaps daily human experience had hit a certain level of complexity). But the human need to organize our lives, our environment, even our thoughts, remains strong.

(C) Dogs have been known to collect their toys and put them in baskets; ants carry off dead members of the colony to burial grounds; certain birds and rodents create barriers around their nests in order to more easily detect invaders.

* method of loci: 장소를 활용한 기억법
** rodent: 설치류 동물

① (A) – (C) – (B) ② (B) – (A) – (C)
③ (B) – (C) – (A) ④ (C) – (A) – (B)
⑤ (C) – (B) – (A)

8. 주어진 글 다음에 이어질 글의 순서로 가장 적절한 것은?

2017학년도 수능 37번

Evolution works to maximize the number of descendants that an animal leaves behind. Where the risk of death from fishing increases as an animal grows, evolution favors those that grow slowly, mature younger and smaller, and reproduce earlier.

(A) Surely these adaptations are good news for species hard-pressed by excessive fishing? Not exactly. Young fish produce many fewer eggs than large-bodied animals, and many industrial fisheries are now so intensive that few animals survive more than a couple of years beyond the age of maturity.

(B) This is exactly what we now see in the wild. Cod in Canada's Gulf of St. Lawrence begin to reproduce at around four today; forty years ago they had to wait until six or seven to reach maturity. Sole in the North Sea mature at half the body weight they did in 1950.

(C) Together this means there are fewer eggs and larvae to secure future generations. In some cases the amount of young produced today is a hundred or even a thousand times less than in the past, putting the survival of species, and the fisheries dependent on them, at grave risk.

① (A) – (C) – (B) ② (B) – (A) – (C)
③ (B) – (C) – (A) ④ (C) – (A) – (B)
⑤ (C) – (B) – (A)

WORD

externalize 외면화하다 imperative 명령 instinctively 본능적으로 digestive 소화의 simultaneous 동시의 explosion 폭발 burial ground 매장지 detect 탐지하다 invader 침입자

WORD

evolution 진화 descendant 후손 reproduce 번식하다, 생식하다 hard-pressed 심한 압박을 받는 fishery 어업 intensive 집중적인 maturity 성숙 cod 대구 sole 가자미 larvae 유충들

4 단계 혼공 개념 마무리

★ 혼공 7일차에 나온 문장들을 해석해 보자.

1 Examining the pleasing features of the Mona Lisa or a snow-capped mountain, for example, would come under aesthetics.

2 So a better definition of aesthetics would be that it is the branch of philosophy that deals with the ways things please people in being experienced.

3 Then I can play the film backward and watch the cat fly down to the floor and see all the splashes of ice cream slurp themselves back into the dish.

4 There are a growing number of examples where the incorrect meaning of relatively commonplace language has become more widespread than the original intention or definition.

5 It is true that they are far more likely than conventional farmers to practice environmentally beneficial forms of biological control, and that they are also more likely to sensibly diversify their crops to reduce infestation.

6 At the same time, they and the Egyptians became experts at externalizing information, inventing the modern library, a grand storehouse for externalized knowledge.

7 In some cases the amount of young produced today is a hundred or even a thousand times less than in the past, putting the survival of species, and the fisheries dependent on them, at grave risk.

단어 PLUS

1
+ pleasing 즐거운
+ feature 특징
+ aesthetics 미학

2
+ definition 정의
+ philosophy 철학

3
+ splahs 물을 튀기다
+ slurp 후루룩 소리를 내다

4
+ relatively 상대적으로
+ commonplace 흔한
+ intention 의도

5
+ conventional 관례적인
+ beneficial 유리한
+ diversify 다양화하다
+ infestation 만연, 횡행

6
+ externalize 표면화하다

7
+ fishery 어업

커피와 에너지 음료가 없으면 집중이 안된다고?

요즘 학생들은 확실히 샘 때보다 여건은 나아진 것 같다는 생각이 들어. 물론 전반적으로 전력 상승된 거라 '경쟁'하는 학생들 입장에서는 체감하기 어렵겠지만.

대표적인 사례로 요즘 일부 학생들은 공부할 때 테이크 아웃 커피나 잠을 달아나게 하는 핫XX라는 음료를 마시더라고. 둘 다 카페인이 들어가 있기 때문에 잠도 덜 오고, 학생들에게는 효자 역할을 하는 것 같아. 시험 기간에는 애용하는 학생들이 더 늘어나는 게 확실히 보이더군.

문제는 과연 이게 몸에 좋을까 하는 거야. 물론 아무리 생각해도 좋을 것 같지는 않지? 잠이 온다는 것은 몸이 보내는 자연스러운 신호잖아. 그런 자연스러운 신호를 거스르는 거니까 몸에 좋을 것 같지는 않아. 그런데, 구체적으로 왜, 그리고 어떻게 몸에 안 좋은지를 알아야 할 것 같아. 그래서 한 티브이 프로그램에서 나온 내용을 가져와봤어.

> 뇌가 쓰는 에너지는 23%,
>
> 뇌를 쓴다는 것은 굉장히 힘든 일.
>
> 몸에서 에너지가 떨어지면 뇌를 천천히 쓰라고 아데노신 이라는 물질이 분비됨.
>
> 근데 카페인이 아데노신을 막음.
>
> 뇌는 카페인 때문에 에너지가 많다고 속아버림.
>
> 우리 사회가 커피를 많이 마신다는 것은 마시지 않으면 하루를 버틸 수 없다는
>
> 굉장히 피로한 사회라는 증거

읽고 보니 우리 참 힘들게 사는구나 싶네. 그런데 샘은 안타깝게도 카페인이 많이 들어가 있는 제품을 마셔도 잠이 그냥 너무 잘 와. 체질이거든. 문득 궁금해졌는데 샘은 아데노신이 상대적으로 잘 안 나오는 건가? 이거 좋은 거야 안 좋은 거야? 그냥 갑자기 슬프다. ㅎㅎ

08일차

요약문 완성

#시험의_거의_마지막_문항 #시간압박 #빈칸+주제

난이도 🌶🌶🌶

A book that is shut is but a block.
by Thomas Fuller

닫혀있기만 한 책은 블록일 뿐이다.

01 문항 특징

- 매년 1문제씩 출제되며(2017 수능 1문제 출제) 5년 평균 정답률 65.6%
- 빈칸에는 글의 핵심어가 들어가는데 본문에서 언급된 단어보다는 유사어나 파생어가 들어감
- 지문보다 제시된 요약문을 먼저 읽어봐서 지문의 성격을 파악하는 것이 유리함
- 요약문의 빈칸 앞에 부정어가 들어갈 경우 반대로 생각해야 함

02 혼공 전략

1 글의 요지를 파악하는 것이 중요. 주제문을 찾아라.

Children are much more resistant to giving something to someone else than to helping them. One can observe this difference clearly in very young children. Even though one-and-a-half-year-olds will support each other in difficult situations, they are not willing to share their own toys with others. ~

Although very young children will ___(A)___ each other in difficult situations, they are unwilling to ___(B)___ their possessions.

Solution 2 맨 앞 문장이 이 글의 주제문에 해당되지. 주제문과 요약문을 비교해봐. 비슷하지? 요약문에 나온 possession은 something 과 비슷하니까 resistant to giving이랑 unwilling to (   ) 도 비슷해야겠지. 그러니 일단 (B)에는 share가 적절해. (A)에는 help라는 단어가 나오니 그게 들어가면 되겠지.

Solution 1 요약문을 먼저 읽어 봐야 해. 전체적인 글의 분위기를 예상할 수 있어. '아이들 + 어려운 상황 + 자신들의 소유물'이 언급되고 있지.

2 세부적인 내용에 얽매이지 말자.

Researchers promised that the students could have one of the ten posters as a reward for their participation. However, when the students finished the task, the researchers said that the students were not allowed to keep the poster that they had rated as the third-most beautiful. Then, they asked the students to judge all ten posters again from the very beginning. What happened was that the poster they were unable to keep was suddenly ranked as the most beautiful. Just like Romeo and Juliet in the Shakespearean tragedy, people become more attached to each other when their love is prohibited.

When people find they cannot ___(A)___ something, they begin to think it more ___(B)___ .

Solution 본문에서 언급된 실험의 내용이 중요한 것이 아니야. 중요한 것은 실험을 통해서 필자가 말하고 싶은 게 중요하지. 여기서는 '가지지 못하게 한 것에 대한 욕구'가 핵심이야. 따라서 (A)에는 '가지다'를 의미하는 have나 own이 들어가면 돼.

Solution 로미오와 줄리엣이 그냥 나온 게 아니겠지? 바로 금지에 대항 열망을 다시 한 번 말하고 있어. 바로 이 부분이 (B)에 들어가면 되니까 attractive가 적절해.

다음 글의 내용을 한 문장으로 요약하고자 한다. 빈칸 (A)와 (B)에 들어갈 말로 가장 적절한 것은?

2015학년도 6월 40번

An ant turns right, left, and moves ahead over a sandy hill. How can we explain the complexity of the path it chose? We can think up a sophisticated program in the ant's brain, but it does not work. What we have overlooked is the ant's environment. The ant may be following a simple rule: get out of the sun and back to the nest. Complex behavior does not imply complex mental strategies. The same holds for humans. The apparent complexity of a man's behavior over time is largely a reflection of the complexity of the environment in which he finds himself. People adapt to their environments much as gelatin does; if you wish to know what form it will have when it solidifies, study the shape of the mold that holds the gelatin. To understand behavior, one has to look at both the mind and the environment.

* gelatin: 젤라틴, 정제한 아교

Although we tend to ___(A)___ complex behavior with complex mental operations, ___(B)___ factors need to be considered as well for a better understanding of such behavior.

	(A)		(B)
①	associate	······	genetic
②	associate	······	environmental
③	identify	······	psychological
④	replace	······	psychological
⑤	replace	······	environmental

An ant turns right, left, and moves ahead over a sandy hill. How can we explain the complexity of the path it chose? We can think up a sophisticated program in the ant's brain, but it does not work. What we have overlooked is the ant's environment. The ant may be following a simple rule: get out of the sun and back to the nest. Complex behavior does not imply complex mental strategies. The same holds for humans. The apparent complexity of a man's behavior over time is largely a reflection of the complexity of the environment in which he finds himself. People adapt to their environments much as gelatin does; if you wish to know what form it will have when it solidifies, study the shape of the mold that holds the gelatin. To understand behavior, one has to look at both the mind and the environment.

↓

Although we tend to __(A)__ complex behavior with complex mental operations, __(B)__ factors need to be considered as well for a better understanding of such behavior.

Solution 2 일반적인 사람들의 생각을 통념이라고 하지. 바로 이 부분이 통념에 해당되는 부분이야. 복잡한 프로그램이 포인트지.

Solution 3 이 모든 부분이 중요한 것은 바로 '환경'이라고 이야기하고 있어. 반복해서 '환경'과 복잡한 행동을 연결하고 있지.

Solution 1 요약문 완성 문제에서 가장 먼저 할 일은 바로 요약문을 읽어보는 거야. 글의 구조를 보니까 not (A), but (B)가 생각나는 구조지? 분명히 글은 (A)로 시작했다가 사실은 (B)라는 형식으로 전개가 될 거야.

Solution 4 지문에서 반복해서 나오는 건 바로 '복잡한 행동'은 '복잡한 정신적 작용'이 아니라 '환경'에서 비롯된 것이라는 내용이야. 따라서 (A)는 '연관이 있다'라는 뜻의 associate, (B)는 '환경'을 의미하는 environmental이 와야 해.

정답: ②

해석 개미는 모래 언덕 위에서 오른쪽으로, 왼쪽으로, 앞으로 움직인다. 개미가 선택한 길의 복잡성을 어떻게 설명할 수 있을까? 우리는 개미의 뇌 속에 있는 정교한 프로그램을 생각해 낼 수 있지만, 그것은 해결책이 되지 않는다. 우리가 간과한 것은 개미의 환경이다. 개미는 단순한 규칙, 즉 태양에서 벗어나서 집으로 돌아가는 규칙을 따르고 있을지도 모른다. 복잡한 행동이 복잡한 정신적 전략을 암시하는 것은 아니다. 똑같은 것이 인간에게도 적용된다. 시간이 흐르면서 복잡한 것 같아 보이는 인간의 행동은 주로 인간이 처한 환경의 복잡성을 반영하는 것이다. 사람들은 젤라틴과 매우 비슷하게 자신의 환경에 적응한다. 젤라틴이 굳어질 때에 어떤 모양이 될 것인지 알고 싶다면, 그것을 담는 틀의 모양을 살펴보라. 행동을 이해하려면, 정신과 환경을 둘 다 살펴보아야 한다.

↓

우리에게는 복잡한 행동을 복잡한 정신적 작용과 관련시키는 경향이 있지만, 그러한 행동을 더 잘 이해하기 위해서는 환경적인 요인들이 또한 고려되어야 한다.

3 단계 고난도 문항 요리하기

1. 다음 글의 내용을 한 문장으로 요약하고자 한다. 빈칸 (A)와 (B)에 들어갈 말로 가장 적절한 것은?

2018학년도 6월 40번

When considered in terms of evolutionary success, many of the seemingly irrational choices that people make do not seem so foolish after all. Most animals, including our ancestors and modern-day capuchin monkeys, lived very close to the margin of survival. Paleontologists who study early human civilizations have uncovered evidence that our ancestors faced frequent periods of drought and freezing. When you are living on the verge of starvation, a slight downturn in your food reserves makes a lot more difference than a slight upturn. Anthropologists who study people still living in hunter-gatherer societies have discovered that they regularly make choices designed to produce not the best opportunity for obtaining a hyperabundant supply of food but, instead, the least danger of ending up with an insufficient supply. In other words, people everywhere have a strong motivation to avoid falling below the level that will feed themselves and their families. If our ancestors hadn't agonized over losses and instead had taken too many chances in going after the big gains, they'd have been more likely to lose out and never become anyone's ancestor.

↓

Our ancestors gave priority to __(A)__ minimum resources rather than pursuing maximum gains, and that was the rational choice for human __(B)__ from an evolutionary perspective.

	(A)		(B)
①	securing	·····	freedom
②	securing	·····	interaction
③	identifying	·····	exploration
④	securing	·····	prosperity
⑤	securing	·····	survival

WORD

evolutionary 진화적인 paleontologist 고생물학자 anthropologist 인류학자 hyperabundant 매우 풍요로운 on the verge of 직전에

2. 다음 글의 내용을 한 문장으로 요약하고자 한다. 빈칸 (A)와 (B)에 들어갈 말로 가장 적절한 것은?

2011학년도 수능 45번

Unlike the modern society, the primitive society has less specialized knowledge to transmit, and since its way of life is enacted before the eyes of all, it has no need to create a separate institution of education such as the school. Instead, the child acquires the heritage of his culture by observing and imitating adults in such activities as rituals, hunts, festivals, cultivation, and harvesting. As a result, there is little or none of that alienation of young from old so marked in modern industrial societies. A further reason for this alienation in modern societies is that in his conception of reality the modern adult owes less to his direct experience and more to the experience of his culture than does primitive man. Clearly, his debt to culture will vary with the nature of his education. Hence, the contemporary child must travel much further than the offspring of primitive man to acquire the world view of his elders. He is, therefore, that much more removed from the adults of his society.

↓

Unlike the primitive child who learns from his __(A)__ surroundings, the modern child learns in educational institutions, which results in __(B)__ from his elders.

	(A)		(B)
①	foreign	·····	interference
②	immediate	·····	sympathy
③	foreign	·····	sympathy
④	imaginary	·····	alienation
⑤	immediate	·····	alienation

WORD

primitive 원시적인 transmit 전달하다 enact 제정하다, 벌어지다 heritage 유산 cultivation 경작 alienation 소외 contemporary 현대의 offspring 자손, 자녀 interference 방해 sympathy 공감

3. 다음 글의 내용을 한 문장으로 요약하고자 한다. 빈칸 (A)와 (B)에 들어갈 말로 가장 적절한 것은?

2016학년도 수능 40번

Performance must be judged in terms of what is under the control of the individuals being evaluated rather than those influences on performance that are beyond their control. There can be broad, influential factors, sometimes of an economic nature, that hold down the performance of everyone being judged. One example is in sales. If there is a general downturn in the economy and products or services are not being purchased with the same frequency as in the previous year, sales could be down, for example, by an average of 15%. This 15% (actually −15%) figure would then represent "average" performance. Perhaps the best salesperson in the year had only a 3% drop in sales over the previous year. Thus, "good" performance in this situation is a smaller loss compared to some average or norm group.

↓

In performance evaluation, we should consider __(A)__ factors affecting the individual's performance rather than __(B)__ figures only.

(A)	(B)
① contextual	put aside
② contextual	rely on
③ controllable	put aside
④ positive	ignore
⑤ positive	rely on

4. 다음 글의 내용을 한 문장으로 요약하고자 한다. 빈칸 (A)와 (B)에 들어갈 말로 가장 적절한 것은?

2015학년도 9월 40번

Experts have found that reading classical texts benefits the mind by catching the reader's attention and triggering moments of self-reflection. The brain activity of volunteers was monitored as they read classical works. These same texts were then "translated" into more straightforward, modern language and again the readers' brains were monitored as they read the words. Scans showed that the more challenging prose and poetry set off far more electrical activity in the brain than the more pedestrian versions. Scientists were able to study the brain activity as it responded to each word and record how it lit up as the readers encountered unusual words, surprising phrases or difficult sentence structures. This lighting up lasts long enough to shift the brain into a higher gear, encouraging further reading. The research also found that reading the more challenging version of poetry, in particular, increases activity in the right hemisphere of the brain, helping the readers to reflect on and reevaluate their own experiences in light of what they have read. The academics said this meant the classics were more useful than self-help books.

↓

Original versions of classical texts are helpful to readers because they contain __(A)__ language that inspires further reading and __(B)__ readers' self-reflection.

(A)	(B)
① challenging	distorts
② demanding	activates
③ comprehensible	increases
④ difficult	hinders
⑤ accessible	stimulates

WORD

performance 성과, 공연   in terms of ~의 면에서   influential 영향력이 있는   downturn 경기 침체   frequency 빈도   norm group 기준 집단, 준거 집단   contextual 상황적인   put aside 한 쪽으로 빼두다

WORD

trigger 촉발하다   straightforward 쉬운   prose 산문   pedestrian 평범한, 단조로운   hemisphere (뇌의) 반구   academic 교수   self-help book 자습서   comprehensible 이해할 수 있는   hinder 방해하다

5. 다음 글의 내용을 한 문장으로 요약하고자 한다. 빈칸 (A)와 (B)에 들어갈 말로 가장 적절한 것은?

2017학년도 수능 40번

The impacts of tourism on the environment are evident to scientists, but not all residents attribute environmental damage to tourism. Residents commonly have positive views on the economic and some sociocultural influences of tourism on quality of life, but their reactions to environmental impacts are mixed. Some residents feel tourism provides more parks and recreation areas, improves the quality of the roads and public facilities, and does not contribute to ecological decline. Many do not blame tourism for traffic problems, overcrowded outdoor recreation, or the disturbance of peace and tranquility of parks. Alternatively, some residents express concern that tourists overcrowd the local fishing, hunting, and other recreation areas or may cause traffic and pedestrian congestion. Some studies suggest that variations in residents' feelings about tourism's relationship to environmental damage are related to the type of tourism, the extent to which residents feel the natural environment needs to be protected, and the distance residents live from the tourist attractions.

* tranquility: 고요함 ** congestion: 혼잡

↓

Residents do not ___(A)___ tourism's environmental influences identically since they take ___(B)___ postures based on factors such as the type of tourism, opinions on the degree of protection, and their distance from an attraction.

	(A)		(B)
①	weigh	……	common
②	weigh	……	balanced
③	weigh	……	dissimilar
④	control	……	favorable
⑤	control	……	conflicting

WORD

evident 명확한 **attribute A to B** A를 B탓으로 돌리다 **mixed** (의견이) 엇갈린 **contribute to** ~에 기여하다 **disturbance** 방해 **alternatively** 그 대신에 **pedestrian** 보행자(의) **identically** 동일하게

6. 다음 글의 내용을 한 문장으로 요약하고자 한다. 빈칸 (A)와 (B)에 들어갈 말로 가장 적절한 것은?

2014학년도 수능 40번

Low-balling describes the technique where two individuals arrive at an agreement and then one increases the cost to be incurred by the other. For example, after the consumer has agreed to purchase a car for $8,000, the salesperson begins to add on $100 for tax and $200 for tires. These additional costs might be thought of as a metaphorical 'low ball' that the salesperson throws the consumer. One explanation for the effectiveness of low-balling is in terms of self-perception theory. When the consumer agrees to purchase the product under the original terms, that behavior might be used by the consumer to infer his sincere interest in the product. This inferred sincere interest in the product may enable him to endure the increased cost. An alternative explanation is in terms of impression management theory. If the consumer were to withdraw from the deal after the 'slight' change in the terms of agreement, he might foster the rather undesirable impression of being an irresponsible consumer unaware of these necessary charges.

↓

Low-balling is effective in sales contexts because the consumer, by not withdrawing from the deal, tends to ___(A)___ his purchase decision or tries to save ___(B)___ .

	(A)		(B)
①	justify	……	time
②	justify	……	face
③	cherish	……	time
④	modify	……	face
⑤	modify	……	trouble

WORD

low-balling 가격을 과소 산정하는 것(고의로 싼 값을 붙이고 나중에 여러 명목으로 값을 올리는 판매 기술) **incur** 초래하다, 당하다 **metaphorical** 비유적인 **in terms of** ~라는 말로 **self-perception** 자기 인식 **infer** 나타내다, 의미하다 **foster** 불러 일으키다, 기르다

7. 다음 글의 내용을 한 문장으로 요약하고자 한다. 빈칸 (A)와 (B)에 들어갈 말로 가장 적절한 것은?

2017학년도 9월 40번

In science one experiment, whether it succeeds or fails, is logically followed by another in a theoretically infinite progression. According to the underlying myth of modern science, this progression is always replacing the smaller knowledge of the past with the larger knowledge of the present, which will be replaced by the yet larger knowledge of the future. In the arts, by contrast, no limitless sequence of works is ever implied or looked for. No work of art is necessarily followed by a second work that is necessarily better. Given the methodologies of science, the law of gravity and the genome were bound to be discovered by somebody; the identity of the discoverer is incidental to the fact. But it appears that in the arts there are no second chances. We must assume that we had one chance each for *The Divine Comedy* and *King Lear*. If Dante and Shakespeare had died before they wrote those works, nobody ever would have written them.

↓

While scientific knowledge is believed to progress through __(A)__ experiments, an artistic work tends to be __(B)__ to its creator with no limitless sequence implied.

	(A)		(B)
①	successive	……	unique
②	successive	……	valuable
③	controlled	……	valuable
④	incidental	……	influential
⑤	incidental	……	unique

WORD

logically 논리적으로 **theoretically** 이론상, 이론적으로 **infinite** 무한한 **progression** 연속, 발전 **underlying** 기저에 놓인, 근본적인, 숨겨진 **myth** 근거 없는 통념 **sequence** 연속 **methodology** 방법론 **gravity** 중력 **bound** ~하게 되어 있는 **incidental** 부수적인, 따라오는

8. 다음 글의 내용을 한 문장으로 요약하고자 한다. 빈칸 (A)와 (B)에 들어갈 말로 가장 적절한 것은?

2017학년도 6월 40번

Lawyers and scientists use argument to mean a summary of evidence and principles leading to a conclusion; however, a scientific argument is different from a legal argument. A prosecuting attorney constructs an argument to persuade the judge or a jury that the accused is guilty; a defense attorney in the same trial constructs an argument to persuade the same judge or jury toward the opposite conclusion. Neither prosecutor nor defender is obliged to consider anything that weakens their respective cases. On the contrary, scientists construct arguments because they want to test their own ideas and give an accurate explanation of some aspect of nature. Scientists can include any evidence or hypothesis that supports their claim, but they must observe one fundamental rule of professional science. They must include all of the known evidence and all of the hypotheses previously proposed. Unlike lawyers, scientists must explicitly account for the possibility that they might be wrong.

↓

Unlike lawyers, who utilize information __(A)__ to support their arguments, scientists must include all information even if some of it is unlikely to __(B)__ their arguments.

	(A)		(B)
①	objectively	……	weaken
②	objectively	……	support
③	accurately	……	clarify
④	selectively	……	strengthen
⑤	selectively	……	disprove

WORD

summary 요약 **conclusion** 결론 **prosecuting attorney** 검찰관 **persuade** 설득하다 **defense attorney** 피고측 변호인 **accused** 피고인; 비난[혐의]를 받은 **be obliged to** ~ 해야 한다 **respective** 각자의, 각각의, 저마다의 **hypothesis** 가설, 가정, 추측 **observe** 준수하다, 관찰하다 **explicitly** 명확하게 **account for** 설명하다

★ 혼공 8일차에 나온 문장들을 해석해 보자.

단어 PLUS

1 Anthropologists who study people still living in hunter-gatherer societies have discovered that they regularly make choices designed to produce not the best opportunity for obtaining a hyperabundant supply of food but, instead, the least danger of ending up with an insufficient supply.

1
+ **anthropologist** 인류학자
+ **hyperabundant** 매우 풍부한
+ **insufficient** 불충분한

2 A further reason for this alienation in modern societies is that in his conception of reality the modern adult owes less to his direct experience and more to the experience of his culture than does primitive man.

2
+ **alienation** 소외, 고립화
+ **conception** 개념
+ **modern** 현대의
+ **primitive** 원시의

3 Performance must be judged in terms of what is under the control of the individuals being evaluated rather than those influences on performance that are beyond their control.

3
+ **performance** 성과
+ **in terms of** ~라는 개념으로

4 The research also found that reading the more challenging version of poetry, in particular, increases activity in the right hemisphere of the brain, helping the readers to reflect on and reevaluate their own experiences in light of what they have read.

4
+ **hemisphere** 반구
+ **in light of** ~라는 점에서

5 Some studies suggest that variations in residents' feelings about tourism's relationship to environmental damage are related to the type of tourism, the extent to which residents feel the natural environment needs to be protected, and the distance residents live from the tourist attractions.

5
+ **resident** 거주자, 주민
+ **extent** 범위, 정도
+ **tourist attraction** 관광명소

6 Given the methodologies of science, the law of gravity and the genome were bound to be discovered by somebody; the identity of the discoverer is incidental to the fact.

6
+ **given** 고려하자면
+ **methodology** 방법학
+ **gravity** 중력
+ **incidental** 부수적인

7 If the consumer were to withdraw from the deal after the 'slight' change in the terms of agreement, he might foster the rather undesirable impression of being an irresponsible consumer unaware of these necessary charges.

7
+ **withdraw** 철회하다
+ **slight** 약간의
+ **undesirable** 바람직하지 않은

한국 출신 배우가 등장한 미드

한 때 영어 공부한다고 미드에 엄청 빠졌던 때가 있었어. 특히 '하와이'라는 섬에 대한 환상에 젖어있던 나에게 '하와이 파이브 오'라는 미드는 너무나 매력적이었지. 극중 형사가 여러 명 나오는데 공교롭게도 두 명이 한국계 출신 배우인거야.

'데니얼 대 킴(Daniel Dae Kim), 그레이스 박(Grace Park)'은 너무 멋지게 나와. 옆의 사진의 가운데 두 명이지.

영어야 당연히 잘 하는 거겠지만 어려운 용어를 술술 쓰면서 사건을 풀어나가고, 액션 신을 거뜬히 소화해 나가는 모습에 눈을 땔 수가 없었어.

하지만 최근에 굉장히 슬픈 소식을 들었어. 두 사람이 이 드라마에서 하차한다는 거야. 물론 하차할 수는 있지. 하지만 그 이유가 충격적이었어. 주연급인데도 불구하고 단지 동양인 이라는 이유만으로 백인 주연들과 받는 출연료 차이가 있었던 거야. 그리고 그것에 대해서 정중하게 항의 했는데도 불구하고 방송사 측에서는 조정의 의지를 보이지 않은 거지.

결국 그 15% 정도의 출연료 차이는 좁혀지지 않았고, 이 두 명은 하차를 선언했지. 지금까지 168편의 에피소드를 함께 해왔기에 샘 역시 너무 아쉽지만 이미 결정은 난 상태더라고. 제작 방송국 CBS의 네트워크 대변인은 아래처럼 말했어.

"우리는 다니엘과 그레이스의 엄청난 재능과 전문성, 그리고 168편에 걸친 에피소드에 담긴 헌신에 대해 정말로 감사하게 생각한다. 하지만 우리는 새로운 하와이 파이브 오의 챕터로 나가야 하고, 그들의 다음 챕터 역시 최고의 성공과 많은 성공이 있길 바란다."

프로의 세계는 참 냉정하다는 생각이 들어. 동시에 샘이라면 15%라는 출연료를 덜 받는 다고 해도 그만두기 쉽지 않았을 것 같아. 왜냐면 여전히 출연료 자체는 어마어마하거든. 그럼에도 이 배우들은 다른 동양이 배우들이 자신과 같은 처우를 받지 않게 하도록 선배로서 용단을 내린다고 했어.

Hats off to you!!

'모자를 벗어 경의를 표한다'라는 영어 표현이 딱 어울리는군!

09일차

장문독해(2문항형)

#진정한_장문독해 #어려운_소재 #제목+빈칸완성

난이도 🌶🌶🌶

elf-confidence is the first requisite to great undertakings.
by Samuel Johnson

자신감은 위대한 과업의 첫째 요건이다.

01 문항 특징

- 2개 문항이 있는 첫 번째 장문독해(2017학년도 기준 2문항 출제)
- 50~60%의 정답률을 보일 정도로 고난도 문항에 속함
- 보통 2개의 단락으로 이루어진 긴 지문을 가지고 2개의 문항이 출제됨
- 글의 제목과 빈칸추론(단어형) 문제로 출제
- 길지만 정답의 힌트가 많이 제시됨
- 문제의 마지막 장에 있어 실제 지문 난이도보다 체감 난이도가 높음

02 혼공 전략

전체 주제를 파악하고 바로 앞 문장과의 관계를 살펴보자.

> **Solution** 지문의 첫 문장(음식은 경영자로서 사용할 수 있는 가장 중요한 수단이다)이 글의 주제문이야. 음식과 비즈니스가 연관된 단어들이 반복해서 나오지. 그럼 이 글의 제목이 금방 떠오르겠지? 바로 Offer Food for Better Relationships 정도라고 할 수 있겠지.

첫 문장이 바로 주제문!!

Food is one of the most important tools you can use as a manager. Having a full stomach makes people feel satisfied and happier. Eating together gives employees time to make connections with each other. Providing an occasional snack or paying for a lunch now and then can help your employees feel appreciated and make the office feel more welcoming. These do not need to be elaborate setups. If you have a small budget, you're not going to want to buy lunch at a restaurant for your entire group. Bringing in some cookies once in a while is enough; you can also encourage employees to bring in food themselves.

음식과 경영과의 좋은 관계

The key to using food effectively is for it not to become a _____ event. If everyone knows you bring donuts to the Friday morning meeting, it becomes an expectation and not a surprise. To create goodwill, the food must appear to be unexpected. It is also a good idea to praise employees who bring food in without being asked; this creates an atmosphere of sharing.

빈칸 앞 부정어 주의!

> **Solution** 두 번째 단락에 빈칸이 있지. 이 경우는 조심해야 되는 게 앞 단락에 힌트가 있는지, 이후에 힌트가 있는지 찾아야 해. 여기서는 후자의 경우야. 이 때, 주의할 것은 빈칸 앞에 부정어인 not이 있으니까 이것을 선택지에 넣어서 생각해야겠지. 따라서 (not) planned(계획되지 않은)가 적절해.

다음 글을 읽고, 물음에 답하시오.

When someone asks us, "How does that work?" or "Why does that happen?" we tend to answer the question directly if we know the answer. After all, it is efficient. Another person asks a question; we provide the answer to the question. It is usually a win-win. The problem with this is that the direct approach can have an unintended consequence: the loss of confidence. Although the question wanted for an *explanation*, what the asker received was a statement of fact. Why does oil float on top of water in a glass? Relative density. What causes climate change? Increased CO_2 in the atmosphere. Why does the ocean have tides? The moon. Giving direct, accurate, and factual answers may seem to solve the problem from the perspective of the answerer. But in reality, it can shut the asker down. A statement of fact with no other context puts the burden on the asker to take the next step. If the asker isn't familiar with relative density or CO_2, he or she is likely to move on rather than ask a follow-up question or probe for related ideas. Any hope of becoming a customer of that idea is lost. This is a failure in the form of a lost opportunity. Although direct answers are often needed and well-placed, they do not work universally. A skilled explainer learns to see the intent behind the question and formulate an answer that focuses on understanding instead of _____.

1. 윗 글의 제목으로 가장 적절한 것은?

① Give Simpler Answers!

② How Can We Ask Questions Properly?

③ Scientific Facts: What the Asker Needs

④ Accurate Answers: A Mirror of Knowledge

⑤ Why Is Giving Direct Answers Problematic?

2. 윗 글의 빈칸에 들어갈 말로 가장 적절한 것은?

① efficiency ② diversity ③ fluency ④ privacy ⑤ honesty

When someone asks us, "How does that work?" or "Why does that happen?" we tend to answer the question directly if we know the answer. After all, it is efficient. Another person asks a question; we provide the answer to the question. It is usually a win-win. The problem with this is that the direct approach can have an unintended consequence: the loss of confidence. Although the question wanted for an *explanation*, what the asker received was a statement of fact. Why does oil float on top of water in a glass? Relative density. What causes climate change? Increased CO_2 in the atmosphere. Why does the ocean have tides? The moon. Giving direct, accurate, and factual answers may seem to solve the problem from the perspective of the answerer. But in reality, it can shut the asker down. A statement of fact with no other context puts the burden on the asker to take the next step. If the asker isn't familiar with relative density or CO_2, he or she is likely to move on rather than ask a follow-up question or probe for related ideas. Any hope of becoming a customer of that idea is lost. This is a failure in the form of a lost opportunity. Although direct answers are often needed and well-placed, they do not work universally. A skilled explainer learns to see the intent behind the question and formulate an answer that focuses on understanding instead of _____.

Solution 필자가 말하고자 하는 것은 직접적인 답변은 하지 말라는 거야. 여러 가지 단점이 있다는 것을 쭉 설명하고 있어. 한 마디로 직접적은 답변은 NO라는 거지.

Solution 앞부분은 숙련된 설명자(필자가 원하는 방향)는 질문 뒤의 의도를 파악한다는 내용인데 instead of(~ 대신에)는 필자가 원하는 방향과 반대의 관계를 가지게 되니까 전체적인 키워드와는 반대되는 어휘를 찾아야 해.

Solution 바로 직접적인 답변이 문제인 이유는 대답하는 사람에게서 문제를 이해할 수 있는 기회를 가져가버리기 때문이라고 지문에서 이야기하고 있지. 따라서 지문의 키워드는 바로 '답변'이야. 이걸 제목에서 찾아야 하는 거야.

1. 윗 글의 제목으로 가장 적절한 것은?

⑤ Why Is Giving Direct Answers Problematic? 왜 직접적인 답변이 문제일까?

2. 윗 글의 빈칸에 들어갈 말로 가장 적절한 것은?

① efficiency 효율성   ② diversity 다양성   ③ fluency 유창성

Solution instead of 다음에 나오는 빈칸은 직접적인 답변을 주는 거지. 문제는 이걸 하지 말라는 거지? 직접적인 답변은 바로 문제를 해결하는 것이니 ① efficiency(효율성)가 적절해.

Solution diversity는 답변을 통해서 얻고자 하는 궁극적인 목표지. 하지만 여기서는 instead of 뒤에 나오므로 여기는 주제와는 반대 관계인 것을 골라야해. diversity는 긍정의 관계지.

정답: 1. ⑤ 2. ①

해석 누군가가 우리에게 "그것이 어떻게 작동되죠?" 혹은 "그것이 왜 발생하죠?"라고 물을 때에, 우리가 답을 알고 있으면 우리는 그 질문에 대해 직접적으로 답변하는 경향이 있다. 어쨌든, 그것은 효율적이다. 또 다른 사람이 질문을 하면 우리는 그 질문에 대한 답변을 제공한다. 그것은 대개 관련된 모든 사람에게 유리하다. 이것의 문제점은 직접적인 접근 방법이 의도하지 않은 결과, 즉 자신감의 상실을 가져올 수 있다는 점이다. 질문이 '설명'을 원했음에도 불구하고, 질문자가 받은 것은 사실에 대한 진술이었다. 왜 기름은 유리컵 속의 물 위에 뜨는가? 상대 밀도 때문이다. 무엇이 기후 변화를 일으키는가? 대기 중에 증가된 이산화탄소 때문이다. 바다에는 왜 조류가 발생하는가? 달 때문이다. 직접적인, 정확한, 사실에 입각한 해답을 제공하는 것은 대답하는 사람의 시각에서 보면 문제를 해결하는 것처럼 보일 수도 있다. 하지만 실제로 그것은 질문자를 차단해 버릴 수 있다. 다른 맥락이 없이 사실을 진술하는 것은 질문자에게 다음 단계로 나아가는 부담을 지게 하는 것이다. 질문자가 상대적 밀도나 이산화탄소에 대해 익숙하지 않다면, 그는 추가적인 질문을 하거나 관련 아이디어들에 대해 조사를 하는 대신에 (다른 곳으로) 넘어가게 될 가능성이 크다. 그러한 아이디어의 고객이 될 가망성이 완전히 상실된다. 이것은 상실된 기회의 형태를 하고 있는 실패이다. 흔히 직접적인 답변이 필요하고 적절하기는 하지만, 그것이 누구에게나 다 좋은 것은 아니다. 숙련된 설명자는 질문 뒤에 있는 의도를 보고 효율성 대신에 이해에 초점을 맞춘 답변을 만들어내는 것을 배운다.

고난도 문항 요리하기

[1–2] 다음 글을 읽고, 물음에 답하시오.

2016학년도 6월 41–42번

It isn't going to be easy making changes to the food your children eat, and even the most careful, patient parents will probably find that the little ones will resist at some point and to some degree. The problem is that many of us were forced to eat in a healthy way as children: we learned the hard way. And the temptation to continue with these parental habits with our own children is strong.

If you were made to sit at the table until you had cleaned your plate, you are not alone: most of the adult population have suffered this at some point – at school if not at home. Forcing your children to eat, especially if they don't like what is on the plate, is completely _____. "Sit there until you finish" may be how we learned, and may also be the only way you feel able to achieve your goal, but think about it: the experience of eating a pile of unwanted cabbage until they feel sick is hardly going to make children jump for joy the next time it is served.

This strict approach is very old-fashioned, and you may win the battle but you definitely won't win the war. Delaying puddings used to be thought of as a good idea too, but guess what? That doesn't work either. "No pudding until you have finished your main course" was the standard line when most parents of today were young and is still commonly used, but it only makes sweet things seem more desirable.

1. 윗 글의 제목으로 가장 적절한 것은?

① Do Old Feeding Habits Work?
② No More Instant Foods for Kids
③ Kids Today Need Table Manners
④ Time to Switch to Organic Food!
⑤ Homemade Pudding Makes Us Perfect

2. 윗 글의 빈칸에 들어갈 말로 가장 적절한 것은?

① counterproductive   ② beneficial
③ invaluable   ④ unconventional
⑤ constructive

WORD

patient 인내심 있는   resist 저항하다   parental 부모의   temptation 유혹   plate 접시   cabbage 양배추   completely 완전히   sick 질린   line 말, 대사   standard 기준   desirable 바람직한, 매력적인

[3-4] 다음 글을 읽고, 물음에 답하시오.

2017학년도 수능 41-42번

Duration refers to the time that events last. If we think of tempo as the speed of events, then duration is the speed of the clock itself. For the physicist, the duration of a "second" is precise and unambiguous: it is equal to 9,192,631,770 cycles of the frequency associated with the transition between two energy levels of the isotope cesium-133. In the realm of psychological experience, however, quantifying units of time is a considerably clumsier operation. When people are removed from the cues of "real" time – be it the sun, bodily fatigue, or timepieces themselves – it doesn't take long before their time sense breaks down. And it is this usually __(A)__ psychological clock, as opposed to the time on one's watch, that creates the perception of duration that people experience.

Theoretically, a person who mentally stretches the duration of time should experience a slower tempo. Imagine, for example, that baseballs are pitched to two different batters. The balls are thrown every 5 seconds for 50 seconds, so a total of 10 balls are thrown. We now ask both batters how much time has passed. Let's say that batter number one (who loves hitting) feels the duration to be 40 seconds. Batter number two (bored by baseball) believes it to be 60 seconds. Psychologically, then, the first person has experienced baseballs approaching every four seconds while the second sees it as every six seconds. The perceived tempo, in other words, is __(B)__ for batter number one.

* isotope: 동위원소 ** clumsy: 서투른

3. 윗 글의 제목으로 가장 적절한 것은?

① What Timepieces Bring to Our Lives
② Research into Time: Precision vs. Duration
③ Flight from Time: A New Direction for Physics
④ The Peaceful Coexistence of Science and Baseball
⑤ How Long, How Fast: A Matter of Time Perception

4. 윗 글의 빈칸 (A), (B)에 들어갈 말로 가장 적절한 것은?

	(A)		(B)
①	delayed	-	faster
②	internal	-	slower
③	accurate	-	slower
④	imprecise	-	faster
⑤	mysterious	-	slower

WORD

duration 지속   tempo 속도   physicist 물리학자   precise 정확한   unambiguous 분명한   cycle 주기   frequency 진동수   associated with ~와 연관된   transition 전이   realm 영역   quantify 수량화 하다   considerably 상당히   operation 작업   fatigue 피로   timepiece 시계   break down 고장 나다   as opposed to ~과 반대되는   perception 인식   theoretically 이론상

[5–6] 다음 글을 읽고, 물음에 답하시오.

2014학년도 9월 41–42번

If you don't get the kind of information failure provides, you'll end up with unrealistic expectations for yourself, explains a psychologist. You could wind up in a position where failure, which has gathered under cover of darkness, reveals itself all at once.

We should hope, then, for exposure to failure, early and often. The sociologist Glen Elder proposed that there is a sensitive period for growth – late teens through early 30s – during which failures are most beneficial. Such a pattern seems to promote the trait sometimes called equanimity. We learn that trauma is survivable, so we don't plunge too deeply following setbacks. Nor, conversely, do we soar too high on our successes. Some businesses in Silicon Valley and on Wall Street make a point of hiring ex-pro athletes to their staffs. It's not just that their high profile draws business. It's because athletes are good at recovering from their failures. "We needed people who could perform and not get emotionally attached to losses," a Chicago oil trader told the *New York Times*, explaining why the firm likes athletes on the trading floor, particularly in ugly economic times like these. The image is of a rider easy in the saddle. Nothing can so surprise her – either for good or ill – that she'll be knocked off.

One way to help keep life's slings and arrows from knocking you off course is to ensure your life is _____, says Stephen Berglas, a California psychologist and personal coach. That way, a setback in any one area won't mean in your mind that you're a failure categorically. Call it spreading your risk across your emotional portfolio – or adding another leg to the furniture for balance, says Berglas.

* equanimity: 마음의 평정

5. 윗 글의 제목으로 가장 적절한 것은?

① Do Not Let Failure Fail You
② Recipe for Attaining Physical Stability
③ Physical Toughness and Mental Flexibility
④ How to Survive Emotional Unrest in Sports
⑤ Failure as an Enemy of Emotional Calmness

6. 윗 글의 빈칸에 들어갈 말로 가장 적절한 것은?

① illusionary   ② predictable
③ convergent   ④ straightforward
⑤ multidimensional

WORD

end up with 결국 ~ 하게 되다   **under cover of darkness** 어둠을 틈타서   **survivable** 살아남을 수 있는   **plunge** 거꾸러지다   **setback** 좌절, 차질
high profile 대중의 높은 관심   **attached to** ~에 집착한   **trading floor** 증권 거래소   **saddle** 안장   **sling** 투석   **categorically** 절대적으로, 단연코

[7–8] 다음 글을 읽고, 물음에 답하시오.

2018학년도 6월 41-42번

According to many sociologists, the study of what our society calls 'art' can only really progress if we drop the highly specific and ideologically loaded terminology of 'art', 'artworks' and 'artists', and replace these with the more neutral and less historically specific terms 'cultural forms', 'cultural products' and 'cultural producers'. These cultural products – be they paintings, sculptures, forms of music or whatever – should be regarded as being made by certain types of cultural producer, and as being used by particular groups of people in particular ways in specific social contexts. By using the more neutral term 'cultural products' for particular objects, and 'cultural producers' for the people who make those objects, the sociologist seeks to break with a view that she/he sees as having dominated the study of cultural forms for too long, namely trying to understand everything in terms of the category 'art'. This is a category that is too limited and context-specific to encompass all the different cultural products that people in different societies make and use. It is a term that is also too loaded to take at face value and to use naively in study of our own society. Since it is in the interests of certain social groups to define some things as 'art' and others as not, the very term 'art' itself cannot be uncritically used by the sociologist who wishes to understand how and why such labelling processes occur. Quite simply, then, in order to study cultural matters, many sociologists believe one has to _____ the terms 'art', 'artwork' and 'artist' as the basis for our analysis. Instead, these terms become important objects of analysis themselves.

7. 윗 글의 제목으로 가장 적절한 것은?

① Art: A Means to Overcome a Cultural Gap
② Interpreting Culture In and Out of Context
③ Different Forms of Art in the World of Culture
④ Cultural Diversity: Cornerstones of Civilizations
⑤ Culture as a Basis of Understanding the Concept of Art

8. 윗 글의 빈칸에 들어갈 말로 가장 적절한 것은?

① reject   ② borrow
③ introduce   ④ stress
⑤ revive

WORD

sociologist 사회학자   progress 발전하다   specific 구체적인   ideologically loaded 관념적인 의미로 가득한   terminology 전문 용어   neutral 중립적인   historically specific 역사적인 면에서 구체적인   namely 말하자면   break with ~와 결별하다   dominate 지배하다   encompass ~을 포괄하다   at face value 액면 그대로, 겉모습 그대로   naively 순진하게   be in the interests of ~에게 이득이 되다   analysis 분석

혼공 개념 마무리

★ 혼공 9일차에 나온 문장들을 해석해 봅시다.

1 It isn't going to be easy making changes to the food your children eat, and even the most careful, patient parents will probably find that the little ones will resist at some point and to some degree.

1
+ **patient** 인내하는
+ **resist** 저항하다

2 If you were made to sit at the table until you had cleaned your plate, you are not alone: most of the adult population have suffered this at some point – at school if not at home.

2
+ **plate** 접시

3 For the physicist, the duration of a "second" is precise and unambiguous: it is equal to 9,192,631,770 cycles of the frequency associated with the transition between two energy levels of the isotope cesium-133.

3
+ **physicist** 물리학자
+ **duration** 지속
+ **unambiguous** 명확한
+ **frequency** 진동수
+ **associated with** ~과 연관된
+ **transition** 전이

4 When people are removed from the cues of "real" time – be it the sun, bodily fatigue, or timepieces themselves – it doesn't take long before their time sense breaks down.

4
+ **cue** 실마리
+ **fatigue** 피로
+ **timepiece** 시계

5 The sociologist Glen Elder proposed that there is a sensitive period for growth – late teens through early 30s – during which failures are most beneficial.

5
+ **sociologist** 사회학자
+ **sensitive** 예민한
+ **beneficial** 유리한

6 These cultural products – be they paintings, sculptures, forms of music or whatever – should be regarded as being made by certain types of cultural producer, and as being used by particular groups of people in particular ways in specific social contexts.

6
+ **sculpture** 조각
+ **specific** 구체적인

7 By using the more neutral term 'cultural products' for particular objects, and 'cultural producers' for the people who make those objects, the sociologist seeks to break with a view that she/he sees as having dominated the study of cultural forms for too long, namely trying to understand everything in terms of the category 'art'.

7
+ **neutral** 중립적인
+ **seek** 추구하다
+ **dominate** 지배하다

C
course
승부수 문항Ⅲ

혼공

10일차

빈칸추론(단어)

#빈칸이다! #단어빈칸은_그래도_낫다 #반복되는_어휘에_주목

난이도 🌶🌶🌶

What you risk reveals what you value.
by Jeanette Winterson

당신이 어떤 위험을 감수하냐를 보면, 당신이 무엇을 가치있게 여기는지 알 수 있다.

01 문항 특징

- 빈칸 중 그나마 쉬운 유형이 바로 단어 빈칸이며 5년간 정답률 60%
- 지문에서 반복되는 어휘에 주목해 키워드를 찾아야 함
- 주제문, 재진술, 반박문, 반대되는 예시문에 빈칸이 뚫림
- 부정어가 빈칸 앞에 있다면 부정어를 선택지에 넣어라
- 선택지를 먼저 보고, 선택지의 단어가 글의 흐름상 +/−인지 파악

02 혼공 전략

1 문장 사이에 갑작스런 방향 전환이 있는 부분이 정답이야.

주제문

What is the essence of law? I think the law takes away the right of revenge from people and gives the right to the community. If someone harmed one of your family members, you must not harm that person's family members. Instead, you must appeal to the court of law, which will _____ the person.

예시문

① punish   ② avoid   ③ trust   ④ free

Solution 글의 핵심은 개인을 처벌할 권리는 사회가 가지고 있다는 거야. 법이라는 것도 사회의 범주에 들어가겠지. 그래서 마지막 빈칸이 있는 문장은 그걸 설명하는 거야. 따라서 법이 하는 일은 범죄자를 '처벌(punish)'하는 것이라는 거지. 그래서 정답은 ① punish가 되는 거야. 이렇게 빈칸은 주제문을 찾고 그것이 말하고자 하는 바에 잘 맞춰야 해.

2 반전이 나온 다음에 빈칸이 나온 다면, 앞보다는 뒤의 전개가 더 중요하지.

If we lived on a planet where nothing ever changed, there would be little to do. There would be nothing to figure out and there would be no reason for science. If we lived in an unpredictable world, where things changed in random or very complex ways, we would not be able to figure things out. Again, there would be no such thing as science. But we live in an in-between universe, where things change, but according to _____. If I throw a stick up in the air, it always falls down. If the sun sets in the west, it always rises again the next morning in the east. And so it becomes possible to figure things out. We can do science, and with it we can improve our lives.

① age   ② rules   ③ belief

Solution 앞부분은 변하지 않거나, 아니면 너무 많이 변하는 세상에서는 살기 힘들다는 이야기를 하고 있어.

Solution But부터 논조가 변하기 시작하지. 너무 변하지 않는 중간의 세상에서 빈칸으로 인해 살아간다고 나오지. 즉, 앞부분은 정답을 유추하는데 있어 크게 도움이 되지 않는 거야! But부터 잘 봐야 하는 거지. 뒤에는 예시가 나오는데 현상들이 어떤 법칙(rule)에 따라 변한다는 내용이니까, 바로 정답은 ② rules가 되겠지.

다음 빈칸에 들어갈 말로 가장 적절한 것은?

2016학년도 6월 31번

In an increasingly globalized world, literature in translation has an especially important role. Increasingly, writers, readers, and publishers are turning to literature as a bridge between cultures, particularly Western and Arab societies. This growing interest is, in turn, driving a boom in translation. However, not surprisingly perhaps, most translations are from English into other languages, not from another language, such as Arabic, into English. Hence, the huge American market is seen as driving the _____. Bookstores in the United States, for example, rarely stock more than Nobel Prize winner Naguib Mahfouz's *Cairo Trilogy*, a masterful, realistic account of life in Cairo and of a merchant family in the mid-20th century. Western readers likely know little of Mahfouz's more experimental work, his political and religious allegories, or his historical dramas. The result is a kind of one-way mirror between America and the rest of the world.

* allegory: 우화, 풍자

① equality　　　　　② diversity　　　　　③ interaction
④ imbalance　　　　　⑤ uncertainty

WORD

translation 번역　　increasingly 점차　　turn to ~에 의존하다　　in turn 결국　　drive a boom 붐을 일으키다　　be seen as ~로 보여지다　　stock 비축하다, 재고를 확보하다　　trilogy 3부작　　account 설명　　political 정치적인　　religious 종교적인

10일차 빈칸추론(단어)　105

In an increasingly globalized world, literature in translation has an especially important role. Increasingly, writers, readers, and publishers are turning to literature as a bridge between cultures, particularly Western and Arab societies. This growing interest is, in turn, driving a boom in translation. However, not surprisingly perhaps, most translations are from English into other languages, not from another language, such as Arabic, into English. Hence, the huge American market is seen as driving the _____. Bookstores in the United States, for example, rarely stock more than Nobel Prize winner Naguib Mahfouz's *Cairo Trilogy*, a masterful, realistic account of life in Cairo and of a merchant family in the mid-20th century. Western readers likely know little of Mahfouz's more experimental work, his political and religious allegories, or his historicalCairo Trilogy, dramas. The result is a kind of one-way mirror between America and the rest of the world.

* allegory: 우화, 풍자

Solution 처음에는 번역 문학의 성장에 대해서 서술하고 있어. 문화 사이의 다리 역할을 하는 등 번역에서 붐을 일으키고 있다고 하고 있지.

Solution 자 그런데, However가 보이지? 글의 논조가 변한다는 신호야. 번역의 방향이 바뀌었다는 거지. 이게 바로 문제가 되고 있다는 게 필자가 말하고 싶은 거야. 이처럼 반전이 나오면 앞의 분위기를 그냥 버려야 돼.

Solution Hence(그래서)를 통해서 글의 흐름의 변화의 결과라는 것을 알 수 있겠지? 글의 분위기가 현재의 번역의 흐름에 대해서 그리 우호적이지 않지? 그럼 일단 빈칸은 (-) 성향을 띈 어휘가 나와야 해.

Solution 이 부분은 모두 예시지. 앞에서 지적한 부정적인 번역의 흐름에 대한 설명이 나오고 있어. 물론 빈칸에 대한 힌트가 많이 나오고 있지. 예시에서는 노벨상을 탄 아랍 작가와 작품에 대한 것이 미국에서는 소개가 안 되고 있다는 거야. 미국과 아랍 세계의 교류가 잘 안되다는 내용이겠지? 자 그렇다면 정답을 찾을 수 있겠어? 바로 ④ imbalance(불균형)가 되겠지.

우선 선택지를 보면 ① 평등성(+) ② 다양성(+) ③ 상호관계(+) ④ 불균형(-) ⑤ 불확실성(-)으로 ①, ②, ③번은 (+), ④, ⑤번은 (-) 성향을 띄고 있어. 이걸 염두에 두는 것이 좋겠지.

① equality　　　② diversity　　　③ interaction
④ imbalance　　　⑤ uncertainty

Solution 일단 빈칸에는 (-) 성향의 어휘가 들어가야 하니까 ④번과 ⑤번이 남지. 그리고 글의 내용은 미국과 아랍 세계의 번역이 한쪽으로만 흐른다고 하고 있으니 당연히 정답은 ④ imbalance가 되겠지.

정답: ④

해석 점차 세계화되는 세상에서 번역에 있어 문학은 특히 중요한 역할을 해왔다. 작가들, 독자들, 출판업자들은 특히 서구 사회와 아랍 사회간의 문화 사이의 가교로서 문학에 점차 의존해 오고 있다. 이러한 증가하는 관심은 결국 번역에 있어 붐을 일으키고 있다. 그러나, 놀랍지 않게도 대부분은 아라비아어 같은 언어에서 영어로의 번역이 아니라 영어에서 다른 언어로의 번역이다. 그러므로, 미국의 거대 시장은 불균형을 초래하고 있는 것으로 보여진다. 예를 들어, 미국의 서점은 20세기 중반의 상인 가정의 모습과 카이로에서의 삶을 꽤 사실적으로 잘 묘사한 노벨상 수상 작가 Naguib Mahfouz의 Cairo Trilogy 작품의 재고를 확보해두지 않는다. 서양의 독자들은 Mahfouz의 실험적 작품과 그의 정치적 종교적 풍자, 또는 그의 역사적인 드라마에 대해 거의 잘 알지 못한다. 이의 결과는 미국과 나머지 국가들 사이의 한 쪽만 보는 거울이 되어버렸다.

1. 다음 빈칸에 들어갈 말로 가장 적절한 것은?

2013학년도 수능 23번

To say that we need to curb anger and our negative thoughts and emotions does not mean that we should deny our feelings. There is an important distinction to be made between denial and restraint. The latter constitutes a deliberate and voluntarily adopted discipline based on an appreciation of the benefits of doing so. This is very different from the case of someone who suppresses emotions such as anger out of a feeling that they need to present a facade of self-control, or out of fear of what others may think. Such behaviour is like closing a wound which is still infected. We are not talking about rule-following. Where denial and suppression occur, there comes the danger that in doing so the individual _____ anger and resentment. The trouble here is that at some future point they may find they cannot contain these feelings any longer.

* facade: 표면, 겉

① fades out　　　　② copes with
③ stores up　　　　④ soothes
⑤ overestimates

2. 다음 빈칸에 들어갈 말로 가장 적절한 것은?

2016학년도 9월 31번

Early human societies were nomadic, based on hunting and gathering, and, in a shifting pattern of life in search of new sources of food, qualities such as lightness, portability, and adaptability were dominant criteria. With the evolution of more settled rural societies based on agriculture, other characteristics, other traditions of form appropriate to the new patterns of life, rapidly emerged. It must be emphasized, however, that tradition was not static, but constantly subject to minute variations appropriate to people and their circumstances. Although traditional forms reflected the experience of social groups, specific manifestations could be adapted in various minute and subtle ways to suit individual users' needs. A chair could keep its basic, accepted characteristics while still being closely shaped in detail to the physique and proportions of a specific person. This basic principle of _____ allowed a constant stream of incremental modifications to be introduced, which, if demonstrated by experience to be advantageous, could be integrated back into the mainstream of tradition.

* manifestation: 외적 형태, 표시
** physique: 체격
*** incremental: (점진적으로) 증가하는

① dedication　　　　② customization
③ cooperation　　　　④ generalization
⑤ preservation

WORD

curb 억제하다　distinction 차이　denial 부인　restraint 자제　the latter 후자　constitute 여겨지다　discipline 규율　suppress 억누르다　infect 감염시키다　rule-following 규칙 따르기　resentment 분노　soothe 달래다

WORD

nomadic 유목의　shifting 이동하는　adaptability 적응성　criteria 기준, 척도　minute 미세한　modification 변형　integrate 통합하다　mainstream 주류

3. 다음 빈칸에 들어갈 말로 가장 적절한 것은?

2017학년도 6월 31번

Once a hand or gripper has been directed to an object by reaching, it can be grasped. Grasping requires that fingers hold an object securely. A secure grip is one in which the object won't slip or move, especially when displaced by an external force. Your grasp on a hammer, for example, would not be secure if knocking against something caused you to drop it. One precondition of a firm grasp is that the forces applied by the fingers balance each other so as not to disturb the object's position. The characteristics of an object such as its geometric configuration and mass distribution may demand that some fingers apply greater force than others to maintain _____. The grasp and support forces must also match overall object mass and fragility. An egg requires a more delicate touch than a rock.

* geometric configuration: 기하학적 형태

** fragility: 부서지기 쉬움

① distance   ② efficiency

③ mobility   ④ direction

⑤ stability

4. 다음 빈칸에 들어갈 말로 가장 적절한 것은?

2016학년도 수능 31번

When two cultures come into contact, they do not exchange every cultural item. If that were the case, there would be no cultural differences in the world today. Instead, only a small number of cultural elements ever spread from one culture to another. Which cultural item is accepted depends largely on the item's use and compatibility with already existing cultural traits. For example, it is not likely that men's hair dyes designed to "get out the gray" will spread into parts of rural Africa where a person's status is elevated with advancing years. Even when a(n) _____ is consistent with a society's needs, there is still no guarantee that it will be accepted. For example, most people in the United States using US customary units (e.g., inch, foot, yard, mile, etc.) have resisted adopting the metric system even though making such a change would enable US citizens to interface with the rest of the world more efficiently.

* metric system: 미터법

① categorization   ② innovation

③ investigation   ④ observation

⑤ specification

WORD

gripper 집게   grasp 붙잡다   securely 안전하게, 단단히   grip 꽉 잡음   displace 옮겨 놓다   precondition 전제 조건   disturb 방해하다   characteristic 특성, 특징   mass distribution 질량 분포, 대량 분배   delicate 섬세한, 민감한

WORD

come into contact 접촉하다   compatibility 양립가능성   trait 특성   dye 염색약   elevate 올리다   with advancing years 나이가 들어감에 따라   be consistent with ~와 일치하다   guarantee 보장   resist 저항하다   interface with ~와 접촉하다   efficiently 효율적으로

5. 다음 글의 빈칸 (A), (B)에 들어갈 말로 가장 적절한 것을 고르시오.

2014학년도 6월 36번

When a company comes out with a new product, its competitors typically go on the defensive, doing whatever they can to __(A)__ the odds that the offering will eat into their sales. Responses might include increasing marketing efforts, offering discounts to channel partners, and even lobbying for regulations that would hinder the rival's expansion. In many cases, though, such actions are misguided. Although the conventional wisdom that a rival's launch will hurt profits is often correct, my research shows that companies sometimes see profits increase after a rival's launch. The underlying mechanism is pretty simple: When a company comes out with a new product, it often raises the prices of its existing products. This might be designed to make the new product look __(B)__ and thus more attractive by comparison. As that company adjusts its pricing, its competitors can do the same without risking customer defections over price.

* defection: 이탈

	(A)		(B)
①	calculate	……	exceptional
②	calculate	……	more striking
③	eliminate	……	more upgraded
④	reduce	……	up-to-date
⑤	reduce	……	cheaper

6. 다음 빈칸에 들어갈 말로 가장 적절한 것은?

2017학년도 수능 31번

The creativity that children possess needs to be cultivated throughout their development. Research suggests that overstructuring the child's environment may actually limit creative and academic development. This is a central problem with much of science instruction. The exercises or activities are devised to eliminate different options and to focus on predetermined results. The answers are structured to fit the course assessments, and the wonder of science is lost along with cognitive intrigue. We define cognitive intrigue as the wonder that stimulates and intrinsically motivates an individual to voluntarily engage in an activity. The loss of cognitive intrigue may be initiated by the sole use of play items with predetermined conclusions and reinforced by rote instruction in school. This is exemplified by toys, games, and lessons that are a(n) _____ in and of themselves and require little of the individual other than to master the planned objective.

* rote: 기계적인 암기

① end　　　　　　② input

③ puzzle　　　　　④ interest

⑤ alternative

7. 다음 글의 빈칸 (A), (B)에 들어갈 말로 가장 적절한 것을 고르시오.

2014학년도 수능 36번

F. Scott Fitzgerald thought that the test of first-rate intelligence was the ability to hold two opposed ideas in mind at the same time and still function. The eons shaped our brains in the __(A)__ direction. Confirmation bias is a term for the way the mind systematically avoids confronting contradiction. It does this by overvaluing evidence that confirms what we already think or feel and undervaluing or simply disregarding evidence that refutes it. Testimony from members of the Crow tribe about the destruction of their culture provides an extreme and tragic example of this. A man named Plenty Coups reported that "when the buffalo went away, the hearts of my people fell to the ground and they could not lift them up again. After this *nothing happened*." He was not alone in describing the depth of despair as the end of history. "Nothing happened after that," another Crow warrior said. "We just lived." The emotion was so strong that the brain __(B)__ evidence of the continued existence of normal, everyday life that might have eased it.

* eon: 무한히 긴 시대, 영겁

	(A)		(B)
①	opposite	······	retained
②	opposite	······	rejected
③	wrong	······	validated
④	same	······	falsified
⑤	same	······	overlooked

8. 다음 글의 빈칸 (A), (B)에 들어갈 말로 가장 적절한 것을 고르시오.

2014학년도 9월 36번

After making a choice, the decision ultimately changes our estimated pleasure, enhancing the expected pleasure from the selected option and decreasing the expected pleasure from the rejected option. If we were not inclined to __(A)__ the value of our options rapidly so that they concur with our choices, we would likely second-guess ourselves to the point of insanity. We would ask ourselves again and again whether we should have chosen Greece over Thailand, the toaster over the coffee maker, and Jenny over Michele. Consistently second-guessing ourselves would interfere with our daily functioning and promote a negative effect. We would feel anxious and confused, regretful and sad. Have we done the right thing? Should we change our mind? These thoughts would result in a permanent halt. We would find ourselves – literally – stuck, overcome by __(B)__ and unable to move forward. On the other hand, reevaluating our alternatives after making a decision increases our commitment to the action taken and keeps us moving forward.

	(A)		(B)
①	disregard	······	indecision
②	disregard	······	decision
③	disclose	······	decision
④	update	······	prejudice
⑤	update	······	indecision

WORD

first-rate 최상의 function 기능하다 bias 편향, 편견 confront 직면하다 contradiction 모순 overvalue 과대평가하다 disregard 무시하다 refute 반박하다 testimony 증언 despair 절망 warrior 전사, 용사

WORD

option 선택 concur with ~와 일치하다 second-guess 사후에 [뒤늦게] 비판하다 insanity 정신 이상 interfere with ~을 방해하다 halt 멈춤, 중단 reevaluate 재평가하다 commitment 전념, 헌신 indecision 우유부단함 update 새롭게 하다

★ 혼공 10일차에 나온 문장들을 해석해 봅시다.

단어 PLUS

1 To say that we need to curb anger and our negative thoughts and emotions does not mean that we should deny our feelings.

1
+ curb 억제하다

2 With the evolution of more settled rural societies based on agriculture, other characteristics, other traditions of form appropriate to the new patterns of life, rapidly emerged.

2
+ evolution 진화
+ agriculture 농업
+ appropriate 적절한
+ emerge 나타나다

3 The characteristics of an object such as its geometric configuration and mass distribution may demand that some fingers apply greater force than others to maintain stability.

3
+ geometric 기하학적인
+ configuration 배열
+ distribution 분배
+ stability 안정성

4 Although the conventional wisdom that a rival's launch will hurt profits is often correct, my research shows that companies sometimes see profits increase after a rival's launch.

4
+ conventional wisdom 통념
+ launch 출시

5 The loss of cognitive intrigue may be initiated by the sole use of play items with predetermined conclusions and reinforced by rote instruction in school.

5
+ cognitive 인지적인
+ intrigue 호기심
+ predetermined 미리 결정된
+ reinforce 보강하다

6 After making a choice, the decision ultimately changes our estimated pleasure, enhancing the expected pleasure from the selected option and decreasing the expected pleasure from the rejected option.

6
+ enhance 향상하다
+ rejected 거부된

7 This is very different from the case of someone who suppresses emotions such as anger out of a feeling that they need to present a facade of self-control, or out of fear of what others may think.

7
+ suppress 억압하다
+ facade 정면

세계적인 희극인 짐 캐리의 마음에 와닿는 말

샘이 학생일 때 '마스크'라는 영화를 본 적이 있었어. 한 남자 배우가 '돌 + 아이'같은 연기를 신들린 듯이 했지. 그 사람이 유명한 희극 배우인 '짐 캐리'야. 최근에 마하리쉬 대학(MUM) 졸업 축사에서 많은 사람들을 감동시킨 말을 했었어.

> 'You can fail at what you don't want. So you might as well take a chance on doing what you love.'
>
> ───────────────
>
> 당신은 당신이 원하지 않는 것으로도 실패할 수 있다. 그래서 당신은 당신이 진정으로 좋아하는 일을 하는 기회를 잡는 것이 나을지도 모른다.

짐 캐리 역시 자신의 미래에 대해 걱정했던 적이 있었어. 하지만 자신의 아버지를 보고 많은 것을 깨달았다고 했어. 아버지께서는 생계를 위해 본인이 하기 싫어하는 소위 어른들이 말하는 좀 더 '안정적인' 일을 선택했어. 하지만 좋지 않은 일이 생겼고 결국 실패하게 되었지. 그때 짐 캐리는 자신이 좋아하는 것을 따라가야 한다고 생각했다고 해. 여러분들이 좋아하는 일을 취미로든 어떤 형태로든 포기하지 않았으면 좋겠어. 물론, 지금 당장 그것이 떠오르지 않을 수도 있어.

그렇다고 해서 너무 좋아하는 일이 생겨야 하거나 꿈을 가져야 한다고 자기 자신을 옭아매지 않았으면 좋겠어. '강제된 꿈'은 오래가지 못하는 법이거든. 자연스럽게 좋아하는 일을 찾고, 그 일을 내 강점으로 발전시킬 수 있도록 노력해야 해. 그러기 위해서 샘이 했던 것은 '말보다는 작은 행동'을, '행동한 것은 글로 옮기기'를 실천했어. 사실 버킷리스트도 이와 같은 원리라고 생각해.

마음 속에 끝없이 맴도는 내 소망, 갈망 등을 가끔 우리도 주체할 수 없잖아? 그것을 행동할 수 있는 단위로 쪼개서 글로 정리해보고 실천하다보면 시간은 우리 편이라고 생각해.

마지막으로 짐 캐리가 찾은 자신의 사명은 무엇이었을까?

궁금하지?

'제 인생의 목적은 사람들을 걱정으로부터 해방시키는 것입니다.'

– 짐 캐리

혼공

11일차

빈칸추론(구/문장)

#진짜가_나타났다 #역대급_난이도는_모두_여기서

난이도 🌶🌶🌶

The greatest lesson in life is to know that even fools are right sometimes.
by Sir Winston Churchill

인생에서 가장 위대한 교훈은, 심지어는 바보도 어떨 때는 옳다는 걸 아는 것이다.

01 문항 특징

- 수능에서 가장 어려운 유형이 바로 빈칸추론(구/문장) 형태임
- 5년간 정답률 45%, But 최고난도 평균 33% 정답률
- 갈수록 내용+문제가 어려워지고 있는 추세
- 1등급을 확실하게 가르는 유형
- 부정어가 빈칸 앞에 있다면 부정어를 선택지에 넣어라
- 선택지를 먼저 보고, 선택지의 단어가 글의 흐름상 +/− 인지 파악

02 혼공 전략

빈칸 앞에 부정어는 선택지에 넣어라.

이 글의 키워드 아님

Consider the "power" of a baseball bat. All the energy gained by the bat is supplied by the batter. The bat is just an instrument that helps send the ball on its way. If it does its job well, then we usually say that the bat is powerful. In physics terms, we should really describe the bat in terms of its efficiency. An efficient bat would be one that allows the batter to transfer the energy in his arms to the ball without _____ in the process. In fact, all bats are very inefficient in the sense that only a small fraction of the energy in the arms is given to the ball. Most of that energy is retained in the bat and in the arms as a result of the "follow through" after the bat strikes the ball.

① any friction to the ball 공에 있는 마찰
② too much loss of energy 너무 많은 에너지 손실
③ decrease of swing speed 스윙 스피드의 감소
④ help from another instrument 또 다른 도구로부터의 도움
⑤ enhancement of physical strength 신체적 강함의 향상

Solution 선택지만 보면 ⑤번이 효율성과 가장 관련이 있어. 빈칸 앞에 있는 부정어 without이 없다면 이것이 정답이 되겠지. 하지만, 부정어가 있으니까 결국 정반대의 내용을 선택해야 해.

Solution 이 글은 야구방망이가 가진 '힘'은 그 자체에서 나오는 것이 아니라 '에너지를 전달하는 효율성'에서 나온다는 이야기야. 앞에 나온 power는 뒤에 나오는 efficiency를 강조하기 위해서 먼저 꺼낸 소재야. 즉 이 글의 KeyWord는 power가 아니라 efficiency야.

Solution 빈칸 앞에 부정어인 without이 있어. 즉 '뒤에 나오는 빈칸 없이'라고 해석을 해서 문제를 풀어야 해. 빈칸에만 집중하면 정작 필요한 것과는 정반대의 선택지를 고를 수 있으니 주의해야 해.

Solution 이 글의 키워드는 efficiency(효율성)야. 빈칸은 언제나 글의 주제문과 키워드와 밀접한 관계가 있지. 그런데 문제는 빈칸 앞에 부정어가 있어. 즉 선택지는 효율성의 정반대. 낭비와 같은 내용이 들어가야 해. 그래서 부정어를 아예 선택지에 넣어서 생각하는 것이 실수를 줄이는 방법이지. 여기서 낭비를 의미하는 것은 ②번이야.

다음 빈칸에 들어갈 말로 가장 적절한 것은?

We tend to assume that the way to get more time is to speed up. But speeding up can actually slow us down. Anyone who has ever rushed out of the house only to realize that their keys and wallet are sitting on the kitchen table knows this only too well. And it's not just our efficiency that is reduced. The quality of the experience suffers too, as we become less aware or 'mindful.' Have you ever eaten an entire meal without tasting any of it? Hurrying up doesn't just give us less time, it can also steal the pleasure and benefit from the time that we do have. For many of us, hurrying is a way of life. Some of us enjoy the thrill that it gives us while others are driven crazy by the constant pressure and feel that their lives are speeding up to an unacceptable degree. Either way, there are almost certainly areas of our life that could be _____.

① affected by temporary sufferings

② disturbed by inconsistent behaviors

③ enhanced by a little go-slow behavior

④ complicated by slow-but-steady actions

⑤ dominated by a little speedy decision making

WORD

assume 가정하다   **efficiency** 효율성   **mindful** 주의 깊은   **constant** 지속적인   **pressure** 압력   **unacceptable** 받아들일 수 없는

We tend to assume that the way to get more time is to speed up. But speeding up can actually slow us down. Anyone who has ever rushed out of the house only to realize that their keys and wallet are sitting on the kitchen table knows this only too well. And it's not just our efficiency that is reduced. The quality of the experience suffers too, as we become less aware or 'mindful.' Have you ever eaten an entire meal without tasting any of it? Hurrying up doesn't just give us less time, it can also steal the pleasure and benefit from the time that we do have. For many of us, hurrying is a way of life. Some of us enjoy the thrill that it gives us while others are driven crazy by the constant pressure and feel that their lives are speeding up to an unacceptable degree. Either way, there are almost certainly areas of our life that could be _____.

① affected by temporary sufferings 일시적인 고통에 영향을 받는
② disturbed by inconsistent behaviors 모순되는 행동에 의해 방해받는
③ enhanced by a little go-slow behavior 천천히 하는 행동에 의해 좋아지는
④ complicated by slow-but-steady actions 느리지만 꾸준한 행동에 의해 복잡해진
⑤ dominated by a little speedy decision making 약간 빠른 결정에 의해 주도되는

Solution 일반적인 상식, 즉 통념이 제시되고 있어. 이것이 글 전반의 분위기인지 아닌지 살펴보는 것이 독해의 핵심이지.

Solution 자 그런데 But이 보이지? 글의 논조가 변한다는 신호야. 속도를 높이는 게 사실은 속도를 낮춘다는 내용이지. 이것이 바로 필자가 말하고자 하는 바야. 이 글의 주제문일 가능성이 높아. 그리고 빈칸도 역시 이런 분위기로 가겠지?

Solution 속도를 높이는 것, 즉 서두름이 주는 단점에 대해서 이야기하고 있어. 역시 앞에서 이야기한 속도 up이 결국 속도 down을 불러온다는 내용이지.

Solution 결국 '속도 up 〈 속도 down'이라는 결론으로 끝맺음이 나와야겠지. 빈칸은 속도 down과 관련된 내용이 나와야 해.

Solution 속도down과 관련된 내용은 ③번뿐이지. 이것이 정답.

Solution slow라는 단어가 나오지만, 이건 함정이야. 앞에 보면 바로 complicated(복잡해진) 라는 다소 부정적인 단어가 나오지. 이 글의 slow는 (+)이기 때문에 (−)의 어휘랑 연결되면 안 되지.

정답: ③

해석 우리는 더 많은 시간을 확보하는 방법이 속도를 높이는 것이라고 생각하는 경향이 있다. 그러나 속도를 높이는 것은 실제로는 속도를 느리게 하는 것이다. 집 밖으로 급히 뛰쳐나와서 열쇠와 지갑을 부엌 테이블에 두고 나왔다는 것을 깨달은 사람은 누구나 이러한 사실을 너무나 잘 알 것이다. 그리고 줄어든 것은 우리의 효율성만이 아니다. 일의 질 또한 우리가 덜 의식하고 신경쓰지 않음으로 떨어진다. 당신은 식사의 맛을 전혀 느끼지 못하고 식사를 해 보신 적이 있는가? 서두르는 것은 우리에게 시간을 줄여주지 못하고 또한 우리가 가진 시간에서 즐거움과 혜택을 빼앗는다. 우리 중 많은 사람들에게 서두르는 것은 삶의 방식이다. 몇몇은 서두르는 것이 우리에게 주는 스릴을 즐기고 반면에 다른 사람들은 지속적인 압박으로부터 미쳐가며 그들의 삶이 수용할 수 없는 정도까지 속도를 내고 있다고 생각한다. 어느 쪽이든, 분명히 천천히 하는 행동에 의해 좋아지는 삶의 영역이 있다.

3 단계 고난도 문항 요리하기

1. 다음 빈칸에 들어갈 말로 가장 적절한 것은?

2015학년도 수능 32번

My friend was disappointed that scientific progress has not cured the world's ills by abolishing wars and starvation; that gross human inequality is still widespread; that happiness is not universal. My friend made a common mistake – a basic misunderstanding in the nature of knowledge. Knowledge is amoral – not immoral but morality neutral. It can be used for any purpose, but many people assume it will be used to further *their* favorite hopes for society – and this is the fundamental flaw. Knowledge of the world is one thing; its uses create a separate issue. To be disappointed that our progress in understanding has not remedied the social ills of the world is a legitimate view, but _____

_____. To argue that knowledge is not progressing because of the African or Middle Eastern conflicts misses the point. There is nothing inherent in knowledge that dictates any specific social or moral application.

① to confuse this with the progress of knowledge is absurd

② to know the nature of knowledge is to practice its moral value

③ to remove social inequality is the inherent purpose of knowledge

④ to accumulate knowledge is to enhance its social application

⑤ to make science progress is to make it cure social ills

WORD

progress 발전, 진보   amoral 도덕과 관계없는   assume 가정하다   further 증진하다   flaw 결함   remedy 치유하다   legitimate 타당한   inherent 내재적인, 타고난   dictate 좌우하다, 지시하다   specific 구체적인

2. 다음 빈칸에 들어갈 말로 가장 적절한 것은?

2014학년도 수능 32번

The success of human beings depends crucially on numbers and connections. A few hundred people cannot sustain a sophisticated technology. Recall that Australia was colonized 45,000 years ago by pioneers spreading east from Africa along the shore of Asia. The vanguard of such a migration must have been small in number and must have traveled comparatively light. The chances are they had only a sample of the technology available to their relatives back at the Red Sea crossing. This may explain why Australian aboriginal technology, although it developed and elaborated steadily over the ensuing millennia, was lacking in so many features of the Old World – elastic weapons, for example, such as bows and catapults, were unknown, as were ovens. It was not that they were 'primitive' or that they had mentally regressed; it was that they _____ and did not have a dense enough population and therefore a large enough collective brain to develop them much further.

* catapult: 투석기

① were too tightly connected to develop new technologies

② focused on developing and elaborating elastic weapons

③ had arrived with only a subset of technologies

④ inherited none of their relatives' technologies in Africa

⑤ failed to transfer their technical insights to the Old World

WORD

crucially 결정적으로   vanguard 선두   aboriginal 원주민의, 토착의   elaborate 정교하게 만들다   ensuing 뒤이은, 다음의   elastic 탄력 있는   regress 퇴보하다   dense 조밀한

3. 다음 빈칸에 들어갈 말로 가장 적절한 것은?

2017학년도 수능 34번

Over a period of time the buildings which housed social, legal, religious, and other rituals evolved into forms that we subsequently have come _____. This is a two-way process; the building provides the physical environment and setting for a particular social ritual such as traveling by train or going to the theater, as well as the symbolic setting. The meaning of buildings evolves and becomes established by experience and we in turn read our experience into buildings. Buildings arouse an empathetic reaction in us through these projected experiences, and the strength of these reactions is determined by our culture, our beliefs, and our expectations. They tell stories, for their form and spatial organization give us hints about how they should be used. Their physical layout encourages some uses and inhibits others; we do not go backstage in a theater unless especially invited. Inside a law court the precise location of those involved in the legal process is an integral part of the design and an essential part of ensuring that the law is upheld.

* empathetic: 공감할 수 있는

① to identify and relate to a new architectural trend

② to recognize and associate with those buildings' function

③ to define and refine by reflecting cross-cultural interactions

④ to use and change into an integral part of our environment

⑤ to alter and develop for the elimination of their meanings

WORD

house ~에 장소를 제공하다   **ritual** 의식   **evolve** 발전하다, 진화하다   **spatial** 공간의   **layout** 배치, 레이아웃   **inhibit** 억제하다   **integral** 필수적인   **uphold** 유지하다

4. 다음 빈칸에 들어갈 말로 가장 적절한 것은?

2014학년도 9월 35번

When confronted by a seemingly simple pointing task, where their desires are put in conflict with outcomes, chimpanzees find it impossible to exhibit subtle self-serving cognitive strategies in the immediate presence of a desired reward. However, such tasks are mastered _____.
In one study, chimps were confronted by a simple choice; two plates holding tasty food items were presented, each with a different number of treats. If the chimp pointed to the plate having more treats, it would immediately be given to a fellow chimp in an adjacent cage, and the frustrated subject would receive the smaller amount. After hundreds and hundreds of trials, these chimps could not learn to withhold pointing to the larger reward. However, these same chimps had already been taught the symbolic concept of simple numbers. When those numbers were placed on the plates as a substitute for the actual rewards, the chimps promptly learned to point to the smaller numbers first, thereby obtaining the larger rewards for themselves.

① as immediate rewards replace delayed ones

② when an alternative symbol system is employed

③ if their desires for the larger rewards are satisfied

④ when material rewards alternate with symbolic ones

⑤ if the value of the number is proportional to the amount of the reward

WORD

subtle 예리한, 교묘한   **self-serving** 자기 이익을 챙기는   **be confronted by** ~에 직면하다   **treat** 특별한 선물, 대접   **adjacent** 인접한   **subject** 피실험자   **withhold** 억제하다   **substitute** 대신하는 것, 대체물   **proportional to** ~에 비례하는

5. 다음 빈칸에 들어갈 말로 가장 적절한 것은?

2018학년도 6월 33번

To make plans for the future, the brain must have an ability to take certain elements of prior experiences and reconfigure them in a way that does not copy any actual past experience or present reality exactly. To accomplish that, the organism must go beyond the mere ability to form internal representations, the models of the world outside. It must acquire the ability to _____. We can argue that tool-making, one of the fundamental distinguishing features of primate cognition, depends on this ability, since a tool does not exist in a ready-made form in the natural environment and has to be imagined in order to be made. The neural machinery for creating and holding 'images of the future' was a necessary prerequisite for tool-making, and thus for launching human civilization.

① mirror accurate images of the world outside

② manipulate and transform these models

③ visualize the present reality as it is

④ bring the models back from memory

⑤ identify and reproduce past experiences faithfully

6. 다음 빈칸에 들어갈 말로 가장 적절한 것은?

2013학년도 수능 26번

By likening the eye to a camera, elementary biology textbooks help to produce a misleading impression of what perception entails. Only in terms of the physics of image formation do the eye and camera have anything in common. Both eye and camera have a lens that focuses light rays from the outside world into an image, and both have a means of adjusting the focus and brightness of that image. Both eye and camera have a light-sensitive layer onto which the image is cast (the retina and film, respectively). However, image formation is only the first step towards seeing. _____ _____ obscure the much more fundamental difference between the two, which is that the camera merely records an image, whereas the visual system interprets it.

① Apparent differences in the focusing power of a lens

② Superficial analogies between the eye and a camera

③ Contrasts in light adaptation between the retina and film

④ Misunderstandings of image formation in the eye and a camera

⑤ Close relationships between image formation and interpretation

WORD

element 요소   reconfigure 재구성하다   internal representation 내적 표상   acquire 습득하다   fundamental 근본적인   distinguishing 독특한   feature 특징   primate 영장류   cognition 인지   neural machinery 신경 기제   prerequisite 전제 조건   launch 시작하다

WORD

liken 비유하다   misleading 잘못된   perception 인지   in terms of ~라는 면에서   adjust 조절하다   retina 망막   respectively 각각   obscure 가리다, 어두운   whereas 반면에   superficial 표면적인, 피상적인   analogy 비유, 유사   adaptation 적응   interpretation 해석, 이해

7. 다음 빈칸에 들어갈 말로 가장 적절한 것은?

2018학년도 6월 34번

Since life began in the oceans, most life, including freshwater life, has a chemical composition more like the ocean than fresh water. It appears that most freshwater life did not originate in fresh water, but is secondarily adapted, having passed from ocean to land and then back again to fresh water. As improbable as this may seem, the bodily fluids of aquatic animals show a strong similarity to oceans, and indeed, most studies of ion balance in freshwater physiology document the complex regulatory mechanisms by which fish, amphibians and invertebrates attempt to _____. It is these sorts of unexpected complexities and apparent contradictions that make ecology so interesting. The idea of a fish in a freshwater lake struggling to accumulate salts inside its body to mimic the ocean reminds one of the other great contradiction of the biosphere: plants are bathed in an atmosphere composed of roughly three-quarters nitrogen, yet their growth is frequently restricted by lack of nitrogen.

* amphibian: 양서류 ** invertebrate: 무척추동물

① maintain an inner ocean in spite of surrounding fresh water

② attain ion balance by removing salts from inside their body

③ return to the ocean to escape from their natural enemies

④ rebuild their external environment to obtain resources

⑤ change their physiology in accord with their surroundings

WORD

composition 성분, 구성 요소   improbable 있을 법하지 않은   fluid 액체   aquatic 수중의   ion 이온   physiology 생리 상태, 생리학   document 상세히 기록하다   regulatory 조절하는   contradiction 모순   mimic 흉내 내다   biosphere 생물권   nitrogen 질소

8. 다음 빈칸에 들어갈 말로 가장 적절한 것은?

2016학년도 수능 34번

Long before Walt Whitman wrote *Leaves of Grass*, poets had addressed themselves to fame. Horace, Petrarch, Shakespeare, Milton, and Keats all hoped that poetic greatness would grant them a kind of earthly immortality. Whitman held a similar faith that for centuries the world would value his poems. But to this ancient desire to live forever on the page, he added a new sense of fame. Readers would not simply attend to the poet's work; they would be attracted to the greatness of his personality. They would see in his poems a vibrant cultural performance, an individual springing from the book with tremendous charisma and appeal. Out of the political rallies and electoral parades that marked Jacksonian America, Whitman defined poetic fame in relation to the crowd. Other poets might look for their inspiration from the goddess of poetry. Whitman's poet sought _____. In the instability of American democracy, fame would be dependent on celebrity, on the degree to which the people rejoiced in the poet and his work.

* rally: 집회

① a refuge from public attention

② poetic purity out of political chaos

③ immortality in literature itself

④ the approval of his contemporaries

⑤ fame with political celebrities

WORD

address oneself to ~에 주의를 기울이다   grant 부여하다   earthly 세속적인, 현세의   attend to ~에 주의하다   vibrant 고동치는, 활력이 넘치는   spring 솟구치다, 튀어 오르다   tremendous 엄청난   appeal 호소력, 매력   rally 집회, 모임   electoral 선거의   mark 특징짓다   inspiration 영감   instability 불안정   celebrity 인기도, 명성   rejoice 기뻐하다

★ 혼공 11일차에 나온 문장들을 해석해 보자.

단어 PLUS

1　To be disappointed that our progress in understanding has not remedied the social ills of the world is a legitimate view, but to confuse this with the progress of knowledge is absurd.

1
+ disappointed 실망한
+ progress 진보
+ legitimate 합법의
+ confuse 혼동을 주다
+ absurd 불합리한

2　This may explain why Australian aboriginal technology, although it developed and elaborated steadily over the ensuing millennia, was lacking in so many features of the Old World.

2
+ aboriginal 원주민의
+ elaborated 정교한
+ ensue 계속 일어나다

3　When confronted by a seemingly simple pointing task, where their desires are put in conflict with outcomes, chimpanzees find it impossible to exhibit subtle self-serving cognitive strategies in the immediate presence of a desired reward.

3
+ confront 직면하다
+ desire 욕망
+ outcome 결과
+ exhibit 전시하다
+ subtle 미묘한

4　We can argue that tool-making, one of the fundamental distinguishing features of primate cognition, depends on this ability, since a tool does not exist in a ready-made form in the natural environment and has to be imagined in order to be made.

4
+ fundamental 근본적인
+ distinguish 구별하다
+ cognition 인지

5　Superficial analogies between the eye and a camera obscure the much more fundamental difference between the two, which is that the camera merely records an image, whereas the visual system interprets it.

5
+ superficial 피상적인
+ obscure 보기 어렵게 하다
+ interpret 이해하다

6　As improbable as this may seem, the bodily fluids of aquatic animals show a strong similarity to oceans, and indeed, most studies of ion balance in freshwater physiology document the complex regulatory mechanisms by which fish, amphibians and invertebrates attempt to maintain an inner ocean in spite of surrounding fresh water.

6
+ improbable 있을 것 같지 않은
+ aquatic 수생의
+ physiology 생리학
+ complex 복잡한
+ regulatory 규제하는
+ invertebrate 무척추동물
+ amphibian 양서류

'공부가 가장 쉬웠어요'라는 책 들어본 적 있니?

없지? 당연하겠지. 샘이 고등학교 때 나왔던 책이거든. 꽤 유명한 책이어서 책 안 읽기로 둘째가라면 서러운 나도 책을 샀어. 제목이 상당히 도발적이니까 안 읽을 수 없더라고.

첫 표지를 넘기고 단숨에 책을 읽어나갔고, 불과 1주일도 걸리지 않아 완독했었어. 책을 읽기 전 내 마음은 저자를 찾아서 혼내주고 싶은 마음이었어. 그런데 책 읽고 나니까 저자가 이해되더라고. 이유는 다음과 같아.

저자에게 공부는 생존이었던 거야. 가난한 환경, 동생들을 먹여 살려야 하는 입장. 이게 어릴 적 글쓴이에게 직면한 환경이었어. 그래서 글쓴이는 어린 나이부터 아르바이트를 전전해야만 했고 비뚤어진 마음에 주먹질을 하기도 했었지. 특히 막노동을 계속 하면서 생계를 유지했기에 공부는 엄두도 못내는 상황이었어. 그러던 어느 날 세상을 돌이켜 보니 자신의 모습이 참 말도 아니었던 거지. 그래서 공부란 것을 해볼까 했다고 해.

막상 공부를 시작하니 당연히 쉽지 않았지. 하지만 그 동안 쌓인 분노를 '오기'로 삼아 무작정 열심히 했다는군. 수능을 보고 원하는 성적이 나오지 않아 또 공부를 했다고 해. 그 와중에도 틈틈이 막노동을 하면서 생계를 유지했어. 크지 않은 체구지만 온몸에 탄탄한 근육이 있었고, 굳은 살도 엄청났겠지? 그 몸으로 새벽까지 공부를 하고 하고 또 했대.

물리에서 나오는 파동을 공부하다가 답답해서 실제 물방울이 튀는 것도 보고, 강에 돌을 떨어뜨려보기도 하면서 공부와 실제를 연결시키려 노력했고. 눈을 감고 시를 느껴보기도 하고, 세상 모든 것을 수학적으로 생각해보기도 했대. 뭐, 어떤 것에 미치다보면 이럴 수 있거든.

결국 수능을 잘 본 글쓴이는 서울대학교 법학과에 입학할 수 있었어. 공사장의 동료 아저씨들이 어마어마하게 축하해줬다고 하더군. 정말 개천에서 용 났다고 해야 하나? 하지만 샘이 볼 때 개천에서 용 날려면 너무너무 어려운 과정을 거쳐야 한다는 생각이 들게 만든 책이었어.

샘이 고 3이 되던 해였어. 샘이 다니던 고등학교에서 서울대 탐방을 가게 되었어. 서울대가 엄청 넓거든. 그런데 세상에! '공부가 가장 쉬웠어요'의 글쓴이를 캠퍼스에서 우연히 보게 된 거야. 나에게 나름 큰 인상을 남긴 책이었기 때문에 그 분의 얼굴을 한 번에 알아볼 수 있었어. 나도 모르게 '아!'라고 외쳤고, 그 사람과 나는 짧은 시간동안 눈빛을 주고 받았어.

굉장히 짧은 시간이었지만, 작은 체구의 그 분은 굉장한 아우라를 풍겼어. 나는 팬의 입장에서 그 분 마음속으로 텔레파시를 남겼어.

'저도 작가님 만큼 훌륭한 사람이 되고 싶어요. 할 수 있겠죠?'

뭔가 대답을 받은 느낌이었어. 그 만큼 눈빛이 강렬했거든. 샘도 누군가에게 이런 영감을 주는 사람이 되고 싶어.

혼공

12일차

빈칸추론(앞부분)

#보통_주제문_빈칸 #상대적으로_쉬움

난이도 🌶🌶🌶

The freethinking of one age is the common sense of the next.
by Matthew Arnold

한 시대의 자유 사상은 다음 세대의 상식이다.

- 앞부분에 빈칸이 있다면 그 문장이 주제문일 확률이 높음
- 뒤에는 주제문에 대한 부연설명, 예시, 반박문이 나옴
- 예시가 나온다면, 예시를 모두 읽어라. 반전이 나올 수도 있음
- 앞부분 빈칸 유형은 뒷부분 빈칸보다는 쉬움
- 부정어가 빈칸 앞에 있다면 부정어를 선택지에 넣어라
- 선택지를 먼저 보고, 선택지의 단어가 글의 흐름상 +/− 인지 파악

02 혼공 전략

앞부분의 빈칸은 주제문을 물어보는 것이다.

주제문

Patients should be aware that _____ about who should be treated for various conditions. For example, expert committees in Europe and the United States set different guidelines about when to treat high blood pressure. The group of American experts believed that for mild elevation of blood pressure the benefits exceeded the risks from treatment. They wrote guidelines suggesting that patients with mild blood pressure elevation take medicine. But in Europe, an expert committee with access to the same scientific data set different guidelines that don't advise treatment for mild elevation of blood pressure. In Europe, people with the same symptoms would not be encouraged to take medicine. Different groups of experts can disagree significantly about what is "best practice."

예시문

① there is a universal guideline 보편적 지침이 있다
② there can be moral considerations 도덕적 고려사항이 있을 수 있다
③ their family is responsible for the decision 가족이 의사결정 책임이 있다
④ there can be differing views among specialists 전문가들 사이에 다른 의견이 있을 수 있다
⑤ they benefit from following their doctors' advice 주치의의 충고를 따르는 데에서 이득을 얻는다

Solution 맨 앞줄 빈칸은 주제문을 물어보는 거야. 글 전체의 흐름만 제대로 파악하면 그리 어렵지 않아. 환자들이 알아야만 하는 내용을 물어보는 것이니 뒤에 나오는 몇 개의 문장만 파악하면 어렵지 않게 답을 선택할 수 있어.

Solution 아래는 주제문에 대한 예시가 나오지. 미국과 유럽에서의 의사들의 판단 기준이 다르다는 내용이 나와. 그렇다면 빈칸도 '판단 기준의 다름'이 핵심이 되겠지.

Solution 글의 예시는 미국과 유럽 의사들의 판단 기준이 다르다는 내용이지. 즉 선택지는 '판단 기준의 다름'과 연관이 있어야 돼. 바로 정답은 ④번이 되겠지.

문항 맛보기

다음 빈칸에 들어갈 말로 가장 적절한 것은?

2015학년도 6월 31번

   The true champion recognizes that excellence often flows most smoothly from _____, a fact that can get lost in these high-tech days. I used to train with a world-class runner who was constantly hooking himself up to pulse meters and pace keepers. He spent hours collecting data that he thought would help him improve. In fact, a good 25 percent of his athletic time was devoted to externals other than working out. Sports became so complex for him that he forgot how to enjoy himself. Contrast his approach with that of the late Abebe Bikila, the Ethiopian who won the 1960 Olympic Marathon running barefoot. High-tech clothing and digital watches were not part of his world. Abebe Bikila simply ran. Many times in running, and in other areas of life, less is more.

① talent   ② patience   ③ simplicity

④ generosity   ⑤ confidence

WORD

recognize 인식하다   excellence 탁월함   flow 흐르다   high-tech 최첨단의   world-class 세계 일류의   constantly 끊임없이   hook oneself up to 자신을 ~에 연결하다   pulse 맥박   pace keeper 평균 속도 계측기 (달린 거리, 시간, 열량 소모량 등 각 종 지표를 보여주는 장치)   good (수, 양적으로) 상당한, 충분한   athletic 운동의, 경기의   devote ~ to … ~을 …에 바치다[쏟다]   external 외적인 것, 외부 사항   complex 복잡한   contrast 대조하다   barefoot 맨발로, 맨발의

The true champion recognizes that excellence often flows most smoothly from _____, a fact that can get lost in these high-tech days. I used to train with a world-class runner who was constantly hooking himself up to pulse meters and pace keepers. He spent hours collecting data that he thought would help him improve. In fact, a good 25 percent of his athletic time was devoted to externals other than working out. Sports became so complex for him that he forgot how to enjoy himself. Contrast his approach with that of the late Abebe Bikila, the Ethiopian who won the 1960 Olympic Marathon running barefoot. High-tech clothing and digital watches were not part of his world. Abebe Bikila simply ran. Many times in running, and in other areas of life, less is more.

① talent 재능
② patience 인내
③ simplicity 단순함
④ generosity 관대함
⑤ confidence 자신감

정답: ③

해석 진정한 챔피언은 탁월함은 흔히 단순함에서부터 가장 부드럽게 흘러나온다는 것을 인식하고 있는데, 이는 요즘과 같은 최첨단 시대에는 놓쳐질 수 있는 사실이다. 나는 맥박 측정기와 평균 속도 계측기에 끊임없이 자신을 연결하는 어떤 세계 일류 선수와 훈련을 하곤 했었다. 그는 자신이 향상되는 데 도움이 되리라 생각되는 자료를 수집하며 여러 시간을 보냈다. 사실 그의 운동시간 중 상당 부분인 25%가 운동이 아닌 외적인 것에 바쳐졌다. 스포츠가 그에게는 너무나 복잡해져서 그는 자신을 즐기는 법을 잊었다. 그의 접근 방식을 1960년 올림픽 마라톤에서 맨발로 달려 우승한 에티오피아 사람, 고 Abebe Bikila의 접근 방식과 대조해 보라. 최첨단 옷과 디지털 시계는 그의 세계의 일부가 아니었다. Abebe Bikila는 그냥 달렸다. 달리기에서 그리고 삶의 다른 영역에서도 흔히 더 모자라는 것이 더 넘치는 것이다.

고난도 문항 요리하기

1. 다음 빈칸에 들어갈 말로 가장 적절한 것은?

2012학년도 9월 27번

_____ is aggravated by the overabundance of information at our disposal. While this is obvious enough in some realms − for example, consider how much information is potentially relevant for estimating the value of Microsoft stock − even when the information set seems less cluttered, information overload, a state of confusion and decision avoidance, can still occur. In one experiment, shoppers in a supermarket were presented with free samples of jams and jellies. In the first treatment, a small selection was available for tasting; in the second, a large selection was available. While everyone likes the idea of abundant choice, and indeed the table with the greater selection attracted larger crowds, it was the table with fewer samples that led to the most sales. The likely reason is that the large selection led to information overload, the feeling that the decision was too complicated for immediate action.

① Difficulty in assessing information
② The shortage of trustworthy informants
③ Mental fatigue caused by misleading information
④ Indeterminacy arising from indirect information
⑤ The complexity of altering consumer behavior

2. 다음 빈칸에 들어갈 말로 가장 적절한 것은?

2017학년도 6월 33번

It is not hard to see that a strong economy, where opportunities are plentiful and jobs go begging, _____. Biased employers may still dislike hiring members of one group or another, but when nobody else is available, discrimination most often gives way to the basic need to get the work done. The same goes for employees with prejudices about whom they do and do not like working alongside. In the American construction boom of the late 1990s, for example, even the carpenters' union – long known as a "traditional bastion of white men, a world where a coveted union card was handed down from father to son" – began openly encouraging women, blacks, and Hispanics to join its internship program. At least in the workplace, jobs chasing people obviously does more to promote a fluid society than people chasing jobs.

* bastion: 요새 ** coveted: 부러움을 사는

① allows employees to earn more income
② helps break down social barriers
③ simplifies the hiring process
④ increases wage discrimination
⑤ improves the productivity of a company

WORD

assess 평가하다 aggravate 악화시키다 overabundance 과다 at one's disposal 마음대로 쓸 수 있는 clutter 어지럽히다 overload 과부하 avoidance 회피 complicated 복잡한 indeterminacy 불확정성

WORD

plentiful 많은 go begging 구걸하다; 찾는 사람이 없다 biased 편견에 빠진 discrimination 차별 give way to ~에 자리를 내주다 prejudice 편견 alongside 나란히 construction 건설 boom 호황 carpenter 목수 union 조합 chase 쫓다

3. 다음 빈칸에 들어갈 말로 가장 적절한 것은?

2014학년도 9월 31번

Wood is a material that is widely acknowledged to be environmentally friendly. It has been welcome as an alternative material for a long time in building houses instead of cement or bricks. However, it is not always easy to _____ of one particular material such as wood over another. Many species of tree are now endangered, including mahogany and teak, and deforestation, particularly in tropical rainforests, has had a severe impact both on local communities and on native plants and wildlife. Where wood is harvested and then transported halfway across the globe, the associated energy costs are high, causing a negative impact on the environment. What is more, where wood is treated with chemicals to improve fire- and pest-resistance, its healthful properties are compromised.

* mahogany: 마호가니(적갈색 열대산 목재)

① increase the inherent resistance

② favor the chemical properties

③ dominate the natural habitats

④ evaluate the relative merits

⑤ deny the cost advantage

4. 다음 빈칸에 들어갈 말로 가장 적절한 것은?

2014학년도 6월 34번

The so-called Mozart effect – listening to Mozart will make your child smarter – is a good example of _____ by the media through hype not warranted by the research. It all started when researchers reported that after exposure to a selection of Mozart's music, college students showed an increase in spatial reasoning for about 10 minutes on tasks like putting together pieces of a jigsaw puzzle. Note first that the research was done on college students, not infants, and that the effect was very brief. In addition, no one's been able to replicate the research. The increase in spatial reasoning, it turns out, can be generated by any auditory stimulation (e.g., listening to a short story or other types of music) that keeps people alert while being tested. However, none of this has stopped eager parents – spurred on by fantastic claims from unethical companies – from purchasing Mozart CDs for their babies.

* hype: 과대 광고(선전)

① the bond between parents and children exaggerated

② a genuine scientific innovation being discarded

③ a scientific finding being distorted

④ the correlation between reasoning and music being rejected

⑤ the convergence of music and physiology made possible

WORD

alternative 대안적인　**endangered** 멸종 위기에 이른　**teak** 티크
deforestation 삼림 벌채　**tropical rainforest** 열대 우림　**harvest** 추수하다　**transport** 운송하다　**fire- and pest-resistance** 내화성과 내충성

WORD

warranted 입증된, 보증된　**selection** 선곡, 선택　**spatial reasoning** 공간 추리(능력)　**jigsaw** 조각 맞추기　**replicate** 반복하다, 복제하다　**spur** 자극하다, 박차를 가하다　**convergence** 융합, 수렴

5. 다음 빈칸에 들어갈 말로 가장 적절한 것은?

2012학년도 9월 25번

_____. If I assign fifty students a five-page essay on the subject of why the Roman Empire fell, most of them are likely to say it was a combination of economic and social causes ultimately leading to a weakening of the frontiers. This would be a fine answer, but after reading forty-five papers all saying the same thing, I'm ready for a change. If you can take a different angle from the rest of the class in a paper, you're more likely to impress your professors. But here's the tricky part − being different is risky, and it only works if you back up your argument very well. If you choose to argue that Rome fell solely because Christianity weakened the fighting spirit of the Romans, you will need persuasive reasoning and arguments against any potential objections.

① Variety is the spice of life

② The essence of writing is in its brevity

③ Don't fix what is not broken

④ The pen is mightier than the sword

⑤ Rome was not built in a day

6. 다음 빈칸에 들어갈 말로 가장 적절한 것은?

2012학년도 6월 27번

Some people believe that _____ is some kind of instinct, developed because it benefits our species in some way. At first, this seems like a strange idea: Darwin's theories of evolution presume that individuals should act to preserve their own interests, not those of the species as a whole. But the British evolutionary biologist Richard Dawkins believes that natural selection has given us the ability to feel pity for someone who is suffering. When humans lived in small clan-based groups, a person in need would be a relative or someone who could pay you back a good turn later, so taking pity on others could benefit you in the long run. Modern societies are much less close-knit and when we see a heartfelt appeal for charity, chances are we may never even meet the person who is suffering – but the emotion of pity is still in our genes.

① not wanting to suffer

② giving to charity

③ drawing pity from others

④ exploring alternatives

⑤ pursuing individual interests

WORD

assign 할당하다 **empire** 제국 **combination** 조화, 조합 **ultimately** 궁극적으로 **impress** 인상을 주다 **tricky** 다루기 어려운 **persuasive** 설득력이 있는 **reasoning** 추론

WORD

instinct 본능 **presume** 추정하다 **preserve** 보존하다 **evolutionary** 진화의 **evolution** 진화 **natural selection** 자연선택 **clan** 씨족 **close-knit** 긴밀히 맺어진 **heartfelt** 진심 어린

7. 다음 빈칸에 들어갈 말로 가장 적절한 것은?

2014학년도 6월 35번

As the structures of our world and the conditions of certainty have yielded to an avalanche of change, the extent of our longing for stable, definitive leadership _____. The fault lies not with leadership but rather with ourselves and our expectations. In the old days, leaders were supposed to make sense of chaos, to make certainty out of doubt, and to create positive action plans for the resolution of paradoxes. Good leaders straightened things out. Should chaos rear its ugly head, the leader was expected to restore normality immediately. But chaos is now considered normal, paradoxes cannot be resolved, and certainty is possible only to the level of high probability. Leadership that attempts to deliver in terms of fixing any of these can only fail. And that is exactly what is happening.

* an avalanche of: 많은, 쇄도하는

① can only be measured by our will to establish it

② has made traditional leadership more irreplaceable

③ can create viable action plans for restoring normality

④ has vastly reduced the probability of resolving paradoxes

⑤ has been exceeded only by the impossibility of finding it

8. 다음 빈칸에 들어갈 말로 가장 적절한 것은?

2011학년도 9월 26번

Unlike deviance in other settings, deviance in sports often involves _____ norms and expectations. For example, most North Americans see playing football as a positive activity. Young men are encouraged to 'be all they can be' as football players and to live by slogans such as "There is no 'I' in t-e-a-m." They are encouraged to increase their weight and strength, so that they can play more effectively and contribute to the success of their teams. When young men go too far in their acceptance of expectations to become bigger and stronger, when they are so committed to playing football and improving their skills on the field that they use muscle-building drugs, they become deviant. This type of 'overdoing-it-deviance' is dangerous, but it is grounded in completely different social dynamics from the dynamics that occur in the 'antisocial deviance' enacted by alienated young people who reject commonly accepted rules and expectations.

① a disciplined control of the desire to avoid

② wasted efforts and resources in establishing

③ ambitious attempts to get independent of and free from

④ a traditional approach of matching slogans and mottos with

⑤ an unquestioned acceptance of and extreme conformity to

WORD

yield to ~에 굴복하다   extent 범위, 정도   definitive 확실한   paradox 모순   straighten out ~을 해결하다   rear its[one's] (ugly) head 고개를 쳐들다   restore 회복시키다, 재건하다

WORD

deviance 일탈   norm 규범, 기준   be committed to ~ing ~하는 것에 전념하다   overdo 과장하다   grounded 기초를 둔, 근거하는   dynamics 역학   enact 행하다, 제정하다

4 혼공 개념 마무리

★ 혼공 12일차에 나온 문장들을 해석해 보자.

단어 PLUS

1 In the American construction boom of the late 1990s, for example, even the carpenters' union – long known as a "traditional bastion of white men, a world where a coveted union card was handed down from father to son" – began openly encouraging women, blacks, and Hispanics to join its internship program.

1
+ construction 건설
+ carpenter 목수
+ bastion 수호자, 요새

2 Many species of tree are now endangered, including mahogany and teak, and deforestation, particularly in tropical rainforests, has had a severe impact both on local communities and on native plants and wildlife.

2
+ endangered 멸종위기에 처한
+ deforestation 산림벌채
+ severe 심각한

3 The increase in spatial reasoning, it turns out, can be generated by any auditory stimulation (e.g., listening to a short story or other types of music) that keeps people alert while being tested.

3
+ spatial 공간적인
+ reasoning 추리, 추론
+ auditory 청각의
+ stimulation 자극

4 This type of 'overdoing-it-deviance' is dangerous, but it is grounded in completely different social dynamics from the dynamics that occur in the 'antisocial deviance' enacted by alienated young people who reject commonly accepted rules and expectations.

4
+ deviance 일탈
+ grounded 근거를 둔
+ dynamics 역학
+ alienated 고립된
+ reject 거절하다

5 As the structures of our world and the conditions of certainty have yielded to an avalanche of change, the extent of our longing for stable, definitive leadership has been exceeded only by the impossibility of finding it.

5
+ yield to 굴복하다
+ an avalanche of 상당히 많은
+ extent 정도, 양
+ definitive 결정적인
+ exceed 초과하다

6 Modern societies are much less close-knit and when we see a heartfelt appeal for charity, chances are we may never even meet the person who is suffering – but the emotion of pity is still in our genes.

6
+ close-knit 긴밀하게 맺어진
+ heartfelt 진심 어린

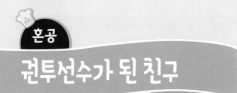
권투선수가 된 친구

샘이 중학교 1학년 때였어. 지금과 비교할 수 없는 환경이었지. 남중이라 '남학생'들만 다니는 학교였는데, 학생들 번호를 키 순서대로 했거든. 체구가 무척 작았던 샘은 거의 45명 중에 4번을 부여 받았어. 까치발이라도 세울 걸 그랬어.

2번 친구가 있었어. 나랑 그리 친하지는 않았지만 이마의 흉터가 좀 무서운 아이였어. 물론 나보다 더 작으니까 당연히 나보다 힘이 약할 거라 생각했었어.

어느 날 나는 짝꿍과 다투게 되었어. 말이 다툼이지, 그 녀석이 새로 산 '자'를 가지고 계속해서 나를 툭툭 치는 거야. 참고로 그 친구는 3번이었어. 나보다 근소하게 작았지. 하하. 그래서 몇 번 싫다고 했는데 그 녀석은 나를 간보는 것 같았어. 계속해서 툭툭 치더라고. 결국 나는 화가 폭발했고 욕설을 했지. 이때다 싶었는지 그 짝꿍 녀석은 안경을 끼고 있던 내 얼굴에 주먹을 날렸고 나는 일방적으로 당했어.

그 날 이후로 나는 반에서 동네 북이 되었고, 2번 친구마저도 나를 괴롭히기 시작했어. 한번 떨어진 사기는 올라올 턱이 없었고 나는 힘겹게 중학교 생활을 했지.

2학년으로 올라갈 때 나는 기도하고 또 기도했어. 제발 이 두 녀석과 같은 반이 되지 말아달라고. 다행히 기존 짝꿍이었던 3번 친구와는 바이바이했어. 너무 좋았지. 그런데 문제는 2번 꼬맹이 친구와 같은 반이 되었다는 거야. 아.. 정말 끔찍한 순간이었어. 그렇게 나의 1년이 시작되었어.

맞기도 맞고, 컨닝을 강요당하기도 했어. 지금 생각해보면 선생님께 일렀어야 하는데 그 당시에는 왕따가 될 수 있는 지름길이라 생각해서 그러지도 못했어. 부모님께도 말씀을 못 드릴 정도였으니까. 여튼 한 학기가 훌쩍 흘렀고 나는 여전히 작았어. 그 녀석도 작았고.

그 녀석이 수업 시간에 한 여자 선생님과 마찰을 빚었어. 거칠게 대들던 그 친구는 급기야 가방을 메고 수업 시간에 밖으로 나가버렸어. 다들 무슨 일인지 영문을 몰랐지만 그렇게 그 친구는 학교를 그만두었어. 다시는 오지 않았어. 내가 졸업할 때까지. 그렇게 한참의 시간이 흘러 나는 교사가 되었고 그 친구의 소식이 끊어진지 엄청나게 오래 되었어.

어느 날, TV를 켜고 채널을 돌리다 보니 권투하는 남편과 아내가 나오더라고. 아내가 권투를 잘해서 권투 선수 출신인 남편도 쩔쩔 매는 이런 이야기였어. 둘 사이에는 귀여운 아이도 둘 있더라고. 참 재미나게 사는 사람들이다 싶었어. 그런데 그 남자 얼굴을 보다 보니 흉터가 딱!! 하고 눈에 들어오는 거야. 문득 옛날 교실을 박차고 나갔던 그 친구의 얼굴이 오버랩 되었어.

혹시나 했는데 확신이 돼서 네이버에 검색해보았지. 그 친구의 기사가 나오더라고. 그리고 권투 선수라는 것도 알게 되었어. 동양 플라이급 챔피언까지 지냈었고, 가명을 쓰고 있었지만 검색해보니 금방 본명을 알 수 있었어. 맞다 맞다! 과거의 분노는 반가움으로 바뀌어 있었고, 지금은 그 친구를 멀리서 응원하게 되었어. 방송을 보니 이제 마음 잡고 잘 살아가는 것 같더라. 건강하고 행복하길 바랄 뿐이야.

13일차

빈칸추론(뒷부분)

#가장_어려운_유형 #모든지문을_읽어라

난이도 🌶🌶🌶

The freethinking of one age is the common sense of the next.
by Matthew Arnold

한 시대의 자유 사상은 다음 세대의 상식이다.

01 문항 특징

- 🌶 뒷부분에 빈칸이 있다면 시간이 소요됨을 의미
- 🌶 모든 지문을 읽어봐야 함
- 🌶 앞부분에 나오는 내용과 중간에 달라지는 내용의 차이를 알아내라
- 🌶 중간에 반전 유무가 키포인트!
- 🌶 부정어가 빈칸 앞에 있다면 부정어를 선택지에 넣어라
- 🌶 선택지를 먼저 보고, 선택지의 단어가 글의 흐름상 +/−인지 파악

02 혼공 전략

중간 반전 포인트가 핵심이야.

주제문

A famous diamond company deals with people's psychology clearly. One component of marketing focuses on the "false expectation" the people's subconsciousness feels about love, the unchanging love: Its ads feature couples using diamonds to express their eternal love or to confirm their devotion after years together. On the contrary, another component of its marketing deals with the consequences of the false expectations, parting or divorce, in a clever manner by emphasizing the investment and resale value of diamonds. In short, both campaigns strongly use psychology, addressing our undying belief in the permanence of romantic love and providing a useful benefit when ▨▨▨▨▨▨▨▨▨▨▨▨.

① that belief is given up 그 믿음이 버려질 때
② couples buy a diamond 커플이 다이아몬드를 살 때
③ love is maintained to the end 사랑이 끝까지 유지될 때
④ the company invests in marketing 회사가 마케팅에 투자할 때
⑤ romantic love ends up in marriage 낭만적인 사랑이 결혼으로 이어질 때

Solution 이 글은 다이아몬드 회사가 사람의 심리를 이용한다는 내용이야. 그 뒤로는 한 가지 방식이 설명되고 있어. 그런데 바로 뒤에 또 다른 방식이 나오지? 이게 핵심일 가능성이 있어. 보통 빈칸은 반전 포인트에 방향을 맞추는 경향이 높아.

반전 포인트 등장

Solution 결론 부분에 빈칸이 있어. 하지만 반전 포인트를 기억해야 해. 다이아몬드 회사는 영원한 사랑을 이야기하지만, 그것이 깨졌을 때도 이용한다는 내용이야.

Solution '영원한 사랑' + '사랑이 깨졌을 때' 라는 이중적 심리를 이용한다는 것인데, 영원한 사랑은 앞에서 언급되니까 빈칸은 '사랑이 깨졌을 때'와 어울릴 만한 ①번이 정답.

Solution 이 글의 핵심인 마케팅이라는 어휘가 보이지만, 이것은 함정이야. 필자가 말하고 싶은 것은 바로 마케팅 전략으로 사람들의 이중적 태도를 이용한다는 거야.

다음 빈칸에 들어갈 말로 가장 적절한 것은?

2016학년도 9월 33번

It is easy to find examples of correlations which are far more systematic than could occur by chance and yet which it would be absurd to treat as evidence of a direct causal link. For instance, there is a high degree of correlation between shoe size and vocabulary size: people with larger shoe sizes tend to have much larger vocabularies than people with smaller shoe sizes. But having larger feet does not *cause* anyone to gain a larger vocabulary; nor does having a large vocabulary *cause* your feet to grow. The obvious explanation of the correlation is that children tend to have much smaller feet than adults, and, because children acquire their vocabularies gradually as they grow older, it is hardly surprising that, on average, people with smaller feet have smaller vocabularies. In other words, foot size and vocabulary size can be explained in terms of _____ _____ from infancy to adulthood: a cause which both observed phenomena have in common.

① by-products of language acquisition

② causal links between uncommon events

③ contrasts between physical and mental growth

④ cultural beliefs derived from social interactions

⑤ features of the process of human development

WORD

correlation 상관관계　**occur** 발생하다　**by chance** 우연히　**absurd** 불합리한　**causal** 인과관계의　**gain** 얻다　**obvious** 분명한　**acquire** 습득하다　**gradually** 서서히　**hardly** 거의 ~않는　**in terms of** ~의 관점에서　**infancy** 유아기　**by-product** 부산물　**acquisition** 습득　**contrast** 대조

It is easy to find examples of correlations which are far more systematic than could occur by chance and yet which it would be absurd to treat as evidence of a direct causal link. For instance, there is a high degree of correlation between shoe size and vocabulary size: people with larger shoe sizes tend to have much larger vocabularies than people with smaller shoe sizes. But having larger feet does not cause anyone to gain a larger vocabulary; nor does having a large vocabulary cause your feet to grow. The obvious explanation of the correlation is that children tend to have much smaller feet than adults, and, because children acquire their vocabularies gradually as they grow older, it is hardly surprising that, on average, people with smaller feet have smaller vocabularies. In other words, foot size and vocabulary size can be explained in terms of_____ from infancy to adulthood: a cause which both observed phenomena have in common.

Solution 이 글의 주제문이라고 할 수 있어. 무언가 연관은 있지만, 합리적이지는 않은 상관관계가 있다는 거지. 분명히 뒤에는 이에 대한 예시가 나올 거야. 여기서의 핵심은 '불합리한'이 될 가능성이 높아.

Solution 발의 크기와 어휘력의 크기와의 상관관계가 예시로 나오고 있어. 발의 크기가 크면 어휘력이 높다는 상관관계가 나오는데, 이건 합리적이는 않다는 거지.

Solution 앞에서 언급한 내용을 재진술 하고 있어. 즉, 발의 크기와 어휘력은 하나의 공통 원인으로 인해 발생한다는 거지. 그게 바로 '나이'를 먹는다는 거야. '나이를 먹는다'와 유사한 개념을 찾는 것이 핵심이지.

① by-products of language acquisition 언어 습득의 부산물
② causal links between uncommon events 흔하지 않은 사건들 사이의 인과관계
③ contrasts between physical and mental growth 신체적 성장과 정신적 성장 사이의 차이
④ cultural beliefs derived from social interactions 사회적 상호 작용에서 비롯된 문화적 신념
⑤ features of the process of human development 인간 발달 과정의 특징

Solution 얼핏 보면 상관관계와 비슷해 보이는 인과관계(causal links)를 보고 답이라고 할 수 있을 것 같은데, 이게 핵심이 아니지. 발 크기와 어휘력은 인과관계가 없다는 것이 핵심이야.

Solution '나이를 먹는다'와 유사한 표현은 '인간 발달과정'이라고 할 수 있겠지? 따라서 정답은 ⑤번이야.

정답: ⑤

해석 우연히 발생할 수 있는 것보다는 훨씬 더 체계적이지만 직접적인 인과관계의 증거로서 다루기에는 불합리한 상관관계의 예를 찾기는 쉽다. 예를 들면, 신발 크기와 어휘 크기 사이에는 상당한 정도의 상관관계가 있는데, 크기가 더 큰 신발을 신는 사람들이 더 작은 신발을 신는 사람들보다 훨씬 더 많은 어휘를 가지는 경향이 있다. 하지만 발의 크기가 더 크다고 해서 누군가 더 많은 어휘를 얻는 것은 아니며, 많은 어휘를 가지고 있다고 해서 발이 자라는 것도 아니다. 그 상관관계에 관한 분명한 설명은 아이들이 어른들보다 발이 훨씬 더 작은 경향이 있다는 것이고, 아이들은 나이가 들어가면서 서서히 어휘를 습득하기 때문에 평균적으로 발이 더 작은 사람들이 더 적은 어휘를 가진다는 것은 거의 놀랄만한 일이 아니다. 다시 말해서, 발 크기와 어휘 크기는 유아기에서 성인기로 가는 인간 발달 과정의 특징의 관점에서 설명될 수 있는데, (그것은) 관찰된 두 현상이 공통으로 가지는 원인이다.

1. 다음 빈칸에 들어갈 말로 가장 적절한 것은?

2014학년도 9월 34번

Researchers asked college student volunteers to think through a fantasy version of an experience (looking attractive in a pair of high-heeled shoes, winning an essay contest, or getting an A on a test) and then evaluated the fantasy's effect on the subjects and on how things unfolded in reality. When participants envisioned the most positive outcome, their energy levels, as measured by blood pressure, dropped, and they reported having a worse experience with the actual event than those who had conjured more realistic or even negative visions. To assess subjects' real life experiences, the researchers compared lists of goals that subjects had set for themselves against what they had actually accomplished and also relied on self-reports. "When we fantasize about it – especially when you fantasize something very positive – it's almost like you are actually living it," says one of the study's co-authors. That _____, draining the incentive to "get energized to go and get it," she explains. Subjects may be better off imagining how to surmount obstacles instead of ignoring them.

① prompts you into assessing the real life as it is

② turns a rosy dream into an actual accomplishment

③ renders your goal independent of the fantasy world

④ tricks the mind into thinking the goal has been achieved

⑤ deceives your mind into believing obstacles are insurmountable

WORD

unfold 전개하다　**envision** 상상하다　**conjure** 마음에 그리다　**render** 만들다　**insurmountable** 극복할 수 없는

2. 다음 빈칸에 들어갈 말로 가장 적절한 것은?

2017학년도 수능 32번

Temporal resolution is particularly interesting in the context of satellite remote sensing. The temporal density of remotely sensed imagery is large, impressive, and growing. Satellites are collecting a great deal of imagery as you read this sentence. However, most applications in geography and environmental studies do not require extremely fine-grained temporal resolution. Meteorologists may require visible, infrared, and radar information at sub-hourly temporal resolution; urban planners might require imagery at monthly or annual resolution; and transportation planners may not need any time series information at all for some applications. Again, the temporal resolution of imagery used should _____. Sometimes researchers have to search archives of aerial photographs to get information from that past that pre-date the collection of satellite imagery.

* meteorologist : 기상학자 ** infrared: 적외선의

① be selected for general purposes

② meet the requirements of your inquiry

③ be as high as possible for any occasion

④ be applied to new technology by experts

⑤ rely exclusively upon satellite information

WORD

temporal 시간의　**resolution** 해상도　**satellite** 위성　**density** 밀도　**remotely** 멀리서　**geography** 지리학　**application** 응용 프로그램　**extremely** 극단적으로　**fine-grained** 결이 고운　**pre-date** (시기가) 앞서다　**exclusively** 오직

3. 다음 빈칸에 들어갈 말로 가장 적절한 것은?

2013학년도 수능 25번

In Belding's ground squirrels, males leave home and females mature in their natal area. This male-biased dispersal creates an imbalance in the way males and females are related to those individuals around them – females find themselves surrounded by relatives, while males are generally in areas with complete strangers. This asymmetry translates into females who warn close kin by emitting alarm calls, while males generally do not emit calls since their dispersal from their natal areas means their blood kin typically do not benefit from such a warning. Further support for the kinship-based alarm-calling hypothesis includes Sherman's finding that in the rare instances when females do move away from their natal groups and into groups with far fewer relatives, they _____.

① end up acquiring the alarm calls of the new group

② make constant attempts to bring their blood kin along

③ display a tendency to become more active an cooperative

④ emit alarm calls less frequently than do native females

⑤ adopt a more elaborate defense mechanism than alarm calls

4. 다음 빈칸에 들어갈 말로 가장 적절한 것은?

2017학년도 6월 34번

One remarkable aspect of aboriginal culture is the concept of "totemism," where the tribal member at birth assumes the soul and identity of a part of nature. This view of the earth and its riches as an intrinsic part of oneself clearly rules out mistreatment of the environment because this would only constitute a destruction of self. Totems are more than objects. They include spiritual rituals, oral histories, and the organization of ceremonial lodges where records of the past travel routes of the soul can be exchanged with others and converted to mythology. The primary motivation is the preservation of tribal myths and a consolidation and sharing of every individual's origins in nature. The aborigines see _____, through a hierarchy of totems that connect to their ancestral origins, a cosmology that places them at one with the earth, and behavior patterns that respect ecological balance.

*aboriginal: 원주민의 **consolidation: 병합, 강화

① themselves as incompatible with nature and her riches

② their mythology as a primary motive toward individualism

③ their identity as being self-contained from surrounding nature

④ their relationship to the environment as a single harmonious continuum

⑤ their communal rituals as a gateway to distancing themselves from their origins

5. 다음 빈칸에 들어갈 말로 가장 적절한 것은?

2013학년도 수능 27번

Recent evidence suggests that the common ancestor of Neanderthals and modern people, living about 400,000 years ago, may have already been using pretty sophisticated language. If language is based on genes and is the key to cultural evolution, and Neanderthals had language, then why did the Neanderthal toolkit show so little cultural change? Moreover, genes would undoubtedly have changed during the human revolution after 200,000 years ago, but more in response to new habits than as causes of them. At an earlier date, cooking selected mutations for smaller guts and mouths, rather than vice versa. At a later date, milk drinking selected for mutations for retaining lactose digestion into adulthood in people of western European and East African descent. _____. The appeal to a genetic change driving evolution gets gene-culture co-evolution backwards: it is a top-down explanation for a bottom-up process.

① Genetic evolution is the mother of new habits

② Every gene is the architect of its own mutation

③ The cultural horse comes before the genetic cart

④ The linguistic shovel paves the way for a cultural road

⑤ When the cultural cat is away, the genetic mice will play

6. 다음 빈칸에 들어갈 말로 가장 적절한 것은?

2017학년도 수능 33번

Grief is unpleasant. Would one not then be better off without it altogether? Why accept it even when the loss is real? Perhaps we should say of it what Spinoza said of regret: that whoever feels it is "twice unhappy or twice helpless." Laurence Thomas has suggested that the utility of "negative sentiments" (emotions like grief, guilt, resentment, and anger, which there is seemingly a reason to believe we might be better off without) lies in their providing a kind of guarantee of authenticity for such dispositional sentiments as love and respect. No occurrent feelings of love and respect need to be present throughout the period in which it is true that one loves or respects. One might therefore sometimes suspect, in the absence of the positive occurrent feelings, that _____. At such times, negative emotions like grief offer a kind of testimonial to the authenticity of love or respect.

* dispositional: 성향적인 ** testimonial: 증거

① one no longer loves

② one is much happier

③ an emotional loss can never be real

④ respect for oneself can be guaranteed

⑤ negative sentiments do not hold any longer

WORD

modern 현대의 **sophisticated** 정교한 **toolkit** 도구 **mutation** 돌연변이, 변화 **digestion** 소화 **descent** 후손 **appeal** 호소 **top-down** 하향식 **bottom-up** 상향식 **linguistic** 언어학적인

WORD

grief 슬픔 **better off** 더 행복한, 형편이 더 나은 **sentiment** 감정 **resentment** 분개함 **guarantee** 보장 **authenticity** 진실성, 진짜 **occurrent** 현재 일어나고 있는, 우연의

7. 다음 빈칸에 들어갈 말로 가장 적절한 것은?

2017학년도 6월 32번

What story could be harsher than that of the Great Auk, the large black-and-white seabird that in northern oceans took the ecological place of a penguin? Its tale rises and falls like a Greek tragedy, with island populations savagely destroyed by humans until almost all were gone. Then the very last colony found safety on a special island, one protected from the destruction of humankind by vicious and unpredictable ocean currents. These waters presented no problem to perfectly adapted seagoing birds, but they prevented humans from making any kind of safe landing. After enjoying a few years of comparative safety, disaster of a different kind struck the Great Auk. Volcanic activity caused the island refuge to sink completely beneath the waves, and surviving individuals were forced to find shelter elsewhere. The new island home they chose _____ in one terrible way. Humans could access it with comparative ease, and they did! Within just a few years the last of this once-plentiful species was entirely eliminated.

* savagely: 잔혹하게

① lacked the benefits of the old

② denied other colonies easy access

③ faced unexpected natural disasters

④ caused conflicts among the refugees

⑤ had a similar disadvantage to the last island

8. 다음 빈칸에 들어갈 말로 가장 적절한 것은?

2013학년도 9월 28번

Guys lost on unfamiliar streets often avoid asking for directions from locals. We try to tough it out with map and compass. Admitting being lost feels like admitting stupidity. This is a stereotype, but it has a large grain of truth. It's also a good metaphor for a big overlooked problem in the human sciences. We're trying to find our way around the dark continent of human nature. We scientists are being paid to be the bus-driving tour guides for the rest of humanity. They expect us to know our way around the human mind, but we don't. So we try to fake it, without asking the locals for directions. We try to find our way from first principles of geography ('theory'), and from maps of our own making ('empirical research'). The roadside is crowded with locals, and their brains are crowded with local knowledge, but we are too arrogant and embarrassed to ask the way. So we drive around in circles, _____ about where to find the scenic vistas that would entertain and enlighten the tourists.

① waiting for the local brains to inquire

② accumulating and examining the locals' knowledge

③ going against the findings of our empirical research

④ relying on passengers' knowledge and experience

⑤ inventing and rejecting successive hypotheses

WORD

ecological 생태학의   tragedy 비극   population 개체군   colony 집단, 군체   vicious 사나운   current 해류   present 일으키다   adapt 적응시키다   seagoing 항해에 알맞은   landing 상륙   refuge 피난처   comparative 비교적인   eliminate 제거하다

WORD

tough out 곤란을 참고 견디다   compass 나침반   grain 기미, 낟알   metaphor 비유, 은유   principle 원리   geography 지리   empirical 경험의   arrogant 거만한   embarrassed 당황한   vista 풍경, 경치   enlighten 계몽하다

★ 혼공 13일차에 나온 문장들을 해석해 봅시다.

단어 + PLUS

1 Researchers asked college student volunteers to think through a fantasy version of an experience (looking attractive in a pair of high-heeled shoes, winning an essay contest, or getting an A on a test) and then evaluated the fantasy's effect on the subjects and on how things unfolded in reality.

1
+ **attractive** 매력적인
+ **evaluate** 평가하다
+ **unfold** 전개되다

2 Further support for the kinship-based alarm-calling hypothesis includes Sherman's finding that in the rare instances when females do move away from their natal groups and into groups with far fewer relatives, they emit alarm calls less frequently than do native females.

2
+ **kinship–based** 친족기반의
+ **hypothesis** 가설
+ **natal** 출생의, 타고난

3 The aborigines see their relationship to the environment as a single harmonious continuum, through a hierarchy of totems that connect to their ancestral origins, a cosmology that places them at one with the earth, and behavior patterns that respect ecological balance.

3
+ **aborigine** 원주민
+ **harmonious** 조화로운
+ **continuum** 연속체
+ **hierarchy** 위계질서
+ **cosmology** 우주론
+ **ecological** 생태학적인

4 Laurence Thomas has suggested that the utility of "negative sentiments" (emotions like grief, guilt, resentment, and anger, which there is seemingly a reason to believe we might be better off without) lies in their providing a kind of guarantee of authenticity for such dispositional sentiments as love and respect.

4
+ **sentiment** 감정
+ **resentment** 분노
+ **seemingly** 외형적으로
+ **authenticity** 진실성
+ **dispositional** 기질의, 기분의

5 So we drive around in circles, inventing and rejecting successive hypotheses about where to find the scenic vistas that would entertain and enlighten the tourists.

5
+ **reject** 거절하다
+ **successive** 연속적인
+ **vista** 경치, 풍경

6 When participants envisioned the most positive outcome, their energy levels, as measured by blood pressure, dropped, and they reported having a worse experience with the actual event than those who had conjured more realistic or even negative visions.

6
+ **participant** 참가자
+ **envision** 상상하다
+ **conjure** 상기하다

D course

승부수 문항
모의고사

14일차

승부수 문항 모의고사

1회

난이도

Concentration comes out of a combination of confidence and hunger.
by Arnold Palmer

집중력은 자신감과 갈망이 결합하여 생긴다.

1. 다음 글의 제목으로 가장 적절한 것은?

When we lived as foragers with earthbound religions, animals were the first beings, world-shapers, and the teachers and ancestors of people. When we became agriculturalists and looked to the heavens for instruction about the seasons and bad weather, we saw animal forms among the stars. Of the forty-eight Ptolemaic constellations, all but a few are organic, and twenty-five are named for animals. Of the twenty-two more that were added in the 17th century, nineteen have animal names. When people built huge earthworks to appeal to the powers of heavens, they built them in animal forms. Some in Peru are over a mile long. One in Ohio is in the shape of a giant snake with an egg in its mouth.

*constellation: 별자리

① Human Fascination with Animal Forms
② Efforts to Record Disappearing Species
③ Origins of the Names of Heavenly Bodies
④ Influence of Animals on Scientific Progress
⑤ Historical Background of Astronomical Progress

2. (A), (B), (C)의 각 네모 안에서 어법에 맞는 표현으로 가장 적절한 것은?

Sometimes perfectionists find that they are troubled because (A) what / whatever they do it never seems good enough. If I ask, "For whom is it not good enough?" they do not always know the answer. After giving it some thought they usually conclude that it is not good enough for them and not good enough for other important people in their lives. This is a key point, because it suggests that the standard you may be struggling to (B) meet / be met may not actually be your own. Instead, the standard you have set for yourself may be the standard of some important person in your life, such as a parent or a boss or a spouse. (C) Live / Living your life in pursuit of someone else's expectations is a difficult way to live. If the standards you set were not yours, it may be time to define your personal expectations for yourself and make self-fulfillment your goal.

	(A)	(B)	(C)
①	what	meet	Live
②	what	be met	Living
③	whatever	meet	Live
④	whatever	meet	Living
⑤	whatever	be met	Live

WORD

forager 수렵 채집인   earthbound 지상의   agriculturalist 농업 전문가
instruction 지시, 가르침   all but 거의 모든 것

WORD

perfectionist 완벽주의자   standard 기준   struggle 애쓰다   pursuit
추구   expectation 기대   self-fulfillment 자기달성

3. 다음 글의 (A)~(C)에서 문맥에 맞는 낱말을 바르게 짝지은 것은?

Entropy is a measure of disorder or randomness. Physicists have given a fully (A) qualitative / quantitative definition to entropy that allows one to describe something's entropy by using a definite numerical value: larger numbers mean greater entropy, smaller numbers mean less entropy. Although the details are a little complicated, this number, roughly speaking, counts the possible rearrangements of the (B) concepts / ingredients in a given physical system that leave its overall appearance intact. When your desk is neat and clean, almost any arrangement – changing the order of the newspapers, books, or articles, moving the pens from their holders – will upset its highly ordered organization. This accounts for its having low entropy. On the contrary, when your desk is a mess, numerous rearrangements of the newspapers, articles, and junk mail will leave it a mess and therefore will not (C) disturb / maintain its overall look. This accounts for its having high entropy.

	(A)		(B)		(C)
①	qualitative	······	concepts	······	disturb
②	qualitative	······	ingredients	······	maintain
③	quantitative	······	ingredients	······	maintain
④	quantitative	······	concepts	······	maintain
⑤	quantitative	······	ingredients	······	disturb

WORD

randomness 무작위 definition 정의 numerical 수의 complicated 복잡한 rearrangement 재배열 intact 온전한 account 설명

4. 다음 빈칸에 들어갈 말로 가장 적절한 것은?

Love is an attitude, an orientation of character which ＿＿＿＿＿＿＿＿＿＿＿＿＿＿＿, not toward one 'object' of love. If a person loves only one other person and is indifferent to the rest of his fellow men, his love is not love but a symbiotic attachment, or an enlarged egotism. Yet, most people believe that love is constituted by the object, not by the faculty. They believe that all that is necessary to find is the right object – and that everything goes by itself afterward. This attitude can be compared to that of a man who wants to paint but who, instead of learning the art, claims that he has just to wait for the right object, and that he will paint beautifully when he finds it. If I truly love one person, I love all persons, I love the world, and I love life. If I can say to somebody else, "I love you," I must be able to say, "I love in you everybody, I love through you the world, and I love in you also myself."

*symbiotic: 공생의, 공생하는

① is closely related to intense attachment to oneself

② directs one's resentment and anger toward oneself

③ has as its ultimate goal to add variety to a person's life

④ primarily serves to guide an individual toward a specific goal

⑤ determines the relatedness of a person to the world as a whole

WORD

orientation 방향성 indifferent 무관심한 attachment 애착 enlarged 확장된 egotism 자기 중심 constitute 구성하다 faculty 능력 ultimate 궁극적인

5. 다음 빈칸 (A)와 (B)에 들어갈 말로 가장 적절한 것은?

Imagine that you are French. You are walking along a busy pavement in Paris and another pedestrian is approaching from the opposite direction. A collision will occur unless you each move out of the other's way. Which way do you step? The answer is almost certainly to the right. Replay the same scene in many parts of Asia, however, and you would probably move to the left. There is no instruction to head in a specific direction. Mehdi Moussaid says this is a behavior brought about by _____(A)_____. If two opposing people guess each other's intentions correctly, each moving to one side and allowing the other past, then they are likely to choose to move the same way the next time they need to avoid a collision. The chance of a successful maneuver increases as more and more people adopt a bias in one direction, until the tendency sticks. Whether it's right or left does not matter; what does is that it is the unspoken will of the _____(B)_____.

	(A)		(B)
①	probabilities	······	authority
②	probabilities	······	majority
③	personalities	······	authority
④	personalities	······	majority
⑤	efficiencies	······	conscience

6. 다음 빈칸에 들어갈 말로 가장 적절한 것은?

Whenever you feel yourself triggered by a passing thought, emotion, or sensation, you have a simple choice: *to identify* or *get identified*. You can observe the thought and "identify" it. Or you can let yourself get caught up in the thought, in other words, "get identified" with it. Naming helps you identify so that you don't get identified. As you observe your passing thoughts, emotions, and sensations, naming them — *Oh, that is my old friend Fear; there goes the Inner Critic* — neutralizes their effect on you and helps you to maintain your state of balance and calm. My friend Donna even likes to give humorous names to her reactive emotions such as "Freddy Fear," "Judge Judy," and "Anger Annie." (Humor, incidentally, can be a great ally in helping you regain perspective from the balcony.) As soon as you name the character in the play, you _____.

① cheer on his or her performance

② adopt him or her as a role model

③ distance yourself from him or her

④ stop yourself from enjoying the play

⑤ become more emotionally expressive

WORD

pavement 보도　pedestrian 보행자　collision 충돌　specific 구체적인　behavior 행동　intention 의도　maneuver 살짝 몸을 피하는 동작, 책략

WORD

trigger 촉발하다　sensation 기분　identify 구별하다　get identified 동일시하다　get caught up in ~에 사로잡히다　neutralize 중화시키다　reactive 반응을 보이는　incidentally 덧붙이자면　perspective 관점

7. 주어진 글 다음에 이어질 글의 순서로 가장 적절한 것은?

Permission marketing is a term coined by Seth Godin, meaning that the customer has given his or her consent to receive marketing messages from an organization.

(A) It is no coincidence that they are commonly referred to in the negative terms 'junk mail' and 'spam,' because they are unwelcome. All too often the final result is a frustrated customer with no intention of buying and a marketer who has wasted his budget 'lose-lose.'

(B) As such, the customer is more receptive to the organization because the messages are anticipated, personal, and relevant. The opposite of permission marketing is interruption marketing, which Godin claims, can lead to a 'lose-lose' situation.

(C) Interruption marketing occurs when the customer receives unrequested direct marketing messages, such as direct mail, telephone calls, e-mails, and text messages. Godin argues that these things often end up wasting the customer's time and therefore lead to frustration.

① (A) – (C) – (B) ② (B) – (A) – (C)

③ (B) – (C) – (A) ④ (C) – (A) – (B)

⑤ (C) – (B) – (A)

8. 글의 흐름으로 보아, 주어진 문장이 들어가기에 가장 적절한 곳은?

An object smaller than the distance between waves is a poor receiver for those waves.

Infrasound has the special characteristic of traveling well in the ground or water; in fact, the waves of an earthquake can be thought of as a form of infrasound. (①) Because sound travels much faster in ground than in air, ground-borne vibrations, if perceived, can serve as an early warning system, arriving well before airborne sound from the same source arrives. (②) Infrasound dissipates less rapidly in air, making it ideal for longdistance communication. (③) Perception of infrasound, however, presents some specific problems. (④) Thus, infrasonic receivers need to be large and tend to be found on the large animals able to generate infrasound. (⑤) This is probably the reason that infrasonic communication is used by only a few animals, and the best understood infrasonic communication system is the African elephants'.

*infrasound: 초저주파음 **dissipate: 소멸하다

WORD

permission 허용 coin 만들다 consent 동의 coincidence 우연의 일치 frustrated 좌절한, 실망한 receptive 수용적인 anticipated 예상된 interruption 방해 unrequested 요청되지 않은

WORD

wave 파동 travel (빛·소리 등이) 전해지다 vibration 진동 perceive 감지하다 serve as ~의 역할을 하다 warning 경고 airborne 공기로 전달되는 specific 특정한 generate 발생시키다

[9–10] 다음을 읽고 물음에 답하시오.

Microsoft senior research fellow Malcolm Slaney and Cambridge University professor Jason Rentfrow advocated dispensing with physical copies of documents and mail, and all the filing, sorting, and locating that they entail. Computer-based digital archives are more efficient in terms of storage space, and generally quicker in terms of retrieval.

But many of us still find something soothing and satisfying about handling physical objects. Memory is multidimensional, and our memories for objects are based on multiple attributes. Think back to your experience with file folders, the physical kind. You might have had an old beatup one that didn't look like the others and that – quite apart from what was inside it or written on it – evoked your memories of what was in it. Physical objects tend to look different from one another in a way that computer files don't. All bits are created equal. The same 0s and 1s on your computer that render junk mail also render the magnificent beauty of Mahler's fifth symphony or Monet's Water Lilies. In the medium itself, there is nothing that _____. So much so that if you looked at the digital representation of any of these, you would not even know that those zeros and ones were representing images rather than text or music. Information has thus become separated from meaning.

9. 윗 글의 제목으로 가장 적절한 것은?

① Why We Still Keep Physical Files
② Digital Culture: Understanding New Media
③ Create Unlimited Space for Your Memories
④ Digital Tools Are a Communication Wizard!
⑤ Challenges of Early Adopters in the Digital Age

10. 윗 글의 빈칸에 들어갈 말로 가장 적절한 것은?

① represents the digital signals
② carries a clue to the message
③ offers userfriendly environments
④ makes information accessible to all
⑤ suppresses your memory from the past

★ 혼공 14일차에 나온 문장들을 해석해 봅시다.

단어 PLUS

1 After giving it some thought they usually conclude that it is not good enough for them and not good enough for other important people in their lives.

1
+ conclude 결론짓다

2 This attitude can be compared to that of a man who wants to paint but who, instead of learning the art, claims that he has just to wait for the right object, and that he will paint beautifully when he finds it.

2
+ attitude 태도

3 If two opposing people guess each other's intentions correctly, each moving to one side and allowing the other past, then they are likely to choose to move the same way the next time they need to avoid a collision.

3
+ intention 의도
+ collision 충돌

4 All too often the final result is a frustrated customer with no intention of buying and a marketer who has wasted his budget 'lose-lose.'

4
+ frustrated 좌절한, 실망한

5 As you observe your passing thoughts, emotions, and sensations, naming them – *Oh, that is my old friend Fear; there goes the Inner Critic* – neutralizes their effect on you and helps you to maintain your state of balance and calm.

5
+ neutralize 중화시키다
+ balance 균형

6 Because sound travels much faster in ground than in air, groundborne vibrations, if perceived, can serve as an early warning system, arriving well before airborne sound from the same source arrives.

6
+ vibration 진동
+ perceive 인지하다

7 So much so that if you looked at the digital representation of any of these, you would not even know that those zeros and ones were representing images rather than text or music.

7
+ represent 나타내다

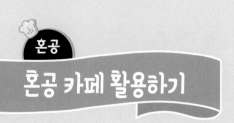
혼공 카페 활용하기

http://cafe.naver.com/junteacherfan

혼공! 혼공이 무슨 의미인지 아니? 아직 모르는 친구들도 있으니 한번 풀어서 설명 해줄게. 혼자서 밥 먹는 것을 '혼밥'이라고 하잖아? 혼자서 공부하는 것을 혼공이라고 해. 하지만 그냥 공부하는 것보다는 '혼신의 힘을 다해 공부하는 것'도 필요하잖아? 그래서 혼공을 만들게 되었어.

2008년부터 시작된 카페인데, 현재 이 문제집과 같이 병행해서 공부할 수 있도록 시스템을 구축해놨어. 혼자서 공부할 수도 있지만, 함께 공부할 수 있도록 만들어 놨단 말씀! 에헴. 네이버에 들어가서 '혼공 영어'라고 검색해봐. '허준석의 혼공영어'라고 상단에 뜰 거야. 가입 엄청 간단하니 바로 해봐. 페이스 북으로도 사실 만들려고 했는데 일부러 하지 않았어. 왜냐고? 페이스 북은 뉴스피드가 너무 재미있어서 한번 영어 공부하러 들어갔다가 다른 쪽으로 빠질 가능성이 높거든. 카페는 그것보다는 좀 더 나을 거라 생각했어. 페이스 북보다는 놀기에 좀 불편하지. 하하.

여하튼 이 책을 공부하다 보면 해설지만으로 안 되는 것이 있을 거야. 그럴 때에는 네이버 혼공 영어 카페를 방문해서 질문을 남겨줘. 짧지만 저자로서 핵심을 찌르는 설명을 해줄게.

그리고 카페에서는 스터디를 종종 해. 온라인이지만 과제를 내주고 검사를 하는 식으로 말이지. 샘과 출판사에서 협심해서 여러분들의 공부를 도와주려고 해. 소소한 상품을 걸기도 하면서 꾸준히 해오고 있지.

한번 가입해두면 손해 볼 것 없는 카페야. 든든한 과외 선생님이 늘 대기하고 있다고 할까. 또한 같은 마음으로 열심히 영어 공부를 하는 사람들이 모여 있으니 마음으로도 위로가 될 거야.

혼공

15일차

승부수 문항 모의고사

2회

난이도 🌶🌶🌶

Use what you have to run toward your best
- that's how I now live my life.
by Oprah Winfrey

최고가 되기 위해 가진 모든 것을 활용하세요. 이것이 바로 현재 제가 사는 방식이랍니다.

1. (A), (B), (C)의 각 네모 안에서 어법에 맞는 표현으로 가장 적절한 것은?

Leonardo da Vinci was one of the most learned and well-rounded persons ever to live. The entire universe from the wing of a dragonfly to the birth of the earth (A) was / were the playground of his curious intelligence. But did Leonardo have some mystical or innate gift of insight and invention, or was his brilliance learned and earned? Certainly he had an unusual mind and an uncanny ability to see (B) that / what others didn't see. But the six thousand pages of detailed notes and drawings present clear evidence of a diligent, curious student – a perpetual learner in laborious pursuit of wisdom who was constantly exploring, questioning, and testing. Expanding your mind is vital to being creative. Therefore, (C) invest / investing regularly in learning opportunities is one of the greatest gifts you can give yourself.

	(A)	(B)	(C)
①	was	what	investing
②	was	that	invest
③	was	what	invest
④	were	what	invest
⑤	were	that	investing

2. (A), (B), (C)의 각 네모 안에서 문맥에 맞는 낱말로 가장 적절한 것은?

Until the twentieth century, when composers began experimenting freely with form and design, classical music continued to follow basic rules relating to structure, not to mention harmony. There still was room for (A) conformity / individuality – the great composers didn't follow the rules, but made the rules follow them – yet there was always a fundamental proportion and logic behind the design. Even after many of the rules were (B) maintained / overturned by radical concepts in more recent times, composers, more often than not, still organized their thoughts in ways that produced an overall, unifying structure. That's one reason the atonal, incredibly complex works by Arnold Schönberg or Karlheinz Stockhausen, to name two twentiethcentury Modernists, are nonetheless (C) approachable / inaccessible . The sounds might be very strange, but the results are still decidedly classical in terms of organization.

*atonal: 무조의, 장조나 단조 등의 조를 따르지 않는

	(A)	(B)	(C)
①	conformity	maintained	approachable
②	individuality	overturned	approachable
③	individuality	maintained	approachable
④	individuality	maintained	inaccessible
⑤	conformity	overturned	inaccessible

WORD

well-rounded 다재다능한, 원만한　innate 타고난　insight 직관력　brilliance 뛰어남　uncanny 묘한　perpetual 계속되는　laborious 힘든　pursuit 추구　constantly 지속적으로

WORD

composer 작곡가　relating to ~와 관련 있는　structure 구조　not to mention ~은 말할 것도 없이　harmony 화음, 조화　fundamental 기본적인　proportion 비율　radical 급진적인　more often than not 대개　unifying 통일적인　incredibly 매우, 엄청나게　nonetheless 그럼에도 불구하고　decidedly 확실히　in terms of ~의 측면에서

3. 다음 빈칸에 들어갈 말로 가장 적절한 것은?

In a study of complimenting behavior in American English, researchers discovered that one of the most striking features of compliments in American English is _____.
An initial examination of a large corpus revealed surprising repetitiveness in both the object of the compliments and the lexical items used to describe them. On closer investigation, it was discovered that regularities exist on all levels and that compliments are in fact formulas. We may categorize 80% of all compliments in the data as adjectival in that they depend on an adjective for their positive semantic value. In all, some seventy-two positive adjectives occur in the data. What is striking, however, is that of these seventy-two adjectives only five (nice, good, beautiful, pretty and great) are used with any frequency. While most adjectives occur only once or twice in the data, these five adjectives occur with such frequency that of all adjectival compliments in the corpus two thirds make use of only five adjectives.

*corpus: 언어 자료

① the foreign sounding qualities

② frequently misused adjectives

③ repetition of pitch patterns

④ an inherent ambiguity in meaning

⑤ the almost total lack of originality

4. 다음 빈칸에 들어갈 말로 가장 적절한 것은?

As the new century begins, the competition between cars and crops for cropland is intensifying. Until now, the paving over of cropland has occurred largely in industrial countries, home to four fifths of the world's 520 million automobiles. But now, more and more farmland is being sacrificed in developing countries with hungry populations, calling into question the future role of the car. Millions of hectares of cropland in the industrial world have been paved over for roads and parking lots. Each U.S. car, for example, requires on average 0.07 hectares of paved land for roads and parking space. For every five cars added to the total number of cars in the U.S., an area the size of a football field is covered with asphalt. More often than not, cropland is paved simply because the flat, well-drained soils that are well suited for farming are also ideal for building roads. Once paved, land is not easily reclaimed. As environmentalist Rupert Cutler once noted, "_____."

* reclaim: 복원하다

① Asphalt is the land's last crop

② Wasteland is a treasure of biodiversity

③ The end of the road leads to another road

④ What comes from soil returns to soil

⑤ The eco-friendly car is our future

WORD

compliment 칭찬하다　reveal 드러내다　repetitiveness 반복성
lexical 어휘의　regularity 규칙성　adjectival 형용사의　semantic
의미의, 의미론의　frequency 빈번도　inherent 내재하는　ambiguity
애매성

WORD

competition 경쟁　intensify 심해지다　pave (도로를) 포장하다　sacrifice
희생하다　well-drained 물이 잘 빠지는　biodiversity 생물의 다양성

5. 다음 빈칸에 들어갈 말로 가장 적절한 것은?

Our kitchens owe much to the brilliance of science, and a cook experimenting with mixtures at the stove is often not very different from a chemist in the lab: we add vinegar to red cabbage to fix the color and use baking soda to counteract the acidity of lemon in the cake. It is wrong to suppose, however, that _____.

It is something more basic and older than this. Not every culture has had formal science – a form of organized knowledge about the universe that starts with Aristotle in the fourth century BC. The modern scientific method, in which experiments form part of a structured system of hypothesis, experimentation, and analysis is as recent as the seventeenth century; the problem-solving technology of cooking goes back thousands of years. Since the earliest Stone Age humans cut raw food with sharpened flints, we have always used invention to devise better ways to feed ourselves.

① science has nothing to do with philosophy
② a hypothesis can be proved by a single experiment
③ technology is just the appliance of scientific thought
④ cooking has always been independent from formal science
⑤ food is cooked only through the problem-solving technology

6. 주어진 글 다음에 이어질 글의 순서로 가장 적절한 것은?

Understanding networks can lead to innovative, non-obvious strategies. Randomly immunizing a population to prevent the spread of infection typically requires that 80 to 100 percent of the population be immunized.

(A) This strategy allows us to exploit a property of networks even if we cannot see the whole structure. Acquaintances have more links and are more central to the network than are the randomly chosen people who named them.

(B) To prevent measles epidemics, for example, 95 percent of the population must be immunized. A more efficient alternative is to target the hubs of the network, namely, those people at the center of the network or those with the most contacts.

(C) However, it is often not possible to discern network ties in advance in a population when trying to figure out how best to immunize it. A creative alternative is to immunize the acquaintances of randomly selected individuals.

① (A) – (C) – (B)   ② (B) – (A) – (C)
③ (B) – (C) – (A)   ④ (C) – (A) – (B)
⑤ (C) – (B) – (A)

WORD

brilliance 훌륭함   chemist 화학자   counteract 중화하다, 대응하다   formal science 형식 과학   hypothesis 가설   analysis 분석   devise 고안하다

WORD

innovative 혁신적인   non-obvious 명시적이지 않은   immunize 면역성을 주다   infection 감염   exploit 이용하다   acquaintance 지인   measles 홍역   epidemic (전염병의) 유행   discern 파악하다, 식별하다

7. 글의 흐름으로 보아, 주어진 문장이 들어가기에 가장 적절한 곳은

Furness was told one family's fei had been lost at sea many years earlier while being transported from a nearby island during a storm.

If you're frustrated by the market and you're looking for a currency that can stand the test of time, look no further. In the Caroline Islands in the South Pacific, there's an island named Yap (or Uap). (①) In 1903 an American anthropologist named Henry Furness III visited the islanders and found they had an unusual system of currency. (②) It consisted of carved stone wheels called fei, ranging in diameter from a foot to 12 feet. (③) Because the stones were heavy, the islanders didn't normally carry their money around with them. (④) After a transaction the fei might remain on a previous owner's land, but it was understood who owned what. (⑤) But that stone was still used as currency, even though it was unseen and irretrievable beneath hundreds of feet of water.

WORD

transport 운송하다   frustrated 좌절한, 실망한   currency 통화   stand 견디다   anthropologist 인류학자   carved 조각된   diameter 지름   transaction 거래   irretrievable 회수할 수 없는

8. 다음 글의 내용을 한 문장으로 요약하고자 한다. 빈칸 (A)와 (B)에 들어갈 말로 가장 적절한 것은?

The main reason you're drawn to novel or surprising things is that it could upset the safe, predictable status quo and even threaten your survival. If you've ever tried to carry on a conversation in a room in which a TV is playing, you know that it's hard not to glance at the screen occasionally. Even if you don't want to watch, your brain is attracted by that constantly shifting stream of images, because change can have life-or-death consequences. Indeed, if our early African ancestors hadn't been good at fixing all their attention on the just-ripened fruit or the approaching predators, we wouldn't be here. For the same reason, a strong sensitivity to the odd detail that doesn't quite correspond with the way things usually are or ought to be is a major asset for a soldier in a war zone. Even in everyday situations, you can't afford to miss that jaywalker darting in front of your car or the single new and important fact in a long, boring list.

*status quo: 현재의 상황 **jaywalker: 무단 횡단자

↓

We are sensitive to _____(A)_____ because that sensitivity gives advantages for our _____(B)_____.

	(A)		(B)
①	change	⋯⋯	safety
②	change	⋯⋯	creativity
③	criticism	⋯⋯	intelligence
④	criticism	⋯⋯	safety
⑤	beauty	⋯⋯	creativity

WORD

novel 새로운   predictable 예측 가능한   threaten 위협하다   survival 생존   glance at ~을 힐끗 보다   occasionally 때때로   consequence 결과   ripen 익다, 익히다   predator 포식자   sensitivity 민감도, 민감성   odd 특이한, 이상한   correspond with ~과 일치하다   dart 쏜살같이 달리다

[9-10] 다음을 읽고 물음에 답하시오.

Have you ever found yourself speaking to someone at length only to realize they haven't heard a single thing you've said? As remarkable as our ability to see or hear is our capacity to _____. This capacity, along with the inherent need to pay attention to something, has dictated the development of the attention industries.

Every instant of every day we are overloaded with information. In fact, all complex organisms, especially those with brains, suffer from information overload. Our eyes and ears receive lights and sounds across the spectrums of visible and audible wavelengths. All told, every second, our senses transmit an estimated 11 million bits of information to our poor brains, as if a giant fiber-optic cable were plugged directly into them, firing information at full speed. In light of this, it is rather incredible that we are even capable of boredom.

Fortunately, we have a valve by which to turn the flow on or off at will. To use another term, we can both "tune in" and "tune out." When we shut the valve, we ignore almost everything, while focusing on just one discrete stream of information out of the millions of bits coming in. In fact, we can even shut out everything external to us, and concentrate on an internal dialogue, as when we are "lost in thought." This ability – to block out most everything, and focus – is what neuroscientists and psychologists refer to as paying attention.

9. 윗 글의 제목으로 가장 적절한 것은?

① How Do Humans Handle Information Overload?

② Increase Your Attention Span with Practice!

③ The More Information, The Better Results

④ Promising Future of the Information Society

⑤ Information Overload: An Obstacle to Remembering

10. 윗 글의 빈칸에 들어갈 말로 가장 적절한 것은?

① criticize   ② intervene

③ sympathize   ④ generalize

⑤ disregard

WORD

at length 상세히, 길게   inherent 내재된   pay attention to ~에 관심을 기울이다   dictate ~에 영향을 주다   instant 순간   be overloaded with ~을 가득 싣다, 부담감을 받다   audible 들리는   wavelength 파장   transmit 보내다   fiber-optics 광섬유   in light of ~을 고려하여   ignore 무시하다   discrete 별개의, 구별된   external 외부의   concentrate on ~에 집중하다   neuroscientist 신경과학자

★ 혼공 15일차에 나온 문장들을 해석해 보자.

단어 PLUS

1 But the six thousand pages of detailed notes and drawings present clear evidence of a diligent, curious student – a perpetual learner in laborious pursuit of wisdom who was constantly exploring, questioning, and testing.

1
+ **evidence** 증거
+ **perpetual** 지속적인
+ **laborious** 힘든
+ **pursuit** 추구
+ **constantly** 지속적으로

2 What is striking, however, is that of these seventy-two adjectives only five (nice, good, beautiful, pretty and great) are used with any frequency.

2
+ **striking** 놀라운
+ **adjective** 형용사
+ **frequency** 빈번

3 More often than not, cropland is paved simply because the flat, well-drained soils that are well suited for farming are also ideal for building roads.

3
+ **cropland** 경작지
+ **pave** (도로)를 포장하다
+ **well-drained** 물이 잘 빠지는

4 The modern scientific method, in which experiments form part of a structured system of hypothesis, experimentation, and analysis is as recent as the seventeenth century; the problem-solving technology of cooking goes back thousands of years.

4
+ **modern** 현대의
+ **hypothesis** 가설
+ **analysis** 분석

5 Randomly immunizing a population to prevent the spread of infection typically requires that 80 to 100 percent of the population be immunized.

5
+ **immunize** 면역화하다
+ **infection** 감염

6 Furness was told one family's fei had been lost at sea many years earlier while being transported from a nearby island during a storm.

6
+ **trasport** 운송하다

7 For the same reason, a strong sensitivity to the odd detail that doesn't quite correspond with the way things usually are or ought to be is a major asset for a soldier in a war zone.

7
+ **correspond with** ~와 일치하다

Count on me

- Bruno Mars

If you ever find yourself stuck in the middle of the sea,
네가 바다 한 가운데서 고전하고 있는 자신을 발견하면

I'll sail the world to find you
너를 찾기 위해 난 세상을 향해 항해할게

If you ever find yourself lost in the dark and you can't see,
네가 어둠속에서 길을 잃고 아무것도 볼 수 없는 자신을 발견할 때,

I'll be the light to guide you
내가 너의 길을 인도할 빛이 되어줄게

Find out what we're made of
우리가 무엇으로 되어있는지 알아봐

What we are called to help our friends in need
어려움에 처한 우리 친구들을 도와줄 때 우리를 부를 수 있는 것 있잖아

You can count on me like 1 2 3
넌 내게 의지할 수 있어 1 2 3 세는 것처럼

I'll be there
나는 네 곁에 있을게

And I know when I need it I can count on you like 4 3 2
그리고 나는 언제 그것을 필요로 하는지 알아 4 3 2 세는 것처럼

And you'll be there
그리고 넌 거기에 있을 거야

Cause that's what friends are supposed to do
왜냐면 그게 친구가 해야 하는 일이기 때문이지

16일차

승부수 문항 모의고사

난이도 🌶🌶🌶

Concentration comes out of a combination of confidence and hunger.
by Arnold Palmer

집중력은 자신감과 갈망이 결합하여 생긴다.

1. 다음 글의 주제로 가장 적절한 것은?

Soil erosion is not new. What is new is the rate of erosion. New soil forms when the weathering of rock exceeds losses from erosion. Throughout most of the earth's geological history, the result was a gradual, long-term buildup of soil that could support vegetation. The vegetation in turn reduced erosion and facilitated the accumulation of topsoil. At some recent point in history, this relationship was reversed – with soil losses from wind and water erosion exceeding new soil formation. The world now is losing soil at a rate of billions of tons per year, and this is reducing the earth's productivity. In many countries, the loss of soil is decreasing the productivity of the land.

① excessive soil erosion and its negative effect
② increased natural rate of topsoil accumulation
③ roles of water in enhancing soil productivity
④ ways to enhance the economic value of soil
⑤ factors that facilitate fertile soil formation

2. 다음 글의 밑줄 친 부분 중, 어법상 틀린 것은?

In some communities, music and performance have successfully transformed whole neighborhoods as ① profoundly as The Guggenheim Museum did in Bilbao. In Salvador, Brazil, musician Carlinhos Brown established several music and culture centers in formerly dangerous neighborhoods. In Candeal, ② where Brown was born, local kids were encouraged to join drum groups, sing, and stage performances. The kids, energized by these activities, ③ began to turn away from dealing drugs. Being a young criminal was no longer their only life option. Being musicians and playing together in a group looked like more fun and was more ④ satisfying. Little by little, the crime rate dropped in those neighborhoods; the hope returned. In another slum area, possibly inspired by Brown's example, a culture center began to encourage the local kids to stage musical events, some of ⑤ them dramatized the tragedy that they were still recovering from.

WORD

erosion 침식   weathering 풍화작용   exceed 초과하다   geological 지질의, 지질학의   gradual 점차적인   buildup 형성   vegetation 식물의 생장   facilitate 용이하게 하다, 촉진하다   accumulation 축적   topsoil 표토   reverse 거꾸로 하다   productivity 생산성   fertile 비옥한

WORD

performance 공연   transform 변형하다   profoundly 심오하게   formerly 이전에   criminal 범죄자   inspired 탁월한   dramatize 극화하다

3. 다음 글의 밑줄 친 부분 중 문맥상 낱말의 쓰임이 적절하지 않은 것은?

The dominance of conclusions over arguments is most pronounced where emotions are involved. The psychologist Paul Slovic has proposed a theory in which people let their likes and dislikes determine their beliefs about the world. Your political ① preference determines the arguments that you find compelling. If you like the current health policy, you believe its benefits are substantial and its costs ② more manageable than the costs of alternatives. If you are a hawk in your attitude toward other nations, you probably think they are relatively weak and likely to ③ submit to your country's will. If you are a dove, you probably think they are strong and will not be easily persuaded. Your emotional attitude to such things as red meat, nuclear power, tattoos, or motorcycles ④ follows your beliefs about their benefits and their risks. If you ⑤ dislike any of these things, you probably believe that its risks are high and its benefits negligible.

4. 다음 빈칸에 들어갈 말로 가장 적절한 것은?

_____ is one of the keys to leadership effectiveness. We want realness in the executive suite, in the superintendent's office, and in our religious leaders. We yearn for leaders who are themselves rather than a copy of someone else. We want leaders who will be fully human with us, men and women who are vulnerable enough to acknowledge their strengths and weaknesses, their gifts and limits, and who are appropriately transparent about their hopes and fears, their motivations and their agendas. We trust leaders who are real, who walk their talk, who act on their core values, and who tell us the truth. We authorize others to lead who author their own life. Those we deem not trustworthy we don't authorize to lead.

① Authenticity
② Tolerance
③ Dedication
④ Compassion
⑤ Responsibility

WORD

dominance 우위 conclusion 결론 pronounced 확연한 determine 결정하다 substantial 상당한 alternative 대안 persuade 설득하다 attitude 태도 tattoo 문신 compelling 설득력 있는, 강렬한 negligible 사소한, 보잘 것 없는

WORD

realness 진실함 executive 간부 superintendent 관리자 vulnerable 약점이 있는 acknowledge 인정하다 transparent 투명한, 명료한 motivation 동기 core 핵심 authorize 권한을 부여하다 trustworthy 믿을 만한 가치가 있는

5. 다음 빈칸에 들어갈 말로 가장 적절한 것은?

In a penalty situation in soccer, the ball takes less than 0.3 seconds to travel from the player who kicks the ball to the goal. There is not enough time for the goalkeeper to watch the ball's trajectory. He must make a decision before the ball is kicked. Soccer players who take penalty kicks shoot one third of the time at the middle of the goal, one third of the time at the left, and one third of the time at the right. Surely goalkeepers have spotted this, but what do they do? They dive either to the left or to the right. Rarely do they stay standing in the middle – even though roughly a third of all balls land there. Why would they jeopardize saving these penalties? The simple answer: _____. It looks more impressive and feels less embarrassing to dive to the wrong side than to freeze on the spot and watch the ball sail past.

① agility
② appearance
③ indecision
④ accuracy
⑤ impatience

6. 다음 빈칸에 들어갈 말로 가장 적절한 것은?

It's a common practice during creativity seminars to give participants a bag full of materials and then a problem to solve. The materials are usually everyday items. Their use is obvious to all. You are then to use those materials in whatever ways you want to solve the problem; however, there isn't usually an obvious connection between the items and your problem. For instance, maybe you have to figure out how to create a communication device using a hammer, tape, a hairbrush, and a bag of marbles. Most people have a cognitive bias called functional fixedness that causes them to see objects only in their normal context. The use of the materials in their ordinary way will generally lead to no workable solutions. The really exciting solutions come from overcoming functional fixedness and using these everyday items in new ways. To see the possibilities it is helpful to take the viewpoint that _____.

① good tools make fine work
② nothing is what you think it is
③ having many options is not a blessing
④ the more we know, the more we want
⑤ deep learning is composed of small parts

WORD

trajectory 궤도, 경로 decision 결정 roughly 대략 jeopardize 위태롭게 하다 impressive 인상적인 embarrassing 당황스런

WORD

common practice 흔히 있는 일 obvious 분명한 figure out ~을 생각해 내다 communication device 통신 장치 marble 구슬 cognitive bias 인지적 편향 functional fixedness 기능적 고착 context 맥락, 상황 workable 실행 가능한 overcome 극복하다 viewpoint 관점, 시각

7. 주어진 글 다음에 이어질 글의 순서로 가장 적절한 것은?

Broad, open-ended questions show your interest in the other person's situation. They often start with "Tell me," "how," "who," "what," or "why."

(A) Our computer salesperson might have a client who says, "I need more control over our order system." He then builds on that response by asking a question using the most important words in the answer – control and order system.

(B) They are much more powerful than closed questions that require a simple answer such as "yes" or "no" or a specific piece of information. After the broad question opens the conversation and begins to build rapport, the artful questioner builds on the responses and increases his understanding of the information being transferred.

(C) For instance, he might ask, "What aspects of your order system would you like to have more control over?" or "Could you tell me more about your order system?" When the client responds, he builds his next question around the response to that question, and so on.

① (A) – (C) – (B) ② (B) – (A) – (C)
③ (B) – (C) – (A) ④ (C) – (A) – (B)
⑤ (C) – (B) – (A)

8. 글의 흐름으로 보아, 주어진 문장이 들어가기에 가장 적절한 곳은?

However, during the same period, there has been no comparable worldwide advance in ethical behavior.

Over the past century, society has witnessed extraordinary advances in medicine, science, and technology. (①) These advances came about because an individual, or many individuals, used the full resources of his or her intellectual imagination to solve problems that had previously been thought to be unsolvable. (②) That is, in part, because human beings rarely use the full resources of their intellect to solve moral problems. (③) Exercising moral imagination means using our intelligence to devise creative and innovative ways to help others. (④) Concerning charity, for example, it means not only providing immediate assistance to the impoverished, but also helping the poor in ways that will enable them to support themselves and no longer need help. (⑤) Therefore, in any situation in which help is required, we should use our intelligence to discover the most effective and loving way to help those in need.

*impoverished: 빈곤한

WORD

open-ended 제약 없는 rapport 친밀한 관계 artful 기교있는, 노련한 transfer 이동하다 aspect 특징, 양상

WORD

comparable 필적하는, 비교할 만한 advance 진보 ethical 윤리적인 witness 이루어지다 extraordinary 엄청난 unsolvable 해결할 수 없는 devise 고안하다 innovative 혁신적인 concerning ~에 관하여 charity 자선 assistance 지원, 도움 effective 효과적인

[9–10] 다음을 읽고 물음에 답하시오.

The overabundance of available storage capacity makes it easy for us to shift our behavioral default regarding external memory from forgetting to remembering. We save different versions of the documents we are working on to our hard disks. And we store images and music files, on the assumption that perhaps some day we might need them. Storing information has become fantastically convenient, but it's more than convenience that makes us preserve. The truth is that the economics of storage have made forgetting brutally expensive. Consider digital cameras: When you connect your camera to your computer to upload the images you took onto your hard disk, you are usually given a choice. You can either select which images to upload, or have your computer copy automatically all images from your camera. Reassured perhaps by the soothing idea that one can always go through them later and delete the images one does not like, invariably most people choose the latter option. Economically speaking, this makes sense. Assuming it takes only three seconds for a person to look at an image and decide whether to preserve it or not, and that she values her own time at a current average wage, the "cost" of the time alone that it takes to decide _____ the cost of storage. With such an abundance of cheap storage, it is simply no longer economical to even decide whether to remember or forget. Forgetting – the three seconds it takes to choose – has become too expensive for people to use.

9. 윗 글의 제목으로 가장 적절한 것은?

① Save Selectively, Save Your Effort!

② Cheap Storage Drives Us to Keep It All

③ How to Cope with Financial Difficulties

④ Benefits of Deleting Your Online History

⑤ Why Is Time More Precious than Money?

10. 윗 글의 빈칸에 들어갈 말로 가장 적절한 것은?

① follows

② creates

③ balances

④ exceeds

⑤ eliminates

WORD

overabundance 과잉, 과다   **available** 이용 가능한   **regarding** ~에 대하여   **default** 초기 설정   **assumption** 추정, 가정   **convenient** 편리한
soothe 완화시키다, 달래다   **invariably** 변함없이, 언제나   **preserve** 보존하다   **storage** 저장   **abundance** 풍부

★ 혼공 16일차에 나온 문장들을 해석해 봅시다.

단어 PLUS

1 In another slum area, possibly inspired by Brown's example, a culture center began to encourage the local kids to stage musical events, some of which dramatized the tragedy that they were still recovering from.

1
+ **inspired** 고양된
+ **dramatize** 극화하다
+ **tragedy** 비극

2 We want leaders who will be fully human with us, men and women who are vulnerable enough to acknowledge their strengths and weaknesses, their gifts and limits, and who are appropriately transparent about their hopes and fears, their motivations and their agendas.

2
+ **vulnerable** 다치기 쉬운
+ **acknowledge** 인정하다
+ **transparent** 명백한, 투명한
+ **motivation** 동기

3 Concerning charity, for example, it means not only providing immediate assistance to the impoverished, but also helping the poor in ways that will enable them to support themselves and no longer need help.

3
+ **concerning** ~에 대하여
+ **charity** 자선
+ **immediate** 즉각적인
+ **impoverished** 빈곤한

4 Reassured perhaps by the soothing idea that one can always go through them later and delete the images one does not like, invariably most people choose the latter option.

4
+ **reassure** 안심시키다
+ **soothe** 완화시키다, 달래다
+ **delete** 지우다
+ **invariably** 변함없이
+ **latter** 후자의

5 If you are a hawk in your attitude toward other nations, you probably think they are relatively weak and likely to submit to your country's will.

5
+ **hawk** 강경파
+ **attitude** 태도

6 Assuming it takes only three seconds for a person to look at an image and decide whether to preserve it or not, and that she values her own time at a current average wage, the "cost" of the time alone that it takes to decide exceeds the cost of storage.

6
+ **assume** 가정하다
+ **current** 현재의
+ **exceed** 초과하다
+ **storage** 저장

자소서 잘 쓰는 방법 #1

자소서를 보면 가장 먼저 보게 되는 게 바로 1번 항목 이야.

고등학교 재학 기간 중 학업에 기울인 노력과 학습 경험에 대해서 자유롭게 기술하시오. (1,000자 이내)

바로 고교재학 시절의 학업역량을 알아보기 위해서 묻는 항목이 바로 1번 항목이야. 대학이 1번 항목을 통해서 알고자 하는 것은 간단해. 과연 이 학생 우리 대학, 학과에 와서 수업을 제대로 소화할 수 있느냐. 그래서 많은 학생들이 선택하는 소재는 자신만의 공부법을 통한 성적상승이라고 할 수 있어. "성적 = 학업역량" 이라고 생각하기 때문이지.

특히 이 소재는 고등학생들이 가장 쓰기 쉬운 소재라고 할 수 있어. 학업역량을 묻기에 자신이 열심히 공부해서 성적이 오른 내용 나쁘다고 할 수 없어. 하지만 이 소재는 장단점이 극명하다고 볼 수 있어. 먼저 장점은 성적이 올랐다면 쓰기 쉬운 소재라는 거야. 자기가 했던 공부법을 술술 풀어 가면 그만이기에 많은 학생들이 선택하게 되지.

하지만 단점은 바로 이점이야. 많은 학생들이 선택한다는.. 즉, 평범한 소재라는 거야. 물론 평범한 소재가 나쁜 건 아니야. 평범하다고 해서 그 학생의 학업역량마저 평범하다는 것은 아니니까.

다면, 이 소재를 쓸 경우 진솔하게 자신의 성실성을 표현해야 해. 지나친 미사어구는 사용하지 않고 담담하게 표현하는 것이 필요하다는 말이야.

자. 여기서 질문. 과연 학업역량은 공부만 해당할까? 정답은 '아니다'야.

학업역량 ＝ 학업성취 ＋ 지적성취 ＋ 태도와 자세

위에서 보듯이 [성취] 가 있다면 그것은 학업역량으로 드러낼 수가 있어. 즉, 고교생활 중 자신이 이 [성취]를 맛본 소재라면 모두 1번 항목의 소재가 될 수 있다는 거야. 성적향상은 물론이거니와 아래와 같은 것도 좋은 소재가 될 수 있어.

> 교내대회 준비과정 (실패도 OK ⇨ 다른 성공으로 이어짐)
> 독서활동으로 인한 지적성장
> 동아리 활동으로 인한 지적/학업 성장

이러한 모든 것들이 1번 항목의 소재가 될 수 있는 거야. 고교시절에 이룬 성취를 통해서 "나는 충분히 대학에서 수학할 수 있다"를 보여주는 것이 중점이야. 그러니 좀 더 넓게 보고 소재를 잘 뽑아내길 바라.

☞ 더 많은 내용은 http://blog.naver.com/sangpia의 '상근'쌤을 찾아오렴

17일차

승부수 문항 모의고사

4회

난이도

Energy and persistence conquer all things.
by Benjamin Franklin

기운과 끈기는 모든 것을 이겨낸다.

1. 다음 글의 밑줄 친 부분 중, 어법상 틀린 것은?

Coming home from work the other day, I saw a woman trying to turn onto the main street and ① having very little luck because of the constant stream of traffic. I slowed and allowed her to turn in front of me. I was feeling pretty good until, a couple of blocks later, she stopped to let a few more cars into the line, causing us both to miss the next light. I found myself completely ② irritated with her. How dare she slow me down after I had so graciously let her into the traffic! As I was sitting there stewing, I realized ③ how ridiculous I was being. Suddenly, a phrase I once read ④ came floating into my mind: 'You must do him or her a kindness for inner reasons, not because someone is keeping score or because you will be punished if you don't.' I realized ⑤ what I had wanted a reward: If I do this nice thing for you, you (or someone else) will do an equally nice thing for me.

*stew: 안달하다

2. 다음 글의 밑줄 친 부분 중, 문맥상 낱말의 쓰임이 적절하지 않은 것은?

The basic task of the preschool years is to establish a sense of competence and initiative. The core struggle is between initiative and guilt. Preschool children begin to initiate many of their own activities as they become physically and psychologically ready to engage in pursuits of their own ① choosing. If they are allowed realistic freedom to make some of their own decisions, they tend to develop a ② positive orientation characterized by confidence in their ability to initiate and follow through. If their choices are ridiculed, however, they tend to experience a sense of guilt and ultimately to withdraw from taking an ③ active stance. One middle-aged woman we talked with still finds herself extremely vulnerable to being seen as ④ foolish. She recalls that during her childhood family members laughed at her attempts to perform certain tasks. She took in certain messages she received from her family, and these messages greatly influenced her attitudes and actions. Even now she vividly carries these pictures in her head, and these messages ⑤ cease to control her life.

3. 다음 빈칸에 들어가기에 가장 적절한 것은?

We tend not to notice how many creative tasks benefit from constraints because they are built-in and have become invisible. For example, almost all popular music is in 4/4 time, four beats in the bar, with the emphasis usually landing on the first beat. Tracks are normally three or four minutes in length, contain a chorus, and so on. These are just a few constraints of many that popular music follows, and yet look at the variation that can be achieved. Many songs break these rules, but they often achieve their effects because there is a rule to break in the first place. Painters, writers, artists, and so on are all influenced by previous styles to various degrees and it's these previous styles that provide constraints. The very limitations we impose on ourselves can be _____.

① the inherent cultural beliefs

② the resistance to taking risks

③ the seeds of our finest creations

④ the obstacles to our future success

⑤ the stepping stone for music education

4. 다음 빈칸에 들어가기에 가장 적절한 것은?

Science and technology degrees are rewarding because they are not designed _____ _____. If you are taking a highly specialized or vocational degree, you may well know what career you are aiming for even before you get to university, but for most science and technology undergraduates university is an adventure in itself; ideas about a career may be in your thoughts, but not completely fixed. This gives you the advantage of knowing that you can develop your career ideas as your course progresses, aware that your degree will be of help to you in many areas of work. It is perhaps with this in mind that science and technology degree programs tend to be wide in scope and flexible in approach. You might go to university to study chemistry and find yourself doing some work within the physics department.

① to represent a socially privileged status

② necessarily to be obtained in the university

③ to force you to follow the established scholars

④ only to grade you and make you feel frustrated

⑤ exclusively to get you into a job and keep you there

WORD

constraint 제약   invisible 보이지 않는   emphasis 강조   variation 변화   impose 부과하다   inherent 내재된   resistance 저항

WORD

degree 학위   rewarding 보람이 있는   specialized 전문적인
vocational 직업상의   undergraduate 학부생   scope 범위
flexible 유연한   approach 접근법   chemistry 화학 physics 물리
exclusively 오직

5. 다음 빈칸에 들어갈 말로 가장 적절한 것은?

Customers' needs are usually expressed as high-level descriptions of the overall quality of a product or service. They are typically stated as adjectives and inherently do not imply a specific benefit to the customer. For instance, customers commonly say they want a product or service to be "reliable," "effective," "robust," "dependable," or "resilient." Razor users may want the product to be "durable and strong." Although these simple statements provide some indication as to what customers are looking for, they have one major drawback. They are _____ _____ and present designers, developers, and engineers with the impossible task of figuring out just what customers really mean by "durable" or "strong." If engineers faced the task of making a razor more "durable," would they try to make the blade last longer, resist bending, or withstand constant moisture? Would any of these actions satisfy the customer's true measure of "durable?"

① not appealing to female customers

② irrelevant to customers making purchases

③ preferable feedback for manufacturers only

④ ineffective in drawing consumers' attention

⑤ imprecise statements open to interpretation

6. 주어진 글 다음에 이어질 글의 순서로 가장 적절한 것은?

Surely since we all have the same visual equipment, we all see something as basic as color in the same way? Wrong. It turns out that color vision isn't a black-and-white issue. It's not nearly that simple.

(A) However, the number of differently labeled segments we use varies. Some languages only distinguish between two basic colors, black and white. Others add green, yellow, blue, and brown.

(B) Language has a significant effect on how we "see" colors – more precisely, on how we divide up and label different parts of the visible spectrum. Our eyes register roughly the same range of light between the aptly named infrared and ultraviolet.

(C) This sort of different color categorization is nicely illustrated by the word "grue." Psychologists use it to describe languages that make no distinction between green and blue.

① (A) – (C) – (B) ② (B) – (A) – (C)
③ (B) – (C) – (A) ④ (C) – (A) – (B)
⑤ (C) – (B) – (A)

WORD

description 묘사, 설명 typically 보통 adjective 형용사 inherently 타고난 reliable 믿을 만한 robust 튼튼한 resilient 복원력이 있는 durable 내구성이 있는 blade 면도날 last 유지하다 satisfy 만족시키다

WORD

equipment 장치 segment 분절, 조각 distinguish 구별하다 significant 상당한 precisely 정확하게 divide up 나누다 roughly 대략 aptly 적절히 infrared 적외선 ultraviolet 자외선 illustrate 설명하다 distinction 구별, 식별

7. 주어진 글 다음에 이어질 글의 순서로 가장 적절한 것은?

The Earth is a somewhat irregular clock. Some years the length of the day is found to vary by as much as one part in 10 million, or three seconds in a year of 31.5 million seconds.

(A) During the winter in the northern hemisphere, water evaporates from the ocean and accumulates as ice and snow on the high mountains. This movement of water from the oceans to the mountaintops is similar to the skater's extending her arms.

(B) In addition, there are also seasonal changes of a few milliseconds per year. In the winter the Earth slows down, and in the summer it speeds up. Think of the Earth as a spinning skater.

(C) So the Earth slows down in winter; by the summer the snow melts and runs back to the seas, and the Earth speeds up again. This effect is not compensated by the opposite effect in the southern hemisphere because most of the land mass is north of the equator.

① (A) – (C) – (B) ② (B) – (A) – (C)
③ (B) – (C) – (A) ④ (C) – (A) – (B)
⑤ (C) – (B) – (A)

8. 글의 흐름으로 보아, 주어진 문장이 들어가기에 가장 적절한 곳은?

It isn't, however, such a hit with police officers and district attorneys, who have criticized the series for presenting a highly misleading image of how crimes are solved.

Since its debut in 2000, an American drama centered around crime scene investigation has become very popular. (①) In 2002, it was the most watched show on American television, and by 2009 the worldwide audience was estimated to be more than 73 million. (②) Their fears have been echoed by Monica Robbers, a criminologist, who found evidence that jurors have increasingly unrealistic expectations of forensic evidence. (③) Bernard Knight, formerly one of Britain's chief pathologists, agrees. (④) Jurors today, he observes, expect clearer proof than forensic science is capable of delivering. (⑤) And he attributes this trend directly to the influence of television crime dramas.

* forensic: 과학 수사의 ** pathologist: 병리학자

[9-10] 다음을 읽고 물음에 답하시오.

What should writers do when they're teased by intriguing but elusive ideas, by hints of thoughts that seem too vague to be expressed in words? Edgar Allan Poe's advice is simple: They should pick up their pens (or, he might add today, power up their laptops). Poe dismisses the argument that any ideas are so deep or subtle that they're "＿＿＿＿＿＿＿＿＿＿＿＿＿＿＿＿＿."

"For my own part," he said in an 1846 article in Graham's Magazine, "I have never had a thought which I could not set down in words, with even more distinctness than that with which I conceived it." The "mere act" of writing, Poe believed, helps writers make their ideas not only clearer but more logical. To use his phrase, the process of writing contributes to "the logicalization of thought." Whenever he felt dissatisfied with a vague "conception of the brain," Poe said, "I resort forthwith to the pen, for the purpose of obtaining, through its aid, the necessary form, consequence and precision." Today's advocates of free-writing would probably agree with Poe on this point. Sometimes, the best way to resolve a dilemma – whether it's a writing dilemma or a thinking dilemma – is simply to start writing.

9. 윗 글의 제목으로 가장 적절한 것은?

① Begin at the End
② Think with Your Pen
③ Pleasure of Freewriting
④ Ideas Too Vague to Be Real
⑤ Make It Clear, Make It Logical

10. 윗 글의 빈칸에 들어갈 말로 가장 적절한 것은?

① incapable of drawing attention
② in danger of being empty
③ against the writer's will
④ beyond the compass of words
⑤ appreciated only by a privileged few

WORD

tease 괴롭히다   **intriguing** 흥미로운   **elusive** 정의하기 어려운   **vague** 애매한   **dismiss** 묵살하다   **subtle** 미묘한   **distinctness** 명료함   **conceive** 고안하다, 상상하다   **contribute to** ~에 공헌하다   **resort to** ~에 의존하다   **forthwith** 즉시   **precision** 정확성   **advocate** 지지자, 변호사   **compass** 범위, 한계

★ 혼공 17일차에 나온 문장들을 해석해 보자.

단어 PLUS

1 Suddenly, a phrase I once read came floating into my mind: 'You must do him or her a kindness for inner reasons, not because someone is keeping score or because you will be punished if you don't.

> **1**
> + **phrase** 문구
> + **float** 떠다니다

2 If they are allowed realistic freedom to make some of their own decisions, they tend to develop a positive orientation characterized by confidence in their ability to initiate and follow through.

> **2**
> + **realistic** 사실적인
> + **orientation** 성향
> + **confidence** 자신감
> + **follow through** 끝까지 해내다

3 If you are taking a highly specialized or vocational degree, you may well know what career you are aiming for even before you get to university, but for most science and technology undergraduates university is an adventure in itself; ideas about a career may be in your thoughts, but not completely fixed.

> **3**
> + **specialized** 특화된
> + **vocational** 직업상의
> + **undergraduates** 대학원
> + **completely** 완전히

4 They are imprecise statements open to interpretation and present designers, developers, and engineers with the impossible task of figuring out just what customers really mean by "durable" or "strong."

> **4**
> + **imprecise** 부정확한
> + **statement** 말
> + **interpretation** 해석,이해
> + **figure out** 이해하다
> + **durable** 내구성이 강한

5 It isn't, however, such a hit with police officers and district attorneys, who have criticized the series for presenting a highly misleading image of how crimes are solved.

> **5**
> + **district attorney** 지역검사
> + **criticize** 비판하다
> + **misleading** 오도하는

6 Some years the length of the day is found to vary by as much as one part in 10 million, or three seconds in a year of 31.5 million seconds.

> **6**
> + **length** 길이
> + **vary** 다르다

7 Whenever he felt dissatisfied with a vague "conception of the brain," Poe said, "I resort forthwith to the pen, for the purpose of obtaining, through its aid, the necessary form, consequence and precision."

> **7**
> + **dissatisfied** 불만족한
> + **conception** 개념
> + **resort to** ~에 의존하다
> + **consequence** 결과
> + **precision** 정확성

자소서 잘 쓰는 방법 #2

자소서 시즌이 도래하면 학생들 선생님들 정말 어마어마하게 바빠지지. 샘도 학교와 자소서 컨설팅지원단에서, 그리고 재능기부 차원에서 진행하는 블로그 자소서 컨설팅까지... 하루에 10개 이상의 자소서를 보니 눈이 뱅뱅 도는 거 같아. (http://blog.naver.com/sangpia)

많은 자소서를 보다보니 잘 쓴 것도 있고 그렇지 않은 것도 접하게 되더라고. 하지만, 많은 학생들이 공통적으로 잊고 있는 것 3가지가 눈에 띄어서, 그것을 커버할 수 있는 꿀 팁을 줄까 해.

❶ 가독성을 높여라!

자소서를 보는 평가관들은 대부분 모니터를 통해서 지원학생의 자소서를 본다는 거 아니? 종이로 봐도 눈이 아픈데 모니터로 본다면, 말 다했지? 고로 아무리 잘 쓴 자소서라도 가독성이 떨어지면 아무래도 마이너스가 돼.

일단 단락이 바뀌면 엔터를 쳐봐. 엔터 2바이트 밖에 안 되거든. 1글자만 잡아먹어. 엔터를 쳐서 한줄 비워두는 센스~ 기억해둬!

ps. 소제목을 쓰는 것도 가독성을 높여주니까 알아둬.

❷ 마지막에 글자 수를 쓰자!

많은 학생들이 자소서 마지막 부분에 글자 수를 잘 쓰지 않아. 글자 수 조정이 필요한 만큼 수정할 때마다 마지막에 글자 수를 써봐. 자소서를 보는 선생님들도 아주 편해. 단 마지막 제출 시에는 꼭 삭제해야해.

❸ 느끼고 배운 점. 무조건 절반에 가깝게!

자소서에서 활동 내역도 중요하지만, 가장 중요한 것은 느끼고 배운 점이야. 느끼고 배운 점의 분량이 적은 자소서는 아무래도 좋은 자소서가 되기 힘들어.

1) 그 활동으로 느낀 점
2) 그 활동으로 내가 배운 점
3) 그 활동 이전과 이후 변화된 나의 모습
4) 그 활동으로 인해 새롭게 시작된 다른 활동

위의 내용들을 공식처럼 활용해봐. 이 항목에 맞추어서 써주기만 해도 무려 4문장이 나오지? 4문장이 지금은 아무것도 아닌 거 같지만, 선배들에게 물어봐. 얼마나 어마어마한 힘을 지니고 있는지.

혼공

18일차

승부수 문항 모의고사

5회

난이도

Why be a man when you can be a success?
by Bertolt Brecht

성공한 사람이 될 수 있는데 왜 평범한 이에 머무르려 하는가?

1. 다음 글의 제목으로 가장 적절한 것은?

In Western culture, playing the masculine role has traditionally required traits such as independence, assertiveness, and dominance. Females are expected to be more nurturing and sensitive to other people. Are these masculine and feminine roles universal? Could biological differences between the sexes lead inevitably to gender differences in behavior? In 1935, anthropologist Margaret Mead compared the gender roles adopted by people in three tribal societies on the island of New Guinea, and her observations are certainly thought-provoking. In the Arapesh tribe, both men and women were taught to play what we would regard as a feminine role: They were cooperative, non-aggressive, and sensitive to the needs of others. Both men and women of the Mundugumor tribe were brought up to be aggressive and emotionally unresponsive to other people – a masculine pattern of behavior by Western standards. Finally, the Tchambuli tribe displayed a pattern of gender-role development that was the direct opposite of the Western pattern: Males were passive, emotionally dependent, and socially sensitive, whereas females were dominant, independent, and assertive.

① Every Tribe Has Its Own Gender Roles

② Changes in Gender Roles Throughout Time

③ Why Do We Have Gender Roles in Human Society?

④ Gender Differences in Temperament: Nature or Culture?

⑤ A Controversial Topic in Anthropology: Gender Discrimination

WORD

masculine 남성적인   assertiveness 단호한 태도   dominance 지배   nurturing 보살피는   inevitably 불가피하게   thought-provoking 생각케하는   aggressive 공격적인   unresponsive 둔감한

2. 다음 글의 밑줄 친 부분 중, 어법상 틀린 것은?

In early modern Europe, transport by water was usually much cheaper than transport by land. An Italian printer calculated in 1550 ① that to send a load of books from Rome to Lyons would cost 18 scudi by land compared with 4 by sea. Letters were normally carried overland, but a system of transporting letters and newspapers, as well as people, by canal boat ② developed in the Dutch Republic in the seventeenth century. The average speed of the boats was a little over four miles an hour, ③ slow compared to a rider on horseback. On the other hand, the service was regular, frequent and cheap, and allowed communication not only between Amsterdam and the smaller towns, but also between one small town and another, thus ④ equalizing accessibility to information. It was only in 1837, with the invention of the electric telegraph, that the traditional link between transport and the communication of messages ⑤ were broken.

*scudi: 이탈리아의 옛 은화 단위(scudo)의 복수형

WORD

modern 현대의   transport 운송하다   overland 육로로   calculate 추정하다   equalize 균등하게 하다   accessibility 접근

3. 다음 글의 밑줄 친 부분 중 문맥상 낱말의 쓰임이 적절하지 <u>않은</u> 것은?

Whether an animal can feel anything resembling the loneliness humans feel is hard to say. However, highly social animals, such as certain types of parrot, seem to be ① <u>adversely</u> affected when kept alone. Some parrots will engage in bizarre behaviors and can severely harm themselves. Some large parrots will even seem to go insane if subjected to long periods of ② <u>isolation</u>. On the other hand, certain animals that are by nature ③ <u>solitary</u> hardly appear to be affected at all. Some fish, in particular some types of cichlids, will even ④ <u>fight</u> viciously with their own kind if more than one is kept in an aquarium. Guam rails, a kind of flightless bird, are ⑤ <u>tolerant</u> of their own kind, which has obviously made breeding them in captivity very difficult.

4. 다음 빈칸에 들어갈 말로 가장 적절한 것은?

_____.
Birds that in the breeding season fight one another to death over territory may end up in the same flock during migration. I know this tendency firsthand from my fish, each time I redo one of my large tropical aquariums. Many fish, such as cichlids, are quite territorial, displaying with spread fins and chasing one another to keep their corner free of intruders. I clean my tanks out every couple of years, during which time I keep the fish in a barrel. After a few days they are released back into the tank, which by then looks quite different from before. I am always amused at how they suddenly seek out the company of their own kind. Like best buddies, the biggest fighters now swim side by side, exploring their new environment together. Until, of course, they start to feel confident again, and claim a piece of real estate.

*intruder: 침입자

① Curiosity is nature's original school of education
② Solitude makes you stronger and more independent
③ Some species suffer disadvantages from living in groups
④ Even bitter rivals seek companionship at times of danger
⑤ Bigger animals tend to feed alone or in small groups

WORD

parrot 앵무새 adversely 해롭게 engage in ~에 관여하다 bizarre 기괴한 severely 심하게 insane 제정신이 아닌 subjected to ~을 당한 isolation 고립 solitary 고독한 viciously 맹렬하게 tolerant 견디는 captivity 포획

WORD

breed 낳다 territory 영역 flock 떼 migration 이동 tendency 경향 firsthand 직접의 fin 지느러미 chase 추적하다 explore 탐구하다 confident 자신감 있는 real estate 부동산 solitude 고독 companionship 동료

5. 다음 글의 빈칸에 들어갈 말로 가장 적절한 것은?

The human brain cannot completely comprehend or appreciate all that it encounters in its lifespan. Even if a music lover kept his headphones on for every minute of every day for an entire year, he wouldn't be able to listen to more than an eighth of all the albums that are released just in the United States in one year. Because we do not possess the capacity to give equal time to every artistic product that might come our way, we must rely on shortcuts. We may look for reviews and ratings of the latest movies before we decide which ones we'd like to see. We often let personal relationships guide our decisions about what art we allow into our lives. Also, we continually rely on the distribution systems through which we experience art – museums, galleries, radio stations, television networks, etc. – to narrow the field of possibilities for us so that we don't have to _____.

① spend all of our energy searching for the next great thing
② know how to turn our artistic talents into profits
③ create artistic products to learn about art
④ satisfy our deeply rooted hunger for art
⑤ avoid buying musical instruments online

6. 다음 글의 빈칸에 들어갈 말로 가장 적절한 것은?

Some people believe that you can't change human nature, and thus they see the idea of an evolving human consciousness as no more than unwarranted idealism. Yet, what is human nature? The dictionary defines nature as the inherent character or basic constitution of a person or thing – its essence. But does the inherent character and essence of a person ever change? We can gain insight into this key issue by asking an analogous question: Does the inherent character of a seed change when it grows into a tree? Not at all. The potential for becoming a tree was always resident within the seed. When a seed grows into a tree, it represents only a change in the degree to which its potential, always inherent in its original nature, is realized. Similarly, human nature does not change; yet, like the seed with the potential of becoming a tree, human nature is _____.
We human beings can grow from a primitive to an enlightened condition without a change in our basic human nature.

① not only an inherent trait but a social product
② not a static thing but a spectrum of potentials
③ fertile soil with the potential to nurture creativity
④ a stepping stone as well as a handicap to the future
⑤ the result of interaction between mankind and nature

7. 주어진 글 다음에 이어질 글의 순서로 가장 적절한 것은?

In experientialism, the body is seen as playing a decisive role in producing the kind of mind we have. The mind is based on the body. In other words, the kind of body humans have influences the kind of mind they have. As a result, thought is taken to be embodied.

(A) A tree is tall relative to our average human size. In this way, categories of mind are defined by the body's interaction with the environment. We call such features of conceptual categories "interactional properties."

(B) As an example, take the conceptual category of TREE. How can the body play any role in our understanding what a tree is? For one thing, we understand a tree as being upright.

(C) This comes from how we experience our own bodies; namely, that we experience ourselves as being erect. For another, we see a tree as tall. The aspect of tallness only makes sense with respect to our standard evaluation of the body's relative height.

① (A) – (C) – (B)　　② (B) – (A) – (C)
③ (B) – (C) – (A)　　④ (C) – (A) – (B)
⑤ (C) – (B) – (A)

8. 글의 흐름으로 보아, 주어진 문장이 들어가기에 가장 적절한 곳은?

In a different paradigm, human health and ecological survival would be paramount, and industrial activities that undermine these goals would be prohibited outright.

Unfortunately many organizations and political leaders working to improve environmental and social conditions operate unquestioningly from within the paradigm. (①) However, to paraphrase Einstein, problems cannot be solved from within the same paradigm in which they were created. (②) A good example is the cap and trade approach to reducing greenhouse gas emissions. (③) In this scenario, private companies are permitted to sell their "right" to pollute to other companies, which can then pollute more, in the belief that the free hand of the market will find the most efficient opportunities for greenhouse gas reductions. (④) But viewing pollution as a "right" and relying on the market to solve environmental problems reinforces the very paradigm that got us into this mess. (⑤) The right to clean air and a healthy climate would win over the right to pollute.

*cap and trade: 배출권 거래제

[9-10] 다음을 읽고 물음에 답하시오.

In the case of a company, it is common to describe culture as the visible elements of a working environment: casual Fridays or free sodas in the cafeteria. But as MIT's Edgar Schein explains, those things don't define a culture. They are just artifacts of it. According to him, culture is a way of working together toward common goals that people have followed so frequently and so successfully that they don't even think about trying to do things another way. If a culture has formed, people will autonomously do what they need to do to be successful.

Those instincts are not formed overnight. Rather, they are the result of shared learning. In every organization, there is that first time when a problem or challenge arises. Those responsible reach a decision together on what to do and how to do it in order to succeed. If that decision results in a successful outcome, then the next time when those employees face a similar type of challenge, they will return to the same decision and same way of solving the problem.

As long as the way they have chosen keeps working to solve the problem, the culture will become an internal set of rules that people will draw upon in making the choices ahead of them. They will just assume that the way they have been doing it is the way of doing it. This causes an organization to become _____. Managers don't need to enforce the rule. People instinctively get on with what needs to be done.

9. 윗 글의 제목으로 가장 적절한 것은?

① Cultural Tolerance: A Way to True Success
② Company Culture: More than What It Seems
③ Widespread Misconceptions about Autonomy
④ Through a Visible Rather than Invisible Hand
⑤ Diversity in a Company: Obligation or Option?

10. 윗 글의 빈칸에 들어갈 말로 가장 적절한 것은?

① vulnerable
② confidential
③ hierarchical
④ non-adaptive
⑤ self-managing

WORD

element 요소　**define** 규정하다　**artifact** 가공품　**autonomously** 자율적으로　**arise** 발생하다　**internal** 내부의　**assume** 가정하다
instinctively 본능적으로　**get on with** 해나가다

★ 혼공 18일차에 나온 문장들을 해석해 보자.

단어 PLUS

1   Finally, the Tchambuli tribe displayed a pattern of gender-role development that was the direct opposite of the Western pattern: Males were passive, emotionally dependent, and socially sensitive, whereas females were dominant, independent, and assertive.

1
+tribe 부족
+gender-role 성역할
+passive 수동적인
+dominant 주도적
+assertive 적극적인

2   It was only in 1837, with the invention of the electric telegraph, that the traditional link between transport and the communication of messages was broken.

2
+invention 발명
+electric telegraph 전보
+transport 운송

3   Birds that in the breeding season fight one another to death over territory may end up in the same flock during migration.

3
+breed 낳다
+territory 영역
+flock 떼
+migration 이동, 이주

4   Also, we continually rely on the distribution systems through which we experience art – museums, galleries, radio stations, television networks, etc. – to narrow the field of possibilities for us so that we don't have to spend all of our energy searching for the next great thing.

4
+continually 계속해서
+distribution 분배

5   As long as the way they have chosen keeps working to solve the problem, the culture will become an internal set of rules that people will draw upon in making the choices ahead of them.

5
+internal 내적인,내부의

6   According to him, culture is a way of working together toward common goals that people have followed so frequently and so successfully that they don't even think about trying to do things another way.

6
+frequently 빈번히

A moment like this
- Kelly Clarkson

What if I told you it was all meant to be?
만일 이 모든 것이 예정된 일이였다고 말한다면

Would you believe me? Would you agree?
그댄 날 믿을 건가요, 내 말에 동의 할 수 있겠어요?

It's almost that feeling that we've met before
우리가 오래전부터 만났던 사이같이 느껴져요

So tell me that you don't think I'm crazy
나를 이상하게 생각하지는 않는다고 말해 주세요

When I tell you love has come here and now
그러니 지금 사랑이 다가온 걸 느낀다고 고백하려고 할 때

A moment like this
이와 같은 순간은

Some people wait a lifetime for a moment like this
사람들이 평생 동안 기다리는 순간인 거죠

Some people search forever for that one special kiss
사람들은 그 한 번의 특별한 입맞춤을 영원히 찾아 헤매곤 해요

Oh I can't believe it's happening to me
오 내게 이런 일이 생겼다는 걸 믿을 수가 없어요

Some people wait a lifetime for a moment like this
사람들이 평생을 기다리는 이런 순간이 말에요

Everything changes but beauty remains
모든 게 변해도 아름다움은 그대로 남아있죠

Something so tender I can't explain
무언가 설명할 수 없을 정도로 달콤하네요

I may be dreaming but until I awake
아마 난 꿈을 꾸고 있는 걸지도 모르죠. 하지만 내가 깰 때까지

Can't we make this dream last forever?
우리의 이 사랑을 영원히 지속할 수 있을까요?

And I'll cherish all the love we share
그럴 수 있다면 나는 우리가 나누고 있는 사랑을
소중히 하려 해요

19일차

승부수 문항 모의고사

6회

난이도 🌶🌶🌶

A wise man will make more opportunities than he finds.
by Sir Francis Bacon

현명한 자라면 찾아낸 기회보다 더 많은 기회를 만들 것이다.

1. 다음 글의 밑줄 친 부분 중, 어법상 틀린 것은?

One of the simplest and most effective ways to build empathy in children ① is to let them play more on their own. Unsupervised kids are not reluctant to tell one another how they feel. In addition, children at play often take on other roles, pretending to be Principal Walsh or Josh's mom, happily forcing ② themselves to imagine how someone else thinks and feels. Unfortunately, free play is becoming rare. Boston College research professor Peter Gray has documented a continuous and ③ ultimately dramatic decline in children's opportunities to play and explore in their own chosen ways over the past fifty years in the United States and other developed countries. The effects have been especially ④ damaged, he argues, to empathy. He concludes that a decline of empathy and a rise in narcissism are exactly ⑤ what we would expect to see in children who have little opportunity to play socially.

*empathy: 공감, 감정 이입

2. (A), (B), (C)의 각 네모 안에서 문맥에 맞는 낱말로 가장 적절한 것은?

Until the mid-20th century, only a few immigrants paid a visit to their homeland once or twice before they died, but most never returned to the land of their birth. This pattern has completely changed with the advent of globalization, coupled with the digital revolution that has (A) enhanced / hindered communication. As a result, immigration is a very different experience from what it was in the past. The ability of immigrant families to (B) object / reconnect to their old culture via phone, television, and the Internet has changed their approach to integration into mainstream American society. This has also greatly influenced immigrant practices of socialization with children. Contacts with the country of origin are now more frequent, and result in more immigrant families being influenced to (C) abandon / maintain cultural patterns from the homeland, and to attempt to influence their children to keep them.

	(A)	(B)	(C)
①	enhanced	object	abandon
②	hindered	object	abandon
③	enhanced	reconnect	maintain
④	hindered	reconnect	maintain
⑤	enhanced	reconnect	abandon

WORD

effective 효과적인　unsupervised 감독을 받지 않는　reluctant 주저하는　pretend ~인 척하다　document 기록하다　continuous 지속적인　ultimately 궁극적으로　dramatic 극적인　decline 감소　explore 탐구하다　conclude 결론 내리다　narcissism 자아도취

WORD

immigrant 이민자　completely 완전히　advent 도래, 출현　revolution 혁명　enhance 향상시키다　hinder 방해하다　integration 통합　socialization 사회화　abandon 버리다

3. 다음 글의 빈칸에 들어갈 말로 가장 적절한 것은?

As essayist Nassim Taleb resolved to do something about the stubborn extra pounds he'd been carrying, he considered taking up various sports. However, joggers seemed skinny and unhappy, and tennis players? Oh, so upper-middle-class! Swimmers, though, appealed to him with their well-built, streamlined bodies. He decided to sign up at his local swimming pool. A short while later, he realized that he had been caught by an illusion. Professional swimmers don't have perfect bodies because they train extensively. Rather, they are good swimmers because of their physiques. Similarly, female models advertise cosmetics and thus, many female consumers believe that these products make them beautiful. But it is not the cosmetics that make these women modellike. Quite simply, the models are born attractive, and only for this reason are they candidates for cosmetics advertising. As with the swimmers' bodies, beauty is _____. Taleb calls the confusions like the cases above the swimmer's body illusion.

* physique 체격

① what triggers gender stereotypes

② a quality with no absolute standard

③ a factor for selection and not the result

④ what helps people boost their selfesteem

⑤ the product of constant care and investment

4. 다음 글의 빈칸에 들어갈 말로 가장 적절한 것은?

The saying that _____ is captured in a study in which researchers wrote up a detailed description of a half inning of baseball and gave it to a group of baseball fanatics and a group of less enthusiastic fans to read. Afterward they tested how well their subjects could recall the half inning. The baseball fanatics structured their recollections around important game-related events, like runners advancing and runs scored. One almost got the impression they were reading off an internal scorecard. The less enthusiastic fans remembered fewer important facts about the game and were more likely to recount superficial details like the weather. Because they lacked a detailed internal representation of the game, they couldn't process the information they were taking in. They didn't know what was important and what was trivial. They couldn't know what mattered. Without a conceptual framework in which to embed what they were learning, they were extremely forgetful.

① it takes knowledge to gain knowledge

② intelligence is much more than mere memory

③ imagination pushes the boundaries of knowledge

④ learning takes place everywhere and at all times

⑤ prejudice is an obstacle to processing information

WORD

essayist 수필가   resolve to 결심하다   stubborn 완고한   take up 시작하다   skinny 비쩍 마른   appeal 관심을 끌다   streamlined 날씬한   illusion 환상   cosmetic 화장품   attractive 매력적인   candidate 후보   confusion 혼동

WORD

detailed 상세한   description 설명, 묘사   fanatic 열광적인 팬   enthusiastic 열광적인   advance 나아가다   superficial 피상적인   internal 내부의   scorecard 세부 경기 기록지   conceptual 개념적인

5. 다음 글의 빈칸에 들어갈 말로 가장 적절한 것은?

In psychology, a 'model' of something should never be taken as an exact copy of the thing being described, but rather as a representation of it. A map of the London Underground, for example, is a representation of the Underground layout that helps us appreciate how it works and where it goes. Of course direction, scale, etc. must be distorted somewhat to make it all fit neatly on the page. A model of memory is also a representation. Based on the evidence available, a model provides us with an analogy of how memory works. Describing memory in terms of 'stores' or 'levels' or 'loops' makes our understanding more concrete, and simply conveys to a reader a(n) _____ of how a particular psychologist has attempted to understand and explain the available evidence. These models change as the available evidence changes, so should not be seen as permanent fixtures.

*analogy: 비유

① approximate idea

② factual experience

③ invariable principle

④ digital representation

⑤ undisputed interpretation

6. 주어진 글 다음에 이어질 글의 순서로 가장 적절한 것은?

A female lawyer working for a prestigious New York law firm once accompanied the male CEO of a major client to Latin America to negotiate a complex deal.

(A) It was the local practice, the colleague suggested, for lawyers to negotiate only with other lawyers, not with the businesspeople. Had the woman lawyer insisted on participating, she would have spoiled the deal and destroyed her credibility.

(B) Before voicing her objections, however, she called a colleague back in New York, who told her that he, too, had been excluded from preliminary talks during his last negotiation in that country. The Latin American executive was just looking for a diplomatic way to get her out of the picture as a lawyer, not as a woman.

(C) Soon after they arrived, the head of the prospective Latin American partner suggested that he and the CEO go off together to discuss business – while his wife and the lawyer go shopping. The lawyer was outraged, assuming this to be an example of Latin American gender bias.

① (A) – (C) – (B)   ② (B) – (A) – (C)

③ (B) – (C) – (A)   ④ (C) – (A) – (B)

⑤ (C) – (B) – (A)

7. 글의 흐름으로 보아, 주어진 문장이 들어가기에 가장 적절한 곳은?

Often, however, someone has an inherent or acquired trait that is foreign to his or her parents and must therefore acquire identity from a peer group, which is called a horizontal identity.

Because of the transmission of identity from one generation to the next, most children share at least some traits with their parents. These are vertical identities. (①) Attributes and values are passed down from parents to child across the generations not only through strands of DNA, but also through shared cultural norms. (②) Language, for example, is usually vertical, since most people who speak Greek raise their children to speak Greek, too. (③) Such identities may reflect recessive genes, or values and preferences that a child does not share with his ancestors. (④) Criminal behavior is often horizontal; most criminals are not raised by gangsters and must invent their own deceptive character. (⑤) So are conditions such as autism and intellectual disability.

* autism: 자폐증

8. 다음 글의 내용을 한 문장으로 요약하고자 한다. 빈칸 (A)와 (B)에 들어갈 말로 가장 적절한 것은?

Online we can hang out in chat rooms with likeminded souls and join social networks that reflect our beliefs and interests, and even read news blogs that reflect our individual ideologies and views of the world. Groups are now formed less on shared activities and more on shared ideologies. We first identify our own values and preferences and then seek out communities that reflect those perspectives and inclinations. This shift that started online has spilled over into retail and business. It has changed the game in how successful products and services are marketed. Our collective mind-set has changed, and mass marketing no longer works. Now the way to get mass support is by microtargeting groups with strong kinship relevancy. Smaller "tribes," where members have the same or almost identical mind-set and a strong sense of kinship, have the power to create global success for a product.

↓

People tend to spend more time online with others who have _____(A)_____ ideas, which makes it necessary for the marketing to _____(B)_____ smaller, more specific groups.

	(A)		(B)
①	creative	……	imitate
②	fresh	……	focus on
③	opposite	……	be independent of
④	similar	……	focus on
⑤	dominant	……	be independent of

WORD

inherent 내재된, 타고난   acquired 습득된, 학습된   identity 정체성   transmission 계승, 전달   vertical 수직적   attribute 속성   recessive gene 열성 유전자   deceptive 사기의, 거짓의   disability 장애

WORD

hang out 시간을 함께 보내다   likeminded 한마음의   reflect 반영하다   perspective 관점   inclination 경향   retail 소매   mind-set 경향   kinship 친족   relevancy 유대감   identical 동일한   specific 특정한

[9–10] 다음을 읽고 물음에 답하시오.

For years, Switzerland had been trying to find a place to store radioactive nuclear waste. One location designated as a potential nuclear waste site was the small village of Wolfenschiessen. In 1993, some economists surveyed the residents of the village, asking whether they would vote to accept a nuclear waste repository, if the Swiss parliament decided to build it there. Although the facility was widely viewed as an undesirable addition to the neighborhood, a slim majority (51 percent) of residents said they would accept it. Apparently their sense of civic duty outweighed their concern about the risks. Then the economists added a sweetener: suppose parliament offered to compensate each resident with an annual monetary payment. Then would you favor it?

The result: support went down, not up. Adding the financial incentive cut the rate of acceptance in half, from 51 to 25 percent. Even when the economists increased the monetary offer, the result was unchanged. Why would more people accept nuclear waste for free than for pay? Standard economic analysis suggests that offering people money to accept a burden would increase, not decrease their willingness to do so. But the economists who led the study point out that the price effect is sometimes invalidated by _____. For villagers, willingness to accept the nuclear waste site reflected public spirit –a recognition that the country as a whole depended on nuclear energy and that the nuclear waste had to be stored somewhere. Against the background of this civic commitment, the offer of cash to residents of the village felt like a bribe, an effort to buy their vote.

9. 윗 글의 제목으로 가장 적절한 것은?

① Money Talks? Not Always!
② Risky Stuff, Not in My Back Yard!
③ Nuclear Waste: Safer than Expected
④ The Price Effect: How the Economy Works
⑤ The Secret of Development in a Small Village

10. 윗 글의 빈칸에 들어갈 말로 가장 적절한 것은?

① irrational fear
② fierce competition
③ egocentric decisions
④ collective intelligence
⑤ ethical considerations

WORD

radioactive nuclear waste 방사능 핵폐기물   designate 지정하다   resident 거주민   repository 저장소   parliament 의회   sweetener 우대조건   compensate 보상하다   monetary 금전의   acceptance 수락   standard 표준   analysis 분석   invalidate 효력을 상실하다   recognition 인식   civic 시민의   commitment 책무   bribe 뇌물

★ 혼공 19일차에 나온 문장들을 해석해 봅시다.

단어 PLUS

1   Boston College research professor Peter Gray has documented a continuous and ultimately dramatic decline in children's opportunities to play and explore in their own chosen ways over the past fifty years in the United States and other developed countries.

1
+ **continuous** 지속적인
+ **explore** 탐구하다

2   Contacts with the country of origin are now more frequent, and result in more immigrant families being influenced to maintain cultural patterns from the homeland, and to attempt to influence their children to keep them.

2
+ **frequent** 빈번한
+ **immigrant** 이민자

3   The saying that it takes knowledge to gain knowledge is captured in a study in which researchers wrote up a detailed description of a half inning of baseball and gave it to a group of baseball fanatics and a group of less enthusiastic fans to read.

3
+ **knowledge** 지식
+ **description** 설명, 묘사
+ **fanatic** 광신자, 열광적인 팬
+ **enthusiastic** 정렬적인

4   Describing memory in terms of 'stores' or 'levels' or 'loops' makes our understanding more concrete, and simply conveys to a reader an approximate idea of how a particular psychologist has attempted to understand and explain the available evidence.

4
+ **in terms of** ~라는 점에서
+ **concrete** 구체적인
+ **convey** 전달하다
+ **approximate** 대략적

5   Had the woman lawyer insisted on participating, she would have spoiled the deal and destroyed her credibility.

5
+ **insist** 주장하다
+ **participate** 참가하다
+ **spoil** 망치다
+ **credibility** 신뢰성

6   Often, however, someone has an inherent or acquired trait that is foreign to his or her parents and must therefore acquire identity from a peer group, which is called a horizontal identity.

6
+ **inherent** 내재된
+ **acquired** 습득된
+ **identity** 정체성
+ **horizontal** 수평적

I need to be in love

- Carpenters

The hardest thing I've ever done is keep believing
여태껏 내가 해왔던 가장 어려운 것은 계속해서 믿는 것이었죠.

There's someone in this crazy world for me
이 미친듯한 세상 속에서 나를 위한 누군가가 있을 거라고

The way that people come and go through temporary lives
일시적인 삶을 통해 사람들이 오고 가는 방식을 보면

My chance could come and I might never know
내게 기회란 것이 온다고 해도 나는 그걸 절대 알지 못할 것 같아요

I used to say "No promises, let's keep it simple"
그동안 자신에게 말하곤 했죠, "약속 따윈 말자, 그저 간단히 보자."

But freedom only helps you say goodbye
그러나 자유는 당신에게 작별만을 고하게 하죠

It took a while for me to learn that nothing comes for free
어떤 것도 거저 오는 것은 없다는 것을 아는데 한참 걸렸죠

The price I paid is high enough for me
내가 치러야할 댓가는 아주 컸구요

I know I need to be in love
나는 사랑이 필요하다는 것을 알아요

I know I've wasted too much time
나는 너무 많은 시간을 낭비한 것을 알아요

I know I ask perfection of a quite imperfect world
나는 아주 불완전한 세상에서 완벽함을 바란다는 것을 알아요

And fool enough to think that's what I'll find
그리고 그것 얻을 수 있다고 생각할 만큼 어리석은 것도 알아요

노래가 절망스러운 것 같지만 실제 '노래'를 찾아서 들어보면 아주 좋아.

지치고 힘들 때 들으면 뭔가 '잠시 내려놓아도 좋아'라고 위로해주는 것 같은 멜로디가 일품이야. 잠시 달리다 지

칠 때, 내가 왜 달리는 지도 모르겠다고 생각될 때 꼭 들어봐. 혼공!

혼공

20일차

승부수 문항 모의고사

7회

난이도 🌶️🌶️🌶️

All you need in this life is ignorance and confidence;
then success is sure.
by Mark Twain

인생에 필요한 것은 무지와 확신 뿐이다. 그러면 성공은 확실하다.

1. 다음 글의 밑줄 친 부분 중, 어법상 틀린 것은?

Humans usually experience sound as the result of vibrations in air or water. Although sound that humans can sense ① is usually carried through these media, vibrations can also travel through soil, including rocks. Thus, sound can travel through a variety of substances with different densities, and the physical characteristics of the medium through which the sound travels have a major influence on ② how the sound can be used. For instance, it requires more energy to make water vibrate than to vibrate air, and it requires a great deal of energy to make soil vibrate. Thus, the use of vibrations in communication ③ depending on the ability of the sender to make a substance vibrate. Because of this, large animals such as elephants are more likely than small animals ④ to use vibrations in the soil for communication. In addition, the speed ⑤ at which sound travels depends on the density of the medium which it is traveling through.

2. 다음 글의 밑줄 친 부분 중, 문맥상 낱말의 쓰임이 적절하지 않은 것은?

One reason conversational life can lack depth and excitement is that we easily fall into using ① formulaic questions to open a dialogue – How are you? What was the weather like? What do you do? How was your weekend? Although such questions can be important social lubricants, in themselves they generally fail to ② spark an engaging and enriching empathic exchange. We answer "Fine" or "OK," then move on down the corridor. The way a conversation ③ begins can be a major determinant of where it goes. So it is worth experimenting with adventurous openings. Instead of greeting a workmate with "How are things?" try taking your conversation in a different direction with something mildly ④ unusual like, "What have you been thinking about this morning?" or "What was the most surprising thing that happened to you over the weekend?" You need to come up with the kinds of questions that suit your own personality. The point is to ⑤ follow conventions so your conversations become energizing, memorable, and vehicles for empathic discovery.

* lubricant: 윤활유

3. 다음 글의 빈칸에 들어갈 말로 가장 적절한 것은?

When scientists describe tool use by human beings, it is usually in terms of mechanical tools. This may apply to tools such as a sharpened flint blade or an electric drill. The key point is that the tool is thought of as passive and with a small number of predetermined uses. The digital revolution has begun to change this landscape in a significant way. Tools are now being developed with a general function in mind, but they are not predetermined in their operations. As a result, _____. For example, the personal computer is designed for the general function of handling and processing information, but exactly how the PC is used is not predetermined. Therefore, for some, it may offer a means of communication; for others, a sophisticated means of managing accounts; and for yet others, an entertainment platform.

*flint: 부싯돌

① you should find the merits of old inventions
② it is not possible to predict the outcome of their use
③ individual digital devices have grown smaller and cheaper
④ you should follow ethical rules when designing tools
⑤ they are not associated with mutual communication

4. 다음 글의 빈칸에 들어갈 말로 가장 적절한 것은?

Dependency never goes away; it just becomes more subtle and systemic. Without someone to feed us, change our diapers, or carry us from place to place, we would never survive to grow up. Later, all these forms of help fade into the background. They no longer look like mommy and daddy putting the spoon in our mouths. They look like the supermarket, the restaurant, the sewer system, the electrical grid, running water, and the emergency room. Help becomes pervasive and invisible, but it's still there. For every one thing we think we have done on our own, there are a dozen things that had to be provided for us by others. We live in a dense fabric of mutual aid. That's what makes us a social species. Even when we go out to compete in the world for money and praise, we never achieve on our own. We build upon parents, relatives, friends, teachers, and neighbors who helped along the way. _____.

① Hope is a wing that gives you victory over obstacles
② Help is to each of us as water is to the fish
③ Heaven helps those who help themselves
④ Humility makes great men twice honorable
⑤ The living person is independent with his individuality

WORD

in terms of ~라는 점에서 apply to ~에 적용되다 blade (칼 따위의) 날 passive 수동적인 predetermined 예정된 revolution 혁명 landscape 풍경, 상황 significant 뚜렷한, 상당한 general 일반적인 process 처리하다 means 수단 sophisticated 정교한 associate 연관시키다 mutual 상호의, 서로의

WORD

dependency 의존 subtle 미묘한 systemic 영향을 주는, 조직의 fade into 희미해져가다 sewer 하수도 electrical grid 전력망 emergency room 응급실 pervasive 널리 퍼지는 dense 밀집한 fabric 구조, 천 compete 경쟁하다 humility 겸손, 비하

5. 다음 글의 빈칸에 들어갈 말로 가장 적절한 것은?

While we like to think that our habits follow our intentions, it's possible for intention and habit to be completely reversed. How the habit started in the first place could be a complete accident, but we can then work out our intentions from our behavior, as long as there's no strong reason for that behavior. Say I take a walk around the park every afternoon and each time I follow a particular route which takes me past a duck pond. When asked why I take this route, I might reply that I like to watch people feeding the ducks. In reality, I just walked that way the first time, completely at random, and saw no reason not to do the same the next day. Now, after the habit is established, I try to come up with a reason and the ducks spring to mind. I end up _____.

① hiding the intention of my previous behavior

② regretting my unconscious behavior in the past

③ being confused about the reason why I started exercising

④ inferring intention from what was essentially just chance

⑤ getting out of my old habits and forming new ones instead

6. 주어진 글 다음에 이어질 글의 순서로 가장 적절한 것은?

Government goods and services are, by and large, distributed to groups of individuals through the use of nonmarket rationing.

(A) The provision of national defense services is one strong example of a good that is freely available to all and not rationed by prices. In other cases, criteria such as income, age, residence, or the payment of certain taxes or charges are used to determine eligibility to receive benefits.

(B) This means that government goods and services are not made available to persons according to their willingness to pay and their use is not rationed by prices. In some cases, the services are available to all, with no direct charge and no eligibility requirements.

(C) For example, to receive Social Security pensions in the United States, individuals must be of a certain age, have worked for a certain period of time (about 10 years) while covered by Social Security, and must have paid their share of Social Security taxes during that time.

*rationing: 배분 **eligibility: 자격

① (A) – (C) – (B)　　② (B) – (A) – (C)

③ (B) – (C) – (A)　　④ (C) – (A) – (B)

⑤ (C) – (B) – (A)

7. 글의 흐름으로 보아, 주어진 문장이 들어가기에 가장 적절한 곳은?

As a result, the first group, thanks to their cooperative tendencies, can take over.

Cooperative tendencies cannot evolve (biologically) unless they present a competitive advantage on the cooperators. Imagine, for example, two groups of herders, one cooperative and one not. (①) The cooperative herders limit the sizes of their individual herds, and thus preserve their commons, which allows them to maintain a sustainable food supply. (②) The members of the uncooperative follow the logic of self-interest, adding more and more animals to their respective herds.(③) Consequently, they use up their commons, leaving themselves with very little food. (④) They can wait for the uncooperative herders to starve, or, if they are more enterprising, they can wage an unequal war of the well fed against the hungry. (⑤) Once the cooperative group has taken over, they can raise even more animals, feed more children, and thus increase the proportion of cooperators in the next generation.

*common: 공유지

---

8. 다음 글의 내용을 한 문장으로 요약하고자 한다. 빈칸 (A)와 (B)에 들어갈 말로 가장 적절한 것은?

Drawing a line is making a distinction between two categories which only differ in degree. Where there is a continuum, such as that between rich and poor, for some purposes, such as deciding who should be eligible for tax relief, it is necessary to draw a line between what is to count as rich and what as poor. Sometimes the fact that a line could have been drawn elsewhere is taken as evidence that we should not draw a line at all, or that the line that has been drawn has no force; in most contexts this view is wrong. For example, in Britain the speed limit in builtup areas is 30 miles per hour (mph); it could have been fixed at 25 mph or 35 mph. However, it in no way follows from this that we should ignore the speed limit, once the line between speeding and driving safely has been set.

↓

The line drawn for telling things apart should be _____(A)_____ even if the line might be to some extent _____(B)_____ .

	(A)		(B)
①	respected	⋯⋯	arbitrary
②	eliminated	⋯⋯	reasonable
③	observed	⋯⋯	outdated
④	ignored	⋯⋯	controversial
⑤	redrawn	⋯⋯	acceptable

WORD

cooperative 협력적인 tendency 경향 biologically 생물학적으로 herder 목동 preserve 보존하다 self-interest 사리사욕 respective 각각의 consequently 결과적으로 use up 다 써버리다 starve 굶주리다 enterprising 진취적인 wage (전쟁, 전투 등을) 벌이다 proportion 비율

WORD

distinction 차이, 구별 continuum 연속성 eligible 적임의 tax relief 세금감면 evidence 증거 builtup area 신시가지 ignore 무시하다

[9-10] 다음을 읽고 물음에 답하시오.

Camping for pleasure is not a direct descendant of nomadic culture. It emerged in the nineteenth century in response to a variety of social forces. First, the Romantic movement encouraged communing with the beauties of nature, while also glorifying the life of the lone outsider who rebelled against organized society. According to the historians of camping, Colin Ward and Dennis Hardy, works like Friedrich Schiller's *The Robbers* and George Borrow's nineteenth-century gypsy tales _____ the gypsy camp whose carefree occupants lived a simple, heroic life under the stars, contemptuous of settled town dwellers in their dull comfort. A second influence was the age of empire. European powers in Africa and Asia were busy trekking into the dark wilderness, pitching their bell tents and erecting barrack huts as they attempted to extend their control over indigenous lands. Camping was necessary for colonial expansion, and became a way of life not only for the troops, but for the explorers and missionaries. A final factor was the rise of emigration. Hundreds of thousands fled Europe in the nineteenth century to create new lives in Australia, the United States, Canada and South Africa, working as trappers, lumberjacks and ranchers, or lured by the gold rushes. A specialist industry grew up to supply their needs – tents, camp beds, stoves, kettles, camp matches and coffee. Their tales of rough adventure were soon popularized in the press back home. Camping was becoming part of the cultural imagination.

9. 윗 글의 제목으로 가장 적절한 것은?

① what made camping popular
② the origin of eco-friendly camping
③ the spirit of adventure nurtured by camping
④ basic necessities for camping on the mountains
⑤ what to consider when choosing good campsites

10. 윗 글의 빈칸에 들어갈 말로 가장 적절한 것은?

① idealized
② ignored
③ isolated
④ criticized
⑤ classified

WORD

descendant 후손 **nomadic** 유목민의 **emerge** 나타나다 **commune** 교감하다, 이야기하다 **glorify** 찬양하다 **historian** 역사가 **carefree** 근심없는 **occupant** 점유자, 거주자 **contemptuous** 경멸하는 **dweller** 거주자 **barrack** 막사, 병영 **colonial** 식민지의 **expansion** 확장 **missionary** 선교사 **emigration** 이민 **trapper** 사냥꾼 **lumberjack** 벌목꾼 **rancher** 목장일꾼

★ 혼공 20일차에 나온 문장들을 해석해 봅시다.

단어 PLUS

1 Thus, sound can travel through a variety of substances with different densities, and the physical characteristics of the medium through which the sound travels have a major influence on how the sound can be used.

1
+ **substance** 물체, 물질
+ **density** 밀집상태, 밀도
+ **medium** 매개체

2 Without someone to feed us, change our diapers, or carry us from place to place, we would never survive to grow up.

2
+ **feed** 먹을 것을 주다
+ **diaper** 기저귀
+ **survive** 살아남다

3 How the habit started in the first place could be a complete accident, but we can then work out our intentions from our behavior, as long as there's no strong reason for that behavior.

3
+ **complete** 완전한
+ **intention** 의도
+ **behavior** 행동

4 In other cases, criteria such as income, age, residence, or the payment of certain taxes or charges are used to determine eligibility to receive benefits.

4
+ **criteria** 기준
+ **residence** 거주
+ **determine** 결정하다
+ **eligibility** 자격

5 The cooperative herders limit the sizes of their individual herds, and thus preserve their commons, which allows them to maintain a sustainable food supply.

5
+ **cooperative** 협동의
+ **herder** 목동
+ **herd** 떼
+ **preserve** 보존하다
+ **commons** 공유지

6 Sometimes the fact that a line could have been drawn elsewhere is taken as evidence that we should not draw a line at all, or that the line that has been drawn has no force; in most contexts this view is wrong.

6
+ **evidence** 증거
+ **context** 문맥, 상황

7 According to the historians of camping, Colin Ward and Dennis Hardy, works like Friedrich Schiller's The Robbers and George Borrow's nineteenth-century gypsy tales idealized the gypsy camp whose carefree occupants lived a simple, heroic life under the stars, contemptuous of settled town dwellers in their dull comfort.

7
+ **historian** 역사가
+ **idealize** 이상화하다
+ **carefree** 근심없는
+ **occupant** 거주자, 점유자
+ **contemptuous** 모욕적인

혼공 책을 마치는 너희들에게

시작이 있으면 끝이 있다. 이 책을 시작하기는 쉬워도, 끝내기는 무척 어려웠을 거야. 아니라고? 비교적 손쉽게 끝낸 학생들도 있겠지. 하지만, 쉽게 느껴졌던 어렵게 느껴졌던 하나의 목표를 시작하고 끝맺는 행위는 대단한 거야. 자기 자신에게 박수를 쳐 줄 수 있도록!

샘도 꽤 오래전엔 문제집을 푸는 입장이었어. 어마어마하게 많이 풀었겠지? 그런데 처음에는 한 번도 책을 쓴 사람에 대해 궁금한 적이 없었어. 기계적으로 풀었던 거지. 하지만, 영어 성적이 조금씩 올라가면서 책과 책마다 스타일이 다르다는 것을 조금씩 느끼기 시작했어. 그리고 친구들에게 각 책의 특징과 장단점을 설명해 줄 수 있었지.

친구들이 내 말을 신뢰하면서 나의 자존감이 올라갔어. 다른 것도 아닌 '영어'에서 말이야. 그리고 그것을 계기로 내가 잘 할 수 있는 것, 즉 영어라는 나름의 적성을 찾은 셈이 되었지. 한 번 확신이 들기 시작하니 사람의 마음이 참 강해지더라.

영어 쪽으로 무엇인가를 해야겠다는 집념이 생기더라고. 그리고 다른 영어를 잘하는 친구와 '난 이런 게 달라'는 하는 점을 내 안에서 찾기 시작했어. 잘하는 것은 좋아하기 쉽고, 곧 나만의 '강점'으로 변하게 되는 것 같아. 거꾸로, 좋아하는 것은 잘하기 쉽고, 시간이 지나면 결국 나만의 '강점'이 될 수 있어.

한 참의 시간이 지났고, 나는 선생님이 되었어. 그리고 책을 쓰고 있는 나 자신을 발견하곤 '어, 신기하다. 내가 책을 쓰네?' 이러고 있다. 하하. 사람의 마음은 때론 육체보다 더 강력한 것 같아. 샘이 오래전 가졌던 단 한 번의 순간이 샘의 직업과 연결되고, 책을 보던 입장에서 쓰는 입장이 되었으니 말이야.

너희들도 이런 한 번의 떨림을 잊지 않길 바라. 남들에게 아무것도 아닌 것 같아도 나에게 소중한 순간이 있다면 소중히 간직하고 어떻게 하면 내 '강점'으로 발전시킬 수 있을지 고민해봐. 그런 고민은 누가 대신해 줄 수 없는 내 인생의 소중한 투자야.

삶은 공평하지 않다고 느낄 때가 많아. 샘도 사회 생활하면서 끝없이 많이 느껴왔어. 하지만, 모두에게 공평한 것, 하루 24시간. 누구에게도 공평하게 주어졌기 때문에 잘 써야해. 어떻게 하면 잘 쓸 수 있냐고? 음.. 일단 내가 좋아하거나 잘 할 수 있는 일을 찾는 게 중요해. 아무래도 그런 일에는 좀 더 집중할 수 있거든. 그리고, 긴 시간을 투자해서 할 공부나 독서, 또는 활동... 반대로 자투리 시간을 활용해서 할 수 있는 활동을 나누어 보자.

그 다음으로 날 위해 할 수 있는 실천 가능한 일들을 계속해서 찾아보자. 지금 당장을 위해 중요한 일과, 앞으로 반드시 해야 할 일들을 적어두고, 생각보다 몸으로 행하자. 그런 행동 하나 하나가 나를 그리고 너를 바꿀 수 있어. 실천하지 않는 몽상가가 아닌, 끝없이 몽상하는 실천가가 될 때 네가 원하는 꿈은 하나씩 하나씩 네 현실이 돼서 널 기다리고 있을 거야. 혼공!

혼공 유형독해
실력(매운맛)

저자 허준석 김상근

정답과 해설

랭기지플러스

유형독해 혼공

실력(매운맛)

정답과 해설

랭기지플러스

01일차 대의 파악 문제

 3 단계 **고난도 문항** 요리하기 p.17

● 정답

> **1.** ⑤ **2.** ⑤ **3.** ① **4.** ① **5.** ③ **6.** ① **7.** ⑤ **8.** ③

1. ⑤

● 전체 해석

인터넷에 있어서 위험한 점은, 그것이 기술이라는 분위기를 두르고 있어서 그것이 전혀 자격도 없으면서 즉각적인 신빙성을 지닌다는 것이다. 정보가 이런 첨단 기술 방식으로 전달된다는 사실이 웬일인지 전달되는 내용에 권위를 더해준다 할지라도, 사실 인터넷은 여과되지 않고, 편집되지 않고, 처리되지 않은 정보를 전 세계에 전하고 있다. 그것은 사람들을 더 빨리 더 똑똑하게 만들기 위한 우리가 가진 가장 좋은 도구에만 그치지 않는다. 그것은 또한 사람들을 더 빨리 더 멍청하게 만들기 위한 우리가 가진 가장 좋은 도구이기도 하다. 인터넷에 발표된 소문들은 오늘날에는 즉시 종종 사실이 된다. 이것은 자신이 인터넷에 접근할 수 없지만, 인터넷에 접속하는 주위 사람들로부터 소식이나 소문을 들을 수 있는 사람들에게는 특히 그러하다.

● 지문분석

> What's dangerous about the Internet / is, because it has the aura of technology around it, / it has a totally undeserved instant credibility.
> 인터넷에 대해서 위험한 것은 / 왜냐하면 그것이 그것을 둘러싼 기술의 아우라를 가지기 때문이다 / 그것은 전체적으로 자격이 없는 즉각적인 신빙성을 가진다
> [The fact / that information is conveyed / in this high-tech manner] / somehow adds authority / to what is conveyed, / when in fact the Internet is a global conveyer / of unfiltered, unedited, untreated information.
> 사실은 / 정보가 전달된다는 / 이러한 첨단 기술방식으로 / 어떻게든 권위를 더한다 / 전달되어지는 것에 / 사실 인터넷이 전 세계적인 전달자일 때 / 걸러지지 않고 편집되지 않고 처리되지 않은 정보의
> It is the greatest tool / we have / not only for making people smarter quicker, / but also for making people dumber faster.
> └ the Internet
> 그것은 가장 대단한 도구이다 / 우리가 가지는 / 사람들을 더 똑똑하고 더 빠르게 만들기 위해서 뿐만 아니라 / 사람들을 더 빨리 멍청하게 만들기 위한
> [Rumors / published on the Internet] / now have a way / of immediately becoming facts.
> 소문들은 / 인터넷에 발표된 / 지금 방식을 가진다 / 즉각적으로 사실이 되는
> This is particularly true / among people / who might not themselves have access to the Internet / but hear a piece of news or gossip / from the people around them / who do

● 2 혼공 유형독해

---

have access.
이것은 특히 사실이다 / 사람들 사이에 / 인터넷에 접속하지 않고 / 뉴스나 소문의 조각을 듣는 / 주변의 사람들로부터 / 접속하는

● 해설

1. 다음 글의 요지로 가장 적절한 것은?

What's dangerous about the Internet is, because it has the aura of technology around it, it has a totally undeserved instant credibility. The fact that information is conveyed in this high-
글의 주제문이야. 딱 봐도 부정적인 면을 부각하고 있어.
tech manner somehow adds authority to what is conveyed, when in fact the Internet is a global conveyer of unfiltered,
인터넷의 부정적인 면 1
unedited, untreated information. It is the greatest tool we have not only for making people smarter quicker, but also for making people dumber faster. Rumors published on the
인터넷의 부정적인 면 2
Internet now have a way of immediately becoming facts. This is particularly true among people who might not themselves have access to the Internet but hear a piece of news or gossip
인터넷의 부정적인 면 3
from the people around them who do have access.

① 신속한 정보 보급을 위해 인터넷 접근성의 개선이 요구된다.
▶ 글의 마지막에 인터넷 접근에 대한 내용이 나오지만 이게 핵심이 아니야.
② 인터넷은 근거 없는 소문을 유포하여 사회 불안을 조장한다.
▶ 인터넷의 부정적인 면이지만 사회 불안까지는 언급이 안 되었어.
③ 인터넷은 다양한 정보를 빠르게 제공하는 훌륭한 도구이다.
▶ 인터넷의 긍정적인 면이므로 NO.
④ 인터넷은 지적 능력의 향상과 저하를 동시에 가져온다.
▶ 지적 능력이 핵심이 아니지.
❺ 인터넷은 검증되지 않은 정보를 사실처럼 믿게 만든다.
▶ 인터넷의 비검증성을 지적하므로 이것이 정답이야.

● 중요 포인트

what절 주어

What's dangerous about the Internet / is, because it
what절 주어는 단수 취급
has the aura of technology around it, / it has a totally undeserved instant credibility.

2. ⑤

● 전체 해석

이야기를 들을 때, 우리는 언급된 신념들을 찾으려고 한다. 모든 이야기는 그 안에 내재된 많은 신념들을 가지고 있다. 그러나 이야기를 듣는 사람들은 이러한 신념들을 어떻게 발견하는 것인가? 우리는 우리가 이미 가지고 있는 신념들을 검토함으로써 이들을 발견한다. 우리는 지금 듣고 있는 것보다는 (듣고 있는 이야기와) 연관된 이미 알고 있는 발견들에 더 많은 관심을 가진다. 이 상황을 다음과 같은 방식으로 생각해 보자. 이해하는 사람으로서, 우리는 주제에 따라 분류된 신념들의 목록을 가지고 있다. 새로운 이야기가 등장하면, 우리는 그것과 연관된 우리의 신념을 찾으려고 노력한다. 이러한 일을 할 때, 우리는 그 신념과 연관된 이야기를 찾고 우리의 기억 속에 있는 이야기를 우리가 지금 처리하고 있는 이야기와 비교한다. 이러한 단계에 이르면, 새로운 이야기에 대한 우리의 이해는 이미 알고 있는 이야기의 기능이 된다. 일단 신념 및 그와 연관된 이

야기를 찾게 되면, 우리는 더 이상의 처리 과정을 필요치 않게 된다. 다시 말해, 다른 신념들에 대한 탐색은 멈추게 된다.

● 지문분석

When we hear a story, / we look for beliefs / that are being commented upon.
우리가 이야기를 들을 때 / 우리는 신념을 찾는다 / 언급되고 있는

Any story has many possible beliefs / inherent in it.
모든 이야기는 많은 가능한 신념을 가진다 / 그 안에 내재된

But how does someone / listening to a story / find those beliefs?
하지만 어떻게 사람은 / 이야기를 듣고 있는 / 그러한 신념을 찾을까?

We find them / by looking through the beliefs / we already have.
우리는 그것들을 찾는다 / 신념들을 검토함으로써 / 우리가 벌써 가지는

We are not as concerned / with what we are hearing / as we are with finding / what we already know / that is relevant.
concerned 생략
우리는 관심이 있는 것은 아니다 / 우리가 듣고 있는 것에 / 우리가 발견하는 것에 관심이 있는 것만큼 / 우리가 이미 알고 있는 것을 / 관련된

Picture it in this way.
그것을 이런 방식으로 그려 봐라

As understanders, / we have a list of beliefs, / indexed by subject area.
이해하는 사람으로서 / 우리는 신념의 목록을 가지고 있다 / 주제 영역에 의해 분류된

When a new story appears, / we attempt to find a belief of ours / that relates to it.
새로운 이야기가 나올 때 / 우리는 우리의 신념을 찾으려고 노력한다 / 그것과 관련된

When we do, / we find a story / attached to that belief / and compare the story in our memory / to the one / we are processing.
a story
우리가 할 때(신념을 찾으려 노력할 때) / 우리는 이야기를 찾는다 / 그런 신념과 연관된 / 그리고 우리 기억속의 이야기를 비교한다 / 이야기에 / 우리가 처리하고 있는

Our understanding of the new story / becomes, at that point, / a function of the old story.
S   V
새로운 이야기에 대한 우리의 이해는 / 그 시점에서 된다 / 옛 이야기의 기능이

Once we find a belief and connected story, / we need no further processing; / that is, the search for other beliefs / stops.
일단 우리가 신념과 연관된 이야기를 찾기만 하면 / 우리는 더 이상 처리할 필요가 없다 / 즉, 다른 신념에 대한 탐색은 / 멈춘다

● 해설

2. 다음 글의 주제로 가장 적절한 것은?

When we hear a story, we look for beliefs that are being commented upon. Any story has many possible beliefs inherent in it. But how does someone listening to a story find those beliefs? We find them by looking through the beliefs we already have. We are not as concerned with what we are
이미 가지고 있는 신념을 이용함
hearing as we are with finding what we already know that is relevant. Picture it in this way. As understanders, we have a list of beliefs, indexed by subject area. When a new story appears, we attempt to find a belief of ours that relates to it. When we do, we find a story attached to that belief and compare the story in our memory to the one we are processing. Our understanding of the new story becomes, at that point, a function of the old story. Once we find a belief and connected story, we need no further processing; that is, the search for other beliefs stops.
→ 글의 핵심이 마지막에 잘 설명되어 있어. 새로운 이야기도 결국 자신의 기존의 이야기와 비교된다는 게 바로 필자가 말하고 싶은 거지.

① the use of a new story in understanding an old story
옛 이야기를 이해할 때 새로운 이야기의 사용
▶ 본문과는 반대되는 이야기야.

② the limits of our memory capacity in recalling stories
이야기를 회상할 때 기억 능력의 한계
▶ 전혀 상관없는 내용이지.

③ the influence of new stories on challenging our beliefs
새로운 이야기가 우리 신념에 도전하는 것에 미치는 영향
▶ 새로운 이야기가 신념에 도전하는 것은 아니야.

④ the most efficient strategy to improve storytelling skills
이야기를 말하는 능력을 개선하는 가장 효율적인 전략
▶ 말하는 능력에 관한 내용이 아니지.

❺ the role of our existing beliefs in comprehending a new story
새로운 이야기를 이해할 때 기존의 우리 신념의 역할
▶ 새로운 이야기도 결국 기존의 과거 이야기를 통해서 판단되므로 이것이 정답.

● 중요 포인트

명사 수식 과거분사
When we do, we find a story attached to that belief and compare the story in our memory to the one we are processing.

3. ①

● 전체 해석

전략적 비전은 그것이 효과적으로 하층의 관리자와 직원들에게 완전하게 전달되지 않으면 조직에 거의 가치를 지니지 못한다. 만일 의사결정자들과 직원들이 비전에 대해 알고서 그 비전에 대한 경영진의 헌신을 주시하지 않는다면, 비전의 진술이 장기적인 전략적 의도를 성취하는 쪽으로 의사결정자들에게 방향을 제공하고 직원들의 열정을 돋우기가 어려울 것이다. 비전을 조직의 구성원들에게 전달하는 것은 거의 항상 '우리가 가는 곳과 이유'를 적어 두고, 그 진술을 조직 전체에 퍼뜨리고, 임원들로 하여

금 가능한 한 많은 사람들에게 비전과 그것의 정당성을 개인적으로 설명하게 하는 것을 의미한다. 이상적으로는, 사람들의 관심에 도달해 그것을 붙잡는 방식으로 임원들이 회사를 위해 그들의 비전을 제시해야만 한다. 사람의 마음을 끌고 설득력 있는 전략적 비전은 엄청난 동기부여의 가치를 지니는데, 석공이 후세에 길이 남을 훌륭한 대성당을 건설하는 데에 고무되는 것과 동일한 이유로 그러하다.

● 지문분석

A strategic vision / has little value / to the organization / unless it's effectively communicated down the line / to
└ a strategic vision
lower-level managers and employees.
전략적 비전은 / 가치가 거의 없다 / 조직에 / 만약 그것이 효과적으로 선까지 전달되지 않으면 / 하층의 관리자와 직원들에게

It would be difficult / for a vision statement / to provide
└가주어   └ 의미상의 주어   └진주어 ❶
direction to decision makers / and energize employees
                                          ❷
/ toward achieving long-term strategic intent / unless they know of the vision / and observe management's commitment / to that vision.
어려울 수도 있다 / 비전의 진술이 / 의사결정권자들에게 방향을 제공하는 게 / 그리고 직원들에게 열정을 주기가 / 장기적인 전략적 의도를 성취하는 쪽으로 / 만약 그들이 비전을 알지 못한다면 / 그리고 관리자의 헌신을 관찰하지 않는다면 / 그 비전에 대한

[Communicating the vision / to organization members]
                S
/ nearly always means / putting "where we are going
              V   ❶
and why" in writing, / distributing the statement
                              ❷
organizationwide, / and having executives personally
                              ❸└ 사역동사
explain / the vision and its justification / to as many people as possible.
비전을 전달하는 것은 / 조직 구성원들에게 / 거의 항상 의미한다 / '우리가 어디로 가고 있으며 왜 그런지'를 적어두는 것을 / 그 진술을 조직 전체로 분배하는 것을 / 그리고 간부들이 개인적으로 설명하도록 하는 것을 / 그 비전과 그 정당성을 / 가능한 한 많은 사람들에게

Ideally, / executives should present their vision / for the company / in a manner / that reaches out and grabs
                                                    ❶   ❷
people's attention.
이상적으로 / 간부들은 그들의 비전을 제시해야 한다 / 회사를 위해서 / 방식으로 / 사람들의 관심에 도달하고 그것을 잡는

An engaging and convincing strategic vision / has
                S   V
enormous motivational value / – for the same reason / that
a stone mason is inspired / by building a great cathedral for the ages.
매력적이며 설득력이 있는 전략적 비전은 / 엄청난 동기적 가치를 가진다 / 같은 이유로 / 석동이 고무되는 것과 / 오랫동안 대성당을 지음으로써

● 해설

3. 다음 글의 제목으로 가장 적절한 것은?
하층 관리자와 직원들에게까지 전략적 비전을 전달해야 한다는 것이 이 글의 포인트야
A strategic vision has little value to the organization unless it's effectively communicated down the line to lower-level managers and employees. It would be difficult for a vision

statement to provide direction to decision makers and energize employees toward achieving long-term strategic intent unless they know of the vision and observe management's commitment to that vision. Communicating the vision to organization members nearly always means putting "where we are going and why" in writing, distributing the statement organizationwide, and having executives personally explain the vision and its justification to as many people as possible. Ideally, executives should present their vision for the company in a manner that reaches out and grabs people's attention. An engaging and convincing strategic vision has enormous motivational value
전략적 비전 전달의 중요성이 나오고 있어
– for the same reason that a stone mason is inspired by building a great cathedral for the ages.

❶ What Makes a Strategic Vision Successful?
무엇이 전략적 비전을 성공적으로 만드는가?
▶ 전략이 성공적이기 위해서는 아래로 전달이 잘되어야 한다고 필자가 이야기하고 있어.
② Why Is Creating a Vision Statement Difficult?
비전의 진술을 하는 것이 왜 어려운가?
▶ 어려운 정도를 언급한 것은 그만큼 힘들다는 것을 강조하는 것이지 핵심은 아니지.
③ Building a Future: Innovative Leadership Training
미래를 건설하기: 혁신적인 리더십 훈련
▶ 리더십에 대한 내용이 아니야.
④ Effective Decision–Making Processes in Organizations
조직에서의 효과적인 의사결정 과정
▶ 의사결정 과정 자체에 대한 글이 아니야.
⑤ Motivating Employees through Organizational Development
조직의 발전을 통하여 직원들에게 동기를 부여하기
▶ 이 글은 전략적 비전에 대한 글이므로 동기 부여와는 상관없어.

● 중요 포인트

동명사의 역할

Communicating the vision to organization members
동명사 주어
nearly always means putting "where we are going
                              동명사 목적어 ❶
and why" in writing, distributing the statement
                              동명사 목적어 ❷
organizationwide, and having executives personally
                              동명사 목적어 ❸
explain the vision and its justification to as many people as possible.

4. ①

● 전체 해석

행동에 관한 어떤 일상적인 규칙이 걸음마를 배우는 아이와 미취학 아동을 사회화하려는 부모의 노력을 인도하는가? 이 질문에 답하기 위해서 Gralinski와 Kopp은 이 연령 집단에 있는 아이들과 그들의 어머니들을 관찰하고 면담했다. 15개월 된 아이들에게 있어서 어머니의 규칙과 요청은 아이들의 안전을 보장하고, 정도는 덜하지만 해로부터 가족의 재산을 보호하고, 기본적으로 사회적인 세부사항들("물어뜯지 마.", "차지 마.")을 존중하고, 그들이 원했던 것을 얻는 걸 미루는 것을 배우는데 중점을 둔다는 것을 그들은 알게 되었다. 아이들의 나이와 인지의 정교함이 증가하면서 금지와 요청의 수와 종류는 아이의 보호와 대인관계에 관련된 이슈

에 원래 초점을 맞추던 것으로부터 가족의 일상적인 일, 자기 스스로 돌보기 그리고 아이의 자립에 관한 여타의 관심으로 확대되었다. 아이들이 3살일 무렵에 새로운 특징의 규칙이 나타났다. 그것은 "음식점에서 비명을 지르지 마라, 함께 있는 사람들 앞에서 벌거벗은 채로 뛰어다니지 마라, 코를 후비지 마라."이다.

● 지문분석

What everyday rules / for behavior / guide parents' efforts / to socialize their toddlers and preschool-age children?
어떤 종류의 매일 매일의 규칙이 / 행동을 위한 / 부모들의 노력을 인도하는가 / 그들의 아이들과 미취학 아동을 사회화하려는

To answer this question, / Gralinski and Kopp / observed and interviewed mothers and their children / in these age groups.
ㄴ 대답하기 위해서
이러한 질문에 답을 하기 위해서 / Gralinski와 Kopp는 / 엄마들과 아이들을 관찰하고 인터뷰했다 / 이 연령 집단의

They found / that for fifteen-month-olds, / mothers' rules and requests / centered on ensuring the children's safety / and, to a lesser extent, / protecting the families' possessions from harm; / respecting basic social niceties ("Don't bite"; "No kicking"); / and learning to delay / getting what they wanted.
그들은 발견했다 / 15개월 된 아이들에게 / 엄마의 규칙과 요구들은 / 그 아이들의 안전을 보장하는 데 집중되었다 / 그리고 더 적은 범위에 있어 / 가족들의 소유물을 위험으로부터 보호하는 데 / 기본적인 사회적 세부사항을 존중하는 데 / (물지 마, 차지 마) / 그리고 미루는 것을 배우는 데 / 그들이 원하는 것을 얻는 것을

As children's ages and cognitive sophistication increased, / [the numbers and kinds / of prohibitions and requests] / expanded from the original focus / on child protection and interpersonal issues / to family routines, self-care, and other concerns / regarding the child's independence.
ㄴ from A to B: A에서 B로
ㄴ ~에 관하여
아이들의 나이와 인지적 복잡성이 증가함에 따라 / 숫자와 종류들은 / 금지와 요구사항에 대한 / 원래의 집중으로부터 확장되었다 / 아이 보호와 상호관계적 이슈에 대한 / 가족의 일상, 자기 돌보기, 그리고 다른 관심로 / 아이들의 독립에 대한

By the time children were three, / a new quality of rule / emerged: / "Do not scream in a restaurant, / run around naked / in front of company, / or pick your nose."
아이들이 3살이 될 무렵 / 새로운 특징의 규칙이 / 나타났다 / "식당에서 소리 지르지 마라 / 벗은 채 뛰지 마라 / 친구들 앞에서 / 코 후비지 마라"

● 해설

4. 다음 글의 주제로 가장 적절한 것은?
아이들의 나이 변화에 따라 규칙이 변한다고 이야기하고 있어.
What everyday rules for behavior guide parents' efforts to socialize their toddlers and preschool-age children? To answer this question, Gralinski and Kopp observed and interviewed mothers and their children in these age groups. They found that for fifteen-month-olds, mothers' rules and requests centered on

ensuring the children's safety and, to a lesser extent, protecting the families' possessions from harm; respecting basic social niceties ("Don't bite"; "No kicking"); and learning to delay getting what they wanted. As children's ages and cognitive sophistication increased, the numbers and kinds of prohibitions and requests expanded from the original focus on child protection and interpersonal issues to family routines, self-care, and other concerns regarding the child's independence. By the time children were three, a new quality of rule emerged: "Do not scream in a restaurant, run around naked in front of company, or pick your nose."

❶ changes in maternal rules according to children's age
아이들의 연령에 따른 어머니의 규칙의 변화
▶ 15개월에서 3세로 변할 때 규칙이 변함을 예로 들고 있어.
② limitations of discipline for children's socialization
아이들의 사회화를 위한 규율의 한계
▶ 규율의 한계가 언급되지는 않았지.
③ parents' concerns about children's independence
아이들의 자립에 대한 부모의 걱정
▶ 걱정 자체는 언급이 되었지만, 그게 핵심이 아니지.
④ importance of parents' anger management skills
부모의 분노 관리 기술의 중요성
▶ 부모의 분노는 상관없는 내용이지.
⑤ effects of thinking ability on children's socialization
아이들의 사회화에 대한 사고 능력의 영향
▶ 아이들의 사회화가 핵심이 아니라 규칙이 핵심이야.

● 중요 포인트

from A to B: A에서 B까지
As children's ages and cognitive sophistication increased, the numbers and kinds of prohibitions and requests expanded from the original focus on child protection and interpersonal issues to family routines, self-care, and other concerns regarding the child's independence.

5. ③

● 전체 해석

1990년대 초반에 노르웨이는 에너지에서 나오는 배출가스에 대해 탄소세를 도입했으며, 그것은 정말 환경적인 혁신을 장려하는 것처럼 보였다. 하지만 그들이 이러한 접근법을 전 세계에 적용하고자 노력했을 때 예상치 못한 상황이 발생했다. 유럽연합이 회원국들의 판매세에 대해 복잡하고도 많은 차이점들을 조정하고자 노력함에 있어서 끔찍한 어려움들을 경험했다는 것을 우리가 이미 알고 있는 것처럼, 배출가스에 대한 국제적인 세금에 동의하는 것도 악평이 날 정도로 힘들었다. 게다가, 비록 스웨덴, 핀란드, 그리고 덴마크가 1990년대에 탄소세를 도입하는 것을 가까스로 결정했지만, 그들은 노르웨이와 그리고 그들 서로 간에 접근 방법들을 일치시키지 못했다. 만약 그러한 비슷한 국가들이 합의에 도달할 수 없다면, 나머지 훨씬 더 다양한 나라들이 그렇게 할(합의에 도달할) 가망이 거의 없다.

In the early 1990s / Norway introduced a carbon tax / on emissions from energy, / and it did seem to encourage / environmental innovation.
1990년대 초 / 노르웨이는 탄소세를 도입했다 / 에너지에서 나오는 배출에 대한 / 그리고 그것은 장려하는 것 같았다 / 환경적 혁신을

However, / unexpected circumstances came / when they tried to apply this approach globally.
하지만 / 예상치 못한 환경이 나타났다 / 그들이 이 접근을 전 세계적으로 적용하려고 노력했을 때

[Agreeing on international taxes / on emissions] / was notoriously hard, / as we already know / that the European Union has experienced terrible difficulties / in trying to regularize / the complex and myriad differences / in its members' sales taxes.
국제적인 세금에 동의하는 것은 / 배출에 대한 / 악명 높을 정도로 어려웠다 / 우리가 이미 아는 것처럼 / EU가 끔찍한 어려움을 경험했다는 것을 / 조정하고자 노력할 때 / 복잡하고 거대한 차이점을 / 구성원의 판매세에서

Besides, / although Sweden, Finland, and Denmark barely decided / to introduce carbon taxes / during the 1990s, / they have not harmonized their approaches / with Norway or with each other.
게다가 / 비록 스웨덴, 핀란드, 그리고 덴마크가 좀처럼 결정하지 않았음에도 불구하고 / 탄소세를 도입하는 것을 / 1990년대에 / 그들은 그들의 접근 방법을 일치시키지 못했다 / 노르웨이나 각 나라와

If such similar countries can't come to an agreement, / there is little hope / for doing so / with the vastly more diverse countries / in the rest of the world.
만약 그런 비슷한 나라들이 동의에 이를 수가 없다면 / 어떠한 희망도 없다 / 그렇게 하는 것에 대한 / 거대하게 더욱 다양한 나라와 / 세계의 나머지에서

●해설

5. 다음 글의 제목으로 가장 적절한 것은?
In the early 1990s Norway introduced a carbon tax on emissions from energy, and it did seem to encourage environmental innovation. However, unexpected circumstances came when they tried to apply this approach globally. Agreeing on international taxes on emissions was notoriously hard, as we already know that the European Union has experienced terrible difficulties in trying to regularize the complex and myriad differences in its members' sales taxes. Besides, although Sweden, Finland, and Denmark barely decided to introduce carbon taxes during the 1990s, they have not harmonized their approaches with Norway or with each other. If such similar countries can't come to an agreement, there is little hope for doing so with the vastly more diverse countries in the rest of the world.

시작은 긍정인데, however 이후로 부정적으로 흐르지

① Reduce Carbon Emission, Rescue Earth
탄소 배출을 줄이고 지구를 구하라
▶ 탄소 배출이 언급되었지만, 핵심은 탄소세지.

② No Exit Out of Fatal Carbon Emissions
치명적인 탄소 배출로의 출구는 없다
▶ 탄소배출이 불가피하다는 내용은 아니지.

❸ Global Carbon Tax: A Long Way to Go
전세계적인 탄소세: 아직 멀었다
▶ 탄소세를 도입했지만 다른 나라와의 동의가 매우 어렵다는 내용이므로 이것이 정답이야.

④ Carbon Emissions: Not in My Backyard
탄소 배출: 님비현상
▶ 각 나라와의 동의가 어려운 원인으로 님비현상은 언급되지 않았어.

⑤ Everlasting Conflict: Taxpayers vs. Collectors
영원한 갈등: 납세자 vs 징수자
▶ 너무 확대했지. 핵심은 탄소세야.

●중요 포인트

barely 구문: 부정문

Besides, although Sweden, Finland, and Denmark barely decided to introduce carbon taxes during the 1990s, they have not harmonized their approaches with Norway or with each other.

6. ①

●전체 해석

우리가 어떤 사람이 그의 생활 연령에 비해 '젊어 보인다'고 놀라면서 말할 때 우리는 우리 모두가 생물학적으로 서로 다른 속도로 나이가 든다는 것을 말하고 있는 것이다. 과학자들은 이 겉으로 보이는 차이가 진짜라는 좋은 증거를 갖고 있다. 나이 변화는 서로 다른 시기에 신체의 서로 다른 부위에서 시작되고 매년의 변화 속도는 사람마다 다른 것은 물론 다양한 세포, 조직 그리고 기관마다 다를 가능성이 있다. 시간의 경과와 달리 생물학적 노화는 쉬운 측정을 방해한다. 우리가 갖고 싶은 것은 예를 들어, 생활 연령으로 80세인 어떤 사람이 생물학적으로 60세라고 말할 수 있도록 시간의 경과와는 관계없이 모든 다른 생물학적 나이 변화를 반영하는 하나 또는 몇 개의 측정 가능한 생물학적 변화이다. 이런 종류의 측정은 80세인 한 사람이 생물학적으로 80 또는 심지어 90세인 또 다른 80세인 사람보다 그렇게 훨씬 더 많은 젊음의 특징을 가진 이유를 설명하는 데 도움을 줄 것이다.

●지문분석

When we remark with surprise / that someone "looks young" / for his or her chronological age, / we are observing / that we all age biologically / at different rates.
우리가 놀라며 말할 때 / 누군가가 어려보인다고 / 그 사람의 생활 연령에 비해 / 우리는 말하고 있다 / 우리 모두가 생물학적으로 나이를 먹는다고 / 다른 속도로

Scientists have good evidence / that this apparent difference is real.
과학자들은 훌륭한 증거를 가지고 있다 / 이 명백한 차이가 사실이라는

It is likely / that age changes / begin in different parts of the body / at different times / and that the rate of annual change / varies / among various cells, tissues, and organs, / as well as from person to person.

가능성이 있다 / 나이 변화는 / 신체의 다른 부분에서 시작될 / 다른 시기에 / 그리고 매년의 변화 속도는 / 다를 / 다양한 세포와 조직, 그리고 기관 가운데서 / 사람마다 다른 것과 마찬가지로

Unlike the passage of time, / biological aging / resists easy measurement.

시간의 경과와는 달리 / 생물학적인 노화는 / 쉬운 측정을 거부한다

What we would like to have / is one or a few measurable biological changes / that mirror all other biological age changes / without reference to the passage of time, / so that we could say, for example, / that [someone / who is chronologically eighty years old] / is biologically sixty years old.

우리가 가지고 싶어 하는 것은 / 한 가지 혹은 몇 가지 측정 가능한 생물학적인 변화이다 / 모든 다른 생물학적인 나이 변화를 반영하는 / 시간의 경과를 언급하지 않고 / 그래서 우리는 예를 들어 말할 수 있도록 / 누군가는 / 생활 연령으로는 80세인 / 생물학적으로 60세라고

This kind of measurement / would help explain / why one eighty-year-old / has so many more youthful qualities / than does another eighty-year-old, / who may be biologically eighty or even ninety years old.

이러한 종류의 측정은 / 설명하는 것을 도울 수도 있다 / 왜 80세인 사람이 / 그렇게나 많은 젊어 보이는 특징을 가지고 있는지 / 다른 80세인 사람보다 / 그 사람은 아마도 생물학적으로 80세 아니면 심지어 90세일 수도 있는

●해설

6. 다음 글의 제목으로 가장 적절한 것은?

When we remark with surprise that someone "looks young" for his or her chronological age, we are observing that we all age biologically at different rates. Scientists have good evidence that this apparent difference is real. It is likely that age changes
이 뒤로는 반전 없이 '젊어 보인다'는 것에 대한 이유를 설명하고 있어.
begin in different parts of the body at different times and that the rate of annual change varies among various cells, tissues, and organs, as well as from person to person. Unlike the passage of time, biological aging resists easy measurement. What we would like to have is one or a few measurable biological changes that mirror all other biological age changes without reference to the passage of time, so that we could say, for example, that someone
필자의 의도가 드러나고 있어. 사람들이 원하는 것은 생물학적인 변화를 측정하는 것이지.
who is chronologically eighty years old is biologically sixty years old. This kind of measurement would help explain why one eighty-year-old has so many more youthful qualities than does another eighty-year-old, who may be biologically eighty or even ninety years old.

❶ In Search of a Mirror Reflecting Biological Aging
생물학적 노화를 반영하는 거울을 찾아서
▶ 생물학적 노화가 글의 핵심이야. 바로 이것이 정답이지.
② Reasons for Slow Aging in the Modern Era
현 시대에서 느린 노화의 이유들
▶ 노화가 느린 이유는 언급이 되지 않았지.
③ A Few Tips to Guess Chronological Age
생활 연령을 짐작할 수 있는 몇 가지 비결
▶ 생활 연령이 아닌 생물학적 나이 변화가 포인트야.
④ Secrets of Biological Aging Disclosed
밝혀진 생물학적 노화의 비밀들
▶ 노화의 비밀을 밝히는 내용이 아니야.
⑤ Looking for the Fountain of Youth
청춘의 샘을 찾기
▶ 젊어지는 비법은 언급이 되지 않았어.

●중요 포인트

that절의 병렬구조

It is likely that age changes begin in different parts of the body at different times and that the rate of annual change varies among various cells, tissues, and organs, as well as from person to person.

7. ⑤

●전체 해석

사바나 지역은 생태학자들에게 약간의 문제를 야기한다. 생태학에는 '완전한 경쟁자들은 공존할 수 없다'라는 격언이 있다. 다시 말해 유기체의 두 개체들이 정확하게 똑같은 자원을 사용하는 곳에서, 한 개체는 다른 개체보다 약간이라도 더 효율적으로 자원을 이용하여 장기적으로 지배적인 위치에 이르게 된다. 세계의 온화한 지역에서 나무가 (숲에서) 지배적인 위치를 차지하거나 풀이 (초원지대에서) 지배적인 위치를 차지한다. 하지만, 사바나 지역에서 나무와 풀이 공존한다. (이 공존 현상을 설명하는) 고전적인 설명에 따르면 나무는 깊은 뿌리를 갖는 반면 풀은 얕은 뿌리를 갖는다는 것이다. 따라서 이 두 식물의 형태는 사실, 서로 경쟁자가 아니므로 서로 공존할 수 있다. 다시 말해 나무는 많은 수분이 깊은 뿌리까지 침투할 수 있으므로 습도가 높은 기후와 모래가 많은 토양에서 성장한다. 사실, 나무는 깊은 곳까지 침투할 수 있는 몇 개의 작은 뿌리를 갖고 있지만, 나무뿌리의 대부분은 풀뿌리가 있는, 토양 상층의 0.5미터 안쪽에 존재한다.

●지문분석

Savannas pose / a bit of a problem / for ecologists.
사바나는 야기한다 / 약간의 문제를 / 생태학자들에게
There is an axiom in ecology / that 'complete competitors cannot coexist': / in other words, / where two populations of organisms / use exactly the same resources, / one would be expected / to do so slightly more efficiently / than the other / and therefore come to dominate in the long term.
생태학에는 격언이 있다 / '완벽한 경쟁자들은 공존할 수 없다'라는 / 다시 말하자면 / 두 생물 개체가 / 정확하게 같은 자원을 사용하는 곳에서 / 하나는 예측된다 / 약간 더 효율적으로 그렇게(사용) 한다고 /

상대방보다 / 그래서 결국 장기적으로 지배하게 된다고

In temperate parts of the world, / either trees dominate (in forests) / or grasses dominate (in grasslands).

세계의 온화한 곳에서는 / 나무가 지배하든 (숲에서) / 아니면 풀이 지배한다 (초원에서)

Yet, in savannas / grasses and trees coexist.

하지만 사바나에서는 / 풀과 나무는 공존한다

The classic explanation proposes / that trees have deep roots / while grasses have shallow roots.

고전적인 설명은 제안한다 / 나무는 깊은 뿌리를 가지며 / 반면에 풀은 얕은 뿌리를 가진다고

The two plant types / are therefore able to coexist / because they are not in fact competitors: / the trees increase / in wetter climates and on sandier soils / because more water is able to penetrate / to the deep roots.

두 개의 식물 형태는 / 그래서 공존할 수 있다 / 그들이 사실은 경쟁자가 아니기 때문에 / 나무는 증가한다 / 습도가 높은 지후에서 그리고 모래가 많은 토양에서 / 왜냐하면 더 많은 물이 침투할 수 있으니까 / 깊은 뿌리 쪽으로

Trees do indeed have a few small roots / which penetrate to great depth, / but most of their roots / are in the top half-metre of the soil, / just where the grass roots are.
└ 동사 강조

나무들은 정말로 몇 개의 작은 뿌리를 가진다 / 엄청난 깊이로 침투하는 / 하지만 대부분의 뿌리는 / 토양 상층의 0.5m 안쪽에 있다 / 단지 풀뿌리가 있는

● 해설

7. 다음 글의 제목으로 가장 적절한 것은?
기본적인 통념이 제시되고 있어. 경쟁자는 공존할 수 없다는 내용이 전개되고 있어.

Savannas pose a bit of a problem for ecologists. There is an axiom in ecology that 'complete competitors cannot coexist': in other words, where two populations of organisms use exactly the same resources, one would be expected to do so slightly more efficiently than the other and therefore come to dominate in the long term. In temperate parts of the world, either trees dominate (in forests) or grasses dominate (in grasslands). Yet, in savannas grasses and trees coexist. The classic explanation
Yet(하지만)의 등장으로 앞에서 제시된 통념이 뒤집어지고 있어. 이후로는 '공존'하는 경우인 나무와 풀이 나오지.
proposes that trees have deep roots while grasses have shallow roots. The two plant types are therefore able to coexist because they are not in fact competitors: the trees increase in wetter climates and on sandier soils because more water is able to penetrate to the deep roots. Trees do indeed have a few small roots which penetrate to great depth, but most of their roots are in the top half-metre of the soil, just where the grass roots are.

① A War at Hand Between Plants in Savannas
사바나 지역에서의 식물들 사이의 직접적 전쟁
▶ 본문에서 언급된 나무와 풀은 직접적 경쟁을 펼치고 있지 않아.
② A Rivalry for Wetter Soils among Savanna Trees
사바나 나무들 사이의 수분이 많은 토양을 위한 경쟁
▶ 나무와 풀의 경쟁을 다루고 있으니까 이것은 아니지.
③ Are Savannas a Hidden Treasure of Bio-Diversity?
사바나가 생물 다양성을 위한 숨겨진 보물인가?
▶ 생물 다양성을 언급하기에는 너무 나아간 것 같아.
④ Cyclic Dominance of Trees over Grasses in Savannas
사바나에서의 나무의 풀에 대한 순환적 지배
▶ 나무와 풀은 공존하는 관계이므로 순환적 지배라는 말은 어울리지 않지.
❺ Strange Companions: Savanna Plants Confuse Ecologists
이상한 친구들: 사바나 식물은 생태계학자들을 혼란스럽게 한다
▶ 동일한 자원을 놓고 경쟁하는 나무와 풀이 사실은 공존한다는 내용이므로 기존의 생각을 뒤집고 있다는 내용이야. 따라서 'strange companions'라는 비유적 표현이 적절하지.

● 중요 포인트

선행사 없는 where

in other words, where two populations of organisms use
                  ~인 곳에서
exactly the same resources, one would be expected to ~

8. ③

● 전체 해석

과학자들은 그들의 실험에서 편견을 줄이기 위해 조심해야 한다. 편견은 과학자들이 기대하는 것이 그 결과가 보여지는 방법을 바꿀 때 발생한다. 이러한 기대는 과학자가 다른 시도들로부터 나온 것들(결과들)을 누르고 (무시하고) 한 시도로부터 나온 결과를 선택하도록 할 수 있다. 과학자들은 가능한 한 많은 시도를 운영해 보는 것에 의하여 그리고 각각의 관찰에서 만들어진 정확한 기록을 유지하는 것에 의하여 편견을 줄일 수 있다. 유효한 실험은 또한 측정되어 질 수 있는 자료를 보유하여야 한다. 이것은 다른 사람들이 유사한 실험에서 그들이 얻은 자료와 비교하는 것을 가능케 하여 준다. 가장 중요한 것은 그 실험은 반복되어질 수 있어야 한다. 발견이라고 하는 것은 다른 과학자들이 똑같은 실험을 수행하고 똑같은 결과를 얻을 수 있어야 지지될 수 있다.

● 지문분석

Scientists should be careful / to reduce bias / in their experiments.

과학자들은 주의를 기울여야 한다 / 편견을 줄이는 데 / 그들의 실험에서

A bias occurs / when what the scientist expects changes / how the results are viewed.
                        S   V

편견은 발생한다 / 과학자가 기대하는 것을 바꿀 때 / 어떻게 결과가 보여지는지를

This expectation might cause / a scientist / to select a result / from one trial / over those / from other trials.
                        V   O   O.C.
                                              └ results

이러한 기대는 유발할 수도 있다 / 과학자가 / 한 결과를 선택하도록 / 한 가지 시도에서 발생한 / 결과들보다도 / 다른 시도에서 발생한

Scientists can lessen bias / by running as many trials as possible / and by keeping accurate notes / of each observation / made.
              ①   ②

과학자들은 편견을 줄 일 수 있다 / 가능한 한 많은 시도를 함으로써 / 그리고 정확한 기록을 유지함으로써 / 각각의 관찰에 대한 / 이루어진

Valid experiments / also must have data / that are measurable.

유효한 실험들은 / 마찬가지로 데이터를 가져야만 한다 / 측정 가능한

This allows / others / to compare the results / to data / they obtain from a similar experiment.
이것은 허용한다 / 다른 사람들이 / 그 결과를 비교하도록 / 데이터와 / 그들이 비슷한 실험에서 얻는
Most importantly, / the experiment must be repeatable.
가장 중요한 것은 / 실험은 반복되어져만 한다
Findings are supportable / when other scientists perform the same experiment / and get the same results.
발견이라는 것은 지지될 수 있다 / 다른 과학자들이 같은 실험을 하고 / 같은 결과를 얻을 때

● 해설

8. 다음 글의 제목으로 가장 적절한 것은?
Scientists should be careful to reduce bias in their experiments. A bias occurs when what the scientist expects changes how the results are viewed. This expectation might cause a scientist to select a result from one trial over those from other trials. Scientists can lessen bias by running as many trials as possible and by keeping accurate notes of each observation made. Valid experiments also must have data that are measurable. This allows others to compare the results to data they obtain from a similar experiment. Most importantly, the experiment must be repeatable. Findings are supportable when other scientists perform the same experiment and get the same results.

① necessary conditions of repeatable experiments
반복 가능한 실험을 위한 필요조건
▶ 반복 가능한 실험은 편견 없는 과학 실험의 한 가지 요건이야. 너무 범위가 좁아.
② importance of identifying bias in scientific research
과학 연구에서 편견을 구별하는 것의 중요성
▶ 편견을 구별하는 것이 아니라 줄여야 하는 거지.
❸ requirements for objective scientific experiments
객관적인 과학 실험을 위한 자격요건
▶ 편견 없는 과학 실험을 위한 여러 가지 조건들이 나열되고 있어. 이것이 정답이야.
④ guidelines for collecting measurable data in experiments
실험에서 측정 가능한 데이터 수집을 위한 지침
▶ 측정 가능한 데이터 수집도 편견 없는 과학 실험의 한 요건이야. 마찬가지고 범위가 좁아.
⑤ effective strategies for keeping accurate notes on data
데이터에 대한 정확한 기록을 하기 위한 효과적인 전략
▶ 마찬가지로 편견 없는 과학 실험의 한 요건으로 범위가 좁아.

● 중요 포인트

대명사 those
This expectation might cause a scientist to select a result from one trial over those from other trials.

---

④ 혼공 개념 마무리   p.21

1. 정보가 이런 첨단 기술 방식으로 전달된다는 사실이 웬일인지 전달되는 내용에 권위를 더해준다 할지라도, 사실 인터넷은 여과되지 않고, 편집되지 않고, 처리되지 않은 정보를 전 세계에 전하고 있다.

2. 만일 의사결정자들과 직원들이 비전에 대해 알고서 그 비전에 대한 경영진의 헌신을 주시하지 않는다면, 비전의 진술이 장기적인 전략적 의도를 성취하는 쪽으로 의사결정자들에게 방향을 제공하고 직원들의 열정을 돋우기가 어려울 것이다.

3. 아이들의 나이와 인지의 정교함이 증가하면서 금지와 요청의 수와 종류는 아이의 보호와 대인관계에 관련된 이슈에 원래 초점을 맞추던 것으로부터 가족의 일상적인 일, 자기 스스로 돌보기 그리고 아이의 자립에 관한 여타의 관심으로 확대되었다.

4. 나이 변화는 서로 다른 시기에 신체의 서로 다른 부위에서 시작되고 매년의 변화 속도는 사람마다 다른 것은 물론 다양한 세포, 조직 그리고 기관마다 다를 가능성이 있다.

5. 생태학에는 '완전한 경쟁자들은 공존할 수 없다'라는 공리가 있다. 다시 말해 유기체의 두 개체들이 정확하게 똑같은 자원을 사용하는 곳에서, 한 개체는 다른 개체보다 약간이라도 더 효율적으로 자원을 이용하여 장기적으로 지배적인 위치에 이르게 된다.

6. 우리가 갖고 싶은 것은 예를 들어, 생활 연령으로 80세인 어떤 사람이 생물학적으로 60세라고 말할 수 있도록 시간의 경과와는 관계없이 모든 다른 생물학적 나이 변화를 반영하는 하나 또는 몇 개의 측정 가능한 생물학적 변화이다.

혼공 02일차 어법 1(선택형)

③ 고난도 문항 요리하기   p.27

● 정답

1. ①	2. ②	3. ①	4. ③	5. ⑤	6. ③	7. ③	8. ①

1. ①

● 전체 해석

사람들은 그들이 의심스러워하는 무엇인가에 말이나 글로 증언을 해 달라고 권유를 받을 때, 종종 그들의 속임수에 관해 나쁜 기분을 느낄 것이다. 그럼에도 그들은 그들이 말하고 있는 것을 믿기 시작한다. 한 사람이 한 말에 대해 설득력 있는 외적인 설명이 없을 때, 말하는 것이 곧 믿는 것이 된다. Tory Higgins와 그의 동료들은 대학생들에게 어떤 사람들의 성격을 기술한 것을 읽게 하고, 그 다음 이 사람을 좋아하거나 싫어한다고 믿어지는 어떤 다른 사람을 위해 그것을 요약해 보게 시켰다. 학생들은 요약문을 받는 사람이 그 사람을 좋아했을 때 더 긍정적인 기술을 했다. 긍정적인 것을 말하고 난 다음, 그들 자신도 그들을 좋아하게 되었다.

그들이 읽은 것을 회상해 보라는 요청을 받았을 때, 그들은 원래의 성격 기술을 더욱 긍정적인 것으로 기억했다. 요약하자면, 우리는 듣는 사람에게 맞춰 메시지를 조정하고, 그렇게 하고 난 다음에는 그 변경된 메시지를 믿는 경향이 있는 것 같다.

● 지문분석

When induced to give / spoken or written witness / to
 접속사 + 분사
something / they doubt, / people will often feel bad / about
their deceit.
주라고 권유를 받았을 때 / 말이나 글로 증언을 / 무언가에 / 그들이
의심스러워하는 / 사람들은 종종 기분이 나빠진다 / 그들의 속임수에
관해서
Nevertheless, / they begin to believe / what they are
saying.
그럼에도 불구하고 / 그들은 믿기 시작한다 / 그들이 말하고 있는 것
을
When there is no compelling external explanation / for
one's words, / saying becomes believing.
                  S   V
어떠한 설득력 있는 외부의 설명이 없다면 / 사람의 말에 대한 / 말은
믿음이 된다
Tory Higgins and his colleagues had / university students
                                L사역동사
/ read a personality description of someone / and then
  ①
summarize it / for someone else / who was believed /
  ②
either to like or to dislike this person.
토리 히긴즈와 그의 동료들은 하게 했다 / 대학생들에게 / 누군가에
대한 성격 묘사를 읽으라고 / 그리고 그것을 요약해보라고 / 다른 누
군가를 위해서 / 믿어지는 / 이 사람을 좋아하거나 싫어한다고
The students wrote a more positive description / when the
recipient liked the person.
그 학생들은 더 긍정적인 묘사를 썼다 / 받는 사람이 그 사람을 좋아
했을 때
Having said positive things, / they also then liked the
 L 이전 사건에 대한 분사구문 having + p.p.
person more themselves.
긍정적인 무언가를 말했을 때 / 그들은 마찬가지로 그 사람을 더 좋
아하게 되었다
Asked to recall / what they had read, / they remembered
=When they were asked to recall ~
the description / as being more positive / than it was.
회상해 보라고 요청받았을 때 / 그들이 무엇을 읽었는지 / 그들은 그
묘사를 기억했다 / 더욱 긍정적으로 / 원래 그랬던 것보다
In short, / it seems / that we are prone to adjust our
                                               ①
messages to our listeners, / and, having done so, / to
believe the altered message.   L having p.p.: 과거의 사건
  ②
요약하자면 / ~인 것 같다 / 우리가 경향이 있는 / 우리의 메시지를
듣는 사람에게 맞추는 / 그리고 그렇게 함으로써 / 바뀐 메시지를 믿
는

● 해설

1. (A), (B), (C)의 각 네모 안에서 어법에 맞는 표현으로 가장 적절한 것
은?
(A) what: say의 목적어가 없으므로 불완전한 문장이 왔어. 따라서 what

이 적절하지.
(B) summarize: summarize는 read와 병렬을 이루며 둘 다 사역동사 had
의 목적 보어로 쓰이고 있어.
(C) Asked: 원래는 When they were asked였지. 이를 분사구문으로 바
꿔서 being asked였는데, being은 생략 가능하므로 asked가 되는 거지.

● 중요 포인트

접속사 + 분사구문

When induced to give spoken or written witness to
  접속사 + 분사: 원래 접속사도 사라지는데, 명확한 의미를 위해서 접속사가 남기도 해.
something they doubt, people will often feel bad about
their deceit.

2. ②

● 전체 해석

많은 나라들의 젊은이들 사이에서, 신문을 읽는 습관이 감소해 오고 있으
며, 전에 신문 광고에 쓰였던 돈의 일부가 인터넷으로 이동해 오고 있다.
물론 신문 읽기가 이처럼 감소하는 까닭의 일부는 우리들이 신문 읽기를
온라인으로 더 많이 하고 있다는 사실 때문이다. 우리는 그날의 뉴스, 사
업계나 연예계의 최신뉴스, 뉴욕타임즈나 가디언이나 또는 세계의 거의
모든 주요 신문의 웹사이트에서 어떤 뉴스든지 읽을 수 있다. 점점 더, 우
리는 컴퓨터는 물론 이동 장비를 사용하여 뉴스와 정보에 무선으로 접근
할 수 있다. 광고에 들어가는 돈은 이러한 새로운 기술에 그 이동경로를
따르고 있다.

● 지문분석

In many countries, / amongst younger people, / [the
habit of reading newspapers] / has been on the decline /
and some of the dollars / previously spent on newspaper
     S
advertising / have migrated to the Internet.
많은 나라에서 / 젊은이들 가운데 / 신문을 읽는 습관은 / 감소하고
있다 / 그리고 그 돈 중 일부가 / 이전에 신문 광고에 소비되었던 /
인터넷으로 이동하고 있다
Of course [some of this decline] / in newspaper reading] /
has been due to the fact / that we are doing / more of our
 V   V
newspaper reading / online.
물론 / 이러한 감소 중 일부는 / 신문 읽기에서의 / 사실 때문이었다
/ 우리가 하고 있다는 / 우리의 신문 읽기를 / 온라인상에서
We can read the news / of the day, or the latest / on
business, entertainment or whatever news / on the
websites of the *New York Times*, the *Guardian* or almost
any other major newspaper in the world.
우리는 뉴스를 읽을 수 있다 / 그날 혹은 최신의 / 비즈니스, 연예, 아
니면 어떤 뉴스든지 간에 / 뉴욕타임즈, 가디언, 아니면 거의 어떤 다
른 주요한 신문 웹사이트에서
Increasingly, / we can access these stories / wirelessly / by
mobile devices / as well as our computers.
점차 / 우리는 이러한 이야기에 접속할 수 있다 / 무선으로 / 모바일
장비에 의해 / 컴퓨터뿐만 아니라

Advertising dollars / have simply been following the migration trail / across to these new technologies.
광고 비용은 / 간단히 이동경로를 따르고 있다 / 이러한 새로운 기술을 가로질러

● 해설

2. (A), (B), (C)의 각 네모 안에서 어법에 맞는 표현으로 가장 적절한 것은?
(A) spent: 뒤에 문장의 본동사 have가 나오므로 주어진 자리는 주어를 수식하는 분사 자리야. 따라서 과거분사인 spent가 적절하지.
(B) whatever: however 뒤에는 형용사나 부사, 혹은 완전한 문장이 나오는데, 주어진 문장은 명사가 나오므로 whatever가 적절해.
(C) following: 뒤에 목적어가 나오므로 능동인 following이 적절해.

● 중요 포인트

분사수식 주어구문

In many countries, amongst younger people, the habit of reading newspapers has been on the decline and some of the dollars previously spent on newspaper advertising have migrated to the Internet.

3. ①

● 전체 해석

어떤 사람이 거짓말을 할 때 그 사람의 평소 행동 양식에서 벗어나는 것을 눈치 채기 위해서는 그것(그 사람의 평소 행동 양식)에 세심한 주의를 기울여야 한다. 때로 그 변화는 잠시 이야기를 중단하는 것만큼 알아채기 힘들다. 또 다른 때는 분명하고 갑작스럽다. 최근에 나는 내가 확신하기에 몇몇 특히 민감한 문제에 대해서 거짓말하려고 하는 지인의 뉴스 인터뷰를 봤는데, 그녀는 정말로 거짓말을 했다. 인터뷰를 하는 대부분의 시간 동안 그녀는 침착했고 솔직했지만, 그녀가 거짓말을 하기 시작하자 그녀의 태도는 돌변했다. 그녀는 머리를 뒤로 젖혔고, '불신'하며 웃었으며, 고개를 앞뒤로 흔들었다. 질문들이 다소 사적인 문제들을 다룬 것은 사실이지만, 나는 일반적으로 질문이 아무리 까다로울지라도 만약 어떤 사람이 사실을 말하고 있다면 대체로 그 사람의 태도가 상당히 또는 갑자기 변하지 않을 것이라는 점을 알게 되었다.

● 지문분석

You have to pay close attention / to someone's normal pattern / in order to notice a deviation from it / when he or she lies.
당신은 세심한 관심을 가져야만 한다 / 누군가의 정상적인 패턴에 / 정상으로부터의 일탈을 알아차리기 위해서 / 그 사람이 거짓말을 할 때
Sometimes the variation is as subtle / as a pause.
때때로 변화는 미미하다 / 중단만큼이나
Other times / it is obvious and abrupt.
다른 때에는 / 그것은 명백하고 갑작스럽다
I recently saw / a news interview with an acquaintance / who I was certain / was going to lie / about a few
= I was certain that an acquaintance ~
who I was certain / was going to lie / about a few
that 생략, that절의 주어인 an acquaintance가 선행사로 나감

particularly sensitive issues, / and lie she did.
목적어 도치, 목적어 lie 강조
나는 최근에 봤다 / 지인과의 뉴스 인터뷰를 / 내가 확신하는 / 거짓말을 하고 있다고 / 몇 가지 구체적인 민감한 이슈들에 대해서 / 그리고 그녀는 정말로 거짓말을 했다

During most of her interview / she was calm and direct, / but when she started lying, / her manner changed dramatically: / she threw her head back, / laughed in 'disbelief,' / and shook her head back and forth.
인터뷰의 대부분 동안 / 그녀는 침착했고 솔직했다 / 하지만 거짓말을 시작하자 / 그녀의 태도는 엄청나게 바뀌었다 / 그녀는 고개를 뒤로 젖혔고 / 불신하며 웃었고 / 그리고 머리를 앞뒤로 흔들었다

It is true / that the questions dealt with very personal
가주어 - 진주어 구문
issues, / but I have found / that in general, / no matter how touchy the question, / if a person is telling the truth / his or her manner will not change significantly or abruptly.
사실이다 / 질문이 매우 개인적인 것을 다룬 것은 / 하지만 나는 발견했다 / 일반적으로 / 아무리 질문이 까다롭더라도 / 만약 사람이 진실을 말하고 있다면 / 그 사람의 태도는 엄청나게 혹은 갑자기 변하지 않을 것이라고

● 해설

3. (A), (B), (C)의 각 네모 안에서 어법에 맞는 표현으로 가장 적절한 것은?
(A) subtle: be동사의 보어 자리로, 주어인 the variation을 설명하는 형용사 subtle이 와야 해.
(B) who: 관계사절의 처음이 I was certain이라서 주어가 있는 것 같지만, 사실 선행사 an acquaintance는 뒤에 오는 was going의 주어야. 일종의 I was certain이 삽입된 형태인데, 원래 문장은 I was certain that an acquaintance was going to ~야. that절의 주어가 선행사로 나갈 경우 해석과 문장 구성에 주의해야 해.
(C) dealt : 본동사가 필요하므로 deal의 과거형인 dealt가 와야 해.

● 중요 포인트

that절의 주어가 선행사인 경우

that절의 주어인 an acquaintance가 선행사로 나감
I recently saw a news interview with an acquaintance who I was certain was going to lie about a few
= I was certain that an acquaintance ~
particularly sensitive issues, and lie she did.

4. ③

● 전체 해석

옛날 일본의 한 전설로 흠잡을 곳 없는 예의범절로 잘 알려진 한 남자가 어느 외딴 마을을 방문한 것에 관한 것이 있다. 마을 사람들은 그를 관찰하고 싶기도 하고 그에게 존경심을 표현하고 싶기도 하여 연회를 준비했다. 식사하러 자리에 앉는 동안 모든 시선은 그들의 고귀한 손님에게로 모아졌다. 모든 사람들은 그 사람이 젓가락을 쥐는 방식을 쳐다보고 그를 따라 할 수 있었다. 그러나 그 때 불행한 사고로 그 예절 바른 사람은 미끄러운 두부 조각을 들어 올려 입에 갖다 대던 중 들고 있던 젓가락에 아주 미세한 정도의 과도한 압력을 행사하여, 그의 두부가 공중에서 움직여 옆에 있던 사람의 무릎 위에 떨어지고 말았다. 연회에 참석한 모든 마을

사람들은 잠깐 놀란 후 그들의 손님이 완벽하다는 믿음을 유지하고 그가 당혹스러워 하지 않도록 하기 위해 서로의 무릎 위에 두부를 던져 놓기 시작했다.

●지문분석

There is an old Japanese legend / about a man / renowned for his flawless manners / visiting a remote village.
<small>about에 걸리는 동명사 「전치사 + 명사 + 동명사」</small>
오래된 일본의 전설이 있다 / 남자에 대한 / 그의 흠없는 태도로 알려진 / 외딴 마을을 방문하는

Wanting to honor / as well as observe him, / the villagers
<small>분사구문 (Because they wanted to ~)</small>
prepared a banquet.
존경심을 표하고 싶어했기에 / 그를 관찰할 뿐만 아니라 / 마을 사람들은 연회를 준비했다

As they sat to eat, / all eyes were on their noble guest.
그들이 먹으려고 앉았을 때 / 모든 눈은 그들의 귀한 손님에게 있었다

Everyone looked at / how the man held his chopsticks, / so that they could imitate him.
모든 사람들은 보았다 / 어떻게 그 남자가 자신의 젓가락을 잡는지를 / 그들이 그를 따라할 수 있기 위해서

But then, / by an unfortunate accident, / as the mannered man raised a slippery slice of tofu / to his lips, / he placed the tiniest bit of excess pressure / on his chopsticks, / propelling his tofu through the air / and onto his
<small>분사구문, 동시상황 (and propelled ~)</small>
neighbor's lap.
하지만 그 때 / 불운한 사건에 의해서 / 예절 바른 남자가 미끄러운 두부 조각을 올렸을 때 / 그의 입술 쪽으로 / 그는 아주 미세한 정도의 초과된 압력을 가했다 / 그의 젓가락에 / 이는 그의 두부가 공중으로 나아가도록 했다 / 그리고 그의 이웃의 무릎에

After a brief moment of surprise, / in order to preserve the myth / of their guest's perfection / and keep him from any embarrassment, / [all the villagers at the banquet] / began
<small>S　　　　　　　　　　　　　　　　　V</small>
to fling tofu / into each other's laps.
짧은 놀람의 순간 이후에 / 신화를 보존하기 위해서 / 그들의 손님의 완벽함에 대한 / 그리고 그가 당황하는 것을 막기 위해서 / 연회의 모든 마을 사람들은 / 두부를 날리기 시작했다 / 각각의 무릎으로

●해설

4. (A), (B), (C)의 각 네모 안에서 어법에 맞는 표현으로 가장 적절한 것은?
(A) how: the man held his chopsticks가 완전한 문장 구조이므로 how가 필요해. * how + 완전문장 / what + 불완전문장
(B) placed: he가 주어이고 뒤에 목적어로 the tiniest bit of excess pressure가 왔으므로 능동형인 과거동사 placed가 와야 하지.
(C) him: keep의 의미상 주어가 all the villagers이므로 목적어와 동일하지 않아. 따라서 재귀대명사 himself를 사용할 수 없어.

●중요 포인트

전치사＋명사＋동명사

There is an old Japanese legend about a man renowned for his flawless manners visiting a remote village.
<small>about에 걸리는 동명사 「전치사 + 명사 + 동명사」</small>

---

5. ⑤

●전체 해석

관찰된 사실들은 공개 검증을 받아야 한다는 과학적인 요구 때문에 측정에서 '객관성'이라는 말은 중요하다. 측정 시스템은 같은 동작을 평가하는 두 명의 관찰자가 같은 (혹은 매우 비슷한) 측정치를 얻게 되는 한 객관적이다. 예를 들어, 투창이 던져진 거리를 판정하기 위해서 줄자를 사용하는 것은 누가 줄자의 눈금을 읽느냐에 상관없이 매우 비슷한 결과를 산출한다. 그에 비해, 정교한 점수 규정이 평가를 더 객관적인 것으로 만드는 데 도움을 주기는 하지만, 다이빙, 체조, 피겨스케이팅과 같은 동작에 대한 평가는 더 주관적이다. 운동 행동을 연구하는 관점에서 볼 때, (운동 동작에 대한 점수를 부여할 때는) 점수 부여가 가능한 객관적으로 이루어질 수 있는 실험실(전문 측정 시스템이 갖추어진 곳) 내의 행동을 사용하는 것이 중요하다.

●지문분석

The term *objectivity* is important / in measurement / because of the scientific demand / that observations be subject to public verification.
<small>'요구'를 의미하므로 that절에는 동사원형</small>
<small>be subject to ~ : '~의 대상이다, ~을 당하다'</small>
객관성이라는 용어는 중요하다 / 측정에서 / 과학적 요구 때문에 / 관찰은 공개 검증을 받아야 한다는

A measurement system is objective / to the extent / that [two observers / evaluating the same performance] / arrive
<small>　　　　　　　　　　　　　　　S</small>
at the same (or very similar) measurements.
측정 시스템은 객관적이다 / 정도로 / 두 명의 관찰자가 / 같은 동작을 평가하는 / 동일한 (혹은 매우 비슷한) 측정에 도달하는

For example, / [using a tape measure / to determine the distance / a javelin was thrown] / yields very similar results / regardless of who reads the tape.
예를 들어 / 줄자를 사용하는 것은 / 거리를 측정하기 위해서 / 창이 던져진 / 비슷한 결과를 만든다 / 누가 줄자를 읽느냐와 상관없이

By comparison, / [evaluation of performances / such as diving, gymnastics, and figure skating] / is more
<small>　　　　　　　　　　S</small>
subjective / – although elaborate scoring rules / help make it more objective.
그에 비해 / 공연의 평가는 / 다이빙, 체조, 피겨스케이팅과 같은 / 더욱 주관적이다 / 비록 정교한 채점 규칙이 / 그것을 더욱 객관적으로 만들어주도록 도와주지만

From the point of view / of research in motor behavior, / it is important / to use performances in the laboratory / for
<small>가주어 – 진주어 구문</small>
which the scoring can be as objective as possible.
관점에서 볼 때 / 운동 행동을 연구하는 / 중요하다 / 실험실에서 행동을 사용하는 것은 / 채점이 가능한 한 객관적일 수 있는

●해설

5. (A), (B), (C)의 각 네모 안에서 어법에 맞는 표현으로 가장 적절한 것은?

(A) evaluating: 뒤에 본동사인 arrive가 나오므로 이 자리에는 본동사가 오지 못해. 따라서 that절의 주어인 two observers를 수식하는 현재분사 evaluating이 적절하지.

(B) was thrown: a javelin이 던지는 동작을 하는 주체가 아니라 던져지는 대상이므로 수동태인 was thrown이 적절해.

(C) it: 문맥상 문장의 주어인 evaluation of performances such as ~ figure skating을 받으므로 대명사 it이 적절해.

● 중요 포인트

현재분사의 수식을 받는 주어

A measurement system is objective to the extent that [two observers / evaluating the same performance] / arrive at the same (or very similar) measurements.

6. ③

●전체 해석

동태평양 북부의 모피 물개들이 캘리포니아에서 알래스카까지 북아메리카의 연안에서 보내는 겨울 동안 어디에서 그리고 무엇을 먹고 사는지는 오랫동안 다소 불가사의한 것이었다. 그것들이 얼마만큼이나 많이 정어리, 고등어 또는 다른 상업적으로 중요한 어류를 먹고 살고 있다는 증거는 없다. 추측컨대, 알려진 사실이 없지만 4백만 마리의 물개들이 같은 종을 놓고 상업을 목적으로 하는 어부들과 다툴 수 없을 것이다. 그러나 모피 물개들의 먹이에 관한 약간의 증거는 있고 그것은 대단히 의미심장하다. 그들의 위에서 살아 있는 채로는 절대 본 적이 없는 한 종의 물고기 뼈가 나왔다. 사실, 물개들의 위속을 제외하고 어느 곳에서도 그것의 잔존물조차 발견된 적이 없었다. 어류학자들은 이 '물개 어류'가 대륙붕 가장자리에서 떨어진 아주 깊은 물에서 보통 서식하는 한 집단에 속한다고 말한다.

●지문분석

It had long been something of a mystery / where, and on what, / [the northern fur seals / of the eastern Pacific] / feed / during the winter, / which they spend / off the coast of North America / from California to Alaska.
가주어 – 진주어 구문

오랫동안 미스터리한 무언가였다 / 어디에서 그리고 무엇을 / 북부의 모피 물개가 / 동태평양의 / 먹는지 / 겨울 동안 / 그들이 보내는 / 북미의 해안가에서 / 캘리포니아에서 알래스카까지

There is no evidence / that they are feeding / to any great extent / on sardines, mackerel, or other commercially important fishes.

어떠한 증거도 없다 / 그들이 먹는다는 / 얼마나 대단한 정도로 / 정어리, 고등어, 아니면 다른 상업적으로 중요한 물고기를

Presumably four million seals / could not compete with commercial fishermen / for the same species / without the fact being known.
without + 명사 + 동명사

추정컨대, 4백만의 물개는 / 상업적인 어부들과 경쟁할 수 없었다 /

같은 종에 대해서 / 알려진 사실없이

But there is some evidence / on the diet of the fur seals, / and it is highly significant.

하지만 몇 가지 증거가 있다 / 모피 물개의 식성에 대한 / 그것은 매우 의미심장하다

Their stomachs / have yielded the bones / of a species of fish / that has never been seen alive.

그들의 위는 / 뼈를 만들어냈다 / 한 종류의 물고기의 / 결코 살아있는 채로 본 적이 없는

Indeed, / not even its remains / have been found / anywhere / except in the stomachs of seals.

사실 / 그것의 잔존물 조차도 / 발견되지 않았다 / 어디에서든 / 물개의 위를 제외하고는

Ichthyologists say / that this 'seal fish' belongs to a group / that typically inhabits very deep water, / off the edge of the continental shelf.

어류학자들은 말한다 / 이 물개 물고기가 그룹에 속한다고 / 전형적으로 매우 깊은 바닷속에 사는 / 대륙붕 가장자리에서 떨어진

●해설

6. (A), (B), (C)의 각 네모 안에서 어법에 맞는 표현으로 가장 적절한 것은?

(A) which: spend의 목적어가 보이지 않으므로 불완전 문장이 와. 따라서 the winter를 선행사로 하는 관계대명사 which가 적절하지.

(B) being: 「전치사 + 명사 + 동명사」 구조 또는 명사 the fact를 수식하는 현재분사의 구조로 봐도 돼. 여하튼 본동사 is는 올 수가 없는 구조야.

(C) have: 주어인 remains가 복수 명사이므로 복수 동사인 have가 와야 해.

● 중요 포인트

it–that 가주어 진주어 구문

It had long been something of a mystery where, and on what, the northern fur seals of the eastern Pacific feed during the winter, which they spend off the coast of North America from California to Alaska.
가주어 – 진주어 구문

7. ③

●전체 해석

처음으로 일일 마감에 맞춰 보도했던 것이 어떤 것이었는지 기억하는가? 혹은 처음으로 시의 공무원을 인터뷰했던 것은? 혹은 컴퓨터 출판 프로그램을 쓰기 시작했던 것이 어떤지를 기억하는가? 우리 대학의 언론학 프로그램이 이런 많은 첫 경험들의 원천이었다는 것을 우리는 알고 있다. 우리는 여전히 이런 중요한 첫 경험들을 젊은 신진 작가들과 편집자들에게 제공하고 있다. 그리고 당신이 이 학생들이 프로그램을 끝낼 수 있도록 기꺼이 도와주기를 바라고 있다. 아시다시피, 최고 수준의 교육을 제공하기 위한 비용은 계속 오르고 있다. 우리는 교육의 질을 손상시키지 않으면서 비용을 억제하기 위해 우리가 할 수 있는 모든 일을 다했다. 그것들 중 하나가 특별한 재정적 지원이 필요한 학생들을 위해 장학기금을 설립하는 일이다. 그리고 우리는 당신이 그 기금에 후하게 기부해 주시기를 바란다. 당신이 이 분야에서 미래의 지도자 양성을 돕고 있다는 것을

알면 정말 기분이 좋아질 것이다.

● 지문분석

Remember / what it was like / to report on a daily deadline / for the first time?
가주어 - 진주어 구문
기억하는가 / 그것이 무엇과 같았는지 / 일일 마감에 맞춰서 보도했던 것이 / 처음으로

Or to interview a city official / for the first time?
아니면 시의 공무원을 인터뷰했던 것은 / 처음으로

Or to begin / to maneuver a desktop publishing program?
아니면 시작했던 것은 / 컴퓨터 출판 프로그램을 사용하는 것을

We know / that [the journalism program at our college] / was a source of many of these firsts / for you.
우리는 알고 있다 / 우리 대학의 언론 프로그램이 / 많은 이러한 최초의 원천이었단 것을 / 당신을 위한

We're still providing / these important first experiences / to budding young writers and editors.
우리는 여전히 제공하고 있다 / 이러한 중요한 첫 번째 경험을 / 새로운 젊은 작가들과 편집자들에게

And we're hoping / you'll be willing to help / these students make it / through the program.
그리고 우리는 희망한다 / 당신이 기꺼이 도울거라고 / 이러한 학생들이 해내도록 / 그 프로그램을 통해서

As you know, / [the costs / of providing first-rate education] / just keep going up.
알다시피 / 비용은 / 일류 수준의 교육을 제공하려는 / 계속 오르고 있다

We've done everything / we can / to contain costs / without compromising quality.
우리는 모든 것을 해왔다 / 우리가 할 수 있는 / 비용을 억제하기 위해서 / 질을 손상시키지 않고

One of those things / is to set up a scholarship fund / for students / with special financial needs.
그러한 것들 중 하나는 / 장학기금을 조성하는 것이다 / 학생들을 위한 / 특별한 재정적 도움이 필요한

We hope / you would consider / contributing generously to our fund.
consider + ~ing
우리는 희망한다 / 당신이 고려하기를 / 관대하게 우리 기금에 기부하는 것을

You'll get a great feeling / knowing / you're helping / support the formation of future leaders / in the profession.
분사구문 (if you know ~)
당신은 엄청난 기분을 얻게 될 것이다 / 알게 된다면 / 당신이 돕고 있다는 것을 / 미래 리더의 양성을 지원하는 것을 / 이 분야에서

● 해설

7. (A), (B), (C)의 각 네모 안에서 어법에 맞는 표현으로 가장 적절한 것은?

(A) many: these firsts에 연결되므로 셀 수 있는 명사 앞에 사용되는 many가 적절해.

(B) to contain: we can은 anything을 수식하는 관계대명사절이야. 내용상 목적을 의미하는 to부정사(억제하기 위해서)가 필요하므로 to contain이 적절하지.

(C) knowing: 뒤에 목적절인 you're helping ~ in the profession이 오므로 능동을 의미하는 현재분사 knowing이 적절해.

● 중요 포인트

조건을 의미하는 분사
분사구문의 주절에 조동사가 있다면, 분사의 원래 의미는 if일 가능성이 높아.

You'll get a great feeling knowing you're helping support the formation of future leaders in the profession.
분사구문 (if you know ~)

8. ①

● 전체 해석

전통 사회의 삶과 마찬가지로, 그러나 다른 팀 스포츠와는 달리, 야구는 시계에 의해 좌우되지 않는다. 미식축구 경기는 정확히 60분 경기로 구성되고, 농구 경기는 40분이나 48분으로 이루어지지만, 야구는 경기가 끝나야 하는 정해진 시간의 길이가 없다. 따라서 정확히 잰 시간, 마감 시간, 일정, 시간 단위로 지급되는 임금 같은 규율이 있기 이전의 세상과 마찬가지로 경기의 속도가 여유롭고 느긋하다. 야구는 사람들이 "저는 시간이 많지 않아요."라고 말하지 않았던 그런 종류의 세상에 속해 있다. 야구 경기는 '정말로' 온종일 경기가 이루어진다. 그러나 그것이 그 경기가 영원히 계속 될 수 있다는 것을 의미하는 것은 아니다. 야구는 전통적인 삶과 마찬가지로 자연의 리듬, 구체적으로 말해 지구의 자전에 따라 진행된다. 그것(야구)의 첫 반세기 동안 경기가 밤에는 이루어지지 않았는데, 그것은 야구 경기가 전통적인 근무일처럼 해가 질 때 끝난다는 것을 의미했다.

● 지문분석

Like life in traditional society, / but unlike other team sports, / baseball is not governed by the clock.
전통적인 사회 속의 삶처럼 / 하지만 다른 팀 스포츠와는 달리 / 야구는 시계에 의해 지배되지 않는다

A football game is comprised / of exactly sixty minutes of play, / a basketball game / forty or forty-eight minutes, / but baseball has no set length of time / within which the game must be completed.
축구는 구성된다 / 정확하게 60분의 경기로 / 농구 경기는 / 40~48분으로 / 하지만 야구는 설정된 시간이 없다 / 게임이 완료되어야만 하는

The pace of the game / is therefore leisurely and unhurried, / like the world / before the discipline of measured time, deadlines, schedules, and wages / paid by the hour.
게임의 속도는 / 그래서 여유롭고 느긋하다 / 세상처럼 / 측정된 시간, 마감시간, 스케쥴, 그리고 월급의 규율이 있기 이전의 / 시간에 의해 지급되는

Baseball belongs to the kind of world / in which people

did not say, / "I haven't got all day."

야구는 그런 종류의 세상에 속한다 / 사람들이 말하지 않았던 / 나는 시간이 많지 않다고

Baseball games do have all day / to be played.

야구는 온종일이 있다 / 경기가 되어지는

But that does not mean / that they can go on forever.

하지만 그것은 의미하지는 않는다 / 그들이 영원히 지속될 수 있다는 것을

Baseball, / like traditional life, / proceeds according to the rhythm of nature, / specifically the rotation of the Earth.

야구는 / 전통적인 삶처럼 / 자연의 리듬에 따라 진행된다 / 특히 지구의 자전

During its first half century, / games were not played / at night, / which meant / that baseball games, / like the traditional work day, / ended / when the sun set.

그것의 첫 번째 반세기 동안 / 게임은 진행되지 않았다 / 밤에는 / 이는 의미했다 / 야구는 / 전통적인 근무일처럼 / 끝난다는 것을 / 해가 질 때

● 해설

8. (A), (B), (C)의 각 네모 안에서 어법에 맞는 표현으로 가장 적절한 것은?

(A) unhurried: be동사의 주격 보어가 와야 하므로 형용사 unhurried를 써야 해. 앞에 있는 leisurely(여유있는) 역시 형용사야.

(B) in which: 뒤에 완전한 문장이 오므로 in which를 써야 해.

(C) ended: 주어인 baseball games의 본동사가 필요하므로 ended가 와야 해.

● 중요 포인트

전치사 + 관계대명사

「전치사 + 관계대명사」 뒤에는 완전한 문장이 와야 한다.

Baseball has no set length of time within which the game must be completed.
+ 완전한 문장

● **4단계 혼공 개념 마무리**　　p.31

1. 그들이 읽은 것을 회상해 보라는 요청을 받았을 때, 그들은 원래의 성격 기술을 더욱 긍정적인 것으로 기억했다.

2. 최근에 나는 내가 확신하기에 몇몇 특히 민감한 문제에 대해서 거짓말하려고 하는 지인의 뉴스 인터뷰를 봤는데, 그녀는 정말로 거짓말을 했다.

3. 질문들이 다소 사적인 문제들을 다룬 것은 사실이지만, 나는 일반적으로 질문이 아무리 까다로울지라도 만약 어떤 사람이 사실을 말하고 있다면 대체로 그 사람의 태도가 상당히 또는 갑자기 변하지 않을 것이라는 점을 알게 되었다.

4. 그러나 그 때 불행한 사고로 그 예절 바른 사람은 미끄러운 두부 조

각을 들어 올려 입에 갖다 대던 중 들고 있던 젓가락에 아주 미세한 정도의 과도한 압력을 행사하여, 그의 두부가 공중에서 움직여 옆에 있던 사람의 무릎 위에 떨어지고 말았다.

5. 동태평양 북부의 모피 물개들이 캘리포니아에서 알래스카까지 북아메리카의 연안에서 보내는 겨울 동안 어디에서 그리고 무엇을 먹고 사는지는 오랫동안 다소 불가사의한 것이었다.

6. 미식축구 경기는 정확히 60분 경기로 구성되고, 농구 경기는 40분이나 48분으로 이루어지지만, 야구는 경기가 끝나야 하는 정해진 시간의 길이가 없다.

7. 그것(야구)의 첫 반세기 동안 경기가 밤에는 이루어지지 않았는데, 그것은 야구 경기가 전통적인 근무일처럼 해가 질 때 끝난다는 것을 의미했다.

● **혼공 03일차 어법 2(밑줄형)**

● **3단계 고난도 문항 요리하기**　　p.37

● 정답

> **1.② 2.② 3.⑤ 4.④ 5.② 6.③ 7.④ 8.③**

1. ②

● 전체 해석

20세기에 냉장고에서부터 고성능 오븐, 신선한 재료를 전 세계에 실어 나르는 항공 수송에 이르기까지 기술의 진보는 제빵과 페이스트리 만드는 것에 헤아릴 수 없을 정도로 기여했다. 21세기 초에 고급 빵과 페이스트리의 인기는 새로운 요리사가 훈련될 수 있는 것보다 훨씬 더 빠르게 상승하고 있다. 아주 흥미롭게도 제빵에서의 많은 기술적 발전은 제빵사와 소비자들 사이에 똑같이 하나의 반응을 촉발했다. 그들은 제빵이 더 산업화하고, 제빵 제품이 더 세련되고, 표준화되고, (어떤 사람들이 말하기를) 맛이 없어지면서 사라진 옛날 빵의 몇 가지 맛을 되찾기를 원하고 있다. 제빵사들은 과거의 시큼한 맛이 나는 수제 반죽으로 만든 빵을 생산하는 방법을 연구하고 있으며, 그들은 맛을 찾기 위한 자신들의 연구에서 특별한 밀가루로 실험하고 있다.

● 지문분석

In the twentieth century, / [advances in technology, / from refrigeration to sophisticated ovens to air transportation / that carries fresh ingredients / around the world,] / contributed immeasurably / to baking and pastry making.

20세기에 / 기술의 발전은 / 냉장고에서 고성능 오븐, 항공 수송에 이르는 / 신선한 재료를 옮기는 / 세계로 / 엄청나게 기여했다 / 제빵과 페이스트리를 만드는 데

At the beginning of the twenty-first century, / [the popularity / of fine breads and pastries] / is growing even faster / than new chefs can be trained.

21세기 초반에 / 인기는 / 고급 빵과 페이스트리의 / 더욱 빠르게 성장하고 있다 / 새로운 요리사가 훈련될 수 있는 것보다

Interestingly enough, / [many of the technological advances / in bread making] / have sparked a reaction / among bakers and consumers alike.

아주 흥미롭게도 / 많은 기술적 발전은 / 빵을 만드는 데 있어 / 반응을 일으켜왔다 / 제빵사와 소비자들 모두에게

They are looking to reclaim / some of the flavors of old-fashioned breads / that were lost / as baking became more industrialized / and baked goods became more refined, standardized, / and – some would say – flavorless.

그들은 되찾기를 기대하고 있다 / 옛날 빵의 맛 중 일부를 / 잃어버린 / 제빵이 더욱 산업화됨에 따라 / 그리고 제빵 제품이 더욱 세련되고 표준화됨에 따라 / 그리고 누군가가 말하듯 맛이 없어짐에 따라

Bakers are researching methods / for producing the handmade sourdough breads / of the past, / and they are experimenting / with specialty flours / in their search for flavor.

제빵사들은 방법을 연구하고 있다 / 시큼한 맛이 나는 수제 반죽으로 만든 빵을 만드는 / 과거의 / 그리고 그들은 실험하고 있다 / 특별한 밀가루로 / 맛을 위한 그들의 연구에서

● 해설

1. 다음 글의 밑줄 친 부분 중, 어법상 틀린 것은?
① that: 앞에 있는 air transportation을 수식하는 주격 관계대명사이므로 적절하지.
❷ are → is: 문장의 주어는 동사 앞에 있는 pastries가 아니라 앞에 있는 the popularity이므로 복수 동사 are를 단수 동사 is로 바꾸어야 해.
③ alike: '한결같이'로 쓰이므로 적절하지.
④ were lost: '사라지다, 잃어버리다'를 의미하므로 수동태가 적절하지.
⑤ producing: 전치사의 목적어로 사용되고 있고, 뒤에 목적어가 나오므로 동명사 producing이 적절하지.

● 중요 포인트

긴 주어 구문

주어와 동사의 거리가 멀 경우, 중간에 삽입된 부분이 많으므로 해석에 주의해야 해.

In the twentieth century, [advances in technology, from refrigeration to sophisticated ovens to air transportation that carries fresh ingredients around the world,] contributed immeasurably to baking and pastry making.

2. ②

● 전체 해석

음악이 신체적, 정신적 기술을 향상시키는 듯하다는 점을 감안할 때, 음악이 작업 수행에 해로운 상황이 있는가? 이것이 상당히 중요한 의미를 갖는 한 영역이 안전하게 운전하는 능력에 해로울 수 있는 음악의 영향이다. 시끄럽고 빠른 음악과 난폭한 운전 사이의 연관성을 제시하는 증거가

있는데, 이런 방식으로 운전하는 데 대한 음악의 영향력이 어떻게 설명될 수 있을까? 한 가지 가능성은 운전자가 음악에 있어서 박자의 규칙성에 적응한다는 것, 그리고 그들의 속도가 그에 따라 영향을 받는다는 것이다. 다시 말해, 보다 빠른 음악이 사람들로 하여금 더 빨리 음식을 먹도록 하는 것과 꼭 마찬가지로 보다 빠른 음악은 사람들로 하여금 계속 반복되는 음악 구조에 정신적, 신체적으로 맞물리면서 더 빠른 속도로 운전하게 한다는 것이다.

● 지문분석

Given / that music appears to enhance physical and mental skills, / are there circumstances / where music is damaging to performance?

고려할 때 / 음악이 신체적 정신적 기술을 향상시키는 것 같다는 점을 / 환경이 있을까 / 음악이 작업 수행에 해를 끼치는

[One domain / where this is of considerable significance] / is music's potentially damaging effects / on the ability / to drive safely.

한 영역은 / 이것이 상당히 중요한 / 음악의 잠재적으로 해로운 영향이다 / 능력에 끼치는 / 안전하게 운전하는

Evidence suggests / an association / between loud, fast music and reckless driving, / but how might [music's ability / to influence driving in this way] / be explained?

증거는 말해준다 / 연관성을 / 크고 빠른 음악과 무모한 운전 사이의 / 하지만 어떻게 음악의 능력이 / 이런 식으로 운전에 영향을 주는 / 설명될까

One possibility / is that drivers adjust / to temporal regularities in music, / and that their speed is influenced accordingly.

한 가지 가능성은 / 운전자가 적응한다는 것이다 / 음악에 있어서 박자의 규칙성에 / 그리고 그들의 속도는 이에 따라 영향을 받는다는 것이다

In other words, / just as faster music causes / people to eat faster, / so it causes / people to drive at faster speeds, / as they engage mentally and physically / with ongoing repeated structures in the music.

다시 말하자면 / 더 빠른 음악이 유발하는 것처럼 / 사람들이 더 빨리 먹도록 / 그래서 그것은 유발한다 / 사람들이 더 빠른 속도로 운전하도록 / 그들이 정신적 신체적으로 연관함에 따라 / 음악 안의 지속적인 반복된 구조에

● 해설

2. 다음 글의 밑줄 친 부분 중, 어법상 틀린 것은?
① damaging: '해로운'이라는 뜻의 형용사로 주격 보어야.
❷ which → where: 뒤에 오는 문장이 완전한 문장이므로 관계 대명사 which를 관계부사 where로 바꾸어야 해.
③ be explained: 의문사 how가 이끄는 의문문의 주어는 music's ability ~ this way이고 동사는 might be explained이야. 의문문이므로 might가 주어 앞으로 도치되었어.
④ that: 접속사 that이 이끄는 that their speed ~ accordingly와 앞에 있는 that drivers ~ music이 서로 병렬구조를 이루고 있어.
⑤ so: 'just as ~, so … (~하는 것과 마찬가지로 그렇게 … 하다)' 구조가 사용되고 있어.

●중요 포인트

관계부사의 수식을 받는 긴 주어 구문

[One domain where this is of considerable significance]
is music's potentially damaging effects on the ability to
drive safely.

3. ⑤

●전체 해석

사람들이 진짜 역경, 즉 질병, 실직, 혹은 연령으로 인한 장애에 직면할 때, 애완동물로부터의 애정은 새로운 의미를 띤다. 애완동물의 지속적인 애정은 고난을 견디고 있는 사람들에게 그들의 핵심적인 본질이 손상되지 않았다고 안심시켜 주기 때문에 매우 중요해진다. 그러므로 애완동물은 우울증이 있거나 만성적인 질병이 있는 환자들의 치료에 중요하다. 게다가, 애완동물은 시설에 수용된 노인들에게 매우 유익하게 이용된다. 그런 시설에서 직원들은 모든 환자가 건강이 쇠퇴하고 있을 때 낙관주의를 유지하기가 힘들다. 방문하는 자녀들은 부모님이나 조부모님이 예전에 어떠했는지를 기억하고 그들의 무능함에 의기소침해할 수밖에 없다. 그러나 동물은 정신적인 능력에 대한 기대를 하지 않는다. 그들은 젊음을 숭배하지 않는다. 그들은 노인들이 예전에 어떠했는지에 대한 기억이 전혀 없어서 그들이(노인들이) 마치 어린이들인 것처럼 그들을 반긴다. 강아지를 안고 있는 노인은 완전히 정확하게 어린 시절을 다시 체험할 수 있다. 그의 기쁨과 그 동물의 반응은 동일하다.

●지문분석

When people face real adversity / – disease,
unemployment, or the disabilities of age / – [affection
from a pet] / takes on new meaning.
사람들이 진짜 역경에 직면할 때 / 질병, 실업, 아니면 나이로 인한 장애와 같은 / 애완동물로부터의 애정은 / 새로운 의미를 띤다

A pet's continuing affection / becomes crucially important
/ for those / enduring hardship / because it reassures them
/ that their core essence has not been damaged.
애완동물의 지속적인 애정은 / 매우 중요해진다 / 사람들에게 / 고통을 견디는 / 왜냐하면 이것은 그들을 안심시켜주기 때문에 / 그들의 핵심 본질이 손상받지 않았다고

Thus pets are important / in the treatment / of depressed or
chronically ill patients.
그래서 애완동물은 중요하다 / 치료에서 / 우울증이 있거나 만성적인 질병이 있는 환자들에게

In addition, / pets are used / to great advantage / with the
institutionalized aged.
더불어 / 애완동물들은 사용된다 / 엄청난 장점으로 / 시설에 수용된 노인들에게

In such institutions / it is difficult / for the staff / to retain
optimism / when all the patients are declining / in health.
그런 시설에서 / 어렵다 / 직원들은 / 낙관주의를 유지하기가 / 모든 환자들이 쇠퇴할 때 / 건강이

Children / who visit / cannot help but remember / what

---

their parents or grandparents once were / and be depressed
/ by their incapacities.
아이들은 / 방문하는 / 기억하지 않을 수 없다 / 그들의 부모나 조부모가 예전에 어떠했는지 / 그리고 우울해질 수밖에 없다 / 그들의 무능함에 의해서

Animals, however, have no expectations / about mental
capacity.
하지만 동물들은 기대감이 없다 / 정신적 능력에 대한

They do not worship youth.
그들은 젊음을 숭배하지 않는다

They have no memories / about what the aged once were /
and greet them / as if they were children.
그들은 기억이 없다 / 노인들이 예전에 어떠했는지에 대해서 / 그리고 그들을 반긴다 / 마치 그들이 아이인 것처럼

[An old man / holding a puppy] / can relive a childhood
moment / with complete accuracy.
노인은 / 강아지를 안고 있는 / 다시 어린 시절을 체험할 수 있다 / 완전히 정확하게

His joy and the animal's response are the same.
그의 기쁨과 동물들의 반응은 동일하다

●해설

3. 다음 글의 밑줄 친 부분 중, 어법상 틀린 것은?
① those: '사람들'의 의미를 나타내는 대명사 those로 어법상 적절하지.
② depressed: depressed는 뒤에 나오는 patients를 수식하는 형용사로 어법상 적절해. 감정동사의 분사의 경우 '느끼면' 수동, '느끼게 하면' 능동을 고르면 돼.
③ used: pets가 use의 주체가 아니라 그 동작을 받는 대상이므로 수동태를 의미하는 과거분사 used는 적절해.
④ what: what은 remember의 목적어 역할을 하는 명사절을 이끌고 있는데, 그 절이 were의 보어가 없는 불완전 문장이므로 what이 적절해.
❺ was → were: 주어인 the aged가 'the + 형용사'의 형태로 '~하는 사람들'의 복수의 의미를 나타내므로 단수 동사 was가 아닌 복수 동사 were이 와야 해.

●중요 포인트

cannot help but 구문

cannot help but 동사원형 : ~하지 않을 수 없다
= cannot help ~ing

Children who visit cannot help but remember what their
parents or grandparents once were and be depressed by
their incapacities.
= cannot help remembering

4. ④

●전체 해석

그리스인은 두드러진 물체와 그것의 속성에 초점을 맞추느라 인과 관계의 근본적인 성질을 이해하지 못했다. 아리스토텔레스는 돌이 공중에서 떨어지는 것은 돌이 '중력'이라는 성질을 가지고 있기 때문이라고 설명했

다. 하지만 물론 물에 던져진 나무 조각은 가라앉는 대신 뜬다. 이 현상을 아리스토텔레스는 나무가 '가벼움'이라는 성질을 가지고 있기 때문이라고 설명했다! 그 물체 밖에 있는 어떤 힘이 관련 있을지도 모른다는 가능성에 주의를 기울이지 않고, 두 경우 모두 초점은 오로지 그 물체에 있다. 그러나 중국인은 세계를 계속적으로 상호 작용하는 물질로 구성된 것으로 보았고, 그래서 그것을 이해하고자 하는 그들의 시도는 그들로 하여금 전체적인 '장(場)', 즉 전체로서의 맥락이나 환경의 복잡성에 중점을 두도록 했다. 사건은 언제나 여러 힘이 작용하는 장에서 발생한다는 개념은 중국인에게 전적으로 직관적이었을 것이다.

● 지문분석

> [The Greeks' focus / on the salient object and its attributes] / led to their failure / to understand the fundamental nature of causality.
> 그리스의 초점은 / 두드러진 물체와 그 속성에 대한 / 실패를 이끌었다 / 근본적인 인과 관계의 본성을 이해하는 것에 대한
>
> Aristotle explained / that [a stone / falling through the air] / is due to the stone having / the property of "gravity."
> 아리스토텔레스는 설명했다 / 돌은 / 공중에서 떨어지는 / 돌이 가지고 있기 때문이라고 / 중력의 속성을
>
> But of course / [a piece of wood / tossed into water] / floats / instead of sinking.
> 하지만 물론 / 나무 조각은 / 물로 던져진 / 뜬다 / 가라앉는 것 대신에
>
> This phenomenon / Aristotle explained / as being due to the wood having / the property of "levity"!
> 이 현상을 / 아리스토텔레스는 설명했다 / 나무가 가지고 있기 때문이라고 / 가벼움이라는 속성을
>
> In both cases / the focus is exclusively on the object, / with no attention / paid to the possibility / that [some force / outside the object] / might be relevant.
> 양쪽 모두의 경우 / 초점은 오로지 물체에게만 있다 / 관심없이 / 가능성에 주어진 / 어떤 힘이 / 대상 바깥에 있는 / 관련이 있을 수도 있는
>
> But the Chinese saw the world / as consisting of continuously interacting substances, / so [their attempts / to understand it] / caused / them to be oriented / toward the complexities of the entire "field," / that is, / the context or environment as a whole.
> 하지만 중국인들은 세상을 보았다 / 지속적으로 상호 작용하는 물질로 구성되어 있다고 / 그래서 그들의 시도는 / 그것을 이해하려는 / 유발했다 / 그들이 방향을 정하도록 / 전체 장의 복잡성을 향해서 / 즉 / 전체로서의 맥락 혹은 환경에
>
> [The notion / that events always occur / in a field of forces] / would have been completely intuitive / to the Chinese.
> 개념은 / 사건은 항상 발생한다는 / 힘의 장에서 / 완벽하게 직관적이었을 것이다 / 중국인들에게는

● 해설

4. 다음 글의 밑줄 친 부분 중, 어법상 틀린 것은?
① their: the Greeks를 대신하는 소유격 대명사이므로 their은 적절해.

② tossed: 주어인 a piece of wood가 뒤에 본동사 floats를 가지므로 주어진 위치는 주어를 수식하는 것이어야 하지. toss와의 관계는 던지는(toss) 행위의 대상에 해당하므로 과거분사 tossed를 사용한 것은 적절해.
③ exclusively: be동사 뒤에 오지만, 전치사구인 on the object를 수식하니까 부사 exclusively가 와야 해.
❹ causing → caused: 문장의 주어인 their attempts를 to understand it이 수식하고 있어. 다음에 나오는 것은 문장의 본동사여야겠지. 따라서 분사인 causing이 아닌 과거동사 caused가 와야 해.
⑤ that: 뒤에 완벽한 문장이 오고 있으니 주어인 The notion을 수식하는 동격의 접속사 that은 적절해.

● 중요 포인트

주어를 수식하는 분사

❶ Aristotle explained that [a stone falling through the air] is due to the stone having the property of "gravity."
❷ But of course [a piece of wood tossed into water] floats instead of sinking.

5. ②

● 전체 해석

중요한 것은 바로 산소이다. 역설적이게도, 우리에게 생명을 주는 것이 결국 그것(생명)을 죽인다. 궁극적인 생명력은 우리가 들이쉬는 거의 모든 산소를 태우는, 미토콘드리아라고 불리는 아주 작은 에너지 세포 공장에 있다. 그러나 호흡에는 대가가 있다. 우리를 살아있게 하고 활동적이게 유지하는 산소 연소는 활성 산소라고 불리는 부산물을 내보낸다. 그것들(활성 산소)은 지킬박사와 하이드 씨의 특징을 가지고 있다(서로 다른 이중적인 특징을 가지고 있다). 한편으로, 그것들은 우리의 생존 보장을 돕는다. 예를 들어, 감염원과 싸워 물리치기 위해 신체가 동원될 때, 그것(신체)은 침입자들을 매우 효율적으로 파괴하기 위해 한바탕 활성 산소를 생산한다. 다른 한편으로, 활성 산소는 통제할 수 없을 정도로 신체를 돌아다니면서 세포를 공격하고, 세포의 단백질을 부식시키고, 세포막을 뚫고 세포의 유전 암호를 변질시켜 마침내 그 세포는 제대로 기능을 하지 못하게 되고 때로는 포기하여 죽어버린다. 보호자인 동시에 보복자로 생명체의 일부가 되어 있는 이런 사나운 활성 산소는 노화의 강력한 동인이다.

● 지문분석

> Oxygen is / what it is all about.
> 산소는 / 그것에 대한 모든 것이다(중요한 것은 산소이다)
>
> Ironically, [the stuff / that gives us life] / eventually kills it.
> 역설적이게도 / 물질은 / 우리에게 생명을 주는 / 결과적으로는 그것을 죽인다
>
> The ultimate life force / lies in tiny cellular factories of energy, / called mitochondria, / that burn nearly all the oxygen / we breathe in.
> 궁극적인 생명력은 / 에너지의 작은 세포 공장에 있다 / 미토콘드리아라고 불리우는 / 거의 모든 산소를 태우는 / 우리가 들이쉬는
>
> But breathing has a price.
> 하지만 호흡은 대가가 있다

[The combustion of oxygen / that keeps us alive and active] / sends out by-products called oxygen free radicals.
산소의 연소는 / 우리를 살아있고 활동적이게 해주는 / 부산물을 내보낸다 / 활성 산소라고 불리우는

They have Dr. Jekyll and Mr. Hyde characteristics.
그들은 지킬박사와 하이드의 특성을 가지고 있다

On the one hand, / they help guarantee our survival.
한편으로는 / 그들은 우리의 생존을 보장하도록 돕는다

For example, / when the body mobilizes / to fight off infectious agents, / it generates a burst of free radicals / to destroy the invaders very efficiently.
예를 들어 / 신체가 동원될 때 / 감염원과 싸우기 위해서 / 그것은 폭발적으로 활성 산소를 발생한다 / 침입자를 매우 효율적으로 파괴하기 위해서

On the other hand, / free radicals move / uncontrollably through the body, / attacking❶ cells, / rusting❷ their proteins, / piercing❸ their membranes / and corrupting❹ their genetic code / until the cells become dysfunctional / and sometimes give up and die.
다른 한편으로 / 활성 산소는 이동한다 / 통제할수 없을 정도로 신체를 / 세포를 공격하며 / 그들의 단백질을 부식시키며 / 그들의 세포막을 뚫으며 / 그리고 그들의 유전자 코드를 변질시키며 / 세포가 기능을 못하게 될 때까지 / 그리고 때때로 포기하고 죽을 때까지

[These fierce radicals, / built into life] / as both protectors and avengers,] / are potent agents of aging.
이러한 격렬한 활성 산소는 / 생명체에 만들어진 / 보호자이자 보복자로서 / 노화의 강력한 동인이다

● 해설

5. 다음 글의 밑줄 친 부분 중, 어법상 틀린 것은?
① that: that은 tiny cellular factories of energy를 선행사로 취하고 관계절에서 주어 역할을 하는 관계사지.
❷ sending → sends: 문장의 주어는 The combustion of oxygen으로 that ~ active의 수식을 받고 있어. 문장의 본동사가 필요하니까 sends가 와야겠지.
③ to fight: to부정사인 to fight가 목적을 나타내어 '싸우기 위해서'로 쓰이고 있어.
④ uncontrollably: 동사 move를 수식하고 있으니까 부사인 uncontrollably는 적절해.
⑤ built: 본동사가 are가 있고, 콤마 사이에 있으니까 삽입된 것으로 봐야 해. 뒤에 목적어가 없으니 수동인 과거분사 built가 적절하겠지.

● 중요 포인트

이중 수식 구조

The ultimate life force / lies in tiny cellular factories of energy, / called mitochondria, / that burn nearly all the oxygen / we breathe in.

---

6. ③

● 전체 해석

수산 양식 산업이 급속하게 팽창하고 있던 초기 단계 동안, 실수들이 발생하였으며 이것들은 직접적인 손실 면에서 그리고 그 산업의 이미지 측면 양쪽 모두에 있어 대가가 컸다. 고밀도의 사육은 몇몇 경우에서 가두리에 있는 어류뿐만 아니라 지역의 야생 어류 개체군 또한 황폐화하는 전염성 질병의 발발을 초래했다. 양식장에 인접한 지역에 서식하고 있는 지역 야생 생물에 미치는 부정적 영향이 계속해서 그 산업에 대한 지속적인 대민 관계의 문제가 되고 있다. 더욱이, 수산 양식용 가두리가 처음 지어졌을 때 일반적인 지식의 부족과 불충분하게 행해지던 관리는 초과 사료와 어류 폐기물로부터 발생하는 오염이 거대한 불모의 해저 사막을 만들어냈다는 것을 의미했다. 이것들은 비싼 대가를 치르고 배우게 된 교훈이었지만, 이제는 양식 가두리를 반드시 어류 폐기물을 제거할 수 있는 물의 흐름이 좋은 장소에 설치하도록 하는 더 엄격한 규제들이 시행되고 있다. 이것은 섭취되지 않은 먹이의 전반적인 양을 줄이는 다른 방법들에 더하여, 수산 양식이 자신의 행위를 깨끗이 청소하는 데 도움이 되어왔다.

● 지문분석

During the early stages / when the aquaculture industry was rapidly expanding, / mistakes were made / and these were costly / both in terms of direct losses / and in respect of the industry's image.
초기 단계 동안 / 양식 산업이 빠르게 확장하는 / 실수가 만들어졌다 / 그리고 이러한 것들은 대가가 컸다 / 직접적 손실 면에서 / 그리고 산업의 이미지 측면에서

High-density rearing / led to outbreaks of infectious diseases / that in some cases / devastated not just the caged fish, / but local wild fish populations too.
높은 밀도의 사육은 / 감염성 질병의 발발을 야기했다 / 몇몇 경우에 / 가두리에 있는 물고기를 황폐화하기 할 뿐만 아니라 / 지역의 야생 어류의 개체군도

[The negative impact / on local wildlife / inhabiting areas / close to the fish farms] / continues to be an ongoing public relations problem / for the industry.
부정적 영향은 / 지역 야생동물에 대한 / 지역에 사는 / 양식장 가까이에 / 지속적인 대민 관계의 문제가 계속 된다 / 산업에 대한

Furthermore, / [a general lack of knowledge and insufficient care / being taken / when fish pens were initially constructed] / meant / that [pollution / from excess feed and fish waste] / created huge barren underwater deserts.
게다가 / 일반적 지식의 부족과 불충분한 관리는 / 행해진 / 물고기 가두리가 처음에 구축되었을 때 / 의미했다 / 오염은 / 과잉 사료와 어류 폐기물로부터의 / 거대한 불모의 해저 사막을 만들었다

These were costly lessons / to learn, / but now stricter regulations / are in place to ensure / that fish pens are placed in sites / where there is good water flow / to remove fish waste.
이러한 것은 비용이 드는 교훈이었다 / 배우게 된 / 하지만 지금 더 엄격한 규제가 / 시행되고 있다 / 물고기 가두리가 지역에 설치되어야

한다는 / 좋은 물의 흐름이 있는 / 어류의 폐기물을 제거할 정도로
This, / in addition to other methods / that decrease the overall amount of uneaten food, / has helped / aquaculture to clean up its act.
이것은 / 다른 방법과 더불어 / 전반적인 섭취되지 않은 먹이의 양을 감소시키는 / 도와왔다 / 수산 양식이 그 행위를 깨끗이 하도록

● 해설

6. 다음 글의 밑줄 친 부분 중, 어법상 틀린 것은?
① devastated: that절의 동사 자리로 내용상 과거시제이니 과거 동사 devastated는 적절하지.
② close: 앞에 있는 area를 수식하는 형용사로 앞에 being 혹은 which is 가 생략되어 있어.
❸ meaning → meant: 문장의 주어가 a general lack of knowledge and insufficient care이고 뒤에서 being taken when fish pens were initially constructed가 수식하는 구조지. 본동사가 필요하니까 시제를 맞추어 meant로 바꾸어야 해.
④ where: 뒤에 오는 문장이 완전한 문장이며, 앞에 있는 장소 명사 sites 를 수식하고 있어.
⑤ has: 문장의 주어는 This로 주어와 동사 사이에 in addition ~ uneaten food의 삽입이 이루어져 있어. 주어가 This이므로 단수 동사 has는 적절하지.

● 중요 포인트

복합적 구조로 길어진 주어

[The negative impact on local wildlife inhabiting areas close to the fish farms] continues to be an ongoing public relations problem for the industry.

7. ④

● 전체 해석

'용기'라는 말이 '심장'을 뜻하는 라틴어의 'cor'에서 파생되었다는 것을 기억한다면, 그 말은 추가되는 의미를 지닌다. 사전은 용기를 '불찬성이나, 적의, 또는 경멸을 유발할 수도 있는 올바른 행동의 과정을 추구하게 되는 특질'로 정의한다. 300년보다 이전에 La Rochefoucauld는 그가 '완전한 용기는 모든 사람 앞에서 당신이 할 수 있는 것을 아무도 보지 않는 데서 하는 것이다'라고 말했을 때 한 걸음 더 나갔다. 무관심이나 반대에 직면하여 도덕적 용기를 보여주기는 쉽지 않다. 그러나 진리를 위한 진심 어린 입장을 취하는 것에 대담한 사람들은 종종 그들의 기대를 능가하는 결과를 성취한다. 반면에, 마지못해 하는 개인들은 그것이 그들 자신의 이익과 연관이 있을 때조차도 용기가 두드러지지 않는다. 모든 상황에서 용감하게 되는 것은 강한 결단력을 필요로 한다.

● 지문분석

The word 'courage' / takes on added meaning / if you keep in mind / that it is derived from the Latin word 'cor' / meaning 'heart.'
'용기'라는 단어는 / 추가된 의미를 지닌다 / 만약 당신이 명심한다면 / 그것은 라틴어 'cor'에서 유래한다는 것을 / 심장을 의미하는

The dictionary defines courage / as a 'quality / which enables / one to pursue a right course of action, / through which one may provoke / disapproval, hostility, or contempt.'
사전은 용기를 정의한다 / 특질로 / 가능케 하는 / 사람이 올바른 행동의 경로를 추구하는 것을 / 사람이 유발할 수도 있는 / 부동의, 적대, 혹은 경멸을

Over 300 years ago / La Rochefoucauld went a step further / when he said: / "Perfect courage / is to do unwitnessed / what we should be capable of doing / before all men."
300년보다 이전에 / La Rochefoucauld는 한 발짝 더 나아갔다 / 그가 말했을 때 / 완벽한 용기란 / 아무도 보지 않는 데서 하는 것이다 / 우리가 할 수 있어야만 하는 것을 / 모든 사람 앞에서

It is not easy / to show moral courage / in the face of either indifference or opposition.
쉽지 않다 / 도덕적 용기를 보여주는 것이 / 무관심이나 반대에 직면하여

But [persons / who are daring / in taking a wholehearted stand / for truth] / often achieve results / that surpass their expectations.
하지만 사람들은 / 대담한 / 진심 어린 자세를 취하는 것에 / 진실을 위해 / 종종 결과를 얻는다 / 그들의 기대를 능가하는

On the other hand, / halfhearted individuals / are seldom distinguished / for courage / even when it involves their own welfare.
반면에 / 마지못해 하는 사람들은 / 좀처럼 두드러지지 않는다 / 용기를 위해 / 심지어 그것이 그들 자신의 이익과 연관있을 때 조차도

[To be courageous / under all circumstances] / requires strong determination.
용기가 있는 것은 / 모든 환경 아래에서 / 강한 결단을 요구한다

● 해설

7. 다음 글의 밑줄 친 부분 중, 어법상 틀린 것은?
① meaning: 앞에 있는 명사 the Latin word 'cor'를 수식하며, 뒤에 목적어가 있으므로 현재분사 meaning이 적절해.
② which: 앞에 있는 quality를 수식하므로 관계사 which는 적절하지.
③ to show: 가주어 It에 해당하는 진주어가 필요하므로 to show는 적절해.
❹ achieving → achieve: 주어인 persons가 뒤에 오는 관계사절 who ~ for truth의 수식을 받고 있어. 본동사가 필요하므로 분사 achieving이 아닌 achieve가 와야 해.
⑤ their: 앞에 있는 halfhearted individuals를 의미하므로 복수 대명사 their은 적절해.

● 중요 포인트

관계대명사의 수식을 받는 주어

But [persons who are daring in taking a wholehearted stand for truth] often achieve results that surpass their expectations.

8. ③

고 추천 링크의

● 전체 해석

인터넷과 통신 기술은 선진사회에 있는 젊은이들의 사회생활에서 점점 더 큰 역할을 수행한다. 청소년들은 대부분 소통하기 위해 인터넷을 사용하면서 빠르게 과학기술에 몰두해 왔다. 젊은이들은 휴대전화를 생활에 꼭 필요한 필수품으로 다루고 친구들과 소통하기 위해 문자 메시지를 사용하기를 보통 선호한다. 젊은이들은 소셜 네트워킹 웹 사이트에도 점점 더 많이 접속한다. 과학기술과 인터넷이 젊은이들에게 친숙한 수단이기에, 그들이 이 정보원에서 도움을 구할 것이라는 것은 논리적이다. 이것은 젊은이들을 위한 치료법 정보를 제공하는 웹 사이트의 증가에서 증명되었다. 많은 수의 '젊은이 친화적인' 정신 건강 웹 사이트들이 개발되어 왔다. 제공되는 정보는 '자주 묻는 질문', 자료표, 추천 링크의 형태를 자주 띤다. 그러므로 젊은이들에게 온라인 상담을 제공해주는 것은 논리적으로 보일 것이다.

● 지문분석

The Internet and communication technologies / play an ever-increasing role / in the social lives / of young people in developed societies.
인터넷과 통신 기술은 / 점점 큰 역할을 하고 있다 / 사회적 삶에서 / 선진사회에서의 젊은이들의

Adolescents have been quick / to immerse themselves in technology / with most using the Internet / to communicate.
청소년들은 빠르게 해오고 있다 / 그들 자신을 기술에 몰두하는 것을 / 대부분 인터넷을 사용하면서 / 소통하기 위해서

Young people treat the mobile phone / as an essential necessity of life / and often prefer to use text messages / to communicate with their friends.
젊은 사람들은 휴대폰을 다룬다 / 삶에서 필수품으로 / 그리고 종종 문자메시지 사용을 선호한다 / 그들의 친구들과 소통하기 위해서

Young people also increasingly access / social networking websites.
젊은 사람들은 또한 점점 접속한다 / 소셜 네트워킹 웹사이트에

As technology and the Internet / are a familiar resource / for young people, / it is logical / that they would seek assistance / from this source.
기술과 인터넷이 / 친숙한 자원이 됨에 따라 / 젊은이들에게 / 논리적이다 / 그들이 도움을 구하는 것이 / 이러한 자원으로부터

This has been shown / by the increase in websites / that provide therapeutic information / for young people.
이것은 보여지고 있다 / 웹 사이트의 증가에 의해서 / 치료 정보를 제공하는 / 젊은 사람들을 위한

A number of 'youth friendly' mental health websites / have been developed.
많은 젊은이 친화적 정신 건강 웹 사이트들은 / 개발되어 왔다

[The information / presented] / often takes the form / of Frequently Asked Questions, fact sheets and suggested links.
정보는 / 제공된 / 종종 형태를 띤다 / 자주 묻는 질문, 자료표, 그리

It would seem, therefore, logical / to provide online counselling / for young people.
그래서 논리적일 수도 있다 / 온라인 상담을 제공하는 것이 / 젊은 사람들에게

● 해설

8. 다음 글의 밑줄 친 부분 중, 어법상 틀린 것은?

① using: 동시상황을 표현하는 'with + 명사 + 분사' 구문이야. 뒤에 목적어가 나오므로 현재분사 using이 와야 해.
② increasingly: 동사 access를 수식하므로 부사인 increasingly가 와야겠지.
❸ what → that: 뒤에 완전한 문장이 오므로 what을 쓸 수가 없어. 가주어 it이 대신하는 진주어 이끌 수 있는 접속사 that이 필요하지.
④ have: 주어는 'youth friendly' mental health websites이므로 복수 동사 have가 적절해.
⑤ presented: 앞에 있는 주어 The information을 수식하며, 뒤에 목적어가 없으므로 과거분사인 presented가 적절해.

● 중요 포인트

가주어-진주어 구문

❶ As technology and the Internet are a familiar resource for young people, it is logical that they would seek assistance from this source.
(가주어) (진주어)

❷ It would seem, therefore, logical to provide online counselling for young people.
(가주어) (진주어)

4 단계 혼공 개념 마무리 p.41

1. 20세기에 냉장고에서부터 고성능 오븐, 신선한 재료를 전 세계에 실어 나르는 항공 수송에 이르기까지 기술의 진보는 제빵과 페이스트리 만드는 것에 헤아릴 수 없을 정도로 기여했다.

2. 다시 말해, 보다 빠른 음악이 사람들로 하여금 더 빨리 음식을 먹도록 하는 것과 꼭 마찬가지로 보다 빠른 음악은 사람들로 하여금 계속 반복되는 음악 구조에 정신적, 신체적으로 맞물리면서 더 빠른 속도로 운전하게 한다는 것이다.

3. 방문하는 자녀들은 부모님이나 조부모님이 예전에 어떠했는지를 기억하고 그들의 무능함에 의기소침해할 수밖에 없다.

4. 그 물체 밖에 있는 어떤 힘이 관련 있을지도 모른다는 가능성에 주의를 기울이지 않고, 두 경우 모두 초점은 오로지 그 물체에 있다.

5. 더욱이, 수산 양식용 가두리가 처음 지어졌을 때 일반적인 지식의 부족과 불충분하게 행해지던 관리는 초과 사료와 어류 폐기물로부터 발생하는 오염이 거대한 불모의 해저 사막을 만들어냈다는 것을 의미했다.

6. 사전은 용기를 '불찬성이나, 적의, 또는 경멸을 유발할 수도 있는 올바른 행동의 과정을 추구하게 되는 특질'로 정의한다.

7. 그러나 중국인은 세계를 계속적으로 상호 작용하는 물질로 구성된 것으로 보았고, 그래서 그것을 이해하고자 하는 그들의 시도는 그들로 하여금 전체적인 '장(場)', 즉 전체로서의 맥락이나 환경의 복잡성에 중점을 두도록 했다.

 혼공 04일차 **어휘 1(선택형)**

③ 단계 고난도 문항 요리하기   p.47

● 정답

1. ⑤ **2.** ① **3.** ② **4.** ③ **5.** ⑤ **6.** ④ **7.** ② **8.** ①

1. ⑤

● 전체 해석

일부 코치들은, 정신 능력 훈련(MST)이 고도로 숙련된 선수들의 기량을 완벽하게 하는 데만 도움이 될 수 있다고 잘못 믿고 있다. 그 결과, 그들은 자신이 엘리트 선수를 지도하고 있지 않으므로 정신 능력 훈련이 덜 중요하다고 합리화하면서 정신 능력 훈련을 피한다. 높은 경쟁 수준에서 정신 능력이 점점 더 중요해지고 있다는 것은 사실이다. 선수들이 경쟁의 사다리를 올라갈수록 신체 능력의 측면에서는 더 동질적이 된다. 사실상 높은 경쟁 수준에서는 모든 선수가 성공할 수 있는 신체 능력을 갖추고 있다. 결과적으로 정신적 요인에서의 어떠한 작은 차이라 하더라도 경기력의 결과를 결정하는 데 지대한 역할을 할 수 있다. 그러나 우리는 개인의 성장과 경기력이, 정신 능력 훈련을 받지 않는 선수에서보다는 정신 능력 훈련을 받는 어리고 성장 중인 선수에게서 더 빠르게 진보할 것이라고 예상할 수 있다. 사실상, 정신 능력 훈련을 도입하기 위한 최적의 시간은, 선수들이 처음 운동을 시작할 때일지도 모른다. 선수생활의 초기에 정신 능력 훈련을 도입하는 것은, 그들이 잠재 능력의 최고치까지 발달하도록 도울 기초를 놓을 수도 있다.

● 지문분석

Some coaches erroneously believe / that mental skills training (MST) / can only help perfect the performance / of highly skilled competitors.
일부 코치들은 잘못 믿고 있다 / 정신 능력 훈련이 / 오직 수행을 완벽하게 하는 데 도움을 줄 수 있다고 / 매우 숙련된 선수들의

As a result, / they shy away from MST, / rationalizing /
                                    분사구문 〈동시상황〉 '합리화하면서'
that because they are not coaching elite athletes, / mental skills training is less important.
결과적으로 / 그들은 MST를 피하고 있다 / 합리화하면서 / 그들은 엘리트 선수들을 코칭하고 있지 않기 때문에 / 정신 능력 훈련은 덜 중요하다고

It is true / that mental skills become increasingly
가주어   진주어
important / at high levels of competition.

사실이다 / 정신 능력이 점차 중요해지고 있다는 것은 / 높은 수준의 경쟁에서는

As athletes move up / the competitive ladder, / they become more homogeneous / in terms of physical skills.
선수들이 올라감에 따라 / 경쟁의 사다리를 / 그들은 더욱 동질해진다 / 신체적 능력에 있어서는

In fact, / at high levels of competition, / all athletes have the physical skills / to be successful.
사실 / 높은 수준의 경쟁에서는 / 모든 선수들은 신체적 능력을 가진다 / 성공할 수 있는

Consequently, / [any small difference in mental factors]
                                                   S
/ can play a huge role / in determining performance outcomes.
결과적으로 / 정신적 요인에서의 어떠한 작은 차이점은 / 커다란 역할을 할 수 있다 / 수행의 결과를 결정짓는

However, / we can anticipate / that personal growth and performance / will progress faster / in young, developing athletes / who are given mental skills training / than in athletes / not exposed to MST.
하지만 / 우리는 기대할 수 있다 / 개인의 성장과 수행은 / 더 빠르게 발전할 것이라고 / 어리고 발전 중인 선수들에게서 / 정신 능력 훈련을 받은 / 선수들에게서보다 / MST에 노출되지 않은

In fact, / [the optimal time for introducing MST] / may be / when athletes are first beginning their sport.
                                            V
사실 / MST를 도입하는 최적의 시간은 / 일 것이다 / 선수들이 처음에 그들의 스포츠를 시작하는 때

[Introducing MST / early in athletes' careers] / may lay
                    S   V
the foundation / that will help them / develop to their full potential.
MST를 도입하는 것은 / 운동 선수의 커리어 초기에 / 기초를 놓을 지도 모른다 / 그들을 도울 수 있는 / 그들의 완전한 잠재력을 발전시키도록

● 해설

1. (A), (B), (C)의 각 네모 안에서 문맥에 맞는 낱말로 가장 적절한 것은?
(A) rationalizing: 일부 코치들이 지도하는 선수들의 정신 능력 훈련을 피하는 것은 그러한 훈련이 고도로 숙련된 선수들에게만 도움이 될 뿐이지, 자신의 선수들에게는 덜 중요하다고 합리화(rationalize)하기 때문이야. deny는 '부정하다'라는 의미지.
(B) mental: 높은 경쟁 수준에서는 모든 선수가 성공할 수 있는 신체 능력을 갖추고 있으므로, 결국 수행의 결과를 결정하는 것은 정신적(mental) 요인이겠지. physical은 '신체적인'을 의미해.
(C) early: 앞에서 어리고 발전 중인 선수들에게 개인적 성장이 더 빠를 것이라고 이야기하고 있어. 즉, 정신 능력 훈련을 도입하기 위한 최적의 시간은 선수들이 처음 운동을 시작할 때일지도 모른다고 언급하고 있지. 따라서 '초기에'라는 뜻의 early가 적절해. later는 '나중에'를 의미하지.

● 중요 포인트

동명사 주어

[Introducing MST early in athletes' careers] may lay the
S   동명사를 분사로 해석하면 안됨
foundation that will help them / develop to their full potential.

2. ①

● 전체 해석

우리 중에서 물질 중심적이지 않다고 주장하는 사람들조차도 특정한 옷에 대한 애착을 형성하지 않을 수 없게 된다. 옛날 노래에 나오는 구절처럼 옷은 소중한 추억과 가슴 아픈 기억을 모두 생각나게 할 수 있다. 닳아서 얇아진 드레스는 여러 해 동안 입지 않았더라도 벽장 뒤편에 걸려 있을 수 있는데, 그 이유는 그 옷에 남아있는 옅은 소나무 향이 바로 어떤 사람의 열여섯 살 여름의 모든 잔존물이기 때문이다. 실용성이 떨어지는 흰색 스카프는 그것의 소유자에게 한때 우아함에 대한 기대였기 때문에 기증품 자루에 들어가는 마지막 순간에 빼내어질 수 있다. 그리고 찢어진 티셔츠는 한때 그 위에 쓰여진 록밴드 이름이 희미해진 지 오래된 후에도 걸레통에서 꺼내어질 수 있다. 화석이 고고학자들에게 시간을 나타내는 것과 같은 방식으로 옷은 우리에게 개인의 이력을 보여준다.

● 지문분석

Even [those of us / who claim not to be materialistic] / can't help but form / attachments to certain clothes.
심지어 우리 중에서 / 물질 중심적이지 않다고 주장하는 / 형성하지 않을 수 없다 / 특정한 형태의 옷에 대한 애착을
(cannot help but 동사원형: '~하지 않을 수 없다' = cannot help ~ing)

Like fragments / from old songs, / clothes can evoke / both cherished and painful memories.
구절처럼 / 옛 노래의 / 옷들은 불러일으킬 수 있다 / 소중하고 고통스런 기억 모두를

A worn-thin dress / may hang in the back of a closet / even though it hasn't been worn / in years / because [the faint scent of pine] / that lingers on it / is all that remains / of someone's sixteenth summer.
닳아서 얇아진 드레스는 / 옷장 뒤편에 걸려있을 수도 있다 / 비록 그것을 입지 않았더라도 / 여러 해 동안 / 왜냐하면 희미한 소나무 향이 / 그것에 남아있는 / 모든 잔여물이기 때문에 / 누군가의 16번째 여름의

An impractical white scarf / might be pulled out of a donation bag / at the last minute / because of the promise of elegance / it once held for its owner.
비실용적인 하얀색 스카프는 / 기부 자루에서 빼내질지도 모른다 / 마지막 순간에 / 우아함에 대한 약속 때문에 / 그것이 한때 소유자를 위해 간직했던

And a ripped T-shirt / might be rescued from the dust rag bin / long after / [the name of the rock band / once written across it] / has faded.
그리고 찢어진 티셔츠는 / 걸레통에서 구해질 지도 모른다 / 오랜 후에도 / 락밴드의 이름이 / 한 때 그 위에 쓰여진 / 희미해진

Clothes document personal history / for us / the same way / that fossils chart time / for archaeologists.
옷은 개인의 기록을 기록한다 / 우리를 위해 / 같은 방식으로 / 화석이 시간을 나타내는 것과 / 고고학자들에게

● 해설

2. (A), (B), (C)의 각 네모 안에서 문맥에 맞는 낱말로 가장 적절한 것은?
(A) evoke: 옷이 소중한 추억과 가슴 아픈 기억을 '생각나게 할 수 있다'라는 의미가 되어야 하므로, evoke((기억·감정을) 불러일으키다)가 적절하지. erase는 '(마음에서) 지우다, 잊어버리다'를 의미해.
(B) impractical: 흰색 스카프가 그것을 소유한 사람에게 한때 우아함의 약속이었다는 내용이 되어야 하므로, impractical(비실용적인)이 적절해. brand-new는 '아주 새로운'을 의미하지.
(C) rescued: 찢어진 티셔츠가 한때 그 위에 쓰여진 록밴드 이름이 희미해진 후에도 걸레통에서 '구해질 수' 있다는 내용이 되어야 하므로, rescued가 적절하지. forget은 '잊다, 소홀히 하다'를 의미해.

● 중요 포인트

복잡한 주어 구문: 주어 + 전치사구 + 과거분사

And a ripped T-shirt might be rescued from the dust rag bin long after [the name of the rock band once written across it] has faded.

3. ②

● 전체 해석

음식을 선택하는 데 있어서 젊은 사람들은 특히 또래의 영향에 취약하다. 십대의 소녀는 상추 샐러드가 그녀의 친구들이 먹는 것이기 때문에 나중에 배가 고플지라도 점심으로 상추 샐러드만 먹을지도 모른다. 레슬링 팀을 만들고 싶어 하는 호리호리한 소년은 자기 학교의 레슬링 선수들처럼 '몸집을 불리기' 위해 판에 박힌 듯이 자기 접시를 탄수화물과 단백질이 많은 음식으로 가득 채울지 모른다. 과체중의 십대는 주변에 친구들이 있을 때는 적당히 먹을지 모르지만, 혼자 있게 되면 많은 양을 게걸스럽게 먹게 된다. 음식과 관련된 압박이 의도적으로 강요된 것이든 혹은 그렇지 않든 또래들로부터 그러한 압박에서 완전히 자유로운 젊은 사람들은 거의 없다.

● 지문분석

When it comes to food choices, / young people are particularly vulnerable / to peer influences.
(when it comes to + 명사: '~에 대하여')
음식 선택에 대해서 / 젊은이들은 특히나 취약하다 / 또래의 영향에

A teenage girl / may eat nothing but a lettuce salad / for lunch, / even though she will become hungry later, / because that is what her friends are eating.
(=only)
십대 소녀는 / 오직 상추 샐러드만 먹을 수도 있다 / 점심으로 / 비록 그녀가 나중에 배가 고파지더라도 / 왜냐하면 그것은 그녀의 친구들이 먹고 있는 것이니까

[A slim boy / who hopes to make the wrestling team] / may routinely overload his plate with foods / that are dense in carbohydrates and proteins / to 'bulk up' / like the wrestlers of his school.
마른 소년은 / 레슬링 팀을 만들고 싶어하는 / 일상적으로 음식으로 그의 접시를 가득 채울지도 모른다 / 탄수화물과 단백질로 가득한 / 몸을 불리기 위해서 / 학교의 레슬링 선수들처럼

An overweight teen may eat moderately / while around his
(while he is around his friends)

friends / but then devour huge portions / when alone.
when he is alone
과체중인 십대는 적절하게 먹지도 모른다 / 그의 친구들 주변에 있
는 동안에는 / 하지만 그러고 나서 게걸스럽게 엄청난 양을 먹을 것
이다 / 혼자 있을 때에는

Few young people are completely free / of food-related
pressures from peers, / whether or not these pressures are
imposed intentionally.
어떠한 젊은 사람들도 완벽하게 자유롭지 못하다 / 음식과 관련된 또
래로 부터의 압박에서 / 이러한 압박이 의도적으로 부여되든 아니든

● 해설

3. (A), (B), (C)의 각 네모 안에서 문맥에 맞는 낱말로 가장 적절한 것은?
(A) vulnerable: 전체적으로 '또래의 영향'을 많이 받는다는 내용이므로
'또래의 영향에 취약한'이라는 의미가 자연스럽지. 따라서 vulnerable(취
약한)이 적절해. immune은 '면역의'를 의미하지.
(B) dense: 레슬링 선수처럼 몸집을 불려야하므로 내용상 '탄수화물과 단
백질이 많은 음식'이라는 의미를 가져야 해. 따라서 dense(밀집한)가 적
절해. deficient는 '모자라는, 불충분한'을 의미하지.
(C) moderately: 친구들이랑 있을 때는 그들로부터 압박을 받으니 상대적
으로 적게 먹어야겠지? 이에 맞는 어휘는 moderately(적당히)가 적절해.
greedily는 '게걸스레, 욕심내어'를 의미해.

● 중요 포인트

접속사 + 전치사구, 형용사

접속사 뒤에는 문장이 와야 하는데, 전치사구나 형용사가 단독으로
올 수도 있어. 그 이유는 시간의 부사절에서는 '주어와 be동사'가 종
종 생략되기도 하거든. 아니면 being이 생략된 분사구문으로 봐도
돼.

An overweight teen may eat moderately while around
his friends but then devour huge portions when alone.
while he is around his friends when he is alone

4. ③

● 전체 해석

Atitlá Giant Grebe는 훨씬 더 널리 퍼져 있던 더 작은 Piedbilled Grebe(얼
룩부리논병아리)에서 진화한 날지 못하는 큰 새였다. 1965년 무렵에는
Atitlá 호수에 약 80마리만이 남아 있었다. 한 가지 직접적인 원인은 알아내
기 매우 쉬웠는데, 현지의 인간들이 맹렬한 속도로 갈대밭을 베어 넘어뜨
리는 것이었다. 이런 파괴는 빠르게 성장하는 매트 제조 산업의 필요에 의
해 추진되었다. 그러나 다른 문제들이 있었다. 한 미국 항공사가 그 호수를
낚시꾼들의 관광지로 개발하는 데 강한 관심을 보였다. 하지만 이 생각에
큰 문제가 있었는데, 그 호수에는 적절한 스포츠용(낚시용) 물고기가 없었
다! 이런 다소 분명한 결함을 보충하기 위해 Large-mouthed Bass(큰입농
어)라 불리는 특별히 선택된 물고기 종이 도입되었다. 그 도입된 개체는 즉
각 그 호수에 사는 게와 작은 물고기에게 관심을 돌렸고, 이리하여 몇 마리
안 남은 논병아리와 먹이를 놓고 경쟁하였다. 또한, 가끔 그들(큰입농어)
이 얼룩말 줄무늬가 있는 Atitlá Giant Grebe 새끼들을 게걸스럽게 먹어치
웠다는 데 의심의 여지가 거의 없다.

● 지문분석

The Atitlán Giant Grebe was a large, flightless bird / that
had evolved / from the much more widespread and smaller
Pied-billed Grebe.
Atitlán Giant Grebe는 커다란 날지 못하는 새였다 / 진화했던 / 훨씬
더 널리 퍼지고 더 작은 Pied-billed Grebe(얼룩부리논병아리)로부터
By 1965 / there were only around 80 birds / left on Lake
Atitlán.
1965년까지 / 겨우 약 80마리의 새가 있었다 / Atitlán 호수에 남겨진
One immediate reason / was easy enough to spot: / the
local human population / was cutting down the reed beds /
at a furious rate.
한 가지 직접적인 이유는 / 알아내기가 충분히 쉬웠다 / 그 지역의 사
람들이 / 갈대밭을 베어버리고 있었다 / 맹렬한 속도로
This destruction was driven / by the needs / of a fast
growing mat-making industry.
이러한 파괴는 추진되었다 / 필요에 의해서 / 빠르게 성장하는 매트
제조 산업의
But there were other problems.
하지만 다른 문제가 있었다
An American airline was intent / on developing the lake /
as a tourist destination for fishermen.
한 미국의 항공사가 관심을 보였다 / 그 호수를 개발하는 데 / 낚시꾼
들을 위한 관광지로
However, / there was a major problem with this idea: /
the lake lacked any suitable sporting fish!
하지만 / 이 생각에는 주된 문제가 있었다 / 호수는 어떠한 적절한 스
포츠용 물고기가 부족했다
To compensate for this rather obvious defect, / [a specially
selected species of fish / called the Large-mouthed Bass] /
was introduced.
S
이 다소 명백한 결점을 보완하기 위해서 / 특별히 선택된 물고기 종
이 / 큰입농어라고 불리는 / 도입되었다
The introduced individuals / immediately turned their
attentions / to the crabs and small fish / that lived in the
lake, / thus competing with the few remaining grebes / for
food.
ㄴ 분사구문, '그리고 경쟁하게 되었다'
도입된 각 개체들은 / 즉각적으로 그들의 관심을 돌렸다 / 게와 작은
물고기에 / 그 호수에 살고 있었던 / 그래서 소수의 남아있는 논병아
리들과 경쟁하게 되었다 / 먹이를 두고
There is also little doubt / that they sometimes gobbled up
/ the zebra-striped Atitlán Giant Grebe's chicks.
또한 의심의 여지가 없다 / 그들이 때때로 먹어치웠다는 / 얼룩말 줄
무늬가 있는 Atitlán Giant Grebe의 새끼들을

● 해설

4. (A), (B), (C)의 각 네모 안에서 문맥에 맞는 낱말로 가장 적절한 것은?
(A) destruction: 인간들이 맹렬한 속도로 갈대밭을 베어버리는 행
위를 의미하는 표현이 와야 하므로 destruction(파괴)이 적절하지.
accommodation은 '적응, 화해'를 의미해.

(B) lacked: 관광지로서 호수가 가지고 있는 결함을 보충하기 위해 큰입
농어를 도입했다고 하고 있으므로 그 호수에는 스포츠용 물고기가 없었
다는 것을 알 수 있어. 따라서 lacked(부족했다)가 적절하지. support는
'지지, 지원하다'를 의미해.
(C) competing: 갑작스럽게 큰입농어가 호수에 들어왔으니 기존의 Atitlá
Giant Grebe와 경쟁(competing)을 해야겠지. cooperate는 '협력하다'를
의미해.

● 중요 포인트

과거분사의 명사 수식

❶ By 1965 there were only around 80 birds left on Lake
Atitlán.

❷ To compensate for this rather obvious defect, [a
specially selected species of fish called the Large-
mouthed Bass] was introduced.

5. ⑤

● 전체 해석

2001년에 Wayne 주립대학의 연구자들은 한 무리의 대학생 지원자들에게
20분간 러닝머신, 고정 자전거, 스테퍼의 세 가지 운동 기구에서 각각 자
신이 선택한 속도로 운동할 것을 요청했다. 심박 수, 산소 소모량과 인지된
운동 강도가 세 가지 운동이 이루어지는 내내 측정되었다. 연구자들은 실
험 대상자들이 세 가지 활동 모두에서 무의식적으로 상대적으로 동일한 생
리학적 강도를 목표로 할 것으로 예상했다. 어쩌면 그들은 어떤 기계를 사
용하는지와 관계없이 무의식적으로 최대 심박 수의 65퍼센트로 운동할 것
이었다. 혹은 어쩌면 그들은 세 가지 운동 모두에서 최대 산소 소모 속도의
70퍼센트라는 리듬에 본능적으로 자리 잡을 것이었다. 그러나 일어난 일은
그렇지 않았다. 사실, 세 가지 종목에서 심박 수와 산소 소모량 측정에서
일관성이 없었다. 대신, 실험 대상자들이 러닝머신, 자전거, 그리고 스테퍼
에서 같은 수준의 인지된 운동 강도를 선택했다는 것이 밝혀졌다.

● 지문분석

In 2001, / researchers at Wayne State University / asked
a group of college volunteers / to exercise for twenty
minutes / at a self-selected pace / on each of three
machines: a treadmill, a stationary bike, and a stair
climber.
2001년에 / Wayne 주립대학의 연구원들은 / 한 그룹의 대학생 지원
자들에게 요구했다 / 20분 동안 운동하라고 / 자신이 선택한 속도로 /
3개의 운동 기구에서 각각 / 러닝머신, 고정 자전거, 그리고 스테퍼의
[Measurements] / of heart rate, oxygen consumption,
and perceived effort] / were taken / throughout all three
workouts.
측정은 / 심장 박동수, 산소 소모량, 그리고 인지된 운동 강도의 / 이
루어졌다 / 3가지 모든 운동 내내
The researchers expected to find / that the subjects
unconsciously targeted / the same relative physiological
intensity / in each activity.

연구원들은 찾기를 기대했다 / 피실험자들이 무의식적으로 목표로
할 것으로 / 같은 상대적인 생리학적 강도를 / 각각의 활동에서
Perhaps they would automatically exercise / at 65 percent
of their maximum heart rate / regardless of which machine
they were using.
아마도 그들은 자동적으로 운동을 할 것이었다 / 최대 심박 수의
65%로 / 어떤 기구를 사용하는지와 상관없이
Or maybe they would instinctively settle into rhythm
/ at 70 percent of their maximum rate / of oxygen
consumption / in all three workouts.
아니면 아마도 그들은 본능적으로 리듬에 자리를 잡을 것이었다 / 최
대 속도의 70%에서 / 산소 소모량의 / 세 가지 모든 운동에서
But that's not what happened.
하지만 그것은 일어나지 않았다
There was, in fact, no consistency / in measurements
of heart rate and oxygen consumption / across the three
disciplines.
사실은 일관성이 없었다 / 심박 수와 산소 소모량의 측정에서 / 세 가
지 종목에서
Instead, / the subjects were found / to have chosen the
same level of perceived effort / on the treadmill, the bike,
and the stair climber.
대신에 / 피실험자들은 밝혀졌다 / 같은 수의 인지된 노력을 선택했
었다는 것이 / 러닝머신, 자전거, 그리고 스테퍼에서

● 해설

5. (A), (B), (C)의 각 네모 안에서 문맥에 맞는 낱말로 가장 적절한 것은?
(A) self-selected: 지문의 마지막에서 심박 수와 산소 소모량에 일관성이
없었다는 것으로 보아 미리 정해진 속도가 아니라 자기가 선택한(self-
selected) 속도로 운동을 했음을 알 수 있어. preset은 '미리 맞춰진'을 의
미해.
(B) automatically: 앞에서 unconsciously(무의식적으로), 그리고 아래에
instinctively(본능적으로)와 같은 의미가 되어야 하니, automatically(자동
적으로)가 적절하지. intentionally는 '의도적으로'를 의미해.
(C) consistency: 실험자가 예측한 것과 같은 일이 일어나지 않았다고 하
고 있어. 따라서 심박 수와 산소 소모량에 일관성이 없어야 하겠지(no
consistency). 앞에 부정어가 있으니 선택지에는 부정어를 넣어서 같이
봐야 해. variation은 '변화'를 의미해.

● 중요 포인트

5형식 수동태 구문

5형식의 수동태 구문에서는 동사 뒤에 목적 보어가 온다는 것을 고
려해야 해.

Instead, / the subjects were found / to have chosen the
same level of perceived effort on the treadmill, the bike,
and the stair climber.

6. ④

● 전체 해석

교사가 홀로 일을 할 때 그들은 오직 한 쌍의 눈, 즉 자기 자신의 눈으로 세상을 보는 경향이 있다. 이런저런 과목이나 혹은 수업을 가르치는 데 있어서 더 성공적일 수 있는 누군가가 '같은 건물 혹은 같은 지역' 어딘가에 있을 수 있다는 사실을, 문을 닫고 거의 혼자서 학교의 연간 행사 계획표를 실천해 나가는 교사는 이해하지 못한다. 일을 더 잘하거나 최소한 다르게 하는 사람들을 벤치마킹할 수 있게 해주는 과정이 없는 상태에서, 교사들은 하나의 시각, 즉 자신의 시각만을 갖게 된다. 나는 사회 과학 분야에 속한 다양한 과목을 가르쳤는데 동일한 과목을 가르치는 나의 동료들이 어떻게 가르치는지에 대해 아는 것이 거의 없었다. 의견이나 정보를 교환하고, 공동 평가를 계획하고, 자신이 잘한 것을 공유하기 위해서 정기적으로 만난다는 생각을 우리는 전혀 해보지 않았다. 오히려 우리는 사회 교과 교무실에서 시간이 부족한 것에 대해 불평하면서 그리고 서로 비난하고 책임 전가를 하면서 많은 시간을 보냈다.

● 지문분석

When teachers work in isolation, / they tend to see the world / through one set of eyes / – their own.
교사들이 혼자서 일할 때 / 그들은 세상을 보는 경향이 있다 / 오직 한 쌍의 눈으로 / 자기 자신의

[The fact / that there might be someone / somewhere in the same building or district / who may be more successful / at teaching this or that subject or lesson] / is lost / on teachers / who close the door / and work their way / through the school calendar / virtually alone.
사실은 / 누군가가 있을 수도 있다는 / 같은 건물이나 구역 안 어딘가에 / 더욱 성공적일 지도 모르는 / 이런 저런 과목이나 수업을 가르치는 데 / 사라진다 / 교사들에게서 / 문을 닫는 / 그리고 그들 방식대로 일하는 / 학교 계획표를 따라 / 거의 혼자서

In the absence of a process / that allows them / to benchmark those / who do things better / or at least differently, / teachers are left / with that one perspective / – their own.
과정의 결여 속에서 / 그들을 허용하는 / 사람들을 벤치마킹하는 것을 / 더 잘하는 / 아니면 최소한 다르게 하는 / 교사들은 남겨진다 / 하나의 시각만을 가지고 / 그들 자신만의

I taught various subjects / under the social studies umbrella / and had very little idea / of how my peers / who taught the same subject / did what they did.
나는 다양한 과목을 가르쳤다 / 사회 과학 분야 속에 / 그리고 아는 것이 없었다 / 어떻게 내 동료들이 / 같은 과목을 가르쳤던 / 그들이 했던 것을 했는지

[The idea / of meeting regularly / to compare notes, / plan common assessments, / and share / what we did well] / never occurred to us.
생각들은 / 정기적으로 만나려는 / 노트를 비교하고 / 공통의 평가를 계획하고 / 그리고 공유하려는 / 우리가 잘 했던 것을 / 거의 우리에게는 떠오르지 않았다

Rather, we spent much time / in the social studies office / complaining about a lack of time / and playing the blame game.
오히려 우리는 많은 시간을 보냈다 / 사회 교과 사무실에서 / 부족한 시간에 대해서 불평하고 / 서로 비난하고 책임 전가를 하는 데

● 해설

6. (A), (B), (C)의 각 네모 안에서 문맥에 맞는 낱말로 가장 적절한 것은?
(A) lost: 주변에 더 성공적일 수 있는 다른 교사가 있을 수 있다는 것을 자기 혼자서만 고립되어 연구하고 작업하는 교사는 알지 못하게 된다는 의미가 되어야 하므로 lost가 적절해. based는 '~을 기반으로 하는'을 의미하지.
(B) allows: 바로 앞에 absence라는 부정 의미 어휘가 있지? 일단 (−)라고 생각해야 해. 혼자 고립된 교사를 비판하는(−) 글이니까, 어휘가 있는 부분은 (+)가 되어야 겠지? 그럼 allow와 forbid 중 (+)인 것은 바로 allow야. 내용상 다른 교사를 벤치마킹할 수 있게 해주는 과정이 없는 상태가 되게 하므로 allows가 적절하지. forbid는 '금지하다'를 의미해.
(C) never: 앞에서 언급되는 것들은 다른 사람을 인정하고 다른 의견을 받아들이는 것인데, 현재의 우리(교사)는 그렇지 않다는 거지. 따라서 never가 적절해. mostly는 '주로, 대체로'를 의미해.

● 중요 포인트

너무 복잡한 구문

[The fact / that there might be someone / somewhere in the same building or district / who may be more successful / at teaching this or that subject or lesson] / is lost / on teachers / who close the door / and work their way / through the school calendar / virtually alone.

7. ②

● 전체 해석

서로의 흥미나 관심거리에 대해 이웃과 이야기할 수 없다면 민주주의 체제를 가질 수 없다. 민주주의에 대해 지속적인 관심이 있었던 Thomas Jefferson은 이와 유사한 결론에 이르렀다. 그는 기업에서든, 정치적 지도자들에게서든, 혹은 배타적인 정치 제도에서든 집중된 권력의 위험성을 이해하는 데 있어서 선견지명이 있었다. 시민의 직접적인 참여는 미국 혁명을 가능하게 하고 새로운 공화국에 활력과 미래에 대한 희망을 부여했던 존재였다. 그러한 참여가 없다면 그 공화국은 멸망할 것이다. 결국, 그는 국가가 '(지방 의회 구성단위가 되는) 구'로 세분되어야 할 필요성을 인식했는데, '구'는 그곳에 사는 모든 사람들이 정치적인 과정에 직접 참여할 수 있을 정도로 작은 정치 단위였다. 수도에 있는 각 구의 대표들은 이런 방식으로 조직된 시민들에게 반응해야 할 것이다. 그런 다음 지역적으로 운영되는 활기찬 민주주의 체제는 공화국의 민주적인 삶을 위한 활발한 기본적 단위를 제공할 것이다. 그런 유형의 참여가 있으면, 공화국은 생존하고 번영할 것이다.

● 지문분석

You can't have a democracy / if you can't talk with your neighbors / about matters of mutual interest or concern.

당신은 민주주의를 가질 수 없다 / 만약 당신이 당신의 이웃과 이야기할 수 없다면 / 상호의 흥미나 관심거리에 대해서

[Thomas Jefferson, / who had an enduring interest / in democracy,] / came to a similar conclusion.

토마스 제퍼슨은 / 지속적인 관심을 가졌던 / 민주주의에 대해서 / 비슷한 결론에 도달했다

He was prescient / in understanding the dangers of concentrated power, / whether in corporations or in political leaders / or exclusionary political institutions.

그는 선견지명이 있었다 / 집중화된 권력의 위험성을 이해하는 데 있어서 / 회사에서든 정치 지도자들이든 / 아니면 배타적인 정치 제도에서든

[Direct involvement of citizens] / was what had made the American Revolution possible / and given the new republic / vitality and hope for the future.

시민의 직접적 관여는 / 미국의 혁명을 가능하게 만들었다 / 그리고 새로운 공화국에 주었던 것이다 / 활력과 미래에 대한 희망을

Without that involvement, / the republic would die.

그러한 참여가 없다면 / 공화국은 죽을 것이다

Eventually, he saw a need / for the nation / to be subdivided into "wards" / – political units / so small / that [everyone / living there] / could participate directly in the political process.

so ~ that …: '너무 ~해서 …하다'

결국 그는 필요를 보았다 / 국가는 / 구로 잘게 쪼개져야 할 / 정치적 단위인 / 너무 작아서 / 모든 사람들이 / 그곳에 사는 / 직접적으로 정치 과정에 참여할 수 있는

[The representatives / for each ward in the capital] / would have to be responsive / to citizens / organized in this way.

대표들은 / 수도에 있는 각 구의 / 반응해야 할 것이다 / 시민들에게 / 이런 식으로 조직된

[A vibrant democracy / conducted locally] / would then provide the active basic unit / for the democratic life of the republic.

활기찬 민주주의는 / 지역적으로 운영되는 / 그러면 활발한 기본 단위를 제공할 것이다 / 공화국의 민주주의적 삶을 위한

With that kind of involvement, / the republic might survive and prosper.

그런 종류의 참여가 있다면 / 공화국은 살아남고 번성할지도 모른다

● 해설

7. (A), (B), (C)의 각 네모 안에서 문맥에 맞는 낱말로 가장 적절한 것은?

(A) concentrated: Thomas Jefferson은 시민들이 직접 참여하는 것을 주장했으므로 이와 반대의 의미로 권력을 집중한다는 의미인 concentrated(집중된)가 적절해. limited는 '제한된'을 의미하지.

(B) subdivided: ward(구)로 더 작아져야 한다는 의미이므로 subdivided(세분된)를 써야 해. blended는 '섞인'을 의미하지.

(C) responsive: 수도에 있는 각 구의 대표들은 직접적으로 참여한 시민들의 의견에 귀를 기울여야 하므로 responsive(반응하는)가 적절해. resistant는 '저항하는'을 의미하지.

● 중요 포인트

전치사구의 수식을 받는 주어

[The representatives / for each ward in the capital] / would have to be responsive / to citizens / organized in this way.

8. ①

● 전체 해석

16세기 말에 시작된, 북미에서 식민지를 설립하려는 잉글랜드의 계획은 그릇된 생각에 기반을 두고 있었다. 잉글랜드가 권리를 주장했던 북미 대륙의 지역인 버지니아는 유럽의 지중해 지역과 비슷한 위도에 놓여 있었기 때문에 그 지역과 똑같은 기후를 가질 것이라고 추정되었다. 그 결과, 아메리카 식민지들이 일단 설립되면 올리브와 과일과 같은 지중해의 물품을 공급하게 되어서 유럽 대륙으로부터의 수입품에 대한 잉글랜드의 의존도를 줄일 수 있기를 잉글랜드 국민들은 희망했다. 한 사업 설명서에서는 식민지들이 "프랑스와 스페인의 포도주, 과일, 소금을... 페르시아와 이탈리아의 비단을" 제공해 줄 것이라고 주장했다. 이와 유사하게 풍부한 목재 가 스칸디나비아로부터 목재를 수입할 필요가 없게 해줄 것이었다. 요컨대, 아메리카는 빨리 이익을 낼줄 풍요의 땅이 될 것으로 잘못 기대되었다.

● 지문분석

[England's plan / to establish colonies in North America, / starting in the late sixteenth century,] / was founded / on a false idea.

잉글랜드의 계획은 / 북미 지역에 식민지를 설립하려는 / 16세기 말에 시작한 / 기반을 두고 있었다 / 잘못된 생각에

It was generally assumed / that [Virginia, / the region of the North American continent / to which England laid claim,] / would have the same climate / as the Mediterranean region of Europe, / since it lay at similar latitudes.

일반적으로 추정되었다 / 버지니아는 / 북미 대륙의 지역인 / 잉글랜드가 권리를 주장한 / 같은 기후를 가지고 있을 것이라고 / 유럽의 지중해와 / 왜냐하면 그것은 비슷한 위도에 있으니까

As a result, the English hoped / that the American colonies, / once established, / would be able to supply Mediterranean goods / such as olives and fruit / and reduce England's dependence / on imports from continental Europe.

└ 삽입절

결과적으로 잉글랜드는 희망했다 / 미국 식민지가 / 일단 설립이 되기만 하면 / 지중해 상품을 공급할 수 있을 거라고 / 올리브나 과일과 같은 / 그리고 잉글랜드의 의존을 줄일 수도 있을 거라고 / 유럽 대륙으로부터의 수입에 대한

One prospectus claimed / that the colonies would provide / "the wines, fruit and salt of France and Spain ... / the silks of Persia and Italy."

한 사업 설명서는 주장했다 / 식민지들은 제공해 줄 것이라고 /

와인, 과일, 프랑스와 스페인의 소금을 / 그리고 페르시아와 이탈리아의 비단들을

Similarly, <u>abundant</u> timber / would do away with the need / to import wood from Scandinavia.
유사하게도 풍부한 원목은 / 필요를 없애줄 것이었다 / 스칸디나비아로부터 나무를 수입할

In short, America was mistakenly expected / to be <u>a land of plenty</u> / <u>that</u> would quickly turn a profit.
요컨대 아메리카는 잘못 기대되었다 / 풍요의 땅이 될 것으로 / 빨리 이익을 가져다 줄지도 모르는

● 해설

8. (A), (B), (C)의 각 네모 안에서 문맥에 맞는 낱말로 가장 적절한 것은?
(A) false: 전체적으로 잉글랜드의 계획은 버지니아의 기후에 대해서 잘못 추정하고 계획을 만들었기 때문에 false가 적절하지. valid는 '타당한, 유효한'이라는 의미를 가지지.
(B) dependence: 버지니아로부터 지중해에서 나오는 물품들을 공급받게 되면 유럽으로부터의 수입품에 대한 의존도가 낮아지지. 따라서 '의존도'를 의미하는 dependence가 적절해. restriction은 '제한'이라는 의미를 가져.
(C) abundant: 스칸디나비아에서 오는 나무를 수입할 필요가 없다는 건 원목이 많다는 거겠지? 따라서 '풍부한'을 의미하는 abundant가 적절하지. scarce는 '희박한'이라는 의미야.

● 중요 포인트

to부정사와 분사의 수식을 받는 주어

[England's plan / to establish colonies in North America, / starting in the late sixteenth century,] / was founded / on a false idea.

4 단계 혼공 개념 마무리   p.51

1. 음식과 관련된 압박이 의도적으로 강요된 것이든 혹은 그렇지 않은 또래들로부터 그러한 압박에서 완전히 자유로운 젊은 사람들은 거의 없다.

2. 그러나 우리는 개인의 성장과 경기력이, 정신 능력 훈련을 받지 않는 선수에서보다는 정신 능력 훈련을 받는 어리고 성장 중인 선수에게서 더 빠르게 진보할 것이라고 예상할 수 있다.

3. 닳아서 얇아진 드레스는 여러 해 동안 입지 않았더라도 벽장 뒤편에 걸려 있을 수 있는데, 그 이유는 그 옷에 남아있는 옅은 소나무 향이 바로 어떤 사람의 열여섯 살 여름의 모든 잔존물이기 때문이다.

4. 십대의 소녀는 상추 샐러드가 그녀의 친구들이 먹는 것이기 때문에 나중에 배가 고플지라도 점심으로 상추 샐러드만 먹을지도 모른다.

5. 이런저런 과목이나 혹은 수업을 가르치는 데 있어서 더 성공적일 수 있는 누군가가 '같은 건물 혹은 같은 지역' 어딘가에 있을 수 있다는

사실을, 문을 닫고 거의 혼자서 학교의 연간 행사 계획표를 실천해 나가는 교사는 이해하지 못한다.

6. 시민의 직접적인 참여는 미국 혁명을 가능하게 하고 새로운 공화국에 활력과 미래에 대한 희망을 부여했던 존재였다.

7. 잉글랜드가 권리를 주장했던 북미 대륙의 지역인 버지니아는 유럽의 지중해 지역과 비슷한 위도에 놓여 있었기 때문에 그 지역과 똑같은 기후를 가질 것이라고 추정되었다.

혼공 05일차 어휘 2(밑줄형)

3 단계 고난도 문항 요리하기   p.57

● 정답

> 1. ④ 2. ④ 3. ④ 4. ④ 5. ⑤ 6. ⑤ 7. ⑤ 8. ⑤

1. ④

● 전체 해석

사람들이 저장된 씨앗 종자를 의도적으로 심기 시작했을 때 그들은 또한 자신들의 식물을 보호하기 시작했다. 이것은 이들 식용 식물이 더 이상 자연환경 속에서 살아 남아야 할 필요성이 없어지면서 그것들이 경험한 진화적 압박을 변화시켰다. 대신에, 사람들은 그것들을 위한 새로운 환경을 창조했고, 자연이 이전에 선택한 것과는 다른 특징들을 선택했다. 고고학적 현장에서 발굴된 씨앗들은 농부들이 더 큰 씨앗과 더 얇은 껍질을 선택했다는 것을 명백히 보여준다. 두꺼운 껍질은 흔히 씨앗이 자연환경에서 생존하는 데 필수적인데, 많은 야생 식물의 씨앗이 겨울이 끝나고 비가 오기 시작할 때까지 여러 달을 휴면 상태로 남아 있어야 하기 때문이다. 하지만 인간의 관리 하에서 두꺼운 씨앗 껍질은 불필요한데, 농부들이 수분과 포식자로부터 씨앗을 보호하여 저장하는 책임을 피하기(→ 넘겨받기) 때문이다. 사실, 더 얇은 껍질을 가진 씨앗은 그것이 먹거나 가루로 가공하기가 더 수월하고 파종되었을 때 묘목이 더 빠르게 발아하기 때문에 선호되었다.

● 지문분석

When people started / to plant stored seed stock deliberately, / they also began protecting their plants.
사람들이 시작할 때 / 저장된 씨앗 종자를 의도적으로 심는 것을 / 그들은 마찬가지로 그들의 식물을 보호하기 시작했다

This changed <u>the evolutionary pressure</u> / <u>that</u> these food plants experienced, / as they no longer had to survive / in a natural environment.
이것은 진화적 압박을 변화시켰다 / 이러한 식용 식물이 경험했던 / 그들이 더 이상 살아남을 필요가 없어지면서 / 자연환경에서

Instead, people created a new environment / for them, / and selected for other characteristics / than nature previously had.

대신에 사람들은 새로운 환경을 만들었다 / 그것들을 위한 / 그리고 다른 특징들을 선택했다 / 자연이 이전에 선택했던 것과는

[Seeds / recovered at archaeological sites] / clearly show / that farmers selected / for larger seeds and thinner seed coats.
씨앗들은 / 고고학적 현장에서 발굴된 / 명백하게 보여준다 / 농부들이 선택했다는 것을 / 더 큰 씨앗과 더 얇은 껍질을

Thick seed coats / are often essential / for seeds / to survive in a natural environment / because the seeds of many wild plants / remain dormant for months / until winter is over / and rain sets in.
두꺼운 씨앗 껍질은 / 종종 중요하다 / 씨앗이 / 자연환경에서 살아남는데 / 왜냐하면 많은 야생 식물의 씨앗은 / 수 개월 동안 휴면 상태로 남아있기에 / 겨울이 끝날 때까지 / 그리고 비가 오기 시작할 때까지

But under human management / thick seed coats / are unnecessary, / as farmers (evade) take over responsibility / for storing seeds / away from moisture and predators.
하지만 인간의 관리하에서 / 두꺼운 씨앗 껍질은 / 불필요하다 / 농부들이 책임을 짐에 따라 / 씨앗을 보관하는 / 습기와 포식자로부터

In fact, [seeds with thinner coats] / were preferred / as they are easier / to eat / or process into flour, / and they allow / seedlings to sprout more quickly / when sown.
사실 더 얇은 껍질을 가진 씨앗들은 / 선호되었다 / 그들이 더 쉬움에 따라 / 먹기가 / 아니면 가루로 가공되는 것이 / 그리고 그들은 허용한다 / 묘목이 더 빠르게 싹이 트도록 / 파종되었을 때

● 해설

1. 다음 글의 밑줄 친 부분 중, 문맥상 낱말의 쓰임이 적절하지 <u>않은</u> 것은?
④ evade → take over: 야생 상태와는 달리 인간의 관리 하에서 두꺼운 씨앗 껍질은 불필요한데, 그것은 농부들이 수분과 포식자로부터 씨앗을 보호하여 저장하는 책임을 넘겨받기 때문이야. 따라서 ④번의 evade(피하다)를 '넘겨받다'라는 의미를 지닌 take over로 바꾸어야 해.

● 중요 포인트

전치사구의 수식을 받는 주어

❶ Thick seed coats / are often essential / for seeds / to survive in a natural environment / because the seeds of many wild plants / remain dormant for months / until winter is over / and rain sets in.
❷ In fact, [seeds with thinner coats] / were preferred / as they are easier / to eat / or process into flour, / and they allow / seedlings to sprout more quickly / when sown.

2. ④

● 전체 해석

인생은 위험으로 가득 차 있다. 질병과 천적, 그리고 기아는 언제나 원시인들을 위협하고 있었다. 경험을 통해 원시인은 약초와 용기, 근면한 노동 등이 종종 아무런 소용이 없다는 것을 배우게 되지만 일반적으로 인간이란 살아남기를 원하며 살아 있는 것이 주는 좋은 것들을 누리고 싶어 한다. 이런 문제에 직면하여 원시인은 자신의 목적에 부합하는 어떤 방법에라도 매달리게 된다. 종종 그 방법은 우리 현대인이 보기에는 믿을 수 없이 투박해 보일 수 있지만 곧 우리는 현대에 살고 있는 우리 이웃 역시 비슷한 위기 상황에서 어떻게 행동하는 지를 깨닫게 된다. 어떤 현대인이 의학에 의해 치료 가능하다는(→ 불치병이란) 선언을 듣게 되면 그 사람은 체념하고 운명을 받아들이지 않고 치료의 희망을 내미는 가장 가까운 돌팔이 의사에게라도 달려 갈 것이다. 자기 보존에 대한 그의 욕구는 전혀 감소하지 않을 것이며 이는 세상의 다른 무지한 사람들의 경우도 마찬가지일 것이다. 생존에 대한 이 압도적인 의지에 바로 초자연에 대한 믿음이 뿌리박고 있으며 이는 과거나 현재나 우리가 알고 있는 그 어떤 사람들에게도 보편적으로 나타난다.

● 지문분석

Life is full of hazards.
삶은 위험으로 가득 차 있다
Disease, enemies and starvation / are always menacing primitive man.
질병과 적, 그리고 기아는 / 항상 원시인을 위협하고 있다
Experience teaches him / that medicinal herbs, valor, the most strenuous labor, / often come to naught, / yet normally he wants to survive / and enjoy the good things of existence.
경험은 그를 가르친다 / 약초, 용기, 근면한 노동은 / 종종 소용이 없어진다는 것을 / 하지만 일반적으로 사람은 살아남기를 원한다 / 그리고 존재가 주는 좋은 것들을 누리기를
Faced with this problem, / he takes to any method / that seems adapted to his ends.
이러한 문제에 직면할 때 / 그는 모든 방법을 강구한다 / 그의 목적에 부합하는
Often his ways appear incredibly crude / to us moderns / until we remember / how our next-door neighbor acts / in like emergencies.
종종 그의 방법은 믿을 수 없을 만큼 투박해 보인다 / 우리 현대인들에게 / 우리가 기억할 때까지 / 어떻게 우리 이웃이 행동하는지를 / 비슷한 위기 상황에서
When medical science pronounces / him (curable) incurable, / he will not resign himself to fate / but runs to the nearest quack / who holds out hope of recovery.
의학이 선언할 때 / 그가 치료 불가능하다고 / 그는 자신을 운명에 체념하지 않을 것이다 / 가장 가까운 돌팔이 의사에게 달려갈 것이다 / 회복할거라는 희망을 내미는
[His urge for self-preservation] / will not down, / nor will that of the illiterate peoples of the world, / and in that [overpowering will to live] / is anchored the belief / in

supernaturalism, / which is absolutely universal / among known peoples, past and present.
자기 보존에 대한 그의 욕구는 / 감소하지 않을 것이고 / 세상의 무지한 사람들의 그것(욕구)도 그렇지 않을 것이다 / 그리고 즉 살고자 하는 압도적인 의지는 / 믿음에 뿌리박고 있다 / 초자연에 대한 / 그리고 그것은 절대적으로 보편적이다 / 과거나 현재나 알려진 사람들에게

● 해설

2. 다음 글의 밑줄 친 부분 중, 문맥상 낱말의 쓰임이 적절하지 않은 것은?

④ curable → incurable: 위기 상황에서 어떤 방법을 쓰더라도 그 상황을 해결하기 위해 매달리는 것이 모든 인간들의 보편적인 반응이라는 것이 글의 주제야. 원시인들의 위기 상황에서의 태도와 마찬가지로 현대인들도 위기 상황에 놓여야 하는 모습이 그려져야 하므로 ④번은 위기 상황이라는 문맥과 어울리게 curable(치료 가능한)을 incurable(불치병의)로 바꾸어야 해.

● 중요 포인트

부정어 도치

His urge for self-preservation will not down, nor will that of the illiterate peoples of the world.

부정 부사어 → 도치

S

---

3. ④

● 전체 해석

캐나다인 손님을 접대한 후에, 한 이집트인 중역이 그에게 새로운 벤처 사업에서의 합작 제휴를 제의했다. 그 제의에 기뻐서, 캐나다인은 세부 사항을 마무리하기 위해 다음 날 아침에 각자의 변호사와 함께 다시 만날 것을 제안했다. 이집트인이 결코 나타나지 않았다. 놀라고 실망한 캐나다인이 무엇이 잘못된 것인지 이해하려고 했다. 이집트인은 시간 엄수 관념이 없었는가? 그 이집트인이 수정 제안을 기대하고 있었는가? 카이로에서는 변호사를 구할 수 없었는가? 이들 설명 중 어떤 것도 올바른 것으로 판명되지 않았다. 오히려, 문제는 캐나다인과 이집트인이 변호사를 불러들이는 것에 두는 서로 다른 의미에 의해 야기되었다. 그 캐나다인은 변호사의 부재(→ 입회)를 협상의 성공적인 마무리를 용이하게 하는 것으로 여겼고, 그 이집트인은 그것을 캐나다인이 그의 구두 약속을 불신하는 것을 암시하는 것이라고 해석했다. 캐나다인은 흔히 합의를 끝내기 위해 변호사의 도움을 받는, 사사로움에 치우치지 않는 형식상의 절차를 이용한다. 이와 대조적으로 이집트인은 같은 목적을 완수하기 위해 거래 상대자 간의 개인적인 관계에 더 자주 의존한다.

● 지문분석

An Egyptian executive, / after entertaining his Canadian guest, / offered him joint partnership / in a new business venture.
　　　S　　　　　　└ 분사구 삽입　　　　V
이집트인 한 간부는 / 그의 캐나다인 손님을 접대한 후에 / 그에게 합작 제휴를 제의했다 / 새로운 벤처 사업에서의

The Canadian, / delighted with the offer, / suggested / that they meet again the next morning / with their respective
　　S　　　　　　　　　　　　　　　V
제안 동사 suggest의 that절에서의 동사원형
lawyers / to finalize the details.

캐나다인은 / 그 제안에 기뻐했던 / 제안했다 / 그들이 다시 다음 날 아침에 만날 것을 / 그들의 각각의 변호사와 함께 / 세부사항을 마무리 짓기 위해서

The Egyptian never showed up.
그 이집트인은 결코 나타나지 않았다

The surprised and disappointed Canadian / tried to understand / what had gone wrong: / Did Egyptians lack punctuality?
놀라고 실망한 캐나다인은 / 이해하려고 노력했다 / 무엇이 잘못되었는지를 / 이집트인이 시간 엄수가 부족한가?

Was the Egyptian expecting a counter-offer?
이집트인이 수정 제안을 기대하고 있었나?

Were lawyers unavailable in Cairo?
카이로에서는 변호사를 구할 수 없었나?

None of these explanations / proved to be correct; / rather, the problem was caused / by the different meaning / Canadians and Egyptians attach / to inviting lawyers.
　　　　　　　　　　　　　　that 생략
이러한 기대 중 어떠한 것도 / 올바르지 않다고 증명되었다 / 오히려 문제는 유발되었다 / 다른 의미에 의해서 / 캐나다인과 이집트인이 두는 / 변호사를 입회하는 것에

The Canadian regarded the lawyers' (absence) presence / as facilitating the successful completion of the negotiation; / the Egyptian interpreted it / as signaling the Canadian's mistrust / of his verbal commitment.
캐나다인은 변호사의 존재를 간주했다 / 협상의 성공적인 마무리를 촉진하는 것으로서 / 그 이집트인은 그것을 해석했다 / 캐나다인의 불신을 나타내는 것으로서 / 그들의 구두 약속에 대한

Canadians often use the impersonal formality / of a lawyer's services / to finalize agreements.
캐나다인은 종종 사사롭지 않은 형식을 이용한다 / 변호사의 서비스의 / 동의를 마무리하기 위해서

Egyptians, by contrast, / more frequently depend on the personal relationship / between bargaining partners / to accomplish the same purpose.
이집트인은 대조적으로 / 더욱 빈번히 개인적 관계에 의존한다 / 거래 상대방 사이의 / 같은 목적을 이루기 위해서

● 해설

3. 다음 글의 밑줄 친 부분 중, 문맥상 낱말의 쓰임이 적절하지 않은 것은?

④ absence → presence: 글의 흐름상 캐나다인은 변호사가 있는 상태에서 협상을 마무리하는 것이 협상을 성공적으로 마무리하는 데 도움이 된다고 생각했지. 따라서, 밑줄 친 ④번의 absence(부재)를 presence(입회)로 바꿔야 해.

● 중요 포인트

제안 동사의 that절의 동사원형

제안/명령/요구/주장 동사가 이끄는 that절의 동사는 「(should) + 동사원형」을 사용한다.

The Canadian, delighted with the offer, suggested that they meet again the next morning with their respective lawyers to finalize the details.

제안 동사 suggest의 that절에서의 동사원형 (suggested 아래)
제안 동사 (meet 아래)

4. ④

● 전체 해석

부동산 임대 시장의 특별한 특징은 그것이 심한 장기적 경기 수축기를 겪는 경향이 있다는 것인데, 공산품보다 그 경향이 더 강하다. 어떤 공산품의 공급이 수요를 초과하면, 수요와 공급의 균형을 맞추기 위해 제조자는 생산량을 줄이고 상인은 재고를 줄인다. 하지만 부동산 소유자는 자신들 건물의 임대 가능한 공간의 양을 줄일 수 없다. 주기의 절정기에 업체와 소비자 요구를 수용하기 위해 건설된 공간은 남아있고, 그래서 공실률은 오르고 하향 추세는 더욱 심해진다. 임대료는 일반적으로 어떤 지점, 즉 운영비를 충당하기 위해 청구되어야 할 최대한의 비용(→ 최소한의 비용) 밑으로는 떨어지지 않는다. 어떤 소유자들은 그것 때문에 돈을 잃으니 그 공간을 시장에서 빼버릴 것이다. 그 부동산의 비용 일부를 지급할 수 없는 소수는 투매 가격에 팔 것이고 대출 기관은 다른 부동산들을 회수할 것이다. 그렇게 되면 이것들은 더 낮은 임대료로 시장에 나올 수도 있는데, 이는 시장을 더욱 침체시킨다.

● 지문분석

[A special feature / of the real estate rental market] / is its tendency / to undergo a severe and prolonged contraction phase, / more so than with manufactured products.
특별한 특징은 / 부동산 임대 시장에서의 / 그 경향이다 / 심각하고 장기적인 경기 수축기를 겪는 / 공산품보다 훨씬 더
When the supply of a manufactured product / exceeds the demand, / the manufacturer cuts back on output, / and the merchant reduces inventory / to balance supply and demand.
공산품의 공급이 / 수요를 초과할 때 / 제조업자는 생산량을 줄인다 / 그리고 상인은 재고를 줄인다 / 공급과 수요의 균형을 맞추기 위해서
However, property owners / cannot reduce the amount of space / available for rent in their buildings.
하지만 자산 소유주는 / 공간의 양을 줄일 수 없다 / 그들의 건물에서 / 임대를 위해서 이용 가능한
[Space / that was constructed / to accommodate business and consumer needs / at the peak of the cycle] / remains, / so vacancy rates climb / and the downward trend becomes more severe.
공간은 / 건축된 / 비즈니스와 소비자의 니즈를 수용하기 위해서 / 주기의 절정기에 / 남아있다 / 그래서 공실률은 오른다 / 그리고 하향 추세는 더욱 심각해진다
Rental rates / generally do not drop below a certain point, / the (maximum) minimum / that must be charged / in order to cover operating expenses.
임대료는 / 일반적으로 특정 지점 아래로 떨어지지 않는다 / 최소 비용인 / 지불되어야만 하는 / 운영 비용을 충당하기 위해서

Some owners / will take space off the market / rather than lose money on it.
일부 소유주들은 / 시장에서 그 공간을 빼버릴 것이다 / 그곳에 돈을 잃어버리느니
A few, / unable to subsidize the property, / will sell at distress prices, / and lenders will repossess others.
소수의 사람들은 / 자산에 보조금을 지급할 수 없는 / 투매 가격에 팔 것이다 / 그리고 대출 기관은 다른 부동산을 회수할 것이다
These may then be placed on the market / at lower rental rates, / further depressing the market.
분사구문 (depressing 아래)
이러한 것은 그때 시장에 나올 수도 있다 / 낮은 임대료로 / 그리고 더 나아가 시장을 침체시킬 것이다

● 해설

4. 다음 글의 밑줄 친 부분 중, 문맥상 낱말의 쓰임이 적절하지 <u>않은</u> 것은?

④ maximum → minimum: 임대료가 일반적으로 운영비를 충당하기 위해 청구되어야 할 최대의 비용이라면 임대자는 망하지 않겠지. 논리적으로 최소한의 비용(minimum) 밑으로는 떨어지지 않는다고 해야 맞게 되지. 따라서 ④번의 maximum을 minimum으로 바꿔야 해.

● 중요 포인트

형용사의 명사 후위 수식

명사나 대명사를 수식하는 형용사구가 길 경우 뒤에서 수식한다.
❶ However, property owners cannot reduce the amount of space available for rent in their buildings.
❷ A few, unable to subsidize the property, will sell at distress prices, and lenders will repossess others.

5. ⑤

● 전체 해석

많은 사람들이 여행이나 휴가 중에 아니면 삶의 중요한 축하를 할 때 미래를 위해 그 경험을 보존해 두려고 수많은 사진을 찍는다. 그러나 사진사의 역할이 현 순간의 즐거움을 실제로 손상시킬 수 있다. 나는 첫 아이이자 외동아이의 탄생 사진을 찍는 데 진지하게 몰두했던 한 아버지를 안다. 사진들은 아름다웠지만 자기 아들의 삶에서 가장 중요한 첫 번째 순간을 놓쳤다는 생각이 들었다고 나중에 그는 탄식했다. 카메라 렌즈를 통해 바라보는 것은 그를 현장에서 분리되도록 만들어 버렸다. 그는 체험자가 아니라 단지 관찰자였다. 사물을 진심으로 바라보고 아름답고 의미있는 것을 발견하는 것을 통해 진행되고 있는 경험을 무시하는(→ 증진시키는) 방법으로 카메라를 사용할 수 있도록 스스로 가르쳐라.

● 지문분석

Many people take numerous photos / while traveling or
접속사 + 분사 / 접속사 + 전치사구
on vacation / or during significant life celebrations / to
전치사 + 명사
preserve the experience for the future.
많은 사람들은 수많은 사진을 찍는다 / 여행이나 휴가 중에 / 또는 특별한 삶의 축하 동안에 / 미래를 위해 그 경험을 보존하기 위해서

But the role of photographer / may actually detract from their delight / in the present moment.
하지만 사진사의 역할은 / 실제로는 그들의 즐거움을 손상시킬 수 있다 / 현재의 순간의

I know a father / who devoted himself earnestly / to photographing / the birth of his first and only child.
나는 한 아버지를 알고 있다 / 진지하게 몰두했던 / 사진을 찍는 데 / 자신의 첫 번째이자 유일한 아이의 탄생을

The photos were beautiful / but, he lamented afterward / he felt / that he had missed out / on the most important first moment of his son's life.
그 사진들은 아름다웠다 / 하지만 그는 나중에 한탄했다 / 그는 느꼈다고 / 그가 놓쳐버렸음을 / 가장 중요한 아들의 인생에서의 첫 번째 순간을

[Looking through the camera lens] / made him detached / from the scene.
카메라 렌즈를 통해서 보는 것은 / 그를 분리되도록 만들었다 / 그 현장과

He was just an observer, / not an experiencer.
그는 단순한 관찰자였다 / 경험자가 아니라

Teach yourself to use your camera / in a way / that (neglects) enhances your ongoing experiences, / by truly looking at things / and noticing / what is beautiful and meaningful.
스스로에게 카메라를 사용하도록 가르쳐라 / 방식대로 / 당신의 지속적인 경험을 증진시키는 / 정말로 사물을 봄으로써 / 그리고 알아차리면서 / 무엇이 아름답고 의미있는 것인지

● 해설

5. 다음 글의 밑줄 친 부분 중, 문맥상 낱말의 쓰임이 적절하지 않은 것은?
⑤ neglects → enhances: 지문에서 사진을 찍다 정작 중요한 아들의 첫 번째 순간의 경험을 놓친 아버지의 예시가 나오고 있지. 이 예를 통해서 사진을 찍느라 실제 중요한 경험을 놓친다고 얘기하고 있으므로 사진을 찍을 때는 경험을 '증진시키는' 방법으로 카메라를 사용하는 방법을 배워야 한다고 하는 것이 글의 흐름상 자연스러워. 따라서 neglects를 enhances로 바꿔야 해.

● 중요 포인트

while vs during

while 뒤에는 문장이, during 뒤에는 명사가 오지. 그런데 while 뒤에는 분사와 전치사구도 올 수가 있어. 특히 전치사구의 경우 being 이 생략된 분사로 보면 이해하기가 쉬울 거야.

Many people take numerous photos while traveling or
접속사 + 분사 / 접속사 + 전치사구
on vacation or during significant life celebrations to
전치사 + 명사
preserve the experience for the future.

6. ⑤

● 전체 해석

유기농 식품 생산이 급속도로 증가하고 있다. 많은 소비자들은 그들이 지구에 도움이 되는 일을 하고 있고 건강에 좀 더 좋은 음식을 먹고 있다고 확신하면서 유기농 식품에 대해 기꺼이 높은 가격을 지불하고 있다. 하지만, 몇몇 전문가들은 유기 농업이 몇 가지 결점을 안고 있다고 말한다. 가장 빈번한 비판 중 하나는, 유기 농가들의 작물 수확량이 전통적인 농가보다 훨씬 낮다는 것이다. 그것은 유기농 경작지가 전통적인 경작지보다 잡초와 벌레들로부터 더 많은 피해를 입기 때문이다. 전문가들이 흔히 제시하는 또 다른 주장은 유기 농업이 틈새시장의 부유한 소비자들에게 먹을거리를 제공해줄 수는 있지만, 전 세계 수십억의 굶주리는 사람들을 먹여 살릴 수는 없다는 것이다. 비용이 많이 드는 유기농법이 아닌 화학적 투입물의 신중한 사용만이 기아에 처한 나라들에서 식량 생산을 크게 감소시키는(→ 증대시키는) 것을 도울 수 있다.

● 지문분석

Organic food production is growing / by leaps and bounds.
유기농 식품 생산은 늘고 있다 / 급속도로

Many consumers are willing / to pay premium prices for organic foods, / convinced / that they are helping the earth / and eating healthier.
분사구문 〈동시상황〉 '확신하면서'
많은 소비자들은 하려고 한다 / 높은 가격을 지불하려고 / 유기농 식품을 위해서 / 확신하며 / 그들이 지구를 돕고 있다고 / 그리고 더 건강하게 먹고 있다고

Some experts say, however, / that organic farming has some drawbacks.
일부 전문가들에 따르면 하지만 / 유기 농업은 몇 가지 단점을 가지고 있다고 한다

[One of the most frequent criticisms] / is that [the crop yields of organic farms] / are much lower / than those of traditional farms.
the crop yields
가장 빈번한 비판 중 하나는 / 유기 농가들의 곡물 생산량은 / 더 낮다는 것이다 / 전통적 농가의 그것들보다

That's because / organic fields suffer more / from weeds and insects / than conventional fields.
'~ 때문이다'
그것은 때문이다 / 유기농 경작지가 더 고통 받기 / 잡초와 벌레로부터 / 전통적 경작지보다

[Another argument / often offered by experts] / is that organic farming can supply food / for niche markets of wealthy consumers / but cannot feed billions of hungry people / around the globe.
또 다른 논쟁은 / 종종 전문가들이 제기하는 / 유기 농업은 식량을 제공할 수 있다는 것이다 / 부유한 소비자의 틈새시장을 위한 / 하지만 수십 억의 배고픈 사람을 먹일 수는 없다 / 전 세계의

[Only the careful use / of chemical inputs, / not the costly organic methods,] / can help (reduce) increase food production significantly / in the countries / facing hunger.
유일한 신중한 사용만이 / 화학 투입물의 / 값비싼 유기농 방법이 아니라 / 식량 생산을 획기적으로 늘리는 데 도울 수 있다 / 나라들에서 / 기아에 직면한

●해설

6. 다음 글의 밑줄 친 부분 중, 문맥상 낱말의 쓰임이 적절하지 <u>않은</u> 것은?

⑤ reduce → increase: 이 글은 유기농 농작에 대한 비판을 다룬 글이야. 따라서 '비용이 많이 드는 유기농법이 아닌 화학적 투입물의 신중한 사용만이 기아에 처한 나라들에서 식량 생산을 크게 증대시키는 것을 도울 수 있다.'라는 내용이 되어야 하겠지. 따라서 ⑤번에 reduce를 increase로 바꿔야 해.

●중요 포인트

that's because ~ 때문이다

that's because 다음에는 이유에 해당하는 구문이 나온다.
That's because organic fields suffer more from weeds
<u>'~ 때문이다'</u> +이유
and insects than conventional fields.

7. ⑤

●전체 해석

지난 40년 동안에 지구상 어떤 나라도 알코올 소비량을 프랑스보다 더 줄이지는 않았다. 프랑스에서 맥주와 독한 술의 소비가 기본적으로 꾸준했던 반면, 1인당 포도주로 인한 알코올 소비는 1962년 20리터에서 2001년 약 8리터로 떨어졌다. 줄어든 포도주 소비에 대한 한 가지 이유는 프랑스인의 식사가 빨라진 것이다. 1978년 프랑스인의 평균 식사는 82분 동안 지속되었다. 한 병까지는 아니지만, 반 병 정도를 마시기에는 충분한 시간이었다. 현재 프랑스인의 평균 식사 시간은 38분으로 뚝 떨어졌다. 포도주는 느긋하게 즐기는 식사가 사라진 것의 희생양이다. 그것이 변화의 목표는 아니지만, 포도주 소비의 감소는 더 빠르고 더 현대적이고 분주한 생활 방식의 출현의 원인(→ 부산물)이다.

●지문분석

Over the course of the past forty years, / no country on earth / has cut its alcohol consumption / more than France.
지난 40년 동안 / 지구상의 어떠한 나라도 / 그것의 알코올 소비량을 줄인 나라는 없다 / 프랑스보다
While [consumption of beer and spirits] / has stayed
                  S   V
basically steady in France, / [the per capita consumption
                                  S
of alcohol / from wine] / fell from 20 liters in 1962 / to
                        V
about 8 in 2001.
맥주와 독한 술의 소비량은 / 프랑스에서 기본적으로 일정하게 유지된 반면 / 1인당 알코올의 소비량은 / 와인의 / 1962년 20리터에서 떨어졌다 / 2001년 약 8리터로
[One reason / for the dwindling wine consumption] / is the
    S   V
acceleration of the French meal.
이유는 / 줄어든 포도주 소비의 / 프랑스인의 식사의 빨라짐이다
In 1978, / the average French meal / lasted 82 minutes.
1978년 / 프랑스인의 평균 식사는 / 82분 동안 지속되었다
Plenty of time for half a bottle, / if not a whole bottle.
반 병을 위해서는 충분한 시간이다 / 1병을 위해서는 아니지만
Today, the average French meal / has been slashed down /

to 38 minutes.
오늘날 평균 프랑스인의 식사는 / 뚝 떨어졌다 / 38분으로
Wine is a victim / of the disappearance / of the leisurely meal.
와인이 피해자다 / 사라짐의 / 여유로운 식사의
It is not the target of the change, / but the decline in wine consumption / is a (cause) by-product of the emergence / of the faster, more modern, on-the-go lifestyle.
그것은 변화의 목표는 아니다 / 하지만 와인 소비의 감소는 / 등장의 부산물이다 / 더 빠르고 더 현대적인 분주한 생활 방식의

●해설

7. 다음 글의 밑줄 친 부분 중, 문맥상 낱말의 쓰임이 적절하지 않은 것은?

⑤ cause → by-product: 포도주의 소비가 줄어든 것은 빨라지고 바빠진 현대의 생활 방식으로 인해 발생한 거야. 따라서 포도주 소비의 감소는 원인이 아닌 결과물로 봐야겠지. 따라서 cause(원인)를 by-product(부산물)로 바꿔야 해.

●중요 포인트

전치사구의 주어 수식으로 복잡해진 구문

While [consumption of beer and spirits] has stayed basically steady in France, [the per capita consumption of alcohol from wine] fell from 20 liters in 1962 / to about 8 in 2001.

8. ⑤

●전체 해석

캄보디아 전설에 따르면 사자들이 한 때 마을 사람들과 그들의 귀중한 물소를 공격하며 시골을 돌아다녔다고 한다. 그러자 9세기 Khmer 제국이 시작되기 오래 전, 농부들이 포식자(사자)에 대항해 자신들을 방어하기 위하여 무시무시한 무술을 개발했다. 이러한 기술들이 bokator(보카도)가 되었다. 사자와 맞서 싸운다는 의미를 가진 bokator는 Ancor Wat 사원 벽에 무술 동작이 그려져 있다. 무술 동작은 원숭이, 코끼리, 심지어 오리들의 동작들을 모방했으며, 기술을 습득하기 위해서는 10,000가지 동작들을 익혀야 한다. 12세기에 캄보디아를 통일한 전사 출신 Jayavarman 7세 왕은 그의 군사들을 bokator로 훈련하도록 시켜 무시무시한 군대로 바꾸어 놓았다. bokator는 캄보디아에서 오랜 전통을 갖고 있음에도 불구하고, Khmer Rouge가 1975년 정권을 잡은 후 4년에 걸쳐 훈련 담당 무술 사범들을 대부분 제거시키면서 거의 자취를 감추었다.

●지문분석

According to Cambodian legends, / lions once roamed
                                             S   V
the countryside / attacking villagers and their precious
                   └분사구문 〈동시상황〉 '공격하면서'
buffalo, / and long before the great Khmer Empire began in the 9th century, / farmers developed a fierce martial art
                             S   V
/ to defend themselves against the predator.
캄보디아의 전설에 따르면 / 사자는 한 때 시골을 돌아다녔다 /

마을 사람들과 그들의 소중한 버팔로를 공격하며 / 그리고 위대한 크메르 제국이 9세기에 시작하기도 오래 전에 / 농부들은 격렬한 무술을 개발했다 / 자신을 포식자로부터 방어하기 위해서

These techniques became *bokator*.

이러한 기술은 보카도가 되었다

Meaning 'to fight a lion,' / *bokator* is a martial art / depicted on the walls of Angkor Wat.

'사자와 싸우는 것'을 의미하는 / 보카도는 무술이다 / 앙코르 와트의 벽에 묘사된

There are 10,000 moves / to master, / mimicking animals / such as monkeys, elephants and even ducks.

만 개의 움직임이 있다 / 습득해야 할 / 동물들을 모방하는 / 원숭이나 코끼리, 심지어 오리까지도

[King Jayavarman VII, / the warrior king / who united Cambodia in the 12th century,] / made his army train / in *bokator*, / turning it into a fearsome fighting force.

Jayavarman 7세는 / 전사 출신 왕이었던 / 12세기 캄보디아를 통일한 / 그의 군대를 훈련시켰다 / 보카도로 / 군대를 무시무시한 군대로 바꿔놓았다

Despite its long tradition in Cambodia, / *bokator* (flourish) disappeared / when the Khmer Rouge took power in 1975 / and executed most of the discipline's masters / over the next four years.

캄보디아에서의 긴 전통에도 불구하고 / 보카도는 사라졌다 / 크메르 루즈가 1975년 정권을 잡았을 때 / 그리고 대부분의 무술 사범들을 처형했을 때 / 4년에 걸쳐

● 해설

8. 다음 글의 밑줄 친 부분 중, 문맥상 낱말의 쓰임이 적절하지 않은 것은?

⑤ flourished → disappeared: 그 이전까지는 무술로서 번성했지만, 크메르 루즈가 정권을 잡은 뒤 무술 사범들을 처형했으므로 flourish(번성했다)가 아니라 disappeared(사라졌다)로 바꿔야 해.

● 중요 포인트

동격 명사 + 관계사절 수식으로 복잡해진 주어

[King Jayavarman VII, / the warrior king / who united Cambodia in the 12th century,] / made his army train / in *bokator*, / turning it into a fearsome fighting force.

4단계 혼공 개념 마무리 p.61

1. 고고학적 현장에서 발굴된 씨앗들은 농부들이 더 큰 씨앗과 더 얇은 껍질을 선택했다는 것을 명백히 보여준다.

2. 자기 보존에 대한 그의 욕구는 전혀 감소하지 않을 것이며 이는 세상의 다른 무지한 사람들의 경우도 마찬가지일 것이다. 생존에 대한 이 압도적인 의지에 바로 초자연에 대한 믿음이 뿌리박고 있으며 이

는 과거나 현재나 우리고 알고 있는 그 어떤 사람들에게도 보편적으로 나타난다.

3. 주기의 절정기에 업체와 소비자 요구를 수용하기 위해 건설된 공간은 남아있고, 그래 서 공실률은 오르고 하향 추세는 더욱 심해진다.

4. 사물을 진심으로 바라보고 아름답고 의미있는 것을 발견하는 것을 통해 진행되고 있는 경험을 증진시키는 방법으로 카메라를 사용할 수 있도록 스스로 가르쳐라.

5. 많은 소비자들은 그들이 지구에 도움이 되는 일을 하고 있고 건강에 좀 더 좋은 음식을 먹고 있다고 확신하면서 유기농 식품에 대해 기꺼이 높은 가격을 지불하고 있다.

6. 12세기에 캄보디아를 통일한 전사 출신 Jayavarman 7세왕은 그의 군사들을 bokator로 훈련하도록 시켜 무시무시한 군대로 바꾸어 놓았다.

7. 두꺼운 껍질은 흔히 씨앗이 자연환경에서 생존하는 데 필수적인데 (그것은) 많은 야생 식물의 씨앗이 겨울이 끝나고 비가 오기 시작할 때까지 여러 달을 휴면 상태로 남아 있어야 하기 때문이다.

 06일차 주어진 문장 넣기

3단계 고난도 문항 요리하기 p.67

● 정답

1. ④ 2. ② 3. ② 4. ③ 5. ② 6. ⑤ 7. ③ 8. ⑤

1. ④

● 전체 해석

연구가 보여주기를, 우리는 자연스럽게 재능, 친절, 정직, 지성과 같은 호의적인 특징을 잘생긴 사람들에게 부여한다고 한다. 더 나아가, 우리는 신체적인 매력 요소가 그 과정에서 중요한 역할을 한다는 것을 깨닫지 않고 이러한 판단을 하게 된다. '잘생긴 것이 좋은 것과 동등한 것'이라는 무의식적인 가정의 몇몇 결과들은 나를 두렵게 한다. 예를 들어, 1974년 캐나다 연방정부의 선거에 대한 한 연구는 매력적인 입후보자들이 그렇지 않은 후보들보다 2.5배 이상의 표를 받았다는 것을 알아냈다. 잘생긴 정치가들에 대한 지나친 애정으로써의 그러한 증거에도 불구하고, 다음의 연구는 유권자들이 자신들의 편견을 깨닫지 못한다는 것을 증명했다. 사실, 설문 조사를 받은 캐나다 유권자들의 73퍼센트가 그들의 투표가 신체적인 외모에 의해 영향을 받았다는 것을 가능한 한 가장 강력한 어조로 부정했다. 그리고 오직 14퍼센트의 유권자들만이 그러한 영향의 가능성을 인정했다. 유권자들은 매력이 선거 가능성에 미치는 영향을 그들이 원하는 만큼 마음껏 부정할 수는 있지만, 증거는 계속해서 그것의 성가신 존재를 확인해 주고 있다.

Research has shown / that we automatically assign / to good-looking individuals / such favorable traits / as talent, kindness, honesty, and intelligence.
연구원들은 보여주었다 / 우리가 자동적으로 부여한다는 것을 / 잘생긴 사람들에게 / 호의적인 특징들을 / 재능이나 친절함, 정직함, 그리고 지성과 같은

Furthermore, we make these judgements / without being aware / that physical attractiveness / plays a role in the process.
더욱이 우리는 이러한 판단을 한다 / 알지 못한 채 / 신체적인 매력이 / 그런 과정에서 역할을 한다는 것을

[Some consequences / of this unconscious assumption] / that "good-looking equals good" / scare me.
일부 결과는 / 이런 무의식적인 가정에 대한 / 잘생긴 것은 좋은 것과 같다는 / 나를 무섭게 한다

For example, a study of the 1974 Canadian federal elections / found / that attractive candidates received / more than two and a half times as many votes / as unattractive candidates.
예를 들어 1974년의 캐나다 연방 선거에 대한 연구는 / 발견했다 / 매력적인 후보자가 받았다고 / 2.5배나 더 많은 표를 / 매력적이지 않은 후보자들보다

Despite such evidence of favoritism / toward handsome politicians, / follow-up research demonstrated / that voters did not realize their bias.
그런 편애에 대한 증거에도 불구하고 / 잘생긴 정치인을 향한 / 다음의 연구는 증명했다 / 투표자들은 그들의 선입견을 깨닫지 못했다고

In fact, 73 percent of Canadian voters / surveyed / denied in the strongest possible terms / that their votes had been influenced / by physical appearance; / only 14 percent / even allowed for / the possibility of such influence.
사실 73%의 캐나다 유권자는 / 조사한 / 가장 강력한 어조로 부인했다 / 그들의 투표가 영향을 받았다는 것을 / 신체적 외모에 의해서 / 오직 14%만이 / 인정했다 / 그런 영향의 가능성을

Voters can deny / the impact of attractiveness / on electability / all they want, / but evidence has continued to confirm / its troubling presence.
유권자들은 부인할 수 있다 / 매력도의 영향을 / 선거 가능성에 미치는 / 그들 모두가 원하는만큼 / 하지만 증거는 계속해서 확인해주고 있다 / 그것의 성가신 존재를

●해설

1. 글의 흐름으로 보아, 주어진 문장이 들어가기에 가장 적절한 곳은?
Despite such evidence of favoritism toward handsome politicians, follow-up research demonstrated that voters did not realize their bias.
└ 이 문장 앞에는 편애에 대한 내용이 나와야겠지?

Research has shown that we automatically assign to good-looking individuals such favorable traits as talent, kindness, honesty, and intelligence. (①) Furthermore, we make these judgements without being aware that physical attractiveness plays a role in the process. (②) Some consequences of this unconscious assumption that "good-looking equals good" scare me. (③) For example, a study of the 1974 Canadian federal elections found that attractive candidates received more than two and a half times as many votes as unattractive candidates.
└ 잘생긴 정치인의 득표율이 높았다는 예시 → 편애
(④) In fact, 73 percent of Canadian voters surveyed denied in the strongest possible terms that their votes had been influenced by physical appearance; only 14 percent even allowed for the possibility of such influence. (⑤) Voters can
└ 유권자들은 자신들의 투표 성향을 인정하지 않음
deny the impact of attractiveness on electability all they want, but evidence has continued to confirm its troubling presence.

●중요 포인트

주어를 수식하는 한 개의 과거분사

In fact, 73 percent of Canadian voters / surveyed / denied
  S   본동사가 아님   V → 본동사
in the strongest possible terms / that their votes had ~

2. ②

●전체 해석
연구자들은 빈정거림의 다양한 비언어적 특성들을 보고했다. 대부분의 연구자들은 비언어적 신호가 빈정거림 또는 그것을 촉발하는 감정을 인지하는 데 필수적인 것인지에 대해 의견이 다르다. 그렇다 하더라도 연구는 특히 언어적 신호와 비언어적 신호가 상충할 때에는 비언어적 신호가 언어적 신호보다 더 신빙성이 있다는 연구 결과를 확증해 준다. 또한, 비언어적 신호가 화자의 의도를 더 잘 보여 준다. 빈정거림의 본질이 의도와 메시지 사이의 모순을 암시하므로, 속임수를 쓸 때 그러는 것처럼 비언어적 신호가 '새어 나와' 말하는 사람의 진정한 기분 상태를 드러낼지도 모른다. 표면적으로 빈정대는 말을 하는 사람은 받아들이는 사람이 그 빈정대는 의도를 알아차리기를 바라지만, 반면에 속임수를 쓸 때는 일반적으로 화자가 듣는 사람이 그 속이려는 의도를 알아차리지 못했으면 하고 바란다는 점에서 표면상으로 빈정거림은 속임과 반대되는 것이다. 따라서 의사 전달자들은 어떤 화자가 빈정대는 것인지 판단하려고 할 때, 언어적 메시지와 비언어적 메시지를 비교하며 두 개가 서로 반대이면 그 화자가 빈정대고 있다는 결론을 내릴 수 있다.

●지문분석

Researchers have reported / various nonverbal features of sarcasm.
연구원들은 보고했다 / 빈정거림의 다양한 비언어적 특징을

Most disagree / as to whether nonverbal cues are essential
  S   └ '~에 대하여'
/ to the perception of sarcasm / or the emotion / that prompts it.
대부분은 동의하지 않는다 / 비언어적 실마리가 중요한지 그렇지 않은지에 대해서 / 빈정거림의 인지에 있어 / 아니면 감정에 있어 / 그것(sarcasm)을 촉발하는

Even so, / research confirms the finding / that nonverbal cues are more credible / than verbal cues, / especially when verbal and nonverbal cues conflict.

그렇다 하더라도 / 연구는 연구 결과를 확인해준다 / 비언어적 실마리가 더 신뢰할 수 있다는 / 언어적 실마리보다 / 특히 언어적 실마리와 비언어적 실마리가 대립할 때

Also, nonverbal cues are better indicators / of speaker intent.

마찬가지로 비언어적 실마리는 더 나은 지표이다 / 화자의 의도에 대한

As the nature of sarcasm / implies a contradiction / between intent and message, / nonverbal cues may "leak" ① / and reveal the speaker's true mood / as they do in deception. ②

빈정거림의 본질이 / 모순을 암시하므로 / 의도와 메시지 사이의 / 비언어적 실마리는 새어나올 수 있다 / 그리고 화자의 진짜 기분 상태를 드러낼 수도 있다 / 그들이 속임수를 쓸 때 그러는 것처럼

Ostensibly, sarcasm is the opposite of deception / in that '~라는 점에서' / a sarcastic speaker typically intends / the receiver to recognize the sarcastic intent; / whereas, in deception / the speaker typically intends / that the receiver not recognize the deceptive intent.
└ intend A to부정사 ┘
└ intend that S + (should) 동사원형 ┘

표면적으로 빈정거림은 속임수의 반대이다 / 빈정거리는 화자가 전형적으로 의도한다는 점에서 / 청자가 빈정대는 의도를 인식하기를 / 반면에 속임수에서는 / 화자는 전형적으로 의도한다 / 청자가 속이려는 의도를 인식하지 않기를

Thus, when communicators are attempting to determine / if a speaker is sarcastic, / they compare the verbal and nonverbal message / and if the two are in opposition, / communicators may conclude / that the speaker is being sarcastic.

그래서 의사 전달자들은 결정하려고 할 때 / 화자가 빈정거리는지 / 그들은 언어적 메시지와 비언어적 메시지를 비교한다 / 그리고 두 개가 서로 반대일 경우 / 의사 전달자들은 결론을 내릴지도 모른다 / 화자가 빈정거리고 있다고

● 해설

2. 글의 흐름으로 보아, 주어진 문장이 들어가기에 가장 적절한 곳은?

Even so, research confirms the finding that nonverbal cues are
└ 앞의 내용과 다른 내용이 전개됨을 암시
more credible than verbal cues, especially when verbal and
비언어적 신호 〉 언어적 신호
nonverbal cues conflict.

Researchers have reported various nonverbal features of sarcasm. (①) Most disagree as to whether nonverbal cues
비언어적 신호에 대해 부정적
are essential to the perception of sarcasm or the emotion that prompts it. (②) Also, nonverbal cues are better indicators of speaker intent. (③) As the nature of sarcasm implies a contradiction between intent and message, nonverbal cues may "leak" and reveal the speaker's true mood as they do in deception. (④) Ostensibly, sarcasm is the opposite of deception in that a sarcastic speaker typically intends the

receiver to recognize the sarcastic intent; whereas, in deception the speaker typically intends that the receiver not recognize the deceptive intent. (⑤) Thus, when communicators are attempting to determine if a speaker is sarcastic, they compare the verbal and nonverbal message and if the two are in opposition, communicators may conclude that the speaker is being sarcastic.

● 중요 포인트

intend 구문

intend는 뒤에 to부정사나 that절이 올 수 있다.

Ostensibly, sarcasm is the opposite of deception in that a sarcastic speaker typically intends the receiver to
intend A to부정사
recognize the sarcastic intent; whereas, in deception the speaker typically intends that the receiver not recognize
intend that S + (should) 동사원형
the deceptive intent.

3. ②

● 전체 해석

과제의 초점이나 상황을 변화시킴으로써 심지어 우리가 완전히 에너지를 고갈했다고 느낄 때조차도 새로워진 에너지를 얻어낼 수 있다. 이것을 입증하기 위해 한 심리학자가 자신이 '반 자유 과제'라고 명명한 것에 사람들이 참여하도록 요청했다. 그 과제에는 그림 그리기, 'abababababababab…'를 반복해서 쓰기, 혹은 짧은 시 읽기가 포함되어 있었다. 참여자는 이러한 과제를 진이 빠진 기분이 될 때까지 수행하도록 요청받았다. 그런 다음 실험자는 참가자가 미묘하게 다른 과제를 수행해야 하도록 상황을 바꿨다. 그림을 그렸던 사람은 얼마나 빨리 그들이 그림을 그릴 수 있는지 증명하기 위해 마지막 그림을 다시 그리도록 요청받았다. 'abab'를 썼던 사람은 이름과 주소를 적어 넣도록 요청받았다. 이러한 새로운 상황에서 그들의 피로는 사라졌다. 원기 회복을 만들어 내는 이러한 현상은 일상에 의해 생기는 피로가 자리 잡는 것을 막기 위해 보안 직원이 다른 위치로 순환하는 공항에서의 조치에서 목격될 수 있다.

● 지문분석

By changing the focus or context of a task, / we can get renewed energy / even when we feel / that we are completely out of energy.

초점이나 일의 상황을 바꿈으로써 / 우리는 새로워진 에너지를 얻을 수 있다 / 심지어 우리가 느낄 때에도 / 우리가 완전히 에너지를 다 썼다고

To demonstrate this, / a psychologist asked / people to
└ ~하기 위해서   └ ask + 목적어 + to부정사
take part in / what she called 'semi-free tasks'.

이것을 설명하기 위해서 / 한 심리학자는 요구했다 / 사람들에게 참여하라고 / 그녀가 반 자유 과제라 부르는 것에

The tasks included drawing, / repeatedly writing 'abababababababab...', / or reading a short poem.

그 과제는 그리기를 포함했다 / 반복적으로 'abababababababab...'를 쓰는 것을 / 아니면 짧은 시를 읽는 것을

The participants were asked / to do these tasks / until they felt exhausted.
참가자들은 요청받았다 / 이러한 과제들을 하라고 / 그들이 지칠 때까지

The experimenter then changed the context / so that the participants had to do / a subtly different task.
실험자는 그때 상황을 바꿨다 / 참가자들이 수행해야 하도록 / 미묘하게 다른 과제를

Those drawing / were asked / to redraw their last picture / to demonstrate / how quickly they could draw.
그리는 사람들은 / 요청되었다 / 그들의 마지막 그림을 다시 그리라고 / 증명하기 위해서 / 얼마나 빠르게 그들이 그릴 수 있는지

Those writing 'abab' / were asked / to sign their name and address.
'abab'를 그리는 사람들은 / 요청받았다 / 그들의 이름과 주소를 적으라는

In this new context / their fatigue disappeared.
이러한 새로운 환경에서 / 그들의 피로는 사라졌다

[This phenomenon / of creating a second wind] / can be seen / in action at airports / where security officers rotate around different stations / to stop routine-induced fatigue from settling in.
stop A from ing: 'A가 ~ing 하는 걸 막다'
이러한 현상은 / 두 번째 바람(원기회복)을 만드는 / 볼 수 있다 / 공항에서의 행동에서 / 안전 요원이 다른 위치로 순환하는 / 일상이 유발한 피로가 자리잡는 것을 막기 위해서

● 해설
3. 글의 흐름으로 보아, 주어진 문장이 들어가기에 가장 적절한 곳은?
The experimenter then changed the context so that the participants had to do a subtly different task.
환경을 바꿈

By changing the focus or context of a task, we can get renewed energy even when we feel that we are completely out of energy. To demonstrate this, a psychologist asked people to take part in what she called 'semi-free tasks'. The tasks included drawing, repeatedly writing 'abababababababab…', or reading a short poem. (①) The participants were asked to do these tasks until they felt exhausted. (②) Those drawing were asked to redraw their last picture to demonstrate how quickly they could draw. (③) Those writing 'abab' were asked to sign their name and address. (④) In this new context their fatigue disappeared. (⑤) This phenomenon of creating a second wind can be seen in action at airports where security officers rotate around different stations to stop routine-induced fatigue from settling in.
다른 일을 함(변화)

● 중요 포인트

~ing의 수식을 받는 주어
❶ Those drawing were asked to redraw their last picture to demonstrate ow quickly they could draw.
❷ Those writing 'abab' were asked to sign their name

---

and address.

4. ③

● 전체 해석
주요한 구조 조정을 겪고 있는 한 전자 회사의 고객 서비스 직원들은 장비를 설치하고 수리하는 것 외에도 장비에 대한 서비스 계약 판매를 시작해야 한다는 말을 들었다. 이것은 많은 저항을 일으켰다. 서비스 직원들에게, 판매하는 것을 배우는 것은 그들이 해 왔던 것과는 아주 다른 일이었다. 하지만 그들은 자신들이 생각 했던 것보다 판매에 대해 이미 훨씬 더 많은 것을 알고 있다는 것이 밝혀졌다. 예를 들면, 장비를 설치하거나 점검할 때의 첫 번째 단계는 고객들이 장비를 어떻게 사용했는지를 알기 위해 고객과 이야기하는 것이다. 똑같은 내용이 판매에도 적용된다. 판매원은 먼저 고객이 필요로 하는 것에 대해 알아야 한다. 서비스 직원들은 또한 제품에 대한 지식과 직접 실무에 참가한 경험을 많이 가지고 있었는데, 이것은 영업에 확실히 중요하다.

● 지문분석

[The customer service representatives / in an electronics firm / under major restructuring] / were told / they had to begin selling service contracts / for their equipment / in addition to installing and repairing them.
in addition to(전치사) + 명사/~ing
고객 서비스 직원들은 / 한 전자 회사의 / 주요한 구조 조정 중인 / 말을 들었다 / 그들이 서비스 계약 판매를 시작해야 한다는 / 그들의 장비를 위한 / 그것들을 설치하고 수리하는 것 외에도

This generated a great deal of resistance.
이것은 엄청난 저항을 만들어냈다

To the service representatives, / [learning to sell] / was a very different game / from what they had been playing.
서비스 직원들에게 있어 / 판매를 배우는 것은 / 매우 다른 게임이었다 / 그들이 해오던 것과는 다른

But it turned out / they already knew a lot more / about sales / than they thought.
비교급 강조
하지만 밝혀졌다 / 그들은 이미 훨씬 많은 것을 알고 있었음을 / 판매에 대해서 / 그들이 생각하던 것보다

For example, [the first step / in servicing or installing equipment] / is talking with the clients / to understand / how they used the equipment.
예를 들어 / 첫 번째 단계는 / 장비를 점검하거나 설치할 때 / 고객들과 이야기하는 것이다 / 이해하기 위해서 / 그들이 장비를 어떻게 사용하는지를

The same is true in selling.
같은 것은 판매할 때도 사실이다

The salesperson first has to learn / about the customer's needs.
판매 직원들은 우선 배워야만 한다 / 고객의 니즈(욕구)에 대해서

The service representatives / also had a great deal of product knowledge and hands-on experience, / which is
앞 문장 전체

obviously important in sales.

서비스 직원들은 / 마찬가지로 엄청난 상품에 대한 지식과 직접 경험을 가지고 있었다 / 그리고 그것은 확실하게 영업에 있어 중요하다

● 해설

4. 글의 흐름으로 보아, 주어진 문장이 들어가기에 가장 적절한 곳은?
For example, the first step in servicing or installing equipment is talking with the clients to understand how they used the equipment. 장비를 설치할 때와 서비스 할 때 필요한 것이 등장

The customer service representatives in an electronics firm
갑작스레 판매를 해야 되는 상황에 대한 부정적 인식
under major restructuring were told they had to begin selling service contracts for their equipment in addition to installing and repairing them. This generated a great deal of resistance. (①) To the service representatives, learning to sell was a very different game from what they had been playing. (②) But it turned out they already knew a lot more about sales than they thought. (③) The same is true in selling. 똑같은 것이 밑줄 친 문장에 있는 내용이라고 하기에는 너무 빈약하지. 이에 해당하는 내용이 앞에 있어야 한다는 것을 알 수 있어.
(④) The salesperson first has to learn about the customer's needs. (⑤) The service representatives also had a great deal of product knowledge and hands-on experience, which is obviously important in sales.

● 중요 포인트

앞 문장 전체를 받는 which
계속적 용법의 which는 때에 따라서 앞 문장 전체를 선행사로 받기도 하니까 해석할 때 조심해야 해.
The service representatives also had a great deal of product knowledge and hands-on experience, which is obviously important in sales.
앞 문장 전체

5. ②

● 전체 해석

언론 매체가 다양하고 상반되는 관점을 제시해서 우리가 가장 나은 선택을 할 수 있도록 하는 것은 중요하다. 전쟁을 시작하는 경우를 예로 들어보자. 전쟁은 분명 다른 모든 선택권이 실패했을 때 착수하는 최후의 수단이어야 한다. 그러므로 누군가가 전쟁을 시작하겠다고 위협하거나 우리를 설득하려고 하면서 엄청난 선전 활동을 벌여 그것을 정당화하려 한다면, 뉴스 매체는 모든 것을 의심해야 할 책임이 있다. 그것(뉴스 매체)은 우리를 대신해 매우 자세히 조사하여, 대중들이 다른 관점도 볼 수 있도록 해야 한다. 그렇지 않으면, 우리는 불필요한 전쟁이나, 정부와 장성들이 제시한 이유 외에 다른 이유로 전쟁을 벌이게 될 수 있다. 대부분의 경우에 언론 매체는 이 중대한 역할을 수행하지 못한다. 심지어 거대한, 소위 "진보적"이라고 불리는 미국의 언론 매체조차도 그들이 항상 대중의 이익을 지키는 파수꾼이 되지는 못했으며, 몇몇 주요 사안에 대한 자사의 보도가 "때로는 눈에 띄게 편향적인 것처럼 보인다"는 것을 인정하였다.

It's important / that the media provide us / with diverse
가주어   진주어
and opposing views, / so we can choose the best available options.
중요하다 / 미디어가 우리에게 제공한다는 것이 / 다양하고 상반되는 관점을 / 그래서 우리는 최상의 이용 가능한 옵션을 선택할 수 있다
Let's take the example of going to war.
전쟁을 시작하는 경우를 예로 들어보자
War should be a last resort, / obviously, undertaken / when all other options have failed.
전쟁은 마지막 수단이어야 한다 / 명백하게 취해지는 / 모든 다른 옵션이 실패했을 때
So, when someone is threatening / to go to war, / or
                          ①
trying to convince us / and mounting a huge public
  ②   ③
relations campaign / to justify it, / the news media have a responsibility / to question everything.
그래서 누군가가 위협을 할 때 / 전쟁을 하겠다고 / 아니면 우리를 설득하려고 할 때 / 그리고 엄청난 선전 활동을 벌이려고 할 때 / 그것 (전쟁을) 정당화하기 위해서 / 뉴스 미디어는 책임이 있다 / 모든 것에 대해 질문을 할
They should be providing / the most intense scrutiny / on our behalf, / so the public can see the other side of things.
그들은 제공해야만 한다 / 매우 자세한 조사를 / 우리를 대신하여 / 그래서 대중들이 사물의 다른 쪽을 볼 수 있도록
Otherwise, / we may be drawn into unnecessary wars, / or wars / fought for reasons / other than those / presented by
                                              └ reasons
governments and generals.
그렇지 않으면 / 우리는 불필요한 전쟁으로 이끌어 질 수도 있다 / 아니면 전쟁으로 / 이유로 벌어진 / 다른 이유로 / 정부나 장성들에 의해서 제기된
Most of the time, / the media fail to perform this crucial role.
대부분의 경우 / 미디어는 이렇게나 중요한 역할을 수행하는 데 실패한다
Even the large, / so-called 'liberal' American media / have admitted / that they have not always been watchdogs / for
                              ①
the public interest, / and that [their own coverage on some
                            S
major issues] / "looks strikingly one-sided at times."
심지어 거대한 / 소위 진보적이라고 불리우는 미국의 미디어도 / 인정해왔다 / 그들이 항상 감시자인 것은 아니라고 / 대중의 이익을 위한 / 그리고 그들 자신의 일부 주된 이슈에 대한 보도는 / 때로는 놀라울 정도로 편향적으로 보인다고

● 해설

5. 글의 흐름으로 보아, 주어진 문장이 들어가기에 가장 적절한 곳은?
So, when someone is threatening to go to war, or trying to convince us and mounting a huge public relations campaign to justify it, the news media have a responsibility to question

everything.

It's important that the media provide us with diverse and opposing views, so we can choose the best available options. Let's take the example of going to war. (①) War should be a last resort, obviously, undertaken when all other options have failed. (②) They should be providing the most intense scrutiny on our behalf, so the public can see the other side of things. (③) Otherwise, we may be drawn into unnecessary wars, or wars fought for reasons other than those presented by governments and generals. (④) Most of the time, the media fail to perform this crucial role. (⑤) Even the large, so-called 'liberal' American media have admitted that they have not always been watchdogs for the public interest, and that their own coverage on some major issues "looks strikingly one-sided at times."

● 중요 포인트

병렬구조로 연결된 접속사 that

Even the large, so-called 'liberal' American media have admitted that they have not always been watchdogs for the public interest, and that their own coverage on some major issues "looks strikingly one-sided at times."

6. ⑤

● 전체 해석

충분히 발달한 시장에서는, 경쟁적 지위들에서의 중요한 변화와 시장의 성장을 가져오는 획기적인 발전이 드물다. 이 때문에, 경쟁은 한 조직이 다른 조직들을 희생해서만 승리할 수 있는 제로섬 게임이 된다. 하지만, 경쟁의 정도가 특히 극심해지는 경우, 제로섬 게임은 시장 내의 모두가 추가적인 비용에 직면하므로, 급속하게 네거티브섬 게임이 될 수도 있다. 이것의 한 가지 예로, 영국의 주요 대형 소매 은행 중 한곳이 토요일 오전에 영업함으로써 경쟁 우위를 점하려고 했을 때, 그 은행은 전통적인 월요일부터 금요일까지의 은행 영업 시간을 제약이라고 여기던 많은 새로운 고객을 끌어 모았다. 하지만 고객의 감소에 직면하자 경쟁 상대도 역시 토요일에 영업함으로써 대응했다. 이것의 최종 결과는, 비록 고객들은 이득을 보았지만, 은행들은 비용은 증가했으나 고객의 총 수는 그대로였기 때문에 손해를 보았다는 것이었다. 본질적으로, 이것은 네거티브 섬 게임으로 판명되었다.

● 지문분석

In mature markets, / [breakthroughs / that lead to a major change / in competitive positions / and to the growth of the market] / are rare.
충분히 발달한 시장에서 / 획기적 발전은 / 주된 변화를 이끄는 / 경쟁적 지위들에서 / 그리고 시장의 성장을 / 드물다

Because of this, / competition becomes a zero sum game / in which one organization can only win / at the expense of others.

이 때문에 / 경쟁은 제로섬 게임이 된다 / 한 조직이 이길 수 있는 / 오직 다른 사람들을 희생해서

However, where the degree of competition / is particularly intense / a zero sum game can quickly become a negative sum game, / in that / everyone in the market / is faced with additional costs.
하지만 경쟁의 정도가 / 특히 심한 곳에서 / 제로섬 게임은 빠르게 네거티브섬 게임이 된다 / ~라는 점에서 / 시장의 모든 사람들이 / 추가적인 비용에 직면하게 된다는

As an example of this, / when [one of the major high street banks in Britain] / tried to gain a competitive advantage / by opening on Saturday mornings, / it attracted a number of new customers / who found / the traditional Monday-Friday bank opening hours / to be a constraint.
이 예로 / 영국의 주요 대형 소매 은행 중 한 곳이 / 경쟁적 이점을 얻으려고 노력했을 때 / 토요일 아침에 문을 열어서 / 그것은 많은 새로운 고객들을 끌어들였다 / 발견한 / 전통적인 월요일에서 금요일까지의 은행의 개장 시간이 / 제약이 있음을

However, faced with a loss of customers, / the competition responded / by opening on Saturdays as well.
하지만 더 많은 고객의 손실에 직면하자 / 경쟁 상대는 반응했다 / 마찬가지로 토요일에 개장함으로써

[The net effect of this] / was that, / although customers benefited, / the banks lost out / as their costs increased / but the total number of customers / stayed the same.
이것의 최종 결과는 / ~였다 / 고객은 이득을 얻었음에도 불구하고 / 은행은 손해를 보았다는 것 / 그들의 비용이 증가함에 따라 / 하지만 전체 고객의 수는 / 동일했다

In essence, / this proved / to be a negative sum game.
본질적으로 / 이것은 증명되었다 / 네거티브섬 게임으로

● 해설

6. 글의 흐름으로 보아, 주어진 문장이 들어가기에 가장 적절한 곳은?

The net effect of this was that, although customers benefited, the banks lost out as their costs increased but the total number of customers stayed the same.

In mature markets, breakthroughs that lead to a major change in competitive positions and to the growth of the market are rare. (①) Because of this, competition becomes a zero sum game in which one organization can only win at the expense of others. (②) However, where the degree of competition is particularly intense a zero sum game can quickly become a negative sum game, in that everyone in the market is faced with additional costs. (③) As an example of this, when one of the major high street banks in Britain tried to gain a competitive advantage by opening on Saturday mornings, it attracted a number of new customers who found the traditional Monday-Friday bank opening hours to be a constraint. (④

) However, faced with a loss of customers, the competition responded by opening on Saturdays as well. (⑤) In essence, this proved to be a negative sum game.

● 중요 포인트

단독으로 접속사로 사용되는 where

However, where the degree of competition is particularly
ㄴ '~인 곳에서, ~인 장소에서'
intense a zero sum game can quickly become a negative sum game, ~

7. ③

● 전체 해석

인간에게는 생체 시계가 우리의 수면-기상 주기뿐만 아니라 혈압, 체온, 호르몬, 배고픔, 갈증에서의 일상의 변화들을 담당하고 있다. 이러한 생물학적 리듬은, 우리가 내부의 시간으로 경험하는 것으로, 아마 수면보다는 더욱 오래 유지된 것인데, 수백만 년의 진화의 과정에서 발달되어 온 것이다. 그것들(생물학적 리듬)은 외부에서 무슨 일이 일어나고 있던지 간에, 즉 한랭전선이 들어오는지 구름이 햇빛을 가리는지 간에, 대략 24시간 주기로 신체와 행동의 변화들을 용이하게 해준다. 그것이 사람들이 시간대를 넘어서 여행할 때 시차증을 겪는 이유이다. 그들의 내부의 시간은 계속하여 그들이 갈 장소가 아닌, 그들이 뒤에 남겨두고 떠난 장소에 상응하여 움직이는데, 그 두 장소들을 재조정하는데 약간의 시간이 걸린다. 가장 주목할 만한 것은 우리의 내부 생체 시계가 환경적인 요인들에 의해 재조정될 수 있다는 것이다. 우리는 우리의 생체 시계가 지구 반대편의 상당히 다른 낮밤 주기의 일정에 적응하도록 요청할 때 며칠 동안 시차증을 겪을 수 있으나 그것은 그렇게 할 수 있다.

● 지문분석

In humans, / body clocks are responsible / for daily changes / in blood pressure, body temperature, hormones, hunger, and thirst, / as well as our sleep-wake cycles.
인간에게 / 생체 시계는 책임이 있다 / 일상의 변화들에 / 혈압에서의, 체온, 호르몬, 배고픔, 갈증에서의 / 우리의 수면-기상 사이클뿐만 아니라

[These biological rhythms, / which we experience /
                    S
as internal time,] / are probably older / than sleep, /
                      V
developed / over the course of millions of years of
ㄴ 분사구문
evolution.
이러한 생물학적 리듬은 / 우리가 경험하는 것으로 / 내부의 시간으로 / 아마도 더 오래되었다 / 수면보다 / 그리고 발전해왔다 / 수백만 년의 진화의 과정에서

They facilitate physiological and behavioral changes / on a roughly twenty-four-hour cycle / no matter what is happening outside, / whether a cold front moves in / or clouds block the light of the sun.
그들은 생리학적 행동적 변화를 용이하게 한다 / 거의 24시간 주기로 / 아무리 외부에서 무언가가 벌어져도 / 한랭전선이 들어오든 / 아니면 구름이 햇살을 가리든

That is why / people experience jet lag / when traveling
                                        ㄴ 접속사 + 분사
across time zones.
그것이 이유이다 / 사람들이 시차증을 경험하는 / 시간대를 넘어서 여행을 할 때

Their internal clocks / continue to run / in accordance with the place / they left behind, / not the one / to which they
          ㄴ the place
have come, / and it can take some time / to realign the
              ㄴ it takes 시간 + to부정사: '~하는 데 시간이 걸리다'
two.
그들의 내부의 시계는 / 계속 움직인다 / 장소에 일치하여 / 그들이 떠난 / 장소가 아니라 / 그들이 가는 / 그리고 그것은 약간의 시간이 걸린다 / 그 두 개를 재조정하는 데

The most remarkable thing / is that our internal body clocks / can be readjusted / by environmental cues.
가장 주목할 만한 것은 / 우리의 내부의 생체 시계는 / 재조정 될 수 있다는 것이다 / 환경적 요인에 따라서

We may get jet lag / for a few days / when we ask / our body clocks / to adapt to a vastly different schedule / of day and night cycles / on the other side of the Earth, / but they can do it.
우리는 시차증을 겪을지도 모른다 / 며칠 동안 / 우리가 요구할 때 / 우리의 신체 시계에게 / 엄청나게 다른 스케쥴에 적응하도록 / 낮과 밤의 주기에 / 지구 반대편에서 / 하지만 그것들은 그것을 할 수 있다

● 해설

7. 글의 흐름으로 보아, 주어진 문장이 들어가기에 가장 적절한 곳은?
That is why people experience jet lag when traveling across
시차증의 이유가 앞에 나와야 하겠지.
time zones.

In humans, body clocks are responsible for daily changes in blood pressure, body temperature, hormones, hunger, and thirst, as well as our sleep-wake cycles. (①) These biological rhythms, which we experience as internal time, are probably older than sleep, developed over the course of millions of years of evolution. (②) They facilitate physiological and behavioral changes on a roughly twenty-four-hour cycle no matter what
                    생체 리듬(biological rhythms)
is happening outside, whether a cold front moves in or clouds block the light of the sun. (③) Their internal clocks continue
                                          Their을 신체 리듬으로 하면 어색하니까 앞에 사람이 나와야 해.
to run in accordance with the place they left behind, not the one to which they have come, and it can take some time to realign the two. (④) The most remarkable thing is that our internal body clocks can be readjusted by environmental cues. (⑤) We may get jet lag for a few days when we ask our body clocks to adapt to a vastly different schedule of day and night cycles on the other side of the Earth, but they can do it.

● 중요 포인트

why vs because

this(that) is why 뒤에는 결과가, because 뒤에는 원인이 와야 해.
종종 어법 시험에 나오니까 문맥상 앞에 있는 것이 원인인지 결과인지 잘 파악해야 해.

They facilitate physiological and behavioral changes on a roughly twenty-four-hour cycle ~. **That is** <u>why</u> people experience jet lag when traveling across time zones.
원인
결과

8. ⑤

● 전체 해석

음식과 거처에 필요한 기본적인 최소한의 범위를 벗어나는 돈은 목적에 대한 수단에 불과하다. 하지만 아주 흔히 우리는 수단을 목적과 혼동하여 돈(수단)을 위해서 행복(목적)을 희생한다. 우리 사회에서 아주 흔히 그렇듯이, 물질적 부유함이 궁극적인 목적의 위치로 높여질 때에 이렇게 하기 쉽다. 이것은 물질적 부의 축적과 생산이 그것 자체로서 잘못된 것이라고 말하는 것이 아니다. 물질적 풍요는 사회뿐만 아니라 개인이 더 높은 수준의 행복을 얻을 수 있도록 도와줄 수 있다. 재정적 안정은 우리가 의미 있다고 생각하지 않는 일로부터 그리고 다음 번 월급에 대해서 걱정해야 하는 것으로부터 우리를 해방시켜 줄 수 있다. 더욱이, 돈을 벌고자 하는 욕구는 우리에게 도전 정신을 심어 주고 영감을 줄 수 있다. 그렇다고 하더라도, 가치가 있는 것은 돈 '그 자체로서'가 아니라 그것이 잠재적으로 더 긍정적인 경험을 만들어 낼 수 있다는 사실이다. 물질적 부유함이 본질적으로 그리고 그 자체로서 의미를 만들어 내거나 감정적인 풍요로움을 반드시 가져오는 것은 아니다.

● 지문분석

[Money / – beyond the bare minimum / necessary for food
 S
and shelter –] / is nothing more than / a means to an end.
돈은 / 기본적으로 최소한의 범위 너머에 있는 / 음식과 거처에 필요
한 / 불과하다 / 목적에 대한 수단에

Yet so often / we confuse means with ends, / and sacrifice
happiness (end) / for money (means).
하지만 너무 종종 / 우리는 수단과 목적을 혼동한다 / 그리고 행복(목
적)을 희생한다 / 돈(수단)을 위해서

It is easy / to do this / when material wealth is elevated /
가주어   진주어
to the position of the ultimate end, / as it so often is / in
our society.
쉽다 / 이것을 하는 것은 / 물질적 부가 올라갈 때 / 궁극적 목표의
위치로 / 그것이 너무 종종 그러하듯이 / 우리 사회에서

This is not to say / that [the accumulation and production
                         / of material wealth] / is in itself wrong.
                                         S   V
이것은 말하는 것이 아니다 / 축적과 생산이 / 물질적 부의 / 그 자체
로 틀렸다고

Material prosperity can help individuals, / as well as
                       V   O
society, / attain higher levels of happiness.
          O.C.
물질적 번영은 사람들을 도울 수 있다 / 사회도 마찬가지로 / 더 높은
수준의 행복을 얻도록

Financial security can liberate us / from work / we do not
find meaningful / and from having to worry about the next
paycheck.
재정적 안정은 우리를 자유롭게 할 수 있다 / 일로부터 / 우리가 유의
미함을 찾을 수 없는 / 그리고 다음의 월급에 대해 걱정해야만 하는

것으로부터

Moreover, [the desire / to make money] / can challenge
            S
and inspire us.
게다가 욕망은 / 돈을 벌고자 하는 / 우리에게 도전감을 주고 영감을
줄 수 있다

                               it–that 강조용법
Even so, / it is not the money *per se* / that is valuable, /
but the fact / that it can potentially yield more positive
experiences.
그렇다고 하더라도 / 돈 그 자체가 아니다 / 가치있는 것은 / 그러나
사실이다 / 그것이 잠재적으로 더 긍정적인 경험을 만들 수 있다는

[Material wealth in and of itself] / does not necessarily
 S
generate meaning / or lead to emotional wealth.
물질적 부유함이 본질적으로 그리고 그 자체로 / 반드시 의미를 발생
시키는 것은 아니다 / 아니면 감정적인 부를 이끄는 것은

● 해설

8. 글의 흐름으로 보아, 주어진 문장이 들어가기에 가장 적절한 곳은?
Even so, it is not the money *per se* that is valuable, but the fact
that it can potentially yield more positive experiences.
돈 그 자체가 가치있는 것이 아니라 다른 것이 가치있는 거야. → 부정적 특징 등장

Money – beyond the bare minimum necessary for food and
shelter – is nothing more than a means to an end. Yet so often
we confuse means with ends, and sacrifice happiness (end) for
money (means). It is easy to do this when material wealth is
elevated to the position of the ultimate end, as it so often is in
our society. (①) This is not to say that the accumulation and
production of material wealth is in itself wrong. (②) Material
prosperity can help individuals, as well as society, attain higher
levels of happiness. (③) Financial security can liberate us
from work we do not find meaningful and from having to
worry about the next paycheck. (④) Moreover, the desire
to make money can challenge and inspire us. (⑤) Material
                                          물질적 부의 긍정적인 면
wealth in and of itself does not necessarily generate meaning
or lead to emotional wealth.
물질적 부의 단점

● 중요 포인트

it ~ that 강조용법

Even so, it is not the money *per se* that is valuable,
        it–that 강조용법
but the fact that it can potentially yield more positive
         강조용법 that이 아닌 the fact 수식 접속사(동격) that임
experiences.

4 혼공 개념 마무리   p.71
  단계

1. 잘생긴 정치가들에 대한 지나친 애정으로써의 그러한 증거에도 불구
하고, 다음의 연구는 유권자들이 자신들의 편견을 깨닫지 못한다는
것을 증명했다.

2. 표면적으로 빈정대는 말을 하는 사람은 받아들이는 사람이 그 빈정
대는 의도를 알아차리기를 바라지만, 반면에 속임수를 쓸 때는 일반

적으로 화자가 듣는 사람이 그 속이려는 의도를 알아차리지 못했으면 하고 바란다는 점에서 표면상으로 빈정거림은 속임과 반대되는 것이다.

3. 원기 회복을 만들어 내는 이러한 현상은 일상에 의해 생기는 피로가 자리 잡는 것을 막기 위해 보안 직원이 다른 위치로 순환하는 공항에서의 조치에서 목격될 수 있다.

4. 주요한 구조 조정을 겪고 있는 한 전자 회사의 고객 서비스 직원들은 장비를 설치하고 수리하는 것 외에도 장비에 대한 서비스 계약 판매를 시작해야 한다는 말을 들었다.

5. 그래서 누군가가 전쟁을 시작하겠다고 위협하거나 우리를 설득하려고 하면서 엄청난 선전 활동을 벌여 그것을 정당화하려 한다면, 뉴스 매체는 모든 것을 의심해야 할 책임이 있다.

6. 충분히 발달한 시장에서는, 경쟁적 지위들에서의 중요한 변화와 시장의 성장을 가져오는 획기적인 발전이 드물다.

7. 그것들(생물학적 리듬)은 외부에서 무슨 일이 일어나고 있던지 간에, 즉 한랭전선이 들어오는지 구름이 햇빛을 가리는지 간에, 대략 24시간 주기로 신체와 행동의 변화들을 용이하게 해준다.

 혼공 **07일차 글의 순서**

3 **고난도 문항** 요리하기 p.77

● 정답

> **1.** ② **2.** ④ **3.** ③ **4.** ③ **5.** ⑤ **6.** ④ **7.** ② **8.** ②

1. ②

● 전체 해석

한 전통적 정의에 따르면, '미학'은 아름다움, 특히 예술에서의 아름다움을 다루는 철학의 분야이다. 예를 들어, '모나리자'나 꼭대기가 눈으로 덮인 산이 주는 즐거운 특징들을 살펴보는 것이 미학의 범위에 포함될 것이다. (B) 그렇지만, 예술 작품들과 자연물들이 아름답다는 것에 의한 것 외에 다른 방식으로 우리의 관심을 끌 수 있으므로 그러한 정의는 너무 좁아 보인다. 아름다움에 대한 감탄을 불러일으키는 대신에, 예술가들은 어리둥절함, 충격, 심지어 혐오감을 불러일으킬 수도 있다. (A) 스페인 내란 동안에 있었던 독일과 이탈리아의 전투기들에 의한 스페인 시민 대량 학살에 대한 반응으로 피카소가 그린 검은색, 흰색, 회색으로 이루어진 거대한(11피트×25.6피트) 그림인 피카소의 '게르니카'에 대해 생각해 보자. 잔인한 전쟁의 이미지가 캔버스를 지배한다. (C) 이 작품은 널리 칭송되고 있으나 아름답기 때문이 아니다. 그러므로 미학에 대한 더 나은 정의는, 미학이란 사물이 경험되면서 사람들을 즐겁게 하는 방식을 다루는 철학의 분야라는 것이 될 것이다.

● 지문분석

According to one traditional definition, / *aesthetics* is the branch of philosophy / that deals with beauty, / especially beauty in the arts.
한 전통적 정의에 따르면 / 미학은 철학의 한 분야이다 / 아름다움을 다루는 / 특히 예술에서의

[Examining the pleasing features / of the *Mona Lisa* / or a snow-capped mountain,] / for example, / would come under aesthetics.
즐거운 특징들을 살펴보는 것은 / 모나리자의 / 아니면 눈으로 덮인 산의 / 예를 들어 / 미학 아래 온다(미학의 범주에 든다)

That definition / seems too narrow, / however, / since [works of art and natural objects] / may interest us / in other ways / than by being beautiful.
그러한 정의는 / 너무 좁은 것 같다 / 하지만 / 예술 작품과 자연물들은 / 우리의 관심이 대상일 수 있으므로 / 다른 방식으로 / 아름답다는 것에 의한 것 외에

Instead of evoking admiration of beauty, / artists may evoke / puzzlement, shock, and even disgust.
아름다움에 대한 감탄을 불러일으키는 것 대신에 / 예술가들은 불러일으킬 수도 있다 / 혼란함과 충격, 그리고 심지어 역겨움을

Consider Picasso's *Guernica*, / a huge (11-ft. × 25.6-ft.) painting / in black, white, and grey / that he made / in response to the slaughter of Spanish civilians / by German and Italian warplanes / during the Spanish Civil War.
피카소의 게르니카를 생각해보자 / 거대한 (11피트 x 25.6피트) 그림인 / 검정과 하얀, 그리고 회색으로 이루어진 / 그가 그렸던 / 스페인 시민의 대량 살상에 대한 반응으로 / 독일과 이탈리아의 전투기들에 의한 / 스페인 내전 동안에

[Images of a cruel war] / dominate the canvas.
잔혹한 전쟁의 이미지는 / 캔버스를 지배한다

This work is widely admired / but not for being beautiful.
이 작품은 널리 칭송된다 / 하지만 아름다워서가 아니다

[So a better definition of aesthetics] / would be that it is the branch of philosophy / that deals with the ways things please people / in being experienced.
그래서 미학에 대한 더 나은 정의는 / 그것은 철학의 한 분야라는 것이 된다는 것이다 / 그러한 방식을 다루는 / 사물이 사람들을 기쁘게 하는 / 경험되어질 때

● 해설

1. 주어진 글 다음에 이어질 글의 순서로 가장 적절한 것은?

According to one traditional definition, aesthetics is the branch of philosophy that deals with beauty, especially beauty in the arts. Examining the pleasing features of the Mona Lisa or a snow-capped mountain, for example, would come under aesthetics.

아름다움의 다루는 것이 미학의 전통적 정의임

(B) That definition seems too narrow, however, since works

of art and natural objects may interest us in other ways than by being beautiful. Instead of evoking admiration of beauty, artists may evoke puzzlement, shock, and even disgust.

(A) Consider Picasso's Guernica, a huge (11-ft. × 25.6-ft.) painting in black, white, and grey that he made in response to the slaughter of Spanish civilians by German and Italian warplanes during the Spanish Civil War. Images of a cruel war dominate the canvas.

(C) This work is widely admired but not for being beautiful. So
'이 작품'이 바로 게르니카를 의미함
a better definition of aesthetics would be that it is the branch of philosophy that deals with the ways things please people in being experienced.

● 중요 포인트

동명사 주어

[Examining the pleasing features of the Mona Lisa or a
S 동명사 주어
snow-capped mountain,] for example, would come under
                                              V
aesthetics.

2. ④

● 전체 해석

우리가 세상과 자신을 바라볼 때 우리는 필터를 통해서 보게 된다. 이 필터가 무엇인지 생각해 보라. 필터는 어떠한 것들은 받아들이고 다른 것들은 걸러내는 심리기제이다. (B) 필터가 무엇으로 이루어졌느냐에 따라서 뭐든지 눈에 띄거나 아니면 지나쳐 버리거나가 바뀔 수도 있다. 선글라스는 시각적 필터의 좋은 예이다. (C) 그러나 안경처럼 썼다 벗을 수 있는 그런 물리적 기구를 말하는 것은 분명 아니다. 사실 내가 의미하는 필터란 실로 내면적이고, 정신적이며, 감정적이고, 언어적이며, 지각적이다. (A) 그것들을 통해서 우리는 모든 사건들을 처리하고 우리 삶에 있어 중요성과 의미를 부여한다. 어떤 것들은 받아들이고 나머지 것들은 걸러내지만, 우리가 '보는' 것뿐 아니라 '듣는' 것과 '믿는' 것까지 이 모든 것들은 서로 영향을 미치게 된다.

● 지문분석

When we look at the world and ourselves, / we do it /
                                          look at the world and ourselves
through a set of filters.
우리가 세상과 우리 자신을 볼 때 / 우리는 그것을 한다 / 필터를 통해서
Think about what a filter is.
필터가 무엇인지 생각해보자
A filter is a mechanism / that lets some things flow in / but
screens other things out.
필터는 기제이다 / 무언가를 받아들이고 / 하지만 다른 것은 걸러내는
Depending on what the filter is made up of, / it can also
└ 분사구문
alter / whatever is looked at / or passes through it.

필터가 무엇으로 만들어지느냐에 따라서 / 그것은 또한 바꿀 수 있다 / 무엇이 보여지든지 / 아니면 지나쳐 버리든
Sunglasses are a good example / of a visual filter.
선글라스는 좋은 예이다 / 시각적 필터의
But, obviously, / I am not talking here / about some physical apparatus / that we can put on / and take off, / like a pair of glasses.
하지만 명백히 / 나는 여기서 말하고 있지는 않다 / 어떤 물리적인 기구에 대해서 / 우리가 착용할 수 있는 / 아니면 벗을 수 있는 / 안경처럼
In fact, [the filters / I am mentioning] / are internal,
            S
mental, emotional, verbal, and perceptual / in nature.
사실 / 필터들은 / 내가 언급하고 있는 / 내면적이고 정신적이며 감정적이고 언어적이며 그리고 지각적이다 / 사실상
Through them, / we process and assign / a weight and meaning / to every event in our lives.
그것들을 통해서 / 우리는 처리하고 부여한다 / 무게와 의미를 / 우리 삶의 모든 사건에 대해서
Some things flow in, / others are screened out, / but
                              not just[only] ~ but (also)
everything is affected: / not just what we 'see,' / but what
we 'hear' and 'believe.'
일부는 받아들이고 / 다른 것들은 차단되고 / 하지만 모든 것들은 영향을 받는다 / 우리가 보는 것 뿐만 아니라 / 우리가 듣고 믿는 것까지

● 해설

2. 주어진 글 다음에 이어질 글의 순서로 가장 적절한 것은?
When we look at the world and ourselves, we do it through a set of filters. Think about what a filter is. A filter is a mechanism that lets some things flow in but screens other things out.
                    필터의 역할에 대한 설명이 나옴
(B) Depending on what the filter is made up of, it can also alter whatever is looked at or passes through it. Sunglasses are a good example of a visual filter. → 필터의 역할에 대한 설명이 나옴

(C) But, obviously, I am not talking here about some physical
      분위기 바뀜, 시각만 해당되는 게 아님
apparatus that we can put on and take off, like a pair of glasses. In fact, the filters I am mentioning are internal, mental, emotional, verbal, and perceptual in nature.

(A) Through them, we process and assign a weight and meaning to every event in our lives. Some things flow in, others are screened out, but everything is affected: not just what we 'see,' but what we 'hear' and 'believe.'

● 중요 포인트

대동사

일반 동사의 대동사는 do로 받지.

When we look at the world and ourselves, we do it through a set of filters.
look at the world and ourselves

3. ③

●전체 해석

엄마와 아빠가 멋진 식당으로 저녁 식사를 하러 가셨다. 혼자 있게 된 그 첫날밤에, 아빠는 자신의 영사기와 모든 필름 통들을 내게 맡기셨다. (B) 그는 그날 밤에 내가 모든 것을 스스로 할 수 있다고 말씀하셨다. 그래서 나는 거실의 한쪽 끝에 영사막을 설치했다. 나는 영사기를 켜고, 전등을 끄고, 무릎에 팝콘 그릇을 놓고는, HATTIE-1951이라는 라벨이 붙은 필름을 보기 위해 자리를 잡았다. (C) 그것은 내가 특히 좋아하는 것 중의 하나인데, 내 세 번째 생일 파티가 들어 있고 우리의 늙은 고양이 Simon이 식당 식탁으로 뛰어올라 아이스크림 접시에 내려앉는 것을 볼 수 있기 때문이다. (A) 그러고 나서 나는 그 필름을 거꾸로 틀어서 그 고양이가 바닥에 뛰어 내리는 것을 지켜보고 모든 아이스크림 방울들이 후루룩 소리를 내며 접시로 돌아가는 것을 볼 수 있다. 필름의 나머지를 보기 전에 나는 Simon이 여러 번 뛰어들었다 뛰어 나오게 하였다.

●지문분석

Mom and Dad went to dinner / at a nice restaurant.
엄마와 아빠는 저녁식사를 하러 갔다 / 멋진 식당에
On that first night to myself, / Dad entrusted me / with his movie projector / and all the reels of film.
혼자 있던 첫날 밤에 / 아빠는 나에게 맡기셨다 / 그의 영화 영사기와 / 모든 필름 통들을
He said / I could do everything myself / that night.
그는 말했다 / 내가 모든 것을 혼자서 할 수 있을 거라고 / 그날 밤에
So I set up the screen / at one end of the living room.
그래서 나는 스크린을 설치했다 / 거실 한쪽 끝에
I turned on the projector, / turned off the light, / put the bowl of popcorn in my lap, / and settled in / to watch the film / labeled HATTIE-1951.
나는 영사기를 켰고 / 불을 껐고 / 팝콘 그릇을 무릎에 놓고 / 그리고 자리를 잡았다 / 영화를 보기 위해서 / HATTIE-1951이라는 라벨이 붙은
It's one of my favorites / because my third birthday party is on it / and I can watch / our old cat Simon / jump up on
지각동사   O.C.
the dining room table / and land in a dish of ice cream.
그것은 내가 좋아하는 것 중 하나였다 / 왜냐하면 나의 세 번째 생일 파티가 그곳에 있고 / 그리고 나는 볼 수 있기 때문이다 / 우리 늙은 고양이 사이먼이 / 식당 식탁으로 뛰어 올라서 / 아이스크림 접시에 내려앉는 것을
Then I can play the film backward / and watch the cat / fly
지각동사   O.C.
down to the floor / and see all the splashes of ice cream /
지각동사
slurp themselves / back into the dish.
O.C.
그리고 나서 나는 영화를 거꾸로 틀 수 있다 / 그리고 고양이를 볼 수 있다 / 바닥에 뛰어내리는 것을 / 그리고 모든 아이스크림 방울들이

/ 후후룩 소리를 내며 / 접시로 돌아가는 것을
I made Simon jump in and out / several times / before I
사역동사   O.C.
watched the rest of the film.
나는 사이먼이 뛰어들었다 나왔다 하도록 했다 / 여러 번 / 내가 영화의 나머지를 보기 전에

●해설

3. 주어진 글 다음에 이어질 글의 순서로 가장 적절한 것은?
Mom and Dad went to dinner at a nice restaurant. On that first night to myself, Dad entrusted me with his movie projector and all the reels of film.

(B) He said I could do everything myself that night. So I set up the screen at one end of the living room. I turned on the projector, turned off the light, put the bowl of popcorn in my lap, and settled in to watch the film labeled HATTIE-1951.

(C) It's one of my favorites because my third birthday party is on it and I can watch our old cat Simon jump up on the dining room table and land in a dish of ice cream.

(A) Then I can play the film backward and watch the cat fly down to the floor and see all the splashes of ice cream slurp themselves back into the dish. I made Simon jump in and out several times before I watched the rest of the film.

●중요 포인트

지각동사

Then I can play the film backward and watch the cat fly
지각동사
down to the floor and see all the splashes of ice cream
지각동사
slurp themselves back into the dish.
O.C.

4. ③

●전체 해석

세월이 지나면서 어휘들의 정의가 변하는 이유는 단순히 잘못된 사용 때문이다. 상대적으로 진부한 언어의 잘못된 의미가 원래 의도나 정의보다 더 널리 퍼지는 수많은 예들이 점차 증가하고 있다. (B) 'peruse'가 그 중의 하나다. 대부분의 사람들은 무언가를 'peruse'한다는 것이 '크게 신경 쓰지 않고, 빠르게 훑어보거나 지나치듯 스쳐감'을 의미한다고 생각한다. 실제로는, 이것의 'peruse'가 실제로 의미하는(어떤 것을 신중하고, 상세하게 연구하거나 읽는다는) 것과 정반대이다. (C) 그러나, 그 단어가 너무 많은 사람들에 의해서 너무 자주 잘못 사용되어서 그 단어의 두 번째 의미 - 실제 의미하는 바의 정반대 - 가 2차 정의로서 마침내 받아들여졌고, 대부분의 사람들이 아는 한, 그것이 유일한 정의이다. (A) 그렇다면, 화난 고객이 당신의 상점 중 한 곳에서 받은 서비스에 대한 편지를 보냈다고 생각해 보라. 만약 당신의 응답이 "그의 편지를 대충 훑어보았다"는 것이라면, 그는 전보다 훨씬 더 화가 날 것이다.

[One reason / why the definitions of words have changed over time] / is simply because of their misuse.
한 가지 이유는 / 왜 단어의 정의가 시간이 지남에 따라 변화하느냐에 대한 / 간단히 그들의 오용 때문이다

There are a growing number of examples / where [the incorrect meaning / of relatively commonplace language] / has become more widespread / than the original intention or definition.
점차 증가하는 많은 수의 예들이 있다 / 잘못된 의미가 / 상대적으로 진부한 언어의 / 더욱 퍼지게 된 / 원래의 의도나 정의보다도

The word 'peruse' is one of them.
'peruse'라는 단어가 그들 중 하나이다

Most people think / that [to 'peruse' something] / means to 'scan or skim it quickly, / without paying much attention.'
대부분의 사람들은 생각한다 / 무언가를 peruse한다는 것은 / 그것을 빠르게 훑어보거나 지나치는 것을 의미한다고 / 많은 주의를 기울이지 않고

In fact, / this is the exact opposite / of what 'peruse' really means: / 'to study or read something carefully, / in detail.'
사실 / 이것은 정확하게 반대이다 / 'peruse'가 정말로 의미하는 것의 / 무언가를 주의깊게 연구하거나 읽는 것 / 세세하게

But the word has been misused / so often / by so many people, / that [this second sense of it / – the exact opposite / of what it actually means] / – has finally been accepted / as a secondary definition / and as far as most people know, / it is the only definition.
하지만 그 단어는 잘못 사용되어 왔고 / 너무 종종 / 너무나도 많은 사람들에 의해서 / 그것의 이 두 번째 의미는 / 정확하게 정반대인 / 그것이 실제로 의미하는 것의 / 마침내 받아들여졌다 / 두 번째 의미로서 / 그리고 대부분의 사람들이 아는 한 / 그것은 유일한 정의이다

Now, imagine / that an angry customer sent you / a letter about the service / he received in one of your stores.
지금 상상해 봐라 / 화난 고객이 당신에게 보냈던 걸 / 서비스의 편지를 / 그가 당신의 점포 중 하나에서 받았던

If your reply / is that you 'perused his letter,' / he is likely to get even more angry / than he was before.
당신의 답장이 / 당신이 그의 편지를 대충 훑어 보았다는 것이라면 / 그는 훨씬 더 화가 날 가능성이 있다 / 그가 이전에 그랬던 것보다

●해설

4. 주어진 글 다음에 이어질 글의 순서로 가장 적절한 것은?
One reason why the definitions of words have changed over time is simply because of their misuse. There are a growing number of examples where the incorrect meaning of relatively commonplace language has become more widespread than the original intention or definition.

(B) The word 'peruse' is one of them. Most people think that to 'peruse' something means to 'scan or skim it quickly, without paying much attention.' In fact, this is the exact opposite of what 'peruse' really means: 'to study or read something carefully, in detail.' peruse의 진짜 의미 등장

화제 전환: 잘못된 용어가 2차 정의가 되고 이것이 유일한 정의가 됨
(C) But the word has been misused so often by so many people, that this second sense of it – the exact opposite of what it actually means – has finally been accepted as a secondary definition and as far as most people know, it is the only definition.

(A) Now, imagine that an angry customer sent you a letter about the service he received in one of your stores. 혼동된 의미로 사용되는 예시가 나옴 If your reply is that you 'perused his letter,' he is likely to get even more angry than he was before.

●중요 포인트

관계부사 why
[One reason why the definitions of words have changed over time] is simply because of their misuse.

5. ⑤

●전체 해석

역사를 공부하는 것은 우리가 들어왔던 것을 암기하는 것에 관한 것이 아니다. 그것은 우리에게 과거를 조사할 것을 요구한다. 탐정처럼 우리는 쉽고, 알려진 정보들로 시작한다. (C) 그런 다음에 그 정보들이 어떻게 서로 들어맞는지를 알아보기 위해서 그것들을 이리저리 바꿔본다. 일단 모든 정보들이 들어맞으면, 우리는 완전한 그림을 갖게 된다. 우리가 모든 정보를 꿰어 맞출 때, 우리는 우리 자신에게 우리가 알고 있는 것을 설명하는 다른 방식을 생각해 볼 것을 요구한다. (B) 예를 들어, 어떤 사람이 당신에게 중국의 황제 진시황이 잔인한 통치자였다고 말한다면, 당신은 이것을 사실로 단순히 받아들이겠는가? 아니면 그 말에 대해서 질문을 하고 그것을 뒷받침할 정보나 증거를 찾겠는가? (A) 당신은 더 나아가 "왜 그는 잔인했을까?" 그리고 "그의 통치의 결과는 무엇이었을까?"와 같은 질문을 해야만 한다. 따라서 역사를 공부하는 것은 우리가 읽거나 들은 모든 것을 사실로 받아들이지 않도록 우리를 훈련시킨다. 대신에, 그것은 과거를 전체적으로 이해할 수 있도록 비판적으로 생각하는 기술을 사용하도록 우리를 훈련시킨다.

●지문분석

Studying history is not about memorizing / what we have been told / – it requires us / to investigate the past.
역사를 공부하는 것은 기억하는 것에 대한 것이 아니다 / 우리가 들어왔던 것을 / 그것은 우리에게 요구한다 / 과거를 조사할 것을

Like a detective, / we start / with the easy, known pieces of information.
탐정처럼 / 우리는 시작한다 / 쉽고 알려진 정보들로

We then shuffle the pieces around / to see / how they fit

together.
그리고 우리는 그 조각들을 이리저리 바꿔본다 / 보기 위해서 / 어떻게 그들이 맞춰지는지

Once all the pieces fit, / we have the full picture.
일단 모든 조각이 맞춰지면 / 우리는 완전한 그림을 갖게 된다

As we put the pieces together, / we challenge ourselves / to think of other ways / to describe what we know.
우리가 조각들을 맞출 때 / 우리는 우리 자신에게 요구한다 / 다른 식으로 생각해보라고 / 우리가 알고 있는 것을 설명하는

For example, / if someone told you / that Chinese Emperor Qin Shihuang / was a cruel ruler, / would you simply accept this / as the truth?
예를 들어 / 만약 누군가가 당신에게 말한다면 / 중국의 황제인 진시황이 / 잔혹한 지배자였다라고 / 당신은 간단히 이것을 받아들이겠는가 / 사실로서

Or, would you ask questions / about the statement / and look for information or evidence / to support it?
아니면 당신은 질문을 하겠는가? / 그 발언에 대해서 / 그리고 정보나 증거를 찾는가 / 그것을 지지할

You have to go further / to ask questions / such as, "Why was he cruel?" / and "What were the results of his rule?"
당신은 더 나아가야만 한다 / 질문을 하러 / 예를 들어 왜 그는 잔혹했는가 / 그리고 그의 통치의 결과가 무엇이었는가

Hence, studying history / trains us / not to accept everything / we read or hear / as the truth.
그래서 역사를 공부하는 것은 / 우리를 훈련시킨다 / 모든 것을 받아들이지는 말라고 / 우리가 읽거나 듣는 / 사실로서

Instead, it trains us / to use our critical thinking skills / to get the full picture of the past.
대신에 그것은 우리를 훈련시킨다 / 우리의 비판적 사고방식을 사용하라고 / 완전한 과거의 그림을 얻기 위해서

● 해설

5. 주어진 글 다음에 이어질 글의 순서로 가장 적절한 것은?
Studying history is not about memorizing what we have been told – it requires us to investigate the past. Like a detective, we start with the easy, known pieces of information.

(C) We then shuffle the pieces around to see how they fit together. Once all the pieces fit, we have the full picture. As we put the pieces together, we challenge ourselves to think of other ways to describe what we know.

(B) For example, if someone told you that Chinese Emperor Qin Shihuang was a cruel ruler, would you simply accept this as the truth? Or, would you ask questions about the statement and look for information or evidence to support it?
(A) You have to go further to ask questions such as, "Why was he cruel?" and "What were the results of his rule?" Hence,
ʰheᵉ 해당하는 사람이 바로 Qin Shihuang이야.
studying history trains us not to accept everything we read or

---

hear as the truth. Instead, it trains us to use our critical thinking skills to get the full picture of the past.

● 중요 포인트

관계사가 생략된 수식어구
Hence, studying history trains us not to accept everything
                                                              ⌐
we read or hear as the truth.
that 생략

6. ④

● 전체 해석

유기농법을 사용하는 농부들은 전통적 재래 농법을 사용하는 농부들의 작물들만큼이나 해충에 시달리는 작물들을 재배하는데, 벌레들은 대개 유기농과 재래 농법을 우리만큼 잘 구별하지 않는다. (C) 그들이 재래 농법을 사용하는 농부들보다 환경적으로 유익한 형태의 생물학적 방제를 실행할 가능성이 훨씬 더 크고, 그들이 또 한 만연하는 것을 줄이기 위해 현명하게 자신들의 작물들을 다양화할 가능성이 더 큰 것이 사실이다. (A) 하지만, 대부분의 유기농법을 사용하는 농부들 은 그들의 작업에 있어서의 필요한 보충물로서 화학물질에 의존할 수밖에 없다. 흔히 해충들이 미국에서 재배되는 작물의 40퍼센트까지 먹어치우기 때문에, 그들은 으레 그렇게 한다. (B) 그들은 이러한 물질들을 "식물성 추출물"이라고 부를지도 모른다. 하지만 소비자 동맹의 수석 과학자인 Ned Groth에 따르면, 이러한 독소들은 "그것들이 천연적이라고 해서 반드시 덜 걱정스러운 것은 아니다."

● 지문분석

Organic farmers grow crops / that are no less plagued / by pests / than those of conventional farmers; / insects
                                                              crops
generally do not discriminate / between organic and conventional / as well as we do.
                                                       discriminate
유기농 농부들은 작물을 키운다 / 고통을 받는 / 해충에 의해서 / 전통적인 기법의 농부들의 그것들(작물)만큼 / 벌레들은 보통 차별하지 않는다 / 유기농과 전통적인 것 사이에 / 우리가 하는 것처럼
가주어 – 진주어 구문
It is true / that they are far more likely / than conventional
            ❶
farmers / to practice environmentally beneficial forms / of biological control, / and that they are also more likely / to
                                                       ❷
sensibly diversify their crops / to reduce infestation.
사실이다 / 그들이 가능성이 더 크다는 것이 / 전통적인 기법의 농부들보다 / 친환경적으로 유익한 형태를 실행할 / 생물학적 통제의 / 그리고 그들은 또한 더 가능성이 크다는 것이 / 그들의 작물을 현명하게 다양화 할 / 벌레들이 많아지는 것을 줄이기 위해서

However, most organic farmers / have no choice but to
                                ㄴ '~하지 않을수 없다'
rely on chemicals / as necessary supplements / to their operations.
하지만 대부분의 유기농 농부들은 / 화학물질에 의존할 수 밖에 없다 / 필요한 보충물로서 / 그들의 작업에서

With pests often consuming / up to 40 percent of the crops
ㄴwith + 명사 + 분사: 동시상황 분사구문
/ grown in the United States, / they do so / as a matter of
                                            rely on chemicals
course.

벌레들이 종종 소비하면서 / 작물의 최대 40%까지 / 미국에서 재배된 / 그들은 그렇게 한다 / 당연히

They might refer to these substances / as "botanical extracts."
그들은 이러한 물질들은 부를지도 모른다 / 식물성 추출물로

But according to Ned Groth, / a senior scientist at Consumers Union, / these toxins "are not necessarily less worrisome / because they are natural."
Ned Groth에 따르면 / 소비자 연맹의 수석 과학자인 / 이러한 독성물질은 꼭 덜 걱정스러운 것은 아니다 / 그들이 천연이기 때문에

● 해설

6. 주어진 글 다음에 이어질 글의 순서로 가장 적절한 것은?
Organic farmers grow crops that are no less plagued by pests than those of conventional farmers; insects generally do not discriminate between organic and conventional as well as we do. → 유기농 농부들도 해충에 시달림

(C) It is true that they are far more likely than conventional farmers to practice environmentally beneficial forms of biological control, and that they are also more likely to sensibly diversify their crops to reduce infestation.
유기농 농부들의 해충 방지 노력

(A) However, most organic farmers have no choice but to rely
유기농 농부들의 해충 방지 노력의 문제점 언급
on chemicals as necessary supplements to their operations. With pests often consuming up to 40 percent of the crops grown in the United States, they do so as a matter of course.

(B) They might refer to these substances as "botanical extracts." But according to Ned Groth, a senior scientist at Consumers Union, these toxins "are not necessarily less worrisome because they are natural."
추가적인 유기농 농부들의 해충 방지 노력의 문제점

● 중요 포인트

with + 명사 + 분사: 동시상황 분사구문

With pests often consuming up to 40 percent of the crops
with + 명사 + 분사: 동시상황 〈분사구문〉, '벌레들이 종종 소비하면서'
grown in the United States, they do so ~

7. ②

● 전체 해석

고대 그리스인들은 기억의 궁전과 장소법과 같은 두뇌 훈련 방법을 통해 기억을 개선하려고 노력했다. 동시에 그들과 이집트인들은 외면화된(형체로 나타난) 지식의 웅대한 저장소인 현대적인 도서관을 처음으로 만들면서 정보를 외면화하는 일에 전문가들이 되었다. (B) 지적 활동이 이렇게 동시에 급증하는 일이 왜 하필 그때에(그렇게 일어났을 때) 일어났는지 우리는 알지 못한다. (아마 인간의 일상적인 경험이 복잡성의 일정한 수준에 이르렀을 것이다.) 하지만 우리의 삶과 우리의 환경과 우리의 사고까지도 정리하려는 인간의 욕구는 여전히 강력하다. (A) 이런 욕구는 단순히 학습되는 것이 아니다. 이것은 생물학적인 명령이다. 즉, 동물은 본능적으로 자기 환경을 정리한다. 대부분의 포유동물은 자신의 소화 관련 배설물을 자신이 먹고 자는 곳으로부터 치우는 생물학적 성향을 타고났다. (C) 개는 자신의 장난감을 모아서 바구니에 넣는다고 알려져 왔고, 개미는 집단의 죽은 구성원을 매장지로 끌고 가고, 특정한 새와 설치류 동물은 침입자를 더 쉽게 발견하기 위하여 자기 보금자리 주변에 대칭적으로 조직된 장애물을 만든다.

● 지문분석

The ancient Greeks sought to improve memory / through brain training methods / such as memory palaces and the method of loci.
고대 그리스인들은 기억력을 개선하고자 노력했다 / 두뇌 훈련 방법을 통해서 / 기억의 궁전과 장소법과 같은

At the same time, / they and the Egyptians became experts / at externalizing information, / inventing the modern
└ 분사구문, '만듦으로서'
library, / a grand storehouse for externalized knowledge.
동시에 / 그들과 이집트인들은 전문가들이 되었다 / 정보를 외면화하는 데 / 현대의 도서관을 만듦으로서 / 외면화된 지식을 위한 거대한 저장소인

We don't know / why [these simultaneous explosions
                                                    S
of intellectual activity] / occurred / when they did /
                              V
(perhaps daily human experience had hit a certain level of complexity).
우리는 알지 못한다 / 왜 이러한 동시에 발생하는 지적 활동의 폭발이 / 발생했는지 / 그들이 했을 때 / 아마도 매일의 인간의 경험이 일정 수준의 복잡한 수준에 도달했을 것이다

But [the human need / to organize our lives, our
                                                S
environment, even our thoughts,] / remains strong.
                                      V
하지만 인간의 욕구는 / 우리의 삶을, 우리의 환경을, 심지어 우리의 생각들을 조직하려는 / 강하게 남아있다

This need isn't simply learned; / it is a biological imperative. — Animals organize their environments instinctively.
이것은 간단히 학습되지 않는다 / 그것은 생물학적인 명령이다 / 동물들은 그들의 환경을 본능적으로 정리한다

Most mammals are biologically programmed / to put their digestive waste / away from where they eat and sleep.
대부분의 포유류는 생물학적으로 프로그램되어 있다 / 그들의 소화관련 분비물을 치우도록 하는 / 그들이 먹고 자는 곳으로부터 떨어져서

Dogs have been known / to collect their toys / and put hem in baskets; / ants carry off dead members of the colony / to burial grounds; / certain birds and rodents create barriers / around their nests / in order to more easily detect invaders.
개들은 알려져 있다 / 그들의 장난감을 모으고 / 바구니에 그것들을 놓는 것으로 / 개미들은 죽은 집단의 구성원을 끌고 간다 / 매장지로 / 어떤 새들과 설치류는 장애물을 만든다 / 그들의 보금자리 주변에 / 침입자들의 발견을 더 쉽게 하려고

7. 주어진 글 다음에 이어질 글의 순서로 가장 적절한 것은?

The ancient Greeks sought to improve memory through brain training methods such as memory palaces and the method of loci. At the same time, they and the Egyptians became experts at externalizing information, inventing the modern library, a grand storehouse for externalized knowledge.

(B) We don't know why these simultaneous explosions of intellectual activity occurred when they did (perhaps daily human experience had hit a certain level of complexity). But the human need to organize our lives, our environment, even our thoughts, remains strong.

(A) This need isn't simply learned; it is a biological imperative. Animals organize their environments instinctively. Most mammals are biologically programmed to put their digestive waste away from where they eat and sleep.

(C) Dogs have been known to collect their toys and put them in baskets; ants carry off dead members of the colony to burial grounds; certain birds and rodents create barriers around their nests in order to more easily detect invaders.

● 중요 포인트

to부정사의 수식을 받는 주어

But [the human need to organize our lives, our environment, even our thoughts,] remains strong.
　　　　　　　　　　S　　　　　　　　　　　　　　　V

8. ②

● 전체 해석

진화는 동물이 남기는 후손들의 수를 최대화하기 위해 작용한다. 동물이 성장할 때에 어로 행위에 의해 죽을 위험이 증가하는 상황에서 진화는 천천히 성장하고, 더 어린 나이에 그리고 더 작을 때에 성숙하고, 더 일찍 번식을 하는 것들을 선호한다. (B) 이것은 정확하게 우리가 현재 야생에서 보는 것이다. 캐나다의 St. Lawrence만에 사는 대구는 현재 네 살쯤 되었을 때 번식을 시작한다. 40년 전에 그것들은 성숙기에 도달하려면 6세 혹은 7세가 될 때까지 기다려야만 했다. 북해의 가자미는 1950년에 그랬던 것에 비해 체중이 절반 정도만 되면 성숙한다. (A) 분명히 이러한 적응은 과도한 어로 행위에 의해 심한 압박을 받는 종들에게는 좋은 소식일까? 꼭 그렇지는 않다. 어린 물고기는 몸집이 큰 동물들보다 훨씬 더 적은 수의 알을 낳으며, 현재 많은 기업적인 어업이 너무나도 집중적이어서 성숙기의 연령을 지나서 2년 넘게 살아남는 동물들이 거의 없다. (C) 동시에 이것은 미래 세대를 보장하는 알이나 유충이 더 적어진다는 것을 의미한다. 어떤 경우에는 오늘날 생산되는 어린 동물의 양이 과거보다 백 배 혹은 심지어 천 배까지도 더 적어서, 종의 생존, 그리고 그것들에 의존하는 어업이 심각한 위기에 처하게 된다.

● 지문분석

Evolution works / to maximize the number of descendants / that an animal leaves behind.
진화는 작용한다 / 후손의 수를 최대화하기 위해서 / 동물이 뒤에 남겨놓는

「~인 상황에서」
Where [the risk of death / from fishing] / increases / as an animal grows, / evolution favors those / that grow slowly, / mature younger and smaller, / and reproduce earlier.
죽음의 위험이 / 어업으로부터 / 증가하는 상황에서 / 동물이 성장할 때 / 진화는 이것들을 선호한다 / 천천히 자라고 / 더 어린 나이에 더 작을 때 성숙하고 / 더 일찍 번식하는

This is exactly what we now see in the wild.
이것은 정확하게 우리가 지금 야생에서 보는 것이다

[Cod in Canada's Gulf of St. Lawrence] / begin to reproduce / at around four today; / forty years ago / they had to wait / until six or seven / to reach maturity.
　S
캐나다의 St. Lawrence 만에 있는 대구는 / 번식하기 시작한다 / 현재 4살 쯤 되었을 때 / 40년 전 / 그들은 기다려야만 했다 / 6~7세까지 / 성숙기에 도달하려면

[Sole in the North Sea] / mature at half the body weight / they did in 1950.
북해 지역의 가자미는 / 체중의 절반 정도로 성숙한다 / 1950년에 그들이 그랬던

Surely these adaptations are good news / for species / hard-pressed / by excessive fishing?
확실히 이러한 적응은 좋은 소식일까 / 종들에게는 / 심한 압박을 받는 / 과도한 어업에 의해서

Not exactly.
정확하게는 아니다

Young fish produce many fewer eggs / than large-bodied animals, / and many industrial fisheries are now so intensive / that few animals survive / more than a couple of years / beyond the age of maturity.
　　　　　　　　　　so ~ that 용법
어린 물고기는 훨씬 더 적은 알을 낳는다 / 몸집이 큰 동물들보다도 / 그리고 많은 산업화된 어업이 지금은 너무 집중적이어서 / 어떠한 동물로 살아남지 못한다 / 2년 이상을 / 성숙기의 연령을 지나서

Together this means / there are fewer eggs and larvae / to secure future generations.
함께 이것은 의미한다 / 알과 유충이 더 적다는 것을 / 미래 세대를 보장하기 위한

In some cases / [the amount of young / produced today] / is a hundred or even a thousand times less / than in the past, / putting the survival of species, / and the fisheries dependent on them, / at grave risk.
　　　　　　　　　　　　　S　　　　V　　　　분사구문
어떤 경우에는 / 어린 동물의 양은 / 오늘날 생산되는 / 백 배 혹은 심지어 천 배 정도 적다 / 과거보다 / 이는 종의 생존을 처하게 한다 / 그리고 그들에 의존하는 어업을 / 심각한 위기에

●해설

8. 주어진 글 다음에 이어질 글의 순서로 가장 적절한 것은?

Evolution works to maximize the number of descendants that an animal leaves behind. Where the risk of death from fishing increases as an animal grows, evolution favors those that grow slowly, mature younger and smaller, and reproduce earlier.

(B) This is exactly what we now see in the wild. Cod in Canada's Gulf of St. Lawrence begin to reproduce at around four today; forty years ago they had to wait until six or seven to reach maturity. Sole in the North Sea mature at half the body weight they did in 1950.

(A) Surely these adaptations are good news for species hard-pressed by excessive fishing? Not exactly. Young fish produce many fewer eggs than large-bodied animals, and many industrial fisheries are now so intensive that few animals survive more than a couple of years beyond the age of maturity.

(C) Together this means there are fewer eggs and larvae to secure future generations. In some cases the amount of young produced today is a hundred or even a thousand times less than in the past, putting the survival of species, and the fisheries dependent on them, at grave risk.

●중요 포인트

복잡한 주어 구문

주어부에 전치사구와 분사가 있을 때 진짜 주어를 찾는 것이 독해의 핵심이야.

In some cases [the amount of young produced today] is a hundred or even a thousand times less than in the past, putting the survival of species, and the fisheries dependent on them, at grave risk.

④ 혼공 개념 마무리 p.81

1. 예를 들어, '모나리자'나 꼭대기가 눈으로 덮인 산이 주는 즐거운 특징들을 살펴보는 것이 미학의 범위에 포함될 것이다.

2. 그래서 미학에 대한 더 나은 정의는, 미학이란 사물이 경험되면서 사람들을 즐겁게 하는 방식을 다루는 철학의 분야라는 것이 될 것이다.

3. 그리고 나서 나는 그 필름을 거꾸로 틀어서 그 고양이가 바닥에 뛰어 내리는 것을 지켜보고 모든 아이스크림 방울들이 후루룩 소리를 내며 접시로 돌아가는 것을 볼 수 있다.

4. 상대적으로 진부한 언어의 잘못된 의미가 원래 의도나 정의보다 더 널리 퍼지는 수많은 예들이 점차 증가하고 있다.

5. 그들이 재래 농법을 사용하는 농부들보다 환경적으로 유익한 형태의 생물학적 방제를 실행할 가능성이 훨씬 더 크고, 그들이 또 한 (벌레들이) 만연하는 것을 줄이기 위해 현명하게 자신들의 작물들을 다양화할 가능성이 더 큰 것이 사실이다.

6. 동시에 그들과 이집트인들은 외면화된(형체로 나타난) 지식의 웅대한 저장소인 현대적인 도서관을 처음으로 만들면서 정보를 외면화하는 일에 전문가들이 되었다.

7. 어떤 경우에는 오늘날 생산되는 어린 동물의 양이 과거보다 백 배 혹은 심지어 천 배까지도 더 적어서, 종의 생존, 그리고 그것들에 의존하는 어업이 심각한 위기에 처하게 된다.

 08일차 요약문 완성

③ 고난도 문항 요리하기 p.87

●정답

1. ⑤ 2. ⑤ 3. ② 4. ② 5. ③ 6. ② 7. ① 8. ④

1. ⑤

●전체 해석

진화적 성공의 관점에서 고려해 볼 때, 사람들이 하는 비이성적인 것처럼 보이는 선택들 중 많은 것들이 결국에는 그다지 어리석어 보이지 않는다. 우리의 조상과 현재의 꼬리감는 원숭이를 포함하여 대부분의 동물들은 생존하는 것이 매우 힘든 상황에서 살았다. 초기 인류 문명에 대해 연구하는 고생물학자들은 우리의 조상들이 빈번한 가뭄과 혹한의 시기에 직면했다는 증거를 찾아냈다. 아사 직전의 위기에서 살고 있을 때에는 양식 저장량이 조금 감소했을 때가 조금 증가했을 때보다 훨씬 더 큰 변화를 가져온다. 아직도 수렵·채집 사회에서 살고 있는 사람들을 연구하는 인류학자들은, 그들이 엄청나게 풍부한 양의 식량을 얻을 수 있는 최상의 기회가 아니라, 오히려 결국 부족한 식량 공급을 초래하게 되는 위험성을 최소화하기 위한 선택을 일관되게 한다는 것을 발견했다. 다시 말해서, 사람들은 어디서나 자신과 가족에게 식량을 공급할 수 있는 수준 아래로 내려가는 것을 피하려는 강한 욕구를 갖고 있다. 우리의 조상들이 손실에 대해 고심하지 않고, 대신에 큰 이득을 얻으려고 너무 많은 모험을 했다면, 그들은 멸망하여 결코 어느 누구의 조상도 되지 못했을 가능성이 더 컸을 것이다.

↓

우리의 조상들은 최대한의 이득을 추구하는 것보다는 최소한의 자원을 확보하기에 우선순위를 두었는데, 그것은 진화적 관점에서 보았을 때 인류 생존을 위해 합리적인 선택이었다.

●지문분석

When considered in terms of evolutionary success, / [many of the seemingly irrational choices / that people make] / do not seem so foolish after all.
진화적 성공의 관점에서 고려되었을 때 / 외형적으로 비이성적인 선

택 중 상당수는 / 사람들이 하는 / 결국 그렇게 멍청해 보이지는 않는다
[Most animals, / including our ancestors and modern-day capuchin monkeys,] / lived very close to the margin of survival.
대부분의 동물들은 / 우리의 조상과 현재의 꼬리감는 원숭이를 포함하여 / 생존하는 것이 매우 힘든 상황에서 살았다
[Paleontologists / who study early human civilizations] / have uncovered evidence / that our ancestors faced / frequent periods of drought and freezing.
고생물학자들은 / 초기 인류의 문명을 연구하는 / 증거를 발견했다 / 우리 조상들이 직면했다는 / 빈번한 가뭄과 혹한의 시기에
When you are living on the verge of starvation, / [a slight downturn in your food reserves] / makes a lot more difference / than a slight upturn.
아사 직전에 살고 있을 때 / 우리 식량의 저장량이 약간 줄어든다는 것은 / 더 많은 차이를 만든다 / 약간의 증가보다는
[Anthropologists / who study people / still living in hunter-gatherer societies] / have discovered / that they regularly make choices / designed to produce / not the best opportunity / for obtaining a hyperabundant supply of food / but, instead, the least danger / of ending up with an insufficient supply.
인류학자들은 / 사람들을 연구하는 / 여전히 수렵•채집 사회에서 살고 있는 / 발견했다 / 그들이 일관되게 선택을 한다는 것을 / 만들기 위해서 고안된 / 최상의 기회가 아니라 / 엄청난 식량의 공급을 얻기 위한 / 대신에 위험을 최소화하는 / 불충분한 식량 공급을 초래하는
In other words, / people everywhere have a strong motivation / to avoid falling below the level / that will feed themselves and their families.
다시 말하자면 / 어디서나 사람들은 강한 동기를 가진다 / 수준 아래로 떨어지는 것을 피하려는 / 자신과 가족들에게 먹일 수 있는
If our ancestors hadn't agonized over losses / and instead had taken too many chances / in going after the big gains, / they'd have been more likely to lose out / and never become anyone's ancestor.
만약 우리 조상이 손실에 대해서 고민하지 않았다면 / 대신에 너무 많은 모험을 했더라면 / 커다란 이익을 얻으려고 / 그들은 손해를 봤을 가능성이 컸을 것이다 / 그리고 결코 누군가의 조상도 되지 못했을 것이다

↓

Our ancestors gave priority / to securing minimum resources / rather than pursuing maximum gains, / and that was the rational choice / for human survival / from an evolutionary perspective.
우리 조상들은 우선순위를 주었다 / 최소한의 자원을 확보하기 위해서 / 최대의 이익을 추구하기 보다는 / 그리고 그것은 합리적인 선택이었다 / 인류의 생존을 위해서 / 진화론적인 관점에서

● 해설

1. 다음 글의 내용을 한 문장으로 요약하고자 한다. 빈칸 (A)와 (B)에 들어갈 말로 가장 적절한 것은?

When considered in terms of evolutionary success, many of the seemingly irrational choices that people make do not seem so foolish after all. Most animals, including our ancestors and modern-day capuchin monkeys, lived very close to the margin of survival. Paleontologists who study early human civilizations have uncovered evidence that our ancestors faced frequent periods of drought and freezing. When you are living on the verge of starvation, a slight downturn in your food reserves makes a lot more difference than a slight upturn. Anthropologists who study people still living in hunter-gatherer societies have discovered that they regularly make choices designed to produce not the best opportunity for obtaining a hyperabundant supply of food but, instead, the least danger of ending up with an insufficient supply. In other words, people everywhere have a strong motivation to avoid falling below the level that will feed themselves and their families. If our ancestors hadn't agonized over losses and instead had taken too many chances in going after the big gains, they'd have been more likely to lose out and never become anyone's ancestor.

Our ancestors gave priority to __(A)__ minimum resources rather than pursuing maximum gains, and that was the rational choice for human __(B)__ from an evolutionary perspective.

이 글은 우리의 조상들은 많은 식량을 얻기 위해 모험을 하는 것보다는 최소한의 식량을 확보하여 생존을 보장받는 방법을 우선적으로 택했다는 내용을 나타내고 있다. 따라서 (A)에는 securing(확보하기), (B)에는 survival(생존)이 들어가야 해.

① 확보하기 – 자유
② 공유하기 – 상호 작용
③ 확인하기 – 탐험
④ 공유하기 – 번영

● 중요 포인트

이중 수식의 주어 구문과 not ~ but 구조

[Anthropologists who study people / still living in hunter-gatherer societies] have discovered that they regularly make choices designed to produce not the best opportunity for obtaining a hyperabundant supply of food but, instead, the least danger of ending up with an insufficient supply.

2. ⑤

● 전체 해석

현대 사회와는 달리, 원시 사회는 전달할 전문 지식이 더 적다. 그리고 생활방식이 모든 사람들의 눈앞에서 행해지기 때문에, 학교와 같은 분리된 교육기관을 만들 필요가 없다. 대신에, 아이는 의식, 사냥, 축제, 경작, 그리고 추수와 같은 활동에서 어른들을 관찰하고 흉내 냄으로써 문화유산

을 획득한다. 그 결과, 현대 산업 사회에서 아주 두드러지는 어른과 아이 간의 소외가 거의 없거나 아예 없다. 현대 사회의 이러한 소외에 대한 더 깊은 이유는 현실에 대한 개념 속에서 현대의 어른은 원시인이 했던 것보다 직접적인 경험에 덜 의존하고, 문화의 경험에 더 의존하기 때문이다. 분명히, 문화에 대한 이런 의존은 그의 교육의 성질에 따라 다를 것이다. 그러므로, 현대의 아이는 어른의 세계관을 획득하기 위해 원시인의 아이보다 더 멀리 여행을 해야 한다. 따라서 그는 그 사회의 어른들로부터 훨씬 더 분리되는 것이다.

↓

가까운 환경으로부터 학습을 하는 원시 시대 아이와 달리 현대의 아이는 교육기관에서 학습을 하는데, 이는 연장자로부터의 소외를 낳는다.

● 지문분석

Unlike the modern society, / the primitive society has less specialized knowledge / to transmit, / and since its way of life is enacted / before the eyes of all, / it has no need / to create a separate institution of education / such as the school.
현대 사회와는 달리 / 원시 사회는 전문화된 지식을 적게 가진다 / 전달할 / 그리고 삶의 방식이 행해지기 때문에 / 모든 사람들의 눈앞에서 / 그것은 필요가 없다 / 분리된 교육기관을 만들 / 학교와 같은

Instead, the child acquires the heritage of his culture / by observing and imitating adults / in such activities / as rituals, hunts, festivals, cultivation, and harvesting.
대신에 아이는 문화유산을 습득한다 / 어른을 관찰하고 모방함으로써 / 그런 활동 속에서 / 의식, 사냥, 축제, 경작, 그리고 추수와 같은

As a result, there is little or none / of that alienation of young from old / so marked in modern industrial societies.
결과적으로 거의 없다 / 어른으로부터의 아이의 소외가 / 현대 산업 사회에서 매우 두드러지는

[A further reason / for this alienation in modern societies] / is that in his conception of reality / the modern adult owes less / to his direct experience / and more / to the experience of his culture / than does primitive man.
더 깊은 이유는 / 현대 사회에서의 이런 소외에 대한 / 현실에 대한 개념속에서 / 현대의 어른들은 덜 의존하기 때문이다 / 그의 직접 경험에 / 그리고 더 의존하기 때문이다 / 문화의 경험에 / 원시인들이 하는 것보다

Clearly, [his debt to culture] / will vary with the nature of his education.
명확하게도 문화에 대한 그의 의존은 / 교육의 성질에 따라 다를 것이다

Hence, the contemporary child must travel much further / than the offspring of primitive man / to acquire the world view of his elders.
그래서 동시대의 아이들은 더 많이 여행해야만 한다 / 원시인의 아이보다도 / 어른들의 세계관을 습득하기 위해서

He is, therefore, that / much more removed / from the adults of his society.
그래서 그는 존재이다 / 더 많이 분리된(제거된) / 그의 사회의 어른들로부터

↓

Unlike the primitive child / who learns from his immediate surroundings, / the modern child learns in educational institutions, / which results in alienation from his elders.
원시인의 아이와는 달리 / 그의 가까운 환경에서 배우는 / 현대의 아이는 교육기관에서 배운다 / 이는 어른으로부터의 소외를 야기한다

● 해설

2. 다음 글의 내용을 한 문장으로 요약하고자 한다. 빈칸 (A)와 (B)에 들어갈 말로 가장 적절한 것은?

Unlike the modern society, the primitive society has less specialized knowledge to transmit, and since its way of life is enacted before the eyes of all, it has no need to create a separate institution of education such as the school. Instead, the child acquires the heritage of his culture by observing and imitating adults in such activities as rituals, hunts, festivals, cultivation, and harvesting. As a result, there is little or none of that alienation of young from old so marked in modern industrial societies. A further reason for this alienation in modern societies is that in his conception of reality the modern adult owes less to his direct experience and more to the experience of his culture than does primitive man. Clearly, his debt to culture will vary with the nature of his education. Hence, the contemporary child must travel much further than the offspring of primitive man to acquire the world view of his elders. He is, therefore, that much more removed from the adults of his society.

↓

Unlike the primitive child who learns from his ___(A)___ surroundings, the modern child learns in educational institutions, which results in ___(B)___ from his elders.

원시의 아이는 어른들로부터 직접적인 학습을 받고 있지. 따라서 직접적인 학생에 해당하는 immediate(가까운)가 (A)에 적합하지. (B)의 경우 현대 사회의 문제니까 바로 alienation(소외)이 적절해.

① 외국의 - 방해
② 가까운 - 동정
③ 외국의 - 동정
④ 가상의 - 소외

● 중요 포인트

문장 전체를 받는 which

Unlike the primitive child who learns from his immediate surroundings, the modern child learns in educational institutions, which results in alienation from his elders.
앞문장 전체를 받음

3. ②

●전체 해석

업무 수행은 개인의 통제 범위를 벗어난 업무 수행에 미친 영향보다는 평가를 받는 개인의 통제 하에 있는 것의 측면에서 평가되어야 한다. 판단을 받고 있는 모든 사람의 업무 수행을 억제하는 때로 경제적 성격을 띠는, 광범위한, 영향을 미치는 요인이 있을 수 있다. 한 가지 예가 매출액에 관한 것이다. 일반적인 경제적 경기 침체가 있어서 상품이나 서비스가 이전 해와 동일한 빈도로 구매되지 않고 있다면, 매출액은 예를 들어 평균 15%만큼 감소될 수 있다. 그렇다면 이 15%(사실은 -5%) 수치는 '평균' 업무 수행을 나타낼 것이다. 아마도 그 해의 가장 우수한 영업사원은 이전 해에 비해서 매출액이 3%만 감소했을 것이다. 따라서 이러한 상황에서 '훌륭한' 업무수행이란 어떤 평균 혹은 기준 집단과 비교했을 때 더 적은 양의 감소를 말한다.

업무 수행 평가에 있어서 우리는 수치에만 의존하기보다는 개인의 업무 수행에 영향을 미치는 상황적 요인들을 고려해야 한다.

●지문분석

Performance must be judged / in terms of what is under the control of the individuals / being evaluated / rather than those influences on performance / that are beyond their control.
업무 수행은 평가되어져야만 한다 / 개인의 통제 하에 있는 측면에서 / 평가 받는 / 수행에 대한 그러한 영향보다는 / 통제를 넘어서는

There can be broad, influential factors, / sometimes of an economic nature, / that hold down the performance of everyone / being judged.
광범위한, 영향을 미치는 요인들이 있을 수 있다 / 때때로 경제적인 성격의 / 모든 사람들의 업무 수행을 억제하는 / 평가받고 있는

One example is in sales.
한 가지 예는 매출액이다

If there is a general downturn in the economy / and products or services are not being purchased / with the same frequency / as in the previous year, / sales could be down, / for example, by an average of 15%.
일반적인 경기 침체가 있고 / 상품이나 재화가 구매되지 않고 있다면 / 같은 빈도로 / 이전 해와 같은 / 매출액은 떨어질 수 있다 / 예를 들어 평균 15% 정도

This 15% (actually -15%) figure / would then represent "average" performance.
이 15%라는 (사실 -15%) 수치는 / 그때 평균 업무 수행으로 나타날 수도 있다

Perhaps the best salesperson in the year / had only a 3% drop in sales / over the previous year.
아마도 그 해의 최고 판매원은 / 매출액에서 3% 정도만 하락했다 / 이전 연도에 비해서

Thus, "good" performance in this situation / is a smaller loss / compared to some average or norm group.
그래서 이 상황에서 좋은 업무 수행은 / 더 적은 감소이다 / 평균 혹은 기준 집단과 비교했을 때

In performance evaluation, / we should consider contextual factors / affecting the individual's performance / rather than rely on figures only.
업무 평가에서 / 우리는 상황적 요인을 고려해야 한다 / 사람의 업무 수행에 영향을 미치는 / 수치에만 의존하기 보다는

●해설

3. 다음 글의 내용을 한 문장으로 요약하고자 한다. 빈칸 (A)와 (B)에 들어갈 말로 가장 적절한 것은?

Performance must be judged in terms of what is under the control of the individuals being evaluated rather than those influences on performance that are beyond their control. There can be broad, influential factors, sometimes of an economic nature, that hold down the performance of everyone being judged. One example is in sales. If there is a general downturn in the economy and products or services are not being purchased with the same frequency as in the previous year, sales could be down, for example, by an average of 15%. This 15% (actually -15%) figure would then represent "average" performance. Perhaps the best salesperson in the year had only a 3% drop in sales over the previous year. Thus, "good" performance in this situation is a smaller loss compared to some average or norm group.

In performance evaluation, we should consider (A) factors affecting the individual's performance rather than (B) figures only.

업무 수행 평가는 겉으로 드러나는 수치에만 의존하기보다는 그것이 처해있는 상황을 고려해야 한다는 것이 필자의 의견이지. 따라서 (A)에는 contextual(상황적인)이, (B)에는 rely on(의존하다)이 적절하다고 할 수 있어.
① 상황적인 – 제쳐놓다
③ 통제할 수 있는 – 제쳐놓다
④ 긍정적인 – 무시하다
⑤ 긍정적인 – 의존하다

●중요 포인트

현재분사의 명사 수식

Performance must be judged in terms of what is under the control of the individuals being evaluated rather than those influences on performance that are beyond their control.

4. ②

●전체 해석

전문가들은 고전 텍스트를 읽는 것이 독자들의 관심을 사로잡아 자기 성찰의 순간을 촉발함으로써 정신에 유익하다는 것을 발견했다. 지원자들

이 고전 작품들을 읽을 때에 그들의 뇌 활동이 추적 관찰되었다. 그런 다음에 이 동일한 텍스트가 더 쉽고 현대적인 언어로 '번역'되어 독자들이 그 글을 읽을 때에 그들의 뇌가 다시 추적 관찰되었다. 정밀 검사는 더 어려운 산문과 시가 더 평범한 버전보다 뇌 속에서 훨씬 더 많은 전기적 활동을 유발한다는 것을 보여주었다. 과학자들은 뇌가 각 단어에 반응할 때에 뇌의 활동을 연구하여 독자들이 특이한 단어, 놀라운 구절, 혹은 어려운 문장 구조를 만났을 때에 그것이 어떻게 점화되는지 기록할 수 있었다. 이 점화는 뇌를 고단 기어로 전환할[더 활발하게 활동하도록 전환할]만큼 충분히 오래 지속되어, 더 심화된 독서를 권장한다. 연구는 또한 더 어려운 버전의 시를 읽는 것이 특히 우뇌의 활동을 증가시켜 서 독자들이 자신이 읽은 것에 비추어 자신의 경험을 되돌아보고 재평가하도록 돕는 다는 것을 발견했다. 교수들은 이것이 고전 작품들이 자습서보다 더 유용하다는 것을 의미한다고 말했다.

↓

고전 텍스트의 원래 버전이 독자의 자아 성찰을 작동시키고 심화된 독서를 고취하는 어려운 언어를 포함하고 있으므로 독자들에게 도움이 된다.

● 지문분석

Experts have found / that [reading classical texts] / benefits the mind / by catching the reader's attention / and triggering moments of self-reflection.
전문가들은 발견했다 / 고전 텍스트를 읽는 것은 / 마음에 유익하다는 것을 / 독자들의 관심을 사로 잡고 / 자아 성찰의 순간을 촉발함으로써

[The brain activity of volunteers] / was monitored / as they read classical works.
지원자들의 두뇌 활동은 / 모니터되었다 / 그들이 고전 작품을 읽을 때

These same texts were then "translated" / into more straightforward, modern language / and again the readers' brains were monitored / as they read the words.
이와 같은 텍스트들은 그런 다음 번역이 되었다 / 더 쉬운 현대 언어로 / 그리고 다시 독자들의 두뇌는 모니터되었다 / 그들이 단어들을 읽을 때

Scans showed / that the more challenging prose and poetry / set off far more electrical activity / in the brain / than the more pedestrian versions.
정밀 검사는 보여주었다 / 더 어려운 산문과 시는 / 훨씬 더 많은 전기적 활동을 유발한다는 것을 / 두뇌에서 / 더 평범한 버전보다

Scientists were able to study the brain activity / as it responded to each word / and record how it lit up / as the readers encountered / unusual words, surprising phrases or difficult sentence structures.
과학자들은 두뇌 활동을 연구할 수 있었다 / 그것이 각각의 단어에 반응할 때 / 그리고 그것이 어떻게 점화되는지 기록할 수 있었다 / 독자들이 직면할 때 / 특이한 단어, 놀라운 구절, 아니면 어려운 문장 구조에

This lighting up lasts long enough / to shift the brain / into a higher gear, / encouraging further reading.
이러한 점화는 충분히 오랫동안 유지된다 / 두뇌를 전환할 만큼 / 더 높은 기어로 / 이는 더 많은 읽기를 장려한다

The research also found / that [reading the more challenging version of poetry,] / in particular, increases

---

activity / in the right hemisphere of the brain, / helping the readers to reflect on / and reevaluate their own experiences / in light of what they have read.
연구는 또한 발견했다 / 더 어려운 버전의 시를 읽는 것은 / 특히 활동을 증가시킨다는 것을 / 두뇌의 우반구에서 / 이는 독자가 성찰하도록 돕는다 / 그리고 자신의 경험을 재평가하도록 / 그들이 읽었던 것에 비추어

The academics said / this meant / the classics were more useful / than self-help books.
교수들은 말한다 / 이것이 의미한다고 / 고전은 더 유용하다는 것을 / 자습서보다도

↓

[Original versions of classical texts] / are helpful to readers / because they contain demanding language / that inspires further reading / and activates readers' self-reflection.
고전 텍스트의 원래 버전은 / 독자들에게 도움이 된다 / 왜냐하면 그들은 어려운 언어를 포함하고 있기 때문에 / 더 많은 독서를 고무시키는, 그리고 독자들의 자기 성찰을 활성화시키는

● 해설

4. 다음 글의 내용을 한 문장으로 요약하고자 한다. 빈칸 (A)와 (B)에 들어갈 말로 가장 적절한 것은?

Experts have found that reading classical texts benefits the mind by catching the reader's attention and triggering moments of self-reflection. The brain activity of volunteers was monitored as they read classical works. These same texts were then "translated" into more straightforward, modern language and again the readers' brains were monitored as they read the words. Scans showed that the more challenging prose and poetry set off far more electrical activity in the brain than the more pedestrian versions. Scientists were able to study the brain activity as it responded to each word and record how it lit up as the readers encountered unusual words, surprising phrases or difficult sentence structures. This lighting up lasts long enough to shift the brain into a higher gear, encouraging further reading. The research also found that reading the more challenging version of poetry, in particular, increases activity in the right hemisphere of the brain, helping the readers to reflect on and reevaluate their own experiences in light of what they have read. The academics said this meant the classics were more useful than self-help books.

↓

Original versions of classical texts are helpful to readers because they contain __(A)__ language that inspires further reading and __(B)__ readers" self-reflection.

어려운 언어들을 포함하고 있는 고전이 독자들에게 독서를 촉진시키고, 자기성찰을 하도록 도와준다는 내용이지. 따라서 (A)에는 demanding(까다로운)이, (B)에는 activates(활성화시키다)가 적절하지.

① 도전적인 – 왜곡하다

③ 이해할 수 있는 – 증가시키다
④ 어려운 – 방해하다
⑤ 접근하기 쉬운 – 자극하다

● 중요 포인트

동명사 주어 – 단수 취급

Experts have found that [reading classical texts] benefits
the mind by catching the reader's attention and triggering
moments of self-reflection.

S 동명사 주어   V 단수 동사

5. ③

● 전체 해석

관광산업이 환경에 미치는 영향은 과학자들에게는 명확하지만, 모든 주
민들이 환경 훼손을 관광산업의 탓으로 돌리지는 않는다. 주민들은 대개
관광산업이 삶의 질에 미치는 경제적인 그리고 몇 가지 사회문화적인 영
향에 대해 긍정적인 견해를 가지고 있지만, 환경적 영향에 대한 그들의
반응은 엇갈린다. 몇몇 주민들은 관광산업이 더 많은 공원과 휴양지를 제
공하고, 도로와 공공시설의 질을 개선하며, 생태계 쇠퇴의 원인이 되지는
않는다고 생각한다. 많은 이들이 교통 문제, 초만원인 야외 오락 활동이
나 공원의 평화로움과 고요함을 방해하는 것에 대해 관광산업을 탓하지
는 않는다. 그 대신에 몇몇 주민들은 관광객들이 현지의 낚시터, 사냥터
및 기타 휴양지에 지나치게 몰리거나 교통과 보행자 혼잡을 초래할지도
모른다는 우려를 표한다. 몇 가지 연구들은 환경 훼손과 관광산업의 관계
에 대해 주민들이 가지는 생각의 차이가 관광산업의 유형, 주민들이 자연
환경이 보호될 필요가 있다고 느끼는 정도, 그리고 주민들이 관광 명소에
서 떨어져 사는 거리와 연관이 있음을 보여 준다.

↓

주민들은 관광산업의 환경에 대한 영향을 동일하게 평가하지 않는데, 왜
냐하면 그들이 관광산업의 유형, 보호 정도에 관한 의견, 그리고 관광 명
소로부터의 거리와 같은 요인을 근거로 다른 태도를 취하기 때문이다.

● 지문분석

[The impacts of tourism on the environment] / are evident
to scientists, / but not all residents attribute environmental
damage to tourism.

환경에 대한 관광의 영향은 / 과학자들에게는 명백하다 / 하지만 모
든 주민들이 환경 훼손을 관광으로 돌리는 것은 아니다

Residents commonly have positive views / on the
economic and some sociocultural influences of tourism /
on quality of life, / but [their reactions to environmental
impacts] / are mixed.

주민들은 일반적으로 긍정적인 견해를 가진다 / 관광의 경제적 그리
고 일부 사회문화적 영향에 대한 / 삶의 질에 미치는 / 하지만 환경적
영향에 대한 그들의 반응은 / 혼재되어 있다

Some residents feel / tourism provides more parks and
recreation areas, / improves the quality of the roads and
public facilities, / and does not contribute to ecological
decline.

일부 주민들은 느낀다 / 관광은 더 많은 공원과 휴양지를 제공하고 /

도로와 공공시설의 질을 개선하며 / 그리고 생태학적인 쇠퇴를 유발
하지 않는다고

Many do not blame tourism / for traffic problems,
overcrowded outdoor recreation, / or the disturbance of
peace and tranquility of parks.

많은 사람들은 관광을 탓하지 않는다 / 교통 문제, 사람으로 붐비는
야외 오락 활동에 대해 / 아니면 공원의 평화로움과 고요함을 방해하
는 것에 대해

Alternatively, some residents express concern / that
tourists overcrowd / the local fishing, hunting, and other
recreation areas / or may cause traffic and pedestrian
congestion.

대신에 일부 주민들은 우려를 표한다 / 관광객들이 붐빈다고 / 현재
의 낚시터, 사냥터, 그리고 다른 휴양지에 / 그리고 교통 혼잡과 보행
자 혼잡을 유발할지도 모른다고

Some studies suggest / that [variations in residents'
feelings / about tourism's relationship / to environmental
damage] / are related to the type of tourism, / the extent /
to which residents feel / the natural environment needs to
be protected, / and the distance / residents live from the
tourist attractions.

S

일부 연구는 제안한다 / 주민들의 감정의 차이가 / 관광의 관계의 /
환경 훼손에 대한 / 관광의 유형과 관련있다고 / 정도와 / 주민들이
느끼는 / 자연 환경이 보호될 필요가 있다고 / 그리고 거리와 / 주민
들이 관광 명소에서 떨어져 사는

↓

Residents do not weigh / tourism's environmental
influences identically / since they take dissimilar postures
/ based on factors / such as the type of tourism, / opinions
on the degree of protection, / and their distance from an
attraction.

주민들은 평가하지 않는다 / 관광의 환경적 영향을 동일하게 / 왜냐
하면 그들은 다른 자세를 취하기 때문에 / 요인들에 근거해서 / 예를
들어 관광의 형태 / 보호의 정도에 대한 의견 / 그리고 관광 명소로
부터의 거리와 같은

● 해설

5. 다음 글의 내용을 한 문장으로 요약하고자 한다. 빈칸 (A)와 (B)에 들어
갈 말로 가장 적절한 것은?

The impacts of tourism on the environment are evident to
scientists, but not all residents attribute environmental damage
to tourism. Residents commonly have positive views on the
economic and some sociocultural influences of tourism on
quality of life, but their reactions to environmental impacts
are mixed. Some residents feel tourism provides more parks
and recreation areas, improves the quality of the roads and
public facilities, and does not contribute to ecological decline.
Many do not blame tourism for traffic problems, overcrowded
outdoor recreation, or the disturbance of peace and tranquility
of parks. Alternatively, some residents express concern

that tourists overcrowd the local fishing, hunting, and other recreation areas or may cause traffic and pedestrian congestion. Some studies suggest that variations in residents' feelings about tourism's relationship to environmental damage are related to the type of tourism, the extent to which residents feel the natural environment needs to be protected, and the distance residents live from the tourist attractions.

↓

Residents do not ___(A)___ tourism's environmental influences identically since they take ___(B)___ postures based on factors such as the type of tourism, opinions on the degree of protection, and their distance from an attraction.

관광지의 주민들은 다양한 요인들에 대해서 다른 자세를 취해서 관광이 가진 환경적 영향을 다르게 평가한다는 내용이지. 따라서 (A)에는 weigh(평가하다)가, (B)에는 dissimilar(상이한, 다른)가 적절해.

① 평가하다 – 공통의
② 평가하다 – 균형 잡힌
④ 통제하다 – 호의적인
⑤ 통제하다 – 상반되는

● 중요 포인트

전치사 + which 구문

Some studies suggest that variations in residents' feelings about tourism's relationship to environmental damage are related to the type of tourism, the extent to which residents feel the natural environment needs to be protected, and the distance residents live from the tourist attractions.
+ 완전한 문장

6. ②

● 전체 해석

가격을 과소 산정하는 것은 두 명이 합의를 한 다음, 한 명이 상대방에 의해 초래된 비용을 증가시키는 기술을 말하는 것이다. 예를 들어, 소비자가 8천 달러를 주고 자동차를 구매하는데 동의한 다음, 판매자가 세금으로 100달러, 그리고 타이어 가격으로 200달러를 추가하기 시작한다. 이러한 부가된 비용은 비유적으로는 판매자가 소비자에게 던지는 '낮은 공'으로 간주될 수 있을 것이다. 가격을 과소 산정하는 것의 효과에 관한 한 가지 설명은 자기인식 이론이라는 말로 할 수 있다. 소비자가 원래의 계약조건 하에서 제품을 구매하는데 동의할 때, 그러한 행위는 그 제품에 진정성 있는 관심을 나타내기 위해 소비자에 의해 이용될 수 있을 것이다. 이렇게 표현된 제품에 대한 진정한 관심은 소비자로 하여금 증가된 비용을 수용하게 할 것이다. 다른 설명은 인상 관리 이론이라는 말로 할 수 있다. 소비자가 합의한 상황에서 '약간의' 변화가 있은 다음 그 거래를 철회한다면, 그는 이러한 불가피한 비용을 모르는 무책임한 사람이 되어 다소 바람직하지 않은 인상을 불러일으키게 될 것이다.

↓

가격을 과소 산정하는 것은 판매 상황에서 효과적인데, 그 이유는 소비자가 거래를 철회하지 않음으로써 자신의 구매 결정을 정당화하는 경향이 있거나 체면을 유지하려고 하기 때문이다.

● 지문분석

Low-balling describes the technique / where two individuals arrive at an agreement / and then one increases the cost / to be incurred by the other.
낮은 공은 기술을 의미한다 / 두 사람이 합의에 이르는 / 그리고 한 쪽이 비용을 올리는 / 다른 상대방에 의해서 초래된

For example, after the consumer has agreed / to purchase a car for $8,000, / the salesperson begins to add on / $100 for tax / and $200 for tires.
예를 들어 소비자가 동의한 이후 / 차를 8천 달러에 구매하기로 / 판매자는 추가하기 시작한다 / 100달러는 세금으로 / 그리고 타이어 비용으로 200달러를

These additional costs might be thought of / as a metaphorical 'low ball' / that the salesperson throws the consumer.
이러한 추가 비용은 간주될 지도 모른다 / 은유적인 '낮은 공'으로 / 판매자가 소비자에게 던지는

[One explanation / for the effectiveness of low-balling] / is in terms of self-perception theory.
한 가지 설명은 / 낮은 공의 효과에 대한 / 자기 인식 이론이라는 말이다

When the consumer agrees / to purchase the product / under the original terms, / that behavior might be used / by the consumer / to infer his sincere interest in the product.
소비자가 동의할 때 / 상품을 구매하기로 / 원래 계약조건 아래에서 / 그러한 행위는 사용될 수 있다 / 소비자에 의해서 / 그의 진정한 상품에 대한 관심을 나타내기 위해

[This inferred sincere interest / in the product] / may enable him to endure the increased cost.
이와 같이 나타난 진정한 관심은 / 상품에 대한 / 그로 하여금 늘어난 비용을 견뎌내도록 할 수 있도록 할 것이다

An alternative explanation / is in terms of impression management theory.
대안적인 설명은 / 인상 관리 이론이라는 말이다

If the consumer were to withdraw from the deal / after the 'slight' change / in the terms of agreement, / he might foster the rather undesirable impression / of being an irresponsible consumer / unaware of these necessary charges.
만약 소비자가 거래에서 물러나야 한다면 / 약간의 변화 이후에 / 합의된 상황에서 / 그는 다소 바람직하지 못한 인상을 불러일으킬지도 모른다 / 무책임한 소비자라는 존재의 / 이러한 필요 경비를 알지 못하는

↓

Low-balling is effective in sales contexts / because [the consumer, / by not withdrawing from the deal,] / tends to justify his purchase decision / or tries to save face.
낮은 공은 판매 상황에서 효과적이다 / 왜냐하면 소비자는 / 거래에서 물러나지 않음으로써 / 그의 구매 결정을 정당화하는 경향이 있거나 / 아니면 체면을 유지하려고 하기 때문이다

6. 다음 글의 내용을 한 문장으로 요약하고자 한다. 빈칸 (A)와 (B)에 들어갈 말로 가장 적절한 것은?

Low-balling describes the technique where two individuals arrive at an agreement and then one increases the cost to be incurred by the other. For example, after the consumer has agreed to purchase a car for $8,000, the salesperson begins to add on $100 for tax and $200 for tires. These additional costs might be thought of as a metaphorical 'low ball' that the salesperson throws the consumer. One explanation for the effectiveness of low-balling is in terms of self-perception theory. When the consumer agrees to purchase the product under the original terms, that behavior might be used by the consumer to infer his sincere interest in the product. This inferred sincere interest in the product may enable him to endure the increased cost. An alternative explanation is in terms of impression management theory. If the consumer were to withdraw from the deal after the 'slight' change in the terms of agreement, he might foster the rather undesirable impression of being an irresponsible consumer unaware of these necessary charges.

↓

Low-balling is effective in sales contexts because the consumer, by not withdrawing from the deal, tends to __(A)__ his purchase decision or tries to save __(B)__.

가격 과소 산정(low-balling)은 제품에 대한 진정한 관심이 있음을 알려 주어서 제품 구매의 정당성을 부여해주지. 여기에 거래를 철회하면 추가 비용을 모르는 무책임한 사람이라는 인상을 주게 되므로 그 거래를 철회하려고 하지 않겠지? 따라서 체면을 살려주게 되는 거야. 그래서 (A)에는 justify(정당화하다), (B)에는 face(save face: 체면을 살리다)가 적절해.

① 정당화하다 – 시간
③ 소중히 하다 – 시간
④ 변경하다 – 체면
⑤ 변경하다 – 고생

● 중요 포인트

주어와 동사 사이에 삽입구가 있는 경우

Low-balling is effective in sales contexts because [the consumer, by not withdrawing from the deal,] tends to justify his purchase decision or tries to save face.

7. ①

● 전체 해석

과학에서 한 가지 실험은 그것이 성공하든 실패하든, 논리적으로는 이론상 무한한 연속 안에서의 또 다른 실험으로 이어진다. 현대 과학의 기저에 놓인 근거 없는 통념에 의하면, 이 연속은 과거의 더 작은 지식을 현재의 더 큰 지식으로 항상 대체하고 있으며, 현재의 더 큰 지식은 미래의 한층 더 큰 지식에 의해 대체될 것이다. 대조적으로 예술에서는 작품의 무한한 연속은 결코 암시되거나 추구되지 않는다. 어떤 예술 작품도 필연적으로 더 나은 제2의 작품으로 반드시 이어지지는 않는다. 과학의 방법론을 고려해 보면, 중력의 법칙과 게놈은 누군가에 의해 반드시 발견되게 되어 있었고, 그 발견자의 신원은 그 사실에 부수적이다. 그러나 예술에서는 제2의 기회란 없는 것처럼 보인다. 우리는 'The Divine Comedy(신곡)'와 'King Lear(리어왕)'에 있어서 각각 한 번의 기회를 가졌었다고 추정해야 한다. 단테와 셰익스피어가 그 작품을 쓰기 전에 사망했더라면 결코 아무도 그것을 쓰지 않았을 것이다.

↓

과학적 지식은 연속적인 실험을 통해 발전되는 것으로 여겨지지만, 예술 작품은 무한한 연속성이 전혀 암시되지 않은 채 그 창작자에게 고유한 경향이 있다.

● 지문분석

In science / one experiment, / whether it succeeds or fails, / is logically followed by another / in a theoretically infinite progression.
과학에서 / 하나의 실험은 / 그것이 성공하든 실패하든 / 논리적으로 또 다른 실험이 뒤따른다 / 이론적으로 무한한 연속 안에서

According to the underlying myth of modern science, / this progression is always replacing / the smaller knowledge of the past / with the larger knowledge of the present, / which will be replaced / by the yet larger knowledge of the future.
현대 과학의 기저에 깔린 근거 없는 통념에 따르면 / 이러한 연속은 항상 대체하고 있다 / 과거의 더 작은 지식을 / 현재의 더 큰 지식으로 / 이는 대체될 것이다 / 미래의 더욱 큰 지식에 의해서

In the arts, / by contrast, / no limitless sequence of works / is ever implied / or looked for.
예술에서 / 대조적으로 / 작품의 어떠한 무제한적인 연속은 / 암시되어지거나 / 추구되어지지 않는다

No work of art / is necessarily followed by a second work / that is necessarily better.
어떠한 예술 작품도 / 꼭 두 번째 작품이 뒤따르지는 않는다 / 반드시 더 나은

Given the methodologies of science, / the law of gravity and the genome / were bound to be discovered by somebody; / the identity of the discoverer / is incidental to the fact.
과학의 방법론을 고려할 때 / 중력의 법칙과 게놈은 / 누군가에 의해서 발견되게 되어 있었다 / 발견자의 신원은 / 그 사실에 부수적이다

But it appears / that in the arts / there are no second chances.
하지만 그런 것 같다 / 예술에서 / 두 번째 기회란 없다

We must assume / that we had one chance each / for *The Divine Comedy* and *King Lear*.
우리는 추정해야만 한다 / 우리가 각각 한 번의 기회만 있다고 / 신곡과 리어왕에 있어서

If Dante and Shakespeare had died / before they wrote those works, / nobody ever would have written them.

단테와 셰익스피어가 죽었다면 / 그들이 그러한 작품을 쓰기도 전에 / 누구도 그것들을 쓰지 않았을 것이다

↓

While scientific knowledge is believed / to progress through successive experiments, / an artistic work tends to be unique / to its creator / with no limitless sequence implied.
　　　　　　　　　　└ with + 명사 + 분사: 동시상황

과학적 지식이 믿어지는 반면 / 연속적인 실험을 통해서 연속된다고 / 예술 작품은 고유의 경향이 있다 / 그 창조자에게 / 어떠한 무제한적인 연속이 암시되지 않고

● 해설

7. 다음 글의 내용을 한 문장으로 요약하고자 한다. 빈칸 (A)와 (B)에 들어갈 말로 가장 적절한 것은?

In science one experiment, whether it succeeds or fails, is logically followed by another in a theoretically infinite progression. According to the underlying myth of modern science, this progression is always replacing the smaller knowledge of the past with the larger knowledge of the present, which will be replaced by the yet larger knowledge of the future. In the arts, by contrast, no limitless sequence of works is ever implied or looked for. No work of art is necessarily followed by a second work that is necessarily better. Given the methodologies of science, the law of gravity and the genome were bound to be discovered by somebody; the identity of the discoverer is incidental to the fact. But it appears that in the arts there are no second chances. We must assume that we had one chance each for The Divine Comedy and King Lear. If Dante and Shakespeare had died before they wrote those works, nobody ever would have written them.

↓

While scientific knowledge is believed to progress through __(A)__ experiments, an artistic work tends to be __(B)__ to its creator with no limitless sequence implied.

과학에서는 또 다른 실험이 이어져서 연속적인 실험이 이루어지는 결과로 발전하게 된다고 하고 있어. 그런데 예술의 경우 똑같은 작품이 연속되지 않고 그 작품으로만 예술가에게 귀속된다고 하고 있지. 따라서 (A)에는 successive(연속적인 *successful 성공적인), (B)에는 unique(고유의)가 적절해.

② 연속적인 – 가치 있는
③ 통제된 – 가치 있는
④ 부수적인 – 영향력 있는
⑤ 부수적인 – 고유한

● 중요 포인트

with + 명사 + 분사: 동시상황

While scientific knowledge is believed to progress through successive experiments, an artistic work tends to be unique to its creator with no limitless sequence implied.
　　　　　　　　　　with + 명사 + 분사: 동시상황

8. ④

● 전체 해석

변호사와 과학자들은 모두 결론에 이르는 증거와 원칙들을 요약하기 위해 논증을 이용한다. 하지만 과학적 논증과 법적 논증은 다르다. 검찰은 재판관이나 배심원들에게 피고가 유죄라는 것을 설득하기 위해 논증을 한다. 반면, 동일한 재판에서 피고측 변호인은 같은 재판관 혹은 배심원들이 반대 방향으로 결론을 내리도록 설득하려 논증을 한다. 검찰이나 변호인 모두 그들 각각의 주장을 약화시킬 수 있는 것을 인정할 의무가 없다. 이와 반대로, 과학자들은 자신들의 생각을 점검하고 자연의 특정 측면에 대해 정확하게 설명하기를 원하기 때문에 논증을 한다. 과학자들은 그들의 주장을 뒷받침하는 증거나 가설을 포함시킬 수 있지만, 전문 과학의 기본적인 원칙은 반드시 준수해야만 한다. 그들은 알려진 모든 증거들과 기존에 제기된 모든 가설들을 포함해야만 한다. 변호사들과 달리, 과학자들은 자신들을 틀릴 수도 있다는 가능성을 명확하게 설명해야만 한다.

↓

자신들의 주장을 받침하기 위해 정보를 선택적으로 사용하는 법률가들과 달리, 과학자들은 그중 일부가 자신들의 주장을 강화시킬 가능성이 없다고 하더라도 모든 정보들을 포함시켜야만 한다.

● 지문분석

Lawyers and scientists use argument / to mean a summary of evidence and principles / leading to a conclusion; / however, a scientific argument is different / from a legal argument.
변호사와 과학자는 논증을 사용한다 / 증거와 원리의 요약을 의미하기 위해서 / 결론에 이르는 / 하지만 과학적 논증은 다르다 / 법적인 논증과는

A prosecuting attorney constructs an argument / to persuade the judge or a jury / that the accused is guilty; / [a defense attorney in the same trial] constructs an
　　　　　　　　　　　　　S　　　　　　　　　　　　　　　V
argument / to persuade the same judge or jury / toward the opposite conclusion.
검찰은 논증을 구축한다 / 재판장이나 배심원을 설득하기 위해서 / 피고인이 유죄라고 / 같은 재판에서 피고측 변호인은 / 논증을 구축한다 / 같은 재판장이나 배심원을 설득하기 위해서 / 반대의 결론을 향해

Neither prosecutor nor defender / is obliged to consider anything / that weakens their respective cases.
검찰이든 변호인이든 / 무엇이든 고려할 의무는 없다 / 그들의 각각의 주장을 약화시키는

On the contrary, scientists construct arguments / because they want to test their own ideas / and give an accurate explanation / of some aspect of nature.
반대로 과학자들은 논증을 구축한다 / 그들이 그들 자신의 생각을 테스트하기를 원하기 때문에 / 그리고 정확한 설명을 주기를 / 자연의 특성에 대해

Scientists can include any evidence or hypothesis / that supports their claim, / but they must observe one fundamental rule / of professional science.

정답 및 해설 **57**

과학자들은 어떠한 증거나 가설을 포함할 수 있다 / 그들의 주장을 뒷받침할 / 하지만 그들은 한 가지 기본적인 규칙은 준수해야만 한다 / 전문 과학의

They must include / all of the known evidence / and all of the hypotheses / previously proposed.

그들은 포함해야만 한다 / 모든 알려진 증거를 / 그리고 모든 가설을 / 이전에 제안된

Unlike lawyers, / scientists must explicitly account for the possibility / that they might be wrong.

변호인과는 달리 / 과학자들은 명확하게 가능성을 설명해야만 한다 / 틀릴 수도 있다는

↓

Unlike lawyers, / who utilize information selectively / to support their arguments, / scientists must include all information / even if some of it is unlikely to strengthen their arguments.

변호인과는 달리 / 정보를 선택적으로 활용하는 / 그들의 논증을 뒷받침할 / 과학자들은 모든 정보를 포함해야 한다 / 비록 그중 일부가 그들의 논증을 강화시킬 가능성이 없다고 하더라도

● 해설

8. 다음 글의 내용을 한 문장으로 요약하고자 한다. 빈칸 (A)와 (B)에 들어갈 말로 가장 적절한 것은?

Lawyers and scientists use argument to mean a summary of evidence and principles leading to a conclusion; however, a scientific argument is different from a legal argument. A prosecuting attorney constructs an argument to persuade the judge or a jury that the accused is guilty; a defense attorney in the same trial constructs an argument to persuade the same judge or jury toward the opposite conclusion. Neither prosecutor nor defender is obliged to consider anything that weakens their respective cases. On the contrary, scientists construct arguments because they want to test their own ideas and give an accurate explanation of some aspect of nature. Scientists can include any evidence or hypothesis that supports their claim, but they must observe one fundamental rule of professional science. They must include all of the known evidence and all of the hypotheses previously proposed. Unlike lawyers, scientists must explicitly account for the possibility that they might be wrong.

↓

Unlike lawyers, who utilize information __(A)__ to support their arguments, scientists must include all information even if some of it is unlikely to __(B)__ their arguments.
└ 부정어 주의

변호인들은 자신에게 유리한 정보만을 사용하는데 반해, 과학자들은 자신에게 불리할 수도 있는 정보도 포함시켜야한다는 내용이야. 따라서 (A)에는 selectively(선택적으로), (B)에는 앞에 부정어(unlikely)를 포함해서 '약화시킨다'라는 의미가 들어가야 하므로 strengthen(강화시키다)이 적절해.

① 객관적으로 – 약화시키다

② 객관적으로 – 지지하다
③ 정확하게 – 명확히 하다
⑤ 선택적으로 – 반증한다

● 중요 포인트

분사의 수식을 받는 명사

❶ Lawyers and scientists use argument to mean a summary of evidence and principles leading to a conclusion; ~

❷ They must include all of the known evidence and all of the hypotheses previously proposed ~

4 단계 혼공 개념 마무리   p.91

1. 아직도 수렵 · 채집 사회에서 살고 있는 사람들을 연구하는 인류학자들은, 그들이 엄청나게 풍부한 양의 식량을 얻을 수 있는 최상의 기회가 아니라, 오히려 결국 부족한 식량 공급을 초래하게 되는 위험성을 최소화하기 위한 선택을 일관되게 한다는 것을 발견했다.

2. 현대 사회의 이러한 소외에 대한 더 깊은 이유는 현실에 대한 개념 속에서 현대의 어른은 원시인이 했던 것 보다 직접적인 경험에 덜 의존하고, 문화의 경험에 더 의존하기 때문이다.

3. 업무 수행은 개인의 통제 범위를 벗어난 업무 수행에 미친 영향보다는 평가를 받는 개인의 통제 하에 있는 것의 측면에서 판단되어야 한다.

4. 연구는 또한 더 어려운 버전의 시를 읽는 것이 특히 우뇌의 활동을 증가시켜 서 독자들이 자신이 읽은 것에 비추어 자신의 경험을 되돌아보고 재평가하도록 돕는다는 것을 발견했다.

5. 몇 가지 연구들은 환경 훼손과 관광산업의 관계에 대해 주민들이 가지는 생각의 차이가 관광산업의 유형, 주민들이 자연환경이 보호될 필요가 있다고 느끼는 정도, 그리고 주민들이 관광 명소에서 떨어져 사는 거리와 연관이 있음을 보여 준다.

6. 과학의 방법론을 고려해 보면, 중력의 법칙과 게놈은 누군가에 의해 반드시 발견되게 되어 있었고, 그 발견자의 신원은 그 사실에 부수적이다.

7. 소비자가 합의한 상황에서 '약간의' 변화가 있은 다음 그 거래를 철회한다면, 그는 이러한 불가피한 비용을 모르는 무책임한 사람이 되어 다소 바람직하지 않은 인상을 불러일으키게 될 것이다.

혼공 09일차 장문독해(2문항형)

3단계 고난도 문항 요리하기   p.97

● 정답

1. ① **2.** ① **3.** ⑤ **4.** ④ **5.** ① **6.** ⑤ **7.** ⑤ **8.** ①

1. ① **2.** ①

● 전체 해석

아이들이 먹는 음식에 변화를 주는 것은 쉬운 게 아닐 것이다. 심지어 가장 신중하고, 인내심 있는 부모들조차 아이들이 어떤 순간에 혹은 어느 정도까지는 저항할 것이라는 것을 발견하게 될 것이다. 문제는 우리가 어렸을 때 건강한 방식으로 먹을 것을 강요받았다는 것인데, 우리는 (그러한 강요 때문에) 어렵게 배웠다. 그리고 아이들에게 부모로서의 습관을 계속(적용)하려는 유혹은 강력하다.

만일 당신이 접시를 다 비울 때까지 식사 테이블에 앉도록 강요받았다면, 당신은 혼자가 아니다(다른 부모들도 마찬가지였다): 어른들 대부분은 이것을 어느 정도까지는 경험을 했다 – 집이 아니더라도 학교에서. 아이들에게 먹도록 강요하는 것은, 특히 그들이 접시에 놓인 음식을 좋아하지 않는 경우에, 완전히 역효과를 낳는다. "다 먹을 때까지 앉아 있어."라는 말은 우리가 배웠던 방식일지도 모른다. 그리고 또한 당신이 목표를 성취했다고 느끼는 유일한 방식일지도 모른다. 그러나 생각을 해보자. 아이들이 질려할 때까지 원치 않는 양배추 더미를 먹는 경험은, 다음에 양배추가 나올 때 아이들이 기뻐하도록 만들 가능성은 거의 없다.

엄격한 접근은 매우 구식이다. 그리고 당신은 전투에는 이기지만, 전쟁에는 지는 것이 될 지도 모른다. 푸딩을 미루는 것 또한 좋은 방법이라고 생각되어졌다. 그러나 중요한 점은, 그것 또한 더 이상 통하지 않는다는 것이다. "식사를 다 할 때까지 푸딩은 없다."라는 말은 대부분 부모가 어렸을 적에 듣던 전형적인 말이었고, 지금도 여전히 흔하게 사용되고 있다. 그러나 그 말은 단지 달콤한 음식이 더 매력적으로 보이도록 만들 뿐이다.

● 지문분석

─── 가주어-진주어 구문 ───
It isn't going to be easy / making changes to the food / your children eat, / and even the most careful, patient parents / will probably find / that the little ones will resist / at some point and to some degree.
쉽지 않을 것이다 / 음식에 변화를 주는 것이 / 당신 아이들이 먹는 / 그리고 심지어 가장 주의 깊고 참을성 있는 부모들은 / 아마도 발견할 것이다 / 작은 아이들은 저항할 것이다라는 것을 / 어느 순간 그리고 어느 정도

The problem / is that many of us were forced to eat / in a healthy way / as children: / we learned the hard way.
문제는 / 우리 중 상당수는 먹어야만 했다는 것이다 / 건강한 방식으로 / 아이였을 때 / 우리가 어렵게 얻었던

And [the temptation / to continue with these parental habits / with our own children] / is strong.
그리고 유혹은 / 계속 이러한 부모의 습관을 가지고 갈 / 우리 자신의 아이들에게 / 강하다

If you were made to sit at the table / until you had cleaned
사역동사의 수동태: be made to부정사
your plate, / you are not alone: / most of the adult

population / have suffered this at some point / – at school if not at home.
만약 당신이 테이블에 앉도록 강요된다면 / 다 먹을 때까지 / 당신은 혼자가 아니다 / 대부분의 어른들은 / 어느 정도까지는 이것을 경험한다 / 학교에서 / 만약 집이 아니라면

[Forcing your children to eat, / especially if they don't like / what is on the plate,] / is completely counterproductive.
당신의 아이가 먹도록 강요하는 것은 / 특히 그들이 좋아하지 않는다면 / 접시에 있는 것을 / 완전히 역효과가 난다

["Sit there / until you finish"] / may be how we learned, / and may also be the only way / you feel / able to achieve your goal, / but think about it: / [the experience of eating a pile of unwanted cabbage / until they feel sick] / is hardly going to make / children jump for joy / the next time it is served.
거기에 앉아라 / 네가 다 먹을 때까지 라는 말은 / 우리가 배웠던 방식일 수도 있다 / 그리고 유일한 방식일 수도 있다 / 당신이 느끼는 / 당신의 목표를 성취할 수 있다고 / 하지만 그것에 대해서 생각해봐라 / 원하지 않는 양배추 더미를 먹는 경험은 / 그들이 질릴 때까지 / 거의 만들지 않는다 / 아이들을 기뻐하도록 / 그것이 다음에 제공되었을 때

This strict approach is very old-fashioned, / and you may win the battle / but you definitely won't win the war.
이 엄격한 방법은 굉장히 구식이다 / 그리고 당신은 전투에서는 이길지도 모른다 / 하지만 당신은 명확하게 전쟁에서는 이기지 못할 것이다

[Delaying puddings] / used to be thought of / as a good idea too, / but guess what?
푸딩을 미루는 것은 / 생각되곤 했다 / 좋은 생각으로 / 근데 그건 아는지

That doesn't work either.
그것은 마찬가지로 효과가 없다

["No pudding / until you have finished your main course"] / was the standard line / when most parents of today were young / and is still commonly used, / but it only makes / sweet things seem more desirable.
푸딩은 없어 / 네가 식사를 끝낼 때까지 라는 말은 / 전형적인 말이었다 / 오늘날의 대부분의 부모들이 어렸을 때에는 / 그리고 여전히 일반적으로 사용된다 / 하지만 그것은 단지 만든다 / 달콤한 음식을 더 매력적으로 보이게

● 해설

[1–2] 다음 글을 읽고, 물음에 답하시오.

It isn't going to be easy making changes to the food your children eat, and even the most careful, patient parents will probably find that the little ones will resist at some point and to some degree. The problem is that many of us were forced to eat in a healthy way as children: we learned the hard way. And the temptation to continue with these parental habits with our own children is strong.

If you were made to sit at the table until you had cleaned your plate, you are not alone: most of the adult population have suffered this at some point – at school if not at home. Forcing your children to eat, especially if they don't like what is on the plate, is completely ＿＿＿＿＿. "Sit there until you finish" may be how we learned, and may also be the only way you feel able to achieve your goal, but think about it: the experience of eating a pile of unwanted cabbage until they feel sick is hardly going to make children jump for joy the next time it is served.

This strict approach is very old-fashioned, and you may win the battle but you definitely won't win the war. Delaying puddings used to be thought of as a good idea too, but guess what? That doesn't work either. "No pudding until you have finished your main course" was the standard line when most parents of today were young and is still commonly used, but it only makes sweet things seem more desirable.

부정적인 내용이 나와야 해.

예전의 밥 먹이는 방식은 이제는 더 이상 효과가 없다는 것이 필자가 하고 싶은 말이지.

1. 윗글의 제목으로 가장 적절한 것은?
❶ Do Old Feeding Habits Work? 예전에 밥을 먹이는 습관이 효과가 있는가?
▶ 예전에 통용되었던 방식이 지금은 효과가 없다는 내용이지.
② No More Instant Foods for Kids 아이에게 더 이상의 인스턴트 음식은 안된다
③ Kids Today Need Table Manners 오늘날의 아이들은 음식 예절이 필요하다
▶ 예전에 강요했던 밥먹이는 방법을 쓰지 말자는 것이지 음식 예절에 대한 내용이 아니야.
④ Time to Switch to Organic Food! 유기농 음식으로 바뀔 때
⑤ Homemade Pudding Makes Us Perfect 수제 푸딩은 우리를 완벽하게 만든다

2. 윗글의 빈칸에 들어갈 말로 가장 적절한 것은?
❶ counterproductive 역효과가 나는 ▶ 이것만 부정적 내용이지.
② beneficial 유익한
③ invaluable 가치로운
④ unconventional 색다른, 독특한
⑤ constructive 건설적인

● 중요 포인트

사역동사의 수동태

사역동사의 수동태에서 목적 보어에 있던 원형동사는 to부정사로 바뀌어야 해.

If you were made to sit at the table until you had
사역동사의 수동태: be made to부정사
cleaned your plate, you are not alone: most of the adult population have suffered this at some point – at school if not at home.

3. ⑤ 4. ④

● 전체 해석

지속 시간은 사건이 지속되는 시간을 말한다. 만약 우리가 템포((움직임, 활동 등의) 속도)를 사건의 속도로 여긴다면, 지속 시간은 시계 자체의 속도이다. 물리학자에게, '1초'의 지속 시간은 정확하고 분명한데, 그것은 동위원소인 세슘-133의 두 개의 에너지 준위 사이의 전이와 연관된

9,192,631,770번의 진동수 주기와 같다. 하지만 심리적 경험의 영역에서, 시간의 단위를 수량화하는 것은 상당히 서투른 작업이다. 사람들에게서 태양이든, 신체적 피로든, 아니면 시계 자체든, '실제' 시간 신호를 제거할 때, 오래지 않아 그들의 시간 감각은 고장이 난다. 그리고 사람들이 경험하는 지속 시간에 대한 인식을 만들어내는 것은 시계에 나타나는 시간이 아니라 일반적으로 부정확한 이 심리적 시계이다.

이론상, 정신적으로 시간의 지속 시간을 늘리는 사람은 더 느린 템포를 경험할 것이다. 예를 들어, 야구공이 두 명의 서로 다른 타자에게 던져진다고 상상해 보라. 공은 50초 동안 5초마다 던져지므로, 합해서 10개의 공이 던져진다. 우리는 이제 두 명의 타자에게 얼마나 많은 시간이 지나갔는지를 묻는다. (치는 것을 좋아하는) 1번 타자는 그 지속 시간이 40초라고 느낀다. (야구가 지루해진) 2번 타자는 그것이 60초라고 믿는다. 그렇다면, 심리적으로, 첫 번째 사람은 야구공이 4초마다 다가오는 것을 경험했지만, 두 번째 사람은 그것을 6초마다 다가온 것으로 여긴다. 다시 말해서, 인식된 템포(속도)는 1번 타자에게 더 빠르다.

● 지문분석

Duration refers to the time / that events last.
지속 시간은 시간을 의미한다 / 사건이 지속되는

If we think of tempo / as the speed of events, / then duration is the speed of the clock itself.
우리가 템포를 생각한다면 / 사건의 속도로 / 그러면 지속 시간은 시계 자체의 속도이다

For the physicist, / [the duration of a "second"] / is precise
S   V
and unambiguous: / it is equal to 9,192,631,770 cycles of the frequency / associated with the transition / between two energy levels / of the isotope cesium-133.
물리학자에게 있어 / '1초'의 지속 시간은 / 정확하고 분명하다 / 그것은 9,192,631,770번의 진동수의 주기와 동일하다 / 전이와 연관된 / 두 개의 에너지 수준 사이의 / 동위원소 세슘-133의

In the realm of psychological experience, / however,
[quantifying units of time] / is a considerably clumsier
S   V
operation.
심리학적 경험의 영역에서 / 하지만 시간의 단위들을 수량화하는 것은 / 엄청나게 서투른 작업이다

When people are removed / from the cues of "real" time
/ – be it the sun, bodily fatigue, or timepieces themselves
= whether it should be ~: whether와 should 생략 후 be it 도치
/ – it doesn't take long / before their time sense breaks down.
사람들이 내보내질 때 / 실제 시간의 신호로부터 / 그것이 태양이든, 신체적 피로든, 아니면 시계 자체이든 / 그것은 오래 걸리지 않는다 / 그들의 시간 감각이 붕괴되기 전까지

And it is this usually imprecise psychological clock, / as
                S
it – that 강조구문
opposed to the time / on one's watch, / that creates the
삽입구   V
perception of duration / that people experience.
그리고 이러한 일반적으로 부정확한 심리학적 시계이다 / 시간과 반대되는 / 사람의 시계 속의 / 지속 시간의 인식을 만드는 것은 / 사람들이 경험하는

Theoretically, / [a person / who mentally stretches the
duration of time] / should experience a slower tempo.
이론적으로 / 사람은 / 정신적으로 시간의 지속 시간을 늘리는 / 더

느린 템포를 경험해야 한다

Imagine, for example, / that baseballs are pitched / to two
different batters.
(V 명령문)

상상해봐라, 예를 들어 / 야구공이 던져진다고 / 두 사람의 다른 타자
에게

The balls are thrown / every 5 seconds for 50 seconds, / so
a total of 10 balls are thrown.

그 공은 던져진다 / 50초 동안 5초마다 / 그래서 전체 10개의 공이
던져진다

We now ask both batters / how much time has passed.

우리는 지금 두 명의 타자에게 묻고 있다 / 얼마만큼의 시간이 흘렀
는지를

Let's say / that [batter number one / (who loves hitting)] /
feels the duration to be 40 seconds.

말해보자 / 1번 타자는 / 치는 것을 좋아하는 / 지속 시간이 40초라고
느낀다

[Batter number two / (bored by baseball)] / believes it to
be 60 seconds.
S   V

2번 타자는 / 야구가 지루해진 / 그것(지속시간)이 60초라고 믿는다

Psychologically, then, / the first person has experienced
/ baseballs approaching every four seconds / while the
second sees it / as every six seconds.

심리학적으로 그때 / 첫 번째 사람은 경험한다 / 야구공이 4초마다
다가오는 것을 / 반면에 두 번째 타자는 그것을 본다 / 6초마다로

The perceived tempo, in other words, / is faster / for batter
number one.

인지된 템포는 다시 말하자면 / 더 빠르다 / 1번 타자에게

●해설

[3~4] 다음 글을 읽고, 물음에 답하시오.

Duration refers to the time that events last. If we think of
tempo as the speed of events, then duration is the speed of
the clock itself. For the physicist, the duration of a "second"
is precise and unambiguous: it is equal to 9,192,631,770
cycles of the frequency associated with the transition between
two energy levels of the isotope cesium-133. In the realm of
psychological experience, however, quantifying units of time is
a considerably clumsier operation. When people are removed
from the cues of "real" time – be it the sun, bodily fatigue, or
timepieces themselves – it doesn't take long before their time
sense breaks down. And it is this usually ___(A)___ psychological
clock, as opposed to the time on one's watch, that creates the
perception of duration that people experience.

Theoretically, a person who mentally stretches the duration of
time should experience a slower tempo. Imagine, for example,
that baseballs are pitched to two different batters. The balls
are thrown every 5 seconds for 50 seconds, so a total of 10
balls are thrown. We now ask both batters how much time has
passed. Let's say that batter number one (who loves hitting)
feels the duration to be 40 seconds. Batter number two (bored
by baseball) believes it to be 60 seconds. Psychologically, then,

the first person has experienced baseballs approaching every
four seconds while the second sees it as every six seconds. The
perceived tempo, in other words, is ___(B)___ for batter number
one.

3. 윗글의 제목으로 가장 적절한 것은?
① What Timepieces Bring to Our Lives 시계가 우리 삶에 가져오는 것
② Research into Time: Precision vs. Duration 시간에 대한 연구: 정확성 vs
지속시간
▶ 시간에 대한 연구는 맞는데, 정확성과 지속 시간에 대한 내용은 아니
지. 지문에서 반복된 단어들이지만, 여기서 중요한 '심리학'적인 내용이
빠졌어.
③ Flight from Time: A New Direction for Physics 시간으로부터의 비행 :
물리학을 위한 새로운 방향
④ The Peaceful Coexistence of Science and Baseball 과학과 야구의 평
화로운 공존
❺ How Long, How Fast: A Matter of Time Perception 얼마나 오랫동안,
얼마나 빠르게: 시간의 인식에 대한 문제
▶ 우리는 일반적으로 심리적 경험의 영역에서 시간 인식을 만들어내므
로 물리적으로 같은 지속 시간에 대해서도 시간의 길이와 속도에 대해 다
른 인식을 하게 된다는 내용이지.

4. 윗글의 빈칸에 들어갈 말로 가장 적절한 것은?
     (A)   (B)
① delayed 지연된 ······ faster 더 빠른
② internal 내적인 ······ slower 더 느린
③ accurate 정확한 ······ slower 더 느린
❹ imprecise 부정확한 ······ faster 더 빠른
⑤ mysterious 불가사의한 ······ slower 더 느린

(A) 심리적 경험의 영역에서, 실제 시간 신호가 사람들에게서 제거될 때
사람들의 시간 감각은 고장이 나게 되지. 이때, 사람들은 일반적으로 이
고장 난 시계를 근거로 시간 인식을 만들어 내지. 따라서 그 시간은 부정
확해질(imprecise) 수밖에 없어.
(B) 야구공을 치는 것을 좋아하는 1번 타자에게 실제 50초는 40초로 짧게
느껴지게 되므로 야구를 지루해하는 2번 타자보다 더 빨라지지. 따라서
faster가 적절해.

●중요 포인트

it-that 강조구문

And it is this usually imprecise psychological clock, as
  it – that 강조구문
opposed to the time on one's watch, that creates ~
                       S   V

5. ① **6.** ⑤

●전체 해석

만약 실패가 제공하는 것과 같은 정보를 얻지 못한다면, 결국 자신에 대
한 비현실적인 기대를 가지게 될 것이라고 어떤 심리학자는 설명한다. 여
러분은 실패가 어둠을 틈타서 모였다가 갑자기 나타나는 위치에 봉착할
수도 있다.

그렇다면 우리는 일찌감치 그리고 자주 실패에 노출되기를 소망해야 한
다. 사회학자 Glen Elder는 10대 후반에서 30대 초반에 이르기까지의 성
장에 민감한 시기가 있는데, 그 기간 동안은 실패가 대단히 유익하다고
하였다. 그러한 패턴은 종종 마음의 평정이라고 불리는 특징을 증진시키

는 것 같다. 우리는 정신적 외상이 (사라지지 않고) 계속 남아있을 수 있다는 것을 알고 있으므로, 좌절을 뒤쫓는데 너무 깊이 뛰어들지 않는다. 반대로, 우리는 성공을 좇아서 너무 높이 날아오르지도 않는다. Silicon Valley와 Wall Street의 몇몇 사업체들은 직원으로 애써 전직 프로 운동선수를 고용한다. 그것은 그들이 가지고 있는 대중의 높은 관심이 사업을 유치하기 때문만은 아니다. 그것은 운동선수들이 실패로부터 잘 회복하기 때문이다. "우리는 일을 수행할 수 있고 손실에 감정적으로 집착하지 않는 사람들이 필요했습니다."라고 어느 Chicago의 석유 상인이 New York Times에 말하면서, 왜 회사들이 특히 이처럼 험난한 경제시기에 증권거래소에 운동선수들을 두는 것을 좋아하는지를 설명했다. 그 이미지는 기수가 안장에 편안히 앉아 있는 것과 같다. 좋든 나쁘든 그 어떤 것도 그 사람을 너무도 깜짝 놀라게 해서 (말에서) 떨어뜨릴 수 없을 것이다.

살면서 날아 오는 돌과 화살이 (인생의) 항로를 벗어나지 못하도록 막는 데 도움이 되는 한 가지 방법은 여러분의 삶이 다차원적이라는 것을 확실하게 하는 것이라고 California의 심리학자이자 개인 코치인 Stephen Berglas가 말한다. 그렇게 하면, 어떤 한 부분에서 좌절하더라도 마음속으로 자신이 절대적으로 실패자라고는 생각하지 않을 것이다. 그것을 감정적 포트폴리오 전반에 위험을 널리 퍼뜨리는 것으로, 다시 말해서 균형을 잡기 위해 가구에 또 하나의 다리를 덧붙이는 것으로 여기라고 Berglas는 말한다.

● 지문분석

If you don't get the kind of information / failure provides, you'll end up with unrealistic expectations / for yourself, / explains a psychologist.
당신이 만약 정보를 얻지 못한다면 / 실패가 제공하는 / 당신은 결국 비현실적인 기대감을 갖게 될 것이다 / 당신 자신에 대한 / 한 심리학자가 설명한다

You could wind up in a position / where [failure, / which has gathered under cover of darkness], reveals itself all at once.
당신은 결국 위치에 있을 수 있다 / 실패가 / 어둠 아래에서 모인 / 갑자기 자신을 드러내는

We should hope, then, / for exposure to failure, / early and often.
우리는 그때 바라야 한다 / 실패에 대한 노출을 / 초기에 그리고 종종

The sociologist Glen Elder proposed / that there is a sensitive period for growth / – late teens through early 30s – / during which failures are most beneficial.
사회학자 Glen Elder는 말했다 / 성장에 민감한 시기가 있다고 / 십대 후반에서 30대 초반이라는 / 그 기간 동안 실패가 가장 유익한

Such a pattern / seems to promote the trait / sometimes called equanimity.
그런 패턴은 / 특성을 촉진하는 것 같다 / 때때로 마음의 여정이라고 불리는

We learn / that trauma is survivable, / so we don't plunge too deeply / following setbacks.
우리는 배운다 / 트라우마는 살아남는다(사라지지 않는다)고 / 그래서 우리는 너무 깊이 뛰어들지 않는다 / 좌절을 따라

Nor, conversely, do we soar too high / on our successes.
부정 부사어 → 도치
대조적으로 우리는 높이 솟지 않는다 / 우리 성공에서

[Some businesses / in Silicon Valley and on Wall Street] /
S

make a point of hiring ex-pro athletes / to their staffs.
일부 사업체는 / 실리콘 밸리와 월 스트리트에서 / 으레 전직 운동선수를 고용한다 / 그들의 직원으로

It's not just / that their high profile draws business.
이것은 단순히 ~인 것만은 아니다 / 그들의 높은 경력이 사업을 끌어들이는 것

It's because athletes are good at recovering / from their failures.
그것은 운동선수들이 회복하는 데 능숙하기 때문이다 / 그들의 실패로부터

"We needed people / who could perform / and not get emotionally attached to losses," / a Chicago oil trader told the New York Times, / explaining / why the firm likes athletes / on the trading floor, / particularly in ugly economic times like these.
ㄴ분사구문 〈동시상황〉 '설명하며'
우리는 사람이 필요하다 / 수행을 할 수 있는 / 그리고 감정적으로 손실에 집착하지 않는 / 시카고의 한 석유 상인이 뉴욕타임지에 말했다 / 설명하면서 / 왜 그 회사가 운동선수를 좋아하는지 / 증권 거래소에 / 특히 이와 같은 경제 불황시기에

The image is of a rider / easy in the saddle.
이미지는 기수와 같다 / 안장에서 편안한

Nothing can so surprise her / – either for good or ill – that she'll be knocked off.
so—that 용법
어떠한 것도 그녀를 너무 놀래켜서 / 좋든 나쁘든 그녀를 떨어뜨릴 것이 없다

[One way / to help keep life's slings and arrows / from knocking you off course] / is to ensure / your life is multidimensional, / says Stephen Berglas, / a California psychologist and personal coach.
한 가지 방법은 / 삶의 돌과 화살을 막는 것을 돕는 / 당신을 항로에서 떨어뜨리는 것을 / 확실하게 하는 것이다 / 당신의 삶이 다차원적이라는 것을 / Stephen Berglas가 말한다 / 캘리포니아의 심리학자이자 개인 코치인

That way, / [a setback / in any one area] / won't mean in your mind / that you're a failure categorically.
S   V
그런 식으로 / 좌절은 / 어떤 한 분야에서의 / 당신의 마음 속에서 의미하지는 않을 것이다 / 당신이 절대적으로 실패자라는 것을

Call it / spreading your risk / across your emotional portfolio / — or adding another leg / to the furniture for balance, / says Berglas.
V 명령문
그것을 불러라 / 당신의 위험을 퍼뜨리는 것으로 / 당신의 감정적인 포트폴리오 전체에 / 아니면 또 다른 다리를 붙여라 / 균형을 위해 가구에 / 라고 Berglas가 말한다

● 해설

[5–6] 다음 글을 읽고, 물음에 답하시오.

If you don't get the kind of information failure provides, you'll end up with unrealistic expectations for yourself, explains a psychologist. You could wind up in a position where failure, which has gathered under cover of darkness, reveals itself all at once.

We should hope, then, for exposure to failure, early and often. 실패는 좋다는 거지. The sociologist Glen Elder proposed that there is a sensitive period for growth – late teens through early 30s – during which failures are most beneficial. Such a pattern seems to promote the trait sometimes called equanimity. We learn that trauma is survivable, so we don't plunge too deeply following setbacks. Nor, conversely, do we soar too high on our successes. Some businesses in Silicon Valley and on Wall Street make a point of hiring ex-pro athletes to their staffs. It's not just that their high profile draws business. It's because athletes are good at recovering from their failures. "We needed people who could perform and not get emotionally attached to losses," a Chicago oil trader told the New York Times, explaining why the firm likes athletes on the trading floor, particularly in ugly economic times like these. The image is of a rider easy in the saddle. Nothing can so surprise her — either for good or ill — that she'll be knocked off.

One way to help keep life's slings and arrows from knocking you off course is to ensure your life is _____ says Stephen Berglas, a California psychologist and personal coach. That way, a setback in any one area won't mean in your mind that you're a failure categorically. Call it spreading your risk across your emotional portfolio — or adding another leg to the furniture for balance, says Berglas.

5. 윗글의 제목으로 가장 적절한 것은?

❶ Do Not Let Failure Fail You 실패로 인해 낙담하지 않도록 해라
▶ 성장에 민감한 시기에서는 실패가 유익하다는 내용이지.
② Recipe for Attaining Physical Stability 신체적 안정에 이르는 비결
③ Physical Toughness and Mental Flexibility 신체의 강인함과 정신의 유연함
④ How to Survive Emotional Unrest in Sports 운동 경기에서 정서적 불안을 견디는 방법
⑤ Failure as an Enemy of Emotional Calmness 서적 평온의 적으로서의 실패
▶ 글은 실패에 대해서 긍정적인 내용인데 이것은 부정적인 면을 의미하지.

6. 윗글의 빈칸에 들어갈 말로 가장 적절한 것은?

① illusionary 환상의
② predictable 예측 가능한
③ convergent 집중적인
④ straightforward 솔직한
▶ 실패가 솔직하면 안되겠지.
❺ multidimensional 다차원적인
▶ 감정적 포트폴리오 전반에 걸쳐 위험을 퍼뜨리고 균형을 위한 또 다른 다리를 만들라고 했지.

● 중요 포인트

수식어구 안의 또 다른 수식어구

관계부사절 안에 관계대명사절이 들어있는 구문이므로 해석에 주의하자.

You could wind up in a position where [failure, which has gathered under cover of darkness,] reveals itself all at once.

7. ⑤ 8. ①

● 전체 해석

여러 사회학자들에 따르면, 매우 특정적이며 관념적인 의미로 가득한 '예술', '예술품', '예술가'라는 전문 용어를 버리고, 이것들을 '문화적 형식', '문화적 산물', '문화 생산자' 등의 더 중립적이고 역사적인 면에서 덜 구체적인 용어로 대체해야만, 우리 사회에서 '예술'이라고 부르는 것에 대한 연구가 진정으로 발전할 수 있다. 이 문화적 산물들은 —그것이 그림이든, 조각이든, 음악의 형태이든, 혹은 무엇이든 —일정한 유형의 문화 생산자에 의해서 만들어지는 것으로, 그리고 특정한 집단의 사람들에 의해 특정한 방식으로 특정한 사회적 맥락에서 사용되는 것으로 간주되어야 한다. 특정한 사물들에 대해 '문화적 산물'이라는 더 중립적인 말을 사용하고, 그러한 사물들을 만들어내는 사람들에 대해 '문화 생산자'라는 말을 사용함으로써, 사회학자는 너무 오랫동안 문화 형태에 대한 연구를 지배해 왔다고 여기는 견해, 즉 모든 것을 '예술'의 범주에서 이해하려는 견해와 결별하려고 한다. 이것은 다양한 사회의 사람들이 만들어내고 사용하는 모든 다양한 문화적 산물을 포괄하기에는 너무 제한적이며 상황에 한정된 범주이다. 그것은 우리 자신의 사회를 연구할 때 액면 그대로 받아들여서 순진하게 사용하기에는 특정한 의미가 너무 많은 용어이기도 하다. 어떤 것들을 '예술'로 규정하고 다른 것들을 아닌 것으로 규정하는 것은 특정한 사회 집단에게 이익이 되므로, '예술'이라는 바로 그 용어 자체는, 그러한 이름을 붙이는 과정이 어떻게 그리고 왜 일어나는지 이해하려는 사회학자에 의해 무비판적으로 사용될 수 없다. 그렇다면, 간단히 말해서, 문화적 문제를 연구하기 위해서는, 우리의 분석의 근거로서 사용되는 '예술', '예술품', '예술가'라는 말을 거부해야 한다고 많은 사회학자들은 믿는다. 대신에 이러한 말들은 그 자체가 중요한 분석의 대상이 된다.

● 지문분석

According to many sociologists, / [the study / of what oursociety calls 'art'] / can only really progress / if we drop / the highly specific and ideologically loaded terminology / of 'art', 'artworks' and 'artists', / and replace these / with the more neutral and less historically specific terms / 'cultural forms', 'cultural products' and 'cultural producers'.

많은 사회학자들에 따르면 / 연구는 / 우리 사회가 '예술'이라고 부르는 것에 대한 / 단지 정말로 발전할 수 있다 / 만약 우리가 버린다면 / 매우 구체적이며 관념적으로 채워진 전문 용어를 / '예술,' 예술작품', '예술가'라는 / 그리고 이러한 것들을 대체한다면 / 보다 중립적이고 덜 역사적이고 덜 구체적인 용어로 / '문화적 형태', '문화적 산물', ' 문화적 생산자'라는

[These cultural products / – be they paintings, sculptures, / forms of music or whatever] / – should be regarded / as being made / by certain types of cultural producer, / and as being used / by particular groups of people / in particular ways in specific social contexts.

이러한 문화적 산물은 / 그들이 그림이든, 조각품이든, 음악의 형태나 무엇이든 / 간주되어야 한다 / 만들어진 존재로 / 특정한 형태의 문화적 생산자에 의해서 / 그리고 사용되어지는 존재로 / 특정한 사람의 그룹에 의해서 / 특정한 사회적 환경에서 특정한 방식으로

By using the more neutral term / 'cultural products' / for particular objects, / and 'cultural producers' / for the people / who make those objects, / the sociologist seeks to break with a view / that she/he sees / as having dominated / the study of cultural forms for too long, / namely trying to understand everything / in terms of the category 'art'.
더 중립적인 용어를 사용함으로써 / '문화적 산물'이라는 / 특정한 물건을 위해 / 그리고 '문화적 생산자'라는 / 사람들을 위해 / 그러한 물건을 만드는 / 사회학자들은 관점과 헤어지려고 한다 / 그 사람이 바라보는 / 지배해왔던 것으로 / 오랫동안 문화적 형태의 학문을 / 말하자면 모든 것을 이해하려고 노력하는 / 예술이라는 범주에서

This is a category / that is too limited and context-specific / to encompass all the different cultural products / that [people in different societies] / make and use.
이것은 범주이다 / 너무 제한적이고 상황에 한정되어서 / 모든 다른 문화적 산물을 포괄할 수 없는 / 다른 사회의 사람들이 / 만들고 사용하는

┌ too ~ to 용법 ┐
It is a term / that is also too loaded / to take at face value / and to use naively / in study of our own society.
그것은 용어이다 / 마찬가지로 너무 실려있어서 / 액면으로 받아들일 수 없고 / 그리고 순진하게 사용할 수 없는 / 우리 자신의 사회의 연구에서는

Since it is in the interests of certain social groups / to define some things as 'art' / and others as not, / the very term 'art' itself / cannot be uncritically used / by the sociologist / who wishes to understand / how and why such labelling processes occur.
특정한 사회 그룹에 이익이기 때문에 / 어떤 것을 '예술'로 규정하는 것이 / 다른 것은 그렇지 않은 것으로 / '예술'이라는 용어는 / 무비판적으로 사용될 수 없다 / 사화학자들에 의해서 / 이해하기를 바라는 / 어떻게 그리고 왜 그런 명칭 붙이기 과정이 발생하는지를

Quite simply, then, / in order to study cultural matters, / many sociologists believe / one has to reject the terms / 'art', 'artwork' and 'artist' / as the basis for our analysis.
아주 간단히 그러면 / 문화적 사실들을 연구하기 위해서 / 많은 사회학자들은 믿는다 / 사람은 용어를 거부해야 한다고 / '예술', '예술 작품', 그리고 '예술가'라는 / 우리 분석의 기본으로서의

Instead, these terms become important objects / of analysis themselves.
대신에 이러한 용어는 아주 중요한 대상이 된다 / 그 자체가 분석의

● 해설

[7-8] 다음 글을 읽고, 물음에 답하시오.
According to many sociologists, the study of what our society calls 'art' can only really progress if we drop the

---

highly specific and ideologically loaded terminology of 'art', 'artworks' and 'artists', and replace these with the more neutral and less historically specific terms 'cultural forms', 'cultural products' and 'cultural producers'. These cultural products –
이 글의 핵심이 바로 나오고 있어.
be they paintings, sculptures, forms of music or whatever – should be regarded as being made by certain types of cultural producer, and as being used by particular groups of people in particular ways in specific social contexts. By using the more neutral term 'cultural products' for particular objects, and 'cultural producers' for the people who make those objects, the sociologist seeks to break with a view that she/he sees as having dominated the study of cultural forms for too long, namely trying to understand everything in terms of the category 'art'. This is a category that is too limited and context-specific to encompass all the different cultural products that people in different societies make and use. It is a term that is also too loaded to take at face value and to use naively in study of our own society. Since it is in the interests of certain social groups to define some things as 'art' and others as not, the very term 'art' itself cannot be uncritically used by the sociologist who wishes to understand how and why such labelling processes occur. Quite simply, then, in order to study cultural matters, many sociologists believe one has to ＿＿＿＿＿ the terms 'art', 'artwork' and 'artist' as the basis for our analysis. Instead,
이것을 하지 말자는 내용이 나와야겠지.
these terms become important objects of analysis themselves.

7. 윗글의 제목으로 가장 적절한 것은?
① Art: A Means to Overcome a Cultural Gap 예술: 문화 격차를 극복하기 위한 수단
② Interpreting Culture In and Out of Context 맥락 안에서 그리고 맥락 밖에서 문화를 이해하기
▶ 언뜻 보면 정답인것 같지만, '맥락'이 핵심이 아니지. 이 지문의 핵심은 바로 '용어'야.
③ Different Forms of Art in the World of Culture 문화계에 존재하는 예술의 다양한 형태
④ Cultural Diversity: Cornerstones of Civilizations 문화적 다양성: 문명의 주춧돌
❺ Culture as a Basis of Understanding the Concept of Art 예술이라는 개념을 이해하기 위한 토대로서의 문화
▶ 사회의 다양한 모습을 있는 그대로 연구하려면 예술, 예술품, 예술가라는 말 대신 문화적 형식, 문화적 산물, 문화 생산자라는 말을 사용해서 이해해야 한다는 내용의 글이지.

8. 윗글의 빈칸에 들어갈 말로 가장 적절한 것은?
❶ reject 거부해야
▶ 사회를 중립적인 입장에서 객관적으로 연구하기 위해서 사회학자들은 예술, 예술품, 예술가라는 말을 버리고 문화적 형식, 문화적 산물, 문화 생산자라는 말을 써야 한다고 하고 있어.
② borrow 빌려야
③ introduce 도입해야
④ stress 강조해야
⑤ revive 되살려야

● 중요 포인트

2개의 구문이 하나의 어휘를 수식하는 구조

관계부사절 안에 관계대명사절이 들어있는 구문이므로 해석에 주의하자.

By using the more neutral term 'cultural products' for particular objects, and 'cultural producers' for the people who make those objects, the sociologist seeks to break with a view that she/he sees as having dominated the study of cultural forms for too long, namely trying to understand everything / in terms of the category 'art'.

4단계 혼공 개념 마무리
p.101

1. 아이들이 먹는 음식에 변화를 주는 것은 쉬운 게 아닐 것이다. 심지어 가장 신중하고, 인내심 있는 부모들조차 아이들이 어떤 순간에 혹은 어느 정도까지는 저항할 것이라는 것을 발견하게 될 것이다.

2. 만일 당신이 접시를 다 비울 때까지 식사 테이블에 앉도록 강요받았다면, 당신은 혼자가 아니다(다른 부모들도 마찬가지였다): 어른들 대부분은 이것을 어느 정도까지는 경험을 했다 – 집이 아니더라도 학교에서.

3. 물리학자에게, '1초'의 지속 시간은 정확하고 분명한데, 그것(1초의 지속 시간)은 동위원소인 세슘-133의 두 개의 에너지 준위 사이의 전이와 연관된 9,192,631,770번의 진동수 주기와 같다.

4. 사람들에게서 태양이든, 신체적 피로든, 아니면 시계 자체든, '실제' 시간 신호를 제거할 때, 오래지 않아 그들의 시간 감각은 고장이 난다.

5. 사회학자 Glen Elder는 10대 후반에서 30대 초반에 이르기까지의 성장에 민감한 시기가 있는데, 그 기간 동안은 실패가 대단히 유익하다고 하였다.

6. 이 문화적 산물들은 —그것이 그림이든, 조각이든, 음악의 형태든, 혹은 무엇이든 —일정한 유형의 문화 생산자에 의해서 만들어지는 것으로, 그리고 특정한 집단의 사람들에 의해 특정한 방식으로 특정한 사회적 맥락에서 사용되는 것으로 간주되어야 한다.

7. 특정한 사물들에 대해 '문화적 산물'이라는 더 중립적인 말을 사용하고, 그러한 사물들을 만들어내는 사람들에 대해 '문화 생산자'라는 말을 사용함으로써, 사회학자는 너무 오랫동안 문화 형태에 대한 연구를 지배해 왔다고 여기는 견해, 즉 모든 것을 '예술'의 범주에서 이해하려는 견해와 결별하려고 한다.

 혼공 10일차 **빈칸추론(단어)**

3단계 고난도 문항 요리하기
p.107

● 정답

1. ③ **2.** ② **3.** ⑤ **4.** ② **5.** ⑤ **6.** ① **7.** ② **8.** ⑤

1. ③

● 전체 해석

우리가 분노와 우리의 부정적인 생각과 감정을 억제할 필요가 있다고 말하는 것은 우리의 감정을 부정해야 함을 의미하지는 않는다. 부정과 자제 사이에는 구분해 두어야 할 중요한 차이점이 있다. 후자는 그렇게 하는 것이 가져오는 이점들을 이해하는 바탕에서 의도적이고 자발적으로 취해진 규율로 여겨진다. 이는 겉으로는 자기 통제를 보일 필요가 있다고 느껴서, 혹은 다른 이들이 어떻게 생각할지에 대한 두려움에서 분노와 같은 감정을 억제하는 사람의 경우와는 매우 다르다. 그러한 행동은 여전히 감염된 상처를 덮어두는 것과 같다. 우리는 규율 준수에 대해서 이야기하고 있는 것이 아니다. 부정과 억압이 일어나는 곳에서, 그렇게 함으로써 그 사람이 분노와 분한 마음을 쌓아 놓는다는 위험성이 오기 마련이다. 여기서 문제는 미래의 어느 시점에 이르게 되면 그들이 더는 이러한 감정을 억누르고 있을 수 없다는 것을 알 수 있다는 것이다.

● 지문분석

[To say / that we need to curb / anger and our negative thoughts and emotions] / does not mean / that we should deny our feelings.
말하는 것은 / 우리가 막을 필요가 있다고 / 분노와 우리의 부정적인 생각과 감정을 / 의미하지는 않는다 / 우리가 우리 감정을 부인해야 한다는 것을

There is an important distinction / to be made between denial and restraint.
중요한 차이점이 있다 / 부인과 억제 사이에 만들어지는

The latter constitutes / a deliberate and voluntarily adopted discipline / based on an appreciation of the benefits of doing so.
후자는 여겨진다 / 의도적이고 자발적으로 채택된 규율로 / 그렇게 하는 것의 이점을 이해하는 바탕에서

This is very different from / the case of someone / who suppresses emotions such as anger / out of a feeling / that they need / to present a facade of self-control, / or out of fear / of what others may think.
이것은 매우 다르다 / 누군가의 경우와는 / 분노와 같은 감정을 억누르는 / 감정으로부터 / 그들이 필요하다고 하는 / 겉으로는 자기 통제를 보여주는 것이 / 아니면 공포로부터 / 다른 사람들이 생각할지도 모르는

Such behaviour is like closing a wound / which is still infected.
그런 행동은 상처를 덮어두는 것과 같다 / 여전히 감염되어 있는

We are not talking about rule-following.
우리는 규칙을 따르는 것에 대해서 이야기하는 것이 아니다

Where denial and suppression occur, / there comes the danger / that in doing so / the individual stores up anger and resentment.
└ '~인 곳에서'
부인과 억압이 발생하는 곳에서 / 위험성이 온다 / 그렇게 함으로써 / 사람이 분노와 분한 마음을 쌓아놓는

The trouble here / is that at some future point / they may find / they cannot contain these feelings any longer.
여기서 문제는 / 미래의 어떤 시점에서 / 그들은 발견할 수도 있다는 것이다 / 그들이 이러한 감정을 더 이상 담아둘 수는 없다는 것을

● 해설

1. 다음 빈칸에 들어갈 말로 가장 적절한 것은?

To say that we need to curb anger and our negative thoughts and emotions does not mean that we should deny our feelings. There is an important distinction to be made between denial and restraint. The latter constitutes a deliberate and voluntarily adopted discipline based on an appreciation of the benefits of doing so. This is very different from the case of someone who suppresses emotions such as anger out of a feeling that they need to present a facade of self-control, or out of fear of what others may think. Such behaviour is like closing a wound which is still infected. We are not talking about rule-following. Where denial and suppression occur, there comes the danger that in doing so the individual _____ anger and resentment. The trouble here is that at some future point they may find they cannot contain these feelings any longer.

① fades out 희미해지다 (+)
② copes with 대처하다 (+)
❸ stores up 쌓아올리다 (−)
④ soothes 완화시키다 (+)
⑤ overestimates 과대평가하다 (+)

이 글은 분노와 같은 부정적인 감정을 숨기다가는 결국 어느 시점에서 그러한 분노가 터지게 되므로 그런 감정을 드러내라는 내용이지. 위에서 밑줄 친 부분으로 봤을 때, 빈칸에 들어갈 말은 결과적으로는 개인으로는 (−)인 내용을 찾아야 해. 주어진 선택지에서는 분노를 부정적으로 만드는 것은 ③ stores up 밖에는 없어. 나머지는 다 개인들에게 (+)적인 내용들이지.

● 중요 포인트

to부정사 주어

[To say that we need to curb anger and our negative thoughts and emotions] does not mean that we should deny our feelings.
S: to부정사 주어
V: 단수

2. ②

● 전체 해석

초기 인간 사회는 수렵과 채집을 기반으로 한 유목 생활이었고, 새로운 식량원을 찾아 이동하는 생활 양식에서는 경량성, 휴대성, 그리고 적응성과 같은 특징이 지배적인 기준이었다. 농업을 기반으로 한 더 정착된 농촌 사회의 발전과 더불어, 다른 특징, 즉 새로운 생활 양식에 적합한 다른 형태의 전통이 빠르게 등장했다. 그러나 전통은 정적인 것이 아니라 사람들과 그들의 환경에 적절한, 아주 작은 변화를 끊임없이 겪었다는 것은 강조되어야 한다. 전통적 형태가 사회 집단의 경험을 반영하더라도, 개개의 사용자의 요구를 충족시키기 위해 특정한 외적 형태가 각양각색의 미세하고 미묘한 방식으로 조정될 수 있었다. 의자는 여전히 특정 개인의 체격과 비율에 맞게 세부적으로 면밀히 모양이 만들어지는 와중에도 그것의 기본적이고 일반적으로 용인되는 특징을 유지할 수 있었다. 맞춤제작의 이러한 기본적 원리에 의해 일련의 끊임없이 증가하는 변형이 도입될 수 있었고, 그것들이 경험에 의해 유익하다고 입증되면 전통의 주류 속으로 다시 통합될 수 있었다.

● 지문분석

Early human societies were nomadic, / based on hunting and gathering, / and, in a shifting pattern of life / in search of new sources of food, / [qualities such as lightness, portability, and adaptability] / were dominant criteria.
초기 인류의 사회는 유목 생활이었다 / 수렵과 채집을 기반으로 한 / 그리고 이동하는 삶의 양식에서 / 새로운 식량 자원을 찾으면서 / 경량성, 휴대성, 그리고 적응성이라는 특징은 / 지배적인 기준이었다

With the evolution of more settled rural societies / based on agriculture, / [other characteristics, other traditions of form / appropriate to the new patterns of life,] / rapidly emerged.
더욱더 정착된 시골 사회의 진화가 / 농경에 기반을 둠과 동시에 / 다른 특징들 / 다른 형태의 전통이 / 새로운 삶의 패턴에 적절한 / 빠르게 나타났다

It must be emphasized, however, / that tradition was not static, / but constantly subject to minute variations / appropriate to people and their circumstances.
가주어 / 진주어
하지만, 강조되어져야 한다 / 전통은 정적이 아니었다는 것이 / 지속적으로 세밀한 변화의 대상이었다는 것이 / 사람들과 그 환경에 적절한

Although traditional forms reflected the experience of social groups, / specific manifestations could be adapted / in various minute and subtle ways / to suit individual users' needs.
비록 전통적인 형태가 사회적 공동체의 경험을 반영함에도 불구하고 / 구체적인 외적 형태가 조정될 수 있었다 / 다양한 세세하고 미묘한 방식으로 / 개개의 사용자의 욕구를 충족시키기 위하여

A chair could keep its basic, accepted characteristics / while still being closely shaped / in detail / to the physique and proportions of a specific person.
접속사 + 분사
의자는 그것의 일반적으로 용인되는 특징을 지닐 수 있었다 / 여전히 면밀히 모양이 만들어지는 와중에도 / 세부적으로 / 특정한 사람의

체격과 비율에 맞게

This basic principle of customization / allowed a constant stream of incremental modifications / to be introduced, / which, if demonstrated by experience / to be advantageous, / could be integrated back / into the mainstream of tradition.
┌─ This basic principle of customization
└─ 일종의 삽입, 접속사 + 분사

이러한 기본적인 맞춤제작의 원리는 / 지속적으로 증가하는 변형의 연속을 허용했다 / 도입되도록 / 그것들이 만약 경험에 의해서 입증된다면 / 유익하다고 / 다시 통합될 수 있었다 / 전통의 주류로

● 해설

2. 다음 빈칸에 들어갈 말로 가장 적절한 것은?

Early human societies were nomadic, based on hunting and gathering, and, in a shifting pattern of life in search of new sources of food, qualities such as lightness, portability, and adaptability were dominant criteria. With the evolution of more settled rural societies based on agriculture, other characteristics, other traditions of form appropriate to the new patterns of life, rapidly emerged. It must be emphasized, however, that tradition was not static, but constantly subject to minute variations appropriate to people and their circumstances. Although traditional forms reflected the experience of social groups, specific manifestations could be adapted in various minute and subtle ways to suit individual users' needs. A chair could keep its basic, accepted characteristics while still being closely shaped in detail to the physique and proportions of a specific person. This basic principle of _____ allowed a constant stream of incremental modifications to be introduced, which, if demonstrated by experience to be advantageous, could be integrated back into the mainstream of tradition.

① dedication 헌신
❷ customization 맞춤제작
▶ 개개인의 특성에 맞추는 것이 바로 이것이지.
③ cooperation 협동
④ generalization 일반화
▶ 정답과는 정반대의 내용이지.
⑤ preservation 보존

사람들과 환경에 적합한 끊임없는 작은 변화가 일어나고 개개인의 사용자의 요구를 충족시키기 위해 특정한 형태가 미세한 방식으로 조정되며 그것이 유익한 것으로 입증되면 전통의 주류 속으로 통합된다는 내용의 글이야. 즉, 전통의 한 분야로 개개인에 특성이 맞는 부분이 들어간다는 것이므로 이므로 빈칸에 들어갈 말로 가장 적절한 것은 ② customization(맞춤제작)이라고 할 수 있어.

● 중요 포인트

관계사절에 삽입구가 들어간 형태

This basic principle of customization / allowed a constant stream of incremental modifications / to be introduced, / which, if demonstrated by experience / to be advantageous, / could be ~
┌─ 일종의 삽입, 접속사 + 분사
= This basic principle of customization

3. ⑤

● 전체 해석

일단 손이나 집게를 내밀어 어떤 물체로 향하게 하면 그것을 붙잡을 수 있다. 붙잡는 것은 손가락이 물체를 안전하게 잡는 것을 필요로 한다. 안전하게 꽉 잡는 것은 특히 외부의 힘에 의해 옮겨질 때 물체가 미끄러지거나 움직이지 않는 것이다. 만약 어떤 것에 부딪혀 망치를 떨어뜨리게 된다면 여러분이 망치를 붙잡고 있는 것은 안정감이 있지 않을 것이다. 단단히 붙잡는 것에 대한 한 가지 전제 조건은 손가락에 의해 가해진 힘이 물체의 위치를 방해하지 않도록 서로 균형을 이룬다는 것이다. 기하학적 구성과 질량 분포와 같은 물체의 특성은 안정을 유지하기 위해 몇몇 손가락이 다른 손가락보다 더 큰 힘을 가하도록 요구할 수도 있다. 붙잡고 지지하는 힘은 또한 전반적인 물체 질량과 연약함에 부합해야 한다. 달걀은 바위보다 더 섬세한 접촉을 요구한다.

● 지문분석

Once a hand or gripper has been directed / to an object / by reaching, / it can be grasped.
일단 손이나 집게가 향하게 된다면 / 물체쪽으로 / 도달함으로써 / 그것은 잡을 수 있게 된다

Grasping requires / that fingers hold an object securely.
잡는 것은 필요하다 / 손가락이 물체를 안전하게 잡는 것이

A secure grip is one / in which the object won't slip or move, / especially when displaced by an external force.
안전한 잡기는 이것이다 / 물체가 미끄러지지 않거나 움직이지 않는 것이다 / 특히 외부의 힘에 의해 옮겨질 때

Your grasp on a hammer, for example, / would not be secure / if knocking against something / caused you to drop it.
예를 들어 당신이 망치를 잡는 것은 / 안정적이지 않을 것이다 / 만약 무언가에 부딪침이 / 당신이 그것을 떨어뜨리도록 한다면

[One precondition of a firm grasp] / is that the forces / applied by the fingers / balance each other / so as not to disturb the object's position.
단단히 붙잡는 것에 대한 한 가지 조건은 / 힘들이 / 손가락에 의해 가해진 / 서로 균형을 이룬다는 것이다 / 물체의 위치를 방해하지 않도록

[The characteristics of an object / such as its geometric configuration and mass distribution] / may demand / that some fingers apply greater force / than others / to maintain stability.
물체의 특징은 / 그것의 기하학적 구성과 질량 분포와 같은 / 요구할 수도 있다 / 일부 손가락이 더 엄청난 힘을 가하도록 / 다른 것들 보다 / 안정감을 유지하기 위해서

The grasp and support forces / must also match overall object mass and fragility.
집기와 지지하는 힘은 / 마찬가지로 전반적인 물체의 질량과 연약함에 부합해야 한다

An egg requires / a more delicate touch / than a rock.
달걀은 필요하다 / 보다 섬세한 접촉이 / 바위보다

3. 다음 빈칸에 들어갈 말로 가장 적절한 것은?

Once a hand or gripper has been directed to an object by reaching, it can be grasped. Grasping requires that fingers hold an object securely. A secure grip is one in which the object won't slip or move, especially when displaced by an external force. Your grasp on a hammer, for example, would not be secure if knocking against something caused you to drop it. One precondition of a firm grasp is that the forces applied by the fingers balance each other so as not to disturb the object's position. The characteristics of an object such as its geometric configuration and mass distribution may demand that some fingers apply greater force than others to maintain _____. The grasp and support forces must also match overall object mass and fragility. An egg requires a more delicate touch than a rock.

① distance 거리
② efficiency 효율성
③ mobility 이동성
④ direction 방향성
❺ stability 안정성

단단히 붙잡는 것에 대한 한 가지 조건은 손가락에 의해 가해진 힘이 물체의 위치를 방해하지 않도록 서로 균형을 이루는 거라고 하고 있지. 즉, 안정적으로 물체가 균형을 이루는 것이 핵심이야. 따라서 빈칸에는 ⑤ stability(안정성)가 가장 적절해.

● 중요 포인트

전치사와 such as로 길어진 주어

[The characteristics of an object / such as its geometric configuration and mass distribution] / may demand / that some fingers apply greater force / than others / to maintain stability.

4. ②

● 전체 해석

두 문화가 접촉할 때, 그 두 문화가 모든 문화 항목을 교환하는 것은 아니다. 만약 그렇다면, 오늘날 세계에는 전혀 문화적 차이가 없을 것이다. 대신에 단지 적은 수의 문화적 요소들만 늘 한 문화에서 다른 문화로 퍼진다. 어떤 문화 항목이 받아들여지는가는 그 항목의 용도 및 이미 존재하는 문화적 특성과의 양립 가능성에 대체로 달려있다. 예를 들어, '흰머리를 피하려고' 고안된 남성용 머리 염색약은 나이가 들어감에 따라 사람의 지위가 올라가는 아프리카의 시골 지역으로 퍼질 것 같지는 않다. 어떤 혁신적인 것이 어떤 사회의 필요와 일치할 때조차도, 여전히 그것이 받아들여질 것이라는 보장은 없다. 예를 들어, 미국의 관습적 단위(예컨대, 인치, 피트, 야드, 마일 등)를 사용하는 미국의 대부분의 사람들은, 그러한 변화를 이루는 것이 미국인들로 하여금 세계의 다른 나라들과 더 효율적으로 접촉할 수 있게 할 터임에도 불구하고, 미터법 채택에 저항해 왔다.

When two cultures come into contact, / they do not exchange every cultural item.
두 개의 문화가 접촉을 하게 될 때 / 그들은 모든 문화적 항목을 교환하지는 않는다

If that were the case, / there would be no cultural differences / in the world today.
만약 그렇다면 / 문화적 차이란 없을 지도 모른다 / 오늘날의 세계에는

Instead, only a small number of cultural elements / ever spread from one culture to another.
대신에 단지 적은 수의 문화적 요소만이 / 한 문화에서 다른 문화로 퍼져나간다

[Which cultural item is accepted] / depends largely on the item's use and compatibility / with already existing cultural traits.
S: 의문사절 주어
어떤 문화 항목이 받아들여지느냐는 / 대개 항목의 사용과 양립 가능성에 달려 있다 / 이미 존재하는 문화적 특성과의

For example, it is not likely / that men's hair dyes / designed to "get out the gray" / will spread into parts of rural Africa / where a person's status is elevated with advancing years.
예를 들어 그럴 가능성이 낮다 / 남자의 머리카락 염색약이 / 흰머리를 피하려고 만들어진 / 아프리카의 시골 지역으로 퍼져나갈 / 사람의 지위가 나이가 들어어 감에 따라 올라가는

Even when an innovation is consistent with a society's needs, / there is still no guarantee / that it will be accepted.
심지어 혁신이라는 것이 사회의 욕구와 부합할 때 조차도 / 여전히 보장은 없다 / 그것이 받아들여질 것이라는

For example, [most people in the United States / using US customary units / (e.g., inch, foot, yard, mile, etc.)] / have resisted adopting the metric system / even though [making such a change] / would enable US citizens / to interface with the rest of the world more efficiently.
S
예를 들어 미국의 대부분의 사람들이 / 미국의 관습적 단위(예를 들어 인치, 피트, 야드, 마일 등)을 사용하는 / 미터법을 받아들이는 데 저항했다 / 비록 그런 변화를 하는 것이 / 미국의 시민들을 가능하게 할지라도 / 세계의 다른 나라들과 더 효율적으로 접촉하는 것을

● 해설

4. 다음 빈칸에 들어갈 말로 가장 적절한 것은?

When two cultures come into contact, they do not exchange every cultural item. If that were the case, there would be no cultural differences in the world today. Instead, only a small number of cultural elements ever spread from one culture to another. Which cultural item is accepted depends largely on the item's use and compatibility with already existing cultural traits. For example, it is not likely that men's hair dyes designed to "get out the gray" will spread into parts of rural Africa where a person's status is elevated with advancing years. Even when a(n) _____ is consistent with a society's needs, there is still no guarantee that it will be accepted. For example, most people in the United States using US customary units (e.g., inch, foot, yard, mile, etc.) have resisted adopting the metric system even though making such a change would enable US citizens to interface with the rest of the world more efficiently.

① categorization 범주화
▶ 범주화란 일종의 분류 체계지. 여기서는 '분류'에 대한 내용은 아니야.
❷ innovation 혁신적인 것
▶ 무언가 도움이 되는 새로운 것에 해당되지.
③ investigation 조사
④ observation 관찰
⑤ specification 설명서

뒤에 나오는 예시를 통해 빈칸에 들어갈 부분을 알 수가 있어. 미국인들에게 있어서 미터법은 굉장히 좋은 것이지. 왜냐하면 다른 나라 사람들과의 효율적 접촉을 도울 수 있으니까. 이에 해당하는 것은 ② innovation(혁신)이라고 할 수 있겠지.

● 중요 포인트

의문사절 주어

[Which cultural item is accepted] depends largely on the item's use and compatibility with already existing cultural traits.

S: 의문사절 주어   V

5. ⑤

● 전체 해석

어떤 회사가 신제품을 출시할 때, 그 회사의 경쟁사들은 일반적으로 그 제품이 자신들의 판매를 잠식할 가능성을 줄이기 위해 할 수 있는 것은 무엇이든 하면서 방어 태세를 취한다. (그들의) 반응들에는 마케팅에 노력을 더 기울이는 것, 유통 체계 협력자들에게 할인 제공하기, 그리고 심지어는 경쟁사의 발전을 방해할 법규를 위해 로비하는 것까지도 포함될 것이다. 그렇지만, 많은 경우 그러한 조치들은 잘못된 것이다. 경쟁사의 (신제품) 출시가 (자사의) 이익에 타격을 줄 것이라는 사회적 통념이 흔히 맞기도 하지만, 내가 연구한 바에 따르면 경쟁사가 (신제품을) 출시한 후에 때로는 회사의 이익이 증가하기도 한다는 것을 보여준다. 그 기저에 깔린 메커니즘은 아주 단순해서 어떤 회사가 신제품을 출시하면, 그 회사는 흔히 기존 제품들의 가격을 올린다. 이것은 신제품이 더 저렴해 보이고, 따라서 (기존 제품들과) 비교하여 (신제품이) 더 매력적으로 보이게 하려고 의도된 것일 것이다. 그 회사가 가격책정을 조정할 때, 경쟁사들도 가격에 대한 고객 이탈 위험 없이 동일한 일을 할 수 있을 것이다.

● 지문분석

When a company comes out with a new product, / its competitors typically go on the defensive, / doing whatever they can to reduce the odds / that the offering will eat into their sales.

동시상황 〈분사구문〉

어떤 회사가 새로운 제품을 출시할 때 / 그 경쟁자들은 전형적으로 방어적이 된다 / 그들이 가능성을 줄이기 위해서 할 수 있는 모든 것을 하면서 / 그 제품이 그들의 판매를 잠식할

Responses might include / increasing marketing efforts, / offering discounts to channel partners, / and even lobbying for regulations / that would hinder the rival's expansion.

반응은 포함할 수도 있다 / 마케팅 노력을 증가시키는 것을 / 유통 협력자들에게 할인 제공하기 / 그리고 심지어 법규를 위한 로비까지 / 경쟁사의 발전을 방해할

In many cases, though, / such actions are misguided.
하지만 많은 경우에 있어 / 그런 행동들은 잘못된 것이다

Although [the conventional wisdom / that a rival's launch will hurt profits] / is often correct, / my research shows / that companies sometimes see profits increase / after a rival's launch.

S   V

비록 사회적 통념이 / 경쟁사의 출시가 이익을 해칠 것이라는 / 종종 맞기는 하지만 / 내 연구는 보여준다 / 회사는 때때로 이익 증가를 본다고 / 경쟁사의 출시 이후에

The underlying mechanism is pretty simple: / When a company comes out with a new product, / it often raises the prices of its existing products.

그 기저에 깔린 메커니즘은 아주 단순하다 / 회사가 새 제품을 출시할 때 / 그것은 종종 기존 제품의 가격을 올린다

This might be designed / to make the new product / look cheaper / and thus more attractive by comparison.

사역동사   사역동사 목적보어

이것은 의도된 것일 것이다 / 새 제품을 만들도록 / 더 저렴하게 보이게 / 그래서 비교해서 더욱 매력적으로 보이게

As that company adjusts its pricing, / its competitors can do the same / without risking customer defections over price.

그 회사가 가격 조정을 할 때 / 경쟁사는 같은 것을 할 수 있다 / 가격에 대한 고객 이탈 위험 없이

● 해설

5. 다음 글의 빈칸 (A), (B)에 들어갈 말로 가장 적절한 것을 고르시오.

When a company comes out with a new product, its competitors typically go on the defensive, doing whatever they can to __(A)__ the odds that the offering will eat into their sales. Responses might include increasing marketing efforts, offering discounts to channel partners, and even lobbying for regulations that would hinder the rival's expansion. In many cases, though, such actions are misguided. Although the conventional wisdom that a rival's launch will hurt profits is often correct, my research shows that companies sometimes see profits increase after a rival's launch. The underlying mechanism is pretty simple: When a company comes out with a new product, it often raises the prices of its existing products. This might be designed to make the new product look __(B)__ and thus more attractive by comparison. As that company adjusts its pricing, its competitors can do the same without risking customer defections over price.

	(A)	(B)
①	calculate 추정하기	······ exceptional 뛰어난
②	calculate 추정하기	······ more striking 더 인상적인
③	eliminate 제거하기	······ more upgraded 더 개선된
④	reduce 줄이기	······ up-to-date 최신식의
❺	reduce 줄이기	······ cheaper 가격이 더 싼

(A) 뒤에 제시되는 마케팅 노력 증가, 할인 제공, 로비는 모두 자신들의 제품 판매를 증진하는 행동이지. 따라서 빈칸에 들어가는 내용은 자신들의 제품 판매를 잠식할 가능성을 '줄이기' 위해 할 수 있는 것이어야 해. 그래서 빈칸에는 reduce(줄이다)가 적절하지.
(B) 기존 제품들의 가격을 올리게 되면 신제품이 상대적으로 '더 싸게' 보이게 되므로, cheaper가 적절하다고 할 수 있지.

● 중요 포인트

사역동사 make

This might be designed to make the new product look
　　　　　　　　　　　　사역동사　　　　　　　사역동사 목적 보어
cheaper and thus more attractive by comparison.

6. ①

● 전체 해석

아이들이 지닌 창의력은 그들의 성장 기간 내내 육성되어야 할 필요가 있다. 연구는 아이의 환경을 지나치게 구조화하는 것이 실제로 창의적 발달과 학문적 발달을 제한할지도 모른다는 것을 보여 준다. 이것은 과학 교육의 많은 부분에서 가장 중요한 문제이다. 연습이나 활동들은 다양한 선택권을 없애고 미리 정해진 결과에 집중하도록 만들어진다. 정답은 수업의 평가에 부합하도록 구조화되고 과학에 대한 경이감은 인지적 호기심과 더불어 상실된다. 우리는 인지적 호기심을 한 개인이 어떤 활동에 자발적으로 참여하도록 자극하고 내재적으로 동기를 부여하는 경이감으로 정의한다. 인지적 호기심의 상실은 미리 정해진 결론을 가지고 놀잇감을 한 가지 방식으로 사용함으로써 시작되고 학교에서의 암기식 교육을 통해 강화되는지도 모른다. 이것은 그 자체로 목적이 되어, 계획된 목표를 숙달하는 것 이외에 개인에게 거의 아무것도 요구하지 않는 장난감, 게임, 그리고 수업에서 전형적인 사례를 보여 준다.

● 지문분석

[The creativity / that children possess] / needs to be
　　　　S　　　　　　　　　　　　　　　　V
cultivated / throughout their development.
창의력은 / 아이들이 가지고 있는 / 육성될 필요가 있다 / 그들의 성장 기간 내내
Research suggests / that [overstructuring the child's
　　　　　　　　　　　　　　　　S
environment] / may actually limit creative and academic
　　　　　　　　V
development.
연구는 보여준다 / 아이들의 환경을 지나치게 구조화하는 것은 / 실제로 창의적이고 학문적인 발달을 제한할지도 모른다는 것을
This is a central problem / with much of science
instruction.
이것은 중요한 문제이다 / 과학 교육의 많은 부분에서

The exercises or activities are devised / to eliminate
　　　　　　　　　　　　　　　　　　　　　　　　①
different options / and to focus on predetermined results.
　　　　　　　　　　　　②
연습이나 활동들은 만들어진다 / 다른 선택을 제거하고 / 미리 정해진 결과에 집중하도록
The answers are structured / to fit the course assessments,
/ and the wonder of science is lost / along with cognitive
intrigue.
정답은 구조화된다 / 수업의 평가에 맞춰지도록 / 그리고 과학의 경이감은 사라진다 / 인지적 호기심과 함께
We define cognitive intrigue / as the wonder / that
stimulates and intrinsically motivates an individual / to
voluntarily engage in an activity.
우리는 인지적 호기심을 정의한다 / 경이감으로 / 한 개인을 자극하고 내재적으로 동기를 부여하는 / 자발적으로 활동에 임하도록
[The loss of cognitive intrigue] / may be initiated / by the
　　S　　　　　　　　　　　　　　　　　　　　①
sole use of play items / with predetermined conclusions /
and reinforced / by rote instruction in school.
인지적 호기심의 상실은 / 시작될지도 모른다 / 놀이 아이템의 한 가지 사용에 의해서 / 미리 정해진 결론을 가지고 / 그리고 강화될지도 모른다 / 학교에서의 암기식 교육에 의해
This is exemplified / by toys, games, and lessons / that
are an end in and of themselves / and require little of the
individual / other than to master the planned objective.
이것은 예시화된다 / 장난감, 게임, 그리고 수업에 의해서 / 그 자체가 목적인 / 그리고 개인에게 어떠한 것도 요구하지 않는 / 계획된 목표를 마스터하는 것을 제외하고는

● 해설

6. 다음 빈칸에 들어갈 말로 가장 적절한 것은?
The creativity that children possess needs to be cultivated throughout their development. Research suggests that overstructuring the child's environment may actually limit creative and academic development. This is a central problem with much of science instruction. The exercises or activities are devised to eliminate different options and to focus on predetermined results. The answers are structured to fit the course assessments, and the wonder of science is lost along with cognitive intrigue. We define cognitive intrigue as the wonder that stimulates and intrinsically motivates an individual to voluntarily engage in an activity. The loss of cognitive intrigue may be initiated by the sole use of play items with predetermined conclusions and reinforced by rote instruction in school. This is exemplified by toys, games, and lessons that are a(n) _____ in and of themselves and require little of the individual other than to master the planned objective.

❶ end 목적
▶ 수업 그 자체가 되어야 하니까 목적이 적절하겠지.
② input 투입
③ puzzle 퍼즐
④ interest 흥밋거리

⑤ alternative 대안
▶ 경이감에 대한 대안이 아니라 수업 그 자체이므로 '대안'이라고 하기에는 좀 그래.

미리 정해진 결론을 가지고 수업을 하고, 암기식 교육을 통해 인지적 호기심의 상실이 이루어진다고 하고 있어. 빈칸이 있는 문장에서는 계획된 목표를 숙달하는 것 이외에 개인에게 아무것도 요구하지 않는 장난감, 게임, 그리고 수업 그 자체가 목적이 되고 있음을 비판하는 글이므로, 빈칸에 들어갈 말로 ① end(목적)가 가장 적절하지.

● 중요 포인트

관계사 that vs 동격의 접속사 that

[The creativity that children possess] needs to be
     S   관계사 + 불완전한 문장   V
cultivated throughout their development.

We define cognitive intrigue as the wonder that
                                              접속사
stimulates and intrinsically motivates an individual to
+ 완전한 문장
voluntarily engage in an activity.

7. ②

● 전체 해석

F. Scott Fitzgerald는 최상의 지능에 대한 평가 기준은 두 가지 상반된 생각을 동시에 머릿속에 담고 있으면서 계속 정상적으로 사고하는 능력이라고 생각했다. 오랜 세월은 우리의 뇌를 반대 방향으로 가도록 맞추었다. 확증편향은 정신이 모순된 사실에 직면하는 것을 조직적으로 회피하는 방식을 설명하는 용어이다. 그것은 우리가 이미 생각하거나 느끼는 것을 확인시켜주는 증거를 과대평가하고 그것에 반대되는 증거를 평가절하하거나 또는 단순히 무시함으로써 그러한 일을 수행한다. Crow 부족의 구성원들의 그들 문화의 파멸에 대한 증언은 이에 대한 극단적이고 비극적인 사례를 제시해준다. Plenty Coups라는 이름의 남자는 "들소가 사라졌을 때 부족 사람들은 몹시 낙담하게 되었고 활기를 되찾을 수 없었습니다. 그 이후에는 '아무 일도 일어나지 않았어요.'"라는 말을 전했다. 그 사람만이 그러한 깊은 절망감을 역사의 종말로 설명한 것은 아니었다. "그 이후에는 아무 일도 일어나지 않았어요. 우리는 그냥 살았어요."라고 또 다른 Crow 부족의 전사가 말했다. 그 감정이 너무나 강렬하여 그것을 누그러뜨릴 수도 있었던 정상적인 일상생활이 지속적으로 존재한다는 증거를 뇌가 거부해버렸다.

● 지문분석

F. Scott Fitzgerald thought / that [the test of first-rate
intelligence] / was the ability / to hold two opposed ideas
                      S
in mind at the same time / and still function.
F. Scott Fitzgerald는 생각했다 / 최상의 지능에 대한 평가 / 능력이라고 / 두 개의 상반된 생각을 마음에 동시에 담고 있는 / 그리고 여전히 작동하는

The eons shaped our brains / in the opposite direction.
오랜 세월은 우리의 두뇌를 형성했다 / 반대의 방향으로

Confirmation bias is a term / for the way / the mind
systematically avoids confronting contradiction.

확증편향은 용어이다 / 방식을 설명하는 / 마음이 체계적으로 모순에 직면하는 것을 피하는

It does this / by overvaluing evidence / that confirms what
                        ①
we already think or feel / and undervaluing or simply
                                     ②
disregarding evidence / that refutes it.
그것은 이것을 한다 / 증거를 과대평가함으로써 / 우리가 벌써 생각하거나 느끼는 것을 확인하는 / 그리고 증거를 평가절하 하거나 단순히 무시함으로써 / 그것에 반대되는

[Testimony from members of the Crow tribe / about the
  S
destruction of their culture] / provides an extreme and
tragic example of this.
Crow 부족의 구성원들의 증거는 / 그들 문화의 파괴에 대한 / 극단적이고 비극적인 이것의 예시를 제공한다

[A man / named Plenty Coups] / reported / that "when the
  S
buffalo went away, / the hearts of my people / fell to the
ground / and they could not lift them up again. / After this
nothing happened."
한 남자는 / Plenty Coups라는 이름을 가진 / 보고했다 / 들소가 사라졌을 때 / 부족 사람들의 마음은 / 땅에 떨어졌고(낙담했고) / 그들을 다시 그것들을 올릴 수가(활기를 찾을 수가) 없었다 / 이후에는 아무것도 벌어지지 않았다

He was not alone / in describing the depth of despair / as
the end of history.
그는 유일한 사람이 아니었다 / 절망의 깊이를 설명한 / 역사의 종말로서

"Nothing happened after that," / another Crow warrior
said. / "We just lived."
어떠한 것도 그 후에 발생하지 않았다 / 또 다른 Crow 전사가 말했다 / 우리는 그냥 살았다

                         so ~ that 용법
The emotion was so strong / that the brain rejected
evidence / of the continued existence of normal, everyday
life / that might have eased it.
그러한 감정은 너무 강해서 / 두뇌는 증거를 거절했다 / 지속된 평범한 일상의 삶의 존재에 대한 / 그것을 누그러뜨릴 수도 있었던

● 해설

7. 다음 글의 빈칸 (A), (B)에 들어갈 말로 가장 적절한 것을 고르시오.

F. Scott Fitzgerald thought that the test of first-rate intelligence was the ability to hold two opposed ideas in mind at the same time and still function. The eons shaped our brains in the (A) direction. Confirmation bias is a term for the way the mind systematically avoids confronting contradiction. It does this by overvaluing evidence that confirms what we already think or feel and undervaluing or simply disregarding evidence that refutes it. Testimony from members of the Crow tribe about the destruction of their culture provides an extreme and tragic example of this. A man named Plenty Coups reported that "when the buffalo went away, the hearts of my people fell to the ground and they could not lift them up again. After this nothing happened." He was not alone in describing the depth of despair as the end of history. "Nothing happened after that," another Crow warrior said. "We just lived." The emotion was so strong that the brain   (B)   evidence of the continued existence of normal, everyday life that might have eased it.

	(A)	(B)
①	opposite 반대	retained 보유했다
❷	opposite 반대	rejected 거부했다
③	wrong 잘못된	validated 유효하게 했다
④	same 같은	falsified 속였다, 위조했다
⑤	same 같은	overlooked 간과했다

(A) 바로 앞에서 오랜 세월 동안 사람들의 두뇌가 두 가지 상반된 생각을 동시에 담고 있다고 하고 있지. 이는 한마디로 우리의 뇌가 반대(opposite) 방향으로 맞춰졌음을 알 수가 있어.

(B) Crow 부족 사람들이 들소가 사라진 것 때문에 절망감에 빠져 헤어나지 못하고 있지. 근데 정상적인 일상생활이 존재한다는 증거가 있음에도 이를 뇌가 거부했다(rejected)는 것을 알 수 있어. 빈칸 뒤에 나오는 부분은 (+)인 것인데, 부족에게 결과는 아무것도 하지 않는 것(−)이 되니 빈칸은 (−)적 성격의 어휘가 되어야 해. 따라서 rejected(거부했다)가 적절하겠지.

● 중요 포인트

전치사구 2개의 수식을 받는 주어

[Testimony from members of the Crow tribe about the destruction of their culture] provides an extreme and tragic example of this.

8. ⑤

● 전체 해석

선택을 한 후에, 그 결정은 결국 우리가 추측하는 즐거움을 변화시키며, 그 선택한 선택사항으로부터 얻을 것으로 기대되는 즐거움을 향상시키고 거부한 선택사항으로부터 얻을 것으로 기대되는 즐거움을 감소시킨다. 우리가 선택한 것과 일치하도록 옵션의 가치를 재빨리 새롭게 하려 하지 않는다면, 우리는 뒤늦게 자신을 비판하여 미칠 지경으로 몰고 갈 가능성이 있다. 우리는 태국보다는 그리스를, 커피메이커보다는 토스터를, Michele보다는 Jenny를 선택해야 했던 것은 아니었는지 자신에게 계속 되풀이하여 물어볼 것이다. 지속적으로 뒤늦게 자신을 비판하는 것은 우리의 일상적인 기능을 방해할 것이고 부정적인 결과를 촉진할 것이다. 우리는 불안하고 혼란스러워 할 것이며, 후회하며 슬퍼할 것이다. 우리가 옳은 일을 한 것일까 우리의 마음을 바꿔야 할 것인가? 이러한 생각들은 영구적인 교착 상태를 초래할 것이다. 우리는 그야말로 옴짝달싹 못하면서, 우유부단함에 사로잡혀 앞으로 나아가지 못하는 자신의 모습을 발견하게 될 것이다. 반면에, 결정을 내린 후에 자신의 선택을 재평가하는 것은 그 취한 행동에 대한 우리의 헌신을 증가시키며 우리를 앞으로 나아가게 해 준다.

● 지문분석

After making a choice, / the decision ultimately changes our estimated pleasure, / enhancing the expected pleasure / from the selected option / and decreasing the expected
분사구문 ❶
분사구문 ❷

pleasure / from the rejected option.
선택을 한 후에 / 결정은 궁극적으로 우리가 예측한 기쁨을 바꾼다 / 이는 기대했던 기쁨을 향상시키고 / 선택한 옵션으로부터의 / 그리고 기대한 기쁨을 감소시킨다 / 거부된 옵션으로부터의

If we were not inclined / to update the value of our options rapidly / so that they concur with our choices, / we would likely second-guess ourselves / to the point of insanity.
만약 우리가 경향이 없다면 / 우리 옵션의 가치를 빠르게 업데이트하려는 / 그것들(옵션)이 우리의 선택과 일치하도록 하기 위해서 / 우리는 자신을 비판하려고 할지도 모른다 / 미칠 지경까지

We would ask ourselves again and again / whether we should have chosen Greece over Thailand, / the toaster over the coffee maker, / and Jenny over Michele.
우리는 반복해서 자신에게 물어볼 지도 모른다 / 우리가 태국보다는 그리스는 선택했어야 했는지를 / 커피 머신보다는 토스터기를 / 그리고 미셀보다는 제니를

[Consistently second-guessing ourselves] / would interfere with our daily functioning / and promote a negative effect.
지속적으로 우리 자신을 비판하는 것은 / 우리의 일상적인 기능을 방해할 것이다 / 그리고 부정적인 결과를 촉진할 것이다

We would feel / anxious and confused, regretful and sad.
우리는 느낄 것이다 / 불안하고 혼동스러우며 후회하고 그리고 슬퍼하는

Have we done the right thing?
우리는 올바른 일을 해왔는가?

Should we change our mind?
우리는 마음을 바꿔야 하나?

These thoughts would result in a permanent halt.
이러한 생각들은 영구적인 교착상태를 불러올 것이다

We would find ourselves / – literally – stuck, / overcome by indecision / and unable to move forward.
우리는 우리 자신을 발견할 것이다 / 말 그대로 꽉 끼어있고 / 우유부단함에 사로잡혀 있고 / 그리고 앞으로 나아가지 못하는

On the other hand, / [reevaluating our alternatives / after making a decision] / increases our commitment / to the action / taken / and keeps us moving forward.
반면에 / 우리의 선택을 재평가하는 것은 / 결정을 한 후에 / 우리의 헌신을 증가시키며 / 행동에 대한 / 취한 / 그리고 우리를 앞으로 나아가도록 한다

● 해설

8. 다음 글의 빈칸 (A), (B)에 들어갈 말로 가장 적절한 것을 고르시오.
After making a choice, the decision ultimately changes our estimated pleasure, enhancing the expected pleasure from the selected option and decreasing the expected pleasure from the rejected option. If we were not inclined to   (A)   the value of our options rapidly so that they concur with our choices, we would likely second-guess ourselves to the point of insanity. We would ask ourselves again and again whether we should have chosen Greece over Thailand, the toaster over the

coffee maker, and Jenny over Michele. Consistently second-guessing ourselves would interfere with our daily functioning and promote a negative effect. We would feel anxious and confused, regretful and sad. Have we done the right thing? Should we change our mind? These thoughts would result in a permanent halt. We would find ourselves – literally – stuck, overcome by __(B)__ and unable to move forward. On the other hand, reevaluating our alternatives after making a decision increases our commitment to the action taken and keeps us moving forward.

　　　　(A)　　　　　　　(B)
① disregard 무시하다 ····· indecision 우유부단함
② disregard 무시하다 ····· decision 결정
③ disclose 밝히다 ····· decision 결정
④ update 새롭게 하다 ····· prejudice 편견
❺ update 새롭게 하다 ····· indecision 우유부단함

(A) 앞에 부정어가 있으므로 이에 주의해야 해. (A)를 하지 않으면 발생하는 결과가 자신을 비판하는 것, 즉 부정적 결과가 나오므로 (A)를 하지 않는 건 (−)지. 따라서 (A) 자체는 (+) 이미지가 있어야 해. 주어진 선택지에서는 (+)인 것은 disclose(밝히다)와 update(새롭게 하다)인데, update가 더 자연스럽지.

(B) 앞에 나온 내용들을 보면, 자신이 한 선택에 대해서 자책하고 고민하는 모습이 나오지. 이도저도 결정하지 못하는 모습이니까 이것은 바로 indecision(우유부단함)이 되겠지.

● 중요 포인트

3가지 목적 보어

We would find ourselves / – literally – stuck, / overcome
　　　　　 V　　O　　　　　　　　　O.C. ❶
by indecision / and unable to move forward.
　　　　　　　　　　　O.C. ❸

4 단계 **혼공 개념 마무리**　　　p.111

1. 우리가 분노와 우리의 부정적인 생각과 감정을 억제할 필요가 있다고 말하는 것은 우리의 감정을 부정해야 함을 의미하지는 않는다.

2. 농업을 기반으로 한 더 정착된 농촌 사회의 발전과 더불어, 다른 특징, 즉 새로운 생활양식에 적합한 다른 형태의 전통이 빠르게 등장했다.

3. 기하학적 구성과 질량 분포와 같은 물체의 특성은 안정을 유지하기 위해 몇몇 손가락이 다른 손가락보다 더 큰 힘을 가하도록 요구할 수도 있다.

4. 경쟁사의 출시가 이익에 타격을 줄 것이라는 사회적 통념이 흔히 맞기도 하지만, 내가 연구한 바에 따르면 경쟁사가 출시한 후에 때로는 회사의 이익이 증가하기도 한다는 것을 보여준다.

5. 인지적 호기심의 상실은 미리 정해진 결론을 가지고 놀잇감을 한 가지 방식으로 사용함으로써 시작되고 학교에서의 암기식 교육을 통해 강화되는지도 모른다.

6. 선택을 한 후에, 그 결정은 결국 우리가 추측하는 즐거움을 변화시키며, 그 선택한 선택사항으로부터 얻을 것으로 기대되는 즐거움을 향상시키고 거부한 선택사항으로부터 얻을 것으로 기대되는 즐거움을 감소시킨다.

7. 이는 겉으로는 자기 통제를 보일 필요가 있다고 느껴서, 혹은 다른 이들이 어떻게 생각할지에 대한 두려움에서 분노와 같은 감정을 억제하는 사람의 경우와는 매우 다르다.

혼공 11일차 빈칸추론(구/문장)

3 단계 **고난도 문항 요리하기**　　　p.117

● 정답

1. ① **2.** ③ **3.** ② **4.** ② **5.** ② **6.** ② **7.** ① **8.** ④

1. ①

● 전체 해석

나의 친구는 과학적인 발전이 전쟁과 기아를 없앰으로써 세상의 불행을 치유하지 못했다는 것과, 엄청난 인간 불평등이 아직도 널리 퍼져 있으며, 행복이 보편적이지 않다는 것에 실망했다. 내 친구는 흔한 실수, 즉 지식의 본질에 있어서 기본적인 오해를 했다. 지식은 도덕과 관계가 없으며 비도덕적인 것이 아니라 도덕 중립적이다. 그것은 어떤 목적으로든 사용될 수 있지만, 많은 사람은 그것이 사회를 위해 '그들이' 선호하는 희망을 증진하는 데 사용될 것이라고 가정하는데, 이것이 근본적으로 잘못된 것이다. 세상의 지식과 그 사용은 별개의 문제이다. 이해에 있어서의 진보가 세계의 사회적인 불행을 치유하지 못해왔다는 것에 실망하는 것은 타당한 견해이지만, 이것을 지식의 진보와 혼동하는 것은 터무니없다. 아프리카나 중동의 갈등 때문에 지식이 진보하지 않는다고 주장하는 것은 요점에서 벗어난다. 지식에는 구체적인 사회적 또는 도덕적 적용을 좌우하는 내재적인 것은 없다.

● 지문분석

My friend was disappointed / that scientific progress
　　　　　　　　　　　　　　 ❶
has not cured the world's ills / by abolishing wars
and starvation; / that gross human inequality is still
　　　　　　　　　 ❷
widespread; / that happiness is not universal.
　　　　　 ❸
나의 친구는 실망했다 / 과학적 진보가 세상의 병을 치료하지 못했다는 것에 / 전쟁과 기아를 없앰으로써 / 엄청난 인간의 불평등이 여전히 널리 퍼져있는 것에 / 행복이 보편적이지 않은 것에

My friend made a common mistake / – a basic
misunderstanding / in the nature of knowledge.
내 친구는 일반적인 실수를 했다 / 기본적인 오해를 / 지식의 본질에 대해서

Knowledge is amoral – / not immoral but morality neutral.
지식은 도덕과 상관이 없다 / 비도덕적이 아닌 도덕 중립적이다

It can be used / for any purpose, / but many people assume

/ it will be used / to further *their* favorite hopes / for society / – and this is the fundamental flaw.
그것(지식)은 사용될 수 있다 / 모든 목적을 위해서 / 하지만 많은 사람들은 추정한다 / 그것은 사용될 것이라고 / 그들이 선호하는 희망을 늘리는 데 / 사회를 위한 / 그리고 이것은 근본적인 잘못이다

Knowledge of the world / is one thing; / its uses create a separate issue.
세상의 지식은 / 하나이다 / 그것의 사용은 별개의 문제를 만든다

[To be disappointed / that our progress in understanding / has remedied the social ills of the world] / is a legitimate view, / but [to confuse this with the progress of knowledge] / is absurd.
실망하는 것은 / 우리의 이해에 있어서의 발전이 / 세상의 사회적 병을 치료하지 못했다는 것에 / 타당한 견해이다 / 하지만 이것을 지식의 발전과 혼동하는 것은 / 터무니 없다

[To argue / that knowledge is not progressing / because of the African or Middle Eastern conflicts] / misses the point.
주장하는 것은 / 지식이 발전하고 있지 않다고 / 아프리카나 중동의 분쟁 때문에 / 핵심을 놓치고 있다

There is nothing / inherent in knowledge / that dictates any specific social or moral application.
어떠한 것도 없다 / 지식에 내재하는 / 어떤 구체적인 사회적 혹은 도덕적 적용을 알려주는

● 해설

1. 다음 빈칸에 들어갈 말로 가장 적절한 것은?

My friend was disappointed that scientific progress has not cured the world's ills by abolishing wars and starvation; that gross human inequality is still widespread; that happiness is not universal. My friend made a common mistake – a basic misunderstanding in the nature of knowledge. Knowledge is amoral – not immoral but morality neutral. It can be used for any purpose, but many people assume it will be used to further their favorite hopes for society – and this is the fundamental flaw. Knowledge of the world is one thing; its uses create a separate issue. To be disappointed that our progress in understanding has not remedied the social ills of the world is a legitimate view, but _____. To argue that knowledge is not progressing because of the African or Middle Eastern conflicts misses the point. There is nothing inherent in knowledge that dictates any specific social or moral application.

❶ to confuse this with the progress of knowledge is absurd 이것을 과학의 발전과 혼동하는 것은 터무니 없다
② to know the nature of knowledge is to practice its moral value 지식의 특성을 아는 것은 그것의 도덕적 가치를 실행하는 것이다
③ to remove social inequality is the inherent purpose of knowledge 사회적 불평등을 제거하는 것은 지식의 내재적 목적이다
④ to accumulate knowledge is to enhance its social application 지식을 축적하는 것은 그것의 사회적 적용을 향상시키는 것이다
⑤ to make science progress is to make it cure social ills 과학을 발전하

게 하는 것은 그것이 사회적 불행을 치유하게 하는 것이다

이 글은 과학적 발전이나 지식의 발전이 세계의 사회적인 문제를 치유해 주는 것이 아니며 이 둘은 서로 별개의 문제라는 내용이지. 서로 다른 문제이니 그것 때문에 다른 문제가 발생한다는 것은 말도 안된다는 내용이 와야 해. 따라서 빈칸에 들어갈 말로 가장 적절한 것은 ①번이지. ②~⑤번은 과학(지식)의 발전이 사회적 문제와 연관이 있다는 것이니 모두 아니야.

● 중요 포인트

to부정사 주어

[To be disappointed that our progress in understanding has not remedied the social ills of the world] is a legitimate view, but [to confuse this with the progress of knowledge] is absurd.

2. ③

● 전체 해석

인류의 성공은 결정적으로 숫자와 관계에 좌우된다. 몇 백 명의 사람들이 정교한 기술을 유지할 수 없다. 호주가 아프리카로부터 아시아의 해안을 따라 동쪽으로 세력을 넓혔던 개척자들에 의해 45,000년 전에 식민지로 개척되었다는 것을 돌이켜 보자. 이러한 이주의 선발대는 숫자가 매우 적었음에 틀림이 없고 비교적 짐을 가볍게 해서 다녔음에 틀림없다. 그들은 홍해를 건널 당시의 동족들이 이용 가능했던 기술의 견본만을 가지고 있었을 것이다. 이는 그들의 기술이 비록 그 뒤로 천 년이 넘게 꾸준히 발전했고 정교해졌지만, 왜 호주 원주민들의 기술에는 구세계의 매우 많은 특징들이 결여되어 있었는지에 대한 이유를 설명해 줄 수 있을 것이다. 예를 들어, 활과 투석기 같은 탄성 무기는 알려지지 않았고, 화덕 또한 그랬다. 그것은 그들이 '원시적'이어서 또는 그들이 정신적으로 퇴보해서도 아니다. 그것은 그들이 단지 기술의 일부분만 가지고 도착했고, 그 기술들을 훨씬 더 발전시키기에 충분히 조밀한 인구와 그로 인해 충분히 거대한 집단적인 뇌를 갖고 있지 않았기 때문이다.

● 지문분석

[The success of human beings] / depends crucially on numbers and connections.
인간의 성공은 / 결정적으로 숫자와 관계에 달려있다

A few hundred people / cannot sustain a sophisticated technology.
수백 명의 사람들은 / 정교한 기술을 유지할 수 없다

Recall / that Australia was colonized 45,000 years ago / by pioneers / spreading east from Africa / along the shore of Asia.
돌이켜 보라 / 호주가 45,000년 전에 식민지로 개척되었다는 것을 / 개척자들에 의해 / 아프리카에서 동쪽으로 펴져나간 / 아시아의 해안을 따라

[The vanguard of such a migration] / must have been small in number / and must have traveled comparatively light.

그런 이주의 선발대는 / 수적인 면에서 적었음에 틀림없다 / 그리고 상대적으로 가볍게 이동했었음에 틀림없다

The chances are / they had only a sample of the technology / available to their relatives / back at the Red Sea crossing.
~일 것 같다 / 그들은 겨우 기술의 견본만 가지고 있었다 / 그들의 동족들에게 이용 가능한 / 홍해를 건널 당시의

This may explain / why [Australian aboriginal technology, / although it developed / and elaborated steadily / over the ensuing millennia,] / was lacking / in so many features of the Old World / – [elastic weapons, for example, / such as bows and catapults, / were unknown, / as were ovens.
이것은 설명할 지도 모른다 / 왜 호주의 원주민들의 기술은 / 비록 그것이 발전했고 / 꾸준히 정교해졌음에도 불구하고 / 천 년 넘게 / 부족했는지 / 구세계의 매우 많은 특징들이 / 예를 들어 탄성무기가 / 활과 투석기 같은 / 알려지지 않았다 / 화덕도 마찬가지였다

It was not / that they were 'primitive' / or that they had mentally regressed; / it was / that they had arrived / with only a subset of technologies / and did not have a dense enough population / and therefore a large enough collective brain / to develop them much further.
아니었다 / 그들이 원시적인 것도 / 그들이 정신적으로 퇴보한 것도 / 맞았다 / 그들이 도착한 것이 / 겨우 일부의 기술만 가지고 / 그리고 충분히 조밀한 인구를 가지고 있지 않았다는 것이 / 그리고 그래서 충분히 거대한 집단적인 뇌를 / 그것들을(기술) 훨씬 더 발전시키기에

●해설
2. 다음 빈칸에 들어갈 말로 가장 적절한 것은?
The success of human beings depends crucially on numbers and connections. A few hundred people cannot sustain a sophisticated technology. Recall that Australia was colonized 45,000 years ago by pioneers spreading east from Africa along the shore of Asia. The vanguard of such a migration must have been small in number and must have traveled comparatively light. The chances are they had only a sample of the technology available to their relatives back at the Red Sea crossing. This may explain why Australian aboriginal technology, although it developed and elaborated steadily over the ensuing millennia, was lacking in so many features of the Old World – elastic weapons, for example, such as bows and catapults, were unknown, as were ovens. It was not that they were 'primitive' or that they had mentally regressed; it was that they _____ and did not have a dense enough population and therefore a large enough collective brain to develop them much further.

① were too tightly connected to develop new technologies 너무 밀접하게 관련을 맺고 있어서 새로운 기술을 개발할 수 없었다
② focused on developing and elaborating elastic weapons 탄성 무기를 개발하고 정교화 하는 것에 집중했다

❸ had arrived with only a subset of technologies 단지 기술의 일부분만 가지고 도착했다
④ inherited none of their relatives' technologies in Africa 아프리카 동족들의 기술을 하나도 물려받지 못했다
▶ 기술의 견본을 가지고 있었어.
⑤ failed to transfer their technical insights to the Old World 그들의 기술적인 안목을 구세계에 전달하지 못했다

첫 문장부터 '숫자'가 중요하다고 하고 있어. 예로 든 호주의 원주민도 결국 가지고 간 기술의 '수'가 부족해서 구세계의 기술보다 못하다고 하고 있어. 따라서 빈칸에 들어갈 말로 ③ '단지 기술의 일부분만 가지고 도착했다'가 가장 적절해.

●중요 포인트

주어와 동사 사이에 끼어든 삽입절

This may explain why [Australian aboriginal technology, although it developed and elaborated steadily over the ensuing millennia,] was lacking in so many features of the Old World.

3. ②

●전체 해석
일정한 시간을 거쳐 오면서 사회적인, 법적인, 종교적인, 그리고 다른 의식들을 위한 장소를 제공한 건물들은 우리가 나중에 인식하고 그러한 건물들의 기능과 결부시키게 된 형태로 발전해왔다. 이것은 양방향의 과정이다. 건물은 상징적인 장소뿐만 아니라 기차 여행을 한다거나 극장에 가는 것과 같은 특별한 사회적 의식을 위한 물리적인 환경과 장소를 제공한다. 건물의 의미는 경험에 의해서 발전하고 확립되며 그런 다음에 우리는 우리의 경험의 의미를 건물에 붙여넣는다. 건물은 이러한 투사된 경험을 통해서 우리 마음속에 공감할 수 있는 반응을 불러일으키며, 이러한 반응의 강도는 우리의 문화, 믿음, 기대에 의해 결정된다. 그것들은 이야기를 들려준다. 왜냐하면 그것들의 형태와 공간 구성이 그것들이 어떻게 사용되어야 하는지에 대한 힌트를 우리에게 주기 때문이다. 그것들의 물리적 배치는 어떤 사용을 권장하고 다른 사용을 억제한다. 우리는 특별히 초대받지 않는다면 극장의 무대 뒤로 가지 않는다. 법정 안에서 법적 절차 과정에서 관련된 사람들의 정확한 위치는 설계의 필수적인 부분이며 법이 유지되는 것을 확실히 하는 꼭 필요한 부분이다.

●지문분석

Over a period of time / [the buildings / which housed social, legal, religious, and other rituals] / evolved into forms / that we subsequently have come to recognize / and associate with those buildings' function.
일정한 시간 동안 / 건물들은 / 사회적, 법적인, 종교적인, 그리고 다른 의식들을 위한 장소를 제공했던 / 형태로 발전했다 / 우리가 계속해서 인식한 / 그리고 그러한 건물들의 기능과 연결된

This is a two-way process; / the building provides the physical environment and setting / for a particular social ritual / such as traveling by train / or going to the theater, / as well as the symbolic setting.

이것은 양방향의 과정이다 / 건물은 물리적인 환경을 제공한다 / 특정한 사회적 의식을 위한 / 예를 들어 기차 여행이나 / 극장에 가는 것처럼 / 상징적인 환경뿐만 아니라

[The meaning of buildings] / evolves and becomes established by experience / and we in turn read our experience into buildings.
건물들의 의미는 / 발전하고 경험에 의해서 확립된다 / 그리고 우리는 우리 경험으로 건물에 의미를 부여한다

Buildings arouse an empathetic reaction in us / through these projected experiences, / and [the strength of these reactions] / is determined / by our culture, our beliefs, and our expectations.
건물들은 공감할 수 있는 반응을 우리에게서 불러일으킨다 / 이러한 투사된 경험들을 통해서 / 그리고 이러한 반응의 강도는 / 결정된다 / 우리 문화와, 신념, 그리고 우리의 기대에 의해서

They tell stories, / for [their form and spatial organization] / give us hints / about how they should be used.
그들은 이야기를 말한다 / 왜냐하면 그들의 형태와 공간 구성은 / 우리에게 힌트를 주기 때문에 / 어떻게 그들이 사용되어져야 하는지

Their physical layout / encourages some uses / and inhibits others; / we do not go backstage in a theater / unless especially invited.
└ 접속사 + 부사
그들의 물리적인 배치는 / 어떤 사용은 촉진하며 / 다른 것들은 억제한다 / 우리는 극장 무대 뒤로 가지 않는다 / 만약 특별히 초대되지 않으면

Inside a law court / [the precise location of those / involved in the legal process] / is an integral part of the design / and an essential part of ensuring / that the law is upheld.
법정 안에서 / 사람들의 정확한 위치는 / 법적 절차 과정에 관련된 / 설계의 필수적 부분이다 / 그리고 확실히 하는 것의 중요한 부분이다 / 법이 유지되는 것을

● 해설

3. 다음 빈칸에 들어갈 말로 가장 적절한 것은?
Over a period of time the buildings which housed social, legal, religious, and other rituals evolved into forms that we subsequently have come _____. This is a two-way process; the building provides the physical environment and setting for a particular social ritual such as traveling by train or going to the theater, as well as the symbolic setting. The meaning of buildings evolves and becomes established by experience and we in turn read our experience into buildings. Buildings arouse an empathetic reaction in us through these projected experiences, and the strength of these reactions is determined by our culture, our beliefs, and our expectations. They tell stories, for their form and spatial organization give us hints about how they should be used. Their physical layout encourages some uses and inhibits others; we do not go backstage in a theater unless especially invited. Inside a

law court the precise location of those involved in the legal process is an integral part of the design and an essential part of ensuring that the law is upheld.

① to identify and relate to a new architectural trend 확인하여 새로운 건축학의 동향과 관련짓게
▶ 새로운 동향과는 상관없지.
❷ to recognize and associate with those buildings' function 인식하고 그러한 건물의 기능에 결부되게
③ to define and refine by reflecting cross-cultural interactions 문화 간의 상호작용을 반영함으로써 규정하고 개선시키게
▶ 문화 간의 상호작용 반영은 위에 언급된 '양방향' 때문인것 같지만, 그게 핵심은 아니지. 실제적인 사용이 언급되어야 해.
④ to use and change into an integral part of our environment 사용하여 우리 환경의 필수적인 부분으로 변화시키게
⑤ to alter and develop for the elimination of their meanings 그것들의 의미를 없애기 위해서 변형시키고 발전시키게

이 글은 사람은 경험을 통해 어떤 건물의 기능을 인식하고 그 건물에 어떤 의미를 결부시키게 된다는 내용이지. 즉, 건물의 물리적 환경과 사회적 의미를 연결시킨다는 거야. 따라서 빈칸이 들어가는 문장이 이 글의 주제문이므로 빈칸에는 ② to recognize and associate with those buildings' function(인식하고 그러한 건물의 기능에 결부되게)이 적절하지.

● 중요 포인트

수식을 받는 부분이 주어가 아닌 경우
Inside a law court [the precise location of those involved in the legal process] is an integral ~

4. ②

● 전체 해석

욕망이 결과와 상충되는, 단순해 보이는 가리키는 과업에 직면했을 때, 침팬지들은 원하는 보상이 바로 옆에 있는 상황에서 자신에게 이익이 되는 예리한 인지 전략을 보여주는 것이 불가능하다는 것을 알게 된다. 그렇지만, 그것을 대신하는 상징 시스템이 이용될 때 그러한 과업이 숙달된다. 한 연구에서, 침팬지들은 단순한 선택에 직면했다. 맛있는 음식물이 담겨 있는 두 개의 접시가 제시되었는데, 각 접시에는 서로 다른 수의 맛있는 먹이가 담겨 있었다. 침팬지가 더 많은 수의 맛있는 먹이가 담겨 있는 접시를 가리키면, 그것은 옆 우리에 있는 동료 침팬지에게 주어지며, 실망한 실험 대상 침팬지는 더 적은 양을 받게 되었다. 수백 번 되풀이 하여 시도해 본 후에도, 침팬지들은 더 큰 보상을 가리키는 것을 억제하는 것을 배우지 못했다. 그렇지만, 이 동일한 침팬지들은 이미 단순한 숫자의 상징 개념을 학습한 상태였다. 실제 보상을 대체하는 것으로서 그 숫자들이 접시에 놓였을 때, 침팬지들은 처음에 작은 숫자를 가리켜서, 자신을 위해 더 큰 보상을 얻는 것을 금방 배웠다.

● 지문분석

┌ 삽입절
When confronted / by a seemingly simple pointing task, / where their desires are put / in conflict with outcomes / chimpanzees find it impossible / to exhibit subtle self-
        └ 가목적어   └ 진목적어

serving cognitive strategies / in the immediate presence of a desired reward.
직면했을 때 / 외형적으로 단순한 가리키는 과업에 / 그들의 욕망이 놓여지는 / 결과와 상충되게 / 침팬지들은 불가능하다는 것을 깨닫는다 / 미묘한 자기에게 이익이 되는 인지적 전략을 보여주는 것이 / 원하는 보상이 바로 옆에 있는 상황에서

However, such tasks are mastered / when an alternative symbol system is employed.
하지만, 그런 과업은 숙달된다 / 대안적인 상징 시스템이 이용될 때

In one study, / chimps were confronted / by a simple choice; / [two plates / holding tasty food items] / were presented, / each with a different number of treats.
한 연구에서 / 침팬지들은 직면했다 / 단순한 선택에 / 두 개의 접시가 / 맛있는 음식이 담겨있는 / 주어졌다 / 각각에는 다른 수의 먹이가 있는

If the chimp pointed to the plate / having more treats, / it would immediately be given / to a fellow chimp in an adjacent cage, / and the frustrated subject would receive the smaller amount.
침팬지가 접시를 가리킨다면 / 더 많은 먹이가 있는 / 그것은 즉시 주어진다 / 인접한 우리에 있는 동료 침팬지에게 / 그리고 실망한 대상자는 더 적은 양을 받게 된다

After hundreds and hundreds of trials, / these chimps could not learn / to withhold pointing to the larger reward.
수백번의 시도 후에 / 이 침팬지들은 배우지는 못했다 / 더 많은 보상을 가리키는 것을 억제하는 것을

However, these same chimps had already been taught / the symbolic concept of simple numbers.
하지만, 이 같은 침팬지들은 벌써 배웠다 / 간단한 숫자의 상징 개념을

When those numbers were placed on the plates / as a substitute for the actual rewards, / the chimps promptly learned / to point to the smaller numbers first, / thereby obtaining the larger rewards for themselves.
└분사구문
그러한 숫자들이 접시 위에 놓여 졌을 때 / 실제 보상의 대체물로서 / 침팬지들은 신속하게 배웠다 / 더 적은 숫자를 우선 가리키는 법을 / 그리고 자신을 위해 더 큰 보상을 얻는 것을

●해설
4. 다음 빈칸에 들어갈 말로 가장 적절한 것은?
When confronted by a seemingly simple pointing task, where their desires are put in conflict with outcomes, chimpanzees find it impossible to exhibit subtle self- serving cognitive strategies in the immediate presence of a desired reward. However, such tasks are mastered _____. In one study, chimps were confronted by a simple choice; two plates holding tasty food items were presented, each with a different number of treats. If the chimp pointed to the plate having more treats, it would immediately be given to a fellow chimp in an adjacent cage, and the frustrated subject would

receive the smaller amount. After hundreds and hundreds of trials, these chimps could not learn to withhold pointing to the larger reward. However, these same chimps had already been taught the symbolic concept of simple numbers. When those numbers were placed on the plates as a substitute for the actual rewards, the chimps promptly learned to point to the smaller numbers first, thereby obtaining the larger rewards for themselves.

① as immediate rewards replace delayed ones 즉각적인 보상이 지연되는 보상을 대체할 때에
▶ 새로운 동향과는 상관없지.
❷ when an alternative symbol system is employed 그것을 대신하는 상징 시스템이 이용될 때
▶ 바로 숫자가 이용되었지.
③ if their desires for the larger rewards are satisfied 더 큰 보상에 대한 그들의 욕망이 충족되면
▶ 욕망을 충족시켜주지 않았어.
④ when material rewards alternate with symbolic ones 물질적인 보상이 상징적인 보상과 번갈아 나올 때
▶ 번갈아 나온 것이 아니라 대신 나왔어.
⑤ if the value of the number is proportional to the amount of the reward 숫자의 가치가 보상의 양과 비례하면
▶ 반비례하고 있지.

접시에 실제 먹이를 담아서 실험을 했을 때에는 침팬지들이 더 많은 먹이를 먹기 위한 전략을 사용할 수 없었어. 그런데 먹이를 숫자로 대체했을 때에는 그것을 금방 배우고 있지. 따라서 상징적인 개념인 숫자를 언급하는 ② when an alternative symbol system is employed(그것을 대신하는 상징 시스템이 이용될 때)가 적절하지.

●중요 포인트

가목적어–진목적어 구문

When confronted by a seemingly simple pointing task, where their desires are put in conflict with outcomes, chimpanzees find it impossible to exhibit subtle self-serving cognitive strategies in the immediate presence of a desired reward.
　　　　　　　가목적어　　　진목적어

5. ②

●전체 해석
미래를 위해 계획을 세우려면, 뇌가 이전 경험의 특정 요소를 받아들여, 어떤 실제적인 과거 경험이나 현실을 있는 그대로 모방하지 않는 방식으로 재구성할 수 있는 능력을 지니고 있어야 한다. 그것을 달성하려면 유기체는 내적 표상, 즉 외부 세계의 모델을 만들어 내는 단순한 능력을 넘어서야 한다. 그것(유기체)은 이러한 모델을 조작하고 변형하는 능력을 습득해야 한다. 우리는 영장류의 인지력의 근본적인 독특한 특징 중의 하나인 도구 제작이 이 능력에 의존한다고 주장할 수 있는데, 왜냐하면 도구는 자연 환경 속에 이미 만들어진 형태로 존재하지 않고, 만들어지려면 상상되어야하기 때문이다. '미래의 이미지'를 만들어 내고 보유하는 신경 기제는 도구 제작을 위한, 따라서 인간 문명의 시작을 위한 필수적인 전제 조건이었다.

● 지문분석

> To make plans for the future, / the brain must have an
> ability / to take certain elements of prior experiences / and
> reconfigure them in a way / that does not copy / any actual
> past experience or present reality exactly.
> 미래를 위한 계획을 세우려면 / 두뇌는 능력이 있어야만 한다 / 이전
> 의 경험의 특정한 요소를 받아들이는 / 그리고 그것을 이런 방식으로
> 재구성할 수 있는 / 모방하지 않는 / 어떤 실제적인 과거 경험이나 현
> 재의 현실을 그대로
>
> To accomplish that, / the organism must go beyond
> the mere ability / to form internal representations, / the
> models of the world outside.
> 그것을 이루기 위해서 / 유기체는 단순한 능력을 넘어서야만 한다 /
> 내적 표상을 형성하는 / 바깥 세상의 모델인
>
> It must acquire the ability / to manipulate and transform
> these models.
> 그것은 능력을 얻어야만 한다 / 이러한 모델들을 조작하고 변형하는
>
> We can argue / that [tool-making, / one of the fundamental
> distinguishing features / of primate cognition,] / depends
> on this ability, / since a tool does not exist / in a ready-
> made form / in the natural environment / and has to be
> imagined / in order to be made.
> 우리는 주장할 수 있다 / 도구를 만드는 것은 / 기본적인 차별화된 특
> 징 중 하나인 / 영장류의 인지력의 / 이러한 능력에 달려있다고 / 왜
> 냐하면 도구는 존재하지 않으니까 / 이미 만들어진 형태로는 / 자연
> 환경에서 / 그리고 상상되어져야만 한다고 / 만들어지기 위해서
>
> [The neural machinery / for creating and holding 'images
> of the future'] / was a necessary prerequisite / for tool-
> making, / and thus for launching human civilization.
> 신경 기제는 / 미래의 이미지를 만들고 보유하기 위한 / 필요한 전제
> 조건이었다 / 도구 만들기와 / 그리고 따라서 인류의 문명을 시작하
> 기 위한

● 해설

5. 다음 빈칸에 들어갈 말로 가장 적절한 것은?

To make plans for the future, the brain must have an ability
to take certain elements of prior experiences and reconfigure
them in a way that does not copy any actual past experience or
present reality exactly. To accomplish that, the organism must
go beyond the mere ability to form internal representations,
the models of the world outside. It must acquire the ability to
_____. We can argue that tool-
making, one of the fundamental distinguishing features of
primate cognition, depends on this ability, since a tool does not
exist in a ready-made form in the natural environment and has
to be imagined in order to be made. The neural machinery for
creating and holding 'images of the future' was a necessary
prerequisite for tool-making, and thus for launching human
civilization.

① mirror accurate images of the world outside 외부 세계의 정확한 이미지
를 반영하는
▶ 외부 세계의 것을 모방하지 않는 방식으로 재구성한다고 하고 있지.

❷ manipulate and transform these models 이러한 모델을 조작하고 변형하
는
▶ 외부 세계의 것을 넘어서는 능력이 필요하므로 이것과 어울리는 것이
바로 ②번이지.

③ visualize the present reality as it is 현실을 있는 그대로의 모습으로 시각
화하는
▶ 현실에 있는 것 이상의 것을 만드는 것이라고 했지.

④ bring the models back from memory 그 모델을 기억에서 되가저오는
▶ 번갈아 나온 것이 아니라 대신 나왔어.

⑤ identify and reproduce past experiences faithfully 과거의 경험을 충실
히 확인하고 재생산하는
▶ 과거의 것을 모방하지 말라고 하고 있지.

이 글은 세상이 존재하는 그 이상의 것을 만들기 위해서는 무언가를 상
상하는 능력이 필요하다고 이야기하고 있어. 예로 든 도구 제작을 통해서
과거의 경험이나 현실을 그대로 모방하지 않고 이를 재구성하는 능력이
필요하다고 하고 있지. 따라서 빈칸에 들어가 말로 가장 적절한 것은 ②
manipulate and transform these models(이러한 모델을 조작하고 변형하
는)야.

● 중요 포인트

동격인 구문이 따라오는 주어

> We can argue / that [tool-making, / one of the
> fundamental distinguishing features / of primate
> cognition,] / depends on this ability ~

6. ②

● 전체 해석

눈을 카메라에 비유함으로써, 기초적인 생물학 교과서는 인식이 수반
하고 있는 것에 대한 잘못된 인상을 만들어내는데 일조하고 있다. 상
(image)을 형성하는 물리학적 관점에서만, 눈과 카메라는 공통적인 것을
갖고 있다. 눈과 카메라 둘 다 외부에서 상(image)으로 들어오는 광선에
초점을 맞추는 렌즈를 갖고 있고, 둘 다 그렇게 들어온 상의 밝기와 초점
을 조절하는 수단을 갖고 있다. 둘 다 상이 맺혀지는 빛에 민감한 막(망막
과 필름)을 갖고 있다. 그러나, 상의 형성은 단지 보기위한 첫 번째 단계
일 뿐이다. 눈과 카메라 간의 표면적(피상적)인 비유는 훨씬 더 많은 근본
적인 차이점, 즉 카메라는 그저 상을 기록할 뿐이지만 시각 체계는 상을
해석한다는 차이점을 가리고 있다.

● 지문분석

> By likening the eye to a camera, / elementary biology
> textbooks / help to produce a misleading impression / of
> what perception entails.
> 눈을 카메라에 비유함으로써 / 초등학교의 생물학 교재는 / 잘못된
> 인상을 만드는 것을 돕고 있다 / 인식이 수반하는 것의
>
> Only in terms of the physics of image formation / do the
> eye and camera / have anything in common.
> 오직 이미지 형성의 물리학점인 관점에서만 / 눈과 카메라는 / 공통

적인 무언가를 가지고 있다

Both eye and camera have a lens / that focuses light rays / from the outside world / into an image, / and both have a means / of adjusting the focus and brightness of that image.

눈과 카메라 둘 다 렌즈를 가지고 있다 / 광선에 초점을 맞추는 / 외부 세계에서 오는 / 이미지로 / 그리고 둘 다 수단을 가진다 / 초점과 그 이미지의 밝기를 조절하는

Both eye and camera / have a light-sensitive layer / onto which the image is cast / (the retina and film, respectively).

눈과 카메라 둘 다 / 빛에 민감한 막을 가지고 있다 / 이미지가 맺혀지는 / (망막과 필름, 각각)

However, image formation / is only the first step towards seeing.

하지만, 이미지 형성은 / 보는 것을 향한 첫 번째 단계일 뿐이다

[Superficial analogies / between the eye and a camera] / obscure the much more fundamental difference / between the two, / which is that the camera merely records an image, / whereas the visual system interprets it.

피상적인 비유는 / 눈과 카메라 사이의 / 훨씬 더 근본적인 차이점을 가리고 있다 / 그 둘 사이의 / 그것은 카메라가 단순히 이미지를 기록한다는 것이다 / 반면에 시각 시스템은 그것을 해석한다는 것이다

● 해설

6. 다음 빈칸에 들어갈 말로 가장 적절한 것은?
눈과 카메라의 유사점
By likening the eye to a camera, elementary biology textbooks help to produce a misleading impression of what perception entails. Only in terms of the physics of image formation do the eye and camera have anything in common. Both eye and camera have a lens that focuses light rays from the outside world into an image, and both have a means of adjusting the focus and brightness of that image. Both eye and camera have a light-sensitive layer onto which the image is cast (the retina and film, respectively). However, image formation is only the first step towards seeing. _____ obscure the much more fundamental difference between the two, which is that the camera merely records an image, whereas the visual system interprets it.
부정적 어휘
눈과 카메라의 실질적 차이

① Apparent differences in the focusing power of a lens 렌즈의 초점에서의 명확한 차이
▶ 외부세계의 것을 모방하지 않는 방식으로 재구성한다고 하고 있지.

❷ Superficial analogies between the eye and a camera 눈과 카메라 사이의 피상적 비유
▶ 이것으로 인해서 눈과 카메라 사이의 차이점이 가려지므로 앞에서 언급한 눈과 카메라의 유사점이 적절하지.

③ Contrasts in light adaptation between the retina and film 망막과 필름 사이의 명순응의 차이점
▶ 현실에 있는 것 이상의 것을 만드는 것이라고 했지.

④ Misunderstandings of image formation in the eye and a camera 눈과 카메라에서의 이미지 형성의 오해
▶ 앞에서 언급한 것은 오해가 아닌 단순한 비슷한 점이지.

⑤ Close relationships between image formation and interpretation 이미지 형성과 이해 사이의 밀접한 관계

지문의 앞부분에서는 눈과 카메라의 유사점을, 뒤부분에서는 실질적인 차이점을 말해주고 있어. 빈칸은 반전을 나타내는 however 뒤에 오고 있지. '빈칸'이 눈과 카메라 사이의 근본적인 차이점을 가리고 있다고 하고 있으니, 앞에서 언급한 눈과 카메라의 유사점이 나와야겠지. 따라서 이를 다르게 표현한 ② Superficial analogies between the eye and a camera(눈과 카메라 사이의 피상적 비유)가 적절해.

● 중요 포인트

only + 부사구 도치

Only in terms of the physics of image formation do the
　　　　　only + 부사구 → V + S (도치)
eye and camera have anything in common.
　S

7. ①

● 전체 해석

생명체는 바다에서 시작되었기 때문에, 담수 생명체를 포함한 대부분의 생명체는 담수보다 바다와 더 흡사한 화학 성분을 지니고 있다. 대부분의 담수 생명체는 담수에서 생겨난 것이 아니라, 바다에서 육지로 그런 다음 다시 담수로 가서 이차적으로 적응한 것처럼 보인다. 이것이 있을 법하지 않게 보일지는 모르지만, 수중 동물의 체액은 바다와의 강한 유사성을 보여주고 있으며, 실제로 담수 생리의 이온 균형에 관한 대부분의 연구는 어류, 양서류, 무척추동물이 주변의 담수에도 불구하고 내부의 바닷물 상태를 유지하려고 하는 복잡한 조절 기제를 상세히 기록하고 있다. 생태학을 매우 흥미롭게 해 주는 것이 바로 이런 종류의 예기치 못한 복잡성과 명백한 모순이다. 담수호에 있는 물고기가 바다를 흉내 내려고 자기 몸속에 염분을 축적하려고 애쓰고 있다는 생각은 우리에게 생물권의 또 다른 거대한 모순, 곧 식물은 대략 3/4에 이르는 질소로 구성된 환경 속에 감싸여 있지만, 그들의 성장은 질소 부족에 의해 제한되는 경우가 빈번하다는 것을 상기시킨다.

● 지문분석

Since life began in the oceans, / [most life, / including freshwater life,] / has a chemical composition / more like the ocean / than fresh water.
생명체가 대양에서 시작한 이후로 / 대부분의 생명체는 / 담수 생명체를 포함한 / 화학 성분을 가진다 / 대양과 비슷한 / 담수보다

It appears / that most freshwater life did not originate in fresh water, / but is secondarily adapted, / having passed from ocean to land / and then back again to fresh water.
　　　　　　　　　　　　　　　　　　　　　분사구문(이전 상황)
~ 인 것 같다 / 대부분의 담수 생명체는 담수에서 생겨난 것이 아니었다 / 하지만 이차적으로 적응한 것 같다 / 대양에서 육지로 갔을 때 / 그리고 다시 담수로 가서

As improbable as this may seem, / the bodily fluids of aquatic animals / show a strong similarity to oceans, / and indeed, most studies of ion balance / in freshwater physiology / document the complex regulatory mechanisms / by which fish, amphibians and invertebrates

attempt to / maintain an inner ocean / in spite of surrounding fresh water.
이것이 있을 법하지 않음에도 불구하고 / 수중 동물의 체액은 / 강한 바다와의 유사성을 보여준다 / 그리고 정말로 이온 균형에 대한 대부분의 연구는 / 담수 생리의 / 복잡한 조절 기제를 기록하고 있다 / 어류, 양서류, 그리고 무척추 동물이 시도하려고 하는 / 내부의 바닷물을 유지하려고 / 주변의 담수에도 불구하고

It is these sorts of unexpected complexities / and apparent
　　it−that 강조 용법
contradictions / **that** make ecology so interesting.
이러한 종류의 예상치 못한 복잡성과 / 명백한 모순이다 / 바로 생태계를 그렇게 흥미롭게 만드는 것은

[The idea / of a fish in a freshwater lake / struggling
　S　　　　전치사 + 명사 + ing: 명사는 S, 동명사는 V로 해석
to accumulate salts / inside its body / to mimic the ocean] / **reminds** one of the other great contradiction
　　　　　　　　　　　　V
of the biosphere: / plants are bathed in an atmosphere / composed of roughly three-quarters nitrogen, / yet their growth is frequently restricted / by lack of nitrogen.
생각은 / 담수 호수에 있는 물고기가 / 소금을 축적하려고 하는 / 신체 내부에 / 바다를 흉내 내기 위해서 / 생물권의 또 다른 거대한 모순중 하나를 상기시킨다 / 식물들은 대기속에 감싸여 있다 / 거의 3/4의 질소로 구성된 / 하지만 그들의 성장은 빈번히 제한된다 / 질소의 부족에 의해서

● 해설

7. 다음 빈칸에 들어갈 말로 가장 적절한 것은?

Since life began in the oceans, most life, including freshwater life, has a chemical composition more like the ocean than fresh water. It appears that most freshwater life did not originate in fresh water, but is secondarily adapted, having passed from ocean to land and then back again to fresh water. As improbable as this may seem, the bodily fluids of aquatic animals show a strong similarity to oceans, and indeed, most studies of ion balance in freshwater physiology document the complex regulatory mechanisms by which fish, amphibians and invertebrates attempt to ＿＿＿＿＿＿＿＿＿. It is these sorts of unexpected complexities and apparent contradictions that make ecology so interesting. The idea of a fish in a freshwater lake struggling to accumulate salts inside its body to mimic the ocean reminds one of the other great contradiction of the biosphere: plants are bathed in an atmosphere composed of roughly three-quarters nitrogen, yet their growth is frequently restricted by lack of nitrogen.

❶ maintain an inner ocean in spite of surrounding fresh water 주변의 담수에도 불구하고 내부의 바닷물 상태를 유지하려고
▶ 앞에서 수중 생물의 내부는 바다와 비슷하다고 했고, 뒤에 나오는 식물과 질소의 관계로 보면 알 수 있어.
② attain ion balance by removing salts from inside their body 자신의 몸 내부에서 염분을 제거함으로써 이온 균형을 획득하려고
▶ 뒤에 나오는 식물−질소의 관계에서는 '제거'라는 의미는 나오지 않고 있어.
③ return to the ocean to escape from their natural enemies 자신의 천적

을 피하기 위해 바다로 되돌아가려고
④ rebuild their external environment to obtain resources 자원을 확보하기 위해 자신의 외부 환경을 재건하려고
⑤ change their physiology in accord with their surroundings 자신의 환경에 맞춰 자신의 생리 상태를 바꾸려고
▶ 자신의 생리를 바꾼다는 말은 나온 적이 없어.

앞부분에서 수중 동물의 체액은 바다와 강한 유사성을 보여주고 있지. 그런데 담수에서 산다는 모순된 상황에 놓여있어. 뒤에 나오는 식물과 질소와의 관계를 통해서도 이런 모순된 상황을 알 수가 있어. 따라서 모순된 상황을 설명하는 ① maintain an inner ocean in spite of surrounding fresh water(주변의 담수에도 불구하고 내부의 바닷물 상태를 유지하려고)가 가장 적절해.

● 중요 포인트

전치사 + 명사 + 동명사

'전치사 + 명사 + ing' 구문에서 ing를 동명사로 보고 명사와 ing를 각각 S와 V로 해석할지, 아니면, ing가 명사를 수식하는 분사로 볼지는 해석의 자연스러움으로 결정해.

[The idea / of a fish in a freshwater lake / struggling to
　S　　　　전치사 + 명사 + ing: 명사는 S, 동명사는 V로 해석
accumulate salts / inside its body / to mimic the ocean] /
reminds one of the other great contradiction of ~
　V

8. ④

● 전체 해석

Walt Whitman이 'Leaves of Grass'를 쓰기 오래전에, 시인들은 명성에 주의를 기울였다. Horace, Petrarch, Shakespeare, Milton, 그리고 Keats는 모두 시의 위대함이 자신들에게 일종의 세속적 불멸을 부여해주기를 바랐다. Whitman도 수 세기 동안 세상이 자신의 시를 가치 있게 여길 것이라는 비슷한 믿음을 갖고 있었다. 그러나 지면 위에서 영원히 살아남고자 하는 이 고대의 열망에다 그는 명성에 대한 새로운 의미를 추가했다. 독자들이 단순히 시인의 작품에만 주목하는 것이 아니라, 그들은 그의 인격적인 위대함에도 이끌릴 것이었다. 그들은 그의 시에서 고동치는 문화적 공연, 즉 엄청난 카리스마와 호소력을 갖고 한 개인이 책에서 솟구쳐 나오는 것을 보게될 것이었다. Jackson주의 미국을 특징지었던 정치 집회와 선거 행진에서 Whitman은 군중과 관련하여 시적 명성을 정의했다. 다른 시인들은 시의 여신으로부터 자신들의 영감을 찾았을지도 모른다. Whitman(이 생각하는) 시인(상)은 자신의 동시대인으로부터의 인정을 추구했다. 미국 민주주의의 불안정 속에 명성은 인기도, 즉 사람들이 그 시인과 그의 작품을 기뻐하는 정도에 의해 좌우될 것이었다.

● 지문분석

Long before Walt Whitman wrote *Leaves of Grass*, / poets had addressed themselves to fame.
Walt Whitman이 Leaves of Grass를 쓰기 오래 전에 / 시인들은 명성에 주의를 기울였다

Horace, Petrarch, Shakespeare, Milton, and Keats all / hoped / that poetic greatness would grant them / a kind of earthly immortality.
Horace, Petrarch, Shakespeare, Milton 그리고 Keats 모두는 / 희망했다 / 시의 위대함이 그들에게 주기를 / 일종의 세속적 불멸을

Whitman held a similar faith / that for centuries / the world would value his poems.
Whitman은 비슷한 신념을 가지고 있었다 / 수 세기 동안 / 세상은 그의 시를 가치있게 여길 것이라는

But to this ancient desire / to live forever on the page, / he added a new sense of fame.
하지만 이러한 고대의 바람에다 / 종이 위에서 영원히 살거라는 / 그는 명성에 대한 새로운 의미를 추가했다

Readers would not simply attend to the poet's work; / they would be attracted / to the greatness of his personality.
독자들은 간단히 시인의 작품에 주의를 기울이지는 않을 것이다 / 그들은 매료될 것이다 / 그의 인격의 위대함에

They would see in his poems / a vibrant cultural performance, / an individual / springing from the book / with tremendous charisma and appeal.
그들은 그의 시에서 볼 것이다 / 고동치는 문화적 공연을 / 한 개인을 / 그의 책에서 뛰쳐나오는 / 엄청난 카리스마와 매력을 지닌

Out of the political rallies and electoral parades / that marked Jacksonian America, / Whitman defined poetic fame / in relation to the crowd.
정치 집회와 선거 행진에서 / Jackson주의 미국을 특징짓는 / Whitman은 시적 명성을 규정했다 / 군중과의 관계에서

Other poets might look for their inspiration / from the goddess of poetry.
다른 시인들은 그들의 영감을 찾았을지도 모른다 / 시의 여신으로부터

Whitman's poet sought / the approval of his contemporaries.
Whitman의 시인상은 추구했다 / 그의 동시대인의 인정을

In the instability of American democracy, / fame would be dependent / on celebrity, / on the degree / to which the people rejoiced / in the poet and his work.
미국의 민주주의의 불안정 속에서 / 명성은 의존했을 것이다 / 인기도에 / 정도에 / 사람들이 기뻐하는 / 시인과 그의 작품에

●해설

8. 다음 빈칸에 들어갈 말로 가장 적절한 것은?

Long before Walt Whitman wrote Leaves of Grass, poets had addressed themselves to fame. Horace, Petrarch, Shakespeare, Milton, and Keats all hoped that poetic greatness would grant them a kind of earthly immortality. Whitman held a similar faith that for centuries the world would value his poems. But to this ancient desire to live forever on the page, he added a new sense of fame. Readers would not simply attend to the poet's work; they would be attracted to the greatness of his personality. They would see in his poems a vibrant cultural performance, an individual springing from the book with tremendous charisma and appeal. Out of the political rallies and electoral parades that marked Jacksonian America, Whitman defined poetic fame in relation to the crowd. Other

poets might look for their inspiration from the goddess of poetry. Whitman's poet sought _____.
In the instability of American democracy, fame would be dependent on celebrity, on the degree to which the people rejoiced in the poet and his work.

① a refuge from public attention 대중의 관심으로부터의 도피
▶ 오히려 정반대지.
② poetic purity out of political chaos 정치적 혼돈에서 나오는 시적 순수성
▶ 앞에 정치와 관련된 어휘가 나오지만, '순수성'이라는 것은 갑자기 튀어나온 거지.
③ immortality in literature itself 문학 그 자체 속에서의 불멸성
▶ 앞에 나오는 세속적 불멸성(earthy immortality)를 보고 만든 오답이지. 문학 자체에 초점이 아니라 시인에게 초점이 맞춰진 글이야.
❹ the approval of his contemporaries 자신의 동시대인으로부터의 인정
▶ 이 글의 핵심은 fame(명성)이지. 명성은 독자들로부터 나오지.
⑤ fame with political celebrities 정치적 유명인사와의 명성

이 글의 마지막에 나오는 말이 핵심이야. Whitman은 시인의 명성은 단순히 훌륭한 시에 의해서가 아니라 대중들이 시인과 시인의 시를 함께 기뻐하는 정도, 즉 대중에 의한 인기도에 의해 결정된다고 생각했어. 즉, 대중들(독자들)에게서 명성이 나온다고 생각하고 있지. 따라서 빈칸에 들어갈 적절한 것은 ④ the approval of his contemporaries(자신의 동시대인으로부터의 인정)야.

●중요 포인트

분사와 전치사의 수식을 받는 명사
They would see in his poems / a vibrant cultural performance, / an individual / springing from the book / with tremendous charisma and appeal.

4단계 혼공 개념 마무리   p.121

1. 이해에 있어서의 진보가 세계의 사회적인 불행을 치유하지 못해왔다는 것에 실망하는 것은 타당한 견해이지만, 이것을 지식의 진보와 혼동하는 것은 터무니없다.

2. 이는 그들의 기술이 비록 그 뒤로 천 년이 넘게 꾸준히 발전했고 정교해졌지만, 왜 호주 원주민들의 기술에는 구세계의 매우 많은 특징들이 결여되어 있었는지에 대한 이유를 설명해 줄 수 있을 것이다.

3. 욕망이 결과와 상충되는, 단순해 보이는 가리키는 과업에 직면했을 때, 침팬지들은 원하는 보상이 바로 옆에 있는 상황에서 자신에게 이익이 되는 예리한 인지 전략을 보여주는 것이 불가능하다는 것을 알게 된다.

4. 우리는 영장류의 인지력의 근본적인 독특한 특징 중의 하나인 도구 제작이 이 능력에 의존한다고 주장할 수 있는데, 왜냐하면 도구는 자연 환경 속에 이미 만들어진 형태로 존재하지 않고, 만들어지려면 상상되어야 하기 때문이다.

5. 눈과 카메라 간의 피상적인 비유는 훨씬 더 많은 근본적인 차이점, 즉 카메라는 그저 상을 기록할 뿐이지만 시각 체계는 상을 해석한다는 차이점을 가리고 있다.

6. 이것이 있을 법하지 않게 보일지는 모르지만, 수중 동물의 체액은 바다와의 강한 유사성을 보여주고 있으며, 실제로 담수 생리의 이온 균형에 관한 대부분의 연구는 어류, 양서류, 무척추동물이 주변의 담수에도 불구하고 내부의 바닷물 상태를 유지하려고 하는 복잡한 조절 기제를 상세히 기록하고 있다.

혼공 12일차 **빈칸추론(앞부분)**

3
단계 **고난도 문항** 요리하기   p.127

● 정답

> **1.** ① **2.** ② **3.** ④ **4.** ③ **5.** ① **6.** ② **7.** ⑤ **8.** ⑤

1. ①

● 전체 해석

정보를 평가하는 것에 있어서의 어려움은 우리 마음대로 쓸 수 있는 정보의 과다함에 의해 악화된다. 이것이 일부 영역에서는 분명하나 – 예를 들어, Microsoft사 주식의 가치를 추산하는데 얼마나 많은 정보가 잠재적으로 관련이 있는지 고려해 보라. – 정보의 집합이 덜 혼란스러워 보일 때조차도, 정보의 과부하, 즉 혼란 및 의사 결정 회피의 상태는 여전히 발생할 수 있다. 한 실험에서, 슈퍼마켓의 구매자들에게 잼과 젤리의 무료 샘플이 제공되었다. 첫 번째 제공에서는, 맛을 보기 위한 약간의 샘플만이 이용 가능했다. 두 번째 제공에서는, 많은 양을 이용할 수 있었다. 모든 구매자들이 풍부한 선택이라는 아이디어를 흡족해하고 실제로 더 많은 제공물이 있는 테이블에 더 많은 구매자들을 끌어들인 반면, 가장 많은 매출로 이어진 것은 가장 적은 샘플이 제공된 테이블이었다. 가능성 있는 이유는, 많은 선택이 정보의 과부하를 초래했다는 것인데, 그것은 즉각적인 행동을 하기에는 의사 결정이 너무 복잡하다는 느낌을 말한다.

● 지문분석

[Difficulty in assessing information] / is aggravated / by
  S
the overabundance of information / at our disposal.
정보를 평가할 때의 어려움은 / 악화된다 / 정보의 과다에 의해서 /
우리 마음대로 쓸 수 있는

While this is obvious enough in some realms / — for
example, consider / how much information is potentially
relevant / for estimating the value of Microsoft stock —
/ even when the information set seems less cluttered, /
[information overload, a state of confusion and decision
avoidance,] can still occur.
                    S
이것이 일부 영역에서 충분히 명확하더라도 / 예를 들어 고려해봐라
/ 얼마만큼의 정보가 잠재적으로 관련이 있는지 / 마이크로소프트사
의 주식 가치를 평가하는 데 / 심지어 정보의 집합이 덜 혼란스러울

때 조차도 / 정보의 과부하, 혼동과 결정 회피의 상태는 / 여전히 발
생할 수 있다

In one experiment, / shoppers in a supermarket / were
presented with free samples of jams and jellies.
한 실험에서 / 슈퍼마켓의 구매자들에게 / 잼과 젤리의 무료 샘플이
제공되었다

In the first treatment, / a small selection was available for
tasting; / in the second, a large selection was available.
첫 번째 제공에서 / 작은 선택은 맛보기 위해서 가능했다 / 두 번째에
서 / 많은 선택이 이용 가능했다

While everyone likes the idea of abundant choice, / and
indeed [the table with the greater selection] / attracted
                        S
larger crowds, / it was the table with fewer samples / that
                    it – that 강조 용법
led to the most sales.
모든 사람들이 과도한 선택의 생각을 좋아한 반면 / 그리고 정말로
엄청난 선택사항이 있는 테이블은 / 더 많은 사람들을 끌어모았지만
/ 바로 더 적은 샘플이 있는 테이블이었다 / 가장 많은 매출액을 야기
했던 것은

The likely reason / is that the large selection / led to
information overload, / the feeling / that the decision was
                    ┌ = ┐
too complicated / for immediate action.
가능성이 있는 이유는 / 많은 선택이 / 정보의 과다를 유발했다는 것
이다 / 이것은 이런 느낌이다 / 결정이 너무 복잡하다는 / 즉각적인
행동을 하기에는

● 해설

1. 다음 빈칸에 들어갈 말로 가장 적절한 것은?

_____ is aggravated by the overabundance
of information at our disposal. While this is obvious enough in
some realms – for example, consider how much information
is potentially relevant for estimating the value of Microsoft
stock – even when the information set seems less cluttered,
information overload, a state of confusion and decision
avoidance, can still occur. In one experiment, shoppers in a
supermarket were presented with free samples of jams and
jellies. In the first treatment, a small selection was available
for tasting; in the second, a large selection was available.
While everyone likes the idea of abundant choice, and indeed
the table with the greater selection attracted larger crowds, it
was the table with fewer samples that led to the most sales.
The likely reason is that the large selection led to information
overload, the feeling that the decision was too complicated for
immediate action.

❶ Difficulty in assessing information 정보를 평가함에 있어 어려움
② The shortage of trustworthy informants 믿을 만한 정보 제공자의 부족
▶ 정보의 신뢰성보다는 양이 문제라는 거야.
③ Mental fatigue caused by misleading information 잘못된 정보로 인한
정신적 피로감
▶ 잘못된 정보가 아니라 많은 정보가 문제인거지.
④ Indeterminacy arising from indirect information 간접 정보에서 발생하는
불확정성

▶ 뒤에 나오는 예가 바로 눈앞에 있는 선택(정보)니까 간접 정보는 아니지.
⑤ The complexity of altering consumer behavior 소비자의 행동을 바꾸는 것의 복잡함
▶ 복잡함은 맞지만, 소비자의 행동 변화는 아니지.

선택사항이 너무 많아서 결국에는 즉각적인 선택이 힘들다는 내용이 지문의 마지막에 나오고 있어. 즉, 정보가 너무 많아서 구매자가 무엇을 고를지 고민한다는 것이니 ① Difficulty in assessing information(정보를 평가함에 있어 어려움)이 적절하겠지.

● 중요 포인트

동격 구문

The likely reason is that the large selection led to information overload, the feeling that the decision was too complicated for immediate action.

2. ②

● 전체 해석

기회가 많고 일자리가 남아도는 튼튼한 경제가 사회적 장벽을 무너뜨리는 데 도움이 된다는 것을 아는 것은 어렵지 않다. 편견에 빠져 있는 고용주는 이런 저런 무리에 속한 구성원을 고용하기를 여전히 싫어할 수 있지만, 다른 어느 누구도 이용할 수 없다면, 차별은 그 일을 끝내야 한다는 기본적인 필요에 자리를 내주게 된다. 자신이 누구와 함께 일하기 좋아하고 싫어하는지에 대한 편견들을 갖고 있는 직원들의 경우도 마찬가지다. 예를 들어, 1990년대 후반의 미국의 건설 경기가 호황일 때, 심지어 "전통적인 백인 남성의 요새, 부러움을 사는 조합증이 아버지에서 아들로 전수되는 세계"로 오랫동안 알려져 있던 목수 조합조차도 여자, 흑인, 히스패닉이 인턴 프로그램에 참여하는 것을 공개적으로 장려하기 시작했다. 작업장에서만큼은 적어도, 사람들을 쫓는 일자리가 유동적인 사회를 진작하는 데 일자리를 쫓는 사람들보다 확실히 더 많이 기여한다.

● 지문분석

It is not hard / to see / that a strong economy, / where opportunities are plentiful / and jobs go begging, / helps break down social barriers.
어렵지 않다 / 보는 것은 / 강한 경제가 / 기회가 풍부하고 / 일자리가 남아도는 / 사회적 장벽을 붕괴시키는 것을 돕는다는 것을
Biased employers may still dislike / hiring members of one group or another, / but when nobody else is available, / discrimination most often gives way to the basic need / to get the work done.
편견에 빠진 고용주는 여전히 싫어할 수도 있다 / 이런 저런 그룹에 속한 구성원을 고용하는 것을 / 하지만 다른 누구도 이용 가능하지 않을 때 / 차별은 종종 기본적인 필요에 굴복한다 / 일을 끝내야 한다는
The same goes for employees with prejudices / about whom they do and do not like / working alongside.
같은 것들이 선입견을 가진 직원들에게 적용된다 / 그들이 좋아하고 좋아하지 않는 / 함께 일하는 것을

In the American construction boom of the late 1990s, for example, / even the carpenters' union / — long known / as a "traditional bastion of white men, / a world / where a coveted union card / was handed down from father to son" / — began openly encouraging / women, blacks, and Hispanics / to join its internship program.
1980년대 후반 미국의 건설붐에서, 예를 들어 / 심지어 목수 조합도 / 오랫동안 알려진 / 백인 남성들의 전통적인 요새로서 / 세계인 / 부러움을 사는 조합카드가 / 아버지에게서 아들에게로 전해졌던 / 공개적으로 장려하기 시작했다 / 여성, 흑인, 그리고 히스페닉계가 / 그 인턴 프로그램에 참여하는 것을
At least in the workplace, / jobs / chasing people / obviously does more / to promote a fluid society / than people / chasing jobs.
최소한 작업장에서는 / 일은 / 사람들을 쫓는 / 명백하게 더 많은 것을 하고 있다 / 유동적인 사회를 촉진하는 데 / 사람들보다 / 일자리를 쫓는

● 해설

2. 다음 빈칸에 들어갈 말로 가장 적절한 것은?
It is not hard to see that a strong economy, where opportunities are plentiful and jobs go begging, _____. Biased employers may still dislike hiring members of one group or another, but when nobody else is available, discrimination most often gives way to the basic need to get the work done. The same goes for employees with prejudices about whom they do and do not like working alongside. In the American construction boom of the late 1990s, for example, even the carpenters' union – long known as a "traditional bastion of white men, a world where a coveted union card was handed down from father to son" – began openly encouraging women, blacks, and Hispanics to join its internship program. At least in the workplace, jobs chasing people obviously does more to promote a fluid society than people chasing jobs.

① allows employees to earn more income 피고용인들이 더 많은 수입을 벌도록 허용한다
❷ helps break down social barriers 사회적 장벽을 붕괴하도록 도와준다
▶ 사람들이 갖는 편견이 호황기로 인해서 작동하기 힘들게 되고 있지.
③ simplifies the hiring process 고용 과정을 단순화한다
▶ 뒤에 나오는 예시를 보면 고용 과정의 단순화가 주제가 아니지.
④ increases wage discrimination 임금 차별을 증가시킨다
⑤ improves the productivity of a company 회사의 생산성을 개선한다

이 글은 일자리를 채울 사람들이 부족할 만큼 호황기일 때는 고용주나 피고용인이 가지고 있는 편견이 힘을 발휘하지 못하고 사회의 유동성이 더 커진다는 글이야. 뒤에 나오는 예시에서 보듯이 호황기일 때 백인 남성들의 전유물인 목수에도 여성이나 다른 인종의 사람들이 들어 올 수도 있다고 하고 있어. 따라서 빈칸에는 ② helps break down social barriers(사회적 장벽을 붕괴하도록 도와준다)가 가장 적절해.

주어와 동사 사이에 삽입구가 있는 구문

In the American construction boom of the late 1990s, for example, / even the carpenters' union / — long known / as a "traditional bastion of white men, / a world / where a coveted union card / was handed down from father to son" / — began openly encouraging / women, blacks, and Hispanics / to join its internship program.

3. ④

●전체 해석

목재는 환경 친화적이라고 널리 인정받고 있는 자재이다. 그것은 시멘트나 벽돌 대신, 집을 지을 때 하나의 대체재로서 오랫동안 환영받아 왔다. 그러나 목재와 같은 특정한 자재가 다른 것들보다 뛰어난 상대적인 장점을 평가하는 것이 반드시 쉬운 일이 아니다. 마호가니와 티크를 포함하여 많은 종의 나무들이 이제 멸종 위기에 놓여 있고, 특히, 열대 우림의 삼림 벌채는 지역 사회뿐만 아니라 토착 식물과 야생 동물에도 심각한 영향을 미친다. 목재가 채취되고 세상을 반이나 가로질러 운반되는 경우, 관련 에너지 비용이 증가하게 되어, 환경에 부정적인 영향을 미친다. 게다가 나무가 내화성(耐火性)과 내충성(耐蟲性)을 향상시키기 위해 화학 물질로 약품 처리되는 경우, 건강에 유익한 목재의 성질을 손상시킨다.

●지문분석

Wood is a material / that is widely acknowledged / to be environmentally friendly.
목재는 재료이다 / 널리 인정받고 있는 / 친환경적이라고

It has been welcome / as an alternative material for a long time / in building houses / instead of cement or bricks.
그것은 환영받아왔다 / 대안 재료로서 오랜 기간 동안 / 집을 지을 때 / 시멘트나 벽돌을 대신하여

However, it is not always easy / to evaluate the relative merits / of one particular material such as wood / over another.
하지만 항상 쉬운 것은 아니다 / 상대적 장점을 평가하는 것은 / 목재와 같은 한 가지 특정한 재료의 / 다른 것보다 뛰어난

[Many species of tree] / are now endangered, / including mahogany and teak, / and [deforestation, / particularly in tropical rainforests,] / has had a severe impact / both on local communities and on native plants and wildlife.
많은 나무 종들이 / 지금 멸종 위기에 처해있다 / 마호가니와 티크를 포함한 / 그리고 산림 벌채는 / 특히 열대 우림에서의 / 심각한 영향을 주고 있다 / 지역 사회와 자연의 식물과 야생 동물 모두에게

Where wood is harvested / and then transported halfway across the globe, / the associated energy costs / are high, / causing a negative impact on the environment.
목재가 채취되고 / 그리고 지구를 반이나 가로질러 운반되는 곳에서 / 연관된 에너지 비용은 / 높다 / 이는 환경에 부정적 영향을 유발한다

What is more, / where wood is treated with chemicals / to improve fire- and pest-resistance, / its healthful properties are compromised.
게다가 / 목재가 화학 물질로 처리되는 곳에서는 / 내화성과 내충성을 개선하기 위해서 / 그것의 건강에 유익한 특성은 손상된다

●해설

3. 다음 빈칸에 들어갈 말로 가장 적절한 것은?

Wood is a material that is widely acknowledged to be environmentally friendly. It has been welcome as an alternative material for a long time in building houses instead of cement or bricks. However, it is not always easy to _____ (목재의 긍정적 측면 / 빈칸 앞 부정어 주의 → 빈칸은 글의 주제와 정반대 성격) of one particular material such as wood over another. Many species of tree are now endangered, including mahogany and teak, and deforestation, particularly in tropical rainforests, has had a severe impact both on local communities and on native plants and wildlife. Where wood is harvested and then transported halfway across the globe, the associated energy costs are high, causing a negative impact on the environment. What is more, where wood is treated with chemicals to improve fire- and pest-resistance, its healthful properties are compromised. (목재의 부정적 측면)

① increase the inherent resistance 내재적인 저항을 증가시키다
▶ 단점
② favor the chemical properties 화학적 특성을 선호하다
▶ 단점
③ dominate the natural habitats 자연적인 서식지를 지배하다
▶ 단점(환경파괴)
❹ evaluate the relative merits 상대적인 장점을 평가하다
▶ 장점
⑤ deny the cost advantage 비용의 이점을 부인하다
▶ 단점

이 글은 친환경 자재로 인식된 목재의 단점을 언급하고 있어. 빈칸이 있는 문장에서 주의할 점은 however로 앞에서 이야기하고 있는 장점이 아닌 이제부터 단점을 이야기하겠다는 거지. 특히나 빈칸 앞에 바로 부정어인 not이 있으므로 빈칸은 필자가 이야기하고자 하는 내용과는 반대의 내용을 선택지에서 골라야겠지. 즉, 선택지에서 목재의 장점이 되는 부분을 선택해야 해. 따라서 유일하게 장점을 이야기하는 ④ evaluate the relative merits(상대적인 장점을 평가하다)가 정답이 되겠지.

●중요 포인트

가주어-진주어 구문

However, it is not always easy to evaluate the relative merits of one particular material such as wood over another.

4. ③

●전체 해석

모차르트 음악을 들으면 아이가 더 영리해진다는 소위 모차르트 효과는, 연구조사에 의해 정당성을 부여받지 못한 과학적 발견이 과대광고를 통

해 방송 매체에 의해 왜곡된 과학적 발견의 한 가지 좋은 예이다. 그것은 순전히, 선곡한 모차르트 음악에 노출된 후에 대학생들이 조각 그림 맞추기와 같은 과제에서 약 10분 동안 공간 추리능력이 상승함을 보여주었다고 연구자들이 보고했을 때 시작되었다. 우선 그 연구가 아이가 아닌 대학생을 대상으로 행해졌고 또 그 효과는 매우 짧았음을 주목하라. 뿐만 아니라, 그와 똑같은 연구를 반복한 사람은 아무도 없었다. 공간 추리능력의 상승은 테스트를 받는 동안 사람들의 정신활동을 기민하게 하는 모든 청각 자극(예를 들어, 짧은 이야기나 그와는 다른 형태의 음악을 듣는 것)에 의해 생길 수 있음이 밝혀지고 있다. 하지만, 이중 어느 것도 비윤리적인 회사가 행하는 그럴듯한 주장에 자극을 받은 열성적인 부모들이 자기 아이들을 위해 모차르트의 음반을 사는 것을 막지는 못하였다.

● 지문분석

[The so-called Mozart effect / – [listening to Mozart] will make your child smarter] – is a good example of a scientific finding / being distorted by the media / through hype / not warranted by the research.

소위 모차르트 효과는 / 모차르트 음악을 듣는 것은 / 당신의 아이를 더 똑똑하게 만들 것이라는 / 과학적 결과의 좋은 예이다 / 미디어에 의해서 왜곡되고 있는 / 과대광고를 통해서 / 연구에 의해 보장받지 못한

It all started / when researchers reported / that after exposure to a selection of Mozart's music, / college students showed an increase / in spatial reasoning / for about 10 minutes / on tasks / like putting together pieces of a jigsaw puzzle.

그것은 모두 시작했다 / 연구원들이 보고할 때 / 선곡한 모차르트의 음악에 노출된 이후 / 대학생들은 증가를 보여주었다고 / 공간적 추론 능력의 / 약 10분 동안 / 과제에서 / 조각을 맞추는 것과 같은

Note first / that the research was done / on college students, / not infants, / and that the effect was very brief.

우선 주목해라 / 그 연구가 이루어졌음을 / 대학생들에게 / 아이가 아닌 / 그리고 그 효과가 매우 짧았음에

In addition, / no one's been able to replicate the research.

게다가 / 어떤 누구도 그 연구를 반복할 수가 없었다

[The increase in spatial reasoning, / it turns out,] can be generated / by any auditory stimulation / (e.g., listening to a short story or other types of music) / that keeps people alert / while being tested.

공간 추론 능력의 증가는 / 밝혀지듯이 / 발생할 수 있다 / 모든 청각적 자극에 의해서 / 예를 들어 짧은 이야기나 다른 형태의 음악을 듣는 것 / 사람들을 정신을 바짝 차리게 만드는 / 테스트를 받는 동안

However, none of this / has stopped eager parents / – spurred on by fantastic claims from unethical companies / – from purchasing Mozart CDs for their babies.

하지만 이중 어느 것도 / 열정적인 부모들을 멈추지 못했다 / 비윤리적인 기업에서 나온 환상적인 주장에 의해 자극받은 / 그들의 아이들을 위한 모차르트 CD를 구매하는 것을

● 해설

4. 다음 빈칸에 들어갈 말로 가장 적절한 것은?

The so-called Mozart effect – listening to Mozart will make your child smarter – is a good example of _____ by the media through hype not warranted by the research. It all started when researchers reported that after exposure to a selection of Mozart's music, college students showed an increase in spatial reasoning for about 10 minutes on tasks like putting together pieces of a jigsaw puzzle. Note first that the research was done on college students, not infants, and that the effect was very brief. In addition, no one's been able to replicate the research. The increase in spatial reasoning, it turns out, can be generated by any auditory stimulation (e.g., listening to a short story or other types of music) that keeps people alert while being tested. However, none of this has stopped eager parents – spurred on by fantastic claims from unethical companies – from purchasing Mozart CDs for their babies.

① the bond between parents and children exaggerated 부모와 자녀 사이의 과장된 유대
② a genuine scientific innovation being discarded 버려진 진정한 과학적 혁신
❸ a scientific finding being distorted 왜곡된 과학적 발견
④ the correlation between reasoning and music being rejected 무시된 추론과 음악의 상관관계
⑤ the convergence of music and physiology made possible 가능해진 음악과 생리학의 융합

모차르트 효과는 모차르트 음악을 틀어준 결과의 효과는 짧았고, 연구를 반복할 수도 없었고, 다른 청각적 자극에 의해서도 비슷한 효과를 나타내는 것으로 보아 과학적으로 입증된 것이 아니지. 그것은 비윤리적인 회사들의 과대 광고로 왜곡되어 이용되었다고 해야겠지. 따라서 빈칸에 들어갈 가장 적절한 표현은 ③ a scientific finding being distorted(왜곡된 과학적 발견)라고 할 수 있어.

● 중요 포인트

분사가 수식하는 명사

명사 수식 현재분사
~ a good example of a scientific finding / being distorted by the media / through hype / not warranted by the research.
명사 수식 현재분사

5. ①

● 전체 해석

다양성은 인생의 양념과 같다. 만일 내가 50명의 학생들에게 왜 로마 제국이 멸망했는지에 관한 5페이지 분량의 글을 과제로 내 준다면, 그들 중 대부분은 궁극적으로 국경선의 약화를 초래한 경제, 사회적 원인들의 복합이라 말할 가능성이 높다. 이것은 훌륭한 답이 되겠지만, 모두 같은 내용을 말하는 45개의 글을 읽은 후에, 나는 뭔가 변화를 위한 준비가 되어 있다. 만일 학생이 하나의 글에서 나머지 학생들과 다른 각도를 취한다면 교수들에게 깊은 인상을 줄 가능성이 더 높아진다. 그러나 여기에 어려운 부분이 있다 – 다르다고 하는 것은 위험을 무릅쓰는 것이고, 주장의 근

거를 매우 잘 뒷받침해 줄 때 만이 효과가 있는 것이다. 만일 로마가 멸망한 것이 오직 기독교가 로마인들의 투쟁 정신을 약화시킨 것 때문만 이라고 주장한다면, 그 어떤 가능성 있는 반대 의견에 대해서도 설득력 있는 추론과 논쟁이 필요할 것이다.

●지문분석

Variety is the spice of life.
다양성은 인생의 양념이다

If I assign fifty students / a five-page essay / on the subject / of why the Roman Empire fell, / most of them are likely to say / it was a combination of economic and social causes / ultimately leading to a weakening of the frontiers.
만약 내가 50명의 학생에게 준다면 / 5페이지짜리 에세이를 / 주제에 대한 / 왜 로마제국이 몰락했는지에 대한 / 그들 대부분은 말할 가능성이 높다 / 그것은 경제적 그리고 사회적 요인의 결합이었다고 / 궁극적으로 국경선의 약화를 불러일으킨

This would be a fine answer, / but after reading forty-five papers all / saying the same thing, / I'm ready for a change.
이것은 좋은 답이 될 수도 있다 / 하지만 45개의 보고서 모두를 읽은 후에 / 모두 같은 것을 말하는 / 나는 변화를 위한 준비가 되어 있다

If you can take a different angle / from the rest of the class / in a paper, / you're more likely to impress your professors.
만약 당신이 다른 관점을 취한다면 / 학급의 나머지와는 다른 / 보고서에서 / 당신은 교수들에게 인상을 줄 가능성이 높다

But here's the tricky part / — being different is risky, / and it only works / if you back up your argument very well.
하지만 여기에 어려운 부분이 있다 / 다르다는 것은 위험하다 / 그리고 그것은 효과가 있다 / 만약 당신이 당신의 주장을 잘 뒷받침한다면

If you choose to argue / that Rome fell / solely because Christianity weakened the fighting spirit of the Romans, / you will need persuasive reasoning and arguments / against any potential objections.
만약 당신이 주장하기로 선택한다면 / 로마제국은 멸망했다고 / 오직 기독교가 로마인들의 투쟁정 신을 약화시켰기 때문에 / 당신은 설득력 있는 추론과 논쟁이 필요할 것이다 / 어떤 잠재적 반대에 대한

●해설

5. 다음 빈칸에 들어갈 말로 가장 적절한 것은?
_____. If I assign fifty students a five-page essay on the subject of why the Roman Empire fell, most of them are likely to say it was a combination of economic and social causes ultimately leading to a weakening of the frontiers. This would be a fine answer, but after reading forty-five papers all saying the same thing, I'm ready for a change. If you can take a different angle from the rest of the class in a paper, you're more likely to impress your professors.

But here's the tricky part – being different is risky, and it only works if you back up your argument very well. If you choose to argue that Rome fell solely because Christianity weakened the fighting spirit of the Romans, you will need persuasive reasoning and arguments against any potential objections.

❶ Variety is the spice of life 다양성은 인생의 양념과도 같다
② The essence of writing is in its brevity 글쓰기의 핵심은 간결함에 있다
③ Don't fix what is not broken 고장나지 않은 것을 고치지 마라
④ The pen is mightier than the sword 펜은 칼보다 강하다
⑤ Rome was not built in a day 로마는 하루 아침에 멸망하지 않았다
▶ 뒤에 나오는 로마에 대한 내용 때문에 나온 선택지야.

남들과 다른 각도로 쓴 글은, 깊은 인상을 남길 가능성이 높다는 요지의 글이지. 물론 뒤에서 자신의 주장을 뒷받침하는 것이 쉽지 않은 일이라고 덧붙이지만 말이야. 따라서 빈칸에 들어가기에 가장 적절한 것은 ① Variety is the spice of life(다양성은 인생의 양념과도 같다)이지.

●중요 포인트

명사 수식 현재분사
most of them are likely to say / it was a combination of economic and social causes / ultimately leading to a weakening of the frontiers.

6. ②

●전체 해석

어떤 사람들은 자선 단체에 기부하는 것이 어떤 면에서는 우리 인류에게 이롭기 때문에 생겨난, 일종의 본능이라고 생각한다. 처음에는, 이것이 이상한 생각으로 보일 수 있다. 다윈의 진화론은 개개인이 전체로서의 종족의 이익이 아닌, 자기 자신의 이익을 보호하기 위해 행동한다고 가정한다. 그러나 영국의 진화생물학자인 Richard Dawkins는 자연선택이 우리에게 고통 받는 타인을 측은히 여기는 능력을 주었다고 믿는다. 인간이 소규모의 씨족 단위로 살았을 때는, 도움을 필요로 하는 사람이 친척이거나 나중에 은혜를 갚을 수 있는 사람일 수 있었다. 그러므로 타인을 측은히 여기는 것은 결국엔 자신에게 이득이 될 수 있었다. 분명 현대 사회는 서로의 관계가 훨씬 덜 긴밀하다. 그리고, 우리는 자선에 대한 진심 어린 호소를 볼 때, 고통을 겪고 있는 당사자를 결코 만나지 못할 수도 있다. 그러나 측은히 여기는 감정은 여전히 우리 유전자 속에 남아 있다.

●지문분석

Some people believe / that [giving to charity] / is some kind of instinct, / developed because it benefits our species in some way.
일부 사람들은 믿는다 / 자선 단체에 기부하는 것은 / 일종의 본능이라고 / 발달된 왜냐하면 그것이 우리 종을 어떤 식으로 돕기 때문에

At first, this seems like a strange idea: / [Darwin's theories of evolution] / presume / that individuals should act / to preserve their own interests, / not those of the species as a whole.
처음에 이것은 이상한 생각인 것 같다 / 다윈의 진화에 대한 이론들은

/ 가정한다 / 개인들은 행동해야 한다고 / 자신의 이익을 보호하기 위해서 / 종족 전체의 이익이 아니라

But the British evolutionary biologist Richard Dawkins believes / that natural selection has given us / the ability / to feel pity for someone / who is suffering.
하지만 영국의 진화생물학자인 Richard Dawkins는 믿는다 / 자연 선택이 우리에게 준다고 / 능력을 / 누군가를 위해 측은함을 여기는 / 고통 받고 있는

When humans lived in small clan-based groups, / a person in need / would be a relative or someone / who could pay you back a good turn later, / so [taking pity on others] / could benefit you / in the long run.
인간이 작은 씨족 단위로 살았을 때 / 어려운 사람은 / 친척이거나 누군가일 수도 있었다 / 당신에게 나중에 은혜를 갚을 수 있는 / 그래서 다른 사람을 측은해 하는 것은 / 당신에게 유익할 수 있었다 / 결국에는

Modern societies are much less close-knit / and when we see a heartfelt appeal / for charity, / chances are / we may never even meet the person / who is suffering – but [the emotion of pity] / is still in our genes.
현대 사회는 훨씬 덜 긴밀하다 / 그리고 우리가 진심 어린 호소를 볼 때 / 자선에 대한 / 가능성이 있다 / 우리가 결코 그 사람을 만나지 못할 / 고통 받는 / 하지만 측은함이라는 감정은 / 여전히 우리 유전자에 있다

● 해설

6. 다음 빈칸에 들어갈 말로 가장 적절한 것은?

Some people believe that _____ is some kind of instinct, developed because it benefits our species in some way. At first, this seems like a strange idea: Darwin's theories of evolution presume that individuals should act to preserve their own interests, not those of the species as a whole. But the British evolutionary biologist Richard Dawkins believes that natural selection has given us the ability to feel pity for someone who is suffering. When humans lived in small clan-based groups, a person in need would be a relative or someone who could pay you back a good turn later, so taking pity on others could benefit you in the long run. Modern societies are much less close-knit and when we see a heartfelt appeal for charity, chances are we may never even meet the person who is suffering — but the emotion of pity is still in our genes.

① not wanting to suffer 고통받기 원하지 않는 것
▶ 본문에 suffering이 나와서 등장한 선택이야.
❷ giving to charity 자선 단체에 기부하는 것
▶ 남을 돕는 것을 의미하는 건 이것 뿐이야.
③ drawing pity from others 다른 사람으로부터 측은함을 끌어내는 것
▶ 측은함을 끌어내는 것이 아니라 측은함을 느끼는 거지.
④ exploring alternatives 대안을 탐구하는 것
⑤ pursuing individual interests 개인적 이익을 추구하는 것

씨족 단위로 살던 인간이 어려움에 처한 사람을 도울 때, 결국 그 도움이 나중에 자신을 이롭게 한다고 하고 있어. 이러한 것은 오늘날도 인간의 유전자 속에 남아 현대 사회에서도 도움이 필요한 다른 사람들을 돕고 있다는 내용이지. 따라서 빈칸은 '남을 돕는다'라는 내용이 나와야 해. 이게 해당하는 것은 ② giving to charity(자선단체에 기부하는 것)이 되겠지.

● 중요 포인트

동명사 주어
❶ Some people believe that [giving to charity] is some kind of ~
❷ So [taking pity on others] could benefit you ~

7. ⑤

● 전체 해석

우리 세계의 구조와 확실성의 조건이 많은 변화에 무너지면서, 안정적이고 확실한 지도력에 대한 우리의 염원의 범위는 단순히 그것을 찾을 수 없다는 것에 의해 능가되어 왔다. 잘못은 지도력에 있는 것이 아니라 오히려 우리 자신과 우리의 기대에 있다. 옛날에는 지도자들이 혼돈을 이해하고, 불확실함에서 확실성을 만들어 내고, 그리고 모순들을 해결하기 위해 적극적인 실행 계획을 만들어 내야만 했다. 훌륭한 지도자들은 상황을 해결했다. 혼돈이 그 추한 고개를 들면 지도자는 즉시 정상으로 되돌릴 것으로 기대되었다. 그러나 혼돈은 이제 정상으로 여겨지고, 모순들은 해결될 수 없고, 확실성은 가망성이 높은 수준으로만 가능하다. 이것들 중 어느 것이라도 바로 잡으려는 견지에서 이끌어내려고 하는 지도력은 실패할 뿐이다. 그리고 그것이 정확히 일어나고 있는 것이다.

● 지문분석

As [the structures of our world / and the conditions of certainty] / have yielded to an avalanche of change, / [the extent of our longing / for stable, definitive leadership] / has been exceeded / only by the impossibility of finding it.
우리 세상의 구조와 / 확실성의 조건은 / 엄청난 변화에 굴복해오면서 / 우리의 바람의 정도는 / 안정되고 명확한 리더십에 대한 / 초과되어 버렸다 / 오직 그것을 찾을 수 없기에

The fault lies / not with leadership / but rather with ourselves and our expectations.
잘못은 놓여있다 / 리더십이 아니라 / 오히려 우리 자신과 우리의 기대에

In the old days, / leaders were supposed to make sense of chaos, / to make certainty out of doubt, / and to create positive action plans / for the resolution of paradoxes.
옛날에는 / 리더들은 혼돈을 이해해야만 했다 / 의심으로부터 확실성을 만들고 / 그리고 긍정적인 행동 계획을 만들기 위해 / 역설의 해결을 위해서

Good leaders straightened things out.
훌륭한 리더들은 일을 해결했다

Should chaos rear its ugly head, / the leader was expected / to restore normality immediately.
혼돈이 그 추악한 머리를 들면 / 리더는 기대되었다 / 정상을 즉시 회복할 것으로

But chaos is now considered normal, / paradoxes cannot be resolved, / and certainty is possible / only to the level of high probability.

하지만 혼돈은 지금 정상으로 고려되고 / 역설은 해결될 리가 없고 / 그리고 확실성은 가능하다 / 높은 가능성의 정도로만

[Leadership / that attempts to deliver / in terms of fixing any of these] / can only fail.

리더십은 / 전달하려고 노력하는 / 이러한 것을 고치려는 점에서 / 실패할 뿐이다

And that is exactly what is happening.

그리고 그것은 정확하게 벌어지고 있는 일이다

●해설

7. 다음 빈칸에 들어갈 말로 가장 적절한 것은?

As the structures of our world and the conditions of certainty have yielded to an avalanche of change, the extent of our longing for stable, definitive leadership _____. The fault lies not with leadership but rather with ourselves and our expectations. In the old days, leaders were supposed to make sense of chaos, to make certainty out of doubt, and to create positive action plans for the resolution of paradoxes. Good leaders straightened things out. Should chaos rear its ugly head, the leader was expected to restore normality immediately.

But chaos is now considered normal, paradoxes cannot be resolved, and certainty is possible only to the level of high probability. Leadership that attempts to deliver in terms of fixing any of these can only fail. And that is exactly what is happening.

① can only be measured by our will to establish it 그것을 확립하기 위한 우리의 의지에 의해서만 평가될 수 있다
▶ 원래부터 우리의 의지와는 상관이 없었지.

② has made traditional leadership more irreplaceable 전통적인 지도력을 더 대체할 수 없도록 만들었다
▶ 대체할 수 없다는 것은 전통적인 지도력이 지금도 유효하다는 거지?

③ can create viable action plans for restoring normality 정상으로 되돌리기 위한 실행 가능한 행동 계획을 만들 수 있다
▶ 이걸 이제는 못한다고 하고 있어.

④ has vastly reduced the probability of resolving paradoxes 모순들이 해결될 가능성을 상당히 감소시켰다
▶ 지금은 '해결'이 주된 목적이 아니지.

❺ has been exceeded only by the impossibility of finding it 단순히 그것 (지도력)을 찾을 수 없다는 것에 의해 능가되어 왔다
▶ 이제는 문제를 해결하는 지도력이 중요한 것이 아니지.

옛날 지도자들은 모든 것을 해결해야하는 절대자 같은 역할을 했었지. 그런데, 이제는 혼돈이 정상으로 여겨지고 모순들도 해결될 수 없으며, 확실성은 높은 가망성 수준으로만 가능하므로 이러한 것들을 바로 잡으려고 하는 지도력은 실패할 뿐이라고 하고 있어. 따라서 빈칸에 들어갈 가장 적절한 말은 ⑤ has been exceeded only by the impossibility of finding it(단순히 그것(→ 지도력)을 찾을 수 없다는 것에 의해 능가되어 왔다)이라고 할 수 있겠지.

● 중요 포인트

that절의 수식을 받는 주어

[Leadership that attempts to deliver in terms of fixing any of these] can only fail.

8. ⑤

● 전체 해석

다른 분야에서의 일탈과는 달리 스포츠에서의 일탈은 종종 규범과 기대에 대한 아무런 의심 없는 수용과 극단적인 순응을 수반한다. 예를 들어, 대부분의 북아메리카 사람들은 미식축구 경기에 참여하는 것을 적극적 활동으로 간주한다. 젊은 사람들은 미식축구 선수로서 자신의 최고의 모습을 보이고, "팀에 '나'라는 존재는 없다"라는 말과 같은 슬로건으로 살아가도록 격려 받는다. 그들은 체중과 힘을 증가시켜서 좀 더 효과적으로 경기를 하고 팀의 성공에 기여하라고 격려 받는다. 젊은 사람들이 좀 더 몸집이 커지고 힘이 세어지리라는 기대를 지나칠 정도로 수용하게 될 때, 그들이 경기장에서 미식축구 경기를 하는 것과 기술을 향상시키는 것에 지나칠 정도로 전념하여 근육을 형성하는 약물을 복용하게 될 때, 그들은 일탈하게 된다. 이러한 유형의 '과잉 행동 일탈'은 위험한 것이지만, 그것은 일반적으로 받아들여지는 규칙과 기대를 거부하는 소외된 젊은 사람들에 의해 이루어지는 '반사회적 일탈'에서 발생하는 역학과는 완전히 다른 사회적 역학에 근거한다.

● 지문분석

Unlike deviance in other settings, / [deviance in sports] / often involves an unquestioned acceptance of / and extreme conformity / to norms and expectations.

다른 환경에서의 일탈과는 달리 / 스포츠에서의 일탈은 / 종종 의심 없는 수용을 수반한다 / 그리고 극단적인 순응을 / 규범과 기대에 대한

For example, most North Americans / see / playing football / as a positive activity.

예를 들어 대부분의 북미 사람들은 / 본다 / 미식축구 경기를 하는 것을 / 긍정적(적극적) 활동으로

Young men are encouraged / to 'be all they can be' / as football players / and to live by slogans / such as "There is no 'I' in t-e-a-m."

젊은 사람들은 격려 받는다 / 그들이 될 수 있는 모든 것이 되라고 / 미식축구 선수로서 / 그리고 슬로건에 의해 살아가도록 / 팀에는 나라는 존재는 없다와 같은

They are encouraged / to increase their weight and strength, / so that they can play more effectively / and contribute to the success of their teams.

그들은 격려 받는다 / 그들의 무게와 힘을 증가시키라는 / 그래서 그들은 더 효과적으로 경기할 수 있다 / 그리고 팀의 승리에 기여할 수 있다

When young men go too far / in their acceptance of expectations / to become bigger and stronger, / when they are so committed / to playing football / and improving
——so-that 용법

their skills on the field / that they use muscle-building drugs, / they become deviant.

젊은 사람들이 너무 멀리 갈 때 / 기대에 대한 수용에 / 더 크고 더 강해지라는 / 그들이 너무 전념해서 / 미식축구 경기에 / 그리고 경기장에서 그들의 기술을 개선시키는 것에 / 그래서 그들이 근육을 형성하는 약물을 사용하게 될 때 / 그들은 일탈하게 된다

This type of 'overdoing-it-deviance' / is dangerous, / but it is grounded in completely different social dynamics / from the dynamics / that occur in the 'antisocial deviance' / enacted by alienated young people / who reject commonly accepted rules and expectations.

이러한 종류의 과잉 행동 일탈은 / 위험하다 / 하지만 그것은 완전히 다른 사회적 역학에 근거를 둔다 / 역학과는 / 반사회적 일탈에서 발생하는 / 소외된 젊은 사람에 의해서 행해지는 / 일반적으로 받아들여지는 규범과 기대를 거부하는

● 해설

8. 다음 빈칸에 들어갈 말로 가장 적절한 것은?

Unlike deviance in other settings, deviance in sports often involves _____ norms and expectations. For example, most North Americans see playing football as a positive activity. Young men are encouraged to 'be all they can be' as football players and to live by slogans such as "There is no 'I' in t-e-a-m." They are encouraged to increase their weight and strength, so that they can play more effectively and contribute to the success of their teams. When young men go too far in their acceptance of expectations to become bigger and stronger, when they are so committed to playing football and improving their skills on the field that they use muscle-building drugs, they become deviant. This type of 'overdoing-it-deviance' is dangerous, but it is grounded in completely different social dynamics from the dynamics that occur in the 'antisocial deviance' enacted by alienated young people who reject commonly accepted rules and expectations.

① a disciplined control of the desire to avoid ~를 피하려는 바람에 대한 단련된 통제
▶ 피하는 것이 아니라 그것을 따르는 거지.
② wasted efforts and resources in establishing ~를 형성함에 있어서 낭비된 노력과 자원
▶ 낭비라는 의미는 언급이 되지 않았지.
③ ambitious attempts to get independent of and free from ~에서 독립되고 자유로워지려는 야심찬 시도
▶ 벗어나는 것이 아니라 그것에 종속되고 있지.
④ a traditional approach of matching slogans and mottos with 슬로건과 표어에 맞추는 전통적인 접근 방법
▶ 전통적이라는 의미 역시 언급되지 않았어.
❺ an unquestioned acceptance of and extreme conformity to ~에 대한 극단적인 수용과 의심없이 수용
▶ 나보다 팀을 위해서 규범과 기대에 종속되고 있지.

다른 분야와는 다르게 스포츠에서는 기대에 대한 반응으로 벌어지는 일탈행위를 미식축구 선수의 약물 복용을 사례로 설명하고 있어. 즉, 자신에게 쏟아지는 기대와 전체를 위한다는 일종의 규범에 철저하게 종속

되다보니 이런 일이 벌어지고 있다고 하고 있지. 따라서 빈칸에 들어갈 가장 적절한 말은 ⑤ an unquestioned acceptance of and extreme conformity to(~에 대한 극단적인 수용과 의심없이 수용)라고 할 수 있겠지.

● 중요 포인트

연속된 수식 구문

This type of 'overdoing-it-deviance' / is dangerous, / but it is grounded in completely different social dynamics / from the dynamics / that occur in the 'antisocial deviance' / enacted by alienated young people / who reject commonly accepted rules and expectations.

4 단계 혼공 개념 마무리 p.131

1. 예를 들어, 1990년대 후반의 미국의 건설 경기가 호황일 때, 심지어 "전통적인 백인 남성의 요새, 부러움을 사는 조합증이 아버지에서 아들로 전수되는 세계"로 오랫동안 알려져 있던 목수 조합조차도 여자, 흑인, 히스패닉이 인턴 프로그램에 참여하는 것을 공개적으로 장려하기 시작했다.

2. 마호가니와 티크를 포함하여 많은 종의 나무들이 이제 멸종 위기에 놓여 있고, 특히, 열대 우림의 삼림 벌채는 지역 사회뿐만 아니라 토착 식물과 야생 동물에도 심각한 영향을 미쳤다.

3. 공간 추리능력의 상승은 테스트를 받는 동안 사람들의 정신활동을 기민하게 하는 모든 청각 자극(예를 들어, 짧은 이야기나 그와는 다른 형태의 음악을 듣는 것)에 의해 생길 수 있음이 밝혀지고 있다.

4. 이러한 유형의 '과잉 행동 일탈'은 위험한 것이지만, 그것은 일반적으로 받아들여지는 규칙과 기대를 거부하는 소외된 젊은 사람들에 의해 이루어지는 '반사회적 일탈'에서 발생하는 역학과는 완전히 다른 사회적 역학에 근거한다.

5. 우리 세계의 구조와 확실성의 조건이 많은 변화에 무너지면서, 안정적이고 확실한 지도력에 대한 우리의 염원의 범위는 단순히 그것을 찾을 수 없다는 것에 의해 능가되어 왔다.

6. 분명 현대 사회는 서로의 관계가 훨씬 덜 긴밀하다. 그리고, 우리는 자선에 대한 진심 어린 호소를 볼 때, 고통을 겪고 있는 당사자를 결코 만나지 못할 수도 있다. 그러나 측은히 여기는 감정은 여전히 우리 유전자 속에 남아 있다.

3 단계 **고난도 문항** 요리하기   p.137

●정답

> **1.** ④ **2.** ② **3.** ④ **4.** ④ **5.** ③ **6.** ① **7.** ① **8.** ⑤

1. ④

●전체 해석

연구원들은 대학생 자원자들에게 판타지 형태의 경험(높은 굽이 달린 신발을 신고 멋있어 보이거나, 에세이 콘테스트에서 우승을 하거나, 시험에서 A학점을 받는 것)을 하는 생각을 하라고 요청하고 나서, 판타지가 실험 대상자와 현실에서 어떻게 일이 전개되는가에 끼친 영향에 대해 평가했다. 참여자들이 가장 긍정적인 결과를 상상했을 때, 혈압으로 측정한 그들의 에너지 수준은 떨어졌고, 그들은 보다 현실적이거나 심지어 부정적인 모습을 떠올렸던 사람보다 실제 사건에서 더 나쁜 경험을 했다고 보고했다. 실험 대상자들의 실생활 경험을 평가하기 위해, 연구원들은 실험 대상자들 스스로가 설정했던 목표들의 목록과 그들이 실제로 성취했던 것을 비교하였고, 또한 자기 보고서에 의존했다. "우리가 그것에 대해 환상을 가질 때, 특히 (여러분이 아주 긍정적인 것에 환상을 가질 때), 그것은 거의 실제로 그것(환상한 것)을 경험하는 것과 같다"라고 그 연구의 공동 저자 중 한 명이 말했다. 그것은 마음을 속여서 목표가 달성되었다고 생각하게 만들고, '그것을 추구하고 달성할 열정이 생길' 동기를 소진시킨다고 그녀는 설명한다. 실험 대상자들은 장애물을 무시하는 대신 극복할 방법을 상상하면서 더 나아질 수 있다.

●지문분석

Researchers asked college student volunteers / to think through a fantasy version of an experience / (looking attractive / in a pair of high-heeled shoes, / winning an essay contest, / or getting an A on a test) / and then evaluated the fantasy's effect / on the subjects / and on how things unfolded in reality.
연구원들은 대학생 지원자들에게 요구했다 / 판타지 형태의 경험을 생각해보라고 / 매력적이게 보이거나 / 높은 힐의 신발을 신고 / 에세이 대회에서 우승하거나 / 아니면 시험에서 A를 받는 것을 / 그러고 나서 판타지의 영향을 평가했다 / 실험 대상자에 대한 / 그리고 어떻게 일이 현실에서 펼쳐졌는지에 대한

When participants envisioned the most positive outcome, / [their energy levels, / as measured by blood pressure,] / dropped, / and they reported / having a worse experience / with the actual event / than those / who had conjured more realistic or even negative visions.
참가자들은 가장 긍정적인 결과를 상상했을 때 / 그들의 에너지 수준은 / 혈압에 의해서 측정되어질 때 / 떨어졌다 / 그리고 그들은 보고했다 / 더 나쁜 경험을 했다고 / 실제 사건에 대해서 / 사람들보다 / 더 현실적이거나 심지어 부정적인 모습을 생각했던

To assess subjects' real life experiences, / the researchers compared lists of goals / that subjects had set for themselves / against what they had actually accomplished / and also relied on self-reports.
실험 참가자의 실제 인생 경험을 평가하기 위해서 / 연구원들은 목표 목록을 비교했다 / 실험 참가자가 스스로 세웠던 / 그들이 실제로 성취했던 것과 / 그리고 또한 자기 보고서에 의존했다

"When we fantasize about it / – especially when you fantasize something very positive / – it's almost like / you are actually living it," / says one of the study's co-authors.
우리가 그것에 대해서 환상을 가질 때 / 특히 우리가 매우 긍정적인 것에 대한 환상을 가질 때 / 그것은 거의 같다 / 그것을 살아가는 것과 / 그 연구의 공동 저자 중 한명이 말한다

That tricks the mind / into thinking / the goal has been achieved, / draining the incentive / to "get energized to go and get it," / she explains.
그것은 마음을 속인다 / 생각하도록 / 목표가 달성되었다고 / 동기를 소진시킨다 / 그것을 추구하고 달성할 에너지가 생길 / 그녀가 설명한다

Subjects may be better off imagining / how to surmount obstacles / instead of ignoring them.
실험 대상자들은 상상하며 더 나아질 수 있다 / 장애물을 극복하는 방법을 / 그것들을 무시하는 것 대신에

●해설

1. 다음 빈칸에 들어갈 말로 가장 적절한 것은?

Researchers asked college student volunteers to think through a fantasy version of an experience (looking attractive in a pair of high-heeled shoes, winning an essay contest, or getting an A on a test) and then evaluated the fantasy's effect on the subjects and on how things unfolded in reality. When participants envisioned the most positive outcome, their energy levels, as measured by blood pressure, dropped, and they reported having a worse experience with the actual event than those who had conjured more realistic or even negative visions. To assess subjects' real life experiences, the researchers compared lists of goals that subjects had set for themselves against what they had actually accomplished and also relied on self-reports. "When we fantasize about it – especially when you fantasize something very positive – it's almost like you are actually living it," says one of the study's co-authors. That _____, draining the incentive to "get energized to go and get it," she explains. Subjects may be better off imagining how to surmount obstacles instead of ignoring them.

① prompts you into assessing the real life as it is 여러분이 실제 삶을 있는 그대로 평가하도록 촉구한다

② turns a rosy dream into an actual accomplishment 장밋빛 희망을 실제의 성취로 변화시킨다
▶ 오히려 반대의 결과가 나왔지.

③ renders your goal independent of the fantasy world 환상의 세계와는 별개인 여러분의 목표를 만들어 준다

▶ 아니. 현실에서는 악영향을 끼쳤어.
❹ tricks the mind into thinking the goal has been achieved 마음을 속여서 목표가 달성되었다고 생각하게 만든다
▶ 그래서 에너지를 소모하도록 만들지.
⑤ deceives your mind into believing obstacles are insurmountable 장애물은 극복할 수 없는 것이라고 여러분의 마음을 속여서 믿게 한다
▶ 극복할 수 있다고 믿게 만들어서 에너지를 소모시키도록 하지.

환상적이고 아주 긍정적인 것을 상상했던 사람들이 현실적이거나 부정적인 것을 상상했던 사람들보다 현실의 사건에서 더 나쁜 경험을 한다는 실험 결과가 나온다고 하고 있어. 빈칸의 결과로 목표를 추구하고 달성할 열정이 생길 동기를 소진시킨다고 하고 있으니, 빈칸은 그 원인이 나와야 하겠어. 따라서 빈칸에는 ④ tricks the mind into thinking the goal has been achieved(마음을 속여서 목표가 달성되었다고 생각하게 만든다)가 가장 적절해.

● 중요 포인트

멀리 떨어져 있는 병렬구조
To assess subjects' real life experiences, / the researchers compared lists of goals / that subjects had set for themselves / against what they had actually accomplished / and also relied on self-reports.
관계사절이 들어가 있음
❶
❷

2. ②

● 전체 해석

시간적 해상도는 위성의 원격 감지의 맥락에서 특히 흥미롭다. 원격으로 감지된 사진의 시간적인 밀도는 크고, 인상적이고, 성장하고 있다. 여러분이 이 문장을 읽을 때에도 위성들은 많은 양의 사진을 모으고 있다. 그렇지만, 지리학과 환경 과학 분야에서의 대부분의 응용 프로그램들은 극단적으로 결이 고운 시간적 해상도를 필요로 하지 않는다. 기상학자들은 눈에 보이는, 적외선, 레이더 정보를 한 시간 이내의 주기로 찍은 시간적 해상도로 필요로 할 것이다. 그리고 도시 계획자들은 한 달에 한 번 혹은 일년에 한 번씩 찍는 해상도의 사진을 필요로 할 것이다. 그리고 교통 계획자들은 어떤 응용 프로그램을 위해서는 어떤 시간적 시차를 두는 일련의 정보를 전혀 필요로 하지 않을 수도 있다. 거기에다가, 사용되는 사진의 시간적 해상도는 여러분이 탐구하는 것의 필요를 충족시켜야 한다. 때로 연구자들은 수집된 위성 사진들보다 앞서는 과거의 정보를 얻기 위해서 항공 사진의 기록 보관소를 뒤져야만 한다.

● 지문분석

Temporal resolution is particularly interesting / in the context of satellite remote sensing.
시간적 해상도는 특히 흥미롭다 / 위성의 원격 감지라는 맥락에서
[The temporal density / of remotely sensed imagery] / is large, impressive, and growing.
S   V
시간적 밀도는 / 원격으로 감지된 이미지의 / 크고 인상적이고 성장하고 있다
Satellites are collecting a great deal of imagery / as you read this sentence.
위성은 엄청난 양의 이미지를 모으고 있다 / 당신이 이 문장을

읽고 있을 때
However, [most applications / in geography and environmental studies] / do not require extremely fine-grained temporal resolution.
                S
하지만, 대부분의 응용 프로그램들은 / 지리학과 환경 과학 분야의 연구에서 / 엄청나게 결이 고운 시간 해상도를 필요로 하지 않는다
Meteorologists may require visible, infrared, and radar information / at sub-hourly temporal resolution; / urban planners might require imagery / at monthly or annual resolution; / and transportation planners may not need any time series information at all / for some applications.
기상학자들은 눈에 보이는, 적외선의 레이더 정보를 원할지도 모른다 / 한 시간 이내로 찍은 시간 해상도로 / 도시 계획자들은 이미지를 요구할 지도 모른다 / 한 달에 한 번, 또는 일년에 한 번 찍은 해상도를 / 그리고 교통 계획자들은 어떤 시간적 연속 정보를 전혀 필요하지 않을지도 모른다 / 어떤 응용 프로그램을 위해서
Again, the temporal resolution / of imagery used / should meet the requirements of your inquiry.
                        S   V
거기다가 시간 해상도는 / 사용된 이미지의 / 당신의 탐구의 요구를 맞춰야만 한다
Sometimes researchers have to search / archives of aerial photographs / to get information from that past / that pre-date the collection of satellite imagery.
때때로 연구원들은 조사해야 한다 / 항공 사진 보관소를 / 과거로부터의 정보를 얻기 위해서 / 위성 사진의 수집보다 앞서는

● 해설

2. 다음 빈칸에 들어갈 말로 가장 적절한 것은?
Temporal resolution is particularly interesting in the context of satellite remote sensing. The temporal density of remotely sensed imagery is large, impressive, and growing. Satellites are collecting a great deal of imagery as you read this sentence. However, most applications in geography and environmental studies do not require extremely fine-grained temporal resolution. Meteorologists may require visible, infrared, and radar information at sub-hourly temporal resolution; urban planners might require imagery at monthly or annual resolution; and transportation planners may not need any time series information at all for some applications. Again, the temporal resolution of imagery used should _____ _____. Sometimes researchers have to search archives of aerial photographs to get information from that past that pre-date the collection of satellite imagery.

① be selected for general purposes 일반적인 목적을 위해 선택되어야
▶ 일반적인 목적이 아니라 특정한 목적이지.
❷ meet the requirements of your inquiry 여러분이 탐구하는 것의 필요를 충족시켜야
▶ 앞의 예에서 경우에 따른 다양한 종류의 해상도가 필요하다고 하고 있지.
③ be as high as possible for any occasion 어떤 경우든 가능한 한 높아야
▶ 쓰이는 용도에 따라 다른 해상도가 필요하다고 하고 있어.

④ be applied to new technology by experts 전문가에 의해 신기술에 적용되어야
▶ 신기술은 언급이 안 되고 있지.
⑤ rely exclusively upon satellite information 오직 위성의 정보에만 의존해야
▶ 위성에만 의존한다는 것은 언급되고 있지 않아. '위성'이라는 것이 나와서 만든 오답지야.

중간에 나오는 예시에서 다양한 경우에 따라 다른 해상도가 필요하다고 하고 있어. 빈칸도 역시 이런 내용이 나와야 해. 따라서 ② meet the requirements of your inquiry(여러분이 탐구하는 것의 필요를 충족시켜야)가 가장 적절하지.

● 중요 포인트

명사 전치사 명사 뒤에 오는 관계사절
「명사 + 전치사 + 명사」 뒤에 오는 관계사절이 어떤 명사를 수식하는지 주의해야 해. 해석은 필수지.
Sometimes researchers have to search / archives of aerial photographs / to get information from that past / that pre-date the collection of satellite imagery.

3. ④

● 전체 해석

Belding 지역의 다람쥐들에게 있어서, 수컷은 집을 떠나고 암컷은 자기가 태어난 곳에서 자란다. 수컷에 치우쳐 있는 확산은, 수컷과 암컷이 그들 주변에 있는 개체들과 맺는 관계의 면에서 불균형을 만들어낸다. 즉 암컷은 자신들 주변에 친척들로 둘러싸여 있게 되고, 반면 수컷은 일반적으로 완전히 다른 낯선 자들과 함께 있게 된다. 이러한 불균형은 다음과 같이 해석된다 – 경고 소리를 냄으로써 가까운 친족에게 경고를 하는 암컷과, 태어난 곳으로부터 멀리 떨어져 있어서 그들의 혈연이 그러한 경고 소리로 혜택을 얻지 못하기 때문에 수컷은 일반적으로 경고 소리를 내지 않는다. 친족에 기반을 둔 경고소리 가설에 대한 추가적 지지는 Sherman의 발견, 즉 암컷들이 태어난 그룹으로부터 벗어나서 친척들이 거의 없는 그룹으로 이동해가는 희귀한 경우라면, 그 암컷들은 원래의 암컷들보다 경고소리를 덜 빈번하게 낼 것이다.

● 지문분석

In Belding's ground squirrels, / males leave home / and females mature in their natal area.
벨딩 지역의 다람쥐들에게서 / 수컷은 집을 떠나고 / 암컷은 그들이 태어난 곳에서 자란다
This male-biased dispersal / creates an imbalance in the way / males and females are related / to those individuals / around them / – females find themselves surrounded by relatives, / while males are generally in areas / with complete strangers.
이러한 수컷에 치우친 확산은 / 방식에서의 불균형을 만든다 / 수컷과 암컷이 관련하는 / 그러한 개개인들에 / 그들 주변의 / 암컷은 자신들이 친척에 둘러싸여 있음을 깨닫는다 / 반면에 수컷은 일반적으로 지역에 있다 / 완전히 낯선 이들과

This asymmetry / translates into females / who warn close kin / by emitting alarm calls, / while males generally do not emit calls / since [their dispersal / from their natal areas] / means / their blood kin typically do not benefit / from such a warning.
이러한 불균형은 / 암컷에게 전달된다 / 가까운 친족에게 경고하는 / 경고음을 냄으로써 / 반면에 수컷은 일반적으로 그런 소리를 내지 않는다 / 왜냐하면 그들의 확산이 / 그들의 자란 지역으로부터의 / 의미하기 때문에 / 그들의 친족은 전형적으로 혜택을 얻지 않는다는 것을 / 그런 경고음으로부터
[Further support / for the kinship-based alarm-calling hypothesis] / includes Sherman's finding / that in the rare instances / when females do move away from their natal groups / and into groups with far fewer relatives, / they emit alarm calls less frequently / than do native females.
추가적 지지는 / 친족 기반의 경고음 가설에 대한 / Sherman의 발견을 포함한다 / 드문 경우에 / 암컷이 그들이 태어난 그룹에게서 떨어지고 / 친척들이 거의 없는 곳으로 갈 때 / 그들은 경고음을 덜 빈번하게 낸다는 / 원래의 암컷들이 하는 것보다

● 해설

3. 다음 빈칸에 들어갈 말로 가장 적절한 것은?
In Belding's ground squirrels, males leave home and females mature in their natal area. This male-biased dispersal creates an imbalance in the way males and females are related to those individuals around them – females find themselves surrounded by relatives, while males are generally in areas with complete strangers. This asymmetry translates into females who warn close kin by emitting alarm calls, while males generally do not emit calls since their dispersal from their natal areas means their blood kin typically do not benefit from such a warning. Further support for the kinship-based alarm-calling hypothesis includes Sherman's finding that in the rare instances when females do move away from their natal groups and into groups with far fewer relatives, they _____.

① end up acquiring the alarm calls of the new group 결국 새로운 그룹의 경고 소리를 얻게 된다
▶ 새로운 그룹에 친척이 없으니까 별로 없겠지.
② make constant attempts to bring their blood kin along 그들의 친족을 데려오려고 지속적으로 노력한다
▶ 데리고 온다는 내용은 나오지 않고 있어.
③ display a tendency to become more active and cooperative 보다 적극적이고 협동적이 되려는 경향을 보여준다
▶ 경고음에 대한 내용이므로 상관없는 이야기야.
❹ emit alarm calls less frequently than do native females 원래의 암컷들보다 덜 빈번히 경고음을 낸다
▶ 친족이 없으니 경고음이 줄어들겠지.
⑤ adopt a more elaborate defense mechanism than alarm calls 경고음보다 더 정교한 방어 기재를 채택한다
▶ 다른 방어 기재는 언급조차 되지 않았어.

암컷들이 경고음을 내는 이유는 주변에 자신들의 친족이 있기 때문이

지. 수컷들은 주변에 친족이 없어서 경고음을 내지 않고 있어. 따라서 암컷이라도 주변에 친족이 없으면 경고음을 내지 않겠지. 빈칸에 들어가기에 가장 적절한 것은 ④ emit alarm calls less frequently than do native females(원래의 암컷들보다 덜 빈번히 경고음을 낸다)야.

● 중요 포인트

주어와 동사 사이에 전치사구가 있는 경우

while males generally do not emit calls / since [their dispersal / from their natal areas] / means ~
S 전치사구 V

4. ④

● 전체 해석

원주민 문화의 한 가지 놀랄만한 측면은, 태어날 때 부족의 구성원들이 영혼과 정체성이 자연의 일부라고 여기는 'totemism'이다. 지구와 지구의 풍요로움을 자기 자신의 고유한 일부분이라는 이 관점이 환경을 잘못 다루는 것을 막아준다. 왜냐하면 이것은 오직 자아 파괴에 해당하기 때문이다. 토템은 물체 이상의 것이다. 토템은 영적인 의식, 구전되는 역사, 그리고 과거 영혼의 여행 경로의 기록이 다른 사람들과 교환되고 신화로 전환되는 의식을 벌이는 공간의 구성을 포함한다. 주된 동기는 부족 신화의 보존과 자연속에서 모든 개인의 기원을 강화하고 공유하는 것이다. 원주민들은 그들의 조상의 기원과 연결시켜주는 토템의 위계, 그들을 지구와 함께 한 지점에 그들을 두는 우주론, 그리고 생태학적 균형을 존중하는 행동 양식을 통해 환경과 그들의 관계를 하나의 조화로운 연속체로 여긴다.

● 지문분석

[One remarkable aspect / of aboriginal culture] / is the
S V
concept of "totemism," / where [the tribal member at
S
birth] / assumes / the soul and identity / of a part of nature.
V
한 가지 놀라운 측면은 / 원주민 문화의 / 토테미즘의 개념이다 / 이곳에서 부족의 구성원은 태어날 때 / 추정한다 / 영혼과 정체성이 / 자연의 부분이라고

[This view / of the earth and its riches / as an intrinsic
S
part of oneself] / clearly rules out mistreatment of the
V
environment / because this would only constitute a
destruction of self.
이러한 관점은 / 지구와 그것의 부유함을 / 자신의 내적 부분이라는 / 명확하게 환경을 잘못 다루는 것을 배제한다 / 왜냐하면 이것은 오직 자아의 파괴를 구성하기 때문이다

Totems are more than objects.
토템은 대상 이상의 것이다

They include / spiritual rituals, oral histories, and the
organization of ceremonial lodges / where [records of the
past travel routes of the soul] / can be exchanged with
V
others / and converted to mythology.
그것들은 포함한다 / 영적인 의식, 구전 역사, 그리고 의식의 공간 구성을 / 과거 영혼의 여행 경로의 기록들이 / 다른 사람들과 교환되고 / 신화로 전환될 수 있는

The primary motivation / is the preservation of tribal
myths / and a consolidation and sharing / of every
individual's origins in nature.
주요한 동기는 / 부족 신화의 보존이다 / 그리고 강화와 공유이다 / 모든 개인의 자연속에서의 기원의

The aborigines see their relationship to the environment /
as a single harmonious continuum, / through a hierarchy
of totems / that connect to their ancestral origins, / a
cosmology / that places them at one with the earth, / and
behavior patterns / that respect ecological balance.
원주민들은 그들의 환경과의 관계를 본다 / 하나의 조화로운 연속체로 / 토템의 위계를 통해서 / 그들의 조상의 기원과 연결하는 / 우주론으로 / 그들은 지구와 함께 한 지점에 놓는 / 그리고 행동 패턴으로 / 생태학적 균형을 존중하는

● 해설

4. 다음 빈칸에 들어갈 말로 가장 적절한 것은?
One remarkable aspect of aboriginal culture is the concept of "totemism," where the tribal member at birth assumes the soul and identity of a part of nature. This view of the earth and its riches as an intrinsic part of oneself clearly rules out mistreatment of the environment because this would only constitute a destruction of self. Totems are more than objects. They include spiritual rituals, oral histories, and the organization of ceremonial lodges where records of the past travel routes of the soul can be exchanged with others and converted to mythology. The primary motivation is the preservation of tribal myths and a consolidation and sharing of every individual's origins in nature. The aborigines see ＿＿＿＿＿＿＿＿＿＿＿, through a hierarchy of totems that connect to their ancestral origins, a cosmology that places them at one with the earth, and behavior patterns that respect ecological balance.

① themselves as incompatible with nature and her riches 그들 자신을 자연과 자연의 부유함과 양립하지 못하는 것으로
▶ 이미 앞에서 한부분이라고 언급하고 있어.

② their mythology as a primary motive toward individualism 그들의 신화를 주된 개인주의의 동기로
▶ 개인주의는 언급되지 않고 있지.

③ their identity as being self-contained from surrounding nature 그들의 정체성을 주변 환경과는 독립적인 존재로
▶ 독립적이기 보다는 서로의 일부로 보고 있어.

❹ their relationship to the environment as a single harmonious continuum 환경과의 관계를 하나의 조화로운 연속체로
▶ 하나의 일부로 보고 있으므로 조화로운 관계가 맞지.

⑤ their communal rituals as a gateway to distancing themselves from their origins 그들의 공동의 의식을 그들의 기원으로부터 자신을 멀어지게 하는 통로로서
▶ 하나의 일부이므로 멀어지는 것이 아니라 가까워져야 하겠지.

원주민 자신이 지구와 지구의 풍요로움을 자기 자신의 타고난 일부분이라 여기고 자연을 잘못 대하는 것을 피한다고 하고 있어. 즉 자연과 자신을 가까운 존재로 보고 있는 거지. 따라서 빈칸에 들어갈 가장 적절한

것은 ④ their relationship to the environment as a single harmonious continuum(환경과의 관계를 하나의 조화로운 연속체로)이겠지.

● 중요 포인트

수식을 받는 병렬구조

The aborigines see their relationship to the environment / as a single harmonious continuum, / through a hierarchy of totems / that connect to their ancestral origins, / a cosmology / that places them at one with the earth, / and behavior patterns / that respect ecological balance.

5. ③

● 전체 해석

최근 연구는, 약 400,000년 전에 살았던 네안데르탈인과 현대 인간들의 공통 조상이 이미 상당히 정교한 언어를 사용하고 있었을 것이라고 시사하고 있다. 만약 언어가 유전자에 근간을 두고 있고 문화적 진화의 핵심이라면, 왜 네안데르탈인의 도구는 거의 문화적 변화를 보여주지 않고 있었나? 게다가 유전자가 의심할 바 없이 200,000년 전 이후 인간 혁명 동안에 변화를 해 왔으나, 새로운 습관(문화)의 원인으로서 보다는 새로운 습관에 대한 반응으로서 더 변화를 해왔다. 초창기에, 요리는 더 작은 창자와 입에 맞추어 돌연변화를 선택했다(그 거꾸로라기 보다는). 나중에, 우유 마시기는 서유럽과 동아프리카 후손들의 성인기에 락토스 소화를 유지하기 위한 변화를 선택했다. 문화적 말이 유전적 마차 앞에 온다.('말 앞에 마차를 두지 마라'라는 속담 비유) 진화를 이끄는 유전적 변화에 대한 호소는 유전자-문화 상호진화의 역행을 가져온다: 즉 상향식의 과정에 대해 하향식의 설명을 하는 것이 되어 버린다.

● 지문분석

Recent evidence suggests / that [the common ancestor of Neanderthals and modern people,] / living about 400,000 years ago, may have already been using pretty sophisticated language.
최근 연구는 시사한다 / 네안데르탈인과 현대 인류의 공통 조상은 / 40만년 전에 살았던 / 벌써 아주 정교한 언어를 상용하고 있었을 것이라고

If language is based on genes / and is the key / to cultural evolution, / and Neanderthals had language, / then why did the Neanderthal toolkit show / so little cultural change?
언어가 유전자에 기반을 두고 / 핵심이라면 / 문화적 진화의 / 그리고 네안데르탈인이 언어를 가지고 있다면 / 그러면 왜 네안데르탈인의 도구는 보여주었나 / 그렇게나 적은 문화적 변화를

Moreover, genes would undoubtedly have changed / during the human revolution / after 200,000 years ago, / but more in response to new habits / than as causes of them.
게다가 유전자는 의심할 여지없이 변해왔을 수도 있다 / 인간의 혁명기간 동안에 / 20만년 전 이후 / 하지만 새로운 습관의 반응으로서

더 많이 / 그것들의 원인으로서 보다는

At an earlier date, / cooking selected mutations / for smaller guts and mouths, / rather than vice versa.
초창기에 / 요리는 변화를 선택했다 / 더 작은 내장과 입에 맞게 / 거꾸로 라기보다는

At a later date, / milk drinking selected for mutations / for retaining lactose digestion / into adulthood in people of western European and East African descent.
나중에 / 우유 마시기는 변화를 선택했다 / 락토스 소화를 유지하기 위한 / 서유럽과 동아프리카 후손들의 성인기에

The cultural horse comes before the genetic cart.
문화적 말은 유전자적 마차 앞에 온다

[The appeal to a genetic change / driving evolution] / gets gene-culture co-evolution backwards: / it is a top-down explanation / for a bottom-up process.
유전적 변화에 대한 호소는 / 진화를 이끄는 / 유전자-문화의 상호진화를 후퇴시킨다 / 그것은 하향식 설명이다 / 상향식 과정에 대한

● 해설

5. 다음 빈칸에 들어갈 말로 가장 적절한 것은?
Recent evidence suggests that the common ancestor of Neanderthals and modern people, living about 400,000 years ago, may have already been using pretty sophisticated language. If language is based on genes and is the key to cultural evolution, and Neanderthals had language, then why did the Neanderthal toolkit show so little cultural change? Moreover, genes would undoubtedly have changed during the human revolution after 200,000 years ago, but more in response to new habits than as causes of them. At an earlier date, cooking selected mutations for smaller guts and mouths, rather than vice versa. At a later date, milk drinking selected for mutations for retaining lactose digestion into adulthood in people of western European and East African descent. _____. The appeal to a genetic change driving evolution gets gene-culture co-evolution backwards: it is a top-down explanation for a bottom-up process.

① Genetic evolution is the mother of new habits 유전자적 진화는 새로운 습관의 어머니다
▶ 새로운 습관은 문화적 진화로 인한거라고 하고 있다.
② Every gene is the architect of its own mutation 모든 유전자는 자신의 변화의 건축가이다
▶ 유전자를 문화의 변화를 뒤따른다고 하고 있어.
❸ The cultural horse comes before the genetic cart 문화적 말이 유전자적 마차 앞에 온다
▶ 문화적 변화가 유전자적 변화를 이끌었다고 하고 있어.
④ The linguistic shovel paves the way for a cultural road 언어적 삽이 문화적 길을 위한 길을 낸다
▶ 언어와 문화는 언급이 되었지만, 언어를 문화의 한 요소로 보고 있지.
⑤ When the cultural cat is away, the genetic mice will play 문화 고양이가 떠날 때 유전자 쥐가 놀 것이다
▶ 문화와 유전자가 서로 적대적인 관계는 아니지.

유전자가 인간 발달에 도움을 주었지만, 새로운 습관(문화)로 인해서 변해왔다고 하고 있어. 즉 유전자가 문화에 종속된다는 이야기지. 따라서 빈칸에 들어가기에 적절한 것은 ③ The cultural horse comes before the genetic cart(문화적 말이 유전자적 마차 앞에 온다)가 되겠지.

● 중요 포인트

전치사와 분사의 수식을 받는 주어
[the common ancestor of Neanderthals and modern
       S
people,] / living about 400,000 years ago, may have
already been using ~
                V

6. ①

● 전체 해석

슬픔은 불유쾌하다. 그렇다면 그것이 완전히 없는 상태라면 더 행복하지 않을까? 손해를 보는 것이 확실한데도 왜 그것을 받아들이는가? 아마도 우리는 스피노자가 후회에 대해 이야기한 말, 즉 누구든지 그것을 느끼는 자는 '두 배 불행하거나 두 배 무기력하다'는 말을 그것에 대해 이야기해야 할 것이다. Laurence Thomas는 '부정적인 감정'(없으면 우리가 더 행복할 것이라고 믿을 이유가 있어 보이는 감정들인 슬픔, 죄책감, 분개함, 분노와 같은 감정들)의 유용성이 그것들이 사랑과 존경심과 같은 그런 성향적인 감정에 대한 일종의 진실성을 보장해 준다는 점에서 찾을 수 있다는 것을 암시했다. 그 어떤 현재 일어나고 있는 사랑과 존경의 감정도 사랑하거나 존경하는 것이 사실인 그 기간 동안 줄곧 존재할 필요는 없다(존재할 수는 없다). 그러므로 때때로 현재 일어나고 있는 긍정적인 감정이 없는 상태에서 더 이상 사랑하지 않는다고 의심을 하게 될 것이다. 그러한 때에, 슬픔과 같은 부정적인 감정이 사랑과 존경심의 진실성에 대한 일종의 증거를 제공한다.

● 지문분석

> Grief is unpleasant.
> 슬픔은 유쾌하지 않다
> Would one not then be better off / without it altogether?
> 그러면 사람은 더 행복하지 않을까 / 그것이 완전히 없다면
> Why accept it / even when the loss is real?
> 왜 그것을 받아들일까 / 심지어 그 상실이 실제일 때 조차도
> Perhaps we should say of it / what Spinoza said of regret:
> / that [whoever feels it] / is "twice unhappy or twice
>   S   V
> helpless."
> 아마도 우리는 그것에 대해서 이야기 해야 한다 / 스피노자가 후회에 대해서 한 말 / 즉 그것을 느끼는 누구든지 / 두 배 덜 행복하거나 두 배 무기력하다는 말을
> Laurence Thomas has suggested / that [the utility of
>   S
> "negative sentiments" / (emotions like grief, guilt,
> resentment, and anger, which there is seemingly a reason
> / to believe / we might be better off without)] / lies in their
>   V
> providing / a kind of guarantee of authenticity / for such
> dispositional sentiments / as love and respect.
> 로렌스 토마스는 암시했다 / 부정적 감정의 유용성은 / 슬픔, 죄책감, 분개, 분노와 같은 감정들 / 외형적으로 이유인 / 믿을 / 우리가

없다면 더 좋을 수 있는 / 그들의 제공에 있다고 / 일종의 진실성의 보장을 / 기질적인 감정에 대한 / 사랑과 존경 같은
> [No occurrent feelings / of love and respect] / need to be
>   S   V
> present / throughout the period / in which it is true / that
> one loves or respects.
> 어떠한 현재 일어나고 있는 감정들은 / 사랑과 존경이라는 / 존재할 필요가 없다 / 기간 내내 / 사실인 / 사람이 사랑하고 존경하는 것이
> One might therefore sometimes suspect, / in the absence
> of the positive occurrent feelings, / that one no longer
> loves.
> 사람은 그래서 때때로 의심할지도 모른다 / 현재 일어나는 긍정적인 감정의 결여 상태에서 / 사람은 더 이상 사랑하지 않음을
> At such times, / [negative emotions / like grief] / offer a
> kind of testimonial / to the authenticity of love or respect.
> 그런 시기에 / 부정적 감정들은 / 슬픔과 같은 / 일종의 증거를 제공한다 / 사랑과 존중의 진실성에 대한

● 해설

6. 다음 빈칸에 들어갈 말로 가장 적절한 것은?
Grief is unpleasant. Would one not then be better off without it altogether? Why accept it even when the loss is real? Perhaps we should say of it what Spinoza said of regret: that whoever feels it is "twice unhappy or twice helpless." Laurence Thomas has suggested that the utility of "negative sentiments" (emotions like grief, guilt, resentment, and anger, which there is seemingly a reason to believe we might be better off without) lies in their providing a kind of guarantee of authenticity for such dispositional sentiments as love and respect. No occurrent feelings of love and respect need to be present throughout the period in which it is true that one loves or respects. One might therefore sometimes suspect, in the absence of the positive occurrent feelings, that _____. At such times, negative emotions like grief offer a kind of testimonial to the authenticity of love or respect.

❶ one no longer loves 더 이상 사랑하지 않는다고
▶ 현재 일어나는 긍정적인 감정이 없으므로 '사랑'의 감정이 없다고 의심하게 되는 거지.
② one is much happier 훨씬 더 행복하다고
▶ 긍정적인 감정이 없는데 행복하지는 않지.
③ an emotional loss can never be real 감정적 손실은 결코 실제일 수 없다고
▶ 앞에 loss(손실)가 나와서 나온 오답지로, 이미 감정적 손실은 긍정적 감정이 없기에 존재하고 있지.
④ respect for oneself can be guaranteed 자신에 대한 존경이 보장될 수 있다고
▶ 앞에 suspect(의심하다)가 나오니 뒤에는 부정적인 내용이 나와야겠지.
⑤ negative sentiments do not hold any longer 부정적인 감정이 더 이상 유지되지 않는다고
▶ 마찬가지로 부정적인 내용이 아니지.

사랑과 존경과 같은 긍정적인 감정의 진실성을 확인해 주는 데서 슬픔,

죄책감, 분개함, 분노와 같은 부정적인 감정의 유용성을 찾을 수 있다는 내용의 글이야. 즉, 부정적 감정은 긍정적 감정이 존재한다는 것을 알려주는 일종의 역설적 상태라는 거지. 따라서 빈칸에서는 긍정적 감정이 없는 상태에서는 그것의 존재여부를 의심하게 되는 거지. 그리고 동사 suspect(의심하다)의 성격으로 봐서 뒤에는 부정적인 내용이 나와야 해. 따라서 빈칸에 들어가기에 가장 적절한 것은 ① one no longer loves(더 이상 사랑하지 않는다고)가 되겠지.

● 중요 포인트

주어와 동사 사이에 긴 부분이 들어간 경우
Laurence Thomas has suggested / that [the utility of "negative sentiments" / (emotions like grief, guilt, resentment, and anger, / which there is seemingly a reason / to believe / we might be better off without)] / lies in ~

7. ①

● 전체 해석

어떤 이야기가 북쪽 대양에서 생태상 펭귄의 위치를 차지했던 흑백의 대형 바닷새인 큰바다쇠오리의 이야기보다 더 가혹할 수 있을까? 그 새의 이야기는 그리스 비극처럼 융성하고 쇠퇴하는데, 거의 모두 사라질 때까지 섬의 개채군은 인간에 의해 잔인하게 죽임을 당했다. 그러고 나서 진짜 마지막 집단이 한 특별한 섬, 사납고 예측할 수 없는 해류에 의해 인간의 파괴로부터 보호를 받았던 것(섬)에서 안전을 찾아냈다. 이런 바다는 완벽하게 적응하여 바다 여행에 알맞은 새에게는 아무 문제도 일으키지 않았지만, 사람들에게는 어떤 종류의 안전한 상륙도 하지 못하게 했다. 몇 년을 비교적 안전하게 지낸 뒤에 다른 종류의 재난이 큰바다쇠오리에게 타격을 주었다. 화산 활동은 그 섬 피난처가 완전히 바다 속에 가라앉게 했고 살아남은 개체들은 하는 수 없이 다른 곳으로 피난해야 했다. 그것들이 선택한 새로운 섬 서식지에는 하나의 끔찍한 측면에서 옛것의 이점들이 없었다. 인간들이 비교적 쉽게 그것(그 서식지)에 접근할 수 있었고, 인간들은 실제로 그렇게 했다! 단지 몇 년 이내에 이 한때 많았던 종의 가련한 마지막 나머지가 완전히 제거되었다.

● 지문분석

What story could be harsher / than that of the Great Auk, /
story
the large black-and-white seabird / that in northern oceans took the ecological place of a penguin?
어떤 이야기가 더 가혹할까 / 큰바다쇠오리의 그것(이야기)보다 / 커다란 흑백의 대형 바닷새인 / 북쪽 대양에서 생태상 펭귄의 위치를 점유했던

Its tale rises and falls like a Greek tragedy, / with island populations savagely destroyed / by humans / until almost
└ with + 명사 + 분사 → 동시상황
all were gone.
그것의 이야기는 그리스 비극처럼 융성하고 쇠퇴한다 / 섬의 개체군이 야만적으로 파괴되면서 / 인간들에 의해서 / 거의 모두가 사라질 때까지

Then the very last colony found safety / on a special island, / one / protected from the destruction of humankind
island

/ by vicious and unpredictable ocean currents.
그러고 나서 바로 마지막 군체는 안전을 찾았다 / 특별한 섬에서 / 섬인 / 인간의 파괴로부터 보호된 / 사납고 예측할 수 없는 대양의 조류에 의해서

These waters presented no problem / to perfectly adapted seagoing birds, / but they prevented humans / from making any kind of safe landing.
이러한 바다는 어떠한 문제도 일으키지 않았다 / 완벽하게 적응한 바다 여행에 적합한 새들에게 / 하지만 그들은 인간을 방해했다 / 어떠한 안전한 상륙을 하지 못하게

After enjoying a few years of comparative safety, / [disaster of a different kind] / struck the Great Auk.
몇 년을 상대적으로 안전하게 보낸 후에 / 다른 종류의 재앙이 / 큰바다쇠오리에게 닥쳤다

Volcanic activity caused / the island refuge to sink completely / beneath the waves, / and surviving individuals were forced to find shelter elsewhere.
화산 활동은 유발했다 / 섬의 피난처가 완전하게 잠기도록 / 바다 아래로 / 그리고 살아남은 개체들은 다른 안식처를 찾아야만 했다

[The new island home / they chose] / lacked the benefits of the old / in one terrible way.
새로운 섬 서식지는 / 그들이 선택한 / 예전 섬의 혜택이 부족했다 / 끔찍한 방식으로

Humans could access it / with comparative ease, / and they did!
인간들은 그 섬에 접근할 수 있었다 / 비교적 쉽게 / 그리고 그들은 해냈다

Within just a few years / [the last of this once-plentiful
S
species] / was entirely eliminated.
단지 몇 년 안에 / 한 때 많았던 종의 나머지가 / 완전히 제거되었다

● 해설

7. 다음 빈칸에 들어갈 말로 가장 적절한 것은?
What story could be harsher than that of the Great Auk, the large black-and-white seabird that in northern oceans took the ecological place of a penguin? Its tale rises and falls like a Greek tragedy, with island populations savagely destroyed by humans until almost all were gone. Then the very last colony found safety on a special island, one protected from the destruction of humankind by vicious and unpredictable ocean currents. These waters presented no problem to perfectly adapted seagoing birds, but they prevented humans from making any kind of safe landing. After enjoying a few years of comparative safety, disaster of a different kind struck the Great Auk. Volcanic activity caused the island refuge to sink completely beneath the waves, and surviving individuals were forced to find shelter elsewhere. The new island home they chose _____ in one terrible way. Humans could access it with comparative ease, and they did! Within just a few years the last of this once-plentiful species was

entirely eliminated.

❶ lacked the benefits of the old 예전의 이점들이 부족했다
▶ 예전에는 인간이 접근하지 못했는데, 이제는 접근이 가능하지.
② denied other colonies easy access 다른 군체들의 쉬운 접근을 허락하지 않았다
▶ 뒤에 보면 인간이 접근하기 쉬웠지.
③ faced unexpected natural disasters 예상치 못한 자연 재해에 직면했다
▶ 자연 재해가 아니라 인간들이 왔어.
④ caused conflicts among the refugees 피해온 자들 사이에서 갈등을 유발했다
▶ 내부갈등이 아닌 인간들이 왔어.
⑤ had a similar disadvantage to the last island 지난번 섬에서와 유사한 단점을 가졌다
▶ 지난번 섬과는 다른 단점(인간의 접근이 쉬움)이 생겼지.

빈칸 뒤에 전개되는 과정을 보면 그 전 섬에서 접근하지 못했던 인간들에게 접근을 허용했다는 내용이 나오지. 그것은 큰바다쇠오리에게는 큰 재앙이었어. 따라서 그 전 섬이 가지고 있었던 최대 장점(인간들의 접근 불허)이 사라지게 되는거야. 빈칸에 가장 적절한 것은 ① lacked the benefits of the old(예전의 이점들이 부족했다)가 맞아.

● 중요 포인트

with + 명사 + 분사: 동사상황 설명

Its tale rises and falls like a Greek tragedy, with island
populations savagely destroyed by humans until ~
with + 명사 + 분사 → 동사상황: 섬의 군체들이 잔인하게 파괴되었다

8. ⑤

● 전체 해석

낯선 거리에서 길을 잃은 사람은 지역 주민으로부터 방향을 묻는 것을 종종 피한다. 우리는 지도와 나침반으로 참고 견딘다. 길을 잃었다고 인정하는 것은 어리석음을 인정하는 것처럼 느껴진다. 이것은 고정관념이지만, 많은 진실을 갖고 있다. 인문 과학에서 간과되는 커다란 문제에 대한 좋은 비유이기도 하다. 우리는 인간 본성의 어두운 대륙에서 길을 찾으려고 노력하고 있다. 우리 과학자들은 나머지 인류를 위해 버스를 운전하는 여행 가이드로서 돈을 받고 있다. 그들은 우리가 인간 마음에서의 길을 알고 있을 거라고 기대하지만, 우리는 모른다. 따라서 우리는 지역 주민들에게 방향을 묻지 않고, 아는 체 하려고 노력한다. 우리는 지리('이론')라는 첫 번째 원리로 그리고 우리 자신이 만든 지도('경험적인 조사')로 길을 찾으려고 한다. 길가는 지역 주민들로 붐비고, 그들의 두뇌는 지역의 지식으로 가득하지만, 우리는 길을 묻기에는 너무 거만하고 당황스럽다. 그래서 우리는 관광객들을 즐겁게 하고 계몽할 멋진 경치를 어디에서 찾을지에 관해서 연속적인 가설을 만들고 버리면서 원을 그리며 주행한다.

● 지문분석

[Guys / lost on unfamiliar streets] / often avoid asking for directions from locals.
사람들은 / 낯선 거리에서 길을 잃은 / 종종 지역 주민으로부터 방향을 묻는 것을 피한다

We try to tough it out / with map and compass.
우리는 그것을 참으려고 노력한다 / 지도와 나침반을 가지고

[Admitting being lost] / feels like admitting stupidity.
길을 잃었다는 것을 인정하는 것은 / 멍청함을 인정하는 것 같다고 느껴진다

This is a stereotype, / but it has a large grain of truth.
이것은 고정관념이다 / 하지만 그것은 많은 진실을 가진다

It's also a good metaphor / for a big overlooked problem / in the human sciences.
그것은 또한 좋은 비유이다 / 간과되는 커다란 문제를 위한 / 인문 과학에서

We're trying to find our way / around the dark continent of human nature.
우리는 우리의 길을 찾으려고 노력하고 있다 / 인간 본성의 어두운 대륙에서

We scientists are being paid / to be the bus-driving tour guides / for the rest of humanity.
우리 과학자들은 돈을 받고 있다 / 버스를 운전하는 여행가이드로서 / 인류의 나머지를 위해서

They expect us / to know our way / around the human mind, / but we don't.
그들은 우리에게 기대한다 / 우리의 길을 알기를 / 인간의 마음 주변에서 / 하지만 우리는 그렇지 않다

So we try to fake it, / without asking the locals for directions.
그래서 우리는 그것을 속이려고 노력한다 / 지역 주민들에게 방향을 묻지 않고

We try to find our way / from first principles of geography ('theory'), / and from maps of our own making ('empirical research').
우리는 우리의 길을 찾으려고 노력한다 / 첫 번째 지리학의 원리에서부터(이론) / 그리고 우리 자신의 만든 지도로부터 (경험적 조사)

The roadside is crowded with locals, / and their brains are crowded with local knowledge, / but we are too arrogant and embarrassed / to ask the way.
길가는 지역 주민들로 붐빈다 / 그리고 그들의 두뇌는 지역의 지식으로 가득하다 / 하지만 우리는 너무 거만하고 당황스러워서 / 그 길을 묻지 않는다

So we drive around in circles, / inventing and rejecting successive hypotheses / about where to find the scenic vistas / that would entertain and enlighten the tourists.
그래서 우리는 원을 그리며 주행한다 / 연속적인 가설을 만들고 거부하면서 / 멋진 경치를 어디서 찾을지에 대해서 / 관광객들을 즐겁게 하고 계몽할

● 해설

8. 다음 빈칸에 들어갈 말로 가장 적절한 것은?
Guys lost on unfamiliar streets often avoid asking for directions from locals. We try to tough it out with map and compass. Admitting being lost feels like admitting stupidity. This is a stereotype, but it has a large grain of truth. It's also a good

metaphor for a big overlooked problem in the human sciences. We're trying to find our way around the dark continent of human nature. We scientists are being paid to be the bus-driving tour guides for the rest of humanity. They expect us to know our way around the human mind, but we don't. So we try to fake it, without asking the locals for directions. We try to find our way from first principles of geography ('theory'), and from maps of our own making ('empirical research'). The roadside is crowded with locals, and their brains are crowded with local knowledge, but we are too arrogant and embarrassed to ask the way. So we drive around in circles, _____ about where to find the scenic vistas that would entertain and enlighten the tourists.

① waiting for the local brains to inquire 묻기 위하여 지역 지식인들을 기다리면서
▶ 묻지 않는다고 앞에서 이야기 하고 있지.
② accumulating and examining the locals' knowledge 지역 주민들의 지식을 축적하고 조사하면서
▶ 지역 주민에게 묻지도 않고, 그들에 대해서 알아보려하지도 않고 있지.
③ going against the findings of our empirical research 우리의 경험적인 조사의 결과를 반대하면서
▶ '반대'라는 의미는 어색하지.
④ relying on passengers' knowledge and experience 승객의 지식과 경험에 의존하면서
▶ 승객은 다른 인류인데, 그들에게 물어보지는 않겠지.
❺ inventing and rejecting successive hypotheses 연속적인 가설을 만들고 버리는
▶ 지역주민에게 물어보지도 않고 자기 스스로가 계속해서 지도와 나침반을 들고 다니고 있으니 이것과 비슷하다고 할 수 있겠지.

과학자들은 길을 알지 못한 채 버스에 태운 사람들을 인도하는 여행 가이드와 같지. 즉, 과학자는 다른 사람들(지역 주민)에게 지식(길)을 구하지 않고 자신들의 가설(지도)을 만들고 버리면서 제자리를 맴돌고 있다는 내용이 되어야 하므로, ⑤ inventing and rejecting successive hypotheses(연속적인 가설을 만들고 버리는)가 적절해.

● 중요 포인트

동명사 주어: 단수 취급

[Admitting being lost] feels like admitting stupidity.
S 동명사 주어   V 단수 동사

④ 혼공 개념 마무리 · p.141

1. 연구원들은 대학생 자원자들에게 판타지 형태의 경험(높은 굽이 달린 신발을 신고 멋있어 보이거나, 에세이 콘테스트에서 우승을 하거나, 시험에서 A학점을 받는 것을 하는 생각을 하라고 요청하고 나서, 판타지가 실험 대상자와 현실에서 어떻게 일이 전개되는가에 끼친 영향에 대해 평가했다.

2. 친족에 기반을 둔 경고 소리 가설에 대한 추가적 지지는 Sherman의 발견, 즉 암컷들이 태어난 그룹으로부터 벗어나서 친척들이 거의 없는 그룹으로 이동해가는 희귀한 경우라면, 그 암컷들은 원래의 암컷들보다 경고 소리를 덜 빈번하게 낼 것이다.

3. 원주민들은 그들의 조상의 기원과 연결시켜주는 토템의 위계, 그들을 지구와 함께 한 지점에 그들을 두는 우주론, 그리고 생태학적 균형을 존중하는 행동 양식을 통해 환경과 그들의 관계를 하나의 조화로운 연속체로 여긴다.

4. Laurence Thomas는 '부정적인 감정'(없으면 우리가 더 행복할 것이라고 믿을 이유가 있어 보이는 감정들인 슬픔, 죄책감, 분개함, 분노와 같은 감정들)의 유용성이 그것들이 사랑과 존경심과 같은 그런 성향적인 감정에 대한 일종의 진실성을 보장해 준다는 점에서 찾을 수 있다는 것을 암시했다.

5. 그래서 우리는 관광객들을 즐겁게 하고 계몽할 과학적인 경치를 어디에서 찾을지에 관해서 연속적인 가설을 만들고 버리면서 원을 그리며 주행한다.

6. 참여자들이 가장 긍정적인 결과를 상상했을 때, 혈압으로 측정한 그들의 에너지 수준은 떨어졌고, 그들은 보다 현실적이거나 심지어 부정적인 모습을 떠올렸던 사람들보다 실제 사건에서 더 나쁜 경험을 했다고 보고했다.

혼공 14일차 승부수 문항 모의고사 1회

1 단계 모의고사 1회 · p.144

● 정답

1. ①	2. ④	3. ⑤	4. ⑤	5. ②
6. ③	7. ③	8. ④	9. ①	10. ②

1. ①

● 전체 해석

우리가 현실적인 지상의 종교를 갖고 수렵·채집인들로 살았을 때, 동물은 최초의 존재이자 세상을 만드는 자이면서 인간을 가르치는 자이자 조상이었다. 본격적으로 농사를 짓게 되고 계절과 궂은 날씨에 대한 정보를 하늘이 주기를 기대했을 때, 우리는 별들 사이에서 동물의 형상을 보았다. 48개의 프톨레마이오스 별자리들 중 몇 개를 제외하고는 모두가 생명체와 관련되어 있고, 25개는 동물의 이름을 따서 지어진 것이다. 17세기에 더 추가된 22개 중에서 19개가 동물 이름이다. 사람들이 하늘의 힘에 호소하기 위해 거대한 지상 구조물을 만들었을 때, 그들은 그것을 동물의 형태로 만들었다. 페루에 있는 몇 개는 길이가 1마일이 넘는다. Ohio에 있는 것은 입에 알을 물고 있는 거대한 뱀의 형상으로 되어 있다.

● 지문분석

When we lived as foragers / with earthbound religions, / animals were the first beings, world-shapers, and the teachers and ancestors of people.
우리가 채집인으로 살았을 때 / 세속적인 종교를 가지고 / 동물들은

최초의 존재였고, 세상을 만드는 자였으며, 그리고 가르치는 자였고 사람의 조상이었다

When we became agriculturalists / and looked to the heavens / for instruction about the seasons and bad weather, / we saw animal forms among the stars.
우리가 농사를 짓게 되었고 / 하늘에 기댔을 때 / 계절과 궂은 날씨에 대한 사용법을 위해서 / 우리는 동물의 형태를 별들 사이에서 보았다

Of the forty-eight Ptolemaic constellations, / all but a few are organic, / and twenty-five are named for animals.
48개의 프톨레마이오스 별자리 중에서 / 몇 개를 제외한 모든 것들은 생명체와 관련된 것이고 / 25개는 동물의 이름을 따서 지어진다

Of the twenty-two more that were added in the 17th century, / nineteen have animal names.
17세기에 추가된 22개 중에서 / 19개는 동물의 이름을 가진다

When people built huge earthworks / to appeal to the powers of heavens, / they built them in animal forms.
사람들이 거대한 지상 구조물을 만들었을 때 / 하늘의 힘에 호소하기 위해서 / 그들은 동물의 형태로 그것들을 만들었다

Some in Peru are over a mile long.
페루에 있는 일부는 1마일이 넘는다

One in Ohio is in the shape of a giant snake / with an egg in its mouth.
오하이오에 있는 하나는 거대한 뱀의 모양이다 / 입에 알을 물고 있는

● 해설

1. 다음 글의 제목으로 가장 적절한 것은?

When we lived as foragers with earthbound religions, animals were the first beings, worldshapers, and the teachers and ancestors of people. When we became agriculturalists and looked to the heavens for instruction about the seasons and bad weather, we saw animal forms among the stars. Of the forty-eight Ptolemaic constellations, all but a few are organic, and twenty-five are named for animals. Of the twenty-two more that were added in the 17th century, nineteen have animal names. When people built huge earthworks to appeal to the powers of heavens, they built them in animal forms. Some in Peru are over a mile long. One in Ohio is in the shape of a giant snake with an egg in its mouth.

❶ Human Fascination with Animal Forms 동물 형태에 대한 인간의 매혹
▶ 언뜻 보면 별자리가 안 나와서 아닌 것 같은데, 결국 동물에 대한 인간의 매혹으로 별자리에까지 이름을 붙이게 되는거지.
② Efforts to Record Disappearing Species 사라지는 종을 기록하려는 노력
③ Origins of the Names of Heavenly Bodies 천체의 이름의 기원
▶ 본문에서 언급이 되기는 했지만, 단순히 동물의 이름을 붙였다는 것이지 기원 자체는 아니야.
④ Influence of Animals on Scientific Progress 동물이 과학 기술의 진보 미친 영향
▶ 과학 기술은 언급이 되지 않았지.
⑤ Historical Background of Astronomical Progress 천문학 발전의 역사적 배경

▶ 천문학이 아닌 별자리의 이름에 관한 내용이지.

이 글은 인간이 동물에게 많은 관심이 있었고 그것이 결국 별자리의 이름에까지 나타났다는 내용이지. ①번의 경우 별자리가 언급이 되지 않았지만, 인간이 동물에게 가진 매혹이 별자리 이름에까지 이르렀으니 제목으로 적당하지.

● 중요 포인트

help 동사의 특징
❶ help는 뒤에 동사원형과 to부정사가 모두 올 수 있어.
Charlie Brown and Blondie help me to start the day ~
= start
❷ 동명사는 다음의 경우에만 올 수 있어.
cannot help ~ing ~하지 않을 수 없다
I cannot help finishing my homework.
나는 내 숙제를 하지 않을 수 없다.

2. ④

● 전체 해석

때때로 완벽주의자들은 무엇을 하든지 결코 만족스럽지 않아 보이기 때문에 자신들이 괴롭다는 것을 알게 된다. 만일 내가 "그것이 누구에게 만족스럽지 않은가?"라고 물으면, 그들은 항상 대답을 아는 것은 아니다. 그것에 대해 생각을 해본 후에 대개 그들은 자신들에게 만족스럽지 못하고, 자신들의 삶 속의 다른 중요한 사람들에게 만족스럽지 못하다는 결론을 내린다. 이것이 중요한 점인데, 왜냐하면 그것은 여러분이 충족시키려고 애쓰고 있을 기준이 실은 여러분 자신의 것이 아닐 수도 있다는 것을 시사하기 때문이다. 대신, 여러분이 자신을 위해 세운 기준이 부모, 사장, 혹은 배우자와 같은 여러분의 삶에서 어떤 중요한 사람의 기준일 수 있다. 다른 누군가의 기대를 추구하며 여러분의 삶을 사는 것은 힘든 삶의 방식이다. 만약 여러분이 세운 기준이 자신의 것이 아니라면, 어쩌면 여러분의 개인적인 기대를 스스로 정하고 자기실현을 여러분의 목표로 삼아야 할 때일 것이다

● 지문분석

Sometimes perfectionists find / that they are troubled / because whatever they do / it never seems good enough.
때때로 완벽주의자들은 발견한다 / 그들이 문제가 있음을 / 그들이 하는 무엇이든지 / 그것은 충분히 좋아 보이지 않기 때문에

If I ask, / "For whom is it not good enough?" / they do not always know the answer.
만일 내가 묻는다면 / 그것이 누구에게 좋지 않으냐 / 그들은 항상 대답을 아는 것은 아니다

After giving it some thought / they usually conclude / that it is not good enough for them / and not good enough for other important people in their lives.
그것에 대해서 생각해 본 후에 / 그들은 보통 결론을 내린다 / 그것은 그들에게 충분히 좋지 않고 / 또한 그들의 삶에 있는 다른 중요한 사람들에게도 좋지 않다는

This is a key point, / because it suggests / that [the standard / you may be struggling to meet] / may not actually be your own.

이것은 중요한 점인데 / 그것이 시사하기 때문이다 / 기준은 / 당신이 맞추려고 애쓰는 / 실제로 당신의 것이 아닐 수도 있다고

Instead, [the standard / you have set for yourself] / may be the standard / of some important person in your life, / such as a parent or a boss or a spouse.

대신에 기준은 / 당신이 당신 스스로를 위해 세운 / 기준일 수도 있다 / 당신의 삶에서 어떤 중요한 사람의 / 부모나, 상사, 아니면 배우자와 같은

[Living your life / in pursuit of someone else's expectations] / is a difficult way to live.

당신의 삶을 사는 것은 / 어떤 다른 누군가의 기대를 추구하며 / 살기 어려운 방식이다

If [the standards / you set] / were not yours, / it may be time / to define your personal expectations for yourself / and make self-fulfillment your goal.

만약 기준이 / 당신이 세운 / 당신의 것이 아니라면 / 때일 것이다 / 당신 자신을 위한 당신 개인적인 기대를 규정할 / 그리고 자기실현을 당신 자신의 목표로 만들어야 할

● 해설

2. (A), (B), (C)의 각 네모 안에서 어법에 맞는 표현으로 가장 적절한 것은?

(A) whatever: because 부사절 안에서 it never seems good enough가 주절이며, 완전한 문장이야. 따라서 불완전한 문장이 와야 하는 what은 올 수가 없지. whatever의 경우 부사절을 이끌 수 있으므로 whatever가 적절해.

(B) meet: the standard가 뒤에 오는 you may be struggling to의 수식을 받고 있으며, 뒤에 동사가 필요하므로 본동사인 meet이 적절해.

(C) Livng: 뒤에 문장의 본동사 is가 나오므로 주어 역할이 가능한 동명사 Living이 적절해.

● 중요 포인트

관계사가 생략된 문장의 수식을 받는 주어

If [the standards / you set] were not yours, it may be time to define your personal expectations for yourself and make self-fulfillment your goal.

which 생략

3. ⑤

● 전체 해석

엔트로피는 무질서와 무작위의 척도이다. 물리학자들은 하나의 명확한 수치 값을 사용하여 누군가로 하여금 어떤 대상의 엔트로피를 설명할 수 있도록 해 주는 전적으로 양적인 정의를 엔트로피에 부여해 왔다. 보다 큰 수치는 보다 큰 엔트로피를, 보다 작은 수치는 보다 작은 엔트로피를 의미한다. 세부 내용은 다소 복잡하지만, 대략적으로 말해서 이 수치는 어떤 특정한 물리적 체계 속에서 그것의 전반적인 외형을 변화시키지 않는 구성 요소의 가능한 재배열의 수를 나타낸다. 당신의 책상이 정돈되고 깨끗한 상태에 있다면, 신문, 책, 혹은 물건들의 순서를 바꾸는 것이나 펜을 홀더에서 이동시키는 것과 같은 거의 어떠한 배열이라도 매우 질서정

연한 이 구성을 뒤엎을 것이다. 이것은 이 책상이 낮은 엔트로피를 가지고 있다는 것을 설명한다. 반면에 당신의 책상이 지저분한 상태에서는 신문과 물건, 쓸데없는 우편물의 무수히 많은 재배열도 이것을 엉망인 상태 그대로 남겨둘 것이고 따라서 이 책상의 전반적인 (지저분한) 외형을 흐트러뜨리지 않을 것이다. 이것은 그 책상이 높은 엔트로피를 가지고 있다는 것을 설명한다.

● 지문분석

Entropy is a measure / of disorder or randomness.
엔트로피는 측정치이다 / 무질서와 무작위의

Physicists have given a fully quantitative definition / to entropy / that allows one to describe something's entropy / by using a definite numerical value: / larger numbers mean greater entropy, / smaller numbers mean less entropy.
물리학자들은 완전한 수량적 정의를 주었다 / 엔트로피에게 / 사람이 무언가의 엔트로피를 설명할 수 있는 / 명확한 수치값을 사용함으로써 / 더 큰 숫자가 더 큰 엔트로피를 의미하고 / 더 작은 숫자가 더 작은 엔트로피를 의미한다

Although the details are a little complicated, / this number, / roughly speaking, / counts the possible rearrangements of the ingredients / in a given physical system / that leave its overall appearance intact.
비록 세부 내용은 약간 복잡하지만 / 이 숫자는 / 대략적으로 말하자면 / 구성 요소의 가능한 재배열의 수를 센다 / 주어진 물리적 시스템에서 / 그것의 전반적인 외형을 온전히 남겨두는

When your desk is neat and clean, / [almost any arrangement / – changing the order of the newspapers, books, or articles, / moving the pens from their holders] / – will upset its highly ordered organization.
여러분의 책상이 정돈되고 깨끗할 때 / 거의 모든 배열은 / 신문이나 책, 물건들의 순서를 바꾸는 것, 펜을 홀더로부터 옮기는 것 / 그것의 매우 정돈된 구성을 뒤엎을 것이다

This accounts for its having low entropy.
이것은 그것 낮은 엔트로피를 가지게 됨을 설명한다

On the contrary, / when your desk is a mess, / [numerous rearrangements] / of the newspapers, articles, and junk mail] / will leave it a mess / and therefore will not disturb its overall look.
반대로 / 여러분의 책상이 엉망일 때 / 많은 재배열은 / 신문과 물건, 우편물의 / 그것을 엉망으로 남겨둘 것이다 / 그래서 그것의 전반적인 모습을 방해하지 않을 것이다

This accounts for its having high entropy.
이것은 그것이 매우 높은 엔트로피를 가지고 있음을 설명한다

● 해설

3. 다음 글의 (A)~(C)에서 문맥에 맞는 낱말을 바르게 짝지은 것은?

(A) quantitative: 바로 뒤에 나오는 문장에서 엔트로피는 무질서를 나타내는 척도로 수치 정보(numerical values)를 사용한다는 내용이 나오므로 '양적인'을 의미하는 quantitative가 적절하지. qualitative는 '질적인'을 의미해.

(B) ingredients: 뒤에 나오는 문장에서 신문, 책, 물건들의 재배열이 나오므로 '구성 요소'를 의미하는 ingredients가 적절하지. concepts는 '개념'을 의미해.

(C) disturb: 어휘 앞에 부정어에 주의해야 해. 지저분한 상태를 그냥 그대로의 지저분한 상태로 두는 것이니 변화는 거의 없다. 따라서 부정어를 넣어서 not disturb(흐뜨러뜨리지 않는다)이 적절하지. maintain은 '유지하다'를 의미해.

● 중요 포인트

삽입으로 인해서 멀어진 주어와 동사

When your desk is neat and clean, [almost any arrangement – changing the order of the newspapers, books, or articles, / moving the pens from their holders] – will upset its highly ordered organization.

4. ⑤

● 전체 해석

사랑은 하나의 사랑의 대상을 향한 것이 아니라, 전체로서의 세계와 한 사람의 관계성을 결정하는 성격의 방향성 즉, 태도이다. 만약 한 사람이 다른 한 사람만을 사랑하고 나머지 다른 사람들에게는 무관심하다면 그의 사랑은 사랑이 아니라 공생적 애착이거나 확대된 자기중심주의이다. 그러나 대부분의 사람들은 사랑은 (사랑하는) 능력이 아니라 그 대상으로 구성된다고 믿는다. 그들이 꼭 찾아야 하는 것은 단지 딱 맞는 대상이고, 그러면 이후 모든 것이 저절로 잘될 것이라고 믿는다. 이러한 태도는 그림을 그리기를 원하지만, 그 기술을 배우는 대신에, 단지 딱 맞는 대상을 기다려야 하며 그것을 발견하게 되면 아름다운 그림을 그리게 될 것이라고 주장하는 사람의 태도에 비유될 수 있다. 만약 내가 진정으로 한 사람을 사랑한다면 나는 모든 사람들을 사랑하는 것이고, 나는 세상을 사랑하는 것이며, 나는 삶을 사랑하는 것이다. 만약 내가 다른 누군가에게, "나는 당신을 사랑합니다."라고 말하면 나는 "나는 당신 안의 모든 이를 사랑하고, 나는 당신을 통해 세상을 사랑하며, 나는 당신 안에 있는 나 자신 또한 사랑합니다."라고 말할 수 있어야 한다.

● 지문분석

Love is an attitude, / an orientation of character / which determines the relatedness of a person to the world / as a whole, / not toward one 'object' of love.
사랑은 태도이다 / 성격의 방향성 / 세계에 대한 사람의 관계성을 결정하는 / 전체로서 / 하나의 사랑의 대상을 향하는 것이 아닌

If a person loves only one other person / and is indifferent to the rest of his fellow men, / his love is not love / but a symbiotic attachment, or an enlarged egotism.
만약 사람이 오직 다른 한 사람만을 사랑한다면 / 그리고 그의 나머지 동료들에게 무관심하다면 / 그의 사랑은 사랑이 아니라 / 공생적인 애착, 혹은 확대된 자기중심주의이다

Yet, most people believe / that love is constituted by the object, / not by the faculty.
하지만, 대부분의 사람들은 믿는다 / 사랑은 대상으로 구성된다고 /

능력이 아니라

They believe / that [all / that is necessary to find] / is the right object / – and that everything goes by itself afterward.
그들은 믿는다 / 모든 것은 / 발견할 필요가 있는 / 올바른 대상이라고 / 그리고 모든 것은 그후에 저절로 잘 된다고

This attitude can be compared / to that of a man / who wants to paint / but who, instead of learning the art, / claims / that he has just to wait for the right object, / and that he will paint beautifully / when finds it.
이러한 태도는 비교될 수 있다 / 사람의 그것과 / 그림을 그리기를 원하는 / 하지만 기술을 배우는 것 대신에 / 주장하는 / 그가 단지 올바른 대상을 기다려야만 한다고 / 그리고 그는 아름답게 그릴 것이라고 / 그가 그것을 발견할 때

If I truly love one person, / I love all persons, / I love the world, / and I love life.
내가 진정으로 한 사람을 사랑한다면 / 나는 모든 사람을 사랑하는 것이다 / 내가 세상을 사랑하는 것이고 / 내가 삶을 사랑하는 것이다

If I can say to somebody else, / "I love you," / I must be able to say, / "I love in you everybody, / I love through you the world, / and I love in you also myself."
내가 다른 누군가에게 말한다면 / 나는 당신을 사랑합니다 라고 / 나는 말할 수 있어야 한다 / 나는 당신 안의 모든 사람을 사랑합니다 / 나는 당신을 통해서 세상을 사랑합니다 / 나는 당신 안에서 내 자신 또한 사랑합니다 라고

● 해설

4. 다음 빈칸에 들어갈 말로 가장 적절한 것은?

Love is an attitude, an orientation of character which _____, not toward one 'object' of love. If a person loves only one other person and is indifferent to the rest of his fellow men, his love is not love but a symbiotic attachment, or an enlarged egotism. Yet, most people believe that love is constituted by the object, not by the faculty. They believe that all that is necessary to find is the right object — and that everything goes by itself afterward. This attitude can be compared to that of a man who wants to paint but who, instead of learning the art, claims that he has just to wait for the right object, and that he will paint beautifully when he finds it. **If I truly love one person, I love all persons, I love the world, and I love life. If I can say to somebody else, "I love you," I must be able to say, "I love in you everybody, I love through you the world, and I love in you also myself."**

① is closely related to intense attachment to oneself 자기 자신에 대한 과도한 애착과 밀접하게 관련된
▶ 자기 자신뿐만 아니라 남들에게로 확장되어야겠지.
② directs one's resentment and anger toward oneself 자기 자신을 향한 사람의 분노로 향하는
▶ 분노가 아니라 애정이겠지.
③ has as its ultimate goal to add variety to a person's life 사람의 삶에

다양성을 더하는 궁극적인 목표로서 가지는
▶ 다양성을 더한다는 것은 약간 추상적이라고 할 수 있겠지.
④ primarily serves to guide an individual toward a specific goal 개개인
을 구체적인 목표로 인도하려고 주로 역할을 하는
▶ 구체적인 목표라고 하기에는 뒤에 나오는 내용과 어울리지 않지.
❺ determines the relatedness of a person to the world as a whole 전
체로서의 세상과 한 사람의 관계성을 결정하는
▶ 뒤에 나오는 전 세계, 다른 사람 모두, 나 자신을 포괄해야 하지.

이 글은 사랑은 하나의 대상에 국한되는 것이 아니라 그 대상을 통한 전
체와의 관계성을 결정하는 태도라고 말하고 있어. 마지막에 나오는 확장
관계에서 이를 확인할 수가 있지. 따라서 빈칸에 들어가기에 가장 적절
한 것은 ⑤ determines the relatedness of a person to the world as a
whole(전체로서의 세상과 한 사람의 관계성을 결정하는)이 되겠지.

● 중요 포인트

관계대명사 2개와 삽입구가 있는 구문
This attitude can be compared / to that of a man / who
wants to paint but who, instead of learning the art,
삽입구
claims that he has just to wait for the right object, and
that he will paint beautifully / when finds it.

5. ②

● 전체 해석

여러분이 프랑스인이라고 상상해 보자. 여러분이 파리의 붐비는 보도를
따라 걷고 있고 또 다른 보행자는 반대 방향에서 다가오고 있다. 여러분
각각이 반대편에서 오는 상대방의 길을 피해 이동하지 않는다면 충돌은
발생할 것이다. 여러분은 어느 길로 걸어가는가? 그 대답은 거의 분명히
오른쪽이다. 그러나 아시아의 많은 지역에서 같은 장면을 재연해보면 여
러분은 아마 왼쪽으로 움직일 것이다. 특정 방향으로 향하라는 지시는 없
다. Mehdi Moussaid는 이것이 확률에 의해 야기된 행동이라고 말한다.
만약 반대 방향에서 오는 두 사람 각각이 한 쪽으로 움직여 다른 사람이
지나가도록 허용하며 서로의 의도를 정확히 추측한다면 그들은 다음에
그들이 충돌을 피해야 할 때 같은 방향으로 움직이는 것을 선택할 가능성
이 높다. 점점 더 많은 사람들이 한쪽 방향으로 이동하는 경향을 채택함
에 따라 성공적으로 몸을 피하는 확률이 그 경향이 받아들여 질 때 까지
증가한다. 그것이 오른쪽이든 왼쪽이든지는 중요한 것이 아니라 중요한
것은 그것이 다수의 암묵적인 의지라는 것이다.

● 지문분석

Imagine that you are French.
여러분이 프랑스인이라고 생각해 보자
You are walking along a busy pavement in Paris / and
another pedestrian is approaching from the opposite
direction.
당신은 파리에서 사람으로 붐비는 보도를 따라 걷고 있다 / 그리고
또 다른 행인이 반대편에서 다가오고 있다
A collision will occur / unless you each move out of the
other's way.
충돌은 발생할 것이다 / 여러분 각자가 상대방의 길에서 피하지 않으면

Which way do you step?
어떤 길로 여러분은 걸어 가는가
The answer is almost certainly to the right.
대답은 거의 확실하게 오른쪽이다
Replay the same scene in many parts of Asia, however, /
and you would probably move to the left.
아시아의 많은 곳에서 같은 장면을 재연해 봐라 하지만 / 그러면 당
신은 아마도 왼쪽으로 움직일 것이다
There is no instruction / to head in a specific direction.
지시는 없다 / 특정 방향으로 향하라는
Mehdi Moussaid says / this is a behavior / brought about
by probabilities.
Mehdi Moussaid는 말한다 / 이것은 행동이라고 / 확률에 의해서 발
생한
If two opposing people guess / each other's intentions
correctly, / each moving to one side / and allowing the
└ 분사구문
other past, / then they are likely to choose to move the
same way / the next time they need to avoid a collision.
두 명의 반대 방향에서 오는 사람이 생각한다면 / 서로의 의도를 정
확하게 / 각각 한 쪽으로 움직이고 / 다른 쪽이 지나가도록 허용하면
서 / 그러면 그들은 같은 방향으로 움직이는 걸 선택할 가능성이 높
다 / 다음에 그들이 충돌을 피할 필요가 있다
[The chance of a successful maneuver] / increases / as
            S   V
more and more people adopt a bias in one direction, / until
the tendency sticks.
성공적인 피하기의 확률은 / 증가한다 / 점점 더 많은 사람들이 한 방
향으로의 선입견을 채택함에 따라 / 그 경향이 받아들여질 때까지
[Whether it's right or left] / does not matter; / [what does]
            S   V
is that it is the unspoken will of the majority.
그것이 오른쪽이냐 왼쪽이냐는 것은 / 중요하지 않다 / 중요한 것
은 그것이 다수의 암묵적인 의지라는 것이다

● 해설

5. 다음 빈칸에 들어갈 말로 가장 적절한 것은?
Imagine that you are French. You are walking along a busy
pavement in Paris and another pedestrian is approaching from
the opposite direction. A collision will occur unless you each
move out of the other's way. Which way do you step? The
answer is almost certainly to the right. Replay the same scene
in many parts of Asia, however, and you would probably
move to the left. There is no instruction to head in a specific
direction. Mehdi Moussaid says this is a behavior brought
about by   (A)   . If two opposing people guess each other's
intentions correctly, each moving to one side and allowing the
other past, then they are likely to choose to move the same way
the next time they need to avoid a collision. The chance of a
successful maneuver increases as more and more people adopt
a bias in one direction, until the tendency sticks. Whether it's
right or left does not matter; what does is that it is the unspoken
will of the   (B)   .

	(A)		(B)	
①	probabilities 확률	……	authority 권위	
❷	probabilities 확률	……	majority 다수	
③	personalities 개성	……	authority 권위	
④	personalities 개성	……	majority 다수	
⑤	efficiencies 효율성	……	conscience 양심	

(A) probabilities: 바로 뒤에 오는 문장에서 서로의 의도를 추측함으로서 피할 확률이 높아지므로 probabilities(확률)이 적절하다.

(B) majority: 점점 더 많은 사람들이 선택하는 쪽으로 몸을 피하는 경향이 짙어지므로, majority(다수)가 적절하다.

● 중요 포인트

whether절 주어

[Whether it's right or left] does not matter; [what does]
　　　　　S → 단수 취급　　　　V → 단수 동사
is that it is the unspoken will of the majority.

6. ③

● 전체 해석

여러분이 지나가는 생각, 감정 또는 기분에 자신이 자극받는다고 느낄 때마다 단순한 선택을 하는데 '구별하기' 또는 '동일시하기'이다. 여러분은 그 생각을 관찰하고 그것을 '구별할' 수 있다. 또는 여러분은 자신을 그 생각에 사로잡히게 둘 수 있는데, 다시 말해서 그것과 '동일시할' 수 있다. 이름을 붙이는 것은 여러분이 동일시하지 않도록 구별하는 것을 도와준다. 여러분이 자신의 지나가는 생각, 감정 그리고 기분을 알아차릴 때, '오, 저것은 나의 오랜 친구 Fear야, 저기 Inner Critic이 가네.'와 같이 그 것들에 이름을 붙이는 것은 그것들이 여러분에게 미치는 영향을 중화시키고 여러분이 자신의 균형과 침착 상태를 유지하도록 돕는다. 내 친구 Donna는 'Freddy Fear', 'Judge Judy' 그리고 'Anger Annie'와 같은 유머러스한 이름을 자신의 감정 반응에 붙이는 것을 좋아하기까지 한다. (덧붙이자면 유머는 여러분이 발코니에서 (연극을 보는 듯한) 관점[객관적 시각]을 되찾는 것을 도와주는 데 훌륭한 협력자가 될 수 있다.) 극 중에서 등장인물에게 이름을 붙이는 순간, 여러분은 그 또는 그녀에게서 자신을 떼어놓게 된다.

● 지문분석

Whenever you feel / yourself triggered by a passing thought, emotion, or sensation, / you have a simple choice: / *to identify* or *get identified.*
여러분이 느낄 때 마다 / 여러분 자신이 지나가는 생각, 감정, 또는 기분에 의해서 자극받는다고 / 여러분은 간단한 선택을 한다 / 구별하기나 혹은 동일시하기

You can observe the thought / and "identify" it.
여러분은 생각을 관찰할 수 있고 / 그것을 구별할 수 있다

Or you can let / yourself get caught up in the thought, / in other words, "get identified" with it.
아니면 여러분은 하게 한다 / 여러분 자신이 생각에 사로잡히게 / 다시 말하자면 그것과 동일시할 수 있다

Naming helps you identify / so that you don't get identified.
이름 붙이기는 여러분이 구별하도록 돕는다 / 여러분이 동일시하지

않도록

As you observe your passing thoughts, emotions, and sensations, / naming them / – *Oh, that is my old friend Fear; / there goes the Inner Critic* / – neutralizes their effect on you / and helps you to maintain your state of balance and calm.
여러분이 여러분의 지나가는 생각, 감정, 그리고 기분을 알아차릴 때 / 이름 붙이기는 / 오 저것은 나의 오랜 친구 Fear야 / 저기 Inner Critic이 가네 / 그들의 당신에 대한 영향력을 중화시킨다 / 그리고 여러분이 여러분의 균형감과 침착 상태를 유지하도록 돕는다

My friend Donna even likes to give humorous names / to her reactive emotions / such as "Freddy Fear," / "Judge Judy," / and "Anger Annie." / (Humor, incidentally, can be a great ally / in helping you regain perspective from the balcony.)
내 친구 Donna는 심지어 유머러스한 이름 붙이기를 좋아한다 / 그녀의 감정 반응에 / Freed Fear / Judge Judy / Anger Annie와 같이 / 유머는 덧붙이자면 엄청난 협력자일 수 있다 / 당신이 발코니에서 관점을 되찾도록 도와줄 때

As soon as you name the character in the play, / you distance yourself from him or her.
여러분이 연극에서 등장 인물에게 이름을 붙이자 마자 / 여러분은 자기 자신을 그 또는 그녀에게서 떨어뜨리게 된다

● 해설

6. 다음 빈칸에 들어갈 말로 가장 적절한 것은?
Whenever you feel yourself triggered by a passing thought, emotion, or sensation, you have a simple choice: *to identify* or *get identified*. You can observe the thought and "identify" it. Or you can let yourself get caught up in the thought, in other words, "get identified" with it. Naming helps you identify so that you don't get identified. As you observe your passing thoughts, emotions, and sensations, naming them – *Oh, that is my old friend Fear; there goes the Inner Critic* – neutralizes their effect on you and helps you to maintain your state of balance and calm. My friend Donna even likes to give humorous names to her reactive emotions such as "Freddy Fear," "Judge Judy," and "Anger Annie." (Humor, incidentally, can be a great ally in helping you regain perspective from the balcony.) As soon as you name the character in the play, you _____.

① cheer on his or her performance 그들의 공연을 응원하다
② adopt him or her as a role model 그 사람을 롤모델로 받아들인다
❸ distance yourself from him or her 그 사람으로부터 자기 자신을 떨어뜨린다
▶ 이름 붙이기의 기능은 중화시키기라는 것을 상기해봐.
④ stop yourself from enjoying the play 여러분 자신이 연극을 즐기는 것을 방해한다
▶ 방해하는 것은 아니지.
⑤ become more emotionally expressive 훨씬 감정적으로 표현하게 된다
▶ 이것과 정반대의 역할을 하게 되지.

이름 붙이기의 기능은 지나가는 생각, 감정, 기분을 중성화시키고, 자신의 균형과 침착 상태를 유지하게 해주지. 또한 유머는 발코니에서 관점, 즉 객관적인 시각을 갖도록 해줘. 이러한 것을 봤을 때, 등장인물로부터 한발자국 떨어지게 만든다는 내용이 나와야 겠지. 따라서 정답은 ③ distance yourself from him or her(그 사람으로부터 자기 자신을 떨어뜨린다)가 적절하겠지.

● 중요 포인트

삽입구가 들어간 주어와 동사

naming them / – *Oh, that is my old friend Fear; there goes the Inner Critic* – neutralizes their effect on you and helps you to maintain your state of balance and calm.

7. ③

● 전체 해석

허용 마케팅은 Seth Godin이 만든 용어이고, 고객이 기관으로부터 온 마케팅 메시지를 받는 데 동의했다는 것을 의미한다. (B) 그럼으로써, 메시지가 기대되고 개인적이고 관련 있기 때문에, 고객은 그 기관에 더 수용적이다. 허용 마케팅의 반대는 끼어들기 마케팅인데, Godin은 이것이 '모두의 손해' 상황을 야기할 수 있다고 주장한다. (C) 끼어들기 마케팅은 고객이 광고용 우편물, 전화, 이메일, 그리고 문자메시지와 같이 요구하지 않은 직접적인 마케팅 메시지를 받을 때 발생한다. Godin은 이것들이 흔히 고객의 시간을 결국 낭비하게 만들고 따라서 불만을 야기한다고 주장한다. (A) 그것들이 흔히 '정크 메일'과 '스팸'이라는 부정적인 용어로 일컬어지는 것은 우연이 아닌데, 왜냐하면 그것들이 환영받지 못하기 때문이다. 너무나 흔하게 그 마지막 결과는 구매 의도가 없는 불만스러워하는 고객과 자신의 예산을 낭비한 마케팅 담당자, '모두의 손해'가 되는 것이다.

● 지문분석

Permission marketing is a term / coined by Seth Godin, / meaning / that the customer has given his or her consent / to receive marketing messages / from an organization.
허용 마케팅은 용어이다 / Seth Godin이 만든 / 의미한다 / 고객이 동의를 했다는 것을 / 마케팅 메시지를 받기 위해서 / 기관으로부터

As such, / the customer is more receptive to the organization / because the messages are anticipated, personal, and relevant.
그럼으로써 / 고객은 기관에 더 수용적이 된다 / 왜냐하면 그 메시지는 기대가 되고, 개인적이며, 관련되어 있기 때문에

[The opposite of permission marketing] / is interruption marketing, / which Godin claims, / can lead to a 'lose-lose' situation.
└ 일종의 삽입
허용 마케팅의 반대는 / 끼어들기 마케팅이다 / Godin이 주장한 / 모두의 손해 상황을 야기할 수 있다고

Interruption marketing occurs / when the customer receives unrequested direct marketing messages, / such as direct mail, telephone calls, e-mails, and text messages.
끼어들기 마케팅은 발생한다 / 고객이 요구하지 않은 직접적인 마케

팅 메시지를 받을 때 / 광고용 우편물, 전화, 이메일, 그리고 문자와 같은

Godin argues / that these things often end up wasting the customer's time / and therefore lead to frustration.
Godin은 주장한다 / 이러한 것들은 종종 고객의 시간을 낭비하게 되며 / 그래서 불만을 야기한다고

It is no coincidence / that they are commonly referred to / in the negative terms 'junk mail' and 'spam,' / because they are unwelcome.
우연은 아니다 / 그것들 공통적으로 일컬어지게 되는 것은 / 부정적인 용어로 정크 메일과 스팸이라는 / 왜냐하면 그것들은 환영받지 못하기 때문에

All too often the final result is a frustrated customer / with no intention of buying / and a marketer / who has wasted his budget 'lose-lose.'
너무나도 종종 마지막 결과는 불만에 찬 고객이다 / 구매 의도가 없는 / 그리고 마케터이다 / 자신의 예산을 낭비한 모두의 손해

● 해설

7. 주어진 글 다음에 이어질 글의 순서로 가장 적절한 것은?
Permission marketing is a term coined by Seth Godin, meaning that the customer has given his or her consent to receive marketing messages from an organization.
(B) As such, the customer is more receptive to the organization because the messages are anticipated, personal, and relevant. The opposite of permission marketing is interruption marketing, which Godin claims, can lead to a 'lose-lose' situation.
(C) Interruption marketing occurs when the customer receives unrequested direct marketing messages, such as direct mail, telephone calls, e-mails, and text messages. Godin argues that these things often end up wasting the customer's time and therefore lead to frustration.
(A) It is no coincidence that they are commonly referred to in the negative terms 'junk mail' and 'spam,' because they are unwelcome. All too often the final result is a frustrated customer with no intention of buying and a marketer who has wasted his budget 'lose-lose.'

허용 마케팅에 대한 소개로 주어진 글 다음에, 허용 마케팅에 대한 부연 설명이 나오는 (B)가 적절하지. (B)의 마지막에 언급되는 끼어들기 마케팅에 대한 설명이 나오는 (C)가 그 다음이 되고, 끼어들기 마케팅의 부정적인 면이 소개되는 (A)가 마지막으로 오게 되겠지.

● 중요 포인트

that절의 주어가 선행사로 나간 경우

❶ Godin claims (that) (interruption marketing) can lead to 〜가 원래 문장이야. that절의 주어인 interruption marketing이 선행사로 나가게 되었고, that도 생략되어서 Godin claims가 can 앞에 있게 되는 거지.

❷ 편하게 생각하려면 Godin claims가 단순하게 삽입되었다고 생각해도 돼.

[The opposite of permission marketing] is interruption marketing, which Godin claims, can lead to a 'lose-lose' situation.
일종의 삽입

8. ④

● 전체 해석

초저주파음은 땅이나 물에서 잘 전해지는 독특한 특징이 있다. 사실, 지진파는 초저주파음의 한 형태라고 여겨질 수 있다. 소리는 공기 중에서보다 땅에서 훨씬 더 빨리 전해지기 때문에, 땅으로 전달되는 진동은, 만약 감지될 수 있다면, 조기 경보 체계의 역할을 하여 똑같은 근원지로부터 공기로 전달되는 소리가 도착하기 훨씬 전에 도달할 수 있다. 초저주파음은 공기 중에서 덜 빠르게 소멸하는데, 그것이 초저주파음을 장거리 소통에 이상적인 것으로 만든다. 그러나 초저주파음의 지각은 몇 가지 특정한 문제를 일으킨다. 파동 사이의 거리보다 작은 물체는 그러한 파동을 잘 수신하지 못한다. 그러므로 초저주파음 수신자는 클 필요가 있으며 초저주파음을 발생시킬 수 있는 큰 동물들에게서 발견되는 경향이 있다. 이것이 아마도 초저주파음 소통이 단지 몇몇 동물들에 의해서만 사용되는 이유일 것이며, 가장 잘 이해되는 초저주파음 소통 체계는 아프리카 코끼리의 것이다.

● 지문분석

Infrasound has the special characteristic / of traveling well in the ground or water; / in fact, [the waves of an earthquake] / can be thought of as a form of infrasound.
초저주파음은 특별한 특징이 있다 / 땅이나 물에서 잘 전해지는 / 사실 지진파는 / 초저주파음의 한 형태로 생각될 수 있다

Because sound travels much faster in ground / than in air, / ground-borne vibrations, / if perceived, / can serve as an early warning system, / arriving well / before [airborne sound from the same source] arrives.
└분사구문
소리는 땅에서 더욱 빠르게 전달되기 때문에 / 공기 중 보다 / 땅에서 전달되는 진동은 / 만약 감지된다면 / 초기 경고 시스템으로 역할을 할 수 있다 / 잘 전달된다 / 같은 근원지에서 나온 공기로 전달되는 소리가 도달하기 전에

Infrasound dissipates less rapidly in air, / making it ideal / for long-distance communication.
└분사구문
초저주파는 공기에서 느리게 소멸한다 / 이는 그것(초저주파)을 이상적으로 만든다 / 장거리 통신에서

[Perception of infrasound,] however, / presents some specific problems.
초저주파의 감지는 하지만 / 약간의 구체적인 문제점을 드러낸다

[An object / smaller than the distance between waves] / is a poor receiver for those waves.
물체는 / 파동들 사이의 거리보다 더 작은 / 그러한 파동을 잘 수신하지 못한다

Thus, infrasonic receivers / need to be large / and tend to be found / on the large animals / able to generate infrasound.
V1   V2

그래서 초저주파음의 수신자는 / 클 필요가 있다 / 그리고 발견되는 경향이 있다 / 큰 동물들에서 / 초저주파를 발생할 수 있는

This is probably the reason / that infrasonic communication is used / by only a few animals, / and the best understood infrasonic communication system / is the African elephants'.
이것은 아마도 이유이다 / 초저주파 통신이 사용되는 / 오직 몇몇 동물에게서만 / 그리고 최고로 잘 이해가 되는 초저주파음 통신 시스템은 / 아프리카 코끼리의 것이다

● 해설

8. 글의 흐름으로 보아, 주어진 문장이 들어가기에 가장 적절한 곳은?
An object smaller than the distance between waves is a poor receiver for those waves. 작은 동물들은 초저주파를 수신하지 못함

Infrasound has the special characteristic of traveling well in the ground or water; in fact, the waves of an earthquake can be thought of as a form of infrasound. (①) Because sound travels much faster in ground than in air, groundborne vibrations, if perceived, can serve as an early warning system, arriving well before airborne sound from the same source arrives. (②) Infrasound dissipates less rapidly in air, making it ideal for longdistance communication. (③) Perception of infrasound, however, presents some specific problems. (④ 초저주파음의 단점이 처음으로 등장하지) Thus, infrasonic receivers need to be large and tend to be found on the large animals able to generate infrasound. (⑤)
커다란 동물들이 초저주파를 잘 받는다고 나오니까, 앞에는 문제점에 해당되는 작은 동물들은 그렇지 않음이 나와야겠지.
This is probably the reason that infrasonic communication is used by only a few animals, and the best understood infrasonic communication system is the African elephants'.

● 중요 포인트

주어를 수식하는 형용사구

[An object smaller than the distance between waves] is ~
S   V

9. ① 10. ②

● 전체 해석

마이크로소프트사의 선임연구원인 Malcolm Slaney와 캠브리지 대학의 교수인 Jason Rentfrow는 서류와 우편물의 물리적인 인쇄물과 그것들이 수반하는 그 모든 정리하기, 분류하기, 찾기 없이 지내는 것을 옹호했다. 컴퓨터에 기반을 둔 디지털 기록 보관소는 저장 공간의 측면에서 더 효율적이고, 검색 측면에서도 일반적으로 더 빠르다.

그러나 우리 중 많은 사람들이 여전히 물리적인 사물을 다루는 것에 대한 무언가가 마음을 달래주고 만족스럽게 해준다고 여긴다. 기억은 다차원적이고, 물건에 대한 우리의 기억은 여러 가지 속성에 기초를 둔다. 물리적 유형의 서류철과의 경험을 떠올려 보라. 여러분은 다른 서류철과는 다르게 생기고, (그 안에 있었던 것이나 위에 쓰여 있던 것과는 완전히 별도로) 그 안에 무엇이 있었는지에 대한 여러분의 기억을 떠올려 주는 오래된 낡은 서류철을 가지고 있었을지 모른다. 물리적인 사물들은 컴퓨터 파일과는 달리 서로 다르게 보이는 경향이 있다. 모든 (컴퓨터) 비트들은

똑같이 만들어진다. 정크 메일을 만드는 당신 컴퓨터 속에 있는 바로 그 똑같은 0들과 1들이 Mahler의 5번 교향곡과 Monet의 수련의 숭고한 아름다움도 만들어낸다. 그 매개물 자체에는 메시지에 대한 단서를 전달해 주는 것이 전혀 없다. 매우 그러하기 때문에, 만약 여러분이 이것들 중 어떤 것의 디지털 표시를 본다면, 여러분은 아마 그 0들과 1들이 텍스트나 혹은 음악이 아닌 이미지를 나타내고 있었다는 것조차도 알지 못할 것이다. 따라서 정보는 의미로부터 분리된다.

● 지문분석

Microsoft senior research fellow Malcolm Slaney and Cambridge University professor Jason Rentfrow / advocated dispensing with physical copies of documents and mail, / and all the filing, sorting, and locating / that they entail.
마이크로소프트사의 선임연구원인 Malcom Slaney와 캠브리지 대학의 교수인 Jason Rentfrow는 / 서류와 메일의 물리적인 복사본들 없이 지내기를 옹호했다 / 그리고 모든 정리하기, 분류하기와 찾기도 / 그들이 수반하는

Compute-based digital archives / are more efficient / in terms of storage space, / and generally quicker / in terms of retrieval.
컴퓨터 기반의 디지털 기록 보관소는 / 보다 더 효율적이다 / 저장 공간 측면에서 / 그리고 일반적으로 더 빠르다 / 검색 측면에서도

But many of us still find / something soothing and satisfying / about handling physical objects.
하지만 우리 중 많은 사람들은 여전히 찾는다 / 마음을 달래주고 만족스러운 무언가를 / 물리적 물건을 다루는 것에 대해서

Memory is multidimensional, / and [our memories for objects] / are based on multiple attributes.
기억은 다차원적이다 / 그리고 물건에 대한 우리의 기억들은 / 다양한 속성에 기초를 둔다

Think back to your experience / with file folders, / the physical kind.
여러분의 기억을 떠올려 봐라 / 파일 폴더에 대한 / 물리적 종류의

You might have had an old beat-up one / that didn't look like the others / and that – quite apart from / what was inside it / or written on it / – evoked your memories / of what was in it.
여러분은 오래된 낡은 파일 폴더를 가지고 있었을지도 모른다 / 다른 것들과 같이 보이지 않았던 / 그리고 아주 다른 / 그 안에 있었던 것과는 / 아니면 그것 위에 쓰여져 있었던 것과는 / 여러분의 기억을 불러일으켰던 / 그 안에 있었던 것의

Physical objects tend to look different from one another / in a way / that computer files don't.
물리적인 물건들은 서로 다르게 보이는 경향이 있다 / 방식에서 / 컴퓨터 파일이 보이는

All bits are created equal.
모든 비트들은 동일하게 만들어 진다

[The same 0s and 1s on your computer / that render junk mail] / also render the magnificent beauty / of Mahler's fifth symphony or Monet's Water Lilies.
여러분의 컴퓨터 속의 같은 0과 1들은 / 정크메일을 만드는 / 역시 엄청난 아름다움을 만든다 / Mahler의 5번 교향곡이나 Monet의 Water Lilies(수련)과 같은

In the medium itself, / there is nothing / that carries a clue to the message.
매개체 자체에서 / 아무것도 없다 / 메시지에 단서를 전달하는

So much so that / if you looked at the digital representation / of any of these, / you would not even know / that those zeros and ones / were representing images / rather than text or music.
매우 그러해서 / 만약 당신이 디지털 표시를 본다면 / 이러한 것 중 어떤 것의 / 당신은 심지어 알지 못할 것이다 / 그러한 0과 1들이 / 이미지들을 나타내고 있다는 것을 / 텍스트나 음악이 아닌

Information has thus become separated / from meaning.
정보는 그래서 분리되어 왔다 / 의미로부터

● 해설

Microsoft senior research fellow Malcolm Slaney and Cambridge University professor Jason Rentfrow advocated dispensing with physical copies of documents and mail, and all the filing, sorting, and locating that they entail. Computerbased digital archives are more efficient in terms of storage space, and generally quicker in terms of retrieval.

But many of us still find something soothing and satisfying about handling physical objects. Memory is multidimensional, and our memories for objects are based on multiple attributes. Think back to your experience with file folders, the physical kind. You might have had an old beatup one that didn't look like the others and that — quite apart from what was inside it or written on it — evoked your memories of what was in it. Physical objects tend to look different from one another in a way that computer files don't. All bits are created equal. The same 0s and 1s on your computer that render junk mail also render the magnificent beauty of Mahler's fifth symphony or Monet's Water Lilies. In the medium itself, there is nothing that _____. So much so that if you looked at the digital representation of any of these, you would not even know that those zeros and ones were representing images rather than text or music. Information has thus become separated from meaning.

9. 윗 글의 제목으로 가장 적절한 것은?
❶ Why We Still Keep Physical Files 왜 우리는 물리적 파일을 여전히 보관하나
▶ 디지털 시대지만, 여전히 물리적 파일들을 다루는 이유에 대해서 이야기하고 있지.

② Digital Culture: Understanding New Media 디지털 문화 : 새로운 미디어 이해하기
▶ 디지털 문화가 아닌 물리적 파일을 가지는 것에 대해서 이야기하고 있어.

③ Create Unlimited Space for Your Memories 여러분의 기억을 위한 무제한적인 공간을 만들어라
▶ 기억에 대한 글이 아니지.

④ Digital Tools Are a Communication Wizard! 디지털 도구는 통신 마법사이다
▶ 디지털 도구는 현재의 상황일 뿐 핵심은 아니야.
⑤ Challenges of Early Adopters in the Digital Age 디지털 시대에서 얼리어답터의 어려움
▶ 얼리 어답터는 언급조차 되지 않았지.

10. 윗글의 빈칸에 들어갈 말로 가장 적절한 것은?
① represents the digital signals 디지털 신호를 나타내는
▶ 0과 1은 그 자체가 디지털 신호이지.
❷ carries a clue to the message 메시지에 단서를 전달하는
▶ 0과 1은 그것이 전달하는 것이 무엇인지 알려주지 않지.
③ offers userfriendly environments 사용자 친화적인 환경을 제공하는
▶ 사용자 친화적인 것과는 상관없어.
④ makes information accessible to all 모두에게 이용 가능한 정보를 만드는
▶ 정보의 공정성과는 상관없는 내용이지.
⑤ suppresses your memory from the past 과거로부터 당신의 기억을 억누르는
▶ 기억을 억누르는 것이 아니라, 그것이 무엇인지 모르고 있지.

● 중요 포인트

주어와 동사 사이에 전치사구와 관계사절이 들어간 경우

[The same 0s and 1s on your computer that render junk
                          전치사구
mail] also render the magnificent beauty of Mahler's
fifth symphony or Monet's Water Lilies.

● 혼공 개념 마무리 p.149

1. 그것에 대해 생각을 해본 후에 대개 그들은 자신들에게 만족스럽지 못하고, 자신들의 삶 속에 다른 중요한 사람들에게 만족스럽지 못하다는 결론을 내린다.

2. 이러한 태도는 그림을 그리기를 원하지만, 그 기술을 배우는 대신에, 단지 딱 맞는 대상을 기다려야 하며 그것을 발견하게 되면 아름다운 그림을 그리게 될 것이라고 주장하는 사람의 태도에 비유될 수 있다.

3. 만약 반대 방향에서 오는 두 사람 각각이 한쪽으로 움직여 다른 사람이 지나가도록 허용하며 서로의 의도를 정확히 추측한다면 그들은 다음에 그들이 충돌을 피해야 할 때 같은 방향으로 움직이는 것을 선택할 가능성이 높다.

4. 너무나 흔하게 그 마지막 결과는 구매 의도가 없는 불만스러워하는 고객과 자신의 예산을 낭비한 마케팅 담당자, '모두의 손해'가 되는 것이다.

5. 여러분이 자신의 지나가는 생각, 감정 그리고 기분을 알아차릴 때, '오, 저것은 나의 오랜 친구 Fear야, 저기 Inner Critic이 가네.'와 같이 그것들에 이름을 붙이는 것은 그것들이 여러분에게 미치는 영향을 중화시키고 여러분이 자신의 균형과 침착 상태를 유지하도록 돕는다.

6. 소리는 공기 중에서보다 땅에서 훨씬 더 빨리 전해지기 때문에, 땅으로 전달되는 진동은, 만약 감지될 수 있다면, 조기 경보 체계의 역할을 하여 똑같은 근원지로부터 공기로 전달되는 소리가 도착하기 훨씬 전에 도달할 수 있다.

7. 매우 그러하기 때문에, 만약 여러분이 이것들 중 어떤 것의 디지털 표시를 본다면, 여러분은 아마 그 0들과 1들이 텍스트나 혹은 음악이 아닌 이미지를 나타내고 있었다는 것조차도 알지 못할 것이다.

혼공 15일차 **승부수 문항 모의고사 2회**

1 모의고사 2회 p.152

● 정답

1. ①	**2.** ②	**3.** ⑤	**4.** ①	**5.** ③	**6.** ③	**7.** ⑤	**8.** ①
9. ①	**10.** ⑤						

1. ①

● 전체 해석

Leonardo da Vinci는 지금껏 살았던 사람 가운데 가장 박식하고 다재다능한 사람 중 한 명이었다. 잠자리 날개부터 지구의 탄생에 이르기까지 전 우주는 그의 호기심 많은 지성의 놀이터였다. 그러나 Leonardo는 신비하거나 타고난 통찰과 발명의 어떤 재능을 가지고 있었는가, 아니면 그의 탁월함이 학습되고 획득된 것인가? 분명 그는 비범한 정신과 다른 사람들이 보지 못하는 것을 보는 예리한 능력을 가지고 있었다. 하지만 6천 쪽의 자세한 메모와 그림은 부지런하고 호기심 많은 학생 즉, 부지런히 지식을 추구하는 가운데, 끊임없이 탐구하고, 의문을 제기하고, 시험하는 끊임없는 학습자에 대한 분명한 증거를 보여준다. 여러분의 지성을 넓히는 것은 창의적으로 되는 것에 필수적이다. 그러므로 학습 기회에 자주 투자하는 것은 여러분이 자신에게 줄 수 있는 가장 멋진 선물 가운데 하나이다.

● 지문분석

Leonardo da Vinci was one of the most learned and well-rounded persons / ever to live.
레오나르도 다빈치는 가장 박식하고 다재다능한 사람들 중 하나였다 / 지금껏 살았던
[The entire universe / from the wing of a dragonfly / to
  S
the birth of the earth] / was the playground of his curious
              V
intelligence.
전체 우주는 / 잠자리의 날개에서부터 / 지구의 탄생에 이르는 / 그의 호기심 많은 지성의 놀이터였다
But did Leonardo have some mystical or innate gift / of
insight and invention, / or was his brilliance learned and
earned?
그런데 레오나르도는 어떤 신비하거나 타고난 재능을 가지고 있었는가 / 통찰과 발명의 / 아니면 그의 탁월함은 학습되고 획득된 것인가?

Certainly he had an unusual mind / and an uncanny ability / to see what others didn't see.
확실히 그는 비범한 정신을 가지고 있었다 / 그리고 묘한 능력을 / 다른 이들이 보지 못하는 것을 보는

But the six thousand pages / of detailed notes and drawings / present clear evidence of a diligent, curious student / – a perpetual learner / in laborious pursuit of wisdom / who was constantly exploring, questioning, and testing.
하지만 6천 페이지의 / 상세한 노트들과 그림들은 / 부지런하고 호기심 많은 학생의 명확한 증거를 보여준다 / 끊임없는 학습자인 / 지혜에 대한 고된 추구를 하는 / 지속적으로 탐구하고 질문하고 테스트하는

[Expanding your mind] / is vital to being creative.
여러분의 정신을 확장하는 것은 / 창의적으로 되는 것에 있어서 필수적이다

Therefore, [investing regularly in learning opportunities] / is one of the greatest gifts / you can give yourself.
그래서 자주 학습 기회에 투자하는 것은 / 가장 대단한 재능 중 하나이다 / 당신이 당신 자신에게 줄 수 있는

● 해설

1. (A), (B), (C)의 각 네모 안에서 어법에 맞는 표현으로 가장 적절한 것은?
(A) was: 문장의 주어는 맨 앞에 있는 The entire universe이므로 단수 주어인 was가 적절하지. [The entire universe from the wing of a dragonfly to the birth of the earth] was ~ 이런 구조야.
(B) what: 뒤에 see의 목적어가 없는 불완전한 문장이 오므로 관계대명사 what이 와야 겠지.
(C) investing: 본동사 is의 주어가 필요하므로 동명사 investing이 와야 해.

● 중요 포인트

관계사의 선행사가 [명사+전치사+명사]의 구조인 경우
문맥을 통해서 수식을 받는 선행사가 무엇인지 파악해야 해. 관계사 바로 앞에 있는 명사(대명사)가 선행사가 아닐 수 있으니까 주의하자.

a perpetual learner in laborious pursuit of wisdom who
선행사   선행사 아님
was constantly exploring, questioning, and testing.

2. ②

● 전체 해석

작곡가들이 형식과 디자인을 자유롭게 실험하기 시작했던 20세기에 이를 때까지, 고전 음악은 화음은 말할 것도 없이, 구조와 관련 있는 기본적인 규칙들을 계속 따랐다. 여전히 개성을 발휘할 여지는 있었지만(위대한 작곡가들은 규칙을 따르지 않고, 규칙이 그들을 따르도록 만들었다), 디자인 이면에는 항상 기본적인 비율과 논리가 있었다. 많은 규칙이 더 최근 들어 급진적인 개념에 의해 뒤집어진 이후에도, 대개 작곡가들은 전체적이고 통일적인 구조를 생산해내는 방식으로 여전히 자신들의 생각을 구성했다. 그것이 20세기 모더니즘 작곡가 두 명을 예로 들면, Arnold

Schönberg나 Karlheinz Stockhausen에 의해 작곡된 무조(無調)의 매우 복잡한 작품들이 그럼에도 불구하고 접근 가능한 한 가지 이유이다. 그 소리는 매우 이상할지 모르지만, 그 결과는 여전히 구성의 측면에서 분명히 고전적이다.

● 지문분석

Until the twentieth century, / when composers began
                              └ 관계부사
experimenting freely with form and design, / classical music continued to follow basic rules / relating to structure, / not to mention harmony.
20세기에 이를 때까지 / 작곡가들이 자유롭게 형식과 디자인을 실험하기 시작했던 / 고전 음악은 계속해서 기본적인 규칙을 따랐다 / 구조와 관련된 / 화음은 말할 것도 없이

There still was room for individuality / – the great composers didn't follow the rules, / but made the rules follow them / – yet there was always a fundamental proportion and logic / behind the design.
여전히 개성을 위한 공간은 있었다 / 위대한 작곡가들은 그 규칙을 따르지 않았다 / 하지만 그 규칙이 그들을 따르도록 만들었다 / 하지만 항상 기본적인 비율과 논리는 있었다 / 디자인 이면에는

Even after many of the rules / were overturned / by radical concepts / in more recent times, / composers, / more often than not, / still organized their thoughts / in ways / that produced an overall, unifying structure.
규칙 중 많은 것들이 / 뒤집어진 후에도 / 급진적인 개념들에 의해서 / 최근 들어 / 작곡가들은 / 대개 / 여전히 그들의 생각을 구성했다 / 방식으로 / 전체적으로 통일적인 구조를 만들었던

That's one reason / the atonal, incredibly complex works / by Arnold Schönberg or Karlheinz Stockhausen, / to name two twentiethcentury Modernists, / are nonetheless approachable.
그것이 한 가지 이유이다 / 무조의 믿을 수 없을 만큼 복잡한 작품들이 / Arnold Schonberg나 Karlheinz Stockhausen에 의한 / 두 가지 20세기 모더니즘 작곡가의 예를 들자면 / 그럼에도 불구하고 접근 가능한

The sounds might be very strange, / but the results are still decidedly classical / in terms of organization.
그 소리는 매우 이상할 수도 있다 / 하지만 그 결과는 여전히 단호하게 고전적이다 / 구성의 측면에서는

● 해설

2. (A), (B), (C)의 각 네모 안에서 어법에 맞는 표현으로 가장 적절한 것은?
(A) individuality: 뒤에 나오는 yet 이하의 문장과 비교했을 때, '여전히 기본적인 비율과 논리가 있다'와는 상반되는 내용이 나와야 해. 따라서 individuality(개성)가 적절하겠지. conformity는 '순응'을 나타내.
(B) overturned: 고전 음악이 주제이므로 급진적인 개념에 의해서는 maintained(유지되다)보다는 overturned(뒤집히다)가 어울리겠지.
(C) approachable: 복잡한 현대의 작품이 구성면에서 고전 음악을 따르고 있으니 이해하기가 쉽다는 거겠지? 따라서 approachable(접근 가능

한)이 적절하지. inaccessible은 '가까이 하기 어려운'을 의미해.

● 중요 포인트

전치사구와 삽입구로 인해 멀어진 주어와 동사

That's one reason / the atonal, incredibly complex works / by Arnold Schönberg or Karlheinz Stockhausen, / to name two twentiethcentury Modernists, / are nonetheless approachable.

3. ⑤

● 전체 해석

미국식 영어로 칭찬하는 행동에 관한 연구에서 연구자들은 미국식 영어로 하는 칭찬의 가장 두드러진 특징 중 하나는 독창성의 거의 완전한 부족이라는 것을 발견했다. 방대한 언어 자료의 초기 연구에서 칭찬의 대상과 그것들을 묘사하기 위해 사용된 어휘 항목 둘 다에 있어서 놀라운 반복성이 드러났다. 좀 더 심도 있는 조사에서 규칙성이 모든 수준에서 존재하고 칭찬은 사실상 공식이라는 것이 발견되었다. 칭찬들이 그것들의 긍정적인 의미론적 가치를 위해 형용사에 의존한다는 점에서 우리는 자료에 있는 모든 칭찬의 80퍼센트를 형용사적인 것으로 분류할 수 있을 것이다. 종합하자면, 72개의 긍정적인 형용사가 자료에 나타난다. 그러나 놀라운 것은 이러한 72개의 형용사들 중에서 단지 5개(멋진, 좋은, 아름다운, 예쁜, 그리고 훌륭한)의 형용사만 빈번하게 사용된다는 사실이다. 대부분의 형용사가 자료에서 단지 한 두 번만 나타나는 반면에 이러한 5개의 형용사는 너무 빈번하게 나타나서 언어자료에 있는 모든 형용사적 칭찬 중에서 3분의 2가 단지 5개의 형용사만을 활용하고 있다.

● 지문분석

In a study of complimenting behavior in American English, / researchers discovered / that [one of the most striking features / of compliments in American English] / is the almost total lack of originality.
미국 영어에서의 칭찬하는 행동에 관한 연구에서 / 연구원들은 발견했다 / 가장 두드러지는 특징 중의 하나는 / 미국 영어에서 칭찬에 대한 / 독창성의 거의 완전한 부족이라는 것을

[An initial examination / of a large corpus] / revealed surprising repetitiveness / in both the object of the compliments and the lexical items / used to describe them.
초기 연구는 / 방대한 언어 자료의 / 놀라운 반복성을 드러냈다 / 칭찬의 대상과 어휘 항목 둘 다에서 / 그들을 묘사하는데 사용된

On closer investigation, / it was discovered / that regularities exist on all levels / and that compliments are in fact formulas.
더 심도 있는 연구에서 / 밝혀졌다 / 규칙성이 모든 수준에서 존재한다는 것과 / 칭찬은 사실상의 공식이라는 것이

We may categorize 80% of all compliments / in the data / as adjectival / in that they depend on an adjective / for their positive semantic value.
우리는 모든 칭찬의 80%를 분류할 지도 모른다 / 데이터상의 /

형용사로서 / 그들이 형용사에 의존한다는 점에서 / 그들의 긍정적인 의미론적 가치를 위해서

In all, / some seventy-two positive adjectives occur / in the data.
모두 합쳐 / 일부 72개의 긍정적인 형용사가 발생한다 / 그 데이터에서

[What is striking,] however, is / that of these seventy-two adjectives / only five (nice, good, beautiful, pretty and great) / are used with any frequency.
놀라운 것은 하지만 / 이 72개의 형용사 중에서 / 오직 5개(멋진, 좋은, 아름다운, 예쁜, 그리고 훌륭한)만이 / 빈번하게 사용된다

While most adjectives occur / only once or twice in the data, / these five adjectives occur / with such frequency / that of all adjectival compliments in the corpus / two thirds make use of only five adjectives.
대부분의 형용사가 발생하는 반면 / 오직 그 데이터에서 1~2번만 / 이 5개의 형용사는 나타난다 / 너무 빈번히 / 그래서 언어 자료에서 모든 형용사적 칭찬 중 / 2/3가 단지 5개의 형용사만을 사용한다

● 해설

3. 다음 빈칸에 들어갈 말로 가장 적절한 것은?
In a study of complimenting behavior in American English, researchers discovered that one of the most striking features of compliments in American English is _____. An initial examination of a large corpus revealed surprising repetitiveness in both the object of the compliments and the lexical items used to describe them. On closer investigation, it was discovered that regularities exist on all levels and that compliments are in fact formulas. We may categorize 80% of all compliments in the data as adjectival in that they depend on an adjective for their positive semantic value. In all, some seventy—two positive adjectives occur in the data. What is striking, however, is that of these seventy—two adjectives only five (nice, good, beautiful, pretty and great) are used with any frequency. While most adjectives occur only once or twice in the data, these five adjectives occur with such frequency that of all adjectival compliments in the corpus two thirds make use of only five adjectives.

① the foreign sounding qualities 이질적인 소리의 질
② frequently misused adjectives 빈번히 잘못 사용되는 형용사
▶ 후반부에 주로 나오는 어휘인 adjectives를 사용한 오답이지.
③ repetition of pitch patterns 높이 패턴의 반복
▶ pitch는 언급조차 되지 않고 있어.
④ an inherent ambiguity in meaning 의미에서의 타고난 애매함
▶ 애매함은 언급조차 되지 않았어.
❺ the almost total lack of originality 독창성의 거의 완전한 부족
▶ 5개의 형용사만 빈번히 사용하므로 독창성이 거의 없지.

미국식 영어의 칭찬은 주로 5개의 형용사만 빈번히 사용하고 있어. 이와 비슷한 어감을 찾는 다면 '독창성의 부족'이라고 할 수 있겠지.

such ~ that

While most adjectives occur only once or twice in the data, these five adjectives occur with such frequency that
_{such ~ that}
of all adjectival compliments in the corpus two thirds make use of only five adjectives.

4. ①

● 전체 해석

새로운 세기가 시작되면서, 농경지를 두고 자동차와 농작물이 벌이는 경쟁이 심해지고 있다. 지금까지, 농경지의 포장은 전 세계의 5억 2천만대의 자동차 중 5분의 4가 있는 산업 국가에서 주로 발생했다. 그러나 이제, 더욱 더 많은 농지가 배고픈 사람들이 있는 개발도상국에서 희생되고 있는데, 그것은 자동차의 미래 역할에 의문을 제기한다. 산업 세계의 수백만 헥타르의 농경지가 도로와 주차장을 만들기 위해 포장되었다. 예를 들어, 미국의 각각의 자동차는 도로와 주차 공간을 위해 평균 0.07헥타르의 포장된 땅이 필요하다. 미국에 있는 전체 자동차 수에 자동차가 다섯 대 더해질 때마다, 축구장 하나 크기의 지역이 아스팔트로 덮인다. 흔히, 농사에 제격인 평평하고 배수가 잘 되는 땅이 도로 건설에도 이상적이라는 이유만으로 농경지가 포장이 된다. 일단 포장이 되면, 땅은 (원 상태로) 쉽게 복원되지 않는다. 환경론자인 Rupert Cutler가 언젠가 (주목하여) 언급했던 것처럼, "아스팔트는 땅의 마지막 작물이다."

● 지문분석

As the new century begins, / [the competition between cars and crops / for cropland] / is intensifying.
새로운 세기가 시작되면서 / 자동차와 농작물 사이의 경쟁은 / 농경지를 위한 / 심화되고 있다

Until now, / [the paving over of cropland] / has occurred largely in industrial countries, / home to four fifths / of the world's 520 million automobiles.
지금까지 / 농경기의 포장은 / 대개 산업국가에서 발생했다 / 5분의 4가 있는 / 전 세계 5억 2천만대의 자동차의

But now, / more and more farmland is being sacrificed / in developing countries / with hungry populations, / calling into question / the future role of the car.
하지만 지금 / 점점 더 많은 농경지가 희생되고 있다 / 개발도상국에서 / 배고픈 사람들이 있는 / 의문을 표하고 있다 / 자동차의 미래 역할에 대한
└ 분사구문

[Millions of hectares of cropland / in the industrial world] / have been paved / over for roads and parking lots.
수백만 헥타르의 농경지가 / 산업 세계의 / 포장되고 있다 / 도로와 주차장을 위해서

Each U.S. car, / for example, requires on average 0.07 hectares of paved land / for roads and parking space.
각각의 미국의 자동차는 / 예를 들어 평균 0.07 헥타르의 포장된 땅이 필요하다 / 도로와 주차 공간을 위해

For every five cars / added to the total number of cars in the U.S., / [an area the size of a football field] / is covered with asphalt.
매 5대의 자동차가 / 미국의 전체 자동차의 수에 더해질 때 / 축구장 크기의 땅이 / 아스팔트로 덮인다

More often than not, / cropland is paved / simply because [the flat, well-drained soils / that are well suited for farming] / are also ideal for building roads.
대개 / 농경지는 포장된다 / 단순히 평평하고 배수가 잘 되는 땅이 / 농사에 적합한 / 역시 도로 건설에도 이상적이기 때문에

Once paved, / land is not easily reclaimed.
일단 포장이 되면 / 땅은 쉽게 복원되지 않는다

As environmentalist Rupert Cutler once noted, / "Asphalt is the land's last crop ."
환경론자인 Rupert Cutler는 예전에 언급했던 것처럼 / 아스팔트는 땅의 마지막 작물이라고

● 해설

4. 다음 빈칸에 들어갈 말로 가장 적절한 것은?
As the new century begins, the competition between cars and crops for cropland is intensifying. Until now, the paving over of cropland has occurred largely in industrial countries, home to four fifths of the world's 520 million automobiles. But now, more and more farmland is being sacrificed in developing countries with hungry populations, calling into question the future role of the car. Millions of hectares of cropland in the industrial world have been paved over for roads and parking lots. Each U.S. car, for example, requires on average 0.07 hectares of paved land for roads and parking space. For every five cars added to the total number of cars in the U.S., an area the size of a football field is covered with asphalt. More often than not, cropland is paved simply because the flat, well-drained soils that are well suited for farming are also ideal for building roads. Once paved, land is not easily reclaimed. As environmentalist Rupert Cutler once noted, "_____."

❶ Asphalt is the land's last crop 아스팔트는 땅의 마지막 작물이다
▶ 포장이 되면 복원이 쉽지 않으므로 아스팔트가 깔리면 그것으로 끝이라는 거지.
② Wasteland is a treasure of biodiversity 황무지는 생물학적 다양성의 보물이다
▶ 황무지는 언급조차 되지 않았어.
③ The end of the road leads to another road 도로의 마지막은 또 다른 도로를 이끈다
▶ 반복되는 단어인 road에서 오는 오답으로 도로가 계속 이어진다는 내용은 아니야.
④ What comes from soil returns to soil 땅에서 온 것은 땅으로 돌아간다
▶ 농경지와 도로의 경쟁에 대한 글이지.
⑤ The eco-friendly car is our future 친환경적인 차는 우리의 미래이다
▶ 친환경적 차에 대한 내용이 아니야.

관계사절의 수식을 받는 주어

More often than not, cropland is paved simply because [the flat, well-drained soils that are well suited for farming] are also ideal for building roads.

5. ③

●전체 해석

우리의 부엌은 과학의 훌륭함의 덕을 많이 보고 있고, 스토브에서 혼합 재료로 실험하는 요리사는 흔히 실험실에 있는 화학자와 크게 다르지 않다. 우리는 색을 유지하기 위해 적양배추에 식초를 첨가하고 케이크에 있는 레몬의 산성을 중화하기 위해 베이킹 소다를 사용한다. 그러나 기술이 단지 과학적 사고를 적용한 것이라고 생각하는 것은 잘못이다. 그것(기술)은 이것(과학적 사고)보다 더 기초적이고 더 오래된 무언가이다. 모든 문화가 기원전 4세기에 Aristotle에게서 시작된 우주에 관한 체계화된 지식의 형태인 형식 과학을 가지고 있지는 않다. 실험이 가설, 실험법, 그리고 분석의 구조화된 체계의 일부를 형성하는 현대 과학 방식은 17세기에 이르러서인 근래의 것이다. 요리의 문제 해결 기술은 수천 년 전으로 거슬러 간다. 최초 석기 시대 인간이 날카롭게 만든 부싯돌로 날 음식물을 잘랐던 이래로, 우리는 항상 우리 자신을 먹여 살리는 더 나은 방법을 고안하기 위해 발명을 사용해왔다.

●지문분석

Our kitchens owe much to the brilliance of science, / and [a cook / experimenting with mixtures at the stove] / is often not very different / from a chemist in the lab: / we add vinegar to red cabbage / to fix the color / and use baking soda / to counteract the acidity of lemon in the cake.
우리의 부엌은 많은 것이 과학의 훌륭함 덕분이다 / 그리고 요리사는 / 스토브에서 혼합 재료를 가지고 실험하는 / 종종 다르지 않다 / 실험실에서의 화학자와 / 우리는 식초를 적양배추에 넣는다 / 색을 유지하기 위해서 / 그리고 베이킹 소다를 사용한다 / 케이크에서 레몬의 산성을 중화하기 위해서

It is wrong / to suppose, however, / that technology is just the appliance of scientific thought.
틀리다 / 가정하는 것은 하지만 / 기술은 단지 과학적 사고의 적용이라고

It is something / more basic and older / than this.
그것은 무언가이다 / 보다 기초적이고 더 오래된 / 이것보다

Not every culture has had formal science / – a form of organized knowledge / about the universe / that starts with Aristotle in the fourth century BC.
모든 문화가 형식적인 과학을 가지는 것은 아니다 / 조직된 지식의 형태인 / 우주에 대한 / 아리스토텔레스와 함께 4세기경 시작된

[The modern scientific method, / in which experiments form part of a structured system / of hypothesis, experimentation, and analysis] / is as recent as / the

seventeenth century; / the problem-solving technology of cooking / goes back thousands of years.
현대의 과학 방식은 / 실험이 구조화된 시스템의 일부를 형성하는 / 가설과 실험, 그리고 분석의 / 최신이다 / 17세기 만큼이나 / 요리의 문제 해결 기술은 / 수천 년 전으로 거슬러 간다

Since the earliest Stone Age humans / cut raw food with sharpened flints, / we have always used invention / to devise better ways / to feed ourselves.
초기 석기 시대의 인간들이 / 날카로운 부싯돌로 날 음식을 잘랐을 때 이후로 / 우리는 항상 발명을 이용했다 / 더 나은 방법을 고안하기 위해서 / 우리 스스로를 먹여살리는

●해설

5. 다음 빈칸에 들어갈 말로 가장 적절한 것은?
요리는 과학적 원리를 이용한다는 내용이지.
Our kitchens owe much to the brilliance of science, and a cook experimenting with mixtures at the stove is often not very different from a chemist in the lab: we add vinegar to red cabbage to fix the color and use baking soda to counteract the acidity of lemon in the cake. It is wrong to suppose, however, that _____. It is something more basic
앞의 내용을 반박. 빈칸의 내용이 틀리다는거지, 즉 앞의 내용을 담는 내용이 빈칸이야.
and older than this. Not every culture has had formal science – a form of organized knowledge about the universe that starts with Aristotle in the fourth century BC. The modern scientific method, in which experiments form part of a structured system of hypothesis, experimentation, and analysis is as recent as the seventeenth century; the problem-solving technology of cooking goes back thousands of years. Since the earliest Stone Age humans cut raw food with sharpened flints, we have always used invention to devise better ways to feed ourselves.
과학이 적용된 것은 얼마 되지 않았음.

① science has nothing to do with philosophy 과학은 철학과 전혀 관계가 없다
▶ 아리스토텔레스가 언급되어서 나온 오답이야.
② a hypothesis can be proved by a single experiment 가설은 하나의 실험에 의해 증명될 수 있다
▶ 실험과 가설이라는 어휘가 본문에 언급되어서 나온 오답이지.
❸ technology is just the appliance of scientific thought 기술은 단순한 과학 기술의 적용이다
▶ 바로 앞문장에 나오는 요리에서의 과학 원리의 적용을 언급하는 것이지.
④ cooking has always been independent from formal science 요리는 항상 형식적 과학으로부터 독립적이다
▶ 아니지. 현재의 요리는 과학적 원리가 적용되고 있어.
⑤ food is cooked only through the problem–solving technology 음식은 오직 문제해결 기술을 통해서 요리되어진다
▶ 문제 해결 기술을 통해서 요리되어진 것은 얼마되지 않았고, 그것이 유일한 것은 아니지.

●중요 포인트

현재분사의 수식을 받는 명사

명사 수식 분사
[a cook experimenting with mixtures at the stove] is often not very different from a chemist in the lab ~

6. ③

●전체 해석

관계망을 이해하는 것은 혁신적이고 명시적이지 않은 전략들을 이끌어낼 수 있는 감염의 확산을 막기 위해서 무작위로 집단을 면역시키는 것은 보통 인구의 80에서 100퍼센트를 면역시킬 것을 요구한다. (B) 예를 들어, 홍역의 확산을 예방하기 위해서는, 인구의 95퍼센트가 면역되어야만 한다. 보다 효과적인 대안은 관계망의 중심을 목표로 하는 것인데, 다시 말하면, 관계망의 중심에 있는 사람들이나 또는 접촉이 가장 많은 사람들이다. (C) 하지만, 어떻게 하면 그 집단을 가장 잘 면역화 시킬 수 있을지 알아내려고 할 때, 그 집단의 관계망 연결을 사전에 파악하는 것이 종종 불가능하다. 창의적인 또 하나의 대안은 무작위로 선발된 사람들의 지인들을 면역화 시키는 것이다. (A) 이 전략은 우리가 그 전체 구조를 볼 수 없을지라도 관계망의 특성을 이용할 수 있게 해 준다. 지인들은 더 많은 연결고리를 가지고 있고 그들을 지명한 무작위로 선발된 사람들보다 관계망에서 좀 더 중심에 있다.

●지문분석

[Understanding networks] / can lead to innovative, non-obvious strategies.
관계망을 이해하는 것은 / 혁신적이고 명시적이지 않은 전략을 이끌어 낼 수 있다

[Randomly immunizing a population / to prevent the spread of infection] / typically requires / that 80 to 100 percent of the population / be immunized.
무작위로 사람들을 면역시키는 것은 / 감염의 확산을 막기 위해서 / 보통 요구한다 / 80~100%의 사람들을 / 면역시키기를

To prevent measles epidemics, / for example, / [95 percent of the population] / must be immunized.
홍역의 확산을 막기 위해서 / 예를 들어 / 95%의 사람들은 / 면역이 되어야만 한다

A more efficient alternative / is to target the hubs of the network, / namely, those people at the center of the network / or those with the most contacts.
더 효율적인 대안은 / 관계망 중심을 목표로 하는 것이다 / 말하자면 네트워크의 중심에 있는 그러한 사람들을 / 아니면 가장 접촉이 많은 사람들을

However, it is often not possible / to discern network ties / in advance in a population / when trying to figure out / how best to immunize it.
하지만 종종 가능하지 않다 / 관계망의 연결을 구별하는 것은 / 사람들 속에서 미리 / 알아내고자 노력할 때 / 그것을 가장 잘 면역화시키는 것을

A creative alternative / is to immunize the acquaintances / of randomly selected individuals.
창조적인 대안은 / 지인들을 면역화 시키는 것이다 / 무작위로 선택된 사람들의

This strategy allows / us to exploit a property of networks / even if we cannot see the whole structure.
이 전략은 허용한다 / 우리가 관계망의 특성을 이용하도록 / 비록 우리가 전체 구조를 볼 수 없음에도 불구하고

Acquaintances have more links / and are more central to the network / than are the randomly chosen people / who named them.
지인들은 더 많은 연결을 가지고 있다 / 그리고 그 관계망에서 더 중심에 있다 / 무작위로 선택된 사람들보다 / 그들을 지명한

●해설

6. 주어진 글 다음에 이어질 글의 순서로 가장 적절한 것은?
Understanding networks can lead to innovative, nonobvious strategies. Randomly immunizing a population to prevent the spread of infection typically requires that 80 to 100 percent of the population be immunized.

(B) To prevent measles epidemics, for example, 95 percent of the population must be immunized. A more efficient alternative is to target the hubs of the network, namely, those people at the center of the network or those with the most contacts.
(C)와 (A)는 중심부가 아닌 주변부(지인)에 초점을 맞추고 있으니, 전환점(however)이 나와야겠지.
(C) However, it is often not possible to discern network ties in advance in a population when trying to figure out how best to immunize it. A creative alternative is to immunize the acquaintances of randomly selected individuals.

(A) This strategy allows us to exploit a property of networks even if we cannot see the whole structure. Acquaintances have more links and are more central to the network than are the randomly chosen people who named them.

●중요 포인트

to부정사로 인해서 멀어진 주어와 동사
[Randomly immunizing a population to prevent the spread of infection] typically requires that 80 to 100 percent of the population be immunized.

7. ⑤

●전체 해석

만일 여러분이 시장에 불만을 갖고 있으면서 오랜 세월에도 끄떡없는 화폐를 찾고 있다면, 더 알아볼 필요가 없다. 남태평양의 Caroline 제도에는 Yap(혹은 Uap)이라는 이름의 섬이 있다. 1903년에 Henry Furness Ⅲ라는 미국의 인류학자가 그 섬사람들을 방문하여 그들이 특이한 화폐 체계를 가지고 있다는 것을 발견했다. 그것은 'fei'라고 불리는 조각된 돌 바퀴들로 구성되었는데, 지름이 1피트에서 12피트에 이르렀다. 그 돌들은 무거웠기 때문에, 그 섬사람들은 평상시에 그들의 돈을 가지고 다니지 않았다. 거래가 이루어진 후 'fei'가 이전 소유자의 땅에 남아 있었을지도 모르지만, 사람들은 누가 무엇을 소유하는지 알고 있었다. Furness는 한 가족의 'fei'가 수년 전에 폭풍우가 치는 동안 근처의 섬으로부터 운반되던 도중에 바다에서 분실되었다는 이야기를 들었다. 그러나 그 돌은 수백 피트의 물 아래에서 보이지도 않고 회수할 수도 없었음에도 불구하고, 여전히 화폐로 사용되었다.

● 지문분석

If you're frustrated / by the market / and you're looking for a currency / that can stand the test of time, / look no further.
당신이 불만을 가지고 있다면 / 시장에 의해서 / 그리고 당신이 화폐를 찾고 있다면 / 시간의 시험을 견딜 수 있는 / 더 알아 보지 마라

In the Caroline Islands in the South Pacific, / there's an island / named Yap (or Uap).
남태평양의 Caroline 제도에는 / 한 섬이 있다 / Yap (또는 Uap) 라는 이름의

In 1903 / [an American anthropologist / named Henry Furness III] / visited the islanders / and found / they had an unusual system of currency.
1903년 / 한 미국인 인류학자가 / Henry Furnes III이라는 / 섬사람들을 방문했다 / 그리고 발견했다 / 그들이 독특한 화폐 체계를 가지고 있음을

It consisted of carved stone wheels / called fei, / ranging in diameter from a foot to 12 feet.
그것은 조각된 돌 바퀴들로 구성되었다 / fei라 불리는 / 직격이 1피트에서 12피트에 이르는

Because the stones were heavy, / the islanders didn't normally carry their money around / with them.
그 돌들은 무겁기 때문에 / 섬사람들은 보통은 그들의 돈을 가지고 다니지 않았다 / 그들과 함께

After a transaction / the fei might remain on a previous owner's land, / but it was understood / who owned what.
거래 이후에 / fei는 이전 주인의 땅에 남아 있었을지도 모른다 / 하지만 이해되었다 / 누가 무엇을 소유했는지는

Furness was told / one family's fei had been lost / at sea many years earlier / while being transported from a nearby island / during a storm.
Furness는 들었다 / 한 가족의 fei가 사라졌었다고 / 바다에서 몇 년 전에 / 가까운 섬으로부터 옮겨지는 동안 / 폭풍우가 치는 동안

But that stone was still used as currency, / even though it was unseen and irretrievable / beneath hundreds of feet of water.
하지만 그 돌은 여전히 화폐로서 사용되었다 / 비록 그것이 보이지도 않고 회수할 수도 없었음에도 불구하고 / 수백 피트 바다 아래에서

● 해설

7. 글의 흐름으로 보아, 주어진 문장이 들어가기에 가장 적절한 곳은?
Furness was told one family's fei had been lost at sea many years earlier while being transported from a nearby island during a storm.

If you're frustrated by the market and you're looking for a currency that can stand the test of time, look no further. In the Caroline Islands in the South Pacific, there's an island named Yap (or Uap). (①) In 1903 an American anthropologist named Henry Furness III visited the islanders and found they had an unusual system of currency. (②) It consisted of carved stone wheels called fei, ranging in diameter from a foot to 12 feet. (③) Because the stones were heavy, the islanders didn't normally carry their money around with them. (④) After a transaction the fei might remain on a previous owner's land, but it was understood who owned what. (⑤) But that stone was still used as currency, even though it was unseen and irretrievable beneath hundreds of feet of water.
돌은 바다 속에 있지만, 사용됨

● 중요 포인트

이중 수식 구조

It consisted of carved stone wheels called fei, ranging in diameter from a foot to 12 feet.

8. ①

● 전체 해석

여러분이 새롭거나 놀라운 것에 끌리는 주된 이유는 그것이 안전하고 예측 가능한 현재의 상황을 엉망진창으로 만들 수 있고 심지어 여러분의 생존을 위협할 수도 있기 때문이다. 만약 TV가 켜져 있는 방에서 여러분이 대화를 계속 하려고 애써 본 적이 있다면, 여러분은 이따금 화면을 힐끗 바라보지 않기가 힘들다는 것을 안다. 비록 여러분이 보고 싶어 하지 않더라도, 여러분의 뇌는 계속 변하는 연속된 이미지들에 이끌리는데, 왜냐하면 변화가 생과 사의 결과를 낳을 수도 있기 때문이다. 실로, 우리의 옛 아프리카 조상들이 그들의 모든 주의력을 막 익은 과일이나 다가오는 포식자들에게 집중하는 것을 잘 하지 못했다면, 우리는 여기에 없을 것이다. 동일한 이유로, 사물이 보통 그러한 혹은 온당히 그래야 하는 방식과 그다지 일치하지 않는 특이한 세부 사항에 대한 강한 민감도는 교전 지역에 있는 군인에게 중요한 자산이다. 일상의 상황에서조차, 여러분은 차 앞으로 휙 달려드는 무단 횡단자 혹은 길고 따분한 목록에 있는 하나의 새롭고 중요한 사실을 놓쳐서는 안 된다.

↓

우리는 변화에 민감한데, 그것은 그 민감함이 우리의 안전에 이점을 주기 때문이다.

● 지문분석

[The main reason / you're drawn to novel or surprising things] / is that it could upset the safe, predictable status quo / and even threaten your survival.
주된 이유는 / 여러분이 참신하거나 놀라운 것에 끌리는 / 그것이 안전하고 예측 가능한 현재의 상황을 뒤집을 수 있기 때문이다 / 그리고 심지어 여러분의 생존을 위협할 수 있기

If you've ever tried to carry on a conversation / in a room / in which a TV is playing, / you know / that it's hard / not to glance at the screen occasionally.
만약 여러분이 대화를 계속 하려고 노력한다면 / 방 안에서 / TV가 켜져있는 / 여러분은 안다 / 어렵다는 것을 / 때때로 화면을 힐끗 바라보지 않기가

Even if you don't want to watch, / your brain is attracted

정답 및 해설 113

/ by that constantly shifting stream of images, / because change can have life-or-death consequences.
비록 여러분이 보고 싶지 않더라도 / 여러분의 두뇌는 이끌린다 / 지속적으로 변화하는 이미지의 흐름에 의해서 / 왜냐하면 변화는 생과 사의 결과를 가질 수 있기 때문이다

Indeed, if our early African ancestors / hadn't been good at / fixing all their attention / on the just-ripened fruit or the approaching predators, / we wouldn't be here.
실제로 우리의 옛 아프리카 조상들이 / 능숙하지 않았었다면 / 그들의 관심을 모두 고정시키는 데 / 막 익은 과일이나 접근하는 포식자에게 / 우리는 여기에 없을지도 모른다

For the same reason, / [a strong sensitivity / to the odd detail / that doesn't quite correspond with the way / things usually are or ought to be] / is a major asset / for a soldier in a war zone.
같은 이유로 / 강한 민감도는 / 특이한 세부사항에 대한 / 방식과 아주 일치하지 않는 / 사물이 보통 그러한 혹은 그래야만 하는 / 주된 자산이다 / 전쟁 지역에 있는 군인들을 위한

Even in everyday situations, / you can't afford to miss / that jaywalker darting / in front of your car / or the single new and important fact / in a long, boring list.
심지어 매일 매일의 상황에서조차 / 여러분은 놓칠 여유는 없다 / 달려드는 무단 횡단자를 / 여러분의 차 앞에서 / 아니면 하나의 새롭고 중요한 사실을 / 길고 따분한 목록에서

●해설

8. 다음 글의 내용을 한 문장으로 요약하고자 한다. 빈칸 (A)와 (B)에 들어갈 말로 가장 적절한 것은?

The main reason you're drawn to novel or surprising things is that it could upset the safe, predictable status quo and even threaten your survival. If you've ever tried to carry on a conversation in a room in which a TV is playing, you know that it's hard not to glance at the screen occasionally. Even if you don't want to watch, your brain is attracted by that constantly shifting stream of images, because change can have life-or-death consequences. Indeed, if our early African ancestors hadn't been good at fixing all their attention on the justripened fruit or the approaching predators, we wouldn't be here. For the same reason, a strong sensitivity to the odd detail that doesn't quite correspond with the way things usually are or ought to be is a major asset for a soldier in a war zone. Even in everyday situations, you can't afford to miss that jaywalker darting in front of your car or the single new and important fact in a long, boring list.

↓

We are sensitive to __(A)__ because that sensitivity gives advantages for our __(B)__.

❶ change 변화 ⋯ safety 안전
② change 변화 ⋯ creativity 창의성
③ criticism 비판 ⋯ intelligence 지능
④ criticism 비판 ⋯ safety 안전
⑤ beauty 아름다움 ⋯ creativity 창의성

새롭고 놀라운 것에 끌리고, 지속적으로 변하는 이미지의 흐름을 의미하는 것은 바로 변화가 되겠지. 그리고 이러한 변화(change)에 관심을 가지는 것은 바로 예부터 생존을 위한 것이라고 했어. 따라서 안전(safety)이 적절하지.

●중요 포인트

수식의 수식을 받는 주어

For the same reason, [a strong sensitivity to the odd detail that doesn't quite correspond with the way things usually are or ought to be] is a major asset for a soldier in a war zone.

9. ① 10. ⑤

●전체 해석

여러분은 누군가에게 길게 이야기를 했는데 그들이 여러분이 한 말을 한 마디도 듣지 않았다는 것을 깨달은 자신을 발견한 적이 있는가? 보거나 듣는 우리의 능력만큼 놀라운 것이 우리의 무시하는 능력이다. 어떤 것에 관심을 기울이는 선천적 욕구와 함께 이 능력은 관심을 활용한 산업의 발달에 영향을 끼쳐 왔다.

매일 매 순간 우리는 정보로 과부하를 겪는다. 사실 모든 복잡한 생명체, 특히 뇌를 가진 것들은 정보 과부하로 고통을 겪는다. 우리의 눈과 귀는 볼 수 있고 들을 수 있는 파장의 스펙트럼 전체에 걸쳐 있는 빛과 소리를 받아들인다. 마치 거대한 광섬유 케이블이 그것들[뇌]에 직접 연결된 것처럼 우리의 감각은 모두 합쳐서 매초 천백만 비트로 추정되는 정보를 우리의 불쌍한 뇌로 전송하여, 전속력으로 정보를 쏘아댄다. 이 점에 비추어 보면 우리가 심지어는 지루해할 수도 있다는 것은 오히려 믿기 힘들다.

다행히도 우리는 마음대로 그 흐름을 지속하게 하거나 차단할 수 있는 밸브를 가지고 있다. 다른 말로 표현하자면 우리는 '(정보를) 받아들일' 수도 '차단할' 수도 있다. 우리가 밸브를 잠그면, 들어오고 있는 수백만 비트 중 단지 하나의 별개 정보 흐름에 집중하면서 우리는 거의 모든 것을 무시한다. 사실, 우리가 '사색에 잠겼을' 때처럼 우리는 심지어 우리 외부에 있는 모든 것을 차단하고 내부의 대화에 집중할 수 있다. 거의 모든 것을 차단하고 집중하는 이 능력은 신경과학자들과 심리학자들이 관심을 기울이는 것이라고 말하는 것이다.

●지문분석

Have you ever found / yourself speaking to someone at length / only to realize / they haven't heard a single thing / you've said?
└ only + to부정사: to부정사의 결과적 용법
당신은 발견한 적이 있는가 / 당신 자신이 길게 누군가에게 이야기하고 있는 것을 / 그리고 깨닫는 것을 / 그들이 한마디도 듣지 않고 있다는 것을 / 당신이 말한

As remarkable as our ability / to see or hear / is our capacity to disregard.
우리의 능력만큼 놀라운 / 보거나 듣는 / 우리의 무시하는 능력이다

[This capacity, / along with the inherent need / to pay attention to something,] / has dictated the development of the attention industries.

이러한 능력은 / 타고난 욕구와 함께 / 무언가에 관심을 가지는 / 관심 산업의 발달에 영향을 끼쳐 왔다

Every instant of every day / we are overloaded with information.

매일 매 순간 / 우리는 정보로 과부화된다

In fact, [all complex organisms, / especially those with brains,] / suffer from information overload.

사실 모든 복잡한 생명체는 / 특히 두뇌를 가진 생명체들 / 정보 과부하로 고통을 겪는다

Our eyes and ears / receive lights and sounds / across the spectrums of visible and audible wavelengths.

우리의 눈과 귀들은 / 빛과 소리를 받는다 / 볼 수 있고 들을 수 있는 파장의 스펙트럼 전체에 걸쳐

All told, / every second, / our senses transmit an estimated 11 million bits of information / to our poor brains, / as if a giant fiber-optic cable / were plugged directly into them, / firing information at full speed.

'모두 합쳐서'

부사구문

모두 합쳐서 / 매초 / 우리의 감각은 천백만 비트로 추정되는 정보를 전달한다 / 우리의 불쌍한 뇌로 / 마치 거대한 광섬유 케이블이 / 직접적으로 그것들에 연결된 것처럼 / 전속력으로 정보를 쏘아댄다

In light of this, / it is rather incredible / that we are even capable of boredom.

가주어 – 진주어

이러한 점에서 / 오히려 믿기 힘들다 / 우리가 심지어 지루해 할 수도 있다는 것은

Fortunately, we have a valve / by which to turn the flow on or off at will.

운이 좋게도 우리는 밸브를 가지고 있다 / 흐름을 마음대로 켜거나 끌 수 있는

To use another term, / we can both "tune in" / and "tune out."

다른 용어로는 / 우리는 받아들일 수 있고 / 차단할 수도 있다

When we shut the valve, / we ignore almost everything, / while focusing on just one discrete stream of information / out of the millions of bits coming in.

우리가 밸브를 닫을 때 / 우리는 거의 모든 것을 무시한다 / 단지 하나의 별개 정보 흐름에 집중하면서 / 들어오는 수백만 개의 비트로부터

In fact, we can even shut out everything / external to us, / and concentrate on an internal dialogue, / as when we are "lost in thought."

사실 우리는 모든 것을 심지어 닫을 수 있다 / 우리 외부에 있는 / 그리고 내부의 대화에 집중할 수 있다 / 우리가 사색에 잠겼을 때처럼

[This ability – / to block out most everything, and focus] / – is what neuroscientists and psychologists refer to / as paying attention.

이러한 능력은 / 거의 모든 것을 차단하고 집중하는 / 신경과학자들과 심리학자들이 언급하는 것이다 / 관심을 기울이는 것이라고

● 해설

Have you ever found yourself speaking to someone at length only to realize they haven't heard a single thing you've said? As remarkable as our ability to see or hear is our capacity to _____. This capacity, along with the inherent need to pay attention to something, has dictated the development of the attention industries.

Every instant of every day we are overloaded with information. In fact, all complex organisms, especially those with brains, suffer from information overload. Our eyes and ears receive lights and sounds across the spectrums of visible and audible wavelengths. All told, every second, our senses transmit an estimated 11 million bits of information to our poor brains, as if a giant fiber-optic cable were plugged directly into them, firing information at full speed. In light of this, it is rather incredible that we are even capable of boredom.

Fortunately, we have a valve by which to turn the flow on or off at will. To use another term, we can both "tune in" and "tune out." When we shut the valve, we ignore almost everything, while focusing on just one discrete stream of information out of the millions of bits coming in. In fact, we can even shut out everything external to us, and concentrate on an internal dialogue, as when we are "lost in thought." This ability — to block out most everything, and focus — is what neuroscientists and psychologists refer to as paying attention.

9. 윗글의 제목으로 가장 적절한 것은?
❶ How Do Humans Handle Information Overload? 어떻게 인간은 정보과부화를 다루는가
▶ 바로 밸브를 잠그는 '무시' 전략을 사용하는 것이지.
② Increase Your Attention Span with Practice! 인내심을 가지고 관심 지속 시간을 늘려라
▶ 정반대의 내용이지. 무시가 핵심이야.
③ The More Information, The Better Results 정보가 많으면 많을수록 결과는 더 좋아진다
▶ 정보가 많으면 정보 과부화에 걸리지.
④ Promising Future of the Information Society 정보 사회의 전도 유망한 미래
▶ 정보사회와 관련된 내용은 아니지.
⑤ Information Overload: An Obstacle to Remembering 정보 과부화: 기억의 장애물
▶ 정보 과부화라는 핵심어를 따왔지만, 기억과는 상관이 없는 내용이지.

10. 윗글의 빈칸에 들어갈 말로 가장 적절한 것은?
① criticize 비판하다
② intervene 간섭하다
③ sympathize 공감하다
④ generalize 일반화하다
❺ disregard 무시하다
▶ 들어오는 정보를 차단하는 것, 즉, 무시하는 방법이 핵심이지.

● 중요 포인트

to부정사의 수식을 받는 주어

[This ability – to block out most everything, and focus] –
is ~

2단계 혼공 개념 마무리 p.157

1. 하지만 6천 쪽의 자세한 메모와 그림은 부지런하고 호기심 많은 학생 즉, 부지런히 지식을 추구하는 가운데, 끊임없이 탐구하고, 의문을 제기하고, 시험하는 끊임없는 학습자에 대한 분명한 증거를 보여준다.

2. 그러나 놀라운 것은 이러한 72개의 형용사들 중에서 단지 5개(멋진, 좋은, 아름다운, 예쁜, 그리고 훌륭한)의 형용사만 빈번하게 사용된다는 사실이다.

3. 흔히, 농사에 제격인 평평하고 배수가 잘 되는 땅이 도로 건설에도 이상적이라는 이유만으로 농경지가 포장이 된다.

4. 실험이 가설, 실험법, 그리고 분석의 구조화된 체계의 일부를 형성하는 현대 과학 방식은 17세기에 이르러서인 근래의 것이다. 요리의 문제 해결 기술은 수천 년 전으로 거슬러 간다.

5. 감염의 확산을 막기 위해서 무작위로 집단을 면역시키는 것은 보통 인구의 80에서 100퍼센트를 면역시킬 것을 요구한다.

6. Furness는 한 가족의 'fei'가 수년 전에 폭풍우가 치는 동안 근처의 섬으로부터 운반되던 도중에 바다에서 분실되었다는 이야기를 들었다.

7. 동일한 이유로, 사물이 보통 그러한 혹은 온당히 그래야 하는 방식과 그다지 일치하지 않는 특이한 세부 사항에 대한 강한 민감도는 교전 지역에 있는 군인에게는 중요한 자산이다.

16일차 승부수 문항 모의고사 3회

1단계 모의고사 3회 p.160

● 정답

1. ① **2.** ⑤ **3.** ④ **4.** ① **5.** ② **6.** ② **7.** ② **8.** ②
9. ② **10.** ④

1. ①

● 전체 해석

토양 침식은 새로운 것이 아니다. 새로운 것은 침식의 속도이다. 암석의 풍화가 침식으로 인한 손실보다 많을 때 새로운 토양이 형성된다. 지구의 대부분의 지질학적 역사 내내, 결과적으로 식물의 생장을 뒷받침할 수 있는 점차적이고 장기적인 토양의 축적이 이루어졌다. 그 결과 식물의 생장은 침식을 줄여 주었고 표토의 축적을 용이하게 했다. 역사의 최근 어느 시점에 바람과 물의 침식으로 인한 토양 손실이 새로운 토양 형성을 앞지르면서 이 관계가 뒤바뀌었다. 오늘날의 세계는 연간 수십억 톤의 속도로 토양이 손실되고 있고, 이것이 지구의 생산성을 감소시키고 있다. 많은 국가에서 토양의 손실은 땅의 생산성을 감소시키고 있다.

● 지문분석

Soil erosion is not new.
토지 침식은 새로운 것이 아니다

[What is new] / is the rate of erosion.
새로운 것은 / 침식의 속도이다

New soil forms / when [the weathering of rock] / exceeds losses from erosion.
새로운 토양은 형성된다 / 암석의 풍화가 / 침식으로 인한 손실을 초과할 때

Throughout most of the earth's geological history, / the result was a gradual, long-term buildup of soil / that could support vegetation.
지구의 대부분의 지질학적 역사 내내 / 결과는 점진적이며 장기적인 토양의 형성이었다 / 식물의 생장을 뒷받침할 수 있는

The vegetation in turn reduced erosion / and facilitated the accumulation of topsoil.
식물의 생장은 그 결과 침식을 줄여주며 / 표토의 축적을 용이하게 했다

At some recent point in history, / this relationship was reversed / with soil losses / from wind and water erosion
with + 명사 + 분사: 동시상황
/ exceeding new soil formation.
역사의 최근 어느 시점에서 / 이러한 관계는 뒤바뀌었다 / 토양의 손실이 / 바람과 물에 의한 침식으로부터 / 새로운 토양 형성을 초과하면서

The world now is losing soil / at a rate of billions of tons per year, / and this is reducing the earth's productivity.
오늘날의 세계는 토양을 잃고 있다 / 1년에 수십억 톤의 속도로 / 그리고 이것은 지구의 생산성을 줄이고 있다

In many countries, / [the loss of soil] / is decreasing the productivity of the land.
많은 나라에서 / 토지의 손실은 / 땅의 생산성을 줄이고 있다

● 해설

1. 다음 글의 주제로 가장 적절한 것은?
❶ excessive soil erosion and its negative effect 초과하는 토양 침식과 그 부정적 영향
▶ 토양 형성보다 토양 침식이 빨라져서 지구의 생산성을 감소시키고 있다는 내용이지.
② increased natural rate of topsoil accumulation 표토 축적의 증가된 자연 속도
▶ 토양 형성보다 토양 침식이 더 빨라.
③ roles of water in enhancing soil productivity 토양의 생산성을 늘리는 데 있어 물의 역할
▶ 여기서 물은 토양 침식의 원인이야.
④ ways to enhance the economic value of soil 토양의 경제적 가치를 늘리는 방법
▶ 토양의 생산성을 경제적 가치라고 볼 수도 있지만, 그것을 늘리는 방법이 아니라 그것이 줄어드는 원인에 대해서 말하고 있어.
⑤ factors that facilitate fertile soil formation 비옥한 토양 형성을 촉진하는 요인
▶ fertile(비옥한)을 futile(무익한)과 헷갈리게 해서 낸 오답지야.

●중요 포인트

with + 명사 + 분사 동시상황 구문

At some recent point in history, this relationship was reversed – with soil losses from wind and water erosion exceeding new soil formation.
　　　　with + 명사 + 분사: 동시상황

2. ⑤

●전체 해석

Bilbao의 Guggenheim 박물관이 그랬던 것만큼이나 완전히, 몇몇 지역사회에서 음악과 공연이 동네 전체를 성공적으로 바꾸어 놓았다. 브라질의 Salvador에서 음악가인 Carlinhos Brown은 이전에 위험했던 동네에 음악과 문화 센터를 여러 개 세웠다. Brown이 태어난 Candeal에서, 지역 아이들은 드럼 동호회에 가입하고, 노래를 부르고, 무대에서 공연하도록 권장되었다. 이러한 활동들을 통해 활력을 얻은 이 아이들은 마약 거래에서 손을 떼기 시작했다. 어린 범죄자가 되는 것이 더 이상 이들의 유일한 삶의 선택은 아니었다. 음악가가 되고 그룹을 이루어 함께 연주를 하는 것이 더 재미있어 보였으며, 보다 만족스러운 것이었다. 조금씩 이들 동네에서 범죄율이 감소했고, 희망이 돌아왔다. Brown의 본보기에 영감을 받았을 다른 빈민가 지역에서, 문화센터가 지역 아이들로 하여금 뮤지컬 공연을 무대에 올리도록 권장하였으며, 이 중 몇몇은 아이들이 아직 회복 중에 있던 비극적인 일을 극화한 것이었다.

●지문분석

In some communities, / music and performance have successfully transformed whole neighborhoods / as profoundly / as The Guggenheim Museum did in Bilbao.
어떤 사회에서는 / 음악과 공연은 성공적으로 동네 전체를 바꾸어 놓았다 / 심오하게 / Bilbao의 Guggenheim 박물관이 그랬던 것처럼

In Salvador, Brazil, / musician Carlinhos Brown established several music and culture centers / in formerly dangerous neighborhoods.
브라질의 Slavador에서 / 음악가인 Carlinhos Brown은 음악과 문화 센터를 설립했다 / 이전에 위험한 동네에

In Candeal, / where Brown was born, / local kids were encouraged to join / drum groups, sing, and stage performances.
Candeal에서 / Brown이 태어났던 / 지역 아이들은 참여하도록 권장되었다 / 드럼 그룹과 노래, 그리고 무대 공연에

[The kids, / energized by these activities,] / began to turn away from dealing drugs.
그 아이들은 / 이러한 활동에 의해서 활력을 얻은 / 마약 거래에서 손을 떼기 시작했다

[Being a young criminal] / was no longer their only life option.
어린 범죄자가 되는 것은 / 더 이상 그들의 유일한 삶의 선택이 아니었다

[Being musicians and playing together in a group] / looked like more fun / and was more satisfying.
음악가가 되고 그룹에서 함께 연주하는 것은 / 더 재미있어 보였고 / 더 만족스러웠다

Little by little, / the crime rate dropped / in those neighborhoods; / the hope returned.
조금씩 조금씩 / 범죄율은 떨어졌다 / 그 동네에서 / 희망이 돌아왔다

In another slum area, / possibly inspired by Brown's example, / a culture center began to encourage / the local kids to stage musical events, / some of which dramatized the tragedy / that they were still recovering from.
또 다른 빈민가 지역에서는 / Brown의 예에 영감을 받았을 / 문화 센터가 권장하기 시작했다 / 지역 아이들로 하여금 뮤지컬 공연을 무대에 올리도록 / 그중 일부는 비극을 극화한 것이었다 / 그들이 여전히 회복 중에 있던

●해설

2. 다음 글의 밑줄 친 부분 중, 어법상 틀린 것은?
① 동사인 transformed를 수식하므로 부사인 profoundly는 옳지.
② 뒤에 오는 문장이 완전하므로 관계부사 where은 적절해.
③ 주어는 the kids이고 사이에 있는 energized by these activities는 주어를 수식하는 분사구야. 본동사가 필요하니 과거동사인 began은 적절해.
④ 수식을 받는 주어 Being musicians and playing together in a group이 '만족감을 주고' 있으므로 능동의 의미를 가진 형용사 satisfying(만족스러운)이 적절하지.
❺ them → which: 문장은 두 개 인데 이를 연결해줄 연결사가 없으므로 관계사가 와야 하지. 선행사가 musical events이므로 which가 와야 해.

●중요 포인트

부정대명사 + which

'문장 + 문장'에서 '+' 역할은 접속사나 관계사가 하지. 그런데 접속사와 관계사는 동시에 나올 수가 없어. 둘 중 하나만 나와야 해. 아래 문장에서는 접속사가 보이지 않으니 관계사가 나와야 하겠지.

In another slum area, possibly inspired by Brown's example, a culture center began to encourage the local kids to stage musical events, some of which dramatized the tragedy that they were still recovering from.

3. ④

●전체 해석

논거에 대한 결론의 우위는 감정이 결부되는 곳에서 가장 두드러진다. 심리학자 Paul Slovic은 사람들이 좋아하는 것과 싫어하는 것이 세상에 대한 그들의 믿음을 결정한다는 이론을 제시했다. 여러분의 정치적 선호는 여러분이 설득력이 있다고 생각하는 논거를 결정한다. 만일 여러분이 현재의 보건 정책을 좋아한다면 여러분은 그것의 이점이 상당히 많고 그것의 비용이 대안들의 비용보다 더 관리할 만하다고 믿는다. 만약 여러분이 다른 나라에 대하여 강경론자의 태도를 취한다면, 여러분은 아마 그들이 비교적 약하고 여러분 나라의 뜻에 굴복하기 쉬울 거라고 생각할 것이다.

만일 여러분이 온건론자라면 여러분은 아마 그들이 강하고 쉽게 설득되지 않을 거라고 생각할 것이다. 육류, 원자력, 문신 또는 오토바이와 같은 것들에 대한 여러분의 감정적인 태도는 그것들의 이점과 위험에 대한 여러분의 믿음을 따른다(→이끈다). 만약 여러분이 이것들 중 어떤 것이라도 싫어한다면 여러분은 아마 그것들의 위험은 높고 이점은 사소하다고 믿을 것이다.

● 지문분석

[The dominance of conclusions over arguments] / is most pronounced / where emotions are involved.
논거에 대한 결론의 우위는 / 가장 두드러진다 / 감정이 수반되는 곳에서

The psychologist Paul Slovic has proposed a theory / in which people let their likes and dislikes determine / their beliefs about the world.
심리학자인 Paul Slovic은 이론을 제시했다 / 사람들은 그들이 좋아하는 것과 싫어하는 것이 결정하도록 한다는 / 세상에 대한 그들의 믿음을

Your political preference / determines the arguments / that you find compelling.
당신의 정치적 선호도는 / 논거를 결정한다 / 당신이 설득력이 있다고 생각하는

If you like the current health policy, / you believe / its benefits are substantial / and its costs more manageable / than the costs of alternatives.
만약 당신이 현재의 보건 정책을 좋아한다면 / 당신은 믿는다 / 그것의 혜택이 상당하다고 / 그리고 그것의 비용은 더 관리할 만하다고 / 대안의 비용들보다

If you are a hawk / in your attitude toward other nations, / you probably think / they are relatively weak / and likely to submit to your country's will.
당신이 강경파라면 / 다른 나라에 대한 당신의 태도에서 / 당신은 아마도 생각할 것이다 / 그들은 상대적으로 약하다고 / 그리고 당신 나라의 의지에 굴복할 가능성이 높다고

If you are a dove, / you probably think / they are strong / and will not be easily persuaded.
당신이 온건파라면 / 당신은 아마도 생각할 것이다 / 그들이 강하다고 / 그리고 쉽게 설득되지 않을 것이라고

[Your emotional attitude / to such things / as red meat, nuclear power, tattoos, or motorcycles] / drives your beliefs / about their benefits and their risks.
당신의 감정적 태도가 / 그건 것들에 대한 / 육류, 원자력, 문신 또는 오토바이와 같은 / 당신의 믿음을 이끈다 / 그들의 이점과 위험에 대한

If you dislike any of these things, / you probably believe / that its risks are high / and its benefits negligible.
당신이 만약 이러한 것 중 어떤 것도 싫다면 / 당신은 아마 믿을 것이다 / 그것의 위험이 높고 / 그리고 그것의 이점이 사소하다고

---

3. 다음 글의 밑줄 친 부분 중 문맥상 낱말의 쓰임이 적절하지 <u>않은</u> 것은?

① 좋아하고 싫어하는 것이니까 선호도(preference)가 적절해.

② 이점이 더 크니까 다른 것의 비용보다 지금드는 비용을 감당할만 하므로 '관리 가능한(more manageable)'이 적절하지.

③ 상대방에 대해서 강경파니까 상대방을 굴복(submit)시킨다는 것이 적절하지.

❹ follows → drives: 글의 내용 전개가 감정으로 인해서 믿음이 결정된다고 하고 있으니까 감정적 태도가 믿음을 따르는(follow) 것이 아니라 이끌어야(drives) 하겠지.

⑤ 위험이 커지고 이점이 사소하다고 했으니 그 대상을 싫어하겠지(dislike).

● 중요 포인트

전치사 + 관계대명사

The psychologist Paul Slovic has proposed a theory in which people let their likes and dislikes determine their beliefs about the world.
전치사 + which + 완전한 문장

4. ①

● 전체 해석

진정성은 리더십의 효과의 비결 중 하나이다. 우리는 임원실에서, 관리자의 사무실에서, 그리고 우리의 종교 지도자에게서 진실함을 원한다. 우리는 다른 어느 누군가의 복사품이 아닌 그들 자신인 지도자를 동경한다. 우리는 우리에게 완전히 인간적일 지도자를, 자신들의 장점과 단점, 자신들의 재능과 한계를 인정할 만큼 약점이 있고, 자신들의 희망과 두려움, 자신들의 동기부여와 자신들의 계획에 있어서 타당하게 솔직한 사람들을 원한다. 우리는 진실하고, 언행이 일치되고, 자신들의 핵심 가치에 따라 행동하고, 그리고 우리에게 진실을 말하는 지도자를 신뢰한다. 우리는 그들 자신의 삶을 써 나가는 다른 사람들에게 (우리를) 이끄는 권한을 부여한다. 우리는 우리가 신뢰할 수 있다고 여기지 않는 사람들에게 (우리를) 이끄는 권한을 부여하지 않는다.

● 지문분석

Authenticity is one of the keys / to leadership effectiveness.
진정성은 핵심 중 하나이다 / 리더십 효과의

We want realness / in the executive suite, / in the superintendent's office, / and in our religious leaders.
우리는 진실함을 원한다 / 임원실에서 / 관리자의 사무실에서 / 그리고 우리의 종교 지도자에게서

We yearn for leaders / who are themselves / rather than a copy of someone else.
우리는 리더들을 동경한다 / 자기 자신인 / 다른 누군가의 복제품이 아닌

We want leaders / who will be fully human with us, / men and women / who are vulnerable enough / to acknowledge their strengths and weaknesses, their gifts and limits, / and who are appropriately transparent / about their hopes and

---

fears, their motivations and their agendas.

우리는 지도자들을 원한다 / 우리에게 완전히 인간적일 / 남자와 여자들을 / 충분히 약한 / 그들의 강점과 약점, 그들의 재능과 한계를 인정할 정도로 / 그리고 타당하게 솔직한 / 그들의 희망과 두려움, 그들의 동기와 계획에 대해서

We trust leaders / who are real, / who walk their talk, / who act on their core values, / and who tell us the truth.

우리는 지도자들을 신뢰한다 / 진실되고 / 언행이 일치되고 / 자신의 핵심 가치에 따라 행동하고 / 우리에게 진실을 말하는

We authorize others / to lead / who author their own life.

우리는 다른 사람들에게 권한을 부여한다 / 우리를 이끌 / 자신의 삶을 써내려가는

Those / we deem not trustworthy / we don't authorize / to lead.
        목적어 도치

사람들에게 / 우리가 믿을 만하지 않다고 여기는 / 우리는 권한을 주지 않는다 / 우리를 이끌

● 해설

4. 다음 빈칸에 들어갈 말로 가장 적절한 것은?

_____ is one of the keys to leadership effectiveness. We want realness in the executive suite, in the superintendent's office, and in our religious leaders. We yearn for leaders who are themselves rather than a copy of someone else. We want leaders who will be fully human with us, men and women who are vulnerable enough to acknowledge their strengths and weaknesses, their gifts and limits, and who are appropriately transparent about their hopes and fears, their motivations and their agendas. We trust leaders who are real, who walk their talk, who act on their core values, and who tell us the truth. We authorize others to lead who author their own life. Those we deem not trustworthy we don't authorize to lead.

❶ Authenticity 진정성
▶ 이 글의 핵심은 과연 '그 사람이 믿을 만한가'야. '믿을 만한가'가 바로 '진정성'이겠지.
② Tolerance 관용
③ Dedication 헌신
▶ 지도자에게 필요한 요건이지만, 여기서는 언급이 되지 않았어.
④ Compassion 동정심
⑤ Responsibility 책임
▶ 권한이라는 내용이 본문에서 나오기 때문에 나온 오답이지.

● 중요 포인트

목적어 도치

Those / we deem not trustworthy / we don't authorize /
        목적어 도치
to lead.

= We don't authorize those we deem not trustworthy to lead.

5. ②

● 전체 해석

축구의 페널티킥 상황에서 공은 공을 찬 선수로부터 골대로 이동하는 데 0.3초도 걸리지 않는다. 골키퍼에게는 공의 경로를 관찰하는데 충분한 시간이 없다. 상대가 공을 차기 전에 골키퍼는 결정을 해야 한다. 페널티킥을 차는 축구 선수들은 각각 3분의 1의 경우로 골대의 중간, 골대의 왼쪽, 골대의 오른쪽으로 공을 찬다. 물론 골키퍼들은 이를 알고 있지만 그들은 무엇을 하는가? 그들은 왼쪽이나 오른쪽으로 몸을 던진다. 비록 대략 모든 공의 3분의 1이 중앙으로 떨어짐에도 불구하고 그들은 좀처럼 중앙에 서 있지 않는다. 왜 그들은 이런 공을 막으려고 하지 않을까? 그 간단한 대답은 모양새다. 그 위치에서 가만히 공이 지나가는 것을 보고 있는 것보다 잘못된 방향으로 몸을 던지는 것이 좀 더 인상적으로 보이고 덜 민망하게 느껴진다.

● 지문분석

In a penalty situation in soccer, / the ball takes less than 0.3 seconds / to travel from the player / who kicks the ball / to the goal.

축구의 페널티킥 상황에서 / 공은 0.3초도 걸리지 않는다 / 선수로부터 떠나는 데 / 골을 차는 / 골대로

There is not enough time / for the goalkeeper / to watch the ball's trajectory.

충분한 시간이 없다 / 골키퍼가 / 공의 경로를 관찰하는데

He must make a decision / before the ball is kicked.

그는 결정을 해야만 한다 / 공을 차기 전에

[Soccer players / who take penalty kicks] / shoot one third
        S   관계대명사   V
of the time at the middle of the goal, / one third of the time at the left, / and one third of the time at the right.

축구 선수들은 / 페널티 킥을 차는 / 1/3은 골대 중간으로 공을 찬다 / 1/3은 왼쪽으로 / 1/3은 오른쪽으로

Surely goalkeepers have spotted this, / but what do they do?

확실히 골키퍼는 이것을 알고 있지만 / 그들은 무엇을 하는가?

They dive either to the left or to the right.

그들은 왼쪽이든 오른쪽이든 몸을 던진다

Rarely do they stay standing in the middle / – even though
부정어 도치 V S
roughly a third of all balls land there.

그들은 거의 중앙에 서 있지는 않는다 / 비록 거의 모든 공의 1/3이 거기에 떨어짐에도 불구하고

Why would they jeopardize saving these penalties?

왜 그들은 위태롭게 이러한 페널티를 막으려고 할까

The simple answer: appearance.

간단한 대답은 외모(모양새)이다

It looks more impressive / and feels less embarrassing /
가주어-진주어
to dive to the wrong side / than to freeze on the spot / and watch the ball sail past.

더욱 인상적으로 보이고 / 덜 민망하게 느껴진다 / 잘못된 쪽으로 던지는 것이 / 그 자리에 가만히 있는 것보다 / 그리고 공이 지나가는 것을 보는 것보다

5. 다음 빈칸에 들어갈 말로 가장 적절한 것은?

In a penalty situation in soccer, the ball takes less than 0.3 seconds to travel from the player who kicks the ball to the goal. There is not enough time for the goalkeeper to watch the ball's trajectory. He must make a decision before the ball is kicked. Soccer players who take penalty kicks shoot one third of the time at the middle of the goal, one third of the time at the left, and one third of the time at the right. Surely goalkeepers have spotted this, but what do they do? They dive either to the left or to the right. Rarely do they stay standing in the middle – even though roughly a third of all balls land there. Why would they jeopardize saving these penalties? The simple answer: _____. It looks more impressive and feels less embarrassing to dive to the wrong side than to freeze on the spot and watch the ball sail past.

① agility 민첩성
▶ 공이 지나가는 걸 가만히 보기보다 움직이는 걸 선택하는 건 민첩성이 아니지.
❷ appearance 모양새(외양)
▶ 가만히 있는 것보다 움직이는 것이 더 인상적이고 덜 당황스러운것과 어울리는 게 바로 '모양새'겠지.
③ indecision 우유부단함
▶ 이도 저도 결정하지 못한 것은 아니지.
④ accuracy 정확성
⑤ impatience 성급함

● 중요 포인트

부정어 도치

Rarely do they stay standing in the middle – even though
부정어 도치 V   S
roughly a third of all balls land there.
부정어인 rarely가 문두에 오니 주어와 동사가 서로 도치가 되지.

6. ②

● 전체 해석

참가자들에게 재료가 가득 찬 가방을 하나 준 다음 해결할 문제를 주는 것은 창의력 세미나를 하는 동안 흔히 있는 일이다. 그 재료는 보통 일상 용품이다. 그것들의 쓰임새는 모두에게 분명하다. 그런데 그 재료를 사용해서 원하는 어떤 방식으로든 그 문제를 해결해야만 한다. 하지만 물품과 문제 사이에는 보통 분명한 연관성이 없다. 예를 들어, 망치, 테이프, 머리 빗는 솔, 그리고 구슬 한 봉지를 사용하여 여러분은 아마도 통신 장치를 만드는 방법을 생각해 내야만 할 것이다. 대부분의 사람에게는 오로지 전형적인 맥락에서만 물체를 보게 하는, 기능적 고착이라는 인지적 편향이 있다. 그 재료를 일상적인 방식으로 사용하면 일반적으로 실행 가능한 해결책이 나오지 않을 것이다. 정말로 흥미진진한 해결책은 기능적 고착을 극복하고 이런 일상 용품을 새로운 방식으로 사용하는 데서 온다. (새로운 쓰임의) 가능성을 알기 위해서는, 그 어떤 것도 여러분이 생각하는 그대로인 것은 없다는 관점을 취하는 것이 도움이 된다.

● 지문분석

It's a common practice / during creativity seminars / to
가주어–진주어
give participants a bag / full of materials / and then a
problem to solve.
일반적인 행위이다 / 창의력 세미나 동안에 / 참가자들에게 가방을 주는 것은 / 재료로 가득 찬 / 그리고 해결할 문제를

The materials are usually everyday items.
그 재료들은 보통 일상 용품이다

Their use is obvious to all.
그것들의 쓰임은 모두에게 명백하다

You are then to use those materials / in whatever ways / you want to solve the problem; / however, there isn't usually an obvious connection / between the items and your problem.
당신은 그때 그러한 재료들을 사용해야만 한다 / 어떤 방식으로든지 / 당신이 문제를 해결하기를 원하는 / 하지만, 보통 명백한 관계는 없다 / 용품들과 당신의 문제 사이에는

For instance, maybe you have to figure out / how to create a communication device / using a hammer, tape, a
└분사구문
hairbrush, and a bag of marbles.
예를 들어 아마도 당신은 생각해 내야만 한다 / 통신 장치를 만드는 방법을 / 망치와 테이프, 빗, 그리고 구슬 한 봉지를 이용해서

Most people have a cognitive bias / called functional fixedness / that causes them to see objects / only in their normal context.
대부분의 사람들은 인지적 편향을 가진다 / 기능적 고착이라고 불리우는 / 그들로 하여금 사물을 보도록 하는 / 오직 그들의 전형적인 맥락에서

[The use of the materials / in their ordinary way] / will generally lead to no workable solutions.
재료들의 사용은 / 그들의 일상적인 방식으로 / 일반적으로 실행 가능한 해결책을 이끌지 못할 것이다

The really exciting solutions / come from overcoming
❶
functional fixedness / and using these everyday items in
❷
new ways.
진짜로 흥미진진한 해결책은 / 기능적 고착을 극복하는 것에서 온다 / 그리고 이러한 일상 용품을 새로운 방식으로 사용하는 데서

To see the possibilities / it is helpful / to take the
가주어–진주어
viewpoint / that nothing is what you think it is.
그 가능성을 알기 위해서 / 도움이 된다 / 관점을 취하는 것이 / 어떠한 것도 당신이 생각하는 그대로인 것은 없다는

● 해설

6. 다음 빈칸에 들어갈 말로 가장 적절한 것은?

It's a common practice during creativity seminars to give participants a bag full of materials and then a problem to solve. The materials are usually everyday items. Their use is obvious to all. You are then to use those materials in whatever ways you want to solve the problem; however, there isn't usually an obvious connection between the items and your problem.

For instance, maybe you have to figure out how to create a communication device using a hammer, tape, a hairbrush, and a bag of marbles. Most people have a cognitive bias called functional fixedness that causes them to see objects only in their normal context. The use of the materials in their ordinary way will generally lead to no workable solutions. The really exciting solutions come from overcoming functional fixedness and using these everyday items in new ways. To see the possibilities it is helpful to take the viewpoint that _____.

① good tools make fine work 좋은 도구는 멋진 작품을 만든다
▶ 도구의 좋고 나쁨이 문제가 아니지.
❷ nothing is what you think it is 생각하는 그대로인 것은 없다
▶ 일상 용품에서 새로운 방식을 생각해야 하는 것이고 기능적 고착을 극복하는 것이므로 새로운 발상을 의미하는 것을 찾아가겠지.
③ having many options is not a blessing 많은 선택지를 가지는 것은 축복이 아니다
▶ 가짓수가 많다는 것이 핵심은 아니야.
④ the more we know, the more we want 우리가 더 많이 알면 알수록 우리는 더 많은 것을 원한다
▶ 욕망에 대한 것이 아니지.
⑤ deep learning is composed of small parts 깊은 학습은 작은 부품들로 구성된다
▶ 작은 지식의 중요성을 의미하는 말인데 창의적인 방식을 의미하기에는 너무 범위가 크지.

● 중요 포인트

연달아 이어지는 수식 구조
                                        분사의 명사 수식
Most people have a cognitive bias called functional
                  관계대명사의 명사 수식
fixedness that causes them to see objects only in their
normal context.

7. ②

● 전체 해석

광범위한 개방형 질문은 여러분이 상대방의 상황에 관심을 갖고 있음을 보여줍니다. 그것들은 흔히 "제게 말씀해주세요", "어떻게", "누가", "무엇을" 혹은 "왜"로 시작됩니다. (B) 그것들은 "네" 혹은 "아니오" 혹은 특정한 정보와 같은 단순한 대답을 요구하는 폐쇄형 질문보다 훨씬 더 강력합니다. 광범위한 질문이 대화를 개시하고 친밀한 관계를 만들어내기 시작한 후에, 노련한 질문자는 그 반응을 기반으로 해서 전달되는 정보에 대한 자신의 이해를 높입니다. (A) 우리의 컴퓨터 판매원은 "저는 우리의 주문 시스템에 대한 더 많은 통제가 필요해요."라고 말하는 의뢰인을 만날지 모릅니다. 그러면 그는 대답에서 가장 중요한 단어인 '통제'와 '주문 시스템'을 사용하여 질문함으로써 그 반응에서 이어나갑니다. (C) 예를 들어, 그는 "당신의 주문 시스템의 어떤 측면에 대해서 더 많은 통제를 하고 싶으신가요?" 혹은 "당신의 주문 시스템에 대해서 좀 더 말씀해 주시겠어요?"라고 질문할 수 있습니다. 그 의뢰인이 대답을 하면, 그는 그 질문에 대한 응답과 관련하여 다음 질문들을 계속 만들어냅니다.

● 지문분석

Broad, open-ended questions show / your interest in the other person's situation.
광범위한 개방형 질문은 보여준다 / 다른 사람의 상황에 대한 당신의 관심을
They often start with / "Tell me," "how," "who," "what," or "why."
그들은 종종 시작된다 / "말해봐요", "어떻게", "누가", "무엇을", 아니면 "왜"로
They are much more powerful / than closed questions / that require a simple answer / such as "yes" or "no" or a specific piece of information.
그들은 훨씬 더 강력하다 / 폐쇄형 질문들보다 / 간단한 대답을 요구하는 / "네" 아니면 "아니요" 혹은 특정한 정보와 같은
After the broad question opens the conversation / and begins to build rapport, / the artful questioner builds on the responses / and increases his understanding of the information / being transferred.
광범위한 질문이 대화를 연 후에 / 그리고 관계 구축을 시작한 후에 / 노련한 질문자는 반응을 쌓고 / 그리고 정보에 대한 그의 이해를 높인다 / 전달되고 있는
Our computer salesperson might have a client / who says, / "I need more control over our order system."
우리의 컴퓨터 판매원은 고객이 있을지도 모른다 / 말하는 / 나는 우리 주문 시스템에 대한 더 많은 통제가 필요하다고
He then builds on that response / by asking a question / using the most important words in the answer / – control
                                              분사구문
and order system.
그는 그때 그러한 반응을 구축한다 / 질문을 물어봄으로써 / 가장 중요한 단어들을 답변에서 사용하면서 / 통제와 주문 시스템을
For instance, he might ask, / "What aspects of your order system / would you like to have more control over?" / or "Could you tell me more / about your order system?"
예를 들어 그는 물어볼지도 모른다 / 당신의 주문 시스템 중 어떤 속성에 대해서 / 당신은 더 많은 통제를 하고 싶으신가요? / 아니면 당신은 나에게 더 많은 걸 말해줄 수 있나요 / 당신의 주문 시스템에 대한
When the client responds, / he builds his next question / around the response to that question, / and so on.
고객이 답변을 할 때 / 그는 다음 질문을 만든다 / 그 질문에 대한 답변과 관련하여 / 그리고 계속해서

● 해설

7. 주어진 글 다음에 이어질 글의 순서로 가장 적절한 것은?
Broad, open-ended questions show your interest in the other person's situation. They often start with "Tell me," "how," "who," "what," or "why."

(B) They are much more powerful than closed questions that require a simple answer such as "yes" or "no" or a specific piece of information. After the broad question opens the conversation and begins to build rapport, the artful questioner builds on the responses and increases his understanding of the information being transferred.

(A) Our computer salesperson might have a client who says, "I need more control over our order system." He then builds on that response by asking a question using the most important words in the answer – control and order system.

(C) For instance, he might ask, "What aspects of your order system would you like to have more control over?" or "Could you tell me more about your order system?" When the client responds, he builds his next question around the response to that question, and so on.

주어진 문장은 개방형 질문에 대한 특징이 설명되고 있어. 이와 반대되는 폐쇄형 질문에 대한 비교우위를 설명하는 (B)가 먼저 나와야 겠지. (B)에서 언급되는 주문 시스템에 대한 내용이 (A)에서 언급되고 있고, (C)에 나오는 he는 (A)의 컴퓨터 판매원이어야 하지. 따라서 (B)−(A)−(C)가 되어야 해.

● 중요 포인트

분사의 수식을 받는 명사

After the broad question opens the conversation and begins to build rapport, the artful questioner builds on the responses and increases his understanding of the information being transferred.
분사의 명사 수식

8. ②

● 전체 해석

지난 세기 동안 사회적으로 의학, 과학, 그리고 기술에서 엄청난 발전이 이루어졌다. 이러한 발전은 한 개인이나 많은 개인들이 이전에는 해결할 수 없다고 생각되었던 문제들을 해결하기 위해 자신의 지적 상상력의 모든 자원을 이용했기 때문에 일어났다. 그러나 바로 그 시기 동안 윤리적 행동에서는 그에 필적하는 전 세계적인 진보가 없었다. 그것은 부분적으로는 인간이 도덕적 문제를 해결하기 위해 자신의 지성의 모든 자원을 거의 사용하지 않기 때문이다. 도덕적 상상력을 발휘하는 것은 다른 사람들을 돕는 창의적이고 혁신적인 방법을 고안하기 위해 우리의 지성을 사용하는 것을 의미한다. 예를 들어, 자선에 관해 말하자면, 그것은 가난한 사람들에게 즉각적인 지원을 제공하는 것뿐만 아니라 그들이 자립하고 더 이상 도움이 필요하지 않도록 해 주는 방식으로 가난한 사람들을 돕는 것을 의미한다. 그렇기에 도움이 필요한 어떤 상황에서든 우리는 어려운 처지의 사람들을 돕는 가장 효과적이고 애정 어린 방법을 찾기 위해 우리의 지성을 사용해야 한다.

● 지문분석

> Over the past century, / society has witnessed extraordinary advances / in medicine, science, and technology.

지난 세기 동안 / 사회는 엄청난 발전을 목격해왔다 / 의학과 과학 그리고 기술에서

These advances came about / because an individual, or many individuals, / used the full resources of his or her intellectual imagination / to solve problems / that had previously been thought to be unsolvable.
이러한 발전을 일어났다 / 개인 혹은 많은 개인들이 / 자신의 지적 상상력의 모든 자원을 사용했기 때문에 / 문제를 해결하기 위해서 / 이전에 해결할 수 없다고 생각되었던

However, during the same period, / there has been no comparable worldwide advance / in ethical behavior.
하지만, 같은 기간 동안에 / 필적하는 전 세계적인 진보가 없었다 / 윤리적 행동에서

That is, in part, / because human beings rarely use the full resources of their intellect / to solve moral problems.
그것은 부분적으로 / 인류가 거의 그들의 지성의 모든 자원을 사용하지 않았기 때문이다 / 도덕 문제를 해결하기 위해서

[Exercising moral imagination] means using our intelligence / to devise creative and innovative ways / to help others.
도덕적 상상력을 발휘하는 것은 / 우리의 지성을 사용하는 것을 의미한다 / 창의적이고 혁신적인 방법을 고안하기 위해서 / 남들을 돕는

Concerning charity, for example, / it means not only providing immediate assistance to the impoverished, / but also helping the poor in ways / that will enable them to support themselves and / no longer need help.
'~에 관하여
예를 들어 자선에 관하여 / 그것은 가난한 사람들에게 즉각적인 지원을 제공하는 것을 의미할 뿐만 아니라 / 방식으로 가난한 사람을 돕는 것을 의미한다 / 그들이 자립하도록 하고 / 더 이상 도움이 필요하지 않도록 해 주는

Therefore, in any situation / in which help is required, / we should use our intelligence / to discover the most effective and loving way / to help those in need.
그래서 어떤 상황에서든지 간에 / 도움이 필요로 한 / 우리는 우리의 지성을 사용해야만 한다 / 가장 효과적이고 애정 어린 방법을 찾기 위해서 / 어려운 처지의 사람들을 돕기 위해서

● 해설

8. 글의 흐름으로 보아, 주어진 문장이 들어가기에 가장 적절한 곳은?

However, during the same period, there has been no comparable worldwide advance in ethical behavior.
윤리적 진보가 없었다는 내용이므로 앞에는 어떠한 형태의 진보가 있었다는 내용이 나와야 하겠지.

Over the past century, society has witnessed extraordinary advances in medicine, science, and technology. (①) These advances came about because an individual, or many individuals, used the full resources of his or her intellectual imagination to solve problems that had previously been thought to be unsolvable. (②) That is, in part, because human beings rarely use the full resources of their intellect to solve moral problems. (③) Exercising moral imagination means
도덕적 문제가 처음으로 언급되고 있지.

using our intelligence to devise creative and innovative ways to help others. (④) Concerning charity, for example, it means not only providing immediate assistance to the impoverished, but also helping the poor in ways that will enable them to support themselves and no longer need help. (⑤) Therefore, in any situation in which help is required, we should use our intelligence to discover the most effective and loving way to help those in need.

● 중요 포인트

동명사 주어

[Exercising moral imagination] means using our intelligence to devise creative and innovative ways to help others.

S → 동명사 주어 → 단수 취급   V → 단수 동사

9. ② 10. ④

● 전체 해석

이용 가능한 저장 용량의 과잉은 우리가 외부 기억 장치와 관련한 우리 행동의 초기 설정을 잊어버리기에서 기억하기로 바꾸는 것을 쉽게 만들어 준다. 우리는 작업 중인 다양한 형태의 문서를 하드 디스크에 저장한다. 그리고 언젠가 우리가 그것들을 필요로 하게 될지도 모른다는 가정하에 우리는 이미지와 음악 파일들을 저장한다. 정보를 저장하는 것이 엄청나게 편리해졌지만 우리로 하여금 보존하도록 만드는 것은 편리함 이상이다. 사실은 저장의 경제적인 측면이 잊어버리기를 너무 값비싸게 만들어 버렸다는 것이다. 디지털 카메라를 생각해 보라. 당신이 찍은 사진을 하드디스크에 올리기 위해 카메라를 컴퓨터에 연결하면, 당신에게 대개 선택권이 주어진다. 당신은 어떤 이미지를 올릴지 선택하거나 혹은 당신의 컴퓨터가 자동으로 모든 이미지를 카메라에서 복사하도록 할 수 있다. 아마도 언제든지 그것들(이미지)을 나중에 살펴보고 자신이 좋아하지 않는 이미지는 삭제할 수 있다는 마음을 달래주는 생각으로 안심하면서, 변함없이 대부분의 사람들은 후자를 선택한다. 경제적으로 말하면 이것은 이치에 맞는다. 한 사람이 이미지 하나를 보고 그것을 보존할지 말지를 결정하는 데 단지 3초가 걸리고 그녀가 현재 평균 임금 대비 자신의 시간 가치를 평가한다고 가정하면, 결정을 하는 데 걸리는 시간만의 '비용'은 저장하는 비용을 초과한다. 그런 저렴한 저장의 풍족함 때문에 기억할지 또는 잊어버릴지를 결정하는 것조차도 더 이상 절대 경제적이지 않다. 잊어버리기, 선택을 하는 데 걸리는 그 3초가 사람들이 사용하기에는 너무나 값비싸졌다.

● 지문분석

[The overabundance / of available storage capacity] / makes it easy / for us / to shift our behavioral default / regarding external memory / from forgetting to remembering.

V   └가목적어   └의미상의 주어 └진목적어

과잉은 / 이용 가능한 저장 능력의 / 쉽게 만든다 / 우리가 / 우리의 행동적 초기 설정을 바꾸는 것을 / 외부 기억에 대한 / 잊어버리는 것에서 기억하는 것으로

We save different versions of the documents / we are working on / to our hard disks.

우리는 자료의 다른 버전을 저장한다 / 우리가 작업하는 / 우리의

하드디스크에

And we store images and music files, / on the assumption / that perhaps some day we might need them.

그리고 우리는 이미지와 음악 파일을 저장한다 / 가정 하에 / 아마도 언젠가 우리가 그것들을 필요할지도 모른다는

[Storing information] / has become fantastically convenient, / but it's more than convenience / that makes us preserve.

S   V

└가주어   └진주어

정보를 저장하는 것은 / 엄청나게 편리해졌다 / 하지만 편리 그 이상이다 / 우리가 보존하도록 만드는 것은

The truth is / that [the economics of storage] / have made forgetting brutally expensive.

사실은 / 저장의 경제적인 측면의 / 잊는 것을 너무 비싸게 만들었다

Consider digital cameras: / When you connect your camera / to your computer / to upload the images / you took / onto your hard disk, / you are usually given a choice.

디지털 카메라를 고려해보자 / 여러분이 카메라를 연결할 때 / 여러분의 컴퓨터에 / 이미지를 업로드하기 위해서 / 여러분이 찍은 / 여러분의 하드디스크로 / 보통은 선택권이 주어진다

You can either select which images to upload, / or have your computer copy automatically all images / from your camera.

여러분은 어떤 이미지를 업로드할지 선택할 수 있거나 / 아니면 여러분의 컴퓨터가 모든 이미지를 자동적으로 복사하도록 할 수 있다 / 여러분의 카메라로부터

Reassured perhaps by the soothing idea / that one can always go through them later / and delete the images / one does not like, / invariably most people choose the latter option.

└분사구문

아마도 마음을 달래주는 생각에 의해 안심하면서 / 사람은 항상 나중에 그것을 살펴볼 수 있고 / 이미지들을 지울 수 있다는 / 사람이 좋아하지 않는 / 변함없이 대부분의 사람들은 후자의 선택사항을 선택한다

Economically speaking, / this makes sense.

경제적으로 말하자면 / 이것은 말이 된다

Assuming / it takes only three seconds / for a person to look at an image / and decide whether to preserve it or not, / and that she values her own time / at a current average wage, / [the "cost" of the time alone / that it takes to decide] / exceeds the cost of storage.

└분사구문

S

가정한다면 / 겨우 3초만 걸린다고 / 사람이 이미지를 보는 데 / 그리고 그것을 보존할지 안할지 결정하는 데 / 그리고 그녀가 자신의 시간의 가치를 매긴다고 / 현재의 평균 임금으로 / 시간만의 비용은 / 결정하는 데 걸리는 / 저장의 비용을 초과한다

With such an abundance of cheap storage, / it is simply no longer economical / to even decide / whether to remember or forget.

└가주어

└진주어

그런 가격이 싼 저장의 풍족함 때문에 / 단순히 더 이상 경제적이지는 않다 / 심지어 결정하는 것이 / 기억할지 잊어버릴지를

Forgetting – the three seconds / it takes to choose / – has
become too expensive / for people to use.
잊어버리는 것은 / 3초가 / 선택하는 데 걸리는 / 너무 비싸서 / 사람들은 이용할 수 없다

인 지원을 제공하는 것뿐만 아니라 그들이 자립하고 더 이상 도움이 필요하지 않도록 해 주는 방식으로 가난한 사람들을 돕는 것을 의미한다.

4. 아마도 언제든지 그것들(이미지)을 나중에 살펴보고 자신이 좋아하지 않는 이미지는 삭제할 수 있다는 마음을 달래주는 생각으로 안심하면서, 변함없이 대부분의 사람들은 후자를 선택한다.

5. 만약 여러분이 다른 나라에 대하여 강경론자의 태도를 취한다면, 여러분은 아마 그들이 비교적 약하고 여러분 나라의 뜻에 굴복하기 쉬울 거라고 생각할 것이다.

6. 한 사람이 이미지 하나를 보고 그것을 보존할지 말지를 결정하는 데 단지 3초가 걸리고 그녀가 현재 평균 임금 대비 자신의 시간 가치를 평가한다고 가정하면, 결정을 하는 데 걸리는 시간만의 '비용'은 저장하는 비용을 초과한다.

● 해설

9. 윗 글의 제목으로 가장 적절한 것은?
① Save Selectively, Save Your Effort! 선택적으로 아껴라. 당신의 노력을 아껴라.
❷ Cheap Storage Drives Us to Keep It All 저렴한 저장은 우리가 그것을 모두 유지하도록 이끈다
▶ 저장하는 데 드는 비용이 저렴하기에 사람들은 거리낌 없이 사진을 저장한다는 내용이지.
③ How to Cope with Financial Difficulties 재정적 어려움에 대처하는 방법
④ Benefits of Deleting Your Online History 당신의 온라인 기록을 지우는 것의 이점
▶ '지우다(deleting)'가 본문에 나오기 때문에 등장한 오답이니까 헷갈리면 안 돼.
⑤ Why Is Time More Precious than Money? 왜 시간은 돈보다 더 소중한가?
▶ 시간이 돈보다 소중한 것이 아니라 그 시간을 돈으로 환산해서 판단하고 있지.

10. 윗글의 빈칸에 들어갈 말로 가장 적절한 것은?
① follows 따르다
② creates 만들다
③ balances 균형을 맞추다
❹ exceeds 초과하다
▶ 걸리는 데 드는 시간 비용이 저장하는 비용보다 비싸야지, 사람들이 그냥 저장하겠지.
⑤ eliminates 제거하다

● 중요 포인트

가목적어-진목적어

The overabundance of available storage capacity makes
it easy for us to shift our behavioral default regarding
가목적어 의미상의 주어 진목적어
external memory from forgetting to remembering.

 17일차 승부수 문항 모의고사 4회

1 단계 모의고사 4회   p.168

● 정답

1. ⑤	2. ⑤	3. ③	4. ⑤	5. ⑤	6. ②	7. ②	8. ②
9. ②	10. ④						

1. ⑤

● 전체 해석

며칠 전 퇴근하면서 나는 어떤 여자가 큰 길로 들어오려고 애쓰는데 계속되는 차량 흐름 때문에 기회가 별로 없는 것을 봤다. 나는 속도를 줄이고 그녀가 내 앞에 들어오게 해주었다. 나는 기분이 꽤 좋았는데, 그 후 두어 블록 간 후에 그녀가 몇 대의 차를 끼워주려고 차를 멈추는 바람에 우리 둘 다 다음 신호를 놓치게 되었다. 나는 그녀에게 완전히 짜증났다. 내가 그렇게 친절하게 그녀가 들어오게 해주었는데 어떻게 감히 그녀가 나를 느리게 가게 한단 말인가! 내가 안달하면서 (자동차에) 앉아 있을 때 나는 내 자신이 참으로 어리석게 굴고 있다는 사실을 깨달았다. 불현듯 언젠가 읽었던 문구 하나가 마음속에 떠올랐다. '누군가 점수를 매기고 있기 때문이거나, 하지 않으면 처벌을 받기 때문이 아니라 내적 동기로 사람들에게 친절을 베풀어야 한다.' 나는 내가 보상을 원하고 있다는 사실을 깨달았다. 내가 당신에게 이런 친절을 베푼다면 당신(또는 어떤 다른 사람)이 나에게 그만한 친절을 베풀 것이라는 생각이었다.

● 지문분석

Coming home from work the other day, / I saw a woman
└ 분사구문
trying / to turn onto the main street / and having very little
luck / because of the constant stream of traffic.
며칠 전 퇴근하면서 / 나는 한 여자가 노력하는 것을 보았다 / 큰 길로 들어오려고 / 그리고 기회가 없는 것을 / 지속적인 차량 흐름 때문에
I slowed / and allowed her to turn / in front of me.

● 혼공 개념 마무리

2 단계 혼공 개념 마무리   p.165

1. Brown의 본보기에 영감을 받았을 다른 빈민가 지역에서, 문화센터가 지역 아이들로 하여금 뮤지컬 공연을 무대에 올리도록 권장하였으며, 이 중 몇몇은 아이들이 아직 회복 중에 있던 비극적인 일을 극화한 것이었다.

2. 우리는 우리에게 완전히 인간적일 지도자를, 자신들의 장점과 단점, 자신들의 재능과 한계를 인정할 만큼 약점이 있고, 자신들의 희망과 두려움, 자신들의 동기부여와 자신들의 계획에 있어서 타당하게 솔직한 사람들을 원한다.

3. 예를 들어, 자선에 관해 말하자면, 그것은 가난한 사람들에게 즉각적

나는 속도를 늦췄고 / 그녀가 들어오도록 허용해주었다 / 내 앞에서

I was feeling pretty good / until, a couple of blocks later, / she stopped / to let a few more cars into the line, / causing us both to miss the next light.
└ 분사구문

나는 아주 기분이 좋았다 / 몇 블록 간 후까지는 / 그녀가 멈추었다 / 그녀가 몇 대의 차들을 끼워주려고 하기 위해서 / 이는 우리 모두가 다음 신호를 놓치도록 했다

I found myself completely irritated with her.

나는 내가 완전히 그녀에게 짜증났음을 알았다

How dare she slow me down / after I had so graciously let her into the traffic!

어떻게 그녀는 나를 느리게 가게 한단 말인가 / 내가 그렇게 친절하게 그녀가 들어오도록 해주었는데

As I was sitting there stewing, / I realized / how ridiculous I was being.

내가 안달하며 앉아있을 때 / 나는 깨달았다 / 얼마나 내가 어리석은지를

Suddenly, [a phrase / I once read] / came floating into my mind: / 'You must do him or her a kindness / for inner reasons, / not because someone is keeping score / or because you will be punished / if you don't.'
              S   S   V   V

갑자기 한 구절이 / 내가 전에 읽었던 / 내 마음에서 떠올랐다 / 너는 그 사람에게 친절히 대해야 한다 / 내적인 동기로 / 누군가가 점수를 매기기 때문이 아니라 / 아니면 네가 처벌을 받기 때문이 아니라 / 하지 않으면

I realized / that I had wanted a reward: / If I do this nice thing for you, / you (or someone else) will do an equally nice thing for me.

나는 깨달았다 / 나는 보상을 원했다고 / 만약 내가 이러한 좋은 것을 당신을 위해 한다면 / 당신도 (아니면 다른 누군가는) 똑같이 좋은 것을 나에게 할 것이라고

● 해설

1. 다음 글의 밑줄 친 부분 중, 어법상 틀린 것은?
① 지각동사 saw의 목적 보어로 앞에 나온 trying과 병렬구조를 보이므로 현재분사 having이 적절하지.
② 목적어인 myself가 짜증남을 느끼므로 irritated가 적절하지.
③ 뒤에 바로 형용사인 ridiculous가 오므로 how가 적절하지
④ 앞에서 I once read의 수식을 주어 a phrase의 본동사가 필요하므로 과거동사 came은 적절하지.
❺ what → that: 뒤에 오는 문장이 완전한 문장이므로 접속사 that이 와야 하지.

● 중요 포인트

지각동사 see

I saw a woman trying to turn onto the main street and
지각동사   O   O.C.1
having very little luck because of the constant stream of
O.C.2
traffic.

---

2. ⑤

● 전체 해석

취학 전 시기의 기본적인 과제는 능력과 (자기) 주도력의 감각을 확립하는 것이다. (자기) 주도력과 죄책감 사이에 핵심 난제가 있다. 취학 전 아동은 자기가 직접 선택한 활동에 신체적으로 그리고 심리적으로 참여할 준비가 되면서 많은 자기 활동들을 주도하기 시작한다. 자기 결정을 얼마간 내릴 실제적인 자유가 허용된다면 그들은 자기가 주도하고 끝까지 완수해 낼 자신의 능력에 대한 자신감을 특징으로 하는 긍정적인 성향을 발달시키게 된다. 그러나 만약 자신들의 선택이 놀림을 받는다면 그들은 죄책감을 겪고 적극적인 태도를 취하는 데서 궁극적으로 손을 떼는 경향을 띠게 된다. 우리와 이야기를 나눈 한 중년 여성은 여전히 자신이 멍청해 보이는 것에 매우 취약하다는 것을 알고 있다. 그녀는 어린 시절 동안 가족 구성원들이 어떤 과제를 수행하는 그녀의 시도에 대해 놀렸다는 것을 상기한다. 그녀는 자기 가족에게서 받은 어떤 메시지를 받아들였고 이 메시지는 그녀의 태도와 행동에 크게 영향을 미쳤다. 지금까지도 그녀는 자기 머릿속에 이런 장면들을 생생하게 지니고 있고 이 메시지들이 그녀의 삶을 통제하기를 멈춘다(→ 계속한다).

● 지문분석

[The basic task / of the preschool years] / is to establish a
 S   V
sense of competence and initiative.

기본적인 과제는 / 취학 전 시기의 / 능력과 자기 주도력의 감각을 확립하는 것이다

The core struggle is between initiative and guilt.

핵심 난제는 자기 주도력과 죄책감 사이에 있다

Preschool children begin to initiate many of their own activities / as they become physically and psychologically ready / to engage in pursuits of their own choosing.

취학 전 아이들은 그들 자신의 활동 중 많은 것을 주도하기 시작한다 / 그들이 신체적으로 심리학적으로 준비가 되면서 / 그들 자신이 선택 활동 추구에 참여하는 것에

If they are allowed realistic freedom / to make some of their own decisions, / they tend to develop a positive orientation / characterized by confidence / in their ability to initiate and follow through.

만약 그들이 실제적인 자유가 허용된다면 / 그들 자신의 결정을 할 / 그들은 긍정적인 성향을 발달시키게 된다 / 자신감의 의해서 특징되는 / 자기가 주도하고 끝까지 완수하려는 능력에서의

If their choices are ridiculed, however, / they tend to experience a sense of guilt / and ultimately to withdraw from taking an active stance.

하지만, 그들의 선택이 놀림을 받는다면 / 그들은 죄책감의 경험을 하게 된다 / 그리고 궁극적으로 적극적인 태도를 취하는 데서 물러나게 된다

[One middle-aged woman / we talked with] / still finds
 S   S   V   V
herself extremely vulnerable / to being seen as foolish.

한 중년 여성은 / 우리가 대화를 한 / 여전히 그녀 자신이 극단적으로 취약하다는 것을 깨닫는다 / 멍청해 보이는 것에

She recalls / that during her childhood / family members laughed at her attempts / to perform certain tasks.

그녀는 회상한다 / 그녀의 어린 시절 동안 / 가족들이 그녀의 시도를 비웃었던 것을 / 어떤 과제를 수행하려는

She took in certain messages / she received from her family, / and these messages greatly influenced her attitudes and actions.

그녀는 어떤 메시지를 받아들였다 / 그녀가 가족들로부터 받았던 / 그리고 이러한 메시지는 엄청나게 그녀의 태도와 행동에 영향을 주었다

Even now she vividly carries these pictures in her head, / and these messages continue to control her life.

심지어 지금도 그녀는 생생하게 이런 그림을 머릿속에 지니고 있고 / 이러한 메시지는 계속해서 그녀의 삶을 통제하고 있다

●해설

2. 다음 글의 밑줄 친 부분 중, 문맥상 낱말의 쓰임이 적절하지 않은 것은?

❺ cease → continue: 여전히 어린 시절의 메시지가 지금의 인생에 영향을 주고 있으므로 continue(계속하다)가 적절하지. cease는 '중단하다'를 의미해.

●중요 포인트

관계사가 생략된 구문

[One middleaged woman we talked with] still finds herself extremely vulnerable to being seen as foolish.
S / whom(that) 생략 / V

3. ③

●전체 해석

제약은 본래 갖추어져 있고 눈에 보이지 않게 되어 있기 때문에, 우리는 얼마나 많은 창의적 과업이 제약에서 도움을 받는지 알아차리지 못하는 경향이 있다. 예를 들어, 거의 대부분의 대중음악은 첫 박자가 대개 강조되는, 한 마디에 네 개의 박자가 있는 4/4 박자이다. 곡은 보통 길이가 3분이나 4분이고, 후렴구를 포함하고, 기타 등등이다. 이것들은 대중음악이 따르는 많은 것 중에서 단지 몇 가지 제약일 뿐이지만, 달성될 수 있는 변화를 봐라. 많은 노래가 이러한 규칙들을 어기지만, 그것들은 애초에 어길 수 있는 규칙이 있기 때문에 그것들의 효과를 흔히 달성하는 것이다. 화가, 작가, 예술가 등은 모두 다양한 정도로 이전 양식에 영향을 받으며, 제약을 제공하는 것이 바로 이러한 이전 양식이다. 우리가 우리 자신에게 부과하는 바로 그 제약은 우리의 가장 훌륭한 창작물의 씨앗이 될 수 있다.

●지문분석

We tend not to notice / how many creative tasks benefit from constraints / because they are built in / and have become invisible.

우리는 알아차리지 못하는 경향이 있다 / 얼마나 많은 창의적인 과제가 제약으로부터 이익을 보는지를 / 왜냐하면 그들은 갖추어져 있고 / 보이지 않게 되어 있어서

For example, almost all popular music is in 4/4 time, /

four beats in the bar, / with the emphasis usually landing on the first beat.
with + 명사 + 분사: 동시상황

예를 들어 거의 모든 대중음악은 4/4박자이며 / 한 마디에 4개의 박자인 / 강조는 보통 첫 박자에 있다

Tracks are normally three or four minutes in length, / contain a chorus, / and so on.

곡은 보통 길이가 3-4분이고 / 후렴구를 포함하며 / 기타 등등이다

These are just a few constraints of many / that popular music follows, / and yet look at the variation / that can be achieved.

이러한 것들은 단지 많은 것들 중 몇 가지 제약이다 / 대중음악이 따르는 / 하지만 변화를 봐라 / 달성될 수 있는

Many songs break these rules, / but they often achieve their effects / because there is a rule to break in the first place.

많은 노래들은 이러한 규칙을 위반하기도 한다 / 하지만 그들은 종종 그들의 효과를 얻는다 / 왜냐하면 애초에 어길 수 있는 규칙이 있어서

Painters, writers, artists, and so on / are all influenced by previous styles / to various degrees / and it's these previous styles / that provide constraints.
it-that 강조구문

화가, 작가, 예술가 등은 / 모두 이전 스타일에 영향을 받는다 / 다양한 정도로 / 그리고 바로 이러한 이전의 스타일이다 / 제약을 제공하는 것은

[The very limitations / we impose on ourselves] / can be the seeds of our finest creations.
S

바로 그 제약은 / 우리가 우리 자신에게 부여하는 / 우리의 가장 훌륭한 창작물의 씨앗이 될 수 있다

●해설

3. 다음 빈칸에 들어가기에 가장 적절한 것은?

We tend not to notice how many creative tasks benefit from constraints because they are built in and have become invisible. For example, almost all popular music is in 4/4 time, four beats in the bar, with the emphasis usually landing on the first beat. Tracks are normally three or four minutes in length, contain a chorus, and so on. These are just a few constraints of many that popular music follows, and yet look at the variation that can be achieved. Many songs break these rules, but they often achieve their effects because there is a rule to break in the first place. Painters, writers, artists, and so on are all influenced by previous styles to various degrees and it's these previous styles that provide constraints. The very limitations we impose on ourselves can be _____.

① the inherent cultural beliefs 내재된 문화적 신념
▶ 말이 아예 안 되는 것은 아니지만, 제약은 인간이 만든 것이므로 내재되었다고 하기는 그렇지.
② the resistance to taking risks 위험감수에 대한 저항
▶ 부정적 이미지이므로 탈락!
❸ the seeds of our finest creations 우리의 가장 훌륭한 창작물의 씨앗

▶ 제약 때문에 작품의 효과가 나타나므로 여기서 제약은 긍정적인 요인이지.

④ the obstacles to our future success 우리 미래 성공의 장애물
▶ 부정적 요인이므로 탈락.

⑤ the stepping stone for music education 음악 교육의 디딤돌
▶ 음악 교육이 아니라 대중음악, 더 나아가 예술 전체로 봐야 해.

● 중요 포인트

it-that 강조구문

Painters, writers, artists, and so on are all influenced by
revious styles to various degrees and it's these previous
styles that provide constraints.
　　　　　　　　　　　　　　　　　it-that 강조구문

4. ⑤

● 전체 해석

과학 기술 학위는 오로지 여러분이 일자리를 잡고 계속 그 일에 종사하도록 고안된 것이 아니므로 가치가 있다. 만약 여러분이 매우 전문적이거나 직업과 관련된 학위를 취득하고 있다면, 대학교에 가기도 전에 어떤 직업을 목표로 하고 있는가를 당연히 알겠지만, 대부분의 과학 기술 학부생들에게 대학교는 그 자체로 모험이다. 즉 어떤 직업에 대한 생각이 머릿속에 있을 수는 있지만, 완전히 확정된 것은 아니다. 이 덕분에 여러분은 학위가 많은 분야의 일에서 도움이 될 것을 인식하면서, 교육 과정이 진행되는 동안 직업에 대한 생각을 발전시킬 수 있다는 것을 알게 되는 이점을 가진다. 과학 기술 학위 프로그램이 범위가 넓고 접근법이 유연한 경향이 있는 것은 아마도 바로 이런 점을 염두에 두고서 일 것이다. 여러분은 화학을 공부하러 대학교에 가서 물리학과 내의 어떤 연구를 하고 있다는 것을 알 수도 있다.

● 지문분석

Science and technology degrees / are rewarding / because
they are not designed exclusively / to get you into a job /
and keep you there.
과학 기술 학위는 / 가치가 있다 / 왜냐하면 그것들은 단지 고안된 것은 아니기 때문에 / 당신이 직업을 얻도록 / 그리고 당신이 거기에 계속 있도록

If you are taking a highly specialized or vocational
degree, / you may well know / what career you are aiming
for / even before you get to university, / but for most
science and technology undergraduates / university is an
adventure in itself; / ideas about a career / may be in your
thoughts, / but not completely fixed.
당신이 매우 전문적이거나 직업과 관련된 학위를 취득하고 있다면 / 당신은 당연히 알 것이다 / 어떤 직업을 당신이 목표로 하고 있는지 / 심지어 당신이 대학에 가기도 전에 / 하지만 대부분의 과학 기술 학부생들에게는 / 대학은 그 자체로 모험이다 / 직업에 대한 생각들은 / 당신 머릿속에 있을 수도 있다 / 하지만 완전히 고정된 것은 아니다

This gives you the advantage of knowing / that you can
develop your career ideas / as your course progresses, /
aware / that your degree will be of help to you / in many
└ being 생략 분사구문

areas of work.
이것은 당신에게 아는 것의 이점을 준다 / 당신이 당신의 직업에 대한 생각을 발전시킬 수 있다는 것을 / 당신의 교육 과정이 진행되는 동안 / 인식하면서 / 당신의 학위가 당신에게 도움이 될 것이라는 것을 / 많은 분야의 일에서

It is perhaps with this in mind / that science and
　　└ 가주어　　　　　　　　　 └ 진주어
technology degree programs / tend to be wide in scope /
and flexible in approach.
아마도 이것을 염두에 둔 것이다 / 과학 기술 학위 프로그램이 / 범위가 넓은 경향이 있다는 것을 / 그리고 접근법이 유연한

You might go to university / to study chemistry / and find
yourself doing some work / within the physics department.
당신은 아마도 대학에 갈 것이다 / 화학을 공부하러 / 그리고 당신 자신이 어떤 일을 하고 있다는 것을 발견할 것이다 / 물리학과 내의

● 해설

4. 다음 빈칸에 들어가기에 가장 적절한 것은?
Science and technology degrees are rewarding because they
are not designed ＿＿＿＿＿＿＿＿＿＿＿＿. If you are taking
a highly specialized or vocational degree, you may well
know what career you are aiming for even before you get to
university, but for most science and technology undergraduates
university is an adventure in itself; ideas about a career may
be in your thoughts, but not completely fixed. This gives you
the advantage of knowing that you can develop your career
ideas as your course progresses, aware that your degree will
be of help to you in many areas of work. It is perhaps with this
in mind that science and technology degree programs tend to
be wide in scope and flexible in approach. You might go to
university to study chemistry and find yourself doing some
work within the physics department.

① to represent a socially privileged status 사회적으로 특권있는 계층을 대표하도록
▶ 계층에 대한 내용은 아니야.

② necessarily to be obtained in the university 대학에서 꼭 얻어지도록
▶ 학위는 대학에서 얻는다고 하고 있어.

③ to force you to follow the established scholars 당신이 인정받은 학자들을 따르도록
▶ 뒤에서도 학자들에 대한 이야기는 안나오지.

④ only to grade you and make you feel frustrated 당신을 등급매기고 당신이 좌절감을 맛보도록
▶ 등급을 매기는 이야기는 나오지 않고 있지.

❺ exclusively to get you into a job and keep you there 오로지 당신이 일자리를 잡고 계속 그 일에 종사하도록
▶ 과학 기술 학위의 역할이 표면적인 이유(직업) 때문이 아니라는 글이지. 계속해서 직업관련된 이야기가 나오고 있어. 단순한 일자리를 위한 것을 넘어서는 글이지.

● 중요 포인트

being 생략 분사구문

This gives you the advantage of knowing that you can develop your career ideas as your course progresses, aware that your degree will be of help to you in many
being 생략 분사구문, '인식하면서'
areas of work.

5. ⑤

●전체 해석

고객의 욕구는 대체로 제품이나 서비스의 전반적인 품질에 대한 상위 수준의 묘사로 표현된다. 그것들은 보통 형용사로 진술되는데 본질적으로 고객에게 돌아가는 구체적인 혜택을 의미하지 않는다. 예를 들어, 고객들은 흔히 제품이나 서비스가 '믿을 수 있는', '효과적인', '튼튼한', '신뢰할 만한' 혹은 '복원력이 있는' 것이기를 원한다고 말한다. 면도기 사용자들은 제품이 '내구성이 있고 튼튼한' 것이기를 원할 것이다. 이 단순한 말들이 고객이 무엇을 찾고 있는지를 나타낼지라도 여기에는 한 가지 중대한 결점이 있다. 그 말들은 (다양한) 해석의 여지가 있는 부정확한 진술이며 디자이너, 개발자, 기술자들에게 고객들이 '내구성이 있는' 또는 '튼튼한'이라는 말을 통해 정말로 무엇을 의미하는 것인지 알아내라는 불가능한 과제를 제시한다. 만약 기술자들이 면도기를 좀 더 '내구성이 있는' 것으로 만들어야 하는 과제에 직면한다면, 과연 그들은 면도날이 더 오래 지속되도록, 휘어짐에 견디도록, 혹은 지속적인 습기에 견딜 수 있도록 만들려고 할 것인가? 이러한 조치들 중 어느 하나라도 "내구성이 있는"이라는 말에 대한 고객들의 진정한 기준을 만족시키겠는가?

●지문분석

Customers' needs are usually expressed / as high-level descriptions / of the overall quality of a product or service.
고객의 욕구는 보통 표현된다 / 높은 수준의 묘사로 / 상품이나 서비스의 전반적인 품질에 대한

They are typically stated / as adjectives / and inherently do not imply / a specific benefit to the customer.
그들은 보통 진술된다 / 형용사로 / 그리고 본질적으로 의미하지 않는다 / 소비자에 대한 구체적인 이점을

For instance, customers commonly say / they want a product or service / to be "reliable," "effective," "robust," "dependable," or "resilient."
예를 들어 고객들은 흔히 말한다 / 그들이 제품이나 서비스를 원한다고 / '믿을 수 있는', '효과적인', '튼튼한', '신뢰할 만한', 아니면 '복원력 있는'이 되기를

Razor users may want / the product to be "durable and strong."
면도기 사용자들은 원할지도 모른다 / 제품이 내구성이 있고 튼튼하기를

Although these simple statements / provide some indication / as to what customers are looking for, / they have one major drawback.
비록 이러한 단순한 진술들이 / 몇 가지 지시사항을 제공할지라도 / 고객들이 무엇을 찾고 있는지에 대해서 / 그들은 한 가지 중대한

결점이 있다

They are imprecise statements / open to interpretation / and present designers, developers, and engineers / with the impossible task / of figuring out just what customers really mean / by "durable" or "strong."
그들은 부정확한 진술이다 / 해석의 여지가 있는 / 그리고 디자이너와 개발자, 그리고 기술자들에게 제시한다 / 불가능한 과제를 / 단지 고객들이 정말로 의미하는 것이 무엇인지 알아내라는 / '내구성이 있는' 혹은 '튼튼한'이라는 말에 의해서

If engineers faced the task / of making a razor more "durable," / would they try to make the blade / last longer, / resist bending, / or withstand constant moisture?
기술자들이 과제에 직면한다면 / 면도날을 더욱 내구성있게 만드는 / 그들은 면도날을 만들려고 노력할까 / 더 오래 지속되고 / 휘어짐에 견디고 / 아니면 지속적인 습기에 견디도록

Would any of these actions / satisfy the customer's true measure of "durable?"
이러한 행동 중 일부가 / 고객의 내구성에 대한 진정한 기준을 만족시킬까

●해설

5. 다음 빈칸에 들어갈 말로 가장 적절한 것은?

① not appealing to female customers 여성 고객들에게 매력적이지 않은
▶ 여성 고객들은 뒤에 나오지도 않아.

② irrelevant to customers making purchases 구매를 하는 고객들과 관련 없는
▶ 고객이 하는 말인데 관계가 없을 리가 없지.

③ preferable feedback for manufacturers only 제조업자들에게만 선호되는 피드백
▶뒤에는 디자이너, 개발자, 기술자들이 언급되었지만 제조업자들은 언급이 안되고 있어.

④ ineffective in drawing consumers' attention 고객의 관심을 끌어들이는 데 효과가 없는

❺ imprecise statements open to interpretation 해석의 여지가 있는 부정확한 진술
▶ 뒤에 기술자들에게 하는 고객들의 말이 다양한 의미로 해석이 가능하다고 하니 이것이 바로 정답이지.

●중요 포인트

뒤에서 명사를 수식하는 형용사

They are imprecise statements open to interpretation and present designers, developers, and engineers with ~

6. ②

●전체 해석

확실히 우리 모두 똑같은 시각 장치를 가지고 있으므로 색과 같은 기본적인 것을 똑같은 방식으로 바라보는가? 그렇지 않다. 색을 보는 것이 흑백 논리의 문제는 아니라는 것이 밝혀졌다. 그것은 거의 그렇게 간단하지 않다. (B) 언어는 우리가 색을 "보는" 방식에 상당한 영향을 미친다. 더 엄

밀히 말하면, 우리가 가시적인 스펙트럼의 여러 부분을 어떻게 나누고 분류하는지에 영향을 준다. 우리 눈은 적절히 이름 붙여진 적외선과 자외선 간의 대략 똑같은 빛의 범위를 인식한다. (A) 그러나 우리가 사용하는 다르게 명명된 (빛의) 분절의 수는 다양하다. 어떤 언어들은 두 가지 기본색, 즉 검은색과 흰색만을 구별한다. 다른 언어들은 녹색, 노란색, 파란색 그리고 갈색을 추가한다. (C) 이와 같이 다양한 종류의 색깔의 분류는 "grue"라는 단어로 잘 설명된다. 심리학자들은 녹색과 파란색을 구분하지 않는 언어를 설명하기 위해서 그 단어를 사용한다.

● 지문분석

Surely since we all have the same visual equipment, / we all see something / as basic as color / in the same way?
확실히 우리 모두가 같은 시각 장치를 가지고 있기 때문에 / 우리 모두는 무언가를 보는 것인가 / 색과 같은 기본적인 것을 / 똑같은 방식으로

Wrong.
그렇지 않다

It turns out / that color vision isn't a black-and-white issue.
밝혀졌다 / 색을 보는 것은 흑백 논리가 아니라는 것이

It's not nearly that simple.
그것은 거의 그렇게 간단하지 않다

Language has a significant effect / on how we "see" colors / – more precisely, / on how we divide up / and label different parts of the visible spectrum.
언어는 상당한 영향을 미친다 / 어떻게 우리가 색을 보는지에 / 보다 정확하게 / 우리가 어떻게 나누고 / 눈에 보이는 스펙트럼의 다른 형태를 분류하는지에 대해서

Our eyes register / roughly the same range of light / between the aptly named infrared and ultraviolet.
우리의 눈은 인식한다 / 대략 같은 빛의 범위를 / 적절히 이름 붙여진 적외선과 자외선 사이의

However, [the number of differently labeled segments / we use] / varies.
하지만, 다르게 분류되는 분절의 수는 / 우리가 사용하는 / 다르다

Some languages only distinguish / between two basic colors, black and white.
일부 언어는 오직 구별한다 / 두 가지 기본적인 색인 검은색과 흰색만을

Others add green, yellow, blue, and brown.
다른 것들은 녹색과 노란색, 파란색, 그리고 갈색을 추가한다

This sort of different color categorization / is nicely illustrated / by the word "grue."
이러한 종류의 다른 색 분류는 / 잘 설명된다 / grue라는 단어에 의해서

Psychologists use it / to describe languages / that make no distinction / between green and blue.
심리학자들은 그것을 사용한다 / 언어를 설명하기 위해서 / 구별을 하지 않는 / 녹색과 파란색을

● 해설

6. 주어진 글 다음에 이어질 글의 순서로 가장 적절한 것은?

Surely since we all have the same visual equipment, we all see something as basic as color in the same way? Wrong. It turns out that color vision isn't a black-and-white issue. It's not nearly that simple.
간단한 것이 아니라 '언어'라는 새로운 영향이 등장하지.

(B) Language has a significant effect on how we "see" colors – more precisely, on how we divide up and label different parts of the visible spectrum. Our eyes register roughly the same range of light between the aptly named infrared and ultraviolet.
눈은 한정된 빛의 범위를 인식하지만, 언어는 다르지.

(A) However, the number of differently labeled segments we use varies. Some languages only distinguish between two basic colors, black and white. Others add green, yellow, blue, and brown.
앞에서 언급한 녹색.노랑, 파랑, 갈색이 바로 다양한 종류의 색깔 분류지.

(C) This sort of different color categorization is nicely illustrated by the word "grue." Psychologists use it to describe languages that make no distinction between green and blue.

주어진 문장에서 우리가 색을 인식하는 것은 실제로 간단한 것이 아니라고 하고, 새로운 기준인 '언어'가 등장하는 (B)가 적절히 이어지지. (B)의 마지막에 눈의 기준이 나오고 (A)에서 언어가 다시 나오고 있어. (A)의 마지막에는 다양한 색이 나오고 (C)의 맨 처음에는 이것을 바로 언급하고 있지.

● 중요 포인트

the number 주어

However, [the number of differently labeled segments / we use] varies.
S → 단수
V → 단수 동사

7. ②

● 전체 해석

지구는 다소 불규칙한 시계이다. 몇 년에 걸쳐 하루의 길이는 1,000만 분의 1, 즉 일 년인 3,150만 초에서 3초만큼 변하는 것으로 드러난다. (B) 게다가 매년 천 분의 몇 초만큼 계절에 따른 변화도 있다. 겨울에 지구는 (회전 속도가) 느려지고, 여름에는 빨라진다. 지구를 회전하는 스케이트 타는 사람이라고 생각해 보라. (A) 북반구에서 겨울 동안에 물은 바다에서 증발하여 높은 산들에 얼음과 눈으로 쌓인다. 바다로부터 산꼭대기로의 이러한 물의 이동은 그 스케이트 타는 사람이 자신의 팔을 뻗는 것과 유사하다. (C) 따라서 지구는 겨울에 느려지고, 여름이 되면 그 눈이 녹아 바다로 다시 흘러가고, 지구는 다시 빨라진다. 이런 효과는 대륙의 대부분이 북반구에 있기 때문에 남반구의 반대 효과에 의해 상쇄되지 않는다.

● 지문분석

The Earth is a somewhat irregular clock.
지구는 다소 불규칙적인 시계이다

Some years / [the length of the day] is found / to vary /
S   V

정답 및 해설   129

by as much as one part in 10 million, / or three seconds / in a year of 31.5 million seconds.

몇 년 동안 / 하루의 길이는 / 발견된다 / 다르다고 / 천만 분의 1 만큼 / 아니면 3초 만큼 / 3,150만 초인 1년 중에서

In addition, there are also seasonal changes / of a few milliseconds per year.

덧붙여, 또한 계절적인 변화도 있다 / 매 해 몇 천 분의 몇 초만큼의

In the winter the Earth slows down, / and in the summer it speeds up.

겨울에 지구는 느려지고 / 여름에 지구는 빨라진다

Think of the Earth / as a spinning skater.

지구를 생각해봐라 / 회전하는 스케이트 타는 사람이라고

During the winter in the northern hemisphere, / water evaporates from the ocean / and accumulates as ice and snow / on the high mountains.

북반구에서 겨울 동안 / 물은 대양으로부터 증발하고 / 얼음과 눈으로 축적된다 / 높은 산위에서

[This movement of water / from the oceans to the mountaintops] / is similar to the skater's extending her arms.

이러한 물의 이동은 / 대양으로부터 산꼭대기로의 / 스케이트 타는 사람의 확장되는 팔과 비슷하다

So the Earth slows down in winter; / by the summer the snow melts / and runs back to the seas, / and the Earth speeds up again.

그래서 지구는 겨울에 느려진다 / 여름이 되면 그 눈은 녹고 / 바다로 다시 흘러간다 / 그리고 지구의 속도는 다시 올라간다

This effect is not compensated / by the opposite effect in the southern hemisphere / because most of the land mass / is north of the equator.

이러한 효과는 상쇄되지 않는다 / 남반구의 정반대 효과에 의해서 / 왜냐하면 대부분의 대륙은 / 적도 북쪽에 있기 때문에

● 해설

7. 주어진 글 다음에 이어질 글의 순서로 가장 적절한 것은?

The Earth is a somewhat irregular clock. Some years the length of the day is found to vary by as much as one part in 10 million, or three seconds in a year of 31.5 million seconds.
지구의 불규칙성을 의미하는 첫 문장에 이어지는 계절적 변화

(B) In addition, there are also seasonal changes of a few milliseconds per year. In the winter the Earth slows down, and in the summer it speeds up. Think of the Earth as a spinning skater.
지구를 회전하는 스케이터에 비유했으니까 그 이유를 설명하는 글이 와야 해.

(A) During the winter in the northern hemisphere, water evaporates from the ocean and accumulates as ice and snow on the high mountains. This movement of water from the oceans to the mountaintops is similar to the skater's extending her arms.

(C) So the Earth slows down in winter; by the summer the snow melts and runs back to the seas, and the Earth speeds up again. This effect is not compensated by the opposite effect in the southern hemisphere because most of the land mass is north of the equator.
물의 이동을 설명한 (A)에 이어서 이를 정리하는 부분이 나오지.

주어진 문장은 지구의 불규칙성을 설명하지. 또다른 불규칙성인 계절적 변화를 다룬 (B)가 바로 이어져야 해. (B)의 마지막에 언급된 스케이터에 대한 설명을 (A)가 이어서 하고 있어. (A)에서 언급된 물의 이동을 다시 설명한 (C)가 마지막으로 오게 되는 거지.

● 중요 포인트

주어를 수식하는 전치사구

[This movement of water from the oceans to the mountaintops] is similar to the skater's extending her arms.

전치사구
주어 아님

8. ②

● 전체 해석

범죄 현장 수사를 다루는 한 미국 드라마가 2000년에 처음 등장한 이후로 매우 인기를 얻어 왔다. 2002년에, 그것은 미국 텔레비전에서 가장 많이 시청된 프로그램이었고, 2009년에는 전 세계적인 시청자가 7천 3백만 명이 넘는 것으로 추정되었다. 그러나 경찰관과 지역 검사들에게는 그 정도로 인기가 많지는 않은데, 그들은 범죄 해결 방식에 대해 크게 오해를 불러일으키는 이미지를 제공한다는 이유로 그 시리즈를 비판했다. 그들의 걱정은 배심원들이 과학 수사 증거에 대해 점점 더 비현실적인 기대를 가지고 있다는 증거를 찾은 범죄학자 Monica Robbers에 의해 거듭 말해졌다. 이전에 영국의 주요 병리학자 중 한 명이었던 Bernard Knight가 (이에) 동의한다. 오늘날 배심원들은 과학 수사가 내놓을 수 있는 것보다 더 명백한 증거를 기대한다고 그는 말한다. 그리고 그는 이런 추세가 텔레비전 범죄 드라마의 영향이 직접적인 원인이라고 여긴다.

● 지문분석

Since its debut in 2000, / [an American drama / centered around crime scene investigation] / has become very popular.

2000년 처음 등장한 이후 / 미국 드라마는 / 범죄 현장 수사를 다루는 / 매우 인기를 얻어왔다

In 2002, / it was the most watched show / on American television, / and by 2009 the worldwide audience / was estimated to be more than 73 million.

2002년에 / 그것은 가장 많이 본 프로그램이었다 / 미국 TV에서 / 그리고 2009년에는 전 세계 시청자가 / 7천 3백만명 이상인 것으로 추정되었다

It isn't, however, such a hit / with police officers and district attorneys, / who have criticized the series / for presenting a highly misleading image / of how crimes are solved.

하지만, 그것은 그렇게나 큰 히트는 아니다 / 경찰과 지역 검사들에
게는 / 그 시리즈를 비판해 온 / 매우 잘못된 이미지를 보여주어서 /
어떻게 범죄가 해결되는지에 대한

Their fears have been echoed / by Monica Robbers,
a criminologist, / who found evidence / that jurors
have increasingly unrealistic expectations / of forensic
evidence.

그들의 두려움은 울려 퍼졌다 / 범죄학자인 Monica Robbers에 의해
서 / 증거를 발견한 / 배심원들이 점차 비현실적인 기대를 가지고 있
다는 / 과학 수사 증거에 대한

Bernard Knight, / formerly one of Britain's chief
pathologists, / agrees.

Bernard Knight는 / 이전 영국의 주요 병리학자 중 한 명인 / 동의한
다

Jurors today, / he observes, / expect clearer proof / than
forensic science is capable of delivering.

오늘날의 배심원들은 / 그는 진술한다 / 더 명백한 증거를 기대한다
고 / 과학 수사가 내놓을 수 있는 것보다

And he attributes this trend / directly to the influence of
television crime dramas.

그리고 그는 이 경향을 돌린다 / 직접적으로 TV 범죄 드라마의 영향
으로

● 해설

8. 글의 흐름으로 보아, 주어진 문장이 들어가기에 가장 적절한 곳은?

It isn't, however, such a hit with police officers and district
attorneys, who have criticized the series for presenting a highly
misleading image of how crimes are solved.

경찰과 검사들에게는 그 시리즈가 인기가 없다는 내용이야. however가 있으니 앞에는 인
기가 있다는 내용이 나오겠지.

Since its debut in 2000, an American drama centered around
crime scene investigation has become very popular. (①) In
범죄 현장 수사 드라마가 전 세계적으로 인기가 있다는 내용이지.
2002, it was the most watched show on American television,
and by 2009 the worldwide audience was estimated to be more
than 73 million. (②) Their fears have been echoed by Monica
Robbers, a criminologist, who found evidence that jurors have
increasingly unrealistic expectations of forensic evidence. (③)
범죄 현장 수사 드라마에 대한 비판이 나오고 있어. 앞 문장과의 비약이 느껴지지.
Bernard Knight, formerly one of Britain's chief pathologists,
agrees. (④) Jurors today, he observes, expect clearer proof
than forensic science is capable of delivering. (⑤) And he
attributes this trend directly to the influence of television crime
dramas.

● 중요 포인트

분사의 수식을 받는 주어

Since its debut in 2000, [an American drama centered
around crime scene investigation] has become very
popular.

---

9. ② 10. ④

● 전체 해석

작가들이 흥미를 자아내지만 파악하기 어려운 아이디어들, 너무나 모
호해서 단어로 표현되기 어려워 보이는 생각들의 암시에 의해 괴롭힘
을 당할 때 무엇을 해야 할까? Edgar Allan Poe의 충고는 간단하다. 즉 그들
은 그들의 펜을 집어야 한다. (혹, 그는 오늘날에는 그들의 노트북을 켜라
고 할 것이다.) Poe는 어떤 생각들이 너무 깊거나 미묘하면 그것들이 말
의 범위를 넘어선다는 주장을 일축한다.

"나로서는" 그가 1846년 Graham's Magazine의 한 기사에서 말하기를,
"내가 그것을 생각했을 때의 명확함보다 더 명확함을 가지고 말로 쓸 수
없는 생각을 해본 적이 없다." Poe가 믿기를, 단순히 쓰는 것의 행위가
작가들로 하여금 그들의 생각들을 더 명확하게 할 뿐만 아니라 더 논리적
으로 하는데 도움을 준다고 한다. 그의 말을 사용하자면, 쓰는 것의 과정
이 생각의 논리화에 기여한다.

그가 뇌의 막연한 개념에 불만족을 느낄 때마다, Poe가 말하길, "나는
곧바로 펜에 의존한다. 펜의 도움을 빌어 필요한 형식, 결과와 정확성을
얻을 목적으로."

오늘날의 자유로운 쓰기의 옹호자들은 아마 이러한 관점에서 포와 의견
이 일치할 것이다. 때때로, 그것이 쓰는 딜레마이던지 생각하는 딜레마이
던지 간에 어떤 딜레마를 해결할 가장 좋은 방법은 단순히 쓰는 것을 시
작하는 것이다.

● 지문분석

What should writers do / when they're teased /
by intriguing but elusive ideas, / by hints of thoughts / that
seem too vague / to be expressed in words?

작가는 무엇을 해야 하나 / 그들이 괴롭힘을 당할 때 / 흥미롭지만,
파악하기 어려운 생각에 의해서 / 생각들의 힌트에 의해 / 너무 애매
해서 / 말로는 표현될 수 없는

Edgar Allan Poe's advice is simple: / They should pick
up their pens / (or, he might add today, power up their
laptops).

Edgar Allan Poe의 조언은 간단하다 / 그들은 펜을 잡아야만 한다 /
아니면 오늘날 그는 그들의 노트북을 켜라고 할지도 모른다

Poe dismisses the argument / that any ideas are so deep
or subtle / that they're "beyond the compass of words."
so~that 용법

Poe는 주장을 일축한다 / 어떤 생각들은 너무 깊거나 미묘해서 / 그
것들이 단어의 범위를 넘는다는

"For my own part," / he said in an 1846 article in
Graham's Magazine, / "I have never had a thought /
which I could not set down in words, / with even more
distinctness / than that with which I conceived it."

나로서는 / 그는 1846년 Graham's Magazine의 한 기사에서 말하기
를 / 나는 결코 생각을 해본 적이 없다 / 내가 말로 쓸 수 없는 / 훨씬
더 명확함을 가지고 / 내가 그것을 생각했던 명확함보다

[The "mere act" of writing,] / Poe believed, / helps writers
make their ideas / not only clearer but more logical.

글쓰기라는 단순한 행위가 / Poe가 믿기를 / 작가들이 그들의 생각을
만들도록 도와준다 / 명확할 뿐만 아니라 더 논리적으로

To use his phrase, / [the process of writing] / contributes to "the logicalization of thought."

그의 말을 사용하면서 / 글쓰는 과정은 / 생각의 논리화에 기여한다

Whenever he felt dissatisfied / with a vague "conception of the brain," / Poe said, / "I resort forthwith to the pen, / for the purpose of obtaining, / through its aid, the necessary form, consequence and precision."

그가 불만족을 느낄 때마다 / 애매한 두뇌의 개념을 가지고 / Poe는 말하기를 / 나는 곧바로 펜에 의존한다 / 얻고자 하는 목적으로 / 그것의 도움, 필요한 형식, 결과와 정확성을 통해서

[Today's advocates of free-writing] / would probably agree with Poe on this point.

오늘날의 자유로운 글쓰기의 옹호자들은 / 아마도 Poe의 이러한 관점에 동의할 것이다

Sometimes, [the best way to resolve a dilemma / – whether it's a writing dilemma or a thinking dilemma] – is simply to start writing.

때때로 딜레마를 해결하는 최고의 방법은 / 그것이 글쓰기의 딜레마든 생각의 딜레마든 / 쓰기를 단순하게 시작하는 것이다

●해설

[9-10] 다음을 읽고 물음에 답하시오.

What should writers do when they're teased by intriguing but elusive ideas, by hints of thoughts that seem too vague to be expressed in words? Edgar Allan Poe's advice is simple: They should pick up their pens (or, he might add today, power up their laptops). Poe dismisses the argument that any ideas are so deep or subtle that they're "_____."

"For my own part," he said in an 1846 article in Graham's Magazine, "I have never had a thought which I could not set down in words, with even more distinctness than that with which I conceived it." The "mere act" of writing, Poe believed, helps writers make their ideas not only clearer but more logical. To use his phrase, the process of writing contributes to "the logicalization of thought." Whenever he felt dissatisfied with a vague "conception of the brain," Poe said, "I resort forthwith to the pen, for the purpose of obtaining, through its aid, the necessary form, consequence and precision." Today's advocates of free-writing would probably agree with Poe on this point. Sometimes, the best way to resolve a dilemma — whether it's a writing dilemma or a thinking dilemma — is simply to start writing.

9. 윗 글의 제목으로 가장 적절한 것은?
① Begin at the End 끝에서 시작해라
❷ Think with Your Pen 너의 펜을 가지고 생각해라
▶ 일단 쓰라는 게 바로 필자와 Poe의 생각이지.
③ Pleasure of Freewriting 자유 기고의 즐거움
▶ 자유기고가 언급되기는 하지만, 즐거움에 대한 것이 아니라 글쓰기 그 자체에 대해서 이야기하고 있지.
④ Ideas Too Vague to Be Real 실제라고 하기엔 너무 애매한 생각
⑤ Make It Clear, Make It Logical 명확하게 하고, 논리적이게 해라
▶ Poe가 한 말 때문에 나온 오답으로, 필자가 원하는 것은 그냥 쓰라는

거야.

10. 윗글의 빈칸에 들어갈 말로 가장 적절한 것은?
① incapable of drawing attention 관심을 끌어들일 수 없는
▶ 관심의 문제가 아니라 글을 어떻게 쓰느냐에 문제지.
② in danger of being empty 공허함의 위험 속에서
③ against the writer's will 작가의 의지에 반해서
▶ 작가의 의지는 언급이 되지 않고 있어. 뒤에 나오는 thought랑은 다르지.
❹ beyond the compass of words 말의 범위를 넘어선
▶ 앞에 있는 dismiss라는 말로 봐서 that절의 내용은 Poe가 반박하는 내용이 나와야 해. 따라서 글을 그냥은 못쓴다는 개념에 맞는 것은 이것이 적절해.
⑤ appreciated only by a privileged few 특권 있는 소수에 의한 인정되는

●중요 포인트

help 동사의 특징

Sometimes, [the best way to resolve a dilemma / whether it's a writing dilemma or a thinking dilemma] / 삽입절
is simply to start writing ~

2 혼공 개념 마무리 p.173

1. 불현듯 언젠가 읽었던 문구 하나가 마음속에 떠올랐다. '누군가 점수를 매기고 있기 때문이거나, 하지 않으면 처벌을 받기 때문이 아니라 내적 동기로 사람들에게 친절을 베풀어야 한다.'

2. 자기 결정을 얼마간 내릴 실제적인 자유가 허용된다면 그들은 자기가 주도하고 끝까지 완수해 낼 자신의 능력에 대한 자신감을 특징으로 하는 긍정적인 성향을 발달시키게 된다.

3. 만약 여러분이 매우 전문적이거나 직업과 관련된 학위를 취득하고 있다면, 대학교에 가기도 전에 어떤 직업을 목표로 하고 있는가를 당연히 알겠지만, 대부분의 과학 기술 학부생들에게 대학교는 그 자체로 모험이다. 즉 어떤 직업에 대한 생각이 머릿속에 있을 수는 있지만, 완전히 확정된 것은 아니다.

4. 그 말들은 (다양한) 해석의 여지가 있는 부정확한 진술이며 디자이너, 개발자, 기술자들에게 고객들이 '내구성이 있는' 또는 '튼튼한' 이라는 말을 통해 정말로 무엇을 의미하는 것인지 알아내라는 불가능한 과제를 제시한다.

5. 그러나 경찰관과 지역 검사들에게는 그 정도로 인기가 많지는 않은데, 그들은 범죄 해결 방식에 대해 크게 오해를 불러일으키는 이미지를 제공한다는 이유로 그 시리즈를 비판했다.

6. 몇 년에 걸쳐 하루의 길이는 1,000만 분의 1, 즉 일 년인 3,150만 초에서 3초만큼 변하는 것으로 드러난다.

7. 그가 뇌의 막연한 개념에 불만족을 느낄 때마다, Poe가 말하길, "나는 곧바로 펜에 의존한다. 펜의 도움을 빌어 필요한 형식, 결과와 정

확성을 얻을 목적으로."

혼공 18일차 승부수 문항 모의고사 5회

 1단계 모의고사 5회 p.176

● 정답

> **1.** ④ **2.** ⑤ **3.** ⑤ **4.** ④ **5.** ① **6.** ② **7.** ③ **8.** ⑤
> **9.** ② **10.** ⑤

1. ④

● 전체 해석

서구 문화에서 남성적 역할을 하는 것은 전통적으로 독립성, 단호한 태도, 지배와 같은 특성을 요구해왔다. 여성은 더 보살피고 남을 잘 헤아리는 것으로 기대된다. 이런 남성과 여성의 역할은 보편적인가? 성별 간의 생물학적인 차이가 필연적으로 행동에서의 성별 차이로 이어지는가? 1935년에 인류학자인 Margaret Mead는 뉴기니 섬의 세 부족 사회의 사람들이 취하고 있는 성 역할을 비교했는데, 그녀의 관찰은 확실히 시사하는 바가 많다. Arapesh 부족에서 남성과 여성 모두는 우리가 여성 역할로 간주할 만한 것의 역할을 하도록 배웠다. 그들은 상호 협조적이고 비공격적이었고 다른 사람들의 요구를 잘 헤아렸다. Mundugumor 부족의 양성 모두는 공격적이고 다른 사람들에게 정서적으로 둔감하도록 길러졌는데, 이것은 서구 기준에서 남성적 행동 유형이다. 마지막으로 Tchambuli 부족은 서구 유형의 정반대인 성 역할 발달 유형을 보여주었다. 남성들은 수동적이고 정서적으로 의존적이며 사교적으로 감수성이 뛰어났고, 반면에 여성들은 지배적이고, 독립적이고 자기 주장이 강했다.

● 지문분석

In Western culture, / [playing the masculine role] / has
traditionally required traits / such as independence,
assertiveness, and dominance.
서구 문화에서 / 남성적 역할을 하는 것은 / 전통적으로 특성을 요구
했다 / 독립성, 공격성, 그리고 지배와 같은

Females are expected / to be more nurturing and sensitive
/ to other people.
여성들은 기대가 된다 / 보다 보살피고 감수성이 강한 것으로 / 다른
사람들에게

Are these masculine and feminine roles universal?
이러한 남성적 그리고 여성적 역할은 보편적인가

Could biological differences / between the sexes / lead
inevitably to gender differences in behavior?
생물학적인 차이가 / 성 사이에서 / 불가피하게 행동에서의 성별 차
이를 이끌까

In 1935, anthropologist Margaret Mead compared the
gender roles / adopted by people in three tribal societies
/ on the island of New Guinea, / and her observations are
certainly thought-provoking.

1935년 인류학자 Margaret Mead는 성 역할을 비교했다 / 3개의 부족 사회의 사람들에 의해 채택된 / 뉴기니 섬에서 / 그리고 그녀의 관찰은 확실히 시사하는 바가 많다

In the Arapesh tribe, / both men and women were taught /
to play / what we would regard as a feminine role: / They
were cooperative, non-aggressive, and sensitive / to the
needs of others.
Arapesh 부족에서 / 남성과 여성 모두 배웠다 / 역할을 하도록 / 우리가 여성적인 역할이라고 간주하는 / 그들은 협동적이고 비공격적이고 그리고 감수성이 강했다 / 다른 사람의 욕구에

[Both men and women of the Mundugumor tribe] /
were brought up / to be aggressive and emotionally
unresponsive to other people / – a masculine pattern of
behavior by Western standards.
Mundugumor 부족의 남성과 여성 모두 / 길러졌다 / 공격적이고 정서적으로 다른 사람들에게 둔감하도록 / 이것은 서구의 기준에 의해서 남성적 행동 패턴이다

Finally, the Tchambuli tribe / displayed a pattern of
gender-role development / that was the direct opposite of
the Western pattern: / Males were passive, emotionally
dependent, and socially sensitive, / whereas females were
dominant, independent, and assertive.
마지막으로 Tchambuli 부족은 / 성 역할 발달 패턴을 보여주었다 / 서구의 패턴과는 정반대인 / 남성은 수동적, 정서적으로 의존적이며 사회적으로 감수성이 풍부했다 / 반면에 여성들은 지배적이고 독립적이며 자기 주장이 강했다

● 해설

1. 다음 글의 제목으로 가장 적절한 것은?

① Every Tribe Has Its Own Gender Roles 모든 부족은 자신만의 성 역할을 가진다
▶ 각자 다른 성 역할을 가지기는 했지만, 이게 포인트가 아니지.

② Changes in Gender Roles Throughout Time 오랜 세월동안 성 역할에서의 변화
▶ 세월에 따른 성 역할의 변화가 아니라 사회에 따른 변화지.

③ Why Do We Have Gender Roles in Human Society? 왜 우리는 인간 사회에서 성 역할을 가지나
▶ 성 역할의 존재 이유가 아니지.

❹ Gender Differences in Temperament: Nature or Culture? 기질에서의 성 차이: 천성인가 문화인가
▶ 남성과 여성의 전형적인 성격은 정해진 것이 아니고 속해있는 문화에 따라 다르다는 내용이지.

⑤ A Controversial Topic in Anthropology: Gender Discrimination 인류학에서의 논쟁 중인 주제: 성차별
▶ 성차별이 아니라 성 역할에 관한 내용이지

● 중요 포인트

과거분사의 수식을 받는 명사

In 1935, anthropologist Margaret Mead compared the
gender roles adopted by people in three tribal societies
on the island of New Guinea, and ~
과거분사 adopted가 앞의 명사 the gender roles를 수식하고 있지.

2. ⑤

● 전체 해석

근대 초기 유럽에서 수로를 통한 운송은 대개 육로를 통한 운송보다 훨씬 더 저렴했다. 1550년에 이탈리아의 한 인쇄업자는 Rome에서 Lyons까지 책 한 짐을 보내는 데 뱃길로는 4스쿠도인 데 비해 육로로는 18스쿠도가 들 것이라고 추정했다. 편지는 보통 육로로 운반되었지만 운하용 배를 통해 사람뿐만 아니라 편지와 신문을 운송하는 시스템이 17세기에 네덜란드 공화국에서 발달했다. 그 배들의 평균 속력은 시속 4마일이 약간 넘었는데 말을 타고 다니는 사람에 비해 느렸다. 반면 그 서비스는 규칙적이고 빈번하고 저렴해서 Amsterdam과 더 작은 마을들 사이뿐만 아니라 작은 마을과 또 다른 작은 마을 간에도 연락이 가능했고, 따라서 정보에 대한 접근을 균등하게 했다. 운송과 메시지 연락 사이의 전통적인 관계가 깨진 것은 바로 1837년 전기 전신의 발명으로 인해서였다.

● 지문분석

In early modern Europe, / [transport by water] / was
usually much cheaper / than transport by land.
근대 초기 유럽에서 / 수로를 통한 운송은 / 보통 더 저렴했다 / 육로에 의한 운송보다

An Italian printer calculated in 1550 / that [to send a load
of books / from Rome to Lyons] / would cost 18 scudi by
land / compared with 4 by sea.
이탈리아의 한 인쇄업자는 1550년에 추정했다 / 책 한 짐을 보내는 것이 / 로마에서 리옹까지 / 육로로는 18스쿠도의 비용이 들거라고 / 해로로 4스쿠도인 데 비해

Letters were normally carried overland, / but [a system of
transporting letters and newspapers, / as well as people,
/ by canal boat] / developed in the Dutch Republic in the
seventeenth century.
편지는 보통 육로로 운반된다 / 하지만 편지와 신문의 운송 시스템은 / 사람뿐만 아니라 / 운하용 배를 통한 / 17세기 네덜란드 공화국에서 발달했다

[The average speed of the boats] / was a little over four
miles an hour, / slow compared to a rider on horseback.
배의 평균 속도는 / 시속 4마일이 약간 넘었다 / 말을 타고 다니는 사람과 비교할 때 느렸다

On the other hand, / the service was regular, frequent and
cheap, / and allowed communication / not only between
Amsterdam and the smaller towns, / but also between one
small town and another, / thus equalizing accessibility to
information.
반면에 / 그 서비스는 규칙적이었고, 빈번했으며, 저렴했다 / 그리고 통신이 가능했다 / 암스테르담과 더 작은 마을 사이 뿐만 아니라 / 작은 마을과 또 다른 마을 사이에서도 / 그래서 정보에 대한 접근을 동등하게 했다

It was only in 1837, / with the invention of the electric
telegraph, / that [the traditional link / between transport
and the communication of messages] / was broken.
바로 1837년에야 / 전기 전신의 발명과 함께 / 전통적인 연결이 /

/ 운송과 메시지 통신 사이의 / 깨졌다

● 해설

2. 다음 글의 밑줄 친 부분 중, 어법상 틀린 것은?

① that: 동사 calcualted의 목적어절을 이끄는 접속사 that이야.

② developed: 문장의 주어인 a system이 뒤에 나오는 of ~ by canal boat의 수식을 받고 있으므로 본동사인 developed는 적절하지.

③ slow: being이 생략된 구문으로 분사구문으로 보면 되겠지.

④ equalizing: 콤마 뒤에 나오는 분사구문으로 보면 돼.

❺ were → was: 문장의 주어는 앞에 있는 messages가 아니라 the traditional link이므로 동사는 단수 동사인 was가 와야 해.

● 중요 포인트

being 생략 분사구문

[The average speed of the boats] was a little over four
miles an hour, slow compared to a rider on horseback.
being 생략 분사구문 = being slow ~, which was slow, and was slow

3. ⑤

● 전체 해석

인간이 느끼는 외로움과 유사한 어떤 것을 동물이 느낄 수 있는지 말하기는 어렵다. 그러나 어떤 종류의 앵무새처럼 매우 사회적인 동물들은 혼자 두었을 때 해로운 방향으로 영향을 받는 것처럼 보인다. 일부 앵무새들은 이상한 행동을 할 것이고 심하게 자신에게 상처를 입힐 수 있다. 몇몇 큰 앵무새들은 오랫동안 고립되면 심지어 미쳐가는 것처럼 보일 것이다. 반면에 천성적으로 무리지어 살지 않는 어떤 동물들은 전혀 영향을 받지 않는 것처럼 보인다. 어떤 물고기들, 특히 어떤 종류의 cichlid는, 수족관에 한 마리 이상 두면 같은 종과 심하게 싸우기까지 할 것이다. 날지 못하는 새의 일종인 Guam rail은 그들과 같은 종을 잘 견뎌낸다(→ 못 참는다). 그리고 그것은 명백하게 포획 상태에서 번식시키는 것을 매우 어렵게 만들었다.

● 지문분석

[Whether an animal can feel anything / resembling the
loneliness / humans feel] / is hard to say.
동물이 무언가를 느낄 수 있느냐는 / 외로움과 유사한 / 인간이 느끼는 / 말하기 어렵다

However, [highly social animals, / such as certain types of
parrot,] / seem to be adversely affected / when kept alone.
하지만 매우 사회적인 동물들은 / 어떤 종류의 앵무새들처럼 / 해로운 방향으로 영향을 받는 것 같다 / 혼자 남겨질 때

Some parrots will engage in bizarre behaviors / and can
severely harm themselves.
어떤 앵무새들은 기괴한 행동을 할 것이고 / 심하게 자기 자신에게 상처를 입힐 수 있다

Some large parrots will even seem to go insane / if
subjected to long periods of isolation.
어떤 큰 앵무새들은 심지어 미쳐가는 것처럼 보일 것이다 / 만약 오랜 기간의 고립에 처하게 되면

On the other hand, / [certain animals / that are by nature solitary] / hardly appear to be affected at all.
반면에 / 어떤 동물들은 / 선천적으로 외톨이인 / 거의 전혀 영향을 받지 않는 것 같다

[Some fish, / in particular some types of cichlids,] / will even fight viciously with their own kind / if more than one is kept in an aquarium.
어떤 물고기들은 / 특히 어떤 타입의 cichlid의 경우 / 심지어 같은 종과 심하게 싸울 것이다 / 만약 한 마리 이상이 수족관에 있다면

[Guam rails, / a kind of flightless bird,] / are intolerable of their own kind, / which has obviously made breeding them in captivity very difficult.
Guam rail은 / 일종의 날지 못하는 새인 / 자신의 종에 못 견딘다 / 이는 명백하게 포획 상태에서의 그들의 번식을 매우 어렵게 만들었다

● 해설

3. 다음 글의 밑줄 친 부분 중 문맥상 낱말의 쓰임이 적절하지 않은 것은?

❺ tolerant → intolerable: 같이 있는 걸 싫어하는 물고기 예시 다음에 나온 또 다른 예시이므로 Guam rail도 같이 있는 걸 싫어하겠지. 따라서 같은 종을 견디지 못해야지(intolerable). 따라서 '견뎌내는'을 의미하는 tolerant는 적절하지 않아.

● 중요 포인트

whether절 주어

[Whether an animal can feel anything resembling the loneliness humans feel] / is hard to say.
S → whether가 이끄는 문장 주어
V → 단수 취급

4. ④

● 전체 해석

심한 적의를 가진 경쟁자라도 위기의 시기에는 (동료와) 어울리려고 한다. 번식기에 영역을 차지하려고 서로 싸워 죽기까지 하는 새들은 (철에 따라) 이동하는 동안 결국 같은 무리에 들어가게 될 수 있다. 내 커다란 열대어 어항 중 하나를 다시 꾸며줄 때마다 나는 이런 경향을 내가 기르는 물고기로부터 직접 알게 된다. cichlid와 같은 많은 물고기는 매우 영역을 고집하는 습성이 있어서 펼친 지느러미로 과시하면서 자신의 구역에 침입자가 없게 하려고 서로를 추적한다. 나는 2년마다 내 어항을 청소하는데 그러는 시간 동안 나는 물고기를 통에 넣어둔다. 며칠 후에 물고기를 어항에 다시 풀어놓는데 그것은 그때쯤에는 이전과는 매우 다르게 보인다. 어떻게 그것들이 갑자기 자기와 같은 종과 어울리려고 하는지를 보는 것이 나는 늘 즐겁다. 가장 잘 싸우는 것들이 이제는 가장 친한 친구처럼 나란히 헤엄치면서 함께 새로운 환경을 탐험한다. 물론 그들은 결국에는 다시 자신감을 느끼기 시작해서 일부의 땅을 (자기 것이라고) 주장하게 된다.

● 지문분석

Even bitter rivals / seek companionship at times of danger.
심한 적의를 가진 경쟁자라도 / 위험의 순간에 교우관계를 추구한다

[Birds / that in the breeding season / fight one another to death / over territory] / may end up in the same flock / during migration.
새들은 / 번식기에 / 서로 죽을 때까지 싸우는 / 영역 때문에 / 결국 같은 무리에 들어가게 될 수 있다 / 이동하는 동안

I know this tendency firsthand from my fish, / each time I redo one of my large tropical aquariums.
나는 이러한 경향을 내 물고기로부터 직접 알게 된다 / 내가 내 가장 커다란 열대어 어항 중 하나를 다시 꾸밀 때마다

Many fish, / such as cichlids, / are quite territorial, / displaying with spread fins / and chasing one another / to keep their corner free of intruders.
많은 물고기들은 / cichlid와 같은 / 매우 영역을 고집하는 습성이 있다 / 펼친 지느러미를 가지고 보여주며 / 그리고 서로를 추적한다 / 그들의 구역을 침입자들로부터 자유롭게 하려고

I clean my tanks out / every couple of years, / during which time / I keep the fish in a barrel.
나는 내 어항을 청소한다 / 2년마다 / 그 시기 동안 / 나는 물고기를 통에 넣어둔다

After a few days / they are released back into the tank, / which by then / looks quite different from before.
며칠 후에 / 그들은 어항으로 다시 풀어놓아진다 / 그때에 / 이전과는 아주 다르게 보인다

I am always amused / at how they suddenly seek out the company of their own kind.
나는 항상 즐겁다 / 어떻게 그들이 갑자기 자기 종의 동료를 추구하는지에 대해서

Like best buddies, / the biggest fighters / now swim side by side, / exploring their new environment together.
부사구문
최고의 친구들처럼 / 가장 큰 싸움꾼들이 / 지금은 나란히 헤엄친다 / 그리고 그들의 새로운 환경을 함께 탐험한다

Until, of course, they start to feel confident again, / and claim a piece of real estate.
물론 그들이 다시 자신감을 느끼기 시작할 때까지는 / 그리고 일부의 땅을 주장하게 된다

● 해설

4. 다음 빈칸에 들어갈 말로 가장 적절한 것은?

_____. Birds that in the breeding season fight one another to death over territory may end up in the same flock during migration. I know this tendency firsthand from my fish, each time I redo one of my large tropical aquariums. Many fish, such as cichlids, are quite territorial, displaying with spread fins and chasing one another to keep their corner free of intruders. I clean my tanks out every couple of years, during which time I keep the fish in a barrel. After a few days they are released back into the tank, which by then looks quite different from before. I am always amused at how they suddenly seek out the company of their own kind. Like best buddies, the biggest fighters now swim side by side, exploring their new environment together. Until, of course, they start to feel confident again, and claim a piece of real estate.

① Curiosity is nature's original school of education 호기심은 교육에 있어 자연의 원래의 학교이다
② Solitude makes you stronger and more independent 고독은 당신을 더 강하게 그리고 더 독립적으로 만든디
③ Some species suffer disadvantages from living in groups 일부 종은 단체 생활로부터의 불리함을 겪는다
❹ Even bitter rivals seek companionship at times of danger 심한 적의를 가진 경쟁자라도 위기의 시기에는 어울리려고 한다
▶ 통으로 갔다가(위기 순간) 다시 돌아온 물고기들이 친구가 되어 있다.
⑤ Bigger animals tend to feed alone or in small groups 더 커다란 동물들은 혼자 혹은 더 적은 무리로 먹이를 먹는 경향이 있다

맨 마지막에 나온 예에서 어항을 옮긴(위험의 순간) 물고기들이 다시 돌아왔을 때, 친한 친구가 되었으므로 빈칸에 들어가기에 가장 적절한 것은 ④ Even bitter rivals seek companionship at times of danger(심한 적의를 가진 경쟁자라도 위기의 시기에는 어울리려고 한다)가 되겠지.

● 중요 포인트

관계대명사절의 수식을 받는 주어
[Birds that in the breeding season fight one another to death over territory] may end up in the same flock during migration.

5. ①

● 전체 해석

인간의 두뇌는 그 일생 동안 그것이 만나게 되는 모든 것을 완전히 이해하거나 인식할 수는 없다. 음악 애호가가 일 년 내내, 매일, 매 순간 헤드폰을 쓰고 있다고 해도 미국에서만 한 해 동안 발매되는 모든 앨범의 8분의 1을 넘게 듣는 것은 불가능할 것이다. 우리는 우리의 수중에 들어올 수 있는 예술 작품 전부에게 동일한 시간을 할애해 줄 능력을 가지고 있지 않기 때문에 손쉬운 방법에 의존해야만 한다. 어떤 영화를 보고 싶은지 결정하기 전에 우리는 최신 영화의 비평과 평점을 찾아보려고 할 수 있다. 우리는 흔히 어떤 예술 작품을 우리 삶 속에 받아들일지에 대해 결정하는 것을 인간관계가 안내하게 한다. 그리고 우리는 우리에게 가능한 것의 범위를 줄이기 위해 박물관, 미술관, 라디오 방송국, 텔레비전 방송국 등과 같이 우리가 예술을 경험하는 통로가 되어 주는 배급 체계에 계속 의존하여 그 결과 그 다음(번에 감상할) 훌륭한 것을 찾는 데 우리의 온 힘을 써버릴 필요가 없다.

● 지문분석

The human brain cannot completely comprehend or appreciate all / that it encounters in its lifespan.
인간의 두뇌는 모든 것을 완벽하게 이해하거나 인식할 수 없다 / 그것이 일생 동안 직면하는

Even if a music lover kept his headphones on / for every minute of every day for an entire year, / he wouldn't be able to listen to more / than an eighth of all the albums / that

are released just in the United States in one year.
비록 음악 애호가가 그의 헤드폰을 끼고 있더라도 / 일 년 내내, 매일, 매 순간 / 그는 더 많은 것을 들을 수 없을 것이다 / 모든 앨범의 1/8보다 / 일 년 동안 미국에서 발매되는

Because we do not possess the capacity / to give equal time / to every artistic product / that might come our way, / we must rely on shortcuts.
우리가 능력을 가지고 있지 않기 때문에 / 동등한 시간을 주려는 / 모든 예술 작품에게 / 우리에게 들어올지도 모르는 / 우리는 쉬운 방법에 의존해야만 한다

We may look for reviews and ratings / of the latest movies / before we decide / which ones we'd like to see.
우리는 리뷰나 평점을 찾을지도 모른다 / 최신 영화의 / 우리가 결정하기 전에 / 어떤 영화를 우리가 보고 싶은지

We often let / personal relationships guide our decisions / about what art we allow into our lives.
우리는 종종 하게 한다 / 개인의 관계가 우리의 결정을 인도하도록 / 어떤 예술을 우리가 우리의 삶에 허용할지에 대해서

Also, we continually rely on the distribution systems / through which we experience art / – museums, galleries, radio stations, television networks, etc. / – to narrow the field of possibilities / for us / so that we don't have to spend all of our energy / searching for the next great thing.
또한 우리는 계속해서 배급 체계에 의존한다 / 우리가 예술을 경험하게 되는 / 박물관, 갤러리, 라디오 방송국, TV 방송국 등 / 가능성의 범위를 줄이기 위해서 / 우리를 위해 / 그래서 우리는 모든 에너지를 쓸 필요가 없다 / 다음 대단한 것을 찾는 데

● 해설

5. 다음 빈칸에 들어갈 말로 가장 적절한 것은?
The human brain cannot completely comprehend or appreciate all that it encounters in its lifespan. Even if a music lover kept his headphones on for every minute of every day for an entire year, he wouldn't be able to listen to more than an eighth of all the albums that are released just in the United States in one year. Because we do not possess the capacity to give equal time to every artistic product that might come our way, we must rely on shortcuts. We may look for reviews and ratings of the latest movies before we decide which ones we'd like to see. We often let personal relationships guide our decisions about what art we allow into our lives. Also, we continually rely on the distribution systems through which we experience art – museums, galleries, radio stations, television networks, etc. to narrow the field of possibilities for us so that we don't have to _____.
빈칸 앞 부정어 주의
위의 것들이 없다면 하게 될 것이 바로 빈칸이겠지.

❶ spend all of our energy searching for the next great thing 그 다음 번에 감상할 훌륭한 것을 찾는데 우리의 온 힘을 다 쓴다
▶ 앞에 나온 손쉬운 방법이 없다면 하게 될 것이 바로 이것이지.
② know how to turn our artistic talents into profits 우리의 예술적 재능을 수익으로 바꾸는 법을 안다

③ create artistic products to learn about art 예술에 대해서 배우기 위해 예술적 상품을 만든다
④ satisfy our deeply rooted hunger for art 예술에 대한 우리의 깊이 숨겨진 허기짐을 채운다
⑤ avoid buying musical instruments online 악기를 온라인에서 구매하는 것을 피한다

모든 것을 다 볼 필요가 없게 끔 해주는 손쉬운 방법이 있으니 어렵게 할 필요는 없겠지. 배급 체계도 손쉬운 방법에 해당되지. 따라서 빈칸 앞에 부정어가 있으니 빈칸은 그런 손쉬운 방법이 없을 때 벌어지는 일을 찾으면 돼. 빈칸에 들어갈 가장 적절한 것은 ① spend all of our energy searching for the next great thing(그 다음번에 감상할 훌륭한 것을 찾는 데 우리의 온 힘을 다 쓴다)이 되겠지.

● 중요 포인트

의문사 which

관계대명사 which와 의문사 which를 구별해야 한다.

We may look for reviews and ratings of the latest movies before we decide which ones we'd like to see.
<u>의문사 which '어떤'</u>

6. ②

● 전체 해석

어떤 사람들은 당신이 인간의 본성을 변화시킬 수 없다고 믿고, 그래서 그들은 진화하는 인간의 의식이라는 개념을 단지 보증되지 않은 이상주의라고 생각한다. 그러나 인간 본성이란 무엇인가? 사전은 본성이 내재적인 특성이나 사람 또는 사물의 기본적인 구성 즉, 그것의 본질이라고 정의한다. 그러나 한 사람의 내재적인 특성이나 본질이 정말로 변하는가? 우리는 다음과 같은 하나의 비유적인 질문을 함으로써 이 중요한 쟁점에 대한 통찰을 얻을 수 있다. 씨앗이 나무로 성장할 때 그것의 내재적인 특성은 변하는가? 전혀 그렇지 않다. 나무가 되기 위한 잠재력은 언제나 씨앗 안에 내재되어 있다. 씨앗이 나무로 성장할 때 그것은 씨앗의 고유한 본성 속에 항상 내재되어 있는 잠재력이 실현되는 정도의 변화만을 나타낸다. 마찬가지로 인간의 본성은 변하지 않는다. 하지만 나무가 될 잠재력을 지닌 씨앗처럼 인간의 본성은 정지 상태에 있는 것이 아니라 잠재적 가능성들의 연속체이다. 우리 인간은 기본적인 본성의 변화 없이 원시적인 상태에서 문명화된 상태로 성장할 수 있다.

● 지문분석

Some people believe / that you can't change human nature, / and thus they see / the idea of an evolving human consciousness / as no more than unwarranted idealism.
└ 단지 = only
어떤 사람들은 믿는다 / 당신이 인간의 본성을 바꿀 수 없다고 / 그래서 그들은 본다 / 진화하는 인간의 의식이라는 개념을 / 단지 보증되지 않은 이상주의라고

Yet, what is human nature?
하지만, 인간의 본성이란 무엇인가

The dictionary defines nature / as the inherent character or basic constitution / of a person or thing / – its essence.
사전은 본성을 정의한다 / 내재된 특성 혹은 기본적 구성이라고 / 인간이나 사물의 / 그것의 본질

But does the inherent character and essence of a person / ever change?
하지만 내재적인 특성과 사람의 본질은 / 변하는가

We can gain insight / into this key issue / by asking an analogous question: / Does the inherent character of a seed / change / when it grows into a tree? / Not at all.
우리는 통찰을 얻을 수 있다 / 이 핵심 문제에 대한 / 비유적인 질문을 함으로써 / 내재된 씨앗의 특성은 / 변하는가 / 그것이 나무로 자랄 때 / 전혀 아니다

[The potential for becoming a tree] / was always resident within the seed.
 S   V
나무가 되는 잠재력은 / 항상 씨앗 내에 존재했다

When a seed grows into a tree, / it represents only a change / in the degree / to which [its potential, / always inherent in its original nature,] / is realized.
                                                                              S
씨앗이 나무로 자랄 때 / 그것은 단지 변화를 나타낸다 / 정도에서만 / 그것의 잠재력이 / 항상 천성 속에 내재되어 있는 / 실현되는

Similarly, human nature does not change; / yet, like the seed / with the potential of becoming a tree, / human nature is not a static thing / but a spectrum of potentials.
마찬가지로 인간의 본성은 변하지 않는다 / 하지만, 씨앗처럼 / 나무가 되려는 잠재력이 있는 / 인간의 본성은 정적인 것이 아니라 / 잠재력의 스펙트럼이다

We human beings can grow / from a primitive to an enlightened condition / without a change in our basic human nature.
우리 인간은 성장할 수 있다 / 원시적인 상태에서 계몽된(문명화된) 상태로 / 우리의 기본적인 인간 본성에서의 변화 없이

● 해설

6. 다음 글의 빈칸에 들어갈 말로 가장 적절한 것은?

Some people believe that you can't change human nature, and thus they see the idea of an evolving human consciousness as no more than unwarranted idealism. Yet, what is human nature? The dictionary defines nature as the inherent character or basic constitution of a person or thing — its essence. But does the inherent character and essence of a person ever change? We can gain insight into this key issue by asking an analogous question: Does the inherent character of a seed change when it grows into a tree? Not at all. The potential for becoming a tree was always resident within the seed. When a seed grows into a tree, it represents only a change in the degree to which its potential, always inherent in its original nature, is realized. Similarly, human nature does not change; yet, like the seed with the potential of becoming a tree, human nature is _____. We human beings can grow from a primitive to an enlightened condition without a change in our basic human nature.

① not only an inherent trait but a social product 내재된 특성뿐만 아니라 사회적 상품

다시 말하자면 / 신체의 종류는 / 인간이 가지는 / 일종의 생각에 영향을 준다 / 인간이 가지는

As a result, / thought is taken to be embodied.
결과적으로 / 사고(생각)는 구체화된다

As an example, / take the conceptual category of TREE.
예로서 / '나무'의 개념적인 범주를 생각해 보자

How can the body / play any role / in our understanding / what a tree is?
어떻게 신체는 / 어떤 역할을 할 수 있을까 / 우리의 이해에서 / 나무가 무엇이냐는

For one thing, / we understand a tree / as being upright.
한 가지 면에서 / 우리는 나무를 이해한다 / 똑바로 서 있는 것으로서

This comes from / how we experience our own bodies; / namely, that we experience ourselves / as being erect.
이것은 발생한다 / 어떻게 우리가 우리 자신의 신체를 경험하느냐로부터 / 말하자면 우리는 우리 자신을 경험한다 / 똑바로 서 있는 것으로서

For another, / we see a tree / as tall.
다른 면에서 / 우리는 나무를 본다 / 키가 큰 것으로

The aspect of tallness / only makes sense / with respect to our standard evaluation / of the body's relative height.
키가 크다는 속성은 / 오직 이해가 된다 / 우리의 기준 평가에 관해서 / 신체의 상대적 높이의

A tree is tall / relative to our average human size.
나무는 키가 크다 / 우리의 평균 인간의 크기에 비해서

In this way, / categories of mind / are defined / by the body's interaction with the environment.
이런 식으로 / 생각의 범주는 / 규정된다 / 신체의 환경과의 상호작용에 의해서

We call such features of conceptual categories / "interactional properties."
우리는 그런 개념적 범주의 속성을 부른다 / 상호적 특성이라고

● 해설

7. 주어진 글 다음에 이어질 글의 순서로 가장 적절한 것은?

In experientialism, the body is seen as playing a decisive role in producing the kind of mind we have. The mind is based on the body. In other words, the kind of body humans have influences the kind of mind they have. As a result, thought is taken to be embodied. 일반론

구체적 예시
(B) As an example, take the conceptual category of TREE. How can the body play any role in our understanding what a tree is? For one thing, we understand a tree as being upright.

(C) This comes from how we experience our own bodies; namely, that we experience ourselves as being erect. For another, we see a tree as tall. The aspect of tallness only makes sense with respect to our standard evaluation of the body's

---

▶ 사회성은 언급이 되지 않고 있어.
❷ not a static thing but a spectrum of potentials 정지 상태가 아니라 잠재성들의 연속체
▶ 기본적인 것은 놔두고 어찌되었던 변화하고 있어.
③ fertile soil with the potential to nurture creativity 창의성을 길러주는 잠재성을 가진 풍요로운 토양
▶ 창의성은 언급조차 되지 않았지.
④ a stepping stone as well as a handicap to the future 미래에 대한 불이익일 뿐만 아니라 디딤돌
▶ 좋으냐 나쁘냐의 문제가 아니지.
⑤ the result of interaction between mankind and nature 인간과 자연 사이의 상호작용의 결과
▶ 상호작용도 역시 언급되지 않았어.

인간의 본질은 변하지는 않지만 잠재력이 실현되는 정도의 변화는 한다고 하고 있어. 그리고 마지막 문장에서 기본적인 본성은 변화없이 원시상태에서 문명화된 상태로 성장한다고 했으니 최소한 변화가 언급된 것이 빈칸에 들어가야 하겠지. 따라서 빈칸에 들어가기에 가장 적절한 것은 ② not a static thing but a spectrum of potentials(정지 상태가 아니라 잠재성들의 연속체)가 되겠지.

● 중요 포인트

전치사 + which 구문

When a seed grows into a tree, it represents only a change in the degree to which its potential, always inherent in its original nature, is realized.
전치사 + which + 완전한 문장

---

7. ③

● 전체 해석

경험주의에서, 신체는 우리가 지닌 생각의 종류를 만들어내는 데 결정적인 역할을 하는 것으로 여겨진다. 생각은 신체에 기초한다. 다시 말해서, 인간이 갖고 있는 신체의 종류가 그들이 갖고 있는 생각의 종류에 영향을 준다. 그 결과, 사고가 구체화된다. (B) 한 예로, '나무'라는 개념의 범주를 생각해 보라. 나무라는 것이 무엇인지를 우리가 이해하는데 신체가 어떤 역할을 할 수 있는가? 한 가지 면에서, 우리는 나무가 똑바로 서 있는 것으로 이해한다. (C) 이것은 우리가 우리 자신의 신체를 어떻게 경험하는가에 기인한다. 즉, 우리는 우리 자신을 똑바로 선 존재로 경험한다는 것이다. 또 다른 면에서, 우리는 나무를 키가 큰 물체로 이해한다. 키가 크다는 측면은 단지 신체의 상대적인 높이에 관한 우리의 기본적인 평가와 관련해서만 이해된다. (A) 나무는 우리 인간의 평균적인 크기에 비해 키가 크다. 이런 식으로, 생각의 범주는 신체와 환경의 상호작용에 의해 정의된다. 우리는 개념 범주의 그러한 특성을 '상호적 특성'이라고 부른다.

● 지문분석

In experientialism, / the body is seen / as playing a decisive role / in producing the kind of mind / we have.
경험주의에서 / 신체는 여겨진다 / 결정적인 역할을 하는 것으로 / 일종의 생각을 만들어내는 데 있어 / 우리가 가지는

The mind is based on the body.
이러한 생각은 신체에 근간을 둔다

In other words, / [the kind of body / humans have] /
S

relative height.

(A) A tree is tall relative to our average human size. In this way, categories of mind are defined by the body's interaction with the environment. We call such features of conceptual categories "interactional properties."

주어진 문장은 경험주의에서 생각과 신체와의 관계를 설명하고 있고, (B)에서 이를 구체적인 예시로 설명하고 있어. (B)의 마지막에 나오는 나무가 똑바로 서 있다라는 것은 (C)의 첫 문장에 나온 우리가 똑바로 서 있다와 연결되지. 그리고 (C)의 마지막에 나온 신체의 상대적인 높이 역시 (A)의 첫 문장에 나오는 인간의 평균적인 크기와 이어져야 하겠지.

● 중요 포인트

관계사가 생략된 구문

In other words, [the kind of body humans have] influences the kind of mind they have.
(which, that 생략)

8. ⑤

● 전체 해석

불행하게도 환경적, 사회적 상황들을 향상시키기 위해 일하는 많은 조직들과 정치적 지도자들은 의심할 나위 없이 패러다임 안에서부터 움직인다. 그러나 Einstein의 말을 바꾸어 말하자면, 문제들은 그것들이 생겨난 같은 패러다임 안에서부터는 해결될 수 없다. 적절한 예가 온실가스 배출을 줄이기 위한 배출권 거래제 접근 방식이다. 이 시나리오에서는 시장의 자유로운 손이 온실가스 감축을 위한 가장 효율적인 기회들을 찾아낼 것이라는 믿음 속에서, 사기업들이 오염시킬 그들의 '권리'를 다른 기업들에게 파는 것이 허락되고, 그러면 그들(권리를 산 다른 기업들)은 더 많이 오염시킬 수 있다. 그러나 오염을 하나의 '권리'로 보고 환경적 문제를 해결하기 위해 시장에 의존하는 것은 우리를 이러한 혼란 속에 빠지게 한 바로 그 패러다임을 강화한다. 다른 패러다임 안에서는 인간의 건강과 생태학적인 생존이 가장 중요할 것이며, 이러한 목표들을 약화시키는 산업 활동들이 전면적으로 금지될 것이다. 깨끗한 공기와 건강에 좋은 기후에 대한 권리가 오염시킬 권리를 이길 것이다.

● 지문분석

Unfortunately [many organizations and political leaders / working to improve environmental and social conditions] / operate unquestioningly / from within the paradigm.
불행하게도 많은 조직과 정치 지도자들은 / 환경적 사회적 상황들을 개선시키고자 일하는 / 의심할 여지없이 움직인다 / 패러다임 내부로부터

However, to paraphrase Einstein, / problems cannot be solved / from within the same paradigm / in which they were created.
하지만, Einstein의 말을 바꾸어 말하자면 / 문제는 해결될 수 없다 / 같은 패러다임 내부로부터 / 그것들이 만들어졌던

A good example is the cap and trade approach / to reducing greenhouse gas emissions.
좋은 예시는 배출권 거래제 접근 방식이다 / 온실가스 배출을 줄이려는

In this scenario, / private companies are permitted / to sell their "right" to pollute / to other companies, / which can then pollute more, / in the belief / that [the free hand of the market] / will find the most efficient opportunities / for greenhouse gas reductions.
이 시나리오에서 / 사기업들은 허용된다 / 오염시킬 권리를 판매하는 게 / 다른 회사에게 / 이는 더 많이 오염시킬 수 있게 된다 / 믿음 하에서 / 시장의 자유로운 손이 / 가장 효율적인 기회들을 찾을 것이라는 / 온실가스 감축을 위한

But [viewing pollution as a "right" / and relying on the market / to solve environmental problems] / reinforces the very paradigm / that got us into this mess.
하지만 오염을 권리로 보고 / 시장에 의존하는 것은 / 환경 문제를 해결하기 위해서 / 바로 그 패러다임을 강화한다 / 우리를 이러한 혼란으로 밀어 넣었던

In a different paradigm, / human health and ecological survival / would be paramount, / and [industrial activities / that undermine these goals] / would be prohibited outright.
다른 패러다임에서 / 인간의 건강과 생태학적인 생존이 / 가장 중요할지도 모른다 / 그리고 기업의 활동은 / 이러한 목표를 약화시키는 / 바로 금지될 지도 모른다

[The right / to clean air and a healthy climate] / would win over the right to pollute.
권리는 / 깨끗한 공기와 건강한 기후에 대한 / 오염시킬 권리를 이길 것이다

● 해설

8. 글의 흐름으로 보아, 주어진 문장이 들어가기에 가장 적절한 곳은?

In a different paradigm, human health and ecological survival would be paramount, and industrial activities that undermine these goals would be prohibited outright.
인간의 권리가 기업의 활동보다 우위라는게 다른 패러다임이지. 그렇다면 앞에는 반대의 패러다임, 즉 기업의 활동을 장려하는 내용이 나와야겠지.

Unfortunately many organizations and political leaders working to improve environmental and social conditions operate unquestioningly from within the paradigm. (①) However, to paraphrase Einstein, problems cannot be solved from within the same paradigm in which they were created. 오염시킬 권리인 오염 배출권에 대한 내용은 '기업의 활동' > '인간의 권리인 상황인거지. (②) A good example is the cap and trade approach to reducing greenhouse gas emissions. (③) In this scenario, private companies are permitted to sell their "right" to pollute to other companies, which can then pollute more, in the belief that the free hand of the market will find the most efficient opportunities for greenhouse gas reductions. (④) But viewing pollution as a "right" and relying on the market to solve environmental problems reinforces the very paradigm that got us into this mess. (⑤) The right to clean air and a healthy climate would win over the right to pollute.
인간의 권리 > 오염시킬 권리

'인간의 권리 > 기업의 활동'인 내용이 나와야 하는데, ⑤번 이후의 문장

이 바로 그러한 내용이지. 그 앞에서는 기업의 활동이 우위에 있는 내용이 나오고 있어.

● 중요 포인트

구문 전체가 주어

But [viewing pollution as a "right" and relying on the market to solve environmental problems] reinforces the very paradigm that got us into this mess.

S → 이 전체를 하나의 주어로 보고 있음

9. ② 10. ⑤

● 전체 해석

회사의 경우 문화를 평상복을 입는 금요일이나 구내식당에서의 무료 소다수와 같이 근무 환경의 눈에 보이는 요소로 설명하는 것은 흔한 일이다. 하지만 MIT의 Edgar Schein이 설명하듯이 그런 것들이 문화를 정의하지는 않는다. 그것들은 단지 그것의 가공품일 뿐이다. 그에 의하면, 문화는 사람들이 매우 자주, 그리고 매우 성공적으로 따라서 그들이 다른 방식으로는 일을 하려는 시도를 생각조차 하지 못하는 공통의 목표를 향해 함께 일하는 방식이다. 문화가 형성되면, 사람들은 성공하기 위해 해야 할 일들을 자율적으로 할 것이다.

그러한 본능들은 하룻밤 사이에 형성되지 않는다. 오히려, 그것들은 공유된 학습의 결과이다. 모든 조직에서 문제나 과제가 발생하는 그 첫 번째 순간이 있다. 책임이 있는 사람들은 성공하기 위해서 무엇을 해야 하고 그것을 어떻게 해야 하는지에 대한 결정에 함께 도달한다. 만약 그 결정이 성공적인 결과를 가져온다면, 그러면 다음 번에 그 직원들이 비슷한 유형의 과제에 직면할 때, 그들은 똑같은 결정과 똑같은 문제 해결 방식으로 돌아갈 것이다.

그들이 선택한 방식이 그 문제를 해결하는데 계속 효과적으로 작용하는 한, 그 문화는 그들 앞에 놓인 선택을 하는데 있어 사람들이 이용하는 내재적인 일련의 규칙들이 될 것이다. 그들은 자신들이 해왔던 방식이 그 일을 하는 방식이라고 생각할 것이다. 이것은 조직이 스스로 운영되도록 만든다. 관리자들은 그 규칙을 강요할 필요가 없다. 사람들은 행해져야 할 일들을 본능적으로 해나간다.

● 지문분석

In the case of a company, / it is common / to describe
　　　　　　　　　　　　　　　└ 가주어　　 └ 진주어
culture / as the visible elements of a working
environment: / casual Fridays or free sodas in the
cafeteria.
회사의 경우 / 일반적이다 / 문화를 묘사하는 것이 / 근무 환경의 눈에 보이는 요소로서 / 평상복을 입는 금요일이나 카페에서의 무료 소다수같은

But as MIT's Edgar Schein explains, / those things don't
define a culture.
하지만 MIT의 Edagar Schein이 설명하듯 / 그러한 것들은 문화를 규정하지 않는다

They are just artifacts of it.
└ the visible elements of a working environment
그것들은 단지 그것의 가공품일 뿐이다

According to him, / culture is a way / of working together

toward common goals / that people have followed so
frequently and so successfully / that they don't even
　　　　　　　　　　　 so-that 용법
think / about trying to do things another way.
그에 따르면 / 문화는 하나의 방식이다 / 함께 공통의 목표를 향해서 일하는 / 사람들이 너무 빈번히 그리고 너무 성공적으로 따라왔던 / 그래서 그들은 심지어 생각하지 않는다 / 또 다른 식으로 그러한 것을 하고자 노력하는 것에 대해서

If a culture has formed, / people will autonomously do /
what they need to do to be successful.
문화가 형성된다면 / 사람들은 자동적으로 할 것이다 / 그들이 성공하기 위해서 할 필요가 있는 것을

Those instincts are not formed overnight.
그러한 본능들은 하룻밤 사이에 형성되지 않는다

Rather, they are the result of shared learning.
오히려 그것들은 공유된 학습의 결과이다

In every organization, / there is that first time / when a
problem or challenge arises.
모든 조직에는 / 최초의 시간이 있다 / 문제나 어려움이 발생하는

Those responsible / reach a decision together / on what to
S
do / and how to do it / in order to succeed.
책임이 있는 사람들은 / 함께 결론에 도달한다 / 무엇을 할지에 대한 / 그리고 어떻게 그것을 할지에 대한 / 성공하기 위해서

If that decision results in a successful outcome, / then
the next time when those employees face a similar type
of challenge, / they will return to / the same decision and
same way / of solving the problem.
만약 그러한 결정이 성공적인 결과를 야기한다면 / 그러면 그러한 직원들이 비슷한 어려움에 직면하게 될 때 / 그들은 되돌아올 것이다 / 같은 결정과 같은 방식으로 / 그 문제를 해결하는

As long as [the way / they have chosen] / keeps working
to solve the problem, / the culture will become an
internal set of rules / that people will draw upon / in
making the choices ahead of them.
방식이 / 그들이 선택한 / 문제를 해결하는 데 계속 효과적으로 작용하는 한 / 문화는 내부의 일련의 규칙이 될 것이다 / 사람들이 이용하게 될 / 그들에 앞서 선택을 할 때

They will just assume / that [the way / they have been
　　　　　　　　　　　　　　　　　　　 S
doing it] / is the way of doing it.
그들은 단지 추정할 것이다 / 방식은 / 그들이 그것을 해왔던 / 그것을 하는 방식이라고

This causes / an organization to become self-managing.
이것은 유발한다 / 조직이 스스로 운영되어지기를

Managers don't need to enforce the rule.
관리자들은 그 규칙을 강요할 필요가 없다

People instinctively get on with / what needs to be done.
사람들은 본능적으로 하게 된다 / 되어질 필요가 있는 것을

● 해설

9. 윗 글의 제목으로 가장 적절한 것은?

① Cultural Tolerance: A Way to True Success 문화적 관용: 진실한 성공의 방식

❷ Company Culture: More than What It Seems 회사의 문화: 보이는 것 이상의 것
▶ 회사의 규칙은 공유된 학습의 결과이고, 내재적 일련의 규칙이라고 하고 있으니 보이는 것과는 다르겠지.

③ Widespread Misconceptions about Autonomy 자율에 대한 널리 퍼진 오해

④ Through a Visible Rather than Invisible Hand 보이지 않는 손보다는 보이는 손을 통해서

⑤ Diversity in a Company: Obligation or Option? 회사 안에서의 다양성: 의무 혹은 선택?

10. 윗 글의 빈칸에 들어갈 말로 가장 적절한 것은?

① vulnerable 상처받기 쉬운

② confidential 은밀한

③ hierarchical 계층적인

④ non-adaptive 비적응적인, 적응하기 힘든

❺ self-managing 스스로 운영하는
▶ 바로 뒤에서 강요할 필요가 없고 본능적으로 해나간다고 하고 있지.

● 중요 포인트

명사를 수식하는 that의 역할

As long as the way they have chosen keeps working to solve the problem, the culture will become an internal set of rules that people will draw upon in making the choices ahead of them.
관계대명사 that

❷ 혼공 개념 마무리 p.181

1. 마지막으로 Tchambuli 부족은 서구 유형의 정반대인 성 역할 발달 유형을 보여주었다. 남성들은 수동적이고 정서적으로 의존적이며 사교적으로 감수성이 뛰어났고, 반면에 여성들은 지배적이고, 독립적이고 자기주장이 강했다.

2. 운송과 메시지 연락 사이의 전통적인 관계가 깨진 것은 바로 1837년 전기 전신의 발명으로 인해서였다.

3. 번식기에 영역을 차지하려고 서로 싸워 죽기까지 하는 새들은 (철에 따라) 이동하는 동안 결국 같은 무리에 들어가게 될 수 있다.

4. 또한 우리는 우리에게 가능한 것의 범위를 줄이기 위해 박물관, 미술관, 라디오 방송국, 텔레비전 방송국 등과 같이 우리가 예술을 경험하는 통로가 되어 주는 배급 체계에 계속 의존하여 그 결과 그 다음 (번에 감상할) 훌륭한 것을 찾는 데 우리의 온 힘을 써버릴 필요가 없다.

5. 그들이 선택한 방식이 그 문제를 해결하는데 계속 효과적으로 작용하는 한, 그 문화는 그들 앞에 놓인 선택을 하는데 있어 사람들이 이용하는 내재적인 일련의 규칙들이 될 것이다.

6. 그에 의하면, 문화는 사람들이 매우 자주, 그리고 매우 성공적으로 따라서 그들이 다른 방식으로는 일을 하려는 시도를 생각조차 하지 못하는 공통의 목표를 향해 함께 일하는 방식이다.

 19일차 승부수 문항 모의고사 6회

❶ 모의고사 6회 p.184

● 정답

1. ④	**2.** ③	**3.** ③	**4.** ①	**5.** ①	**6.** ⑤	**7.** ③	**8.** ④
9. ①	**10.** ⑤			

1. ④

● 전체 해석

아이들의 공감 능력을 길러줄 수 있는 가장 간단하고도 효과적인 방법 중 하나는 스스로 더 놀도록 내버려 두는 것이다. 감독 없이 노는 아이들은 그들이 어떻게 느끼는지를 서로에게 주저 없이 말한다. 게다가, 놀고 있는 아이들은 흔히 다른 역할을 맡아서 Walsh 교장 선생님이나 Josh 엄마인 척하고, 즐거운 마음으로 다른 누군가가 어떻게 생각하고 느끼는지를 스스로 상상하게 만든다. 불행하게도, 자유로운 놀이는 드물어지고 있다. Boston 대학의 연구 교수인 Peter Gray는 미국과 다른 선진국에서 지난 50년에 걸쳐서 아이들이 자기 자신들이 선택한 방식으로 놀면서 탐구할 기회가 지속적이고, 궁극적으로는 급격한 감소를 보이고 있음을 상세히 기록해 왔다. 그 결과는 공감 능력을 특히 훼손해 왔다고 그는 주장한다. 사회적으로 놀 기회를 거의 갖지 못하는 아이들에게서 우리가 볼 것으로 예상하는 것은 바로 공감 능력의 감소와 자아도취의 증가라고 그는 결론 내린다.

● 지문분석

[One of the simplest and most effective ways / to build
 S
empathy in children] / is to let them play more on their
        V
own.
가장 간단하고 가장 효과적인 방법 중 하나는 / 아이들에게서 공감 능력을 길러 줄 / 그들에게 스스로 더 많이 놀도록 하는 것이다

Unsupervised kids / are not reluctant to tell one another / how they feel.
감독받지 않는 아이들은 / 서로에게 말하는 걸 주저하지 않는다 / 그들이 느끼는 것을

In addition, / children at play / often take on other roles, / pretending to be Principal Walsh or Josh's mom, / happily
└분사구문
forcing themselves to imagine / how someone else thinks and feels.
덧붙여 / 놀이 중의 아이들은 / 종종 다른 역할을 맡는다 / Walsh 교장 선생님이나 Josh의 엄마인 척 하면서 / 행복하게 자신이 상상하도록 한다 / 어떻게 다른 누군가가 생각하고 느끼는지에 대해서

Unfortunately, free play is becoming rare.
불행하게도 자유 놀이는 드물어지고 있다

Boston College research professor Peter Gray / has documented a continuous and ultimately dramatic decline / in children's opportunities / to play and explore / in their own chosen ways / over the past fifty years / in the United States and other developed countries.

보스턴 대학의 연구 교수인 Peter Gray는 / 지속적인 그리고 궁극적으로 지나치게 감소하는 것을 기록했다 / 아이들의 기회에서 / 놀고 탐구할 / 그들 자신이 선택한 방법에서 / 지난 50년에 걸쳐서 / 미국과 다른 선진국에서

The effects have been especially damaging, / he argues, / to empathy.

그 결과는 특히 훼손해 왔다 / 그가 주장하길 / 공감에 있어

He concludes / that [a decline of empathy and a rise in narcissism] / are exactly what we would expect / to see in children / who have little opportunity to play socially.

그는 결론을 내린다 / 공감의 감소와 자아도취의 증가는 / 정확하게 우리가 기대한 것이라고 / 아이들에게서 볼 것으로 / 사회적으로 놀 기회가 거의 없는

● 해설

1. 다음 글의 밑줄 친 부분 중, 어법상 틀린 것은?

① is: 문장의 주어는 one이며 뒤에 오는 of the simplest ~ in children의 수식을 받고 있어. 따라서 동사는 단수 동사인 is가 적절하지.

② themselves: 주어인 children을 지칭하므로 재귀대명사가 목적어로 와야겠지.

③ ultimately: 바로 뒤에 나오는 형용사 dramatic를 수식하므로 부사인 ultimately는 적절하지.

❹ damaged → damaging: 주어인 the effects가 공감에 손상을 주므로 능동을 의미하는 형용사인 damaging이 와야 하지.

⑤ what: 뒤에 see의 목적어가 없는 불완전 문장이 오므로 관계대명사 what은 적절하지.

● 중요 포인트

one of the ~ 주어 구문

[One of the simplest and most effective ways to build empathy in children] is to let them play more ~
주어 아님   V → 단수 동사

2. ③

● 전체 해석

20세기 중반까지는 단지 소수의 이민자만이 죽기 전에 한두 번 고국을 방문했을 뿐, 대부분은 자기가 태어난 땅으로 다시는 돌아가지 못했다. 이러한 경향은 의사소통을 향상시킨 디지털 혁명과 더불어 세계화의 도래로 완전히 바뀌었다. 결과적으로 이민은 과거의 모습과는 매우 다른 경험이 되었다. 이민자 가족들이 전화와 텔레비전과 인터넷을 통하여 그들의 옛 문화에 다시 연결될 수 있다는 것은 주류 미국 사회 속으로의 통합에 대한 그들의 접근 방식을 바꾸었다. 이것은 또한 어린이들에게 있어 사회화에 대한 이민자 관행에도 크게 영향을 미쳤다. 출신 국가와의 접촉은 이제 더 빈번해졌으며, 더 많은 이민자 가족들이 고국에서 가져온 문화 양식을 유지하고 그들의 자녀들도 그것을 유지하도록 영향을 주려고 시도하게끔 영향 받게 되는 결과를 초래한다.

● 지문분석

Until the mid-20th century, / only a few immigrants paid a visit to their homeland / once or twice before they died, / but most never returned to the land of their birth.

20세기 중반까지 / 오직 소수의 이민자들만이 그들의 고국을 방문했다 / 그들이 죽기 전 한 번 내지는 두 번 / 하지만 대부분은 그들의 태어난 땅으로 돌아가지 못했다

This pattern has completely changed / with the advent of globalization, / coupled with the digital revolution / that has enhanced communication.

이러한 패턴은 확실하게 변했다 / 세계화의 출현과 함께 / 디지털 혁명과 더불어 / 의사소통을 향상시킨

As a result, / immigration is a very different experience / from what it was in the past.

결과적으로 / 이민은 매우 다른 경험이다 / 과거에 그랬던 것과는 달리

[The ability of immigrant families / to reconnect to their old culture / via phone, television, and the Internet] / has changed their approach / to integration into mainstream American society.

이민자 가족의 능력은 / 그들의 오래된 문화에 다시 연결되는 / 전화와 TV, 그리고 인터넷을 통하여 / 그들의 접근 방식을 바꾸었다 / 주류 미국 사회로의 통합에 대한

This has also greatly influenced / immigrant practices / of socialization with children.

이것은 또한 엄청난 영향을 주었다 / 이민자들의 관행에도 / 아이들에게 있어 사회화의

[Contacts with the country of origin] are now more frequent, / and result in / more immigrant families / being influenced / to maintain cultural patterns / from the homeland, / and to attempt to influence their children / to keep them.

출신 국가와의 접촉은 / 지금 더 빈번해졌고 / 그리고 야기한다 / 더 많은 이민자 가족들이 / 영향을 받도록 / 문화적 패턴을 유지하도록 / 고국에서 가져온 / 그리고 그들의 아이들에게 영향을 주려고 시도하게끔 / 그것을 유지하도록

● 해설

2. (A), (B), (C)의 각 네모 안에서 문맥에 맞는 낱말로 가장 적절한 것은?

(A) enhanced: 바로 뒤에 나오는 디지털 혁명의 예시인 전화와 TV, 인터넷은 의사소통을 향상시키지(enhance). hinder는 '방해하다'를 의미해.

(B) reconnect: 디지털 혁명의 결과로 손쉽게 고국과 통신이 되므로 그들의 옛 문화와도 재연결(reconnect) 되겠지. object는 '방해하다'를 의미해.

(C) maintain: 출신 국가와의 접촉은 당연히 고국에서 가져온 문화적 양식을 유지시키겠지(maintain). abandon은 '버리다'를 의미해.

● 중요 포인트

연속되는 수식 구조

This pattern has completely changed with the advent of globalization, coupled with the digital revolution that has enhanced communication.

3. ③

● 전체 해석

수필가인 Nassim Taleb은 그가 지녀왔던 고질적인 과다 체중에 대해 무언가를 하기로 결심하면서, 다양한 스포츠를 시작할 것을 고려했다. 그러나 조깅을 하는 사람들은 비쩍 마르고 행복하지 않아 보였고, 테니스를 하는 사람들은? 오, 너무나 상위 중산층처럼 보였다! 그러나 수영을 하는 사람들은 체격이 좋고 날씬한 몸으로 그의 흥미를 끌었다. 그는 그의 동네에 있는 수영장에 등록하기로 결정했다. 얼마 후, 그는 자신이 착각에 사로잡혀 있었음을 깨달았다. 전문적인 수영 선수들은 그들이 엄청나게 훈련하여 완벽한 몸을 가진 것이 아니다. 오히려, 그들은 그들의 체격 때문에 좋은 수영 선수인 것이다. 마찬가지로, 여성 모델이 화장품을 광고하는데, 그래서 많은 여성 소비자들은 이러한 상품들이 자신들을 아름답게 만들어준다고 믿는다. 그러나 이 여성들을 모델처럼 만들어주는 것은 화장품이 아니다. 단지, 모델들이 매력적으로 태어난 것이며, 오직 이러한 이유로 그들이 화장품 광고를 위한 후보인 것이다. 수영 선수의 몸과 같이, 아름다움은 선택을 위한 하나의 요인이지 결과는 아니다. Taleb은 위의 경우들과 같은 혼동을 'swimmer's body illusion'이라 부른다.

● 지문분석

As essayist Nassim Taleb resolved / to do something about the stubborn extra pounds / he'd been carrying, / he considered taking up various sports.
수필가인 Nassim Taleb가 결심했을 때 / 고질적인 과다 체중에 대한 무언가를 하기로 / 그가 지녀왔던 / 그는 다양한 스포츠를 하기를 고려했다

However, joggers seemed skinny and unhappy, / and tennis players?
하지만, 조깅을 하는 사람들은 마르고 행복해 보이지 않았고 / 테니스 선수들은?

Oh, so upper-middle-class!
오 너무 상위 중산층이야

Swimmers, though, appealed to him / with their well-built, streamlined bodies.
수영을 하는 사람들은 하지만, 그의 흥미를 끌었다 / 그들의 잘 다져진 날씬한 몸으로

He decided to sign up / at his local swimming pool.
그는 등록하기로 결심했다 / 동네 수영장에

A short while later, / he realized / that he had been caught by an illusion.
얼마 후 / 그는 깨달았다 / 그가 환상에 사로잡혔음을

Professional swimmers don't have perfect bodies / because they train extensively.

프로 수영 선수들은 완벽한 몸을 가지고 있는 것이 아니다 / 엄청나게 훈련을 했기 때문에

Rather, they are good swimmers / because of their physiques.
오히려 그들은 좋은 수영 선수이다 / 그들의 체격 때문에

Similarly, female models advertise cosmetics / and thus, many female consumers believe / that these products make them beautiful.
마찬가지로 여성 모델들은 화장품을 광고한다 / 그래서 많은 여성 소비자들은 믿는다 / 이러한 제품이 그들을 아름답게 만들 것이라고

But it is not the cosmetics / that make these women model-like.
　　　　　　　it - that 강조구문
하지만 화장품이 아니다 / 이러한 여성들을 모델처럼 만들어 주는 것은

Quite simply, / the models are born attractive, / and only for this reason / are the candidates for cosmetics advertising.
아주 단순히 / 모델들은 매력적으로 태어났고 / 오직 이런 이유 때문에 / 화장품 광고의 후보들인 것이다

As with the swimmers' bodies, / beauty is a factor for selection / and not the result.
수영 선수들의 몸과 마찬가지로 / 아름다움은 선택의 요인이지 / 결과가 아니다

Taleb calls the confusions like the cases above / the swimmer's body illusion.
Taleb는 위와 같은 경우의 혼동을 부른다 / swimmer's body illusion 이라고

● 해설

3. 다음 글의 빈칸에 들어갈 말로 가장 적절한 것은?

As essayist Nassim Taleb resolved to do something about the stubborn extra pounds he'd been carrying, he considered taking up various sports. However, joggers seemed skinny and unhappy, and tennis players? Oh, so uppermiddle-class! Swimmers, though, appealed to him with their well-built, streamlined bodies. He decided to sign up at his local swimming pool. A short while later, he realized that he had been caught by an illusion. Professional swimmers don't have perfect bodies because they train extensively. Rather, they are good swimmers because of their physiques. Similarly, female models advertise cosmetics and thus, many female consumers believe that these products make them beautiful. But it is not the cosmetics that make these women modellike. Quite simply, the models are born attractive, and only for this reason are they candidates for cosmetics advertising. As with the swimmers' bodies, beauty is _____.
Taleb calls the confusions like the cases above the swimmer's body illusion.

① what triggers gender stereotypes 성에 대한 고정관념을 유발하는 것
▶ 성과는 상관없어.

② a quality with no absolute standard 절대적 기준이 없는 품질
▶ 기준이 중요한 게 아니지.
❸ a factor for selection and not the result 선택에 대한 요인이지 결과가 아닌
▶ 수영선수의 몸을 보고, 모델들이 광고하는 화장품을 보고 수영과 화장품을 선택했지. 수영을 해서, 화장품을 발라서 몸이 좋아지고 아름다워진 것은 아니지.
④ what helps people boost their self-esteem 사람들이 자신감을 올리게 도와주는 것
⑤ the product of constant care and investment 지속적인 관심과 투자에 대한 상품

수영선수의 몸과 모델의 아름다움은 수영과 화장품으로 발생한 결과가 아니라 수영과 상품을 선택하게 만든 원인이지. 따라서 빈칸에 들어갈 가장 적절한 것은 ③ a factor for selection and not the result(선택에 대한 요인이지 결과가 아닌)가 되겠지.

● 중요 포인트

it-that 강조구문

But it is not the cosmetics that make these women model
　　　　　　　　　　it - that 강조구문
-like.

4. ①

● 전체 해석

지식을 얻으려면 지식이 필요하다는 말은 연구자들이 야구 경기 반 이닝을 자세히 묘사하여 그것을 열성적인 야구 팬 한 집단과 덜 열성적인 야구 팬 한 집단에게 읽도록 주었던 한 연구에서 드러났다. 이후에 그들은 피실험자들이 그 반 이닝을 얼마나 잘 기억해 낼 수 있었는지를 시험했다. 열성적인 야구 팬들은 주자가 진루하고 주루 플레이가 득점으로 이어지는 것과 같은 경기와 관련된 중요한 사건을 중심으로 그들의 기억을 구조화하였다. 어떤 이는 거의 그들이 마음속의 세부 경기 기록지를 읽어내는 것 같은 인상을 받았다. 덜 열성적인 팬들은 경기에 대한 중요한 정보를 보다 적게 기억했고 날씨와 같은 피상적인 사항을 보다 자세히 이야기하는 경향을 보였다. 그들은 경기에 대한 상세한 내적 개념 작용이 부족했기 때문에 그들이 받아들이는 정보를 처리할 수 없었다. 그들은 무엇이 중요하고 무엇이 사소한지 몰랐다. 그들은 무엇이 중요한지 알 수 없었다. 그들이 학습하고 있는 것을 내면화하는 개념적 구성 체계 없이는 그들은 매우 잘 잊어버렸다.

● 지문분석

[The saying / that it takes knowledge / to gain knowledge]
　　　　S
/ is captured in a study / in which researchers wrote up
　V
a detailed description / of a half inning of baseball / and
gave it / to a group of baseball fanatics / and a group of
less enthusiastic fans / to read.
말은 / 지식이 필요하다는 / 지식을 얻기 위해서는 / 연구에서 드러난다 / 연구원이 세세한 묘사를 한 / 야구 경기의 반 이닝에 대하여 / 그리고 그것을 주었다 / 야구의 팬 집단과 / 덜 열성적인 팬들에게 / 읽으라고

Afterward / they tested / how well their subjects could
recall the half inning.

이후 / 그들은 시험했다 / 얼마나 잘 그들의 실험 대상자들이 반 이닝을 기억해 낼 수 있는지

The baseball fanatics structured their recollections /
around important game-related events, / like runners
advancing and runs scored.
야구의 팬들은 그들의 기억을 구조화했다 / 중요한 게임 관련 사건을 중심으로 / 주자의 진루와 점수가 난 주루와 같은

One almost got the impression / they were reading off an
internal scorecard.
어떤 사람은 거의 인상을 받았다 / 그들이 내부 경기 기록지를 읽고 있다는

The less enthusiastic fans / remembered fewer important
facts / about the game / and were more likely to recount
superficial details / like the weather.
덜 열성적인 팬들은 / 훨씬 적은 중요한 사실을 기억했다 / 경기에 대한 / 그리고 피상적인 사상들을 더 이야기하는 경향이 있었다 / 날씨와 같은

Because they lacked / a detailed internal representation of
the game, / they couldn't process the information / they
were taking in.
그들은 부족했기 때문에 / 경기에 대한 세세한 내적 개념 작용이 / 그들은 정보를 처리할 수 없었다 / 그들이 받아 들이는

They didn't know / what was important / and what was
trivial.
그들은 알지 못했다 / 무엇이 중요하고 / 무엇이 사소한지를

They couldn't know what mattered.
그들은 무엇이 중요한지를 알지 못했다

Without a conceptual framework / in which to embed
what they were learning, / they were extremely forgetful.
개념적인 구조 없이 / 그들이 학습하고 있는 것을 내면화하는 / 그들은 극단적으로 잘 잊어버렸다

● 해설

4. 다음 글의 빈칸에 들어갈 말로 가장 적절한 것은?
The saying that _____ is captured in a study
in which researchers wrote up a detailed description of a half
inning of baseball and gave it to a group of baseball fanatics
and a group of less enthusiastic fans to read. Afterward they
tested how well their subjects could recall the half inning.
The baseball fanatics structured their recollections around
important game-related events, like runners advancing
and runs scored. One almost got the impression they were
reading off an internal scorecard. The less enthusiastic fans
remembered fewer important facts about the game and were
more likely to recount superficial details like the weather.
Because they lacked a detailed internal representation of the
game, they couldn't process the information they were taking
in. They didn't know what was important and what was trivial.
They couldn't know what mattered. Without a conceptual
framework in which to embed what they were learning, they

were extremely forgetful.

❶ it takes knowledge to gain knowledge 지식을 얻으려면 지식이 필요하다
▶ 야구 경기를 기억하는 실험에서 야구 지식을 알고 있는 사람들이 더 잘 기억했지.
② intelligence is much more than mere memory 지식은 단순 기억 그 이상이다
③ imagination pushes the boundaries of knowledge 상상력은 지식의 경계를 밀어낸다
④ learning takes place everywhere and at all times 학습은 어디서든 언제든지 이루어진다
⑤ prejudice is an obstacle to processing information 편견은 정보를 처리하는 장애물이다

어떤 정보를 받아들이고 이를 처리하기 위해서는 기존의 지식이 필요하다는 글이지. 야구 경기를 예로 들어서 이를 설명하고 있어. 따라서 빈칸에 들어가기에 가장 적절한 것은 ① it takes knowledge to gain knowledge(지식을 얻으려면 지식이 필요하다)라고 할 수 있겠지.

● 중요 포인트

동격절의 수식을 받는 주어
[The saying that it takes knowledge to gain knowledge]
    S   동격을 이끄는 접속사 that
is captured ~
V

5. ①

● 전체 해석

심리학에서 어떤 것의 '모델'은 설명되고 있는 그것의 정확한 복제로 결코 간주되어서는 안 되고, 오히려 그것의 표상으로 간주되어야 한다. 예를 들어, 런던 지하철 지도는 그것이 어떻게 운행되고 어디로 가는지 우리가 이해하도록 도와주는 지하철 지면 배치도의 표상이다. 물론 방향, 축척 등은 그 페이지에 모두 깔끔하게 들어맞도록 다소 왜곡된 것이 틀림없다. 기억의 모델 역시 표상이다. 이용 가능한 증거를 바탕으로 모델은 우리에게 기억이 어떻게 작용하는지에 대한 비유를 제시한다. '저장소' 또는 '단계' 또는 '회로'라는 용어로 기억을 설명하는 것은 우리의 이해를 더욱 구체적으로 만들어주고, 어떤 특정한 심리학자가 이용 가능한 그 증거를 어떻게 이해하고 설명하려고 시도했는지에 대한 대략적 개념을 독자에게 간단하게 전달한다. 이 모델들은 이용 가능한 증거가 바뀜에 따라 변화하고 따라서 불변의 고정된 것들로 여겨져서는 안 된다.

● 지문분석

In psychology, / a 'model' of something / should never be taken / as an exact copy of the thing / being described, / but rather as a representation of it.
심리학에서 / 무언가의 모델은 / 결코 간주되어서는 안 된다 / 사물의 정확한 복제로 / 묘사되어지는 / 오히려 그것의 표상으로서 (간주되어야 한다)
[A map of the London Underground,] for example, / is a
    S   V
representation of the Underground layout / that helps us appreciate / how it works / and where it goes.
런던 지하철의 지도는 예를 들어 / 지하철 지면 배치도의 표상이다 /

우리가 이해하도록 도와주는 / 어떻게 그것이 운행하며 / 어디로 가는지
Of course direction, scale, etc. / must be distorted somewhat / to make it all fit neatly on the page.
물론 방향, 축적 등이 / 다소 왜곡된 것은 틀림없다 / 그것을 지면에 깔끔하게 맞도록 하기 위해서
A model of memory / is also a representation.
기억의 모델도 / 역시 표상이다
Based on the evidence available, / a model provides us / with an analogy of how memory works.
이용 가능한 증거를 바탕으로 / 모델은 우리에게 제공한다 / 어떻게 기억이 작동하는 지에 대한 비유를
[Describing memory / in terms of 'stores' or 'levels' or
    S
'loops'] / makes our understanding more concrete, / and
       V1
simply conveys to a reader / an approximate idea / of how
       V2
a particular psychologist has attempted / to understand and explain the available evidence.
기억을 묘사하는 것은 / 저장이나 단계, 회로라는 용어로 / 우리의 이해를 더욱 구체적으로 만든다 / 그리고 간단히 독자에게 전달한다 / 대략적인 개념을 / 어떻게 특정한 심리학자가 시도했는지를 / 이용 가능한 증거를 이해하고 설명하려고
These models change / as the available evidence changes, / so should not be seen as permanent fixtures.
이러한 모델은 변한다 / 이용 가능한 증거가 변함에 따라 / 그래서 영구적인 고정물로서 간주되어서는 안 된다

● 해설

5. 다음 글의 빈칸에 들어갈 말로 가장 적절한 것은?
In psychology, a 'model' of something should never be taken as an exact copy of the thing being described, but rather as a representation of it. A map of the London Underground, for example, is a representation of the Underground layout that helps us appreciate how it works and where it goes. Of course direction, scale, etc. must be distorted somewhat to make it all fit neatly on the page. A model of memory is also a representation. Based on the evidence available, a model provides us with an analogy of how memory works. Describing memory in terms of 'stores' or 'levels' or 'loops' makes our understanding more concrete, and simply conveys to a reader a(n) _____ of how a particular psychologist has attempted to understand and explain the available evidence. These models change as the available evidence changes, so should not be seen as permanent fixtures.

❶ approximate idea 대략적인 개념
▶ 지도에 나오는 것도 100% 정확하게 나오는게 아니라 틀에 들어 맞게끔 다소 왜곡된 채 표현되지.
② factual experience 사실적 경험
▶ 정확하게 100% 들어맞지는 않아.
③ invariable principle 불변의 원리
▶ 근거에 따라 변한다고 하고 있지.

④ digital representation 디지털 표상
⑤ undisputed interpretation 확실한 이해
▶ 바로 앞에 이해를 구체적으로 만들어준다는 내용에서 나온 오답으로 이해를 하기 위한 도움으로 일종의 '표상'을 사용한다는 것이니 확실한 이해는 거리가 멀지.

어떤 지식에 대한 이해를 돕기 위해 100%는 아닌 어떤 틀에 들어맞게 만들어진 정보를 표상으로서 제공한다는 내용이지. 표상이란 예로 든 지도처럼 핵심 정보만 들어있는 거야. 따라서 빈칸에 들어갈 가장 적절한 것은 ① approximate idea(대략적인 개념)가 되겠지.

● 중요 포인트

동명사 주어와 이에 걸리는 동사
[Describing memory in terms of 'stores' or 'levels' or 'loops'] makes our understanding more concrete, and simply conveys to a reader an approximate idea ~

6. ⑤

● 전체 해석
뉴욕의 한 명망 있는 법률회사에서 일하는 한 여성 변호사가 복잡한 거래를 협상하기 위해 언젠가 라틴 아메리카로 주 고객사의 남성 최고 경영자와 동행했다. (C) 그들이 도착한 직후에 라틴 아메리카의 사업 상대가 될 수도 있는 업체의 책임자가 자신과 그 최고 경영자가 함께 사업에 대한 논의를 하는 동안 자신의 아내와 그 변호사는 쇼핑을 하러 갈 것을 제안했다. 그 변호사는 격분을 하며, 이것이 라틴 아메리카의 성에 대한 편견의 한 예라고 추측했다. (B) 하지만 자신이 반대한다는 것을 말로 표현하기 전에 그녀는 뉴욕에 있는 한 동료에게 전화를 했는데, 그 동료는 지난번 그 나라에 갔을 때 했던 협상 중에 있었던 사전 협의에서 자신도 배제되었다는 말을 그녀에게 했다. 그 라틴 아메리카 경영자는 그녀를 여성으로서가 아니라 단지 '변호사로서' 그 상황에서 빠지도록 할 수 있는 외교적인 방법을 찾고 있었던 것이다. (A) 변호사는 사업가들과 협상하는 것이 아니라 다른 변호사들과 협상하는 것이 현지의 관행이라고 그 동료는 말했다. 그 여성 변호사가 (협의에) 참석하겠다고 우겼다면 그녀는 그 거래를 망치고 자신의 신뢰도를 해쳤을 것이다.

● 지문분석

[A female lawyer / working for a prestigious New York law firm] / once accompanied the male CEO of a major client / to Latin America / to negotiate a complex deal.
한 여성 변호사는 / 명망 있는 뉴욕의 법률 회사에서 일하는 / 언젠가 고객의 남성 최고 경영자와 동행한 적이 있다 / 라틴 아메리카로 / 복잡한 거래를 협상하기 위해서

Soon after they arrived, / [the head of the prospective Latin American partner] / suggested / that he and the CEO go off together / to discuss business / – while his wife and the lawyer go shopping.
그들이 도착하자 곧 / 사업 상대가 될 수도 있는 라틴 아메리카 파트너의 수장이 / 제안했다 / 그와 그 최고 경영자가 함께 할 것을 / 사업을 논의하기 위해서 / 그의 부인과 변호사는 쇼핑을 하러 가는 동안

The lawyer was outraged, / assuming this to be an example / of Latin American gender bias.
ㄴ 분사구문
변호사는 격분했다 / 이를 한 예로 추측하며 / 라틴 아메리카의 성에 대한 편견의

Before voicing her objections, however, / she called a colleague back in New York, / who told her / that he, too, had been excluded from preliminary talks / during his last negotiation in that country.
그녀의 반대를 표현하기 전에 하지만 / 그녀는 뉴욕에 있는 한 동료에게 전화를 했다 / 그 동료는 그녀에게 말했다 / 그도 또한 사전 협의에서 배제되었다고 / 그 나라에서의 그의 지난번 협상에서

The Latin American executive / was just looking for a diplomatic way / to get her out of the picture / as a lawyer, / not as a woman.
라틴 아메리카의 경영자는 / 단지 외교적인 방법을 찾고 있었을 뿐이었다 / 그녀를 그 상황에서 빠지도록 할 / 변호사로서 / 여성으로서가 아니라

It was the local practice, / the colleague suggested, / for
ㄴ 가주어
lawyers / to negotiate only with other lawyers, / not with
ㄴ 의미상의 주어 ㄴ 진주어
the businesspeople.
그 지역의 관행이었다 / 동료가 말했다 / 변호사는 / 오직 다른 변호사와 협상하는 것이라고 / 사업가들이 아니라

Had the woman lawyer insisted on participating, /
ㄴ if 구문의 생략=If the woman lawyer had insisted on participating
she would have spoiled the deal / and destroyed her credibility.
만약 그 여성 변호사가 참여하기를 고집했더라면 / 그녀는 거래를 망쳤을 것이고 / 그녀의 신뢰도를 해쳤을 것이다

● 해설
6. 주어진 글 다음에 이어질 글의 순서로 가장 적절한 것은?
A female lawyer working for a prestigious New York law firm once accompanied the male CEO of a major client to Latin America to negotiate a complex deal.
CEO와 라틴아메리카로 떠났으니 바로 도착하는 문장이 연결되어야겠지.

(C) Soon after they arrived, the head of the prospective Latin American partner suggested that he and the CEO go off together to discuss business – while his wife and the lawyer go shopping. The lawyer was outraged, assuming this to be an example of Latin American gender bias.
여성 변호사가 배제된 것에 대해서 화가 났지만, 사실 확인을 하는 내용이 이어지는 것이 자연스럽지.

(B) Before voicing her objections, however, she called a colleague back in New York, who told her that he, too, had been excluded from preliminary talks during his last negotiation in that country. The Latin American executive was just looking for a diplomatic way to get her out of the picture as a lawyer, not as a woman.
사실 확인의 결과를 다시 설명해주고 있어.

(A) It was the local practice, the colleague suggested, for lawyers to negotiate only with other lawyers, not with the businesspeople. Had the woman lawyer insisted on participating, she would have spoiled the deal and destroyed her credibility.

주어진 문장에서 여성 변호사가 CEO와 출장지로 떠났으니 도착 장면이 있는 (C)가 바로 연결되어야겠지. (C)에 나온 여성 변호사의 배제로 인해서 화가 난 그녀가 동료에게 확인 전화를 하는 (B)가 자연스럽게 이어지고 있어. 그리고 (B)에 마지막 나타난 사실 확인에 대한 추가 설명이 이어지는 (A)가 뒤에 이어지는 것이 자연스럽지.

● 중요 포인트

if의 생략 구문

if가 생략될 경우, had, should, were의 동사가 문장의 앞으로 도치 도는 구문이지.

if 구문의 생략=If the woman lawyer had insisted on participating

Had the woman lawyer insisted on participating, she
$\underset{V}{\quad}$ $\underset{S \rightarrow if 생략, 도치 구문}{\qquad}$
would have spoiled the deal ~

7. ③

● 전체 해석

정체성의 세대 간 계승으로 인해, 대부분의 아이들은 그들의 부모와 최소한 몇 가지 특징을 공유한다. 이러한 것이 수직적 정체성이다. 고유한 특성과 가치는 DNA뿐만 아니라 함께 경험한 문화 규범을 통해서 세대에 걸쳐 부모로부터 아이에게 전달된다. 예를 들어, 언어는 대개 수직적인데 왜냐하면 그리스어를 말하는 대부분의 사람들은 그들의 아이들도 그리스어를 말하도록 키우기 때문이다. 하지만, 어떤 사람들은 그들의 부모와는 다른 선천적 혹은 후천적 특성을 갖는 경우가 종종 있어서 정체성은 그들의 또래 집단으로부터 습득되었을 것인데, 이는 수평적 정체성이라 불려진다. 그러한 정체성은 아이가 그의 조상들과 공유되지 않는 열성 유전자, 가치관, 선호도를 반영할 수 있다. 범죄 행동은 종종 수평적인데, 이는 대부분의 범죄자들이 폭력배에게 길러진 것은 아니므로 그들이 스스로 범죄적 특성을 만들어 냈을 것이다. 자폐증이나 지적 장애 역시 그런 경우이다.

● 지문분석

Because of the transmission of identity / from one
generation to the next, / most children share / at least some
traits / with their parents.
정체성의 전달 때문에 / 한 세대에서 다음 세대로의 / 대부분의 아이들은 공유한다 / 최소한 몇 가지 특성을 / 그들의 부모들과
These are vertical identities.
이것이 수직적 정체성이다
Attributes and values / are passed down / from parents to
child / across the generations / not only through strands of
DNA, / but also through shared cultural norms.
속성과 가치는 / 전달된다 / 부모로부터 아이에게로 / 세대에 걸쳐 / DNA 타래를 통해서 뿐만 아니라 / 공유된 문화적 규범을 통해서
Language, for example, / is usually vertical, / since [most
people / who speak Greek] / raise their children / to speak
Greek, too.
예를 들어 언어는 / 보통 수직적이다 / 왜냐하면 대부분의 사람들이 / 그리스어를 말하는 / 그들의 아이를 키우기 때문에 / 마찬가지로

그리스어를 말하도록
Often, however, someone has an inherent or acquired **trait**
/ **that** is foreign to his or her parents / and must therefore
acquire identity / from a peer group, / which is called a
horizontal identity.
종종 하지만 누군가는 선천적 혹은 후천적 특성을 가진다 / 부모와는 다른 / 그래서 정체성을 습득할 것이다 / 또래 집단으로부터 / 이는 수평적 정체성이라고 불리운다
Such identities may reflect / recessive genes, or values and
preferences / that a child does not share with his ancestors.
그런 정체성은 반영할 수도 있다 / 열성 유전자나 가치, 그리고 선호도를 / 아이들이 조상들과 공유하지 않는
Criminal behavior is often horizontal; / most criminals
are not raised by gangsters / and must invent their own
deceptive character.
범죄적 행동은 보통 수평적이다 / 대부분의 범죄자들은 폭력배에게 길러진 것이 아니다 / 그리고 그들 자신의 범죄적 특성을 만들었음에 틀림없다
So are conditions / such as autism and intellectual
disability.
└ so 도치
상황도 그러하다 / 자폐증이나 지적 장애 역시

● 해설

7. 글의 흐름으로 보아, 주어진 문장이 들어가기에 가장 적절한 곳은?
Often, however, someone has an inherent or acquired trait
that is foreign to his or her parents and must therefore acquire
identity from a peer group, which is called a horizontal
identity.
앞과는 다른 내용이 전개되지. 즉 이후부터는 전과는 다른 내용이 나온다는 거야. 갑작스럽게 바뀌는 구간을 찾아야 해.
Because of the transmission of identity from one generation
수직적 정체성에 대한 내용이야.
to the next, most children share at least some traits with
their parents. These are vertical identities. (①) Attributes
and values are passed down from parents to child across
the generations not only through strands of DNA, but also
through shared cultural norms. (②) Language, for example, is
usually vertical, since most people who speak Greek raise their
children to speak Greek, too. (③) Such identities may reflect
recessive genes, or values and preferences that a child does
not share with his ancestors. (④) Criminal behavior is often
조상, 즉, 부모와는 공유되지 않는 정체성이 언급되고 있어. 즉, 분위기가 비뀐거지.
horizontal; most criminals are not raised by gangsters and must
invent their own deceptive character. (⑤) So are conditions
such as autism and intellectual disability.

● 중요 포인트

so 도치

앞에 나오는 내용을 그대로 받을 때, so를 사용하는데, 보통 주어와 동사가 도치가 된다.

So are conditions such as autism and intellectual
so 도치 V $\qquad$ S
disability.

8. ④

●전체 해석

우리는 온라인 채팅 룸에서 비슷한 생각을 가진 사람들과 함께 시간을 보내고 우리의 믿음과 흥미를 반영하는 사회적 네트워크에 가입하며 우리의 개인적인 이념과 세계관을 반영하는 뉴스 블로그를 읽기도 한다. 이제 집단은 공유된 활동보다는 공유된 이념을 바탕으로 형성된다. 우리는 우선 우리 자신의 가치관과 좋아하는 것을 확인하고 그 관점과 성향을 반영하는 공동체를 찾아낸다. 온라인에서 시작된 이 변화는 소매와 사업까지 영향을 미쳤다. 그것은 성공적인 제품과 서비스가 어떻게 마케팅 되는가에 있어서 경기 방식을 바꾸었다. 우리의 집단적인 사고방식이 변했고, 일반 대중을 상대로 한 마케팅은 더 이상 효과가 없다. 이제 일반 대중의 지지를 얻는 방법은 강한 친족 유대감을 지닌 집단에 대한 마이크로 마케팅(소집단을 파악하여 그들의 개별적인 욕구와 관련하여 마케팅 하는 기술)에 의한 것이다. 구성원들이 똑같거나 거의 동일한 사고방식과 강한 유대감을 가진 더 작은 '부족들'이 제품의 세계적인 성공을 창출하는 힘을 갖고 있다.

↓

사람들은 비슷한 생각을 가진 다른 사람들과 온라인에서 더 많은 시간을 보내는 경향이 있고, 그것은 마케팅이 더 작고 더 특정한 집단에 초점을 두는 것을 필요하게 한다.

●지문분석

Online we can hang out in chat rooms / with likeminded souls / and join social networks / that reflect our beliefs and interests, / and even read news blogs / that reflect our individual ideologies and views of the world.
온라인에서 우리는 채팅룸에서 시간을 보낸다 / 비슷한 생각을 가진 사람들과 / 그리고 소셜네트워크에 참여한다 / 우리의 신념과 흥미를 반영하는 / 그리고 심지어 뉴스 블로그를 읽기도 한다 / 우리의 개인적인 이념과 세계관을 반영하는

Groups are now formed / less on shared activities / and more on shared ideologies.
집단은 이제 형성된다 / 공유된 활동에서라기 보다 / 공유된 이념을 바탕으로

We first identify our own values and preferences / and then seek out communities / that reflect those perspectives and inclinations.
우리는 처음에 우리 자신의 가치와 선호도를 확인하고 / 그러고 나서 공동체를 찾아나선다 / 그러한 관점과 성향을 반영하는

[This shift / that started online] / has spilled over into retail and business.
이러한 변화는 / 온라인에서 시작한 / 소매업과 사업에도 흘러들어왔다

It has changed the game / in how successful products and services are marketed.
그것은 게임을 바꿔 놓았다 / 어떻게 성공한 제품과 서비스가 마케팅 되어지느냐에 있어

Our collective mind-set has changed, / and mass marketing no longer works.
우리의 집단적인 사고방식이 변하고 있고 / 일반 대중 마케팅은 더 이상 효과가 없다

Now [the way / to get mass support] / is by microtargeting groups / with strong kinship relevancy.
지금 방식은 / 일반 대중들의 지지를 얻는 / 마이크로 마케팅 집단에 의한다 / 강한 친족 유대감을 지닌

[Smaller "tribes," / where members have the same or almost identical mind-set / and a strong sense of kinship,] / have the power / to create global success for a product.
더 작은 부족들은 / 구성원이 같거나 거의 동일한 사고방식을 지닌 / 그리고 강한 유대감을 지닌 / 힘을 가지고 있다 / 제품의 세계적인 성공을 만드는

●해설

8. 다음 글의 내용을 한 문장으로 요약하고자 한다. 빈칸 (A)와 (B)에 들어갈 말로 가장 적절한 것은?

Online we can hang out in chat rooms with likeminded souls and join social networks that reflect our beliefs and interests, and even read news blogs that reflect our individual ideologies and views of the world. Groups are now formed less on shared activities and more on shared ideologies. We first identify our own values and preferences and then seek out communities that reflect those perspectives and inclinations. This shift that started online has spilled over into retail and business. It has changed the game in how successful products and services are marketed. Our collective mind-set has changed, and mass marketing no longer works. Now the way to get mass support is by microtargeting groups with strong kinship relevancy. Smaller "tribes," where members have the same or almost identical mind-set and a strong sense of kinship, have the power to create global success for a product.

↓

People tend to spend more time online with others who have __(A)__ ideas, which makes it necessary for the marketing to __(B)__ smaller, more specific groups.

(A) similar: 비슷한 흥미와 관점을 가진 사람들끼리 모이는 온라인 문화가 소매와 사업에까지 영향을 미치고 있으므로 '비슷한'을 의미하는 similar가 적절하지.
(B) focus on: 대세가 영향력이 더 큰 더 작은 집단이 되고 있으니 마케팅의 대상이 이들이 되어야 하겠지. 따라서 '집중하다'를 의미하는 focus on이 적절하지.

●중요 포인트

긴 문장의 병렬구조

Online we can hang out in chat rooms with likeminded souls and join social networks that reflect our beliefs and interests, and even read news blogs that reflect our individual ideologies and views of the world.

9. ① 10. ⑤

● 전체 해석

수년 동안, 스위스는 방사능 핵폐기물을 저장하기 위한 장소를 찾기 위해 노력해 왔다. 핵폐기물 처리장 후보로 지정된 한 장소는 Wolfenschiessen이라는 작은 마을이었다. 1993년에, 몇몇 경제학자들은 만약 스위스 의회가 그 마을에 핵폐기물 처리장 건설을 결정할 경우 찬성표를 던질지 묻는 설문조사를 지역 주민들에게 실시하였다. 비록 그것이 그 지역에 달갑지 않은 추가 시설물로 널리 여겨졌지만, 과반수가 약간 넘는 수(51%)의 지역 주민들은 핵폐기물 처리장을 수용하겠다고 했다. 이는 분명 그들의 시민 의식이 위험에 대한 우려보다 더 높았던 것이다. 그 후, 그 경제학자들은 의회가 지역 주민들에게 매년 보상금을 지급하는 것과 같은 우대조건을 제공하는 경우 찬성할 것인가를 물었다.

그 결과 찬성률은 상승하지 않고 (오히려) 하락했다. 추가적으로 제시한 금전적인 유인책은 찬성률을 51%에서 25%까지 절반으로 하락시켰다. 경제학자들이 금전적인 보상금을 높였을 때에도, 그 결과는 변하지 않았다. 왜 금전적인 보상이 있을 때 보다, 대가가 없을 때 더 많은 사람들이 핵폐기물을 수용하려 했을까? 일반적인 경제 분석은 사람들에게 부담을 수용하는 것에 대한 대가를 제공하는 것이 부담을 수용하려는 의지를 감소시키는 것이 아니라 증가시킬 것이라고 시사한다. 하지만, 이 연구를 주도했던 경제학자들은 가격 효과가 때로는 윤리적 고려 사항들에 의해 효력을 발휘하지 못한다고 지적한다. 마을 사람들에게, 핵폐기물 처리장을 수용하겠다는 의지는 그 나라 전체가 핵에너지에 의존하고 있고 핵폐기물은 어딘가에는 저장되어야 한다는 인식인 공공 정신을 반영한 것이었다. 이러한 시민의 책무에 대한 의식을 바탕으로, 마을주민들에게 현금을 제공하는 것은 뇌물, 그들의 표를 사려는 노력으로 느껴졌다.

● 지문분석

For years, / Switzerland had been trying to find a place / to store radioactive nuclear waste.
수년 동안 / 스위스는 장소를 찾고자 노력하고 있다 / 핵폐기물을 저장하기 위한

[One location / designated as a potential nuclear waste site] / was the small village of Wolfenschiessen.
한 장소는 / 핵폐기물 처리장 후보로 지정된 / Wolfenschiessen의 작은 마을이었다

In 1993, / some economists surveyed the residents of the village, / asking / whether they would vote to accept a nuclear waste repository, / if the Swiss parliament decided to build it there.
1993년 / 일부 경제학자들은 그 마을의 주민들에게 조사를 실시했다 / 물어보는 / 그들이 핵폐기물 처리장에 투표를 할 것인지 / 만약 스위스 의회가 그것을 거기에 짓기로 결정한다면

Although the facility was widely viewed / as an undesirable addition to the neighborhood, / a slim majority (51 percent) of residents said / they would accept it.
비록 그 시설이 널리 여겨졌지만 / 달갑지 않은 추가 시설물로 그지역에 / 과반수가 약간 넘는 수(51%)의 주민들이 말했다 / 그들은 그것을 받아들이겠다고

Apparently their sense of civic duty / outweighed their concern about the risks.
명백하게 그들의 시민 의식은 / 그들의 위험에 대한 염려보다 높았다

Then the economists added a sweetener: / suppose / parliament offered to compensate each resident / with an annual monetary payment.
그러자 경제학자들은 우대조건을 추가했다 / 가정해보라고 / 의회가 각각의 주민들에게 보상을 제안했다고 / 매년 보상금을 지급하는 것과 같은

Then would you favor it?
그러면 당신은 찬성할 것인가?

The result: support went down, / not up.
결과는 찬성은 내려갔다 / 오르지 않고

[Adding the financial incentive] cut the rate of acceptance in half, / from 51 to 25 percent.
재정적인 보상금을 추가하는 것은 / 찬성 비율을 절반으로 줄였다 / 51%에서 25%로

Even when the economists increased the monetary offer, / the result was unchanged.
심지어 경제학자들이 금전적인 보상금을 올렸을 때 조차 / 결과는 변하지 않았다

Why would more people accept / nuclear waste for free / than for pay?
왜 더 많은 사람들이 받아들였을까 / 공짜로 핵폐기물을 / 보상이 있을 때보다

Standard economic analysis suggests / that [offering people money / to accept a burden] / would increase, / not decrease their willingness to do so.
일반적인 경제 분석은 시사한다 / 사람들에게 돈을 제공하는 것은 / 부담을 수용하는 것에 대해 / 증가시킬 것이라고 / 그들의 하려는 의지를 감소시키기보다는

But [the economists / who led the study] / point out / that the price effect is sometimes invalidated / by ethical considerations.
하지만 경제학사들은 / 연구를 이끌었던 / 지적한다 / 가격 효과는 때때로 효력이 없다고 / 윤리적 고려사항에 의해서

For villagers, / [willingness to accept the nuclear waste site] / reflected public spirit / – a recognition / that the country as a whole / depended on nuclear energy / and that the nuclear waste had to be stored somewhere.
마을 주민들에게 있어 / 핵폐기물 처리장을 수용하겠다는 의지는 / 공공 정신을 반영했다 / 인식인 / 전체로서의 나라가 / 핵에너지에 의존하고 있다는 / 그리고 핵폐기물은 어딘가에는 저장되어야만 한다는

Against the background of this civic commitment, / [the offer of cash / to residents of the village] / felt like a bribe, / an effort to buy their vote.
이런 시민의 책무에 대한 배경에 반해 / 현금의 제공은 / 마을 주민들에게 / 뇌물처럼 느껴졌다 / 그들의 투표를 사려는 노력인

9. 윗 글의 제목으로 가장 적절한 것은?

❶ Money Talks? Not Always! 돈이 효과가 있다? 항상 그렇지는 않다
▶ 돈을 주었더니 찬성이 절반으로 줄었지.
② Risky Stuff, Not in My Back Yard! 위험한 것은 내 마당에는 안 돼(님비현상)
▶ 스위스 주민들은 그렇지 않다고 하고 있지.
③ Nuclear Waste: Safer than Expected 핵폐기물: 생각보다 더 안전하다
▶ 안전하다는 내용은 나오지 않고 있어.
④ The Price Effect: How the Economy Works 가격효과: 어떻게 경제가 작동하는가
▶ 경제에 관한 내용이 아니지.
⑤ The Secret of Development in a Small Village 작은 마을에서의 발전의 비밀

10. 윗글의 빈칸에 들어갈 말로 가장 적절한 것은?

① irrational fear 비합리적인 두려움
② fierce competition 심한 경쟁
③ egocentric decisions 이기적 결정
④ collective intelligence 집단 지성
▶ 집단 지성은 여럿이 생각하면 더 나은 생각이 나온다는 것인데, 그런 내용은 아니지.
❺ ethical considerations 윤리적 고려사항
▶ 공공정신이 빛을 발한 상황인데, 돈의 경우는 뇌물처럼 생각된다고 하고 있어.

●중요 포인트

동격절이 2개인 구문

For villagers, willingness to accept the nuclear waste site reflected public spirit – a recognition that the country as a whole depended on nuclear energy and that the nuclear waste had to be stored somewhere.

2단계 혼공 개념 마무리　　p.189

1. Boston 대학의 연구 교수인 Peter Gray는 미국과 다른 선진국에서 지난 50년에 걸쳐서 아이들이 자기 자신이 선택한 방식으로 놀면서 탐구할 기회가 지속적이고, 궁극적으로는 급격한 감소를 보이고 있음을 상세히 기록해 왔다.

2. 출신 국가와의 접촉은 이제 더 빈번해졌으며, 더 많은 이민자 가족들이 고국에서 가져온 문화 양식을 유지하고 그들의 자녀들도 그것을 유지하도록 영향을 주려고 시도하게끔 영향 받게 되는 결과를 초래한다.

3. 지식을 얻으려면 지식이 필요하다는 말은 연구자들이 야구 경기 반이닝을 자세히 묘사하여 그것을 열성적인 야구 팬 한 집단과 덜 열성적인 야구 팬 한 집단에게 읽도록 주었던 한 연구에서 드러났다.

4. '저장소' 또는 '단계' 또는 '회로'라는 용어로 기억을 설명하는 것은 우리의 이해를 더욱 구체적으로 만들어주고, 어떤 특정한 심리학자가 이용 가능한 그 증거를 어떻게 이해하고 설명하려고 시도했는지

에 대한 대략적 개념을 독자에게 간단하게 전달한다.

5. 그 여성 변호사가 (협의에) 참석하겠다고 우겼다면 그녀는 그 거래를 망치고 자신의 신뢰도를 해쳤을 것이다.

6. 하지만, 어떤 사람들은 그들의 부모와는 다른 선천적 혹은 후천적 특성을 갖는 경우가 종종 있어서 정체성은 그들의 또래 집단으로부터 습득되었을 것인데, 이는 수평적 정체성이라 불려진다.

혼공 20일차 **승부수 문항** 모의고사 7회

1단계 **모의고사 7회**　　p.192

●정답

1. ③ **2.** ⑤ **3.** ② **4.** ② **5.** ④ **6.** ② **7.** ④ **8.** ①
9. ① **10.** ①

1. ③

●전체 해석

인간은 대개 공기 또는 물의 진동의 결과로 소리를 경험한다. 인간이 감지할 수 있는 소리가 대개 이러한 매질을 통해 전달된다 할지라도, 진동은 바위를 포함하여 흙을 통해서도 이동할 수 있다. 이와 같이, 소리는 다른 밀도를 가진 다양한 물질을 통해 이동할 수 있고, 그 소리가 이동하는 매질의 물리적 특성들이 그 소리가 어떻게 사용될 수 있는지에 주된 영향을 미친다. 예를 들어, 공기를 진동시키는 것보다 물이 진동하도록 만드는 것이 더 많은 에너지를 필요로 하고, 흙이 진동하도록 만드는 것은 엄청난 에너지를 필요로 한다. 따라서, 의사소통에서 진동을 사용하는 것은 물질이 진동하도록 만드는 발송자의 능력에 달려있다. 이 때문에 코끼리와 같은 큰 동물들이 작은 동물보다 의사소통을 위해 흙의 진동을 사용하는 경향이 더 크다. 게다가 소리가 이동하는 속도는 그것이 이동하는 매질의 밀도에 달려있다.

●지문분석

Humans usually experience sound / as the result of vibrations in air or water.
인간은 보통 소리를 경험한다 / 대기나 물에서의 진동의 결과로서
Although [sound / that humans can sense] / is usually carried through these media, / vibrations can also travel through soil, / including rocks.
비록 소리가 / 인간이 감지할 수 있는 / 보통 이러한 매개체를 통해 이동하지만 / 진동은 또한 토양을 통해서 이동할 수 있다 / 바위를 포함한
Thus, sound can travel through a variety of substances / with different densities, / and [the physical characteristics of the medium / through which the sound travels] / have a major influence / on how the sound can be used.
그러므로 소리는 다양한 물질을 통해 이동할 수 있다 / 다른 밀도를 지닌

/ 그리고 매개체의 물리적인 특성은 / 소리가 이동하는 / 주된 영향을 미친다 / 어떻게 소리가 사용될 수 있느냐에

For instance, / it requires / more energy to make water vibrate / than to vibrate air, / and it requires / a great deal of energy / to make soil vibrate.
예를 들어 / 그것은 요구한다 / 더 많은 에너지가 물을 진동하게 만들도록 / 대기를 진동하게 하는 것보다 / 그리고 그것은 요구한다 / 엄청난 에너지가 / 토양을 진동하게 하도록

Thus, [the use of vibrations in communication] / depends on the ability of the sender / to make a substance vibrate.
그래서 의사소통에서 진동의 사용은 / 전달자의 능력에 달려있다 / 물질을 진동하게 만드는

Because of this, / [large animals such as elephants] / are more likely than small animals / to use vibrations in the soil / for communication.
이 때문에 / 코끼리와 같은 커다란 동물들은 / 작은 동물들보다 더 가능성이 높다 / 토양에서 진동을 사용하려는 / 의사소통을 위해서

In addition, [the speed / at which sound travels] / depends on the density of the medium / which it is traveling through.
게다가 속도는 / 소리가 이동하는 / 매개체의 밀도에 달려있다 / 그것이 이동하게 되는

● 해설

1. 다음 글의 밑줄 친 부분 중, 어법상 틀린 것은?
① is: 주어는 sound이며 that humans can sense의 수식을 받고 있어. 따라서 본동사가 필요하므로 is가 적절하지.
② how: 뒤에 완전한 문장이 오므로 how는 적절하지
❸ depending → depends: 주어인 the use가 of vibrations in communication의 수식을 받고 있어. 본동사가 필요하므로 분사인 depending이 아닌 본동사 depends가 적절하지.
④ to use: be likely to 구문으로 be more likely to use로 연결되지.
⑤ at which: 뒤에 오는 문장이 완전하므로 「전치사 + which」는 적절하지.

● 중요 포인트

which vs 전치사 + which

In addition, the speed at which sound travels depends on
+ 완전한 문장
the density of the medium which it is traveling through.
+ 불완전한 문장 (through의 목적어가 없음)

2. ⑤

● 전체 해석

대화를 하며 사는 삶에 깊이와 흥이 부족할 수 있는 한 가지 이유는 '잘 지내죠?', '날씨가 어땠나요?', '무슨 일을 해요?', '주말은 어땠어요?'와 같은 상투적인 질문을 사용하여 대화를 쉽게 시작해 버린다는 것이다. 그런 질문들이 사회 생활에 중요한 윤활유가 될 수는 있지만, 그것들은 자체로는 매력적이고 풍요로운 감정 이입의 대화를 대체로 촉발하지 못한다. 우리는 "좋아요."라거나 "알았어요."라고 대답하고는 복도를 걸어간다. 대화가 시작되는 방식은 대화가 어디로 흘러갈지에 대한 주요 결정 요인일 수 있다. 그러므로 대담한 첫 마디로 대화를 시도해볼 가치가 있

다. "어떻게 지내요?"라는 말로 동료에게 인사를 하는 대신, "오늘 아침에 무슨 생각을 하고 있었나요?" 또는 "주말에 당신에게 일어난 가장 놀라운 일은 무엇인가요?"와 같은 약간 색다른 질문을 하면서 다른 방향으로 대화를 시도해보라. 여러분은 여러분 자신의 개성에 맞는 그런 질문을 생각해 낼 필요가 있다. 요점은 여러분의 대화가 활기를 띠고, 기억할 만하고, (서로가) 공감하는 발견의 수단이 되게 하도록 관행을 따르는(→깨는) 것이다.

● 지문분석

[One reason / conversational life can lack depth and excitement] / is that we easily fall into using formulaic questions / to open a dialogue / – How are you? / What was the weather like? / What do you do? / How was your weekend?
한 가지 이유는 / 대화를 하며 사는 삶은 깊이와 흥미가 부족할 수 있다는 / 우리가 쉽게 상투적인 질문을 사용하게 된다는 것이다 / 대화를 시작하기 위해서 / 잘 지내죠? / 날씨가 어땠어요? / 무슨 일을 하나요? / 주말 어땠어요?

Although such questions can be important social lubricants, / in themselves / they generally fail to spark / an engaging and enriching empathic exchange.
비록 그런 질문들이 중요한 사회적 윤활유가 될 수 있음에도 불구하고 / 그 자체로 / 그들은 보통 불러일으키는 데 실패한다 / 매력적이고 풍요로운 감정 이입의 교환을

We answer "Fine" or "OK," / then move on down the corridor.
우리는 '좋아요' 또는 '알았어요'라고 대답한다 / 그리고 복도를 걸어간다

[The way / a conversation begins] / can be a major determinant / of where it goes.
방식은 / 대화가 시작되는 / 주된 결정 요인이 될 수 있다 / 대화가 어디로 가는지에 대한

So it is worth experimenting / with adventurous openings.
그래서 그것은 실험할 만한 가치가 있다 / 모험적인 첫 마디를 가지고

Instead of greeting a workmate / with "How are things?" / try taking your conversation / in a different direction / with something mildly unusual / like, "What have you been thinking about this morning?" / or "What was the most surprising thing / that happened to you over the weekend?"
동료에게 인사를 하는 대신 / 어떻게 지내요?라고 / 여러분의 대화를 시작해 봐 / 다른 방향으로 / 약간 색다른 것을 가지고 / 오늘 아침에 무슨 생각을 하고 있었어요? 같은 / 아니면 가장 놀라운 것이 무엇인가요? / 주말에 당신에게 일어난

You need to come up with the kinds of questions / that suit your own personality.
당신은 그런 종류의 질문을 생각해낼 필요가 있다 / 당신 자신의 개성에 맞는

The point is to break conventions / so your conversations

become energizing, memorable, and vehicles / for empathic discovery.
요점은 관행을 깨는 것이다 / 그래서 당신의 대화가 활기를 띠고, 기억할 만하고, 매개체가 되도록 / 공감하는 발견을 위해

● 해설
2. 다음 글의 밑줄 친 부분 중, 문맥상 낱말의 쓰임이 적절하지 <u>않은</u> 것은?
❺ follow → break: 이 글은 상투적인 질문으로 시작하는 대화를 하지 말고 활기를 띠고, 기억할 만하고, 공감하는 발견의 수단이 되게하는 질문을 만들라는 이야기야. 따라서 관행을 따르는(follow) 질문이 아니라 그러한 관행을 깨는(break) 질문을 해야겠지.

● 중요 포인트

주어를 수식하는 관계사 생략 문장
[One reason conversational life can lack depth and excitement] is that we easily fall into using formulaic questions to open a dialogue.
(관계부사 why, that 생략 / S)

3. ②

● 전체 해석
과학자들이 인간에 의한 도구 사용을 설명할 때 그것은 대개 기계적 도구라는 면에서이다. 이것은 예리하게 연마된 부싯돌 날 혹은 전기 드릴과 같은 도구에 적용될 수 있다. 요점은 도구가 수동적인 것이고 소수의 예정된 용도를 가진다고 간주된다는 것이다. 디지털 혁명은 이런 상황을 뚜렷하게 바꾸기 시작했다. 도구는 이제 일반적 기능을 염두에 두고 개발되고 있지만 그것의 작동에 있어서는 미리 예정되지는 않는다. 그 결과, 그것들이 최종적으로 어떻게 사용되는지를 예측하는 것은 불가능하다. 예를 들어, 개인용 컴퓨터는 정보를 다루고 처리하는 일반적 기능을 가지도록 만들어지지만 그 컴퓨터가 정확히 어떻게 사용되는지는 예정되어 있지는 않다. 따라서 그것이 어떤 사람들에게는 의사소통 수단을 제공할 수 있고, 또 어떤 사람들에게는 계좌를 관리하는 고성능 수단을 제공하며, 또 다른 어떤 사람들에게는 오락 플랫폼을 제공할 수도 있다.

● 지문분석

When scientists describe tool use / by human beings, / it is usually in terms of mechanical tools.
과학자들이 도구 사용을 설명할 때 / 인간에 의한 / 그것은 보통 기계적 도구라는 측면에서이다

This may apply to tools / such as a sharpened flint blade or an electric drill.
이것은 도구들에 적용될 지도 모른다 / 날카로운 부싯돌 날이나 전기 드릴과 같은

The key point is / that the tool is thought of as passive / and with a small number of predetermined uses.
요점은 / 도구는 수동적이라는 간주된다는 것이다 / 그리고 적은 수의 예정된 사용법을 가진다고

The digital revolution has begun to change / this landscape in a significant way.
디지털 혁명은 변화시키기 시작했다 / 엄청난 방식으로 이러한 상황을

Tools are now being developed / with a general function in mind, / but they are not predetermined / in their operations.
도구들은 지금 개발되고 있다 / 일반적인 기능을 염두에 두고 / 하지만 그것들은 예정되지 않는다 / 그들의 작동에 있어서

As a result, / it is not possible / to predict the outcome of their use.
(ㄴ 가주어 / ㄴ 진주어)
결과적으로 / 가능하지 않다 / 그들의 사용의 결과를 예측하는 것은

For example, / the personal computer is designed / for the general function / of handling and processing information, / but [exactly how the PC is used] / is not predetermined.
(S)
예를 들어 / 개인용 컴퓨터는 고안된다 / 일반적인 기능을 위해서 / 정보를 다루고 처리하려는 / 그러나 정확하게 PC를 어떻게 사용하는지는 / 예정되어 있지 않다

Therefore, for some, / it may offer a means of communication; / for others, / a sophisticated means of managing accounts; / and for yet others, / an entertainment platform.
그래서 어떤 이들에게 있어 / 그것은 통신의 수단을 제공할지도 모른다 / 다른 이들에게는 / 계좌를 관리하는 복잡한 수단으로 / 또 다른 사람들에게는 / 오락 플랫폼의 수단으로서

● 해설
3. 다음 글의 빈칸에 들어갈 말로 가장 적절한 것은?
When scientists describe tool use by human beings, it is usually in terms of mechanical tools. This may apply to tools such as a sharpened flint blade or an electric drill. The key point is that the tool is thought of as passive and with a small number of predetermined uses. The digital revolution has begun to change this landscape in a significant way. Tools are now being developed with a general function in mind, but they are not predetermined in their operations. As a result, _____. For example, the personal computer is designed for the general function of handling and processing information, but exactly how the PC is used is not predetermined. Therefore, for some, it may offer a means of communication; for others, a sophisticated means of managing accounts; and for yet others, an entertainment platform.

① you should find the merits of old inventions 당신은 옛 발명품의 장점을 발견해야만 한다
❷ it is not possible to predict the outcome of their use 그것들이 최종적으로 어떻게 사용되는지 예측하는 것은 불가능하다
▶ 바로 앞에서 작동이 미리 예정되어있지 않다고 하고 있고, 그 뒤에 나오는 PC의 예시에서도 사용법이 예정되어 있지 않다고 하고 있지.
③ individual digital devices have grown smaller and cheaper 개개의 디지털 장치들은 더 작고 더 저렴하게 되었다
④ you should follow ethical rules when designing tools 당신은 도구를 디자인하기 전에 윤리적인 규칙을 지켜야 한다

⑤ they are not associated with mutual communication 그것들은 상호 의사소통과 연관되어 있지 않다
▶ 의사소통이 문제가 아니라 기능이 예정되어 있지 않다는 것이지.

이 글은 도구의 사용이 디지털 혁명으로 인해서 그 기능이 미리 예정되지 않는다는 내용이다. 즉 도구의 기능에 대한 사용법이 다 다르다는 거야. 따라서 빈칸에 들어가기에 가장 적절한 것은 ② it is not possible to predict the outcome of their use(그것들이 최종적으로 어떻게 사용되는지 예측하는 것은 불가능하다)가 되겠지.

● 중요 포인트

반복 구문의 생략

Therefore, for some, it may offer a means of
　　　　　　　　　　반복되는 구문
communication; for others, (it may offer) a sophisticated
means of managing accounts; and for yet others, (it may
offer) an entertainment platform.

4. ②

● 전체 해석

의존은 결코 사라지지 않으며 단지 더 포착하기 힘들어지고 (어떤) 체제 전체에 영향을 주게 된다. 음식을 먹이거나 기저귀를 갈아주거나 또는 이곳저곳으로 데리고 다니는 사람이 없다면 우리는 결코 생존해서 성장하지 못할 것이다. 이후에 이런 모든 형태의 도움은 배경 속으로 사라진다. 더 이상 그것은 우리의 입 속에 숟가락을 넣어주는 엄마와 아빠처럼 보이지 않는다. 그것은 슈퍼마켓, 식당, 하수도 체계, 전력망, 수돗물, 응급실처럼 보인다. 도움은 널리 퍼져서 보이지 않게 되지만 그것은 여전히 거기에 있다. 혼자서 했다고 우리가 생각하는 모든 것에 있어서 다른 사람에 의해 우리에게 제공되어야 했던 것이 십여 가지가 된다. 우리는 상호 도움의 촘촘한 조직 속에서 산다. 그것이 우리를 사회적 종으로 만드는 것이다. 돈과 칭찬을 얻으려고 밖에 나가 세상에서 경쟁할 때조차 우리는 결코 혼자서 성취하지 못한다. 우리는 도중에 도움이 되어준 부모, 친척, 친구, 교사, 그리고 이웃을 기반으로 한다. 우리 모두에게 도움은 물고기에게 물과 같은 것이다.

● 지문분석

Dependency never goes away; / it just becomes more
subtle and systemic.
의존은 결코 사라지지 않는다 / 그것은 단지 더 미묘해지고 체계적이
된다
Without someone / to feed us, / change our diapers, / or
carry us from place to place, / we would never survive to
grow up.
누군가 없이 / 우리에게 밥을 줄 / 우리의 기저귀를 갈아줄 / 아니면
우리를 여기저기 데려다줄 / 우리는 생존해서 성장할 수 없다
Later, [all these forms of help] / fade into the background.
　　　　　　　　　　S　　　　　　　　　　V
나중에 이러한 형태의 도움은 / 배경 속으로 사라진다
They no longer look like mommy and daddy / putting the
spoon in our mouths.
그들은 더 이상 엄마나 아빠처럼 보이지 않는다 / 우리 입에 숟가락을

넣어주는
They look / like the supermarket, the restaurant, the
sewer system, the electrical grid, running water, and the
emergency room.
그들은 보인다 / 슈퍼마켓, 식당, 하수도 체계, 전력망, 수돗물, 응급
실처럼
Help becomes pervasive and invisible, / but it's still there.
도움은 널리 퍼지고 보이지 않게 된다 / 하지만 그것은 여전히 존재
한다
For every one thing / we think / we have done on our own,
/ there are a dozen things / that had to be provided for us /
by others.
모든 것에 있어 / 우리가 생각하는 / 우리가 스스로 해왔다고 / 십여
가지가 있다 / 우리에게 제공되어야 했던 / 다른 이들에 의해서
We live in a dense fabric / of mutual aid.
우리는 밀집된 조직에서 살고 있다 / 상호적인 도움의
That's what makes us a social species.
그것이 우리를 사회적 동물로 만드는 것이다
Even when we go out / to compete in the world / for
money and praise, / we never achieve on our own.
심지어 우리가 밖에 나갈 때 조차도 / 세상에서 경쟁하려고 / 돈과 칭
찬을 위해서 / 우리는 결코 스스로 얻지 못한다
We build upon parents, relatives, friends, teachers, and
neighbors / who helped along the way.
우리는 부모와 친척, 친구, 선생님, 그리고 이웃을 기반으로 한다 / 그
길 도중에 도왔던
Help is to each of us / as water is to the fish.
도움은 우리에게 있어 / 물고기에게의 물과 같은 것이다

● 해설

4. 다음 글의 빈칸에 들어갈 말로 가장 적절한 것은?
Dependency never goes away; it just becomes more subtle and systemic. Without someone to feed us, change our diapers, or carry us from place to place, we would never survive to grow up. Later, all these forms of help fade into the background. They no longer look like mommy and daddy putting the spoon in our mouths. They look like the supermarket, the restaurant, the sewer system, the electrical grid, running water, and the emergency room. Help becomes pervasive and invisible, but it's still there. For every one thing we think we have done on our own, there are a dozen things that had to be provided for us by others. We live in a dense fabric of mutual aid. That's what makes us a social species. Even when we go out to compete in the world for money and praise, we never achieve on our own. We build upon parents, relatives, friends, teachers, and neighbors who helped along the way.
_____.

① Hope is a wing that gives you victory over obstacles 도움은 당신에게 장애물을 넘어서는 승리를 줄 날개이다
▶ 도움이 나에게 좋은 것이라는 것은 맞는데, 이 글의 중점은 단순히 도

움이 된다는 것을 넘어 필수적인 내용이니까 이건 아니지.

❷ Help is to each of us as water is to the fish 우리 모두에게 도움은 물고기에게 물과 같은 것이다
▶ 도움은 우리에게 필수적이라는 내용이므로 이것이 적절하지.
③ Heaven helps those who help themselves 하늘은 스스로 돕는 자를 돕는다
▶ help라는 단어 때문에 나온 오답지야.
④ Humility makes great men twice honorable 겸손은 위대한 사람을 더욱 명예롭게 만든다
⑤ The living person is independent with his individuality 살아있는 사람은 자신의 개성으로부터 독립적이다

●중요 포인트

A is to B as C is to D

A is to B as (what) C is to D: A와 B의 관계는 C와 D의 관계와 같다.

Help is to each of us as water is to the fish.
도움과 우리각자와의 관계는 물과 물고기와의 관계와 같다.

5. ④

●전체 해석

우리는 습관이 의도를 뒤따른다고 생각하기를 좋아하지만, 의도와 습관이 완전히 뒤바뀌는 것도 가능하다. 습관이 애초에 어떻게 시작되었는지는 완전한 우연일 수 있으나, 우리는 그러고 나서 그 행동에 대한 확실한 이유가 없는 한, 우리의 행동으로부터 의도를 알아낼 수 있다. 예를 들어서 내가 매일 오후 공원 주변을 걷고, 매번 오리 연못을 지나가는 특정한 길을 따른다고 하자. 내가 왜 이 길을 택했는지에 대한 질문을 받을 때, 나는 사람들이 오리에게 먹이를 주고 있는 것을 보는 것이 좋다고 대답할지도 모른다. 실제로, 나는 처음에 완전히 임의로 그저 그 길을 걸었고, 다음 날 똑같이 하지 않아야 할 이유를 생각해 내지 못했다. 이제 습관이 형성된 후, 내가 한 가지 이유를 생각해 보려고 하니 오리가 갑자기 마음에 떠오른 것이다. 나는 결국 본질적으로 그저 우연이었던 것으로부터 의도를 추론한 것이다.

●지문분석

While we like to think / that our habits follow our intentions, / it's possible / for intention and habit / to be completely reversed.
　　　　└ 가주어　　　└ 의미상의 주어　　　└ 진주어
우리가 생각하고 싶어하지만 / 우리의 습관이 우리의 의도를 따른다고 / 가능하다 / 의도와 습관이 / 완전히 뒤바뀌는 것이

[How the habit started in the first place] could be a complete accident, / but we can then work out our intentions / from our behavior, / as long as there's no strong reason / for that behavior.
어떻게 습관이 처음에 시작되었는지는 / 완전히 우연일 수 있다 / 하지만 우리는 그때 우리의 의도를 알아낼 수 있다 / 행동으로부터 / 어떠한 강한 이유가 없는 한 / 그런 행동에 대한

Say / I take a walk around the park / every afternoon / and
 V→ 명령문
each time / I follow a particular route / which takes me past a duck pond.

말해보자 / 내가 공원 주변을 산책하고 있다고 / 매일 오후 / 그리고 매번 나는 특정한 길을 따른다고 / 오리 연못을 지나가는

When asked / why I take this route, / I might reply / that I like to watch people feeding the ducks.
질문을 받았을 때 / 왜 내가 이 길을 가냐고 / 나는 대답할 지도 모른다 / 나는 사람들이 오리에게 먹이를 주는 것을 보고 싶어 한다고

In reality, / I just walked that way the first time, / completely at random, / and saw no reason / not to do the same the next day.
사실 / 나는 단지 처음에 그 길을 걸었다 / 완전히 임의로 / 그리고 어떠한 이유도 알지 못했다 / 다음 날 똑같이 하지 말아야 할

Now, after the habit is established, / I try to come up with a reason / and the ducks spring to mind.
지금 그 습관이 형성된 이후 / 나는 이유를 생각해내려고 노력하고 / 그리고 오리가 내 마음에 떠오른다

I end up inferring intention / from what was essentially just chance.
나는 결국 의도를 추론해 낸다 / 본질적으로 단지 우연이었던 것으로부터

●해설

5. 다음 글의 빈칸에 들어갈 말로 가장 적절한 것은?
① hiding the intention of my previous behavior 내 이전 행동의 의도를 숨긴다
② regretting my unconscious behavior in the past 과거 내 무의식적인 행동을 후회한다
③ being confused about the reason why I started exercising 내가 운동을 시작한 이유에 대해서 혼동스럽다
❹ inferring intention from what was essentially just chance 본질적으로 그저 우연이었던 것으로부터 의도를 추론한다
▶ 산책길을 선택한 이유는 우연이었고, 나중에 오리가 갑자기 생각이 난 것이지.
⑤ getting out of my old habits and forming new ones instead 오랜 습관에서 나오고 대신 새로운 습관을 형성한다

●중요 포인트

접속사 + 분사

「접속사 + 분사」는 문장의 의미를 명확하게 해주기 위한 표현법이지.

When asked why I take this route, ~.
　질문을 받았을 때

6. ②

●전체 해석

정부의 재화와 용역은 대체로 비시장적 배분을 이용하여 개인들의 집단에 분배된다. (B) 이것은 정부의 재화와 용역에 기꺼이 그 값을 내는 사람들의 의사에 따라 그들에게 이용 가능해지는 것이 아니며, 그것들의 이용이 가격에 의해 배분되지 않는다는 것을 의미한다. 어떤 경우에는, 용역이 직접적인 요금과 자격 요건 없이 모두에게 이용 가능하다. (A) 국가 방위 서비스의 제공은 모두에게 무료로 이용 가능하며 가격에 의해 배분되지 않는 재화의 확실한 한 가지 예이다. 또 다른 경우에는, 수입, 나이, 거주, 또는 특정 세금이나 요금의 납부와 같은 기준이 혜택을 받기 위한 자

격을 결정하기 위해 사용된다. (C) 예를 들어, 미국에서 사회보장 연금을 받으려면, 개인들은 일정 나이가 되어야 하고, 사회보장 제도의 보장을 받으면서 특정 기간(대략 10년 정도) 일해 왔고, 그 기간 동안 그들의 사회보장세 부담금을 반드시 납부했어야 한다.

● 지문분석

Government goods and services are, / by and large, / distributed to groups of individuals / through the use of nonmarket rationing.
정부의 재화와 용역은 / 대체로 / 개인들의 집단에 분배된다 / 비시장적 배분의 사용을 통해서

This means / that government goods and services / are not made available / to persons / according to their willingness to pay / and their use is not rationed by prices.
이것은 의미한다 / 정부의 재화와 용역은 / 이용 가능하게 만들어지지 않는다 / 개인들에게 / 그들의 지불할 의도에 따라서 / 그리고 그들의 사용은 가격에 의해서 배분되지 않는다

In some cases, / the services are available to all, / with no direct charge and no eligibility requirements.
어떤 경우에는 / 그 용역은 모두에게 이용 가능하다 / 어떠한 직접적인 비용 없이 그리고 자격 요건 없이

[The provision of national defense services] / is one strong example of a good / that is freely available to all / and not rationed by prices.
국가 방위 서비스의 제공은 / 재화의 한 가지 강력한 예이다 / 자유롭게 모두에게 이용 가능하며 / 가격에 의해 배분되지 않는

In other cases, / [criteria / such as income, age, residence, or the payment of certain taxes or charges] / are used to determine eligibility / to receive benefits.
다른 경우에 / 기준들은 / 수입, 나이, 거주지, 아니면 특정 세금이나 요금 지불과 같은 / 자격을 결정하는 데 이용된다 / 혜택을 받기 위한

For example, / to receive Social Security pensions in the United States, / individuals must be of a certain age, / have worked for a certain period of time / (about 10 years) / while covered by Social Security, / and must have paid their share of Social Security taxes / during that time.
예를 들어 / 사회 보장 연금을 미국에서 받기 위해서 / 개개인들은 특정한 나이가 되어야 하고 / 특정한 기간 동안 일해야 하며 / (약 10년 정도) / 사회 보장 제도의 보장을 받으면서 / 그리고 사회 보장 부담금을 지불해야 한다 / 그 기간 동안

● 해설

6. 주어진 글 다음에 이어질 글의 순서로 가장 적절한 것은?
Government goods and services are, by and large, distributed to groups of individuals **through the use of nonmarket rationing**.
여기서 언급한 비시장적 배분이 잘 설명된 부분이 있는 (B)로 가야 해.

(B) This means that government goods and services are **not made available to persons according to their willingness to pay and their use is not rationed by prices.** In some cases,

the services are available to all, with no direct charge and no eligibility requirements.
요금이나 자격 요건 없이 모두에게 이용 가능한 용역의 대표적인 예가 국가 방위 서비스지.

(A) The provision of national defense services is one strong example of a good that is freely available to all and not rationed by prices. In other cases, criteria such as income, age, residence, or the payment of certain taxes or charges are used to determine eligibility to receive benefits.
특정 자격요건이 있는 서비스의 예로 사회보장 연금이 나오고 있어.

(C) For example, to receive Social Security pensions in the United States, individuals must be of a certain age, have worked for a certain period of time (about 10 years) while covered by Social Security, and must have paid their share of Social Security taxes during that time.

주어진 문장에서 언급된 '비시장적 배분'에 대한 설명이 (B)에 바로 설명이 나오므로 첫 번째 문단이 되어야 해. 마지막에 언급된 요금과 자격요건없이 가능한 서비스의 예로 (A)에서 언급되는 국가 방위 서비스가 나오고 있지. (A) 마지막에 언급된 특정한 자격있는 서비스의 예로 (C)에서 언급되는 사회보장 연금이 연결되면 자연스럽지.

● 중요 포인트

be used to + 동사원형: ～하는 데 이용된다

In other cases, criteria such as income, age, residence, or the payment of certain taxes or charges are used to determine eligibility to receive benefits.
결정하는 데 이용된다

7. ④

● 전체 해석
협력적인 성향은 그것이 협력자들에게 경쟁 우위를 주지 않으면 (생물학적으로) 진화할 수 없다. 예를 들어, 하나는 협력적이고 하나는 그렇지 않은 두 목동 집단을 상상해 보라. 협력적인 목동들은 자신들 각각의 가축 떼 규모를 제한하고, 이렇게 하여 자신들의 공유지를 보존하는데, 이는 그들이 지속 가능한 식량 공급을 유지하는 것을 가능하게 한다. 비협력적인 집단의 구성원들은 자신들 각자의 가축 떼에 점점 더 많은 동물들을 추가하며 사리사욕의 논리를 따른다. 결과적으로 그들은 자신들의 공유지를 다 소모하고 자신들에게 식량을 거의 남기지 않게 된다. 그 결과 첫번째 집단은 자신들의 협력적인 성향 덕분에 우위를 점할 수 있다. 그들은 비협력적인 목동들이 굶주리기를 기다릴 수 있고, 혹은 그들이 더 진취적이라면 굶주린 사람들에 맞서 잘 먹은 사람들의 불공평한 전쟁을 벌일 수 있다. 일단 그 협력적인 집단이 우위를 점하게 되면, 그들은 훨씬 더 많은 동물들을 기르고, 더 많은 아이들을 먹여서 그리하여 다음 세대 협력자들의 비율을 증가시킬 수 있다.

● 지문분석

Cooperative tendencies cannot evolve (biologically) / unless they present a competitive advantage / on the cooperators.
협력적인 성향은 진화할 수 없다 (생물학적으로) / 그들이 경쟁 우위를 보여주지 못하면 / 협력자들에게

Imagine, for example, / two groups of herders, / one cooperative / and one not.
예를 들어 상상해 봐라 / 두 목동 집단을 / 하나는 협력적이고 / 하나는 그렇지 않은

The cooperative herders limit / the sizes of their individual herds, / and thus preserve their commons, / which allows them / to maintain a sustainable food supply.
협력적인 목동은 제한한다 / 그들 개개의 가축 떼 규모를 / 그래서 그들의 공유지를 보존한다 / 이는 그들에게 허용한다 / 지속 가능한 식량 공급 유지를

[The members of the uncooperative group] / follow the logic of self-interest, / adding more and more animals / to their respective herds.
└ 분사구문
비협력적인 그룹의 구성원들은 / 사리사욕의 논리를 따른다 / 이는 점점 더 많은 동물들을 추가한다 / 그들의 각각의 떼에

Consequently, / they use up their commons, / leaving themselves with very little food.
└ 분사구문
결과적으로 / 그들은 그들의 공유지를 다 소모한다 / 그리고 자기 자신에게 어떠한 식량도 남겨두지 못한다

As a result, / the first group, / thanks to their cooperative tendencies, / can take over.
결과적으로 / 첫 번째 그룹은 / 그들의 협력적인 성향 덕분에 / 우위를 점할 수 있다

They can wait / for the uncooperative herders / to starve, / or, if they are more enterprising, / they can wage an unequal war of / the well fed against the hungry.
그들은 기다릴 수 있다 / 비협력적인 목동들이 / 굶주리기를 / 아니면 그들이 보다 진취적이라면 / 그들은 불평등한 전쟁을 벌일 수 있다 / 잘 먹는 사람들 대 배고픈 사람의

Once the cooperative group has taken over, / they can raise even more animals, / feed more children, / and thus increase the proportion of cooperators / in the next generation.
일단 협력적인 그룹이 우위를 점하기만 한다면 / 그들은 훨씬 많은 동물을 기를 수 있고 / 더 많은 아이들을 먹일 수 있고 / 그래서 협력자의 비율을 증가시킬 수도 있다 / 다음 세대의

● 해설

7. 글의 흐름으로 보아, 주어진 문장이 들어가기에 가장 적절한 곳은?
As a result, the first group, thanks to their cooperative tendencies, can take over. 결국 경쟁에서 우위를 점한다는 내용이지.

Cooperative tendencies cannot evolve (biologically) unless they present a competitive advantage on the cooperators. Imagine, for example, two groups of herders, one cooperative and one not. (①) The cooperative herders limit the sizes of their individual herds, and thus preserve their commons, which 협력적 집단 vs 비협력적 집단의 경쟁 과정 allows them to maintain a sustainable food supply. (②) The members of the uncooperative group follow the logic of self-interest, adding more and more animals to their respective

herds. (③) Consequently, they use up their commons, leaving themselves with very little food. (④) They can wait for the uncooperative herders to starve, or, if they are more enterprising, they can wage an unequal war of the well fed against the hungry. (⑤) Once the cooperative group has taken 우위의 내용이 나오고 있지. over, they can raise even more animals, feed more children, and thus increase the proportion of cooperators in the next generation.

● 중요 포인트

문장 뒤에 오는 분사구문

❶ The members of the uncooperative group follow the logic of self-interest, adding more and more animals to their respective herds.
분사구문. '추가하면서'

❷ Consequently, they use up their commons, leaving themselves with very little food.
분사구문. '그리고 남긴다'

8. ①

● 전체 해석

선을 긋는다는 것은 정도의 차이만 있는 두 개의 범주를 구분하는 것이다. 예를 들어, 부유함과 가난함 사이같이 연속성의 개념이 있는 곳에, 누가 세금 감면에 적합할 지를 결정해하는 것과 같은 목적이 있을 경우, 부유하다고 여겨지는 것과 가난하다고 여겨지는 것 사이에 선을 긋는 것이 필요하다. 때때로 선이 어떤 다른 곳에 그어질 수 있었다는 사실은 우리가 선을 그을 필요가 전혀 없거나 혹은 이미 그어진 선이 아무런 효력이 없다는 증거로 여겨질 수 있지만, 대부분의 경우에 이러한 관점은 잘못된 것이다. 예를 들어, 영국에서 신시가지의 제한 속도는 시속 25마일 혹은 35마일로 정해질 수도 있었지만 시속 30마일로 정해졌다. 하지만, 일단 과속과 안전 운행 사이에 선이 그어지고 나면, 우리는 어떤 경우에도 그 제한 속도를 무시해서는 안 된다.

● 지문분석

[Drawing a line] / is making a distinction / between two categories / which only differ in degree.
선을 긋는 다는 것은 / 구분을 한다는 것이다 / 두 개의 범주 사이에 / 오직 정도의 차이만 있는

Where there is a continuum, / such as that between rich
└ '~인 곳에서'
and poor, / for some purposes, / such as deciding / who should be eligible for tax relief, / it is necessary / to draw a line / between what is to count as rich / and what as poor.
└ 가주어   └ 진주어
연속성이 있는 곳에서 / 부유함과 가난함 사이의 그것처럼 / 어떤 목적이 있을 경우 / 결정하는 것과 같은 / 누가 세금 감면에 적합한지를 / 필요하다 / 선을 긋는 것이 / 부유하다고 여겨지는 것과 / 가난하다고 여겨지는 것 사이에

Sometimes [the fact / that a line could have been drawn elsewhere] / is taken as evidence / that we should not draw a line at all, / or that the line / that has been drawn / has no force; / in most contexts / this view is wrong.

때때로 사실은 / 선이 어떤 다른 곳에서 그려질 수 있었다는 / 증거로서 여겨진다 / 우리가 선을 전혀 그어서는 안 된다는 / 아니면 그 선은 / 그려진 / 효력이 없다는 / 대부분의 상황에서 / 이 견해는 틀리다

For example, in Britain / [the speed limit in builtup areas] / is 30 miles per hour (mph); / it could have been fixed / at 25 mph or 35 mph.
예를 들어 영국에서 / 신시가지의 제한속도는 / 시속 30마일로 정해졌다 / 그것은 정해질 수도 있었지만 / 25마일이나 35마일로

However, it in no way follows from this / that we should ignore the speed limit, / once [the line between speeding and driving safely] / has been set.
(걸코 ~이 아니다 / 가주어 / 진주어)
하지만, 이것에서부터 뒤따라서는 안된다 / 우리가 속도 제한을 무시해야만 하는 것을 / 일단 과속과 안전 운행 사이의 선이 / 설정되기만 하면

↓

[The line / drawn for telling things apart] / should be respected / even if the line might be to some extent arbitrary.
선은 / 어떤 것을 구별하기 위해서 그어진 / 존중되어야 한다 / 비록 그 선이 어느 정도 임의적일지라도

● 해설

8. 다음 글의 내용을 한 문장으로 요약하고자 한다. 빈칸 (A)와 (B)에 들어갈 말로 가장 적절한 것은?

Drawing a line is making a distinction between two categories which only differ in degree. Where there is a continuum, such as that between rich and poor, for some purposes, such as deciding who should be eligible for tax relief, it is necessary to draw a line between what is to count as rich and what as poor. Sometimes the fact that a line could have been drawn elsewhere is taken as evidence that we should not draw a line at all, or that the line that has been drawn has no force; in most contexts this view is wrong. For example, in Britain the speed limit in builtup areas is 30 miles per hour (mph); it could have been fixed at 25 mph or 35 mph. However, it in no way follows from this that we should ignore the speed limit, once the line between speeding and driving safely has been set.

↓

The line drawn for telling things apart should be ___(A)___ even if the line might be to some extent ___(B)___.

	(A)	(B)
❶	respected 존중받는	arbitrary 임의적인
②	eliminated 제거되는	reasonable 합리적인
③	observed 관찰되는	outdated 구식의
④	ignored 무시되는	controversial 논쟁의
⑤	redrawn 다시 그려진	acceptable 받아들일 만한

(A) respected: 지문의 마지막에는 어떤 경우라도 그 기준이 지켜져야 한다고 하고 있으니 이를 의미하는 respected(존중하다)가 와야 해.
(B) arbitrary: 지문 중간에 선이 어떤 다른 곳에 그어질 수 있었다라는 사

실은 한마디로 마음대로 그어질 수있다는 걸 의미하겠지? 그렇다면 이에 걸맞는 단어는 arbitrary(임의적인)가 적절하겠지.

● 중요 포인트

관계사로 인해서 매우 복잡한 지문

Sometimes [the fact / that a line could have been drawn elsewhere] / is taken as evidence / that we should not draw a line at all, / or that the line / that has been drawn / has no force; / in most contexts / this view is wrong.

9. ① 10. ①

● 전체 해석

즐거움을 얻기 위한 캠핑은 유목 문화의 직계 후손이 아니다. 그것은 19세기에 다양한 사회적 영향에 반응하여 나타났다. 우선, 낭만주의 운동은 자연의 아름다움과 교감하는 것을 권장했고 또한 조직화된 사회에 반항하는 외로운 아웃사이더의 삶을 찬양했다. 캠핑에 관한 역사가인 Colin Ward와 Dennis Hardy에 따르면, Friedrich Schiller의 '강도들'과 같은 작품들과 George Borrow의 19세기 집시 이야기들은 근심없는 거주자들이 단조로운 편안함 속에 살고 있는 도시에 정착한 거주자들을 경멸하면서, 별을 보며 단순하고 영웅적인 삶을 살아가는 집시 캠프를 이상화했다. 두 번째 영향은 제국의 시대였다. 아프리카와 아시아에서 유럽 열강들은 원주민들의 땅에 대한 지배력을 확장하려고 하면서, 어두운 야생 지역으로 전진하고 원추형 텐트를 치고 병영 임시 막사를 세우느라 바빴다. 캠핑은 식민지 확장을 위해 필요했고 군대뿐만 아니라 탐험가들과 선교사들을 위한 생활 방식이 되었다. 마지막 요소는 이민의 증가였다. 수십만 명의 사람들이 덫 사냥꾼, 벌목꾼, 목장 일꾼으로 일을 하거나 골드러시에 유인되어 호주와 미국, 캐나다와 남아프리카에서 새로운 삶을 살기 위해 19세기에 유럽을 떠났다. 텐트, 간이침대, 난로, 주전자, 캠프용 성냥과 커피와 같은 그들이 필요로 하는 것을 공급하기 위해 전문가를 위한 산업이 성장했다. 그들의 거친 모험담은 고국 언론에서 금방 인기를 얻게 되었다. 캠핑은 문화적 상상력의 일부가 되어가고 있었다.

● 지문분석

Camping for pleasure / is not a direct descendant / of nomadic culture.
즐거움을 위한 캠핑은 / 직계 후손은 아니다 / 유목 문화의

It emerged in the nineteenth century / in response to a variety of social forces.
그것은 19세기에 나타났다 / 다양한 사회적 영향에 반응하여

First, the Romantic movement / encouraged communing with the beauties of nature, / while also glorifying the life of the lone outsider / who rebelled against organized society.
우선, 낭만주의 운동은 / 자연의 아름다움과의 교감을 장려했다 / 또한 외로운 아웃사이더의 삶을 찬양했다 / 조직화된 사회에 반항하는

According to the historians of camping, Colin Ward and Dennis Hardy, / [works / like Friedrich Schiller's *The Robbers* / and George Borrow's nineteenth-century gypsy

tales] / idealized the gypsy camp / whose carefree
occupants lived a simple, heroic life / under the stars,
/ contemptuous of settled town dwellers / in their dull
comfort.
ㄴ being 생략 분사구문
캠핑의 역사가들인 Colin Ward와 Dennis Hardy에 따르면 / 작품들
은 / Friedrich Schiller의 강도들 같은 / 그리고 George Borrow의 19
세기 집시 이야기들은 / 집시의 캠프를 이상화 했다 / 근심 없는 거주
자들이 단순하며 영웅적인 삶을 살아가는 / 별 아래에서 / 그리고 정
착한 도시 거주자들을 경멸하면서 / 그들의 단조로운 편안함 속에 있
는

A second influence was the age of empire.
두 번째 영향은 제국의 시대이다

[European powers in Africa and Asia] were busy /
              S   V
trekking into the dark wilderness, / pitching their bell tents
/ and erecting barrack huts / as they attempted to extend
their control / over indigenous lands.
아프리카와 아시아에서 유럽 열강들은 / 바빴다 / 어두운 야생 지역
으로 들어가는 데 / 그들의 원추형 텐트를 치느라 / 그리고 병영 임시
막사를 세우느라 / 그들이 그들의 통제력을 확장하고자 시도함에 따
라 / 원주민들의 땅으로

Camping was necessary for colonial expansion, / and
became a way of life / not only for the troops, / but for the
explorers and missionaries.
캠핑은 식민지 확장을 위해서 필요했다 / 그리고 삶의 방식이 되었다
/ 군대를 위해서 뿐만 아니라 / 탐험가와 선교사들을 위해서도

A final factor was the rise of emigration.
마지막 요인은 이민의 성장이었다

Hundreds of thousands / fled Europe in the nineteenth
century / to create new lives / in Australia, the United
States, Canada and South Africa, / working as trappers,
                                    ㄴ 분사구문, '일하면서'
lumberjacks and ranchers, / or lured by the gold rushes.
                              ㄴ 분사구문, '유인되어서'
수십만 명의 사람들이 / 유럽을 19세기에 떠났다 / 새로운 삶을 만들
기 위해서 / 호주와 미국, 캐나다와 남아프리카에서 / 덫 사냥꾼, 벌
목꾼, 목장 일꾼으로 일하면서 / 아니면 골드러쉬에 유인되어서

A specialist industry / grew up to supply their needs /
– tents, camp beds, stoves, kettles, camp matches and
coffee.
전문가 산업이 / 그들의 욕구를 제공하기 위해서 성장했다 / 텐트, 캠
핑 침대, 난로, 주전자, 캠핑용 성냥과 커피와 같은

[Their tales of rough adventure] / were soon popularized /
 S   V
in the press back home.
그들의 거친 모험에 대한 이야기들은 / 곧 인기를 얻게 되었다 / 고국
언론에서

Camping was becoming part / of the cultural imagination.
캠핑은 한 부분이 되어가고 있었다 / 문화적 상상력의

●해설
9. 윗 글의 주제로 가장 적절한 것은?
❶ what made camping popular 캠핑을 대중적으로 만든 것

▶ 캠핑이 유럽에서 문화의 일부가 된 내용을 이야기하고 있어.
② the origin of eco-friendly camping 친환경적인 캠핑의 기원
③ the spirit of adventure nurtured by camping 캠핑을 통해서 길러진 모험
심
▶ 모험심 때문에 캠핑을 하게 되었지.
④ basic necessities for camping on the mountains 산에서 캠핑하기 위한
기본적 물품
▶ 물품에 관한 내용이 아니지.
⑤ what to consider when choosing good campsites 좋은 캠핑지를 선택
할 때 고려해야 하는

10. 윗 글의 빈칸에 들어갈 말로 가장 적절한 것은?
❶ idealized 이상화 했다
▶ 집시 캠프에 대한 긍정적인 말이 나와야 하지.
② ignored 무시했다
③ isolated 고립시켰다
④ criticized 비판했다
⑤ classified 분류했다

●중요 포인트

소유격 관계대명사 whose

works like Friedrich Schiller's The Robbers and George
Borrow's nineteenth-century gypsy tales idealized the
gypsy camp whose carefree occupants lived a simple,
heroic life under the stars ~
                              whose + 명사 / + 완전한 문장

2 단계 **혼공 개념 마무리**   p.197

1. 그러므로 소리는 다른 밀도를 가진 다양한 물질을 통해 이동할 수
있고, 그 소리가 이동하는 매질의 물리적 특성들이 그 소리가 어떻게
사용될 수 있는지에 주된 영향을 미친다.

2. 음식을 먹이거나 기저귀를 갈아주거나 또는 이곳저곳으로 데리고 다
니는 사람이 없다면 우리는 결코 생존해서 성장하지 못할 것이다.

3. 습관이 애초에 어떻게 시작되었는지는 완전한 우연일 수 있으나, 우
리는 그러고 나서 그 행동에 대한 확실한 이유가 없는 한, 우리의 행
동으로부터 의도를 알아낼 수 있다.

4. 또 다른 경우에는, 수입, 나이, 거주, 또는 특정 세금이나 요금의 납
부와 같은 기준이 혜택을 받기 위한 자격을 결정하기 위해 사용된다.

5. 협력적인 목동들은 자신들 각각의 가축 떼 규모를 제한하고, 이렇게
하여 자신들의 공유지를 보존하는데, 이는 그들이 지속 가능한 식량
공급을 유지하는 것을 가능하게 한다.

6. 때때로 선이 어떤 다른 곳에 그어질 수 있었다는 사실은 우리가 선
을 그을 필요가 전혀 없거나 혹은 이미 그어진 선이 아무런 효력이
없다는 증거로 여겨질 수 있지만, 대부분의 경우에 이러한 관점은 잘
못된 것이다.

7. 캠핑에 관한 역사가인 Colin Ward와 Dennis Hardy에 따르면, Friedrich Schiller의 '강도들'과 같은 작품들과 George Borrow의 19세기 집시 이야기들은 근심없는 거주자들이 단조로운 편안함 속에 살고 있는 도시에 정착한 거주자들을 경멸하면서, 별을 보며 단순하고 영웅적인 삶을 살아가는 집시 캠프를 이상화했다.